Marketing and Consumer Behavior in East and South-East Asia

Anthony Pecotich
PhD University of Wisconsin–Madison
Associate Professor, Department of Information Management and Marketing, University of Western Australia

Clifford J Shultz II
PhD Columbia University
Associate Professor, School of Management, Arizona State University West

EDITORS

The McGraw-Hill Companies, Inc.

Sydney New York San Francisco Auckland
Bogotá Caracas Lisbon London Madrid
Mexico City Milan New Delhi San Juan
Singapore Toronto Kuala Lumpur

To the memory of my mother, Mara Pecotic, and my cousins Andrea and Katica Gavranic A.P.

To Katherine, Matthew, Marilyn and my parents, Clifford Sr and Kathryn. You make the struggle worthwhile C.J.S. II

McGraw·Hill Australia

*A Division of The **McGraw·Hill** Companies*

National Library of Australia Cataloguing-in-Publication data:

Marketing and Consumer Behavior in East and South-East Asia

Bibliography.
ISBN 0 07 470480 X.

1. Marketing—Asia, Southeastern. 2. Consumers—Asia, Southeastern. 3. Asia, Southeastern—Commerce. 4. Asia, Southeastern—Economic conditions. I. Pecotich, A. (Anthony), 1937–. II. Shultz, C. J. II. III. Asia Pacific centre. IV. Title.

381.095

Published in Australia by
McGraw-Hill Book Company Australia Pty Limited
4 Barcoo Street, Roseville NSW 2069, Australia
Acquisitions Editors: Kristen Baragwanath, John Rowe
Production Editors: Anna Crago, Avril Janks
Cover design: Miller Hare Design
Illustrators: Diane Booth/Steve Miller, Miller Hare Design
Typeset by Post Pre-press Group, Brisbane
Printed in Australia by Australian Print Group

Foreword

In spite of recent events, the East and South-East Asia region (ESEA) has not lost its importance for companies aiming to be global players. But the very diversity of cultures both among and within the countries or strategic locations of ESEA presents three problems: learning about the cultures and how they interact; anticipating the future for market growth within each country; and adapting the company's offerings to the cultures and subcultures when need be. It is with these problems that this book offers help.

And help is needed when cultures are very distant from our own. While it is true that certain brands such as Coca-Cola sell around the world virtually unchanged and products such as drugs, radios, airplanes, tanks and dyes may meet the same needs in all countries, this is not the case for many goods and services.

At present, companies can be helped in finding out about another country by, for example, the relevant state department's 'Background Notes,' which provide a broad survey of a nation's people, geography, economy, government and foreign-policy pursuits. But these are the bare facts, not an insightful analysis made by experts who do not have to consider whether to be politically discreet. What is so distinctive about this book is the recognition that, by looking at a whole region, we get a much greater understanding of, and ability to interpret, what is said about the individual constituent parts. It is a sad fact that few (if any) university business schools try to look at ESEA as a whole, and as a region in world markets. It is difficult enough being an "expert" on just one country (usually either Japan or China) without studying neighboring economies, even when it is acknowledged that such a study could provide a deeper understanding of one's own area of specialization. This is another reason this book is important.

Each chapter in this book focuses on a specific ESEA country or strategic location, and considers eight causal or influencing factors. These are the natural forces, such as geography and resources; the political system; the economic system; the social system; the knowledge system; the education system; the marketing mix; and potential for marketers. If we accept a broad definition of culture as the sum total of a country's laws, dress, architecture, religion, ceremonies, rituals, sexual practices and technologies, and values and beliefs for interpreting experience, making decisions and taking action, then, except for the natural forces described, the rest of the factors are all cultural.

This is as it should be. David Landes,[1] while also taking some account of geographical influences, points out that rich resources, without the relevant cultural traits, do not make a nation wealthy. Landes argues that, if we learn anything at all from the history of economic development, it is that culture does make all the difference: economic success or failure is ultimately determined from within and not imposed from outside. The values of work, thrift, honesty, patience and tenacity can be key, as can the absence of religions that elevate authority and cramp initiative and creative thinking. The reader will want to bear this thesis in mind when reading this book.

And, perhaps more important, this book should be read even if it is just to remind us that there are no universal laws in economic or marketing systems, but only rules—rules that can be broken as they are not true or false, but, simply, either effective or ineffective.

John O'Shaughnessy, April 1998
The Judge Institute of Management Studies
University of Cambridge

Notes

1. Landes, David (1998), *The Wealth and Poverty of Nations*, W. W. Norton.

Brief contents

Acknowledgments xxiv
Notes on our contributors xxv
Map: The East and South-East Asia region xxviii
Introduction 1
CHAPTER 1—**Australia** by JANET R. McCOLL-KENNEDY 25
CHAPTER 2—**Brunei** by SARA U. DOUGLAS 63
CHAPTER 3—**Cambodia** by CLIFFORD J. SHULTZ, II & NARANHKIRI TITH 93
CHAPTER 4—**China** by LAUREN SWANSON 123
CHAPTER 5—**China, Part II** by PIA POLSA & BAI CHANG HONG 161
CHAPTER 6—**Hong Kong** by MARK W. SPEECE & STELLA L.M. SO 213
CHAPTER 7—**Indonesia** by LAWRENCE H. WORTZEL & IGNAS G. SIDIK 257
CHAPTER 8—**Japan** by TSUTOMU OKAHASHI, N. CLAY GARY & STEVEN CORNISH-WARD 315
CHAPTER 9—**Korea** by JAMES W. GENTRY, SUNKYU JUN, GYUNGTAI KO & HEESUK KANG 371
CHAPTER 10—**Laos** by WILLIAM J. ARDREY IV, CLIFFORD J. SHULTZ, II & PHONESAVANH CHANTHAVILAY 413
CHAPTER 11—**Malaysia** by ALIAH HANIM MOHD. SALLEH, BIANCA TEO & ANTHONY PECOTICH 451
CHAPTER 12—**Myanmar** by MAY LWIN & ANTHONY PECOTICH 493
CHAPTER 13—**New Zealand** by ROGER MARSHALL, CHRISTINA KWAI-CHOI LEE & KIM MARSHALL 523
CHAPTER 14—**Papua New Guinea** by GABRIEL O. OGUNMOKUN 549
CHAPTER 15—**The Philippines** by BIANCA TEO, ANTHONY PECOTICH & ALBERT F. CELOZA 561
CHAPTER 16—**Singapore** by JOCHEN WIRTZ 585
CHAPTER 17—**Taiwan** by Y. EDWIN TANG & JEANNE LIU 633
CHAPTER 18—**Thailand** by NITTAYA WONGTADA, OROSE LEELAKULTHANIT & ANUSORN SINGHAPAKDI 667
CHAPTER 19—**Vietnam** by CLIFFORD J. SHULTZ II, NGUYEN XUAN QUE, ANTHONY PECOTICH & WILLIAM ARDREY 715
Acronyms 745

Contents

Acknowledgments xxiv

Notes on our contributors xxv

Map: The East and South-East Asia region xxviii

Introduction 1

CHAPTER 1—Australia

Changing consumer behavior

JANET R. McCOLL-KENNEDY 25

Abstract 26

Introduction 27

Overview 27

Brief historical background 27

Economic factors 28

Introduction 28

Gross Domestic Product 29

Consumer Price Index 29

Inflation 30

Employment 30

Imports and exports 32

Balance of payments 32

Summary 32

Demographic factors 32

Introduction 32

Population size and growth 33

Population distribution 33

Gender distribution 35

Age distribution 35

Aboriginal and Torres Strait Islander population 37

Household composition 38

Immigration 40

Summary 40

Social structure 42
Income 43
Education 45
Occupation 46
Summary 49
Cultural factors 49
Yuppies 51
Teenagers 51
Gays 51
Nationality groups 52
Religious groups 53
Mature consumers 53
REEVS 54
Summary 54
Changes in consumer behavior 54
Implications for marketing management 55
Conclusion 60
References 60

CHAPTER 2—Brunei

Consumers in a monarchical market
SARA U. DOUGLAS 63
Abstract 64
Introduction 65
The demographic environment 65
Brunei's government and political environment 67
The economic environment 68
Income and GDP 69
Primary industries 73
The future 73
Employment 74
Trade 76
Social and cultural environment 77
Human development 77
Education 81
Consumers in a unique marketplace 82
Imports of consumer goods 82
Similarities in consumer behavior and attitudes 84
The monarchy and the consumer 86
References 89

CHAPTER 3—Cambodia

Transition, and the consequences for future consumption and marketing
CLIFFORD J. SHULTZ, II & NARANHKIRI TITH 93
Abstract 94
Introduction 95
A period of systemic change after Independence 96
Sihanouk's monarchy 96
The Khmer Republic 97
The Khmer Rouge and Democratic Kampuchea 97
The People's Republic of Kampuchea 98
UNTAC and constitutional monarchy 99
Economic environment 100
Inflation and other pressures 102
Structure of the economy 103
Geographic and cultural influences 104
Societal structure and demographics 105
Education 107
Public health 108
Implications for marketing and consumer behavior 108
Changes in consumer behavior: Segments and consumer values 109
Changes in the macromarketing mix 110
Products 110
Distribution 111
Promotion 112
Prices 113
Market research 114
Future trends and expectations: Whither Cambodia? 115
Marketing in Cambodia: Go vs no-go decision making 118
References 119

CHAPTER 4—China

The changing consumer: Economic, demographic and social trends and their marketing implications
LAUREN SWANSON 123
Abstract 124
Introduction 125
History 125
Geography 125
Population 125
Language 126
Economy 126

An overview 126
  Population 127
  Daily consumption 128
  "Real" consumers 128
The economic environment 129
  Income 129
  Employment 132
  Unemployment 132
  Consumer price index 133
  Imports and exports 133
The demographic environment 133
  Population size and growth 133
  Age distribution 135
  Households 135
  Family life cycle 136
Cultural environment 137
  Education, literacy, and gender 137
  Health 139
  Economic expectations 139
Changes in consumer behavior 140
  Savings 140
  Household consumption 142
  Household possession of durables 142
Changes in the macromarketing mix 145
  Products and price reaction 145
  Brands 145
  Market segments 146
  Distribution 147
  Advertising 150
  Marketing research 154
Trends and Chinese commerce–into the 21st century 155
  Markets 155
  Transportation 155
  Economic sectors 156
  Foreign investment liberalization 156
  Structural shifts in the economy 156
  Economic expansion and the new China 157
  Future research on marketing in China 158
References 158

CHAPTER 5—China, Part II

Markets within the market
PIA POLSA & BAI CHANG HONG 161
Abstract 162
Introduction 163
A brief introduction to geography and climate 164
A brief introduction to the economic history of China 165
Current government structure and the political situation 165
The socio-economic environment 167
The demographic environment—population: Size and distribution 172
Geographic distribution 173
Urban versus rural population 173
Age distribution 173
The Chinese household 175
Culture and cultural change 177
Basic features of Chinese culture 177
The national language: Putonghua 180
Education 180
Gender issues 181
Health 182
Employment and consumer income 184
Unemployment 186
Socio-economic classes 186
Consumption patterns 190
Savings 191
The single-child market 192
Housing 193
The household's bundle of goods 194
Nutrition and eating habits 195
Leisure activities 195
The macromarketing mix 197
Branding 197
Packaging 197
Price 198
Distribution 198
Retailing 201
Word of mouth 202
Advertising 203
Market research 206
Expected changes in the macromarketing mix 206
References 207

CHAPTER 6—Hong Kong

The consumer market in the 1990s
MARK W. SPEECE & STELLA L.M. SO 213
Abstract 214
Introduction 215
Structure of the economy 215
Demographics 219
Employment, income, and housing 222
Cultural environment 226
  Education 227
  Women 227
Environment 229
Expectations 230
Prices and expenditure 231
Consumers and health care 234
Food-consumption patterns 236
Retailing 238
  Food retailing 239
Advertising 243
Future trends 247
Conclusion 249
References 250

CHAPTER 7—Indonesia

An emerging market with great potential
LAWRENCE H. WORTZEL & IGNAS G. SIDIK 257
Abstract 258
Introduction 259
A brief introduction to Indonesia's geography and climate 259
The demographic environment—population: Size and distribution 260
  Geographic distribution 260
  Age distribution 263
  The Indonesian household 263
  Additional household residents 265
  Marketing implications of Indonesian demography 265
The economic environment 267
Social welfare 269
The Indonesian sociopolitical environment 269
  Government structure 270
  The national language: Bahasa Indonesia 271
  The growing role of the English language 271

Consumer income and socio-economic class 272
  Economic class 273
  The Jakarta income bulge 275
  Social class 275
  Marketing implications 279
  Employment 279
  Gender issues 282
  Education 283
Culture and cultural change 284
  Dress and food 286
  Ethnic origins 286
  Who are the innovators of cultural change in Indonesia? 286
  Marketing implications of cultural change 287
Consumption patterns 287
  Housing 287
  The household's bundle of goods 289
  Health and fitness 293
  Nutrition and eating habits 294
  Leisure activities 296
  Consumer credit and consumer banking 299
The macromarketing mix 299
  Branding 299
  Price 300
  Distribution 301
  Direct marketing and telemarketing 306
  Advertising 306
  Sales promotion 307
  Market research 308
Expected changes in the macromarketing mix 309
Conclusion 310
References 311

CHAPTER 8—Japan

High noon for the rising sun—new realities and forces of change in a mature consumer market

TSUTOMU OKAHASHI, N. CLAY GARY & STEVEN CORNISH-WARD 315
Abstract 316
Introduction 317
  The Japanese consumer: The conventional wisdom 318
  The Bubble Economy 318
The economic environment 320
  Economic growth 320

Decline of lifetime employment 320
Current employment outlook 321
The future 322
Income 322
Inflation 324
The demographic environment 325
Age distribution 325
The "Dankai" Generations 325
Cultural environment 327
Education 327
Education reform 329
Liberalization 329
The traditional family 329
Changes in household composition 330
Gender issues 332
Back to the family 333
Materialism, the environment and health 334
Internationalism and materialism 336
Environment 338
Health 338
Expectations 340
Changes in consumer behavior 341
Consumer credit 341
Consumption 343
Overseas travel 345
Changes in the macromarketing mix 346
Products 346
Dankai Juniors and the product mix 348
Consumer reactions to price 348
Distribution 350
Vending machines 353
Direct marketing 354
Advertising 354
Television advertising–content, tone and manner 356
Comparative advertising 357
Price in advertising 357
Corporate branding 358
Sales promotion 359
Market research 359
Future trends and expectations 359
Economic trends 359
Demographic trends 360
Cultural trends 361

Consumption 361
Marketing management in the 1990s 362
Internationalization 362
Packaging 362
Price consciousness 363
Distribution 363
Advertising and the media 363
Conclusion 364
References 364

CHAPTER 9—Korea

Changing consumer trends and implications for marketers
JAMES W. GENTRY, SUNKYU JUN, GYUNGTAI KO & HEESUK KANG 371
Abstract 372
Introduction 373
A brief historical perspective 373
Political environment 374
The economies of the Koreas 377
Income 377
Employment 378
Prices and credit policy 380
Government/business interface 380
Barriers to trade 382
Korean–Japanese trade relations 385
The demographic and social environments 386
Population 386
Immigrants 387
Education 387
Health care 387
Family relations 388
Gender relations 389
Crime 390
The cultural environment 390
Religion 390
Confucianism 391
Korea and Japan: Cultural similarities and differences 392
Comparisons using Hofstede's cultural dimensions 392
Interpersonal interactions 392
Respect for age 393
Relationship with nature 394
Changes in the macromarketing mix 394
Comparison of the two Koreas 394

Basic consumption in the two Koreas 395
Food 395
Housing 396
A journalist's view of North Korea 397
Advertising 397
Context in advertising 399
Use of humor 399
Distribution 399
Changing trends 400
Intellectual property protection 400
Changing technology 401
Consumer issues 401
Information search 401
Innovativeness 402
Gift giving 402
Social role 403
The future 403
Reunification 403
Korea's role in a global economy 405
Conclusion 406
References 406

CHAPTER 10—Laos

From Marx to market—marketing and consumer behavior in the heart of the golden quadrangle
WILLIAM J. ARDREY IV, CLIFFORD J. SHULTZ, II & PHONESAVANH CHANTHAVILAY 413
Abstract 414
Introduction 415
The economic environment 415
The emergence of modern Laos 416
Income and employment 419
Inflation 423
The demographic and cultural environments 424
Population 424
Sex roles 426
Ethnicity 426
Religion 428
Cultural protectionism 428
Household size 429
Immigrants and returning refugees 430
Education 430

Health 431
Environment 432
Changes in consumer behavior 433
Materialism 433
Consumer expectations 434
Market-segmentation trends 435
Consumer credit 437
Changes to the macromarketing mix 438
Products 438
Services 440
Entertainment 440
Prices 441
Distribution 441
Marketing communications 443
Market research 444
Future trends and expectations 444
Consumer behavior 445
Changing government role 446
Implications for marketing management 446
Broadly defining the market 447
Riding the demographic wave 447
Extending brands to Laos 447
Expecting government involvement 447
Seeking good local partners 448
Investment in training 448
References 448

CHAPTER 11–Malaysia

Consumer behavior and the future

ALIAH HANIM MOHD. SALLEH, BIANCA TEO & ANTHONY PECOTICH 451
Abstract 452
Introduction 453
Physical environment 453
Demography 454
Political environment 457
Investment climate 458
Introduction 458
Government policy on investment 460
Exchange controls 461
Protection 461
Investment regulatory agencies 462
Employment policy 463
Investment incentives 464

Free Trade Zones 464
Business organization 465
Infrastructure 466
Economic environment 467
Culture 471
Marketing infrastructure 476
The market 476
Distribution 477
Advertising 480
Market research 481
Important trends and their marketing implications 481
Dominance of the young population 481
Increasing women's role in purchasing decisions 482
Ethnically segmented/differentiated consumer markets 483
Other business-economic developments 486
The development of new "alternative Islamic" products 486
The post-Proton era of heavy industrial growth 487
The future 488
References 490

CHAPTER 12—Myanmar

From an isolated past to a golden future?
MAY LWIN & ANTHONY PECOTICH 493
Abstract 494
Introduction 495
Background 495
Environment 496
Natural environment 496
Economic environment 497
Demographic environment 503
Cultural environment 506
Consumer behavior 510
Myanmar people abroad 511
Knowledge of English 511
Intact brand profiles 511
Thriving black market 511
Trends in the macromarketing mix 512
Consumer products 512
Pricing 513
Distribution: The retail market 515
Promotion and advertising 516
Future trends: The potential 519
References 520

CHAPTER 13—New Zealand

Consumers in their market environment—profiles and predictions
ROGER MARSHALL, CHRISTINA KWAI-CHOI LEE & KIM MARSHALL 523
Abstract 524
The economic environment 525
Trading 526
Finance 527
Regional differences 527
Employment 527
Income 528
The residential sector 528
The retail sector 529
The demographic environment 529
Population 529
Age distribution 532
Household size 532
Cultural environment 533
Women in New Zealand 534
Education 534
Social-class structure 535
Changes in family structure and decision making 536
The marketing environment 536
Distribution 536
Pricing 538
Communications 538
Product 541
Consumer lifestyles 541
Discussion 544
References 547

CHAPTER 14—Papua New Guinea

An overview of the marketing environment
GABRIEL O. OGUNMOKUN 549
Abstract 550
Introduction 551
Historical background 551
Population, languages and education 551
Geographical environment and climatic conditions 553
Political environment and system 553
Legal system 554
Investment climate and the economy 554

Mineral and energy resources 554
Population issues 554
Agriculture, industries and exports 555
High-technology, service and manufacturing industries 555
Living standards 555
Transport and communications 555
Religion and social activities 556
The macromarketing mix 556
Marketing research 556
Promotion and pricing 557
Distribution 558
Summary and conclusion 559
References 560

CHAPTER 15—The Philippines

Marketing and consumer behavior, past, present and future
BIANCA TEO, ANTHONY PECOTICH & ALBERT F. CELOZA 561
Abstract 562
Introduction 563
Physical environment 563
Demographics 564
Culture and religion 566
Government and politics 569
Historical background 569
Economic position 574
An overview of the major industrial sectors 576
Agriculture, fishing, and the environment 576
Mining and energy 577
Manufacturing 578
Tourism 578
International trade 579
Elements of the macromarketing mix 580
Product 580
Channels of distribution 580
Promotion 582
Conclusion 583
References 583

CHAPTER 16–Singapore

An analysis of changes in the marketing environment and their implications for marketing management

JOCHEN WIRTZ 585
Abstract 586
Introduction 587
Political and historical background information 588
Political structure 588
Some explanations for Singapore's rapid economic development 588
Singapore's position in the region 590
Background information–summary and conclusions 591
Economic environment 591
Income 592
Employment 593
Inflation 594
Trends in trade policy 594
Future trends in the economic environment 595
Summary–economic environment 596
Demographic environment 597
Population size 597
Age distribution 597
Cultural environment 599
Ethnicity 599
Languages 599
Religions 600
Education 602
Households 603
Other aspects of Singapore's cultural environment 604
Cultural environment–summary and conclusions 605
Consumer behavior 606
Consumption 606
Expectations in terms of consumer values and lifestyles 607
Tourism 609
Consumer behavior–summary 610
Changes in the macromarketing mix 611
Products and services 612
Consumer reactions to price and promotions 613
Distribution 614
Advertising 617
Market research 617
Marketing mix–a summary 619
Implications for marketing management into the next century 620
Conclusions on Singapore's marketing environment 620

Implications for the marketing mix 624
Implications for overall marketing strategies 625
Conclusion 627
References 628

CHAPTER 17—Taiwan
Changing marketing and consumer behavior
Y. EDWIN TANG & JEANNE LIU 633
Abstract 634
Introduction 635
Economic environment 636
Changes in income 637
Changes in saving rate and credit spending 637
Changes in consumer consumption patterns 638
Inflation and unemployment 639
The demographic environment 640
Changes in population size 640
Age distribution 640
Household size 641
Ethnicity 642
Cultural environment 643
Education 643
Liberalization 644
The identity of Taiwanese culture 645
The environment and public health 645
Changes in consumer behavior 647
Consumption of durable goods 647
Transportation vehicles 647
Mass-media services 649
Changes in the macromarketing mix 650
Trademark and patent protection 650
Products 651
Distribution 652
Price 653
Advertising 654
Direct marketing 655
Market research 656
Future trends and expectations 656
Economic trends 656
Demographic trends 657
Cultural trends 658
Consumption 658

Political and diplomatic trends 659
Marketing management in the late 1990s 659
Internationalization 659
Products 661
Distribution 661
Advertising 662
Conclusion 662
References 663

CHAPTER 18—Thailand

Consumer behavior and marketing
NITTAYA WONGTADA, OROSE LEELAKULTHANIT & ANUSORN SINGHAPAKDI 667
Abstract 668
Introduction 669
General overview 669
Geography 669
History 670
Prevailing culture 670
Changes in the environment 672
Economic environment 672
Demographic environment 680
Changes in the cultural environment 681
Health 685
Changes in consumer behavior 686
Changes in marketing practice 688
Product 689
Channels of distribution 692
Modern wholesale distribution 694
Promotion 696
Price 697
Marketing management in the 1990s 698
Precise demographic segments 698
The value of retail space 699
Increasing efficiency 701
"Green" marketing 701
Symbiotic marketing 702
Globalization 702
Implications for marketing management 704
Conclusions 706
References 707

CHAPTER 19—Vietnam

Market socialism, marketing and consumer behavior
CLIFFORD J. SHULTZ II, NGUYEN XUAN QUE, ANTHONY PECOTICH &
WILLIAM ARDREY 715
Abstract 716
Introduction 717
Historical and cultural background 717
Economic environment 721
Rebirth through *Doi Moi* 721
Administrative practices and regulations 722
Progressive economic results 725
Political and ideological reform 727
Marketing environment 728
Marketing institutions and infrastructure 728
International trade 729
Consumer markets 730
Demographics 730
Social structure 731
Foreign invasion 733
The new generation 733
Implications for marketing management 734
Adapting to changing regulations 734
Entry strategies 735
The channel decision 736
Researching the market 737
Developing human resources 737
Motivation and persistence 738
Conclusion 739
References 740

ACRONYMS 745

Acknowledgments

As with all endeavors of this kind, there have been many people without whose assistance the completion of this work would have been much more difficult, if not impossible. We therefore wish to express our sincere appreciation to all of them, and in particular the following.

To the authors of the individual chapters, thank you for your contributions and your positive reactions throughout the revision and updating processes.

Thanks are also due to John Rowe, Avril Janks and the editorial staff at McGraw-Hill, who were particularly helpful and supportive, and were instrumental in the completion of the project.

The Editors and the Publisher wish to thank Europa Publications for permission to reproduce their material.

The faculty and secretarial staff in our respective departments at Arizona State and the University of Western Australia are thanked for their support and encouragement. Particular thanks is due to Carole Duffield and the library staff at the University of Western Australia, who greatly facilitated the research on which some of this text is based.

We also thank the faculty, staff and students in the Marketing Departments at the University of Innsbruck, University College Dublin and the University of Zagreb, where Anthony Pecotich was located at various periods during the completion of this text, Tom Vallely and his associates at the Harvard Institute for International Development (HIID) for their assistance during Clifford Shultz's visits to HIID, and the Arizona State University SRCA program.

Finally, we owe a major debt to our families, Katherine and Matthew Shultz, and Jan, Kathrine and Jennifer Pecotich, who helped us to survive the difficult and sometimes frantic efforts to meet the deadlines–thank you.

Notes on our contributors

William Ardrey is a lecturer at the University of Western Australia.

Bai Chang Hong is a faculty member in the Department of International Business Management, Nankai University, Tianjin.

Albert F. Celoza is a faculty member in Social Science at Phoenix College, Phoenix, Arizona. He is also affiliate faculty, Program for South-East Asian Studies, Arizona State University and Adjunct Professor, Thunderbird, American Graduate School of International Management.

Phonesavanh Chanthavilay is with the Permanant Mission of the Lao PDR to the United Nations, New York.

Stephen Cornish-Ward is a Faculty Member in the Department of Marketing, Murdoch University, Murdoch, Western Australia.

Sara U. Douglas is Associate Professor at the Department of Agricultural and Consumer Economics, University of Illinois, Urbana, Illinois.

N. Clay Gary is Marketing Planner, Dentsu Inc., Tokyo.

James W. Gentry is Professor in the College of Business Administration, University of Nebraska, Lincoln, Nebraska.

Sunkyu Jun is a faculty member in the Marketing Department at Han Nam University, South Korea.

HeeSuk Kang is a faculty member in the Marketing Department at WooSuk University, South Korea.

Gyungtai Ko is a faculty member in the Marketing Department at Chonbuk National University, South Korea.

Christina Kwai-Choi Lee is a faculty member in the Marketing Department at the University of Auckland.

Jeanne Liu is a faculty member at National Chengchi University, Taiwan.

Orose Leelakulthanit is a faculty member at the National Institute of Development Administration, Bangkok.

Janet R. McColl-Kennedy is a Senior Lecturer in Marketing at the Graduate School of Management, University of Queensland.

Kim Marshall is associated with the Marketing Department at the University of Auckland.

Roger Marshall is Senior Lecturer in the Marketing Department at the Nanyang Technological University, Singapore.

Gabriel Ogunmokun is a Senior Lecturer at the Department of Information Management and Marketing, University of Western Australia, Perth.

Tsutomu Okahashi is Deputy Director, Marketing Management Division, Dentsu Inc., Tokyo.

Anthony Pecotich is an Associate Professor of Marketing at the Department of Information Management and Marketing, University of Western Australia, Perth. Email: tpecotic@ecel.uwa.edu.au

Pia Polsa is a faculty member in the Department of Marketing and Corporate Geography, Swedish School of Economics and Business Administration, Helsinki.

Nguyen Xuan Que is Director of the Ho Chi Minh City College of Marketing, Ho Chi Minh City.

Aliah Hanim Mohd. Salleh is Lecturer of Marketing at Universiti Kebangsaan Malaysia, Faculty of Business Management, Malaysia.

Clifford J. Shultz, II is an Associate Professor of Marketing at the Arizona State University School of Management, Phoenix, Arizona, and affiliate faculty at the Arizona State Program for South-East Asian Studies. Email: atcjs@asu.edu.

Ignas G. Sidik is a faculty member at Prasetiya Mulya, Graduate School of Business Administration, Indonesia.

Anusorn Singhapakdi is Associate Professor of Marketing in the Department of Management and Marketing, College of Business & Public Administration, Old Dominion University, Norfolk, Virginia.

Mark W. Speece is Professor at the School of Management, Asian Institute of Technology, Bangkok.

Stella L.M. So is a faculty member in the Department of Marketing, Chinese University of Hong Kong, Hong Kong.

Lauren Swanson is a Senior Lecturer in Marketing at the Chinese University of Hong Kong, Hong Kong.

Y. Edwin Tang is a faculty member at the Chinese University of Hong Kong, Hong Kong.

Bianca Teo was a faculty member in the Department of Information Management and Marketing, University of Western Australia, Nedlands, Western Australia.

Naranhkiri Tith is a faculty member, School of Advanced International Studies, International Economics, Russian, and Asian Studies, Johns Hopkins University, Washington, DC.

Jochen Wirtz is Lecturer in Marketing, Faculty of Business Administration, National University of Singapore.

Nittaya Wongtada is a faculty member in the Graduate School of Business Administration, National Institute of Development Administration, Bangkok.

Lawrence H. Wortzel was Professor of Marketing, Boston University, and Senior Faculty Member, Prasetiya Mulya Graduate School of Business Administration, Indonesia.

The East and South-East Asia region

Introduction

The economic rollercoaster that is East and South-East Asia (ESEA) has been brought sharply into focus by the 1997 economic and financial crisis. Prior to this, the extraordinary progress of ESEA was well documented in both the academic and the popular press. The nations have been labelled, individually and collectively, as "the awakening giants," the sources of a "new world economic order," "the little tiger," and "the four tigers," and the period has been hailed as "the Pacific century." This progress is particularly impressive when we consider that, immediately after the Second World War in 1945, ESEA was a scene of devastation and disorder, imbued with the potential for further conflict. The notion that the region was "going nowhere" was not based simply on the jaundiced assessment of those without vision, but was rather the calculated evaluation of the well informed. To accentuate the true nature of the situation, Leger (1995, p. 46) uses the example of Korea's per-capita GNP, which at the time was "roughly equal to that of Ethiopia, and Yemen and about a third less than that of India and Pakistan."

In the first two decades that followed the Second World War there was little immediate improvement. The region continued to be characterized by the rise of brutal centrally controlled forms of government, civil wars (e.g. Korea, Vietnam), poverty and other damaging forms of internal disorder (e.g. corruption, black markets, insurrections and various forms of political and economic repression).

Today, though the process is not complete, and some of the world's poorest nations still exist within the region, both the transformation and the potential are imposing.

The full magnitude of the changes is described by Schwab and Smadja (1994, pp. 40–1) as the rise of the "new economic world order," on whose nature they elaborate as follows:

> Perhaps the most spectacular component of the current revolution is the shift in the world economy's center of gravity to Asia. The extraordinary process of fast and steady growth in East Asia since the end of the 1960s has led to an overall redistribution of the world's economic power, the impact and implications of which are just beginning to be felt. In 1960, East Asia accounted for just 4% of world economic output. Today its share amounts to 25%. While GNP in Europe and the United States has grown at an average of 2.5% to 3% per year over the past 25 years, many East Asian countries have managed an annual average of 6.5% to 7.5%–a trend that is expected to continue beyond the turn of the century. Between 1992 and the year 2000, 40% of all

> the new purchasing power created in the world will be in East Asia, and the region will absorb between 35% and 40% of the global increase in imports. East Asian central banks now hold close to 45% of the world's foreign reserves, and while the United States and the major European countries keep piling up foreign debt, Japan, Taiwan, Singapore, and Hong Kong are in the remarkable position of not having any.

Indeed, trends suggest that "the 'pacific century' is approaching" (Forbes 1997, p. 24). With the renaissance of Japan's economic power, the emergence of the newly-industrializing countries (NICs) and the growth of a group of "near NICs," it seems likely that the Pacific will replace the Atlantic Ocean as the center of world trade. In essence, ESEA will become the world's most formidable market; the reciprocal relationship between marketing and consumers will be its catalyst. Given this ascent and importance, the purpose of this text is to provide insights into the present conditions and the future trends of marketing and consumer behavior in the various countries of the region.

East and South-East Asia: An integrative and systemic overview

As a prelude to the country-specific chapters, it is necessary to address the region of East and South-East Asia as a whole and to extract those aspects that are critical to the explanation of its progress. The contributors, in their presentations for each of the nations, have tended to take a regional perspective. It is not our purpose to reiterate their contributions; we will attempt instead to distill and to describe the major unifying themes and trends in a conceptual context. But, before doing so, two issues should be addressed. The first issue is the question of regional definition, and the second is the nature of the statistical data.

The alert reader would have already noted that our region description, "East and South-East Asia," is somewhat cumbersome (hence the acronym ESEA), and that we appear to move from South-East Asia to East Asia to the Pacific Basin with little apparent distinction. Unfortunately, the literature and common usage are such that this geographic ambiguity cannot be avoided. Many country and region demarcations are possible. Some of these classifications overlap and do not have unique contexts, except in those circumstances where they describe a formal alliance or association such as the Association of South-East Asian Nations (ASEAN) or Asia-Pacific Economic Co-operation (APEC). Further, the history of the region has been characterized by numerous attempts to form regional alliances, and the existence of contradictory (divisive and unifying) forces.

The nations differ on the bases of ethnicity, culture, language, and political and economic systems. Some of the animosities between them have deep historical roots spanning thousands of years. These animosities may be hard to overcome, particularly when one notes the fairly recent military hostilities among some of them, the memory of which is deeply ingrained in the national psyche of the country affected, and is always a factor in international relations. The possibility of further territorial disputes is very real. Consider, for example: China with the status of Hong Kong, Taiwan, Macao and the wide ranging dispute over the Spratly Islands; border tensions between Myanmar and Thailand, the "Timor question" in Indonesia; the still unresolved Korean conflict; and the Khmer Rouge problem in Cambodia, to name just a few potential flash points. However, the forces for integration and co-operation are also very strong, and are further energized by the pragmatic attitude of the leadership, which recognizes that true progress can only be achieved through intra-regional co-operation. The major trends within the region are toward international accommodation, although the conditions within many nations have not been characterized by political stability, and internal turmoil has often been the norm. The movement towards regional integration has been slow but steady (e.g. Chia & Pecotich 1988; Pecotich & Chia 1992), and proposals for groupings have been relatively frequent. For these reasons, the terminology and acronyms have been numerous and confusing.

The choice we have made is based on the broad grouping of countries that are not only in relatively close geographic proximity, but whose economic and marketing futures are also inextricably intertwined. ESEA, therefore, comprises the economically developed nations of Japan, Australia and New Zealand (countries whose futures will increasingly coincide with that of Asia); the NICs such as the Republic of Korea (South Korea), Taiwan and Hong Kong; the states of ASEAN (Indonesia, the Philippines, Thailand, Malaysia, Singapore, Brunei and Vietnam, and the "observer" cum-participant nations, Cambodia, Laos and Myanmar); the evolving socialist economies of the region, the People's Republic of China, Cambodia, Laos, Vietnam, Myanmar, and the Democratic Republic of Korea (North Korea); and the newly developing nation Papua New Guinea. The order of presentation of the chapters could have been based on various criteria such as political systems (e.g. democratic vs centrally planned vs dictatorial), the level of economic development (developed vs developing) or immediate geographic proximity (e.g. Indochina: Vietnam, Cambodia and Laos). Again, readers will note nations fall into multiple categories. We decided to avoid classification difficulties by presenting the states in alphabetical order. This method provides an objective, unambiguous, non-overlapping classification scheme that should be non-controversial. The reader may then, in conjunction with this introduction, read and/or discuss the states in whatever sequence is most suitable for his or her objectives.

This text contains many statistics that are used to support its assertions and enumerate trends. Before discussing these figures, it is necessary to provide a cautionary and exculpatory note. While statistical data even in highly developed nations suffer from inaccuracies and inconsistencies, in the ESEA region there are major problems. Even when data exist, they may be unavailable, outdated, and sometimes distorted or deliberately misreported for political purposes. Statistics will vary according to the source and the compilers' definitions and assumptions. So, for example, in the case of Cambodia the population figures are literally anyone's best guess (see Table A.1); in the case of Indonesia, GNP will vary according to whether East Timor is included or not: it *is* included in Table A.1. These inconsistencies help to illustrate the nature of the problem: ESEA is a complex and multifaceted entity comprised of numerous forces that affect the accuracy of many measures. While this reality can be disconcerting for scholars and practitioners who need accurate data, the inconsistencies should not be allowed to cloud the overall statistical picture, whose power is sufficiently strong to overcome modest variances among indicators presented throughout the text.

The conceptual basis for the discussion to follow is shown as Figure A.1, "Interactive systems affecting ESEA progress" (cf. Shultz & Pecotich 1997). The figure consists of a network of elements in constant interaction. Each of these elements in turn has three aspects that are critical for its influence on

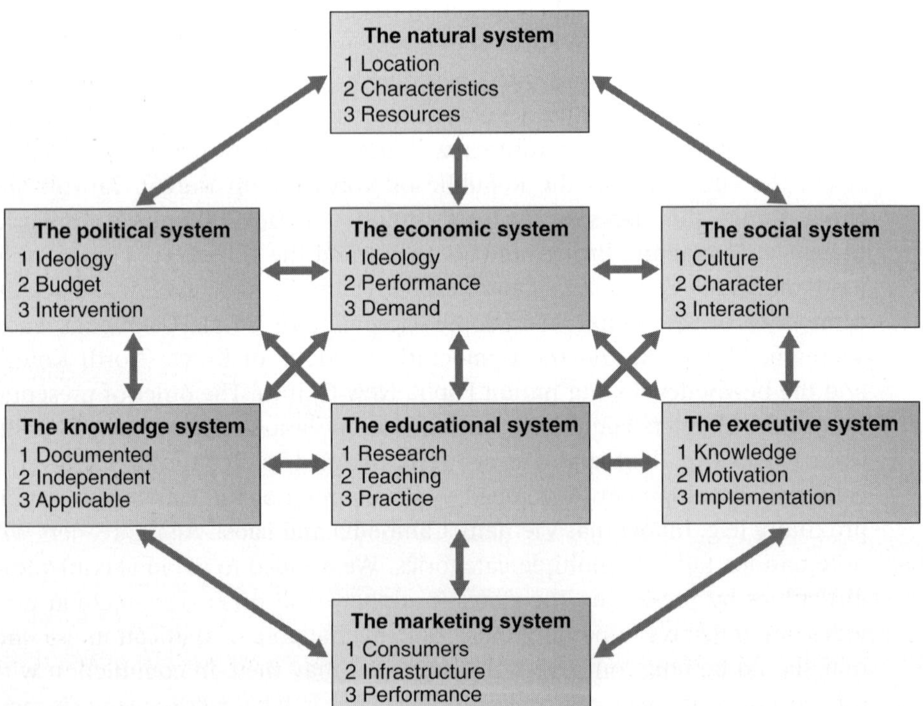

Fig. A.1 Interactive systems affecting ESEA progress

The system is totally interactive, and for reasons of clarity not all arrows are shown.

Table A.1 Basic demographic statistics for East and South-East Asian countries

Country	*Population estimates (million)*			*Annual population increase (%) 1994*	*Doubling time at current growth rate (years)*	*GNP per head (US$) (1992)*	*Exchange rates (March 1998) $1US=*
	1994	*1996*	*2010*				
Australia	17.8	18.3	20.9	0.8	85	17 070	A$1.50
Brunei	0.3	0.3	0.4	2.6	27	–*	B$1.60
Cambodia	10.3	10.9	13.0	2.9	24	200	Riel 3590
China	1 192.0	1 217.6	1 397.8	1.1	61	380	Yuan 8.28
Hong Kong	5.8	6.4	6.3	0.7	99	15 380	HK$7.74
Indonesia	199.7	201.4	238.8	1.6	43	670	Rupiah 10700
Japan	124.8	125.8	130.4	0.3	267	28 220	Yen 128.3
Korea North	23.1	23.9	28.5	1.9	37	–*	–*
Korea South	44.6	45.3	51.7	1.0	67	6 790	Won 1 629
Laos	4.7	5.0	7.2	2.9	24	250	Kip 1 138
Malaysia	19.5	20.6	26.0	2.3	30	2 790	Ringgit 4.04
Myanmar	45.4	46.0	57.7	1.9	36	–*	Kyat 6.35
New Zealand	3.5	3.6	3.9	0.9	76	12 060	NZ$1.73
Papua New Guinea	4.0	4.3	5.7	2.3	30	950	Kina 1.8
Philippines	68.7	72.0	85.5	2.4	29	770	Peso 40.13
Singapore	2.9	3.0	3.2	1.2	56	15 750	S$1.65
Taiwan	21.1	21.4	23.8	1.0	68	–*	NT$32.22
Thailand	59.4	60.7	69.2	1.4	50	1 840	Baht 44.95
Vietnam	73.1	76.6	91.7	2.3	30	–*	Dong 12 978
Total	**1 920.6**	**1 963.1**	**2 262.2**				

Note:
* not available

Source: Extracted from *Asia Pacific Marketing & Media Yearbook* (1997), NTC Publications Ltd, Henley-on-Thames; Michael Williams (1997), "Population in Asia and the Pacific", *The Far East and Australasia*, 28th edn, Europa Publications Ltd, London, pp. 3–14.

the social system. This model is dynamic, and is used here to illuminate and to introduce factors germane to individual chapter on individual country rather than to make a final and causal theoretical statement.[1]

Natural forces

The historical basis of national wealth has emanated from natural forces, the determining elements of which are *location, characteristics* and *resources*. The central location of ESEA within the patterns of world trade, as well as the region's vast resources, have incited intense competition and colonial exploitation. However, the individual nations vary in the characteristics and extent of their natural resources, which form important constraints affecting the economies, markets and consumers. Consider, for example, China's size, topography and arable-land-to-population ratio, which raise questions about this nation's ability to administer its economy and to feed its people. Singapore, on the other hand, is densely populated with virtually no natural resources, but due to location and an organized, hard-working population, is rapidly approaching the living standards of the highly developed nations.

Although the regional resources are plentiful and varied, centuries of exploitation and tremendous population pressures have inevitably led to degradation. The condition of the environment presents serious problems in most of the nations, and will affect their ability to enhance and to sustain life quality. Further economic progress will lead to greater stresses on air and water quality, traffic congestion, forest and fishery depletion, and soil erosion, thus creating a growth-preservation conundrum for these nations. This is one of the major challenges facing the region.

Political system

The second element is the political system, which, guided by its *ideological orientation* toward the correct nature of the values and structures of the society, will determine the *budget* or financial allocations to various uses, and will finally decide the extent of *intervention* in the system.

ESEA is a unique crucible of political processes and social change. Within its ambit may be found the extremes of the political spectrum, from the democratic (e.g. Australia and New Zealand) to the Stalinist authoritarian (e.g. the Democratic People's Republic of Korea, a.k.a. North Korea). In between, we finds various forms of government, some of which have vestiges of military rule (e.g. Indonesia, Thailand and the Republic of Korea, a.k.a. South Korea). Market socialism, market economics under the direction of single-party authoritarian rule (e.g. the Chinese Communist Party, Vietnamese Communist Party and the State Law and Order Restoration Council of Myanmar (SLORC)), is the new experiment in the region. Although in some cases the progress is slow and faltering, it is not a distortion to state that tolerance for personal freedoms is a trend in most parts of the region. The non-communist nations such as Thailand, South Korea and even Indonesia have moved in the direction of greater individual freedoms and liberties, and this, as institutions develop, suggests a more prosperous and peaceful future. The communist/socialist nations, between periods of repression, and motivated by the disintegration of Eastern Europe and the Soviet Union, are liberalizing their institutions and in turn enabling more personal freedoms. Japan provides an interesting departure from the other models. Despite continuous political instability at home, it has managed to progress without any apparent damage to its social harmony or economic interests.

Irrespective of the trend toward political systems that enable greater personal liberties, the unsettling condition of North Korea, for example, should not be overlooked, and further uncertainty within the region may cause problems that could have a negative effect on political reforms and, ultimately, market development. Nevertheless, the growing pragmatism of the political leadership throughout ESEA suggests that the trend toward liberalization will continue. If the process is managed and the various political transitions occur without open conflict, an auspicious future for the region is assured.

It would be a misrepresentation, however, not to state that the region contains some of the most repressive and closed regimes existing in the world today, and these are not simply those labelled "communist." Many of the citizens of ESEA find themselves living in political climates that are not conducive to dissent or the kind of "free" speech enjoyed by some of the more well-developed nations with longer democratic traditions. These same climates also affect the marketing and business environments. Government interference beyond the scope of agreed-upon conditions, corruption, bribery and unethical business practices generally still exist. However, as stated earlier, the movement is toward economic and political systems that are more conducive to expressions of personal liberty and stable business environments. We are reluctant to categorize these trends as "democratic" in the Western sense, but it seems inevitable that further development of economic structures and greater dependence on information technologies will lead to greater freedom of interaction and expression, as well as increased levels of trust within these societies.

Economic system

The economic system is the third element of the model. Again the nature and influence of this system is determined by three factors: (1) the *ideology*, which determines the nature, structure and operation of the system; (2) the *performance* of the system; and (3) the *demand* for the products within the system. The dominant theme in the region is best captured by a headline from *Asian Business* (1992): "The Road to Prosperity Leads to the Market." This headline was designed to describe the process as socialist countries in the region liberalized their economies in an effort to achieve prosperity while retaining power. However, the metaphor is more broadly applicable. Continuing political and economic reform are characteristic of the region as nations attempt to liberalize their economies. China, Vietnam, Cambodia,

Laos and Myanmar have, in different ways, sought to liberalize their economic systems and cautiously implemented reforms to move the nations toward the market system. China in particular has been transforming itself from a centrally planned economy into a form of decentralized market system. The moves have been hesitant and often accompanied with clampdowns on dissidents, but, despite detractors, economic progress has been made. This spread of economic liberalism, facilitated in part by the collapse of Eastern Europe, has brought these previously isolated nations into the world economy. Other countries, such as Indonesia, the Republic of Korea and Thailand, on whose governments the military retain a strong influence, have shown flexibility in both moving toward civilian government and liberalizing the economies.

Accompanying this general trend toward the market have been the related trends of privatization, deregulation, and trade and foreign-investment liberalization. Privatization and deregulation have increased the level of internal competition and placed considerable pressure on previously protected institutions such as telecommunications and energy suppliers. While the attitude to foreign investment is ambivalent in many parts of the world, the consistent economic growth in ESEA has been attained through policies to stimulate foreign investment. Entry of these nations with their 1.9 billion people into the international market-place has increased competitive pressure for global financial sources. Further, the rise of the vast economic power of the region is not only being fuelled by the big players such as Japan, China and Indonesia, with their exports to Europe and the USA, but from within Asia by the four "Tigers" (Hong Kong[2], Singapore, South Korea and Taiwan). Indeed, it appears that the time of region-based prosperity is fast approaching. ESEA nations are increasingly looking to their neighbors for sources of funds and, conversely, for good investment opportunities. Therefore, as they grow wealthy, they look to invest in their neighbors and so help them to move toward affluence. Although Japan's influence is well documented, newer capital exporters such as Singapore, Malaysia and Hong Kong have also emerged. The consistent high economic growth of these nations has resulted in an increase in their capacity to exert an influence both within ESEA and externally. At the present time about half of Asian exports are to other nations within the region. For example, Japan's share of exports to the US has dropped from 40% to less than 33% in ten years, because of intensified investment in ESEA. Hong Kong's wealth has influenced the prosperity of the nearby Guangdong province, Taiwan is the biggest investor in Malaysia and Australia the second biggest investor in Indonesia (Leger 1995).

This welcoming attitude to foreign investment, accompanied by a continuing deregulation of trade, has resulted in a high degree of interdependence amongst the economies of the region. Intra-regional imports as well as exports were over 60% in 1992, and are growing at a rate of 8.1% per year (Forbes 1997). This intra-regional interdependence is being increased by the pragmatic, innovative search for new ventures that contribute to the prosperity and security of the region. Consider, for example, the recent Singaporean push for a growth triangle and the formation of localized trilateral links. There is also a general recognition for the need to form strategic alliances and other types of partnerships in an effort to gain a technological edge. In conjunction with this trend is the exhortation that executives must look at the market as both region and country specific. There is already considerable posturing and competition for the location of the region's center, both internationally and within nations.

Concern has been expressed, however, that trade barriers may be coming down much faster than desired or expected. AFTA (ASEAN Free Trade Area) is in the process of "reducing its trade liberalization period from 15 to 10 years and Asia Pacific Economic Cooperation forum (APEC) intends to abolish all trade barriers by 2010 for industrialized countries and 2020 for all others" (*Asian Business* 1995, p. 24).

Domestic political realities may even curb this general trend, and the progress toward the free trade goals may be uneven, but it seems unlikely that it will be permanently reversed. Indeed, these domestic perceptions of internal and external conditions will largely determine the pace of change. For example, the apparent desynchronization of world economic cycles (ESEA has been booming despite a mercurial Japanese economy, while Europe always seems to be on the cusp of slipping into recession) has made many of the ESEA nations more self-reliant and confident in themselves. In many respects these nations now see themselves as proactive forces for economic change and development.

The implications for the worldwide delocalization of industrial production have also precipitated another area for concern. On the positive side, countries that were previously condemned to simple, labor-intensive manufacturing are now able to produce cost-effective and sophisticated high-tech products. Malaysia, for example, has become the world's leading producer of semi-conductors, and now discourages labor-intensive industries (Schwab & Smadja 1994), thus making the leap to high-tech, high-productivity, high-quality industries and high wages for its citizens. On the negative side, countries that have made the strategic choice to rely on cheap labor as a competitive advantage will likely be forced to rethink and to revise their strategy. The labor-cost edge may be retained, in the short term and in relation to some external competition such as the USA and Europe, but it is not a viable foundation for a sound future within the ESEA region, where the flexible corporation may move from Taiwan to China to Vietnam and so on. Further, in some of the countries of the region labor-cost advantages seems to vanish in the face of realities (e.g. poor infrastructure, local bureaucracy and "voluntary payments") that accompany daily business operations. Nonetheless, the persistent growth, the size of the population and the inevitable increase of wealth will have a strong impact on the demand for products and services.

Social system

Fourth is the social system, which consists of *culture, character,* and *interaction.* Culture determines the most general, enduring set of values within the community. The community may, for example, place a great value on business acumen and education, or it may not; it may value conspicuous consumption and wealth accumulation, or it may not. Character refers to the characteristics of the society, for example, the demographic structure. Interaction is used here as a term to indicate the extent to which the society is open or closed; that is, whether freedom of interaction is afforded to members of society.

The following chapters will demonstrate to readers the vast diversity of ESEA. And while some countries (e.g. Korea) are more ethnically homogenous than others within all the nations there exist important differences in, for example, culture, language, and religion, which preclude a simple enumeration (see, e.g., Parrinder 1995). As suggested earlier, some of the differences are the sources of animosities that have deep historical roots, and that may be difficult to overcome. These differences present challenges to further progress of not only the region, but some of the nations themselves. It is possible that hostilities based on cultural differences and national aspirations could erupt (e.g. Indonesia and the problem of East Timor). However, it is equally true that a visible degree of cultural harmony and accommodation exists among some of the nations in the region (e.g. Singapore and Malaysia), at least on the surface. Further, the pragmatism, and the positive cultural attitudes to business and education, of some of the cultural groupings suggests that a slow evolution toward cultural reconciliation may be possible. The existence of immigrant groups (e.g. the overseas Chinese) may serve not only, in the economic sense, as a source of investment, but more importantly as a cultural bridge between nations. The desire to minimize the potential for religious conflict (e.g. the high degree of religious tolerance in Australia, New Zealand, and Singapore) is another positive manifestation.

Concerning the "character" of the region, there are broad overarching regional tendencies that need to be mentioned. There is little doubt that the size, density and growth rates of many ESEA nations make them of critical importance to the world. The region may–depending upon which nations are included–contain as much as 60% of the world's population while occupying only about 30% of the total area (23%, if Australia and New Zealand are excluded). The region contains the world's most populous country (China, with 1.2 billion people) and 7 other nations with populations greater than 40 million people (South Korea 44.6, Myanmar 45.4, Thailand 59.4, Philippines 68.7, Vietnam 73.1, Japan 124.8 and Indonesia 199.7; see Table A.1). The average annual population increase varies from 0.3% (Japan) to 2.9% (Cambodia and Laos). Although this latter rate may not seem excessive when compared to the 0.38% of Europe, a stark contrast becomes evident, especially when the enormous population base of ESEA is considered.

Although the region contains some of the world's poorest nations (Cambodia, Laos, Myanmar and Vietnam), also included are several of the world's fastest growing and most powerful economies (China, Hong Kong[3], Japan, Korea, Singapore and Taiwan). Hong Kong and Singapore are of particular interest to scholars because their progress may illustrate the importance of trade for overcoming the problems of population density. The population of the region is predominantly rural (Australia, Hong Kong, Japan, Singapore and New Zealand are notable exceptions), and there has been a rapid rural–urban drift that strains infrastructure and often leads to a disenfranchized, poor underclass.

Other important demographic developments include the emergence of sex and age as determinants of future growth. Women are increasingly likely to be factors in the workforce, and women's issues generally are likely to become influential when making policy. Regarding age, although the proportion of those over the age of 65 is increasing (particularly in Japan and Singapore), the "youth group" (i.e. those from 15 to 24 years of age) is also larger than in other parts of the world, hence ESEA overall is younger than other parts of the world. More than half of the people are under 25, compared to the USA and Europe, where the proportion is about one third and one quarter, respectively, so the demographic base for further economic growth also exists. Regional forces that typically affect population changes include migration patterns, fertility rates, and mortality and life expectancy rates. All are changing, and will have an impact on the development of ESEA.

Other problems that remain to be resolved include the movement of "guest" workers and refugees. Rising, balanced prosperity for the region may provide the solution to both of these problems.

Knowledge system

The knowledge system is the fifth element enumerated in Figure A.1. The three components of this system are: the *extent* to which knowledge is well *documented*—that is, the degree to which knowledge in written form, as well as the technological facilities that serve as conduits to knowledge, are readily available; the degree to which it is *independent* (i.e. how it can be relied upon to be objective and free of *ideological* influence); and finally the degree to which guidelines for application (*applicability*) may be distilled from the knowledge base. It is this system, and the three systems to follow—the education, executive and marketing systems—that present some of the greatest challenges for ESEA. The leadership of the region has recognized that the passing on of "concentrated experience" in the form of recorded knowledge is critical to progress. It is becoming clear that intra-regional investment needs will have to be accompanied by the development of an intra-regional knowledge base. Indeed, it is the purpose of this text to contribute toward this development.

Education system

The education system, presented as element six, consists of *teaching, research* and *practice*. The "practice" component is emphasized because marketing is an applied discipline; a test of the applicability or relevance of "knowledge" is the extent to which research findings are useful and information is taught/learned. Education is also a major challenge facing the region because the present growth has not been based on co-ordinated and integrated intra-regional educational foundations. Education mimicry has tended to be the norm whereby, as often as not, "European models" have been adopted. Some countries—Australia, Hong Kong, Singapore and New Zealand—have used their existing systems to provide the education base for others in the region. In some instances overseas education, whether in the better developed regional institutions or in Europe and North America, has been encouraged. Greater economic development and the concomitant need for highly skilled workers will require even greater emphasis on and resource allocation for education, and the ESEA governments face some critical decisions in this area.

Executive system

This leads to the seventh component of the system, which has been labeled the "executive system." Essentially, this refers to the professional practice of marketing. Professionalism depends on the *knowledge* level of the executive population, their *motivation*, and the extent to which they actually *implement* modern marketing practices. In many respects, the rapid growth in the region is testimony to an adequate understanding of marketing practice. The individual chapters provide ample intra-nation evidence of the progress that has been made. There is little doubt that the regional orientation is toward the attainment of greater professionalism in this area.

Marketing system

The final component is the marketing system. This component is shown to consist of the *consumers*, the *infrastructure* and *performance*. The region possesses some of the most well developed marketing systems in the world—and some of the least well developed. As stated above, the growth of ESEA occurred largely because of foreign investment, cheap labor and export development. Now the region is beginning to see itself as its own market, regionally independent and self-sustaining. This inward or regional focus is partly explained by a substantial consumer base that already exists; when larger numbers of consumers join the middle classes, the ESEA market may dwarf all others. Purchase patterns and consumption practises throughout ESEA suggest that this transformation is occurring much more rapidly than many observers thought was possible.

If this potential is to be achieved fully, the infrastructure needs are enormous. Further, and perhaps most importantly, the related specific developments *vis-à-vis* the marketing mix are critical: without a keen understanding of consumer needs and wants, and the market contexts in which marketers must introduce, promote, distribute, price and support products, marketing efforts are destined to fail. Therefore, transregional development will have to include a keen awareness of specific markets and consumers, and a mastery of marketing skills. Moreover, to attain acceptable and sustainable levels of marketing performance, environmental concerns (e.g. the need for clean technology and the protection of forests and fisheries), national and regional interests will have to be balanced. The administrative and organizational challenges are immense, and could, without resolution, destroy the potential of ESEA.

Analysis of countries

Each chapter gives an overview of marketing and consumer developments for a specific country. Many of the analyses are first attempts to examine phenomena from marketing and consumer-behavior perspectives. Furthermore, each chapter has been written by a recognized expert and/or an indigenous scholar from the country of focus. Contributors have attempted to present a balanced and focused view of the trends in each nation, while keeping a regional perspective.

To assure some uniformity among chapters, throughout the review process authors were encouraged to follow rough guidelines when organizing their manuscripts. More specifically, authors were encouraged, first, to describe environmental or exogenous variables such as those discussed in Fig. A.1 (e.g. political, economic and social forces and systems), and to indicate their implications for marketing. Second, authors were instructed to analyze ensuing changes in consumer developments and behavior. Third, authors were encouraged to describe developments in the macromarketing mix—that is, the aggregate trends in products, brands, services, prices, distribution and promotion (cf. Leeflang & van Raaij 1993, p. 345). Authors were then requested to discuss future trends and expectations, as well as to recommend guidelines for marketing management into the next millennium.

We hasten to add, however, that authors also were encouraged to accentuate arcane issues and factors that profoundly affect, and will continue to affect, marketing and consumers in their respective countries of analysis. It would be inappropriate, for example, to use precisely the same template of analysis for both Japan and Cambodia. Each chapter provides material most relevant to current and future marketing and consumer issues. Consequently, some chapters (e.g. those on Cambodia and Laos) have proportionately larger amounts of text that address political forces and the resultant emergence of fledgling marketing institutions. Other chapters (e.g. those on Singapore and Japan), which provide analyses of more "predictable" and economically developed countries with extensive databases that provide specific insights into marketing and consumer trends, focus more directly on specific and traditional marketing and consumer issues. Some chapters were handicapped by the absence of sound information concerning consumer behavior and marketing in the nation concerned.

In summary, we believe that this text will provide readers with an introduction to the most compelling marketing and consumer issues in ESEA, today and in the foreseeable future.

Australia

The first chapter presents Janet McColl-Kennedy's extensive evaluation of Australian consumer behavior, in terms of the present situation, trends and future possibilities. It is perhaps appropriate that Australia is listed first in this book, because, with New Zealand, it is the most southerly of the ESEA nations, and is in some respects a fringe member of the region. Australia, "the Southern Tiger," is endowed with natural resources, a small population and a well-developed infrastructure. It has a Western democratic tradition that provides a stable political environment with well-established, peaceful transitory processes. The nation's down-to-earth, deeply ingrained egalitarianism, with its associated freedom of speech, is sometimes difficult for Australia's near neighbors in the north to comprehend. Nonetheless, Australia is genuinely interested not only in being a member of the region, but also in contributing constructively to the progress of its neighbors, which it has done historically. McColl-Kennedy's evaluation of economic indicators suggests that, after a period of difficulty, the Australian consumer may be gaining confidence, and that the economy may be moving forward again. The demographic and cultural make-up of the nation suggest there are changes to come in both the structure and content, changes that may have long-term implications for marketing practitioners.

Brunei

In describing the consumer characteristics of Negara Brunei Darussalam, Sara Douglas provides an introduction to a small but exceptional state that is undergoing controlled change as its government seeks to ensure a prosperous future. A monarchy founded on Islam, Brunei is nonetheless a modern, oil-rich welfare state with an orientation that is both contemporary and directed toward the future. While some may question the entrepreneurial spirit of its citizens, it is well located for taking advantage of the development in the region. As a nation, it seems to be teetering on the brink of a major transformation. Its global presence is becoming more visible, as is its participation in ASEAN. Domestically, it seems to be moving cautiously toward greater democratization and economic diversification. Brunei is another ESEA nation that, within its unique context, is seeking a formula for a transition into a viable future, and as such it should not be overlooked by the marketing community.

Cambodia

In Chapter 3, Clifford Shultz and Naranhkiri Tith describe Cambodia's horrific past, and the present conditions that are affecting the country's struggle to rise from the ashes of genocide and profound economic mismanagement. The instability of Cambodia has caused many managers and investors to overlook the country as a market opportunity. Tith and Shultz contend that, despite the atrocities of the killing fields and on-going political discord and instability, newly implemented policies may lead to a brighter future. Government reform, substantial foreign investment and consumer responses to market economics are helping to transform this war-torn nation into a viable market. Cambodian consumers remain hopeful their country will continue to progress, but internal discord and some cynical investment practices suggest that long-term prognoses are not entirely optimistic. Nevertheless, the authors indicate that Cambodia, despite significant risks, is a strategically located and promising market of almost 10 million consumers who are receptive to many goods and services.

China

Owing to its importance and size China has been allocated two chapters (in effect four, given the chapters on Hong Kong and Taiwan). Lauren Swanson, and Pia Polsa and Bai Chang Hong provide two contrasting and overlapping overviews of the consumer evolution in the world's most populous nation and, potentially, largest economy. Their reasoned arguments suggest that China, after about 5000 years of history, has entered another period of social and economic change. The direction of the change appears to be toward the market system, democratization and liberalization. The pace of the transformation may not be quick or consistent enough for some outside observers; however, there is no doubt that the economic reforms of 1978 have brought continuous growth of GDP, and that China is one of the fastest growing countries in the world. As is to be expected, the consumer markets have also shown immense expansion. The accompanying social movements (e.g. from the country to the city) and other changes present both a major challenge and opportunity both for China and the region. The management of the transformation will require consummate skills, but, whatever the final outcome, there is little doubt that events in China will have a major influence on the shape of the future in the region. These two incisive chapters provide a basis for an understanding of the marketing and consumer trends in this potentially world-dominating market.

Hong Kong

In Chapter 6, Mark Speece and Stella So discuss the present and the future of one of the last bastions of British colonialism that has returned to Chinese control. Despite some pessimism, and the uncertainty concerning the long-term future, the inevitable take-over by China has taken place, and the people of Hong Kong have to continue to operate within the new constraints. Hong Kong, as China's door to the West, has benefited from being at the interface. In particular, the consumers, with ever-increasing incomes and purchasing power, have become imbued with materialistic values. It is unlikely that this will change under Chinese rule in the short term. It is, however, equally unlikely that Hong Kong will again see the high growth rates characteristic of the 1970s and the 1980s, although this may still be a possibility. Its unique position as a gateway to China may be diluted; however, observers should not be too seduced by the pessimistic view. Hong Kong is a treasury of business and marketing knowledge that the pragmatic Chinese leadership will not disregard. It is a realistic possibility that the two partners will coalesce in a reciprocal relationship that will benefit all of their people. As Speece and So state, in their chapter, Hong Kong will "remain China's most important warehouse and distribution center, port, and financial center, and there is no doubt that it will retain an important role into the foreseeable future."

Indonesia

Lawrence H. Wortzel and Ignas G. Sidik, in their chapter titled "Indonesia: An emerging market with great potential," provide a picture of the marketing situation in another giant undergoing transformation. Indonesia, one of the largest and most populous nations in ESEA, has made a transition from a poor less-developed country to an NIC. Accompanying this change has been the usual rural-to-urban drift, increasing purchasing power and the rise of a new middle class. The government has also attempted to initiate movements of population by providing incentives for resettlement from the highly dense island of Java to less populated areas. The projected increase in working-age population means that it is necessary for growth to continue. All of this makes for a vibrant, dynamic environment with considerable potential. However, the road to true prosperity, although now open, is still long, and many problems will have to be overcome if this destination is to be attained.

In particular, considerable investment will be necessary in marketing education and infrastructure. Nonetheless, Wortzel and Sidik present an optimistic portrait of a nation moving forward to take a place on the world stage that is commensurate with its size.

Japan

Tsutomu Okahashi, N. Clay Gary and Stephen Cornish-Ward in the title of their chapter on Japan use the evocative phrase "high noon for the rising sun." The phrase is appropriate both symbolically and metaphorically. Japan has risen from the ashes of the Second World War to become a dominant economic power. However, it seems that, with the recent recession, the sun has paused in its rising; whether this pause is temporary or not is yet to be determined. The suggestion by the authors is that Japan is undergoing a shift from a production-oriented fast growth to a "slow-growth consumption-led mature economy." This change has confused the Japanese consumer and eroded confidence. The occurrence of the recession, which has come to end a period of unprecedented growth and cultural change, has accentuated this confusion. While it is clear that Japan is facing a period of turbulence, the authors conclude that "there are no grounds for arguing that Japan's economic prosperity is over." The major trends of liberalization and internationalization that are also evident in Japan suggest that the nation will become more accessible to regional market entry, and so perhaps increase the level of integration. The authors of this chapter have provided a highly original treatment that will challenge some of the conceptions of the nature of consumer behavior in Japan. Both the tyro and the expert on Japan will find something of value in this chapter.

Korea

According to James W. Gentry, Sunkyu Jun, Gyungtai Ko and HeeSuk Kang, Korea is an enigma not only because of its long history of isolationism but also on account of the stark contrast in the economic developments of its two constituent parts (North and South). Although culturally among the most homogenous nations in the region, both Koreas have undergone radical changes. The communist North, while pursuing its socialist goals, has become one of the most isolated, underdeveloped nations in the world. The South, in contrast, despite political problems and limits on foreign control, has in the last decade shown remarkable economic progress. While the reunification is presented as almost inevitable, its achievement will not be easy and if it occurs it will herald profound changes. The strong desire to retain cultural identity and traditions may be a delaying factor in future economic development. This chapter provides a rich source of information on these and other consumer-behavior trends in the Koreas.

Laos

William Ardrey, Clifford Shultz, and Phonesavanh Chanthivaly contend that Laos' strategic location, natural wealth and emerging consumer culture make it an opportune market as well as an integral link to regional welfare and development. However, because Laos is landlocked, has a large land-to-population ratio and is a relatively small market of less than 5 million consumers, it is often the "forgotten" country of ESEA. Furthermore, the government and consumers are adjusting to the New Economic Mechanism–Laos' implementation of market socialism–and policies designed to maintain cultural and economic sovereignty in response to the influences of its larger neighbors (e.g. Thailand, China, and Vietnam). Hence, successful marketing in Laos is not without challenges. Laos, however, has a tenable market in Vientiane, and other communities along the Mekong are easily accessible. It is located in the heart of the "Golden Quadrangle," and so is vital to many transportation and distribution networks of the greater Mekong subregion; it must therefore be included as part of regional strategy.

Malaysia

Aliah Salleh, Bianca Teo and Anthony Pecotich conclude their evaluation of Malaysia's marketing practices and consumer behavior by suggesting that, despite the financial crisis of 1997, there exists within the nation a great optimism, and that the feeling of national unity has never been stronger. This optimism seems well founded, for, after 7 years of growth above 8%, the nation has ample reason for confidence. Its economic successes have been hailed in both the national and international press. In the cultural context, the ethnic groups while still seeking to maintain their unique traditions, appear to have a strong desire for harmonious co-existence that can only lead to greater cultural understanding. However, prosperity is bringing cultural change and a new kind of consumer, and is presenting the nation with major problems. To take full advantage of economic progress, a nation must develop an infrastructure and a trained workforce that will animate and direct future growth. In this, Malaysia faces its biggest challenge, and is in some respects at the crossroads. It may continue with uncontrolled growth and face the resultant chaos, traffic jams, pollution and environmental devastation, or recognize that the future does not have to imitate the worst excesses of the west, and proceed to invest in infrastructure and people. As the authors of this chapter demonstrate, there is evidence to suggest that Malaysia is already addressing these problems. Those interested in understanding the developments of this culturally rich and economically rapidly developing nation will find this chapter indispensable.

Myanmar

In Chapter 12, May Lwin and Anthony Pecotich provide an overview of Myanmar, another of the ESEA nations moving with hope from a problematical past to a better future. Despite continuing political problems and trade embargoes, few would disagree that Myanmar is potentially a very promising and exciting market. While the West has been negative about Myanmar's efforts to join the world trading community, its ESEA neighbors, taking a more long-term view, have been encouraging. In particular, the members of ASEAN have taken a pragmatic, welcoming posture toward the nation. The government of Myanmar itself has given a strong indication that it intends to join the emerging developing economies in South-East Asia by emphasizing market reform as it moves its economy into a transitional phase. The nation is undergoing radical changes, and, as one of the region's richest and least exploited countries, must have a promising future.

New Zealand

An evolutionary appraisal of the consumer behavior in New Zealand, once known as "the England of the south," is provided by Roger Marshall, Christina Kwai-Choi Lee and Kim Marshall. This most southerly of the nations covered in this text has undergone startling economic and social change as necessity forced it to de-emphasize economic links with England and Europe, and focus its attention on ESEA. Culturally European (particularly Anglo-Saxon) in orientation, New Zealand has undergone restructuring not only in the much vaunted economic sense, but also in its internal and external relationships, social attitudes and institutions. Internally, the increase of influence of the minorities (Maori) and Asian immigration is leading to the formation of a more worldly society. This internal change has been reinforced by the necessity of turning to and understanding ESEA, with its cultural richness and variety. Marshall, Lee and Marshall provide a current, up-to-date enumeration of the forces operating in this small but intrinsically interesting market.

Papua New Guinea

Gabriel Ogunmokun provides a pioneering description of marketing and consumer behavior in Papua New Guinea, a nation that, while being on the fringes of the region, can nonetheless benefit from regional interaction. Its unexploited resources and relatively stable political structure mark it as a market of future potential. To take full advantage of regional synergy, Papua will have to develop its infrastructure and institutions. However, the demand for capital by other, more "attractive" parts of ESEA may reduce the availability of this important resource. Nevertheless, with vision there is little doubt that Papua can join in the general economic development of the region.

The Philippines

In Chapter 15, Bianca Teo, Anthony Pecotich and Albert F. Celoza refer to the Philippines as "Asia's next tiger." Perhaps a more apt description is "Asia's democratic tiger," to emphasize not only economic progress, but also the positive political basis for that progression. The Philippines has emerged from colonialism and political turmoil and is showing signs of long-promised economic expansion. The most recent economic figures offer hope, and it appears that the nation is transforming itself from "one of the world's problem areas" to a growing ordered democratic state with considerable promise for potential investors.

Singapore

Jochen Wirtz, in his chapter titled "Singapore: An analysis of changes in the marketing environment and their implications for marketing management," characterizes the nation as a progressive, "wealthy society with good future prospects." Singapore's economic progress has been unmatched in the region. The small island nation, with virtually no natural resources but with a central location, political stability, good management and a resourceful people, has advanced to becoming the new vanguard of economic development in the region. Wirtz suggests that a major reason for the progress may be attributed to the pragmatic orientation of the dominant ethnic group, the Chinese, with their strong commitment to education, discipline and industriousness. Singapore is a small market that, despite the ageing of its population, will continue to grow, although perhaps at a slower rate. Wirtz's evaluation of the consumer and marketing trends provides an excellent resource for practitioners and academics in the region.

Taiwan

Taiwan, which could be labelled "the fractious Tiger," is another ESEA nation whose progress in the last decades has been unprecedented. Y. Edwin Tang and Jeanne Liu, in their accomplished treatment of the changing market and consumer behavior of this nation, provide a sound basis for an understanding of both the present position and possible future directions. From their evaluation it becomes clear that, if political problems can be overcome, Taiwan's position as a part of greater China (a coming superpower) will assure its progress well into the 21st century. Indeed, it is expected that Taiwan, with its large foreign reserves, will play a major part in regional growth. However, this optimistic assessment of possibilities in relation to the external environment should not be allowed to obscure the existence of internal problems and challenges that go beyond the simply political. At least in part the existence of the large foreign reserves can be attributed to the lack of investment in internal infrastructure and social development. The time is rapidly approaching when Taiwan will have to address internal conditions before the forces of cultural and social change, and consumer demand, restrain future progress. This chapter should assist both those seeking an understanding of the nation for marketing purposes and Taiwanese scholars and policy makers interested in the progress of their nation.

Thailand

The emergence of Thailand as an important ESEA market serves as a point of departure for the chapter titled "Consumer behavior and marketing in Thailand" by Nittaya Wongtada, Orose Leelakulthanit and Anusorn Singhapakdi. In a very thorough, informative chapter, these authors present a cogent picture of a dynamic nation in the throes of almost uncontrolled change. They point out that, although economic progress has been made, it has produced serious problems. Despite the cultural self-confidence of the Thais concerning their resilience and capacity to absorb and cope with change, the challenges emanating from pollution, poor infrastructure and the AIDS epidemic provide very ominous threats to the fabric of their society. The authors, however, present a future scenario based on the expectation that prudent marketing management may contribute positively to the evolution of an organized and progressive society.

Vietnam

Once a country that conjured images of war and destruction, Vietnam, with its abundant natural resources, over 75 million consumers, and shift towards a market economy has become a progressive force among the communist states of ESEA. Clifford Shultz, Nguyen Xuan Que, Anthony Pecotich and William Ardrey provide an overview of the historical events that led to the transformation, and the emergence of one of the most compelling markets in the region. The authors also assess the current marketing and consumer trends and portray a country whose consumers have embraced the market economy. For all the changes, however, including foreign investment, the proliferation of goods and retail outlets, and the explosion of consumer culture, Vietnam remains a relatively difficult country in which to be successful on a large scale. In this sense the authors refer to Vietnam as a country full of promise, but with changing laws and practices that confuse investors and render difficult the process of successful market penetration. Despite the difficulties, the authors conclude that visionary marketers who understand the commercial, political and legal idiosyncrasies of this market and invest for the long term stand to prosper in Vietnam.

Conclusion

Despite our initial reference to a "rollercoaster," our approach to the nations and the region has been both positive and optimistic. The reader has no doubt detected, even in the cautionary exculpations, a strong belief that the region has a bright future and will weather the storms, to become a major force on the world stage. Nonetheless, recent events have led Malkiel and Mei (1997, p. A6) to emphasize the negative as follows:

> Many who heralded the Asian miracle a year ago now suggest that it was an Asian Mirage. The four tigers that were so formidable only recently—Hong Kong, South Korea, Singapore, and Taiwan—may to varying degrees look like paper tigers today, while the so-called tiger cubs, notably Malaysia and Indonesia, look like kittens . . . Could Asian markets replay the Japanese market crash of 1990, with an initial decline followed by years of stagnation in economic activity and stocks? Are the Asian tigers dead?

While recognizing these possibilities, and the present financial and economic crisis notwithstanding, we, like Malkiel and Mei (1997), believe that economic strength and demographics will carry the region through. Further, while restructuring is essential and will cause some stress, the fundamental economic basics exist. The population is large and growing, the labor costs are low, and many entrepreneurial opportunities are still apparent. It is possible that the lack of processes and institutions for ordered political and economic change in some nations (e.g. Indonesia) could lead to instability and even bloodshed. Our hope is that the developing crises will be resolved, and that the nations in the region will take the necessary steps to continue the impetus to further prosperity. The individual nations in the region have no choice—the alternative is not acceptable to their peoples, or indeed the world (*Business Week* 1997) . It is inevitable that, as in all texts of this kind, events may overtake us and perhaps even prove us wrong. Nonetheless, the chapters should provide scholars and practitioners with an understanding of the underlying forces that affect marketing and consumer behavior in this rich, dynamic region.

References

Asia Pacific Marketing & Media Yearbook (1997), NTC Publications Ltd, Henley-on-Thames.

Asian Business (1992), "The Road to Prosperity Leads to the Market", April, pp. 18–23.

— (1995), "The Challenge of Change", January, pp. 20–4.

Business Week (1997), "Rescuing Asia", 17 November, pp. 4–6.

Chia, Hock Hwa & Pecotich, A. (1988), "Multinational Management and ASEAN Regional Development", *Asia Pacific Journal of Management,* vol. 6, no. 1, pp. 161–74.

Forbes, Dean (1997), "Towards the 'Pacific Century': Integration and Disintegration in the Pacific Basin", *The Far East and Australasia*, 28th edn, Europa Publications Ltd, London, pp. 24–38.

Leeflang, Peter & van Raaij, Fred (1993), "The Changing Consumer in The Netherlands", *International Journal of Research in Marketing*, vol. 10, pp. 345–63.

Leger, John M. (1995), "Rags to Riches", *Far Eastern Economic Review*, October 5, pp. 46–52.

Malkiel, Burton G. & Mei, J.P. (1997), "Why Asia's Tigers will Roar Again", *The New York Times*, December, p. A6.

Parrinder, Geoffrey (1997), "The Religions of Asia", *The Far East and Australasia*, 28th edn, Europa Publications Ltd, London, pp. 15–24.

Pecotich, A. & Chia Hock Hwa (1992), "The Role of Multinational Corporation Characteristics and Strategic Actions in the Development of ASEAN Regionalism", *Journal of Global Marketing*, 5(3), pp. 63–87.

Schwab, Klaus & Smadja, Claude (1994), "Power and Policy: The New Economic World Order", *Harvard Business Review*, November–December, pp. 40–50.

Shultz, C. & Pecotich, A. (1997), "Marketing and Development in the Transition Economies of Southeast Asia: Policy Explication, Assessment and Implications", *Journal of Public Policy & Marketing*, vol. 16, Spring, pp. 55–68.

Williams, Michael (1997), "Population in Asia and the Pacific", *The Far East and Australasia*, 28th edn, Europa Publications Ltd, London, pp. 3–14.

Notes

1 This model and the discussion of it in this chapter include excerpts from a more intricate model and discussion in Shultz & Pecotich (1997). Readers interested in more detailed analysis and elaboration, particularly in the context of transition economies, are encouraged to consult this publication.

2 Now a part of China.

3 Again, we will treat Hong Kong as a separate entity, even though it is now a part of China.

CHAPTER 1

Australia

Changing consumer behavior

JANET R. McCOLL-KENNEDY[1]

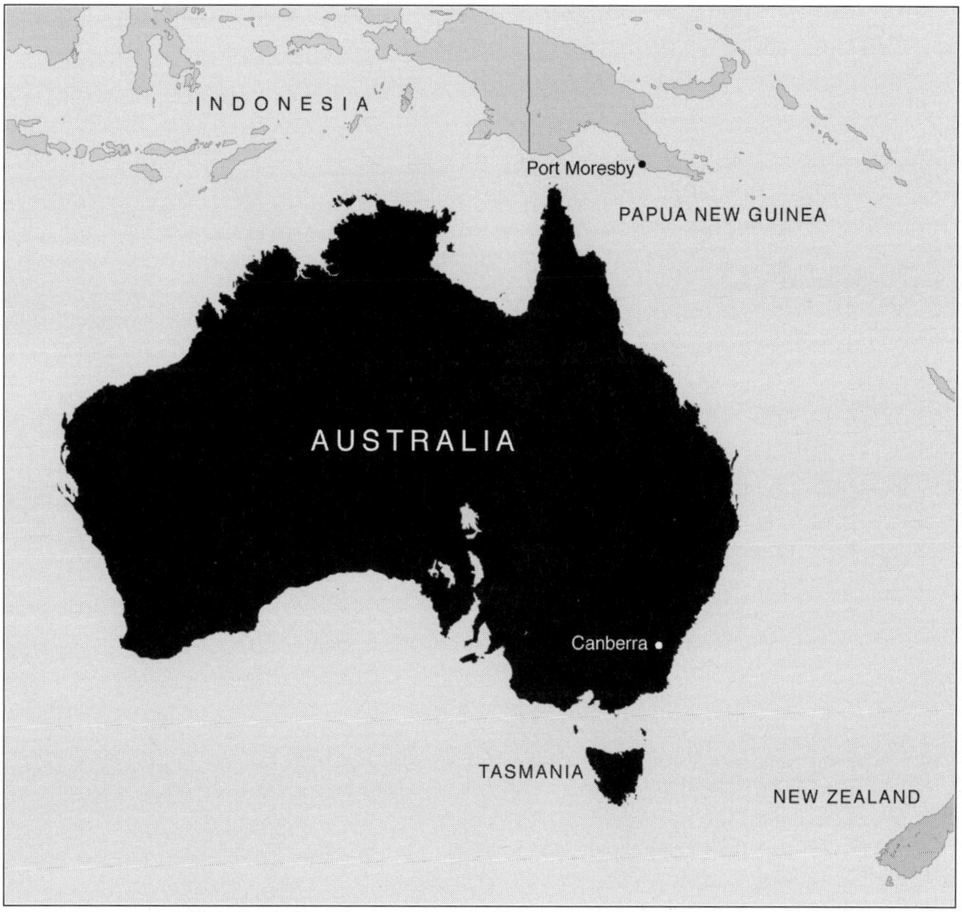

Abstract

After a brief historical introduction, an overview is presented of Australian consumer behavior–its present situation, trends and future possibilities. An evaluation of economic indicators suggests that, after a period of difficulty, the Australian consumer may be gaining confidence, and the economy may be on the way up again. The demographic and cultural make-up of the nation suggest changes in both the structure and content of the population, changes that may have long-term implications for marketing management.

Introduction

Overview

Australia–the "land down under"–is located in the South Pacific immediately south of Indonesia and north of Antarctica. In area, Australia is approximately equal to the USA (minus Alaska). However, its population is only around 18 million (McQueen 1995). The vast majority of Australians trace their origins to Europe, and the indigenous Aboriginal community represents only around 1.6% of the population.

This chapter provides an overview of consumer behavior in Australia in the 1990s. In doing so, it describes the trends in consumer behavior, together with their implications for marketing management.

However, before discussing consumer behavior per se, it is important to examine the historical development of Australia, as many of the trends evidenced today have their origins in the past. Following this introduction, the nature of the Australian economy is outlined, and changes noted for the period from 1971 to the present. In the next section, the demographic environment is discussed. Factors considered include:

- population size and growth
- population distribution (in terms of geography, gender and age)
- Aboriginal and Torres Strait Islander population
- household composition
- immigration

Further discussions center on the social structure, cultural factors and ongoing changes in consumer behavior are discussed, with the final section focusing on marketing implications.

Brief historical background

To understand consumer behavior in the 1990s, it is helpful to consider the historical development of Australia. European settlement began in 1788 with the establishment of a British penal colony. In 1840, the transportation of convicts was abolished in New South Wales. The bulk of the free white population consisted of skilled Protestant artisans from England and Scotland whose prime objective was material self-improvement (Hancock 1995). By the late 1800s, two distinct classes were emerging–the urban upper class and the highly unionized labor force.

During the great depression of the 1890s, unemployment rose as high as 30%, and living standards were lowered considerably. At this time the Labor government combined with middle-class liberals to develop political reforms. Thus the notion of Australia as the "working man's paradise" was born. A basic minimum wage was established to protect the working man and his family. National identity also became a major issue, so much so that the Commonwealth of Australia was formally established in 1901, uniting all the individual colonies into one Federation (Hancock 1995).

During this time the "White Australia" policy was introduced, restricting the right of settlement to Europeans. This white migration policy continued until the 1960s, when immigrants from the Middle East were admitted. In the 1970s, Asian migration commenced; Australia can therefore be regarded today as having a multicultural migration policy (Hancock 1995). Indeed, despite its detractors and the obvious imperfections of its systems, today's Australians can be proud of their democratic traditions, which include freedom of speech and a tolerant lifestyle. In many respects these can act as a model for the world at large.

Much has happened since the early days of settlement. But the interest of Australians in improving their lot has remained. This desire was particularly evident during the 1960s and 1970s when thousands migrated to Australia in search of their dreams. This quest for the "good life" culminated, for many, in the "time of excess" of the early 1980s. During this period there was relatively high inflation, and spending was up. The prevailing attitude was "spend and enjoy."

However, in the late 1980s the economy went into recession, and this recession still prevailed in the early 1990s.

Today, for many Australians, there remains a reluctance to over-spend, and a tendency to conserve and even recycle. The issues of the mid- to late 1990s are concern about the environment, maintaining personal relationships, obtaining value for money where goods and services are concerned, and getting back to basics—this includes a re-focus on the family and home. While all of these issues could be regarded as aspects of improving one's own lot in life, they do show signs of a greater interest in the non-material aspects. This is particularly so when we compare this attitude to that prevailing in the 1980s.

Economic factors

Introduction

In order to understand consumer behavior, it is useful to gain some understanding of the economy of the country—a number of economic factors either directly or indirectly influence consumer behavior. Among the more significant are the measures of a country's economic well-being, including gross domestic product, the level of inflation, employment rates, imports and exports, and the balance of payments.

This section outlines each of these factors in turn before providing a summary of the discussion.

Gross Domestic Product

There is no single measure of an economy's well-being. Rather, performance of an economy may be measured by a variety of factors. One commonly used measurement is growth in gross domestic product (GDP). Australian GDP per capita rose from AU$18 700[2] in 1982 to AU$21 000 in 1992. Although this represents an increase of AU$2300 (12.3%) over 10 years, the annual growth in GDP has been relatively low, with growth rates of generally under 5%.

There were two periods of negative growth during this 10-year period. The first occurred in 1982–1983 (GDP per capita decreased from AU$18 700 to AU$17 900 during this time), and the second in 1990–1992 (there was a decrease from AU$21 700 to AU$21 000 over 2 years) (ABS 1994b, p. 132).

Consumer Price Index

The Consumer Price Index (CPI) is "a general measure of the rate of change in prices paid by household consumers for the goods and services they buy" (ABS 1995b, p. 579). The CPI uses the unit of a "basket" of goods and services bought by Australian households. As prices vary, the total price of the basket of goods and services varies. The CPI is a record of this change in total price. It includes a range of goods and services from the following categories:

- Food (Dairy products, Cereal products, Meat and seafood, Fresh fruit and vegetables, Processed fruit and vegetables, Soft drinks, ice cream and confectionery, Meals out and take away foods, and Other food)
- Clothing (Men's and boys' clothing, Women's and girls' clothing, Fabrics and knitting wool, Footwear, and Dry cleaning and shoe repairs)
- Housing (Rents and Home ownership)
- Household equipment and operation (Fuel and light, Furniture and floor coverings, Appliances, Household textiles, Household utensils and tools, Household supplies and services, Postal and telephone services, and Consumer credit charges)
- Transportation (Private motoring and Urban transport fares)
- Tobacco and alcohol (Alcoholic drinks and Cigarettes and tobacco)
- Health and personal care (Health services, Personal care products, and Hairdressing services)
- Recreation and education (Books, newspapers and magazines, Recreational goods, Holiday travel and accommodation, Recreational services and Education and childcare) (ABS 1995b, p. 581)

Australia's CPI has stabilized in recent years; the figure for 1993–1994 was a 1.8% change over the previous year, whereas the change for 1989–1990—the recession period—was 8.0% (ABS 1995b).

Inflation

The rate of underlying inflation is often considered to be a better measure of a country's economic condition than GDP or CPI (ABS 1995b). This measure is an index defined by the Commonwealth Treasury, and is used extensively by economists. The rate is derived by excluding items from the CPI basket on the basis that changes in their respective prices are "highly volatile, exhibit marked seasonal patterns, or are largely affected by policy decisions" (ABS 1994c, p. 17). As such, this index seeks to measure price movements that are predominantly influenced by market forces. The following items are excluded:

- Meat and seafood
- Fresh fruit and vegetables
- Clothing
- Government-owned dwelling rents
- Mortgage interest charges
- Local government rates and charges
- Household fuel and light
- Postal and telephone services
- Consumer credit charges
- Automotive fuel
- Urban transport fares
- Tobacco and alcohol
- Health services
- Pharmaceuticals
- Holiday travel and accommodation
- Education and childcare

As shown in Table 1.1, the underlying rate of inflation has fluctuated over the past 20 years, from the relatively low figure of around 5.5% in 1972 to a high of 21.4% in 1975, and back down to a very low rate of around 2% in 1993 and 1994.

Employment

Participation and unemployment rates of workers are two more measures of economic well-being. As shown in Table 1.1, unemployment for both males and females has risen over the last 20 years from the very low rate of just around 1% in the early 1970s to around 10% in the 1990s. Indeed, unemployment for males in 1971 was only 1.2%, and for females only 2.2%, whereas by 1993 these figures had risen to 11.7% and 10.0%, respectively. The participation rate in the workforce for males has been steadily declining, from 82.9% in 1971 to 73.6% in 1994, whereas the participation rate for females has been steadily increasing. In 1971 only 39.4% of adult females were employed in the workforce, but by 1994 this figure had risen to 52.2%.

Table 1.1 The Australian economy, 1971–1994 (AU$ million)

Year	*Under-lying inflation rate (%)*	*Unemp. rate (%) Males*	*Unemp. rate (%) Females*	*Particpn rate (%) Males*	*Particpn rate (%) Females*	*Exports ($ million)*	*Imports ($ million)*	*Excess exports – imports ($ million)*	*Balance of payments ($ million)*
1971	N/A	1.2	2.2	82.9	39.4	4 376	4 150	+226	-749
1972	5.5	1.6	2.7	82.5	38.6	4 893	4,008	+885	-293
1973	5.7	1.3	2.6	81.9	40.1	6 214	4,121	+2,093	+754
1974	12.5	1.2	2.5	81.8	41.5	6 914	6 085	+829	-921
1975	21.4	3.2	5.1	81.1	41.7	8 673	8 083	+590	-1 195
1976	13.1	3.5	6.0	81.0	43.8	9 640	8 241	+1 399	-1 423
1977	11.3	4.5	7.3	80.5	44.4	11 652	10 410	+1 241	-2 445
1978	7.3	5.1	8.0	78.9	43.9	12 245	11 167	+1 078	-2 990
1979	6.1	5.1	8.0	78.4	43.1	14 247	13 752	+495	-3 624
1980	8.9	5.2	7.9	78.6	44.7	18 606	16 045	+2 561	-1 994
1981	9.2	4.5	7.3	78.1	44.7	18 949	18 790	+159	-5 465
1982	10.9	6.3	7.5	76.6	44.0	19 294	22 767	-3 473	-8 801
1983	8.8	9.9	9.9	75.9	44.0	21 454	21 216	+238	-6 520
1984	6.2	8.7	8.3	75.7	44.6	24 013	23 540	+473	-7 386
1985	6.1	7.8	8.0	75.2	45.7	29 708	29 049	+659	-10 826
1986	9.9	7.7	8.4	75.2	47.6	32 148	35 691	-3 543	-14 624
1987	9.0	7.9	8.8	75.6	48.7	36 038	37 152	-1 114	-11 715
1988	6.8	7.3	8.4	75.3	49.4	41 515	40 386	+1 129	-10 275
1989	6.1	6.2	7.3	75.2	50.4	43 894	47 012	-3 118	-17 329
1990	6.4	5.8	6.7	75.5	51.8	48 564	50 992	-2 428	-21 657
1991	3.9	8.4	8.2	75.4	52.3	52 155	49 244	+2 911	-15 579
1992	2.7	10.8	9.7	74.4	51.9	54 874	51 055	+3 819	-11 677
1993	1.8	11.7	10.0	73.9	51.7	60 022	59 427	+595	-14 967
1994	2.0	10.9	10.0	73.6	52.2	63 896	64 400	-504	-15 399

Sources: ABS (1994c), *Consumer Price Index, September Quarter 1994*, p. 18 (Catalog No. 6401.0); ABS (1975), *Year Book Australia 1974*, p. 696 (Catalog No. 1301.0); ABS (1977), *Year Book Australia 1975–76*, p. 692 (Catalog No. 1301.0); ABS (1982), *Year Book Australia 1982*, p. 138 (Catalog No. 1301.0); ABS (1988), *Year Book Australia 1988*, pp. 297, 879 (Catalog No. 1301.0); ABS (1995a), *Australian Economic Indicators*, March 1995, pp. 19, 85, 86 (Catalog No. 1350.0).

Imports and exports

The excess of exports over imports is yet another measure of how well the economy is faring. Throughout the 1970s and well into the 1980s, with the exception of 1982, Australia's economy experienced excesses of exports over imports. However, the late 1980s and early 1990s saw negative figures. More recently, relatively high positive balances have been experienced.

Balance of payments

The balance of payments, which measures transactions with the rest of the world, is often considered to be a more useful measure than excess of exports over imports, in that it takes into account external influences on the domestic economy. It includes the following:

1 transactions in goods, services and income between residents of Australia and non-residents
2 financial transactions involving claims and liabilities to the rest of the world
3 unrequited transfers, for example gifts in cash and kind
4 changes in Australia's official reserve assets through the International Monetary Fund (IMF)
5 the monetization of gold (ABS 1995b)

Table 1.1 shows that, in all years except 1973, there was a deficit in the balance of payments. This deficit increased to a maximum in 1990, but is now showing signs of leveling out, at around AU$15 000 million.

Summary

Australia had some problems in the late 1980s, which continued into the 1990s; however, there now appear to be signs of growth in the economy. Unemployment is still relatively high, with rates around 10%, and unemployment is somewhat of a concern for males. Yet there is evidence that the Australian community is starting to spend again, particularly on large ticket items (e.g. automobiles), and this typically indicates that there is a higher level of consumer confidence in the community than was evident in the early 1990s.

The next section outlines the characteristics of the demography of Australia, showing the structure of the population, growth patterns, where the population is located (distribution), household composition and immigration patterns.

Demographic factors

Introduction

Knowing the population, its numbers, location, and content is the key to understanding the demography of a country. Consumer buying patterns are largely influenced by consumer characteristics. For instance, households with young children are typically interested in purchasing family-related goods and services such as nursery furniture, toys, children's clothing and childcare services, while households where there are two adults both of whom are earning income and who do not have any children are more likely to spend their money on "luxury" items such as travel, adult clothing and expensive home furnishings.

However, other factors—family size, social class and cultural background—will also influence the above two scenarios. Hence, it is critical that both the demographic factors and the social factors are considered. In this section, therefore, we outline Australia's population size and growth, population distribution, gender distribution, age distribution, Aboriginal and Torres Strait Islander population, household composition, and immigration, as a basis for understanding the social factors covered in the following section.

Population size and growth

The Australian consumer market as a whole totals around 18 million people. Figures from the Australian Bureau of Statistics (ABS) suggest that the estimated resident population is 17.8 million. Table 1.2 provides a summary not only of Australia's population, but also of growth rates for each year from 1972 through 1994, and projected future population levels up to 2041.

Australia's growth rates are relatively low, and in line with those of other Western developed nations. Over the last 20 years, growth rates have tended to be around 1.5%, with slightly higher figures occurring in the late 1980s. Generally, population growth has eased in the 1990s, and has fallen to the lowest levels experienced in the recent past (Craig-Lees et al. 1995, p. 439). The population of Australia is expected to have reached 20 million by 2006, and just under 25 million by 2041.

Fluctuations in the population growth rate in Australia over the past two decades have been a product of the differing policies on migration. The natural increase rate of the population declined during the 1980s, but in the 1990s it appears to have stabilized, at a rate of approximately 0.79%. Overall, these figures suggest that, compared with other countries in the Asia-Pacific Rim, Australia has a relatively small population, which is expected to grow slowly over the next few years.

Due consideration should be given by marketers to the actual size of the population when considering exporting to Australia. However, despite being relatively small in number, the population is highly concentrated, as outlined below; this makes it more attractive to marketers.

Population distribution

The total land area of Australia is 7 682 300 km^2, which is almost as great as that of the USA (9 363 000 km^2) and China (9 590 000 km^2). By comparison,

Table 1.2 Population growth in Australia, 1972–1994

Year	*Males ('000)*	*Females ('000)*	*Persons ('000)*	*Growth rate (%)*
1972	6 735.7	6 673.6	13 409.3	1.81
1973	6 835.5	6 678.9	13 514.4	1.51
1974	6 941.9	6 890.0	13 832.0	1.61
1975	7 002.2	6 966.6	13 968.9	1.24
1976	7 065.8	7 044.3	14 110.1	1.01
1977	7 145.4	7 136.1	14 281.5	1.13
1978	7 213.6	7 217.3	14 430.8	1.18
1979	7 293.3	7 309.1	14 602.5	1.09
1980	7 391.4	7 415.9	14 807.4	1.24
1981	7 514.3	7 539.8	15 054.1	1.55
1982	7 633.2	7 655.7	15 288.9	1.75
1983	7 770.4	7 753.1	15 483.5	1.38
1984	7 826.4	7 850.9	15 677.3	1.21
1985	7 940.0	7 960.5	15 900.6	1.34
1986	8 055.0	8 079.1	16 134.1	1.46
1987	8 176.5	8 207.6	16 384.1	1.53
1988	8 317.5	8 354.6	16 672.1	1.65
1989	8 438.9	8 482.4	16 921.4	1.71
1990	8 559.8	8 609.6	17 169.4	1.49
1991	8 677.5	8 736.8	17 414.3	1.28
1992	8 714.9	8 774.1	17 489.1	1.19
1993	8 795.8	8 860.6	17 656.4	0.96
1994	8 887.9	8 956.3	17 843.3	1.06
2001[a]	9 537.6	9 631.9	19 169.5	N/A
2011[a]	10 405.0	10 547.4	20 952.4	N/A
2021[a]	11 153.3	11 374.7	22 528.0	N/A
2031[a]	11 767.7	12 106.4	23 874.0	N/A
2041[a]	12 210.3	12 648.1	24 858.4	N/A

[a] projected

Sources: ABS (1994a), *Australian Demographic Statistics, June Quarter 1994*, pp. 5–7 (Catalog No. 3101.0); ABS (1994g), *Year Book Australia 1994*, p. 801 (Catalog No. 1301.0); ABS (1992b), *Year Book Australia 1992*, p. 147 (Catalog No. 1301.0); ABS (1994f), *Projections of the Populations of Australia, States and Territories, 1993 to 2041* (Catalog No. 3222.0).

the population of the USA is currently estimated at 253.7 million people, and China at 1.156 billion (ABS 1995b, p. 92). Not only is Australia's population small relative to the total size of the country, but it is also concentrated into just two regions. Furthermore, the population within these two areas is largely concentrated in the cities, and particularly in the capital cities of each state.

There are six states—New South Wales, Victoria, Queensland, Western Australia, South Australia and Tasmania—and two territories, the Northern Territory and the Australian Capital Territory, the latter of which houses the Australian Capital, Canberra. Sydney, the capital of New South Wales, is Australia's largest city, and comprises over 3.7 million people. Melbourne, the capital of Victoria, has 3.1 million. The third largest city is Brisbane, the capital of Queensland, with 1.4 million people, and the next largest is Perth, the capital of Western Australia, with 1.2 million people (see Table 1.3). A total of 63.4% of Australia's population lives in the seven capital cities. The greatest concentration of a state/territory's population is in the Australian Capital Territory, with 99.9% of the territory living in Canberra. The next greatest in concentration is Adelaide, with 73.2%, followed by Perth, with 72.9%, and Melbourne, with 71.4%. Brisbane has the lowest percentage of its state's population—almost 45%.

All capital cities have experienced growth, as shown in Table 1.3, with the greatest growth occurring in Sydney and Brisbane. There has been a marked decline in rural population since the 1970s, with increasing numbers moving to the capital cities.

While the overall population density of Australia is low, the population is largely concentrated in urban centres, making it very attractive for marketers, as it is easier (and usually less costly) to reach consumers who are geographically concentrated than those who are spread throughout a large area.

Gender distribution

The ratio of males to every 100 females has been in decline since the 1950s, as the overseas migration intake has become less male dominated. In 1992, the sex ratio was 99.3 males for every 100 females. At birth this rate is much higher (105 males/100 females); however, higher male mortality causes a drop in the ratio. But in general, in practical terms, the number of males to females is now about the same.

Age distribution

The median age of the Australian population has been rising since the beginning of the 1970s, as a result of lower birth rates and lower mortality rates for most age groups. As shown in Table 1.4, the median age of the population in 1971 was 27.5 years, while in 1993 it was 33.0, the highest on record. Women are marrying later in life, and married women are postponing their childbearing until later in the marriage. Consequently, fewer children are

Table 1.3 Estimated resident population of capital cities ('000)

	1977	*1982*	*1987*	*1988*	*1989*	*1990*	*1991*	*1992*	*1993*
Population (persons)									
Sydney	3 168.1	3 318.7	3 528.5	3 591.0	3 622.9	3 643.7	3 672.9	3 699.8	3 719.0
Melbourne	2 740.8	2 833.8	3 004.5	3 043.6	3 086.6	3 126.9	3 156.7	3 177.9	3 187.5
Brisbane	1 012.2	1 128.7	1 238.4	1 264.5	1 300.2	1 330.9	1 358.0	1 385.5	1 421.7
Perth	851.8	952.4	1 079.6	1 110.5	1 147.4	1 175.4	1 188.5	1 205.3	1 221.3
Adelaide	933.9	962.5	1 011.9	1 021.1	1 033.5	1 044.6	1 057.2	1 065.8	1 070.2
Hobart	165.8	172.2	183.3	184.2	185.9	189.0	191.0	192.3	193.3
Darwin	N/A	61.8	77.0	75.9	76.0	76.5	76.7	77.2	77.4
Canberra	212.6	231.9	263.9	270.1	274.2	279.7	288.2	294.1	298.6
Total	9 085.2	9 662.0	10 387.1	10 560.9	10 726.7	10 866.7	10 989.5	11 098.1	11 189.0
Proportion of state population (%)									
Sydney	63.3	62.6	62.8	62.9	62.7	62.5	62.3	62.1	62.0
Melbourne	71.4	71.0	71.4	71.4	71.4	71.4	71.4	71.4	71.4
Brisbane	47.5	46.6	46.3	46.2	46.0	45.9	45.9	45.7	45.6
Perth	70.7	71.1	72.2	72.3	72.7	72.9	72.7	72.7	72.9
Adelaide	72.6	72.3	72.7	72.7	72.8	72.9	73.1	73.1	73.2
Hobart	39.9	40.1	40.1	40.8	40.8	40.9	40.9	40.9	41.0
Darwin	N/A	47.4	48.7	47.7	47.2	46.7	46.3	46.1	45.7
Canberra	99.5	99.5	99.4	99.3	99.2	99.1	99.6	99.9	99.9
Total	64.0	63.6	63.9	63.9	63.8	63.7	63.6	63.5	63.4

Source: ABS (1995b), *Year Book Australia 1995*, p. 95 (Catalog No. 1301.0).

being born. The percentage of persons under 15 years has declined steadily—from 28.7% in 1971 to 21.7% in 1993. Australians are also living longer. Indeed, the proportion of persons over 64 years is steadily increasing, with the percentage rising from 8.3% in 1971 to 11.7% in 1993. All of these factors indicate an ageing population, and this trend is expected to continue.

For marketers, these figures suggest that they should bear in mind that the population is ageing, and modify their product and service offerings accordingly. However, the younger age groups should not be neglected because, although relatively few children are being born per family, parents and other family members appear to be spending a greater number of dollars per child

Table 1.4 Age distribution in Australia, 1971–1993 (%)

Year	*0–14*	*15–44*	*45–64*	*>64*	*Median (years)*
1971	28.7	43.0	20.0	8.3	27.5
1976	27.0	44.1	20.0	8.9	28.4
1977	26.5	44.5	19.9	9.1	28.7
1978	26.1	45.0	19.7	9.2	28.9
1979	25.6	45.4	19.5	9.4	29.1
1980	25.3	45.8	19.4	9.6	29.6
1981	25.0	46.1	19.2	9.7	29.6
1982	24.7	46.4	19.1	9.9	29.9
1983	24.4	46.6	19.0	10.0	30.2
1984	24.0	46.8	19.1	10.1	30.5
1985	N/A	N/A	N/A	N/A	30.8
1986	23.1	47.3	19.1	10.5	31.1
1987	22.7	47.6	19.0	10.7	31.3
1988	22.4	47.8	19.0	10.8	31.6
1989	22.2	47.9	19.0	10.9	31.8
1990	22.0	47.8	19.2	11.0	32.2
1991	21.9	47.6	19.3	11.2	32.3
1992	21.8	47.2	19.6	11.4	32.6
1993	21.7	46.7	20.0	11.7	33.0

Sources: ABS (1994e), *Estimated Resident Population by Sex and Age: States and Territories of Australia, Preliminary June 1992 and June 1993*, p. 19 (Catalog No. 3201.0); ABS (1983), *Year Book Australia 1983*, p. 124 (Catalog No. 1301.0); ABS (1986), *Year Book Australia 1986*, p. 100 (Catalog No. 1301.0); ABS (1994g), *Year Book Australia 1994*, p. 120 (Catalog No. 1301.0); ABS (1995b), *Year Book Australia 1995*, p. 99 (Catalog No. 1301.0).

compared with the dollars spent per child in the past. This would suggest greater market potential overall within the younger-age-group market.

Aboriginal and Torres Strait Islander population

The 1991 Census revealed an Aboriginal and Torres Strait Islander population of 265 459 (ABS 1995b). This represents 1.6% of the total Australian population. This 1991 figure is an increase of 16.6% over that of the previous census (1986). The indigenous population in the Northern Territory makes up 22.7% of the total population; the indigenous population does not exceed 3% of the total population of any other state or territory of Australia.

The age distribution of the indigenous population differs greatly from the non-indigenous population in the younger and older age groups. Almost 40% of indigenous people are less than 15 years old, and only 6% are over 55 years old. These figures compare with 22% and 20%, respectively, for the non-indigenous population.

These figures suggest that the Aboriginal people are considerably younger than the rest of the population, and that they typically have very different needs and wants to those of the rest of the population.

Household composition

It is estimated that there are 5.8 million households in Australia. Table 1.5 details their composition, showing that approximately 70% of households are comprised of married couples (with or without children). Around 35% are two-parent households, with dependent children and adult children living at home. Another 9% of households are made up of single-parent families.

As shown in Table 1.6, the rate of household formation has grown steadily, but the number of people per household has decreased over the years, from 3.47 persons in 1966 to 2.79 in 1991. If we were to go back to 1911, the change in household size would seem rather dramatic: 4.53 persons in that year, as compared with 2.79 in 1991. This reduction can be attributed to smaller completed family sizes, and a growth in one-person and two-person households. The baby-boom years following the Second World War resulted in a large number of young adults in the age group 15 to 29 in the 1970s, and this meant an increase in the number of potential young families and small households.

There has also been a greater number of widowed and elderly individuals living as separate households due to the influence of government policy and funding that has been directed at maintaining the elderly in private accommodation.

The latest available figures indicate that 73% of households contain families. Only 51.7% of families had dependent children in 1992, and among those, 36.4% had only one child (ABS 1995b, p. 100). The 1982 Family Survey found the average number of offspring present in family households to be 2.1; this figure has continued to decrease in the past decade (ABS 1988, p. 266).

The number of marriages in Australia peaked in 1971 (117 600 marriages). However, this peak was followed by a rapid decline—despite population growth. The decrease coincides with an increase in the number of de facto relationships. In 1982 there were 168 600 de facto couples in Australia, making up 5% of all couples. By 1992, that number had increased to 344 400 couples, or 8% of all couples. Fewer marriages are taking place, and the median age at first marriage for both men and women is rising, from 23.3 years in 1972 to 26.9 years in 1992 for men, and from 21.0 to 24.7 years for females (ABS 1995b). This seems to suggest that younger Australians are living at home with their parents for a longer time, and also that some are

Table 1.5 Household composition in Australia

Household type		*Total households ('000)*	*%*
Young singles		240	4
Young married (no children)		1 326	23
Married couples		2 002	
Young with children (20–35)	660		35
Middle-aged with children (35–60)	1 342		
Single-parent families		531	9
Young with children (20–35)	158		
Middle-aged with children (35–60)	316		
Older families (65+)	57		
Mature couples		325	5.6
Mature singles		433	7.4
Elderly couples (no children at home)		360	6
Elderly singles		460	8
Unrelated		123	2
Total		**5 800**	**100**

Source: ABS (1993a), *Census Characteristics of Australia 1991, Census of Population and Housing,* Catalog No. 2710.0.

Table 1.6 Households in Australia, 1911–1991

Year	*1911*	*1921*	*1933*	*1947*	*1954*	*1966*	*1971*	*1976*	*1981*	*1986*	*1991*
Persons per private household	4.53	4.40	4.08	3.75	3.55	3.47	3.31	3.12	2.98	2.88	2.79
No. of private households ('000)	894	1 107	1 509	1 873	2 343	3 155	3 670	4 140	4 668	5 187	5 825
Percentage of one-person households	N/A	N/A	N/A	N/A	9.1	10.3	11.8	13.6	15.7	18.0	22.0

Sources: ABS (1988), *Year Book Australia 1988* (Catalog No. 1301.0); ABS (1995b), *Year Book Australia 1995*, pp. 100–1 (Catalog No. 1301.0).

living in independent households before marriage and deciding either not to get married at all, or to wait longer before getting married than previous generations.

Marketers should note, from these figures, that households may take a variety of forms. Accordingly, it is important that they incorporate, in their marketing campaigns, a range of household types—the traditional two-adult, two-children household, the two-adults-and-no-children household, the single-adult household, and so on.

There appear to be a growing number of single-person households, and consumers of this type clearly have very different needs and wants to the two-adult, two-children household. For example, single-serve meals, including desserts and individual cup cakes, are more appropriate for these household units than the standard-sized packaging, which is more suited to the "traditional family" of two adults and two children.

Immigration

Overseas migration rates have been somewhat erratic over the years. The migration rates increased dramatically at the end of the 1970s when a large number of Indo-Chinese refugees were accepted as settlers. Between 1982 and 1988, the levels of migration returned to previous levels, but in 1988 and 1989 the population growth rate rose sharply again as migration intake increased. Net overseas migration is estimated to have directly contributed 50.7% of the total population increase between 1981 and 1991. Despite the increase in Indo-Chinese immigrants, migrants from the UK and New Zealand still remain the largest population of long-term arrivals.

However, since the mid-1980s, the proportion of migrants from European countries such as the UK, Ireland, Italy, Greece, Germany, Croatia/Serbia, and the Netherlands has decreased. There has also been a marked increase in the numbers of settlers arriving from South-East, North-East, and Southern Asia (see Table 1.7).

Australia has experienced a considerable amount of immigration over the years. As stated above, immigration was initially principally from the UK and Europe, but more recently there has been a significant rise in Asian immigration; today Australia could be described as "multicultural." Generally speaking, Australians are accepting of the fact that other Australians may have a very different cultural heritage to their own. There is also a growing awareness of differences in customs, religious beliefs, values, foods and clothing. As a result, Australian consumers are generally interested in trying out new foods and new ways of doing things.

Summary

This section has described Australia's population, pointing out that it is relatively small, yet highly concentrated in urban centres, particularly the

Table 1.7 Immigrant population of Australia

Birthplace	*Prior to 1981*	*1981–1985*	*1986–1987*	*1988–1989*	*1990–1991*	*Not stated*	*Total*
Main English-speaking countries							
Canada	12 825	3 122	1 549	1 918	2 668	364	22 446
Ireland	33 456	4 414	3 921	5 952	2 756	1 232	51 731
New Zealand	117 027	47 306	31 484	42 917	19 156	6 169	264 059
South Africa	21 614	10 429	7 318	5 626	3 228	721	48 936
United Kingdom	884 796	83 986	33 249	41 593	35 470	24 620	1 103 714
USA	21 808	6 047	3 161	4 725	7 088	861	43 690
Total	1 091 526	155 304	80 682	102 731	70 366	33 967	1 534 576
Other countries							
China	22 274	10 056	9 214	22 818	11 977	1 566	77 905
Germany	94 901	8 472	2 122	2 273	2 119	2 005	111 892
Greece	126 431	2 643	1 374	1 160	845	3 422	135 875
Hong Kong	13 808	10 283	6 981	13 696	12 104	689	57 561
India	34 395	7 728	4 837	5 966	6 951	1 099	60 976
Italy	241 211	3 063	1 059	1 029	999	6 088	253 449
Lebanon	44 347	6 411	6 150	5 443	3 921	2 604	68 876
Malaysia	24 994	12 720	8 932	14 933	9 170	1 004	71 753
Malta	49 360	1 859	579	363	178	1 447	53 786
Netherlands	85 155	4 714	1 060	1 098	859	1 676	94 562
Philippines	13 260	16 327	14 317	17 025	10 539	1 507	72 975
Poland	43 396	13 655	3 366	3 794	2 662	1 677	68 550
Former USSR	36 777	1 318	485	2 217	2 126	1 016	43 939
Vietnam	32 689	42 178	12 639	14 156	17 568	2 629	121 859
Former Yugoslavia	135 846	6 658	4 700	5 235	3 224	4 987	160 650
Other	364 087	101 412	67 179	83 236	68 848	16 083	700 845
Total	1 362 931	249 497	144 994	194 442	154 090	49 499	2 155 453
Overall total	2 454 457	404 801	225 676	297 173	224 456	83 466	3 690 029

Source: M. Craig-Lees, S. Joy & B. Browne (1995), *Consumer Behaviour,* John Wiley and Sons, Brisbane, p. 342.

capital cities. There is roughly the same percentage of males as females, and the population is ageing. Households typically range from the more traditional (two-adult, two-children) household to single-person households, and there are many different types in between these two extremes. Immigration was the final aspect discussed, and the fact highlighted that, while Australia's immigrants have traditionally come from the UK and Europe, there have been significant numbers migrating from Asian countries, and this trend is likely to continue. This has resulted in a multicultural society, with people more tolerant of others than they have traditionally been, and increasingly open to new ideas. This prevailing attitude obviously augurs well for the introduction of new products and services.

Social structure

Having outlined the economy and the basic demographic characteristics, it is vital now to consider the social structure of the country.

In most Western cultures, social class is closely associated with wealth. Wealth has direct links to property ownership, and this in turn leads to prestige (status by the consumption of goods and services—Craig-Lees et al. 1995). We will first provide an overview of social class before going on to consider income, education and occupation, all of which have a significant bearing on consumption.

Social class can be measured by two methods:

1 through self-allocation
2 by ranking

With the self-allocation method, people are asked to identify the class to which they feel they belong. Few studies of this nature have been undertaken in Australia. The latest available figures (these are for 1984) show that 1% identified themselves as being upper class, 53% as middle class, 43% as working class, and 3% as lower class (Baxter et al. 1991). Using an objective approach, for example the Australian Standard Classification of Occupations (ASCO), the following breakdown is obtained: 34% of Australians could be classified as professionals, approximately 40% could be placed in the middle cluster, and 25% in the working cluster (Table 1.8).

Formal research studies of class in Australia have found that no more than 10% of Australians think that Australia is a classless society (Craig-Lees et al. 1995). Wealth (including income) appears to be the major contributing factor to class. Associated with wealth (and, in particular, income) are education and occupation. It is seen as possible to move from one class to another through self-improvement. Indeed, it is believed that upward mobility can be achieved through higher education, and subsequently the obtaining of a higher status occupation.

Table 1.8 Socio-economic groups in Australia

Group no.	*% of total*	*Description*
I	10.5%	Upper service, higher professional administrative and managerial, large proprietors
II	23.5%	Lower service, lower professional administrators, managers etc.; higher grade technicians, supervisors of non-manual employees
IIIa	10.3%	Routine non-manual higher grade
IIIb	11.8%	Routine non-manual lower grade; personal-service workers
IVa,b	8.9%	Small proprietors, own-account workers, non-agricultural
IVc	1.6%	Farmers, smallholders
V	7.8%	Lower-grade technical, manual supervisory
VI	11.6%	Skilled manual workers
VIIa	13.3%	Semi-skilled and unskilled workers, non-agricultural
VIIb	0.7%	Agricultural workers

Source: M. Craig-Lees, S. Joy & B. Browne (1995), *Consumer Behaviour,* John Wiley and Sons, Brisbane, p. 274.

Income

The inequality in income distribution for full-time adult employees has increased in the last decade, although the increase is small, and comparable to that of other countries such as Japan and Canada (ABS 1994b). Income differs across Australia between rural and urban areas and between capital cities. In addition, variations in income occur between suburbs of cities and towns. As shown in Table 1.9, average weekly earnings rose from AU$89.90 in 1971 to AU$525.72 in 1994. This represents an increase of almost 500%. If we adjust earnings to changes in the Consumer Price Index (CPI), we see that incomes rose considerably in the early 1980s and then devalued in real terms such that, by 1987, earnings in the top and middle-income brackets had returned to 1983 values. Since 1990, real earnings have increased (ABS 1994b).

Two factors are considered to be critical in this trend toward the greater dispersion of earnings. They are:

1 the decentralization of wage bargaining
2 a shift toward more highly skilled, and therefore higher earning, occupations (ABS 1994g)

In the area of wage bargaining, in 1983 the Wages Accord, a centralized wage-fixing system, took into account economic policies and the CPI. This wage indexation was abandoned in 1987, and replaced with a two-tier system that distributed a flat increase to all workers and made additional increases on the basis of efficiency. Then, in 1988, this was replaced by award restructuring and training provisions.

The other important factor is the trend toward higher education and higher earning occupations. Between 1986 and 1993, the number of persons employed as managers and administrators and in professional occupations increased by 17% and 26% respectively (ABS 1994b).

Table 1.9 Average weekly earnings, 1971–1994 (AU$)

Year	*1971*	*1972*	*1973*	*1974*	*1975*	*1976*	*1977*	*1978*
Average	89.90	97.30	122.20	143.90	163.70	182.10	198.00	212.70
Year	*1979*	*1980*	*1981*	*1982*	*1983*	*1984*	*1985*	*1986*
Average	231.90	270.00	296.00	337.60	362.00	389.50	413.90	446.30
Year	*1987*	*1988*	*1989*	*1990*	*1991*	*1992*	*1993*	*1994*
Average	380.72	403.75	431.07	459.70	486.65	500.75	510.95	525.72

Sources: ABS (1988), *Year Book Australia 1988*, p. 294 (Catalog No. 1301.0); ABS (1995a), *Australian Economic Indicators, March 1995*, p. 98 (Catalog No. 1350.0).

As shown in Table 1.10, the highest weekly total earnings for full-time adult employees were recorded for managers and administrators (males AU$929.20, females AU$708.40), professionals (males AU$866.20, females AU$707.00), and para-professionals (males AU$738.80, females AU$666.60). This table also shows that income distribution is not the same for males and females. Although the gap has decreased significantly, there is still a large difference between the earnings of men and women. In 1989–1990, average earnings for women were still only 61% of those for men. In 1973–74, women working full time for the full year earned 64% of the amount that men earned on the same basis, while in 1989–1990 this figure rose to 76% (see Table 1.11). Some of the contributing factors for this gap between the earnings of men and women include a younger age structure (i.e. women in the workforce are younger), lower educational qualifications (for older women), occupational bias, and fewer hours worked.

> Women do not progress as far as men in their career paths, are more likely than men to interrupt their working lives to care for children, and are more likely than men to be in lower paid occupations (ABS 1993b, p. 181).

However, in time, with increasing education, Australian women are likely to catch up to men's earnings.

Table 1.10 Average weekly total earnings for full-time employees in major occupation groups, May 1993 (AU$)

Occupation	*Males*	*Females*
Managers and administrators	929.20	708.40
Professionals	864.30	706.00
Para-professionals	735.70	664.00
Tradespersons	577.40	412.40
Clerks	593.60	491.40
Salespersons and personal-service workers	582.30	455.60
Plant and machine operators, and drivers	658.10	431.90
Laborers and related workers	526.60	437.50
Total	674.50	538.60

Source: ABS (1995b), *Year Book Australia 1995*, pp. 174–5 (Catalog No. 1301.0).

Table 1.11 Comparison of earnings by males and females, 1989–1990

Proportion of workers	*Females (%)*	*Males (%)*	*Female–male earnings ratio*
With post-school qualifications	49.6	56.3	78.5
With degree	12.9	13.4	72.7
With certificate (non-trade)/diploma	33.8	14.0	72.9
With trade certificate	2.8	28.2	68.1
Without post-school qualifications	50.4	43.7	76.2

Source: ABS (1993b), *Women in Australia*, p. 182 (Catalog No. 4113.0).

Education

The Australian population is becoming more and more qualified. In the late 1980s, as part of national economic policy, higher education institutions in Australia were combined into a unified national system which expanded enrollment capacity. This was part of a wider initiative to train Australia's labor force to meet the needs of a changing economy with growth in the skilled occupational sectors (ABS 1994b).

As the level of higher education in Australia has risen, so too has the percentage of adults who have completed high school. Almost 70% of secondary (high) school students stay on to complete their secondary school education. In conjunction with the Commonwealth Government's policies on increasing the level of education and training, the proportion of the population aged

15–69 holding post-school qualifications has increased over the last decade from 36% in 1984 to 42% in 1992 (see Table 1.12). This increase is more pronounced when the percentage of tertiary qualifications for 1969 (20.3%) is compared with that for 1992 (43.9%). There is still, however, a disparity between the educational attainment of men and women in Australia. Forty-seven per cent of males held post-school qualifications in 1992, as opposed to 37% of females. Of these males with post-school qualifications, 23% held degrees, 51% held trade qualifications and 26% held a certificate or diploma. Around 22% of females held degrees, but only 8% held trade qualifications, and the majority of women (70%) held certificates or diplomas.

Access to and participation in education for women has increased markedly in the last decade, owing to society's changing views of women, as well as government reforms and labor-market changes. In 1992, the overall number of women participating in education was roughly comparable to the number of men; however, the courses of study and qualifications gained were different. Generally, women gained qualifications in fields such as the arts, teaching, and social sciences, while men gained qualifications in the physical sciences and engineering.

Occupation

One of the most important developments in the Australian labor market in the last few decades has been the substantial growth in part-time work. Total employment grew by 1.8 million, or 32%, between 1973 and 1993. Just over one million of the new jobs were part time, an increase in part-time employment of 164% over the 20-year period. The high growth in the service industries has been the reason cited most often for this growth in demand for part-time workers. In 1993, 79% of all part-time workers were employed in service industries. Both the demand and supply side of the labor market have influenced the growth in part-time work (ABS 1994b).

The number of white-collar workers in Australia has grown faster than the number of blue-collar workers. Table 1.13 shows the percentages of workers in blue collar and white collar occupations in 1986 and 1992. It is clear that greater proportions of women than men are engaged in white-collar occupations, and that these proportions are increasing over time. Increased participation of women in the workforce, as well as the recognition and acceptance of women's rights to education and a career, have drastically altered the characteristics of Australia's labor force. Labor-force participation rates for married women increased from 29% in 1966 to 53% in 1992; participation rates for non-married women were maintained at approximately 50% from 1966 to 1992; and the participation rates for men in the labor force declined from 84% to 74% over the same period. It is projected that, by the year 2005, the participation rate for women in the workforce will reach 60%.

Table 1.12 Educational attainment, persons aged 15–69, 1969–1992 ('000)

With post-school qualifications

Year	*Degree*	*% with degrees*	*Trade qualification*	*Certificate or diploma*	*Other*	*Total*
1969	173.9	13.3	573.2		560.3	1 307.4
1982	581.8	16.0	1 445.8		1 600.0	3 627.4
1984	737.2	19.56	2 935.1		96.4	3 768.6
1985	782.4	20.57	2 889.1		131.8	3 803.3
1986	826.1	20.81	3 004.1		137.8	3 968.0
1987	816.6	19.25	1 527.7	1 854.8	41.7	4 240.8
1988	868.4	20.02	1 551.8	1 930.8	35.8	4 386.7
1989	928.6	20.16	1 563.8	2 083.7	30.1	4 606.2
1990	987.7	21.02	1 557.5	2 089.7	64.1	4 699.0
1991	1 047	21.38	1 571.5	2 229.2	47.9	4 896.1
1992	1 140	22.45	1 620.2	2 272.8	44.0	5 076.5

Without post-school qualifications

Year	*Highest level of secondary school*	*% reaching highest level*	*Not highest level of secondary school*	*Total*	*Still at school*
1969	624.7	12.15	4 514.6	5 139.3	N/A
1982	941.1	19.09	3 986.7	4 927.8	N/A
1984	1 211.8	19.03	5 118.3	6 367.8	466.5
1985	1 266.0	19.55	5 173.4	6 475.6	469.2
1986	1 274.1	19.92	5 088.5	6 394.8	501.4
1987	1 308.3	20.65	4 962.1	6 334.3	525.0
1988	1 360.3	21.26	4 962.9	6 396.0	586.3
1989	1 405.3	21.87	4 950.7	6 423.0	568.1
1990	1 535.7	23.50	4 928.7	6 534.0	565.3
1991	1 607.1	24.75	4 819.6	6 491.9	597.8
1992	1 708.7	26.34	4 711.3	6 485.2	593.4

Sources: ABS (1992a), *Education and Training in Australia*, p. 59 (Catalog No. 4224.0); ABS (1984), *Social Indicators No. 4*, 1984, p. 140 (Catalog No. 4101.0).

Nevertheless, although the participation rates for women are increasing, the type of employment for women is still different from that of men. Women are more likely than men to be part-time or casual employees. In August 1992, women accounted for 42% of all employees, but only 32% of all full-time employees and 75% of all part-time employees were women. The major differences are as follows—women tend to be employed as:

- clerks (30.6%, compared to 6.5% for men)
- salespersons and personal-service workers (23.7%, compared to 9.1% for men)

Table 1.13 Blue-collar and white-collar occupations, 1986 and 1992

	Women (%)		*Men (%)*	
	1986	*1992*	*1986*	*1992*
White-collar occupations	79.2	81.6	47.4	49.7
Blue-collar occupations	20.7	18.5	52.5	50.3

Source: ABS (1993), *Women in Australia*, p. 125 (Catalog No. 4113.0).

The major category for males is tradespersons—23.3% of male workers are in this category, compared to a very low 3.7% of female workers. The two areas where there are only small differences in percentage are the professional and para-professional occupations—13.9% for women and 13.8% for men, and 6.7% for women and 5.6% for men respectively.

Table 1.14 Percentages of men and women in each profession, 1986 and 1992

	Women (%)		*Men (%)*	
	1986	*1992*	*1986*	*1992*
Managers and administrators	6.3	6.7	14.0	14.7
Professionals	11.9	13.9	12.1	13.8
Para-professionals	6.4	6.7	5.5	5.6
Tradespersons	4.3	3.7	24.8	23.3
Clerks	32.6	30.6	7.4	6.5
Salespersons and personal-service workers	22.0	23.7	8.4	9.1
Plant and machine operators and drivers	3.3	2.4	10.8	10.6
Laborers and related workers	13.1	12.4	16.9	16.4
Total numbers ('000)	2 716.0	3 245.8	4 202.6	4 433.4

Source: ABS (1993b), *Women in Australia*, p. 125 (Catalog No. 4113.0).

Summary

In this section, Australia's social structure has been outlined in terms of social class, income distribution, educational levels and occupational status. No more than 10% of Australians still think that Australia is a classless society. Rather, the vast majority are seeing evidence that there are real differences in social status; with this perception comes different buying tastes and preferences.

The disparity in income distribution is clearly evident, and although it is small compared with other countries in the Asia-Pacific Rim, the differences do exist, and they appear to be increasing. The rich are getting richer and the poor poorer. Particularly in the most recent years, this trend appears to have been fuelled by migration—principally that from Asian countries—as the majority of immigrants are relatively wealthy.

With higher levels of education there is generally an associated higher status occupation. There appears to be an increasing percentage employed in higher status occupations, particularly managerial and administrative occupations.

Women's education and income levels have increased, but not to the same level as those for males. Indeed, there is still a gap between men's and women's earnings. Much of this gap can be explained by the fact that a large percentage of women choose to work on a part-time basis so that they can handle family responsibilities as well as paid work. There is evidence, however, that more and more women are not taking time out of the paid workforce to care for children, and, given that increasing numbers of men are sharing in family and home-related responsibilities, in time it is highly likely that women's earnings will catch up to those of men. With dual-income households, the spending power of the household unit has increased greatly, and this increase is likely to continue.

The Australian population is certainly much more highly qualified than ever before, and is much more inclined to ask questions of retailers and manufacturers. Furthermore, Australians are more likely than ever before to expect high quality service, and to complain if they do not receive it or to vote with their feet and go to another retailer or supplier. This attitude runs contrary to the traditional more accepting cultural attitudes that characterized Australians in the past. The next section outlines the major facets of Australia's culture, highlighting the major changes that have a bearing on consumer behavior.

Cultural factors

In this section are outlined, first, the key cultural attitudes that have characterized Australia over the years. Those attitudes that have undergone significant modification are also noted. Next are presented the major subgroups evident in the population, and the section concludes with a summary of the key points discussed.

In terms of traditional attitudes, while Australian society has undergone significant change since the 1950s, and particularly in the last 20 years, there is considerable agreement that the following are still core values of Australian society:

- egalitarianism
- respect for the underdog
- autonomy
- democracy
- family life
- humanitarianism
- mateship
- individualism
- informality
- freedom

Australians have been strong believers in the rights of individuals, so much so that many would still hold to the view that they have just as much right as the person next to them on any given matter. This attitude is captured in the saying "Jack is as good as his master." This attitude has prevailed for much of Australia's history, and stems from the early efforts to make Australia a classless society, as referred to in the introduction to this chapter.

This attitude is being modified by education, and by the fact that there are increasing differences in income-earning ability and occupational status among Australians today. Another traditional attitude, "She'll be right, mate,"[3] is gradually being replaced by a certain pessimism, largely as a result of higher levels of education and an increase in the interest in environmental issues. More and more Australians are reaching the conclusion that everything won't be all right if they don't start acting to conserve and protect the environment.

Greater interest is also developing in issues related to morality, ethics, total well-being (i.e. that of both mind and body), and spiritual matters. There has also been a trend toward a less formal lifestyle. This is evident in many facets of life, including increased demand for more informal dress (even in business), simpler home furnishings, and light entertainment (Kotler et al. 1994). While these trends are evident across the population, to gain a fuller understanding of the Australian culture it is important to recognize that there are a number of subgroups, each with their particular characteristics, which impact on the whole culture. These include the following:

- yuppies
- teenagers

- gays
- nationality and religious groups
- mature consumers
- REEVS

Yuppies

This much-discussed group has been sought after by many marketers over the years—not only in Australia, but also in most parts of the world. Their spending power and interest in material possessions, and their sheer numbers, have made them particularly attractive as a group. They often form part of a dual-professional-career household, in which their combined household income is greater than AU$100 000. But yuppies in Australia are becoming more and more concerned with recycling, conservation issues in general, and getting "back to basics." This generally means being interested in such things as personal relationships, the family, home activities, natural foods, home cooking, and natural building materials such as native timbers, terracotta tiles, and solid but understated furniture. When they consume, they are generally concerned about getting value for money, and about understated appeal.

Teenagers

These young adults are sometimes referred to as "Generation X," or the "13th generation." They are primarily the children of the "baby-boomers," and, as such, many are also the children of yuppies. They have grown up in a time of rapid technological change and mass communication. They have experienced much in terms of material possessions. They are characterized as being self-centred and materialistic, and generally fairly self-reliant, determined to carve out their own destinies (Gray et al. 1989). But they also tend to be concerned about the problems facing the world. They are more likely than the previous generations to see through marketers' gimmicks, particularly contrived advertising. Moreover, these consumers tend to be more highly educated than their previous counterparts in other generations, and are generally not shy when it comes to demanding good customer service. They are familiar with the latest technological advancements, and are very comfortable with electronic selling, including using the Internet to shop. Above all, they tend to know their rights as consumers, and to exercise them.

Gays

Another subculture is the gay community. Although small in absolute numbers, they represent a significant segment in terms of their spending power, with an individual household income approximately 70% higher than the national average (*Marketing* 1992). Homosexual males spend 50% more on travel and 250% more on grooming and fitness products than do heterosexual males. They also spend more on alcohol, homewares and entertainment (*Marketing* 1992).

Nationality groups

The Australian government's multiculturalism policy has resulted in a diverse society that holds varying racial and ethnic beliefs, yet still accepts Australia's laws and regulations, and shares its interests. Government policies have been built upon three underlying principles:

1. **cultural identity**—the right of all Australians to express and share their individual cultural heritage
2. **social justice**—the right of all Australians to equality of treatment and opportunity, regardless of race, ethnicity, culture, religion, language, gender or place of birth
3. **economic efficiency**—the need to maintain, develop, and utilize the skills and talents of all Australians, regardless of their background (ABS 1994g)

In all capital cities in Australia there are sections that can be easily identified as Italian, Greek and Asian. This concentration of individual ethnic groups is particularly noticeable in parts of Melbourne and Sydney. However, this segmentation is not apparent only in capital cities; for example, Shepparton East in Victoria is known for its Southern European heritage, while the Barossa Valley in South Australia is known for its German influence.

The ethnic background of these groups influences consumer behavior in a number of ways. First, consumers from these groups often have different tastes in and preferences for particular goods and services, such as food items and food-preparation items. For example, some ethnic groups will not eat certain foods, such as pork. Others prefer different ways of serving food—for instance, Japanese people like to eat raw fish and seaweed. Certain cooking utensils such as rice cookers are now widely available. Having these foods and cooking utensils available has certainly changed many Australians' perceptions of food options and combinations. Second, the manner in which products and services are presented has been influenced by different cultural groups. For instance, the Japanese place considerable value on the presentation itself as well as the service provided with the purchase of the product. The appearance of a large department store of Japanese origins (Daimaru) has influenced the way products are presented to customers. Third, the way in which customers arrive at a final price for both products and services has been influenced by Asian consumers. Australians are now more willing to argue over prices for some goods, and are more willing to ask, "Is that your best price?" This is a relatively new philosophy among the Australian consumer public, and one that still does not have full acceptance.

Religious groups

While Australia is predominantly a Christian country, in the last census (1991) 2.6% of the population identified themselves as non-Christian, and 13% said they did not have any religious affiliation. The major non-Christian groups are Muslims, Buddhists, Jews and Hindus. Generally these religious groups concentrate in particular suburbs or areas, and have a significant impact on the culture in that particular area (Craig-Lees et al. 1995). For example, they tend to observe certain religious days, and eat or abstain from eating certain types of food. They may wear certain types of clothes, such as veils.

Associated with each religious group are various beliefs, taboos and mores, which influence not only product offerings but also the manner in which they are presented to consumers—for instance, in terms of colors used in packaging and in promotional campaigns. Clearly, certain religious groups use particular colors and/or symbols to signify certain religious events. Jewish religious days and customs are now fairly common in the community, as are Chinese New Year celebrations. There are special product offerings associated with each festival.

Mature consumers

Researchers have defined the mature consumer in various ways. In Australia, women receive the age pension at 60 years and men at 65 years, so 60 years is often regarded as an appropriate threshold for entry into the mature-consumer group.

Mature consumers represent the fastest growing consumer group in Australia (McColl-Kennedy et al. 1994). As the population ages, more and more attention is given to health issues, and personal well-being is increasingly identified as important. Australians are living longer, with life expectancy for males being 74.99 years and for females 80.86 years in 1993 (ABS 1994d, p. 10). But it would be a mistake to think that all mature consumers behave alike. Rather, there is evidence to suggest that there may well be subgroups even within this category of mature consumers, segmented according to lifestyle and measure of health. Some marketers have found it useful to segment into "old," "medium," and "young" matures. But sometimes this segmentation is still too broad, as some "old" matures may be chronologically older than some others but, in terms of their mental attitude and overall health, in a far better situation than some of the "young" mature consumers.

However mature consumers are segmented, it is important to remember that they constitute a significant group in terms of their purchasing power, and that the size of the group is likely to increase over time. Mature consumers certainly cannot be ignored.

REEVS

As we have moved through the 1990s, another important group has been emerging in the Australian community—the REEVS. These consumers are concerned about:

- relationships (R)
- ethics (E)
- the environment (E)
- getting value for money (V)
- exercising self-discipline (S) (McColl-Kennedy et al. 1994)

Some of these people suffered the excesses of the 1980s, and have been forced into a life of self-restraint, often as a result of losing their jobs or seeing a partner or close associate lose theirs. Little detailed research has been carried out on these consumers to date. It could well be that many of today's yuppies and a good number of the yuppies of the 1980s fall into this category. Obviously the REEVS group is worth researching further to determine who its members are, how many they number, and what their tastes and preferences are.

Summary

This section has outlined some core Australian cultural values, and has shown how they have been modified over the years. Next, the major subgroups and their patterns of consumer behavior have been described, together with the major influences they have had on consumer behavior in Australia.

The next section elaborates further on the major changes in consumer behavior that have occurred as a result of the changes in the economy, and in the demographic, social and cultural environments.

Changes in consumer behavior

The changes in demographics observed in the previous sections have resulted in changes in consumer behavior. First, as the number of women in the workforce is increasing, more household decisions are being made jointly by several members of the household. Historically, males were thought to influence the purchase of cars, insurance and property, while females dominated choices for food, clothing and home decorating. However, there now appears to be a move away from role-specific purchasing to more joint decisions across the range of products and services. More and more males are engaging in grocery shopping. Teenagers and pre-teens are another important influence, particularly for household items. Indeed, over 70% of breakfast-cereal purchases have been influenced by children (Harrison 1983).

Second, more emphasis is being placed on convenience: for example, families are eating out more in family-style restaurants which offer fast food at reasonable prices, and/or are buying take-aways and frozen meals. Shopping and banking by phone are further examples of the importance being placed on convenience, particularly in households where both adults work full time.

Third, with smaller households and an increase in the number of married women in the workforce, there is a greater demand for smaller packaging, even single-serve packaging and individual meals which can easily be heated for one member of the household if required. Indeed, marketers have responded to this with full meals for individual persons, and single-serve cakes and desserts such as those made by Sara Lee.

Fourth, with more married women in the workforce, there has been a growing demand for services such as childcare, drycleaning, house cleaning and gardening. Table 1.15 summarizes household expenditure surveys, and shows that expenditure increases were particularly significant for household services and operation. This indicates an increased use of house-care services such as house cleaning and gardening maintenance.

Fifth, there appears to be an increasing interest in the environment, and the subsequent demand for "environmentally friendly" products and Australian-made products (Mackay 1992). Products made in Australia with recycled materials are particularly sought after.

Sixth, with higher levels of education, Australians are requesting more information on products, packaging and warranties. They are also shopping around more, making comparisons between products and services, and seeking advice from the Australian Consumers Association and the Department of Consumer Affairs. Retailers and manufacturers will need to take more notice of customer complaints, and make it their business to find out customer-satisfaction levels, pinpoint exactly what customers are unhappy with, and work out specific measures to win back these customers. Recent industry figures suggest that most households had a complaint with a product or service within the previous 12 months, and were dissatisfied with the way in which the complaint was handled and/or the outcome (TARP 1995).

Implications for marketing management

The trends discussed in this chapter have several implications for marketing management. Over the last decade, Australia has experienced a slowed economy, with relatively high unemployment and low growth rates. The impact of these economic factors is seen in the changes in demographic trends: there are now smaller households, fewer children, and dual-income households. The slowed economy has also led to greater retention rates at secondary schools and the trend toward higher levels of education for both males and females, which in turn has increased the percentages of white-collar and service-related occupations. These demographic trends, together

Table 1.15 Household expenditure surveys, Australia, 1984 and 1988–1989 (AU$)

Target of average weekly expenditure	*1984*	*1988–1989*
Commodities and services	361.84	502.71
Current housing costs	46.46	71.80
Fuel and power	10.56	12.87
Food and non-alcoholic beverages	71.22	95.83
Alcoholic beverages	12.30	16.90
Tobacco	5.73	6.89
Clothing and footwear	23.46	30.73
Household furnishings and equipment	27.69	37.37
Household services and operation	15.70	24.11
Medical care and health expenses	14.07	21.68
Transport	59.00	76.13
Recreation	43.13	59.37
Personal care	6.60	9.95
Miscellaneous commodities and services	25.93	39.08
Income tax	80.07	127.02
Mortgage payments	6.49	7.01
Other capital housing costs	18.01	19.91
Superannuation and life insurance	11.51	16.86

Sources: ABS (1990b), *1988–89 Household Expenditure Survey, Australia: Summary of Results,* p. 1 (Catalog No. 6530.0); ABS (1985), *1984 Household Expenditure Survey, Australia: Summary of Results,* p. 11 (Catalog No. 6530.0).

with the cultural norms and values of Australians as a whole, and those specific to certain cultural groups, influence the behavior patterns of consumers.

Marketers need to recognize that the Australian consumer market has become more sophisticated, more demanding, more aware of its rights, and generally not afraid to question retailers and manufacturers. They will need to respond accordingly, providing consumer groups with appropriate information, good customer service and backup, and, above all, will need to be prepared to listen to what the market is asking for.

Consumers are looking for greater information on products and services, and expect that this information will be easily available. Increasingly, this will involve the use of electronic media. Furthermore, consumers want their complaints addressed both honestly and quickly. If they do not receive satisfactory outcomes they will look for another supplier. Marketers should recognize the importance of customer complaints. It is not sufficient, with this market, to acknowledge the complaint and use the information within the organization to enhance future product/service offerings; it is also necessary that individual consumers' complaints be addressed, and resolved satisfactorily. Furthermore, the manner in which complaints are handled can influence the perceptions of the firm, and the overall outcome for the customer.

It is important for marketers to recognize that, although the Australian population is relatively small by world standards, it is not homogeneous. A mistake that is frequently made, particularly by US companies, is to assume that Australians are just like Americans, and that little or no product modification is necessary when entering the Australian market. This can bring about disastrous results. Researching consumer needs and wants on a continuous basis and developing ongoing relations with customers is a necessity if companies are to be successful in the 1990s.

Marketers in the late 1990s and beyond will need to recognize that Australia is located in the Asia-Pacific region, with increasing migration from neighboring Asian countries, and with direct trade linkages into Asia, particularly Indonesia. At the same time, marketers will need to think of Australia as being very much a part of the world scene, with increasing emphasis being placed on internationalization. The Internet makes it possible for Australians to be up to date with the very latest information on products and services. A significant number of Australian consumers are already part of the World Wide Web, and more and more are likely to take up the subscription.

Australia is a multicultural country despite its largely British heritage. There are distinct segments of the population, including the mature consumers, yuppies, and the REEVS group. Within each of these segments, however, there are subgroups of consumers who are concerned about a number of issues, for instance the environment, and wish to purchase "environmentally sound" products. Marketers should note this, and look particularly at the content of the product and its packaging. In addition, across the community there appears to be concern about value for money. Yuppies in particular are no longer so interested in conspicuous consumption. What is important is that the product is well produced, is made of environmentally sound materials, represents value for money, and where possible, is Australian made or Australian designed.

Product packaging will need to be suitable for small households, and single serves in particular will need to be available. Labels must contain information about the product that can be understood by the consumer. That is, the labeling should be meaningful, helping the consumer to choose between competing products. Environmental issues need to be addressed, and it is likely that consumers will expect more use to be made of recycled and recyclable materials.

Marketers should take note of the increasing numbers of mature consumers. But clearly these cannot simply be grouped together into one homogenous group. They are not all alike. Rather, they represent different segments requiring individual attention, and products and services should be adapted accordingly to meet their special needs and wants.

More Australians are shopping from home using their telephones and personal computers, and this trend is likely to continue over the next ten years. There is likely to be more use of interactive home shopping in the future. Consumers will have access to on-line video banking, finance, weather, news, classified, horoscope and travel information by using on-line computer networks or interactive television. But this is not to say that large retail centres will cease to exist. Rather, these retail centres are likely to become more focused on a theme, provide more entertainment, and be true community centers. We are already seeing this trend emerge, with movie houses and entertainment parlors appearing within these centers. The use of virtual-reality equipment is likely to increase, with consumers of all ages able to simulate many different types of situations (without the cost or risk of the real thing), such as skydiving and skiing.

"Category-killer" stores, such as Toys "R" Us, often classified as single-story warehouses concentrating on one or few lines, are likely to continue to emerge. The major advantage of these stores is that they provide a low-cost structure, high turnover, an almost inexhaustible supply, discount incentives, and a constant availability of goods (Elliott 1995a). Within one year of the entry of Toys "R" Us into the Australian market in 1993, 17 stores had been established. Each store, totalling up to 4000 m^2, carries some 15 000 toy lines, including 400 different boardgames (Elliott 1995a).

When promoting products and services, marketers must ensure that the advertisements and messages contained in promotional campaigns are realistic. The persons portrayed in the advertisements need to reflect the varying lifestyles of Australians. Specifically, they should represent the various cultural and social groups, including, among others, Asians, Aboriginals, single-person households, single-parent families and gays. Furthermore, the people portrayed should be credible.

Loyalty schemes are likely to continue and even increase in number. Qantas and Ansett Australia, the two major Australian airlines, offer "Frequent-Flier" programs which give rewards for kilometres traveled by the consumer, along with dollars spent in participating organizations, such as hotels and rental car companies. American Express operates a loyalty scheme, Membership Miles, which offers points to participating consumers on the basis of dollars spent using their American Express card. "Fly Buys," the result of a partnership between Shell Australia, the Coles Myer Group,

National Australia Bank and Telstra, represents a huge force. Within a few months of the launch in 1994, "Fly Buys" had 1.25 million households fully signed up (Elliott 1995b). Australian Profit Sharing Organisation (APSO), founded in 1993, offers incentives such as money-back rebates to loyal customers. To the retailers, APSO claims to offer the following benefits: retailing training programs, promotion, retail association forums, support consultants, data collection terminals, and technology and support (APSO 1995).

Direct marketing has been used widely in Australia in the 1990s, and is expected to increase with the various loyalty schemes in operation. More and more organizations have access to detailed personal information, which can make direct marketing better targeted and, in many cases, more effective. This is likely to be associated with electronic media such as the World Wide Web. The key to success will be the extent to which the marketer is able to make the product/service information and the actual product offerings realistic and appropriate to the consumer.

Changes in the workforce, higher unemployment (in particular for men), early retirement, healthier and older consumers, and longer life expectancies are likely to mean that larger numbers of the Australian population will wish to participate in leisure activities. Again, as consumers are becoming more and more sophisticated and demanding, leisure activities will need to be more and more individualized, with adequate follow-up service and appropriate guarantees.

As illustrated in Table 1.16, expenditure on recreation in Australia is already significant, with the latest available figures suggesting average household expenditure on recreation to be over AU$560 per annum. However, this is expected to increase in the years ahead, and it is anticipated that customers of recreational products and services will be looking for increased quality, service, variety, and up-to-date information on leisure, recreation and travel experiences.

With increasing unemployment and greater disparity in income, increased polarization of the population is likely. This will create a demand for:

1 high priced goods and services that offer quality, but despite their high price tag also offer value
2 lower priced products and services that offer value for money

It is likely that discount malls will develop that offer "seconds," end-of-the-line stock and special lines. It is also likely that recycled goods outlets will continue to increase in number, as consumers can purchase relatively high quality goods for lower prices. These stores have the added appeal of being "in tune" with the environment, a feature highly prized by many Australians.

Table 1.16 Average household expenditure on recreation, selected items, 1988–1989

Expenditure item	*Weekly (AU$)*	*Annual (AU$)*
Camping equipment	0.36	18.72
Sports equipment	1.98	102.96
Recreational equipment	1.54	80.08
Gambling	3.55	184.60
Health & fitness studio charges	0.55	28.60
Sporting club subscriptions	0.75	39.00
Sports lessons	0.51	26.52
Sports services charges	1.05	54.60
Spectator admission fees to sports	0.49	25.48
Total	10.78	560.56

Source: ABS (1990a), *1988–1989 Household Expenditure Survey, Australia: Detailed Expenditure Items* (Catalog No. 6535.0).

Conclusion

The late 1990s and beyond will be both an exciting and a challenging time for marketers. To be successful in such turbulent times, marketers must keep abreast of these important changes, and will need to research the market constantly, endeavoring to develop meaningful and ongoing relationships with their clients.

To maintain these relationships, marketers need to exercise consideration, put in sufficient time getting to know the customer, handle their complaints sensitively, and above all to listen to what customers are saying. Marketers should not fall into the trap of believing that, because Australians generally behave and dress informally, even in business, they have "laid-back" attitudes toward service and product/service quality. To think this will only spell disaster. With a more sophisticated customer base, the "She'll be right, mate" attitude that has prevailed for much of Australia's history is dead.

References

Australian Bureau of Statistics (1975), *Year Book Australia 1974*, Catalog No. 1301.0.

— (1977), *Year Book Australia 1975–76*, Catalog No. 1301.0.

— (1982), *Year Book Australia 1982*, Catalog No. 1301.0.

— (1983), *Year Book Australia 1983*, Catalog No. 1301.0.

— (1984), *Social Indicators No. 4,* 1984, Catalog No. 4101.0.

— (1985), *1984 Household Expenditure Survey, Australia: Summary of Results,* Catalog No. 6530.0.

— (1986), *Year Book Australia 1986,* Catalog No. 1301.0.

— (1988), *Year Book Australia 1988,* Catalog No. 1301.0.

— (1990a), *1988-89 Household Expenditure Survey, Australia: Detailed Expenditure Items,* Catalog No. 6535.0.

— (1990b), *1988-89 Household Expenditure Survey, Australia: Summary of Results,* Catalog No. 6530.0.

— (1992a), *Education and Training in Australia,* Catalog No. 4224.0.

— (1992b), *Year Book Australia 1992,* Catalog No. 1301.0.

— (1993a), *Census Characteristics of Australia 1991, Census of Population and Housing,* Catalog No. 2710.0.

— (1993b), *Women in Australia,* Catalog No. 4113.0.

— (1994a), *Australian Demographic Statistics,* June Quarter 1994, Catalog No. 3101.0.

— (1994b), *Australian Social Trends,* Catalog No. 4102.0.

— (1994c), *Consumer Price Index,* September Quarter 1994, Catalog No. 6401.0.

— (1994d), *Deaths, Australia, 1993,* Catalog No. 3302.0.

— (1994e), *Estimated Resident Population by Sex and Age: States and Territories of Australia, Preliminary June 1992 and June 1993,* Catalog No. 3201.0.

— (1994f), *Projections of the Populations of Australia, States and Territories, 1993 to 2041,* Catalog No. 3222.0.

— (1994g), *Year Book Australia 1994,* Catalog No. 1301.0.

— (1995a), *Australian Economic Indicators, March 1995,* Catalog No. 1350.0.

— (1995b), *Year Book Australia 1995,* Catalog No. 1301.0.

APSO (1995), *"The Card That Pays You To Shop",* APSO brochure.

Baxter, J., Emmison, M., Western, J. & Western, M. eds (1991), *Class Analysis and Contemporary Australia,* Macmillan, South Melbourne.

Craig-Lees, M., Joy, S. & Browne, B. (1995), *Consumer Behaviour,* John Wiley and Sons, Brisbane.

Elliott, Tim (1995a), "Five blockbuster marketing ideas: Big, bigger, best", *Australian Professional Marketing,* 4 (2), p. 10.

— (1995b), "Five blockbuster marketing ideas: Frequent buyers", *Australian Professional Marketing,* 4 (2), p. 11.

Gray, C. et al. (1974), *Literature Review of Studies of Youth Views and Attitudes,* Australian Government Publishing Service, Canberra.

Hancock, I.R. (1995), "Australia: History", *The Far East and Australasia 1995,* 26th edn, Europa Publications, London, pp. 78–83.

Harrison, P. (1983), *Teen Power: A Harrison Report on the Unique Potential of the 10–17-year-old Market,* Harrison Communications, Sydney.

Kotler, P., Chandler, P., Brown, B. & Adam, S. (1994), *Marketing: Australia and New Zealand,* 3rd edn, Prentice Hall, Australia.

McColl-Kennedy, J.R., Kiel, G., Lusch, R. & Lusch, V. (1994), *Marketing: Concepts and Strategies,* 2nd edn, Thomas Nelson, Melbourne.

Mackay, H. (1992), *The Mind and Mood of Australia in the 90s,* Angus & Robertson, Sydney.

McQueen, A.E. (1995), "Australia: Physical and Social Geography", *The Far East and Australasia 1995,* 26th edn, Europa Publications, London, pp. 77–8.

Marketing (1992), "Niche Marketing", June, pp. 16-19.

TARP (1995), *American Express-SOCAP Study of Complaint Handling in Australia, Report 1: Consumer Complaint Behaviour in Australia,* SOCAP, Geelong West, Vic.

Notes

1 The assistance of Eric Manners, Kelly Schultz and Kerrie Unsworth, especially in the compiling of tables, is gratefully acknowledged.

2 All dollar values in this chapter are given in Australian dollars ($1(AU) = US$0.63 (approx.) at time of writing).

3 This is a colloquial Australian phrase meaning, approximately, "Don't worry, things will turn out all right."

CHAPTER 2

Brunei

Consumers in a monarchical market

SARA U. DOUGLAS

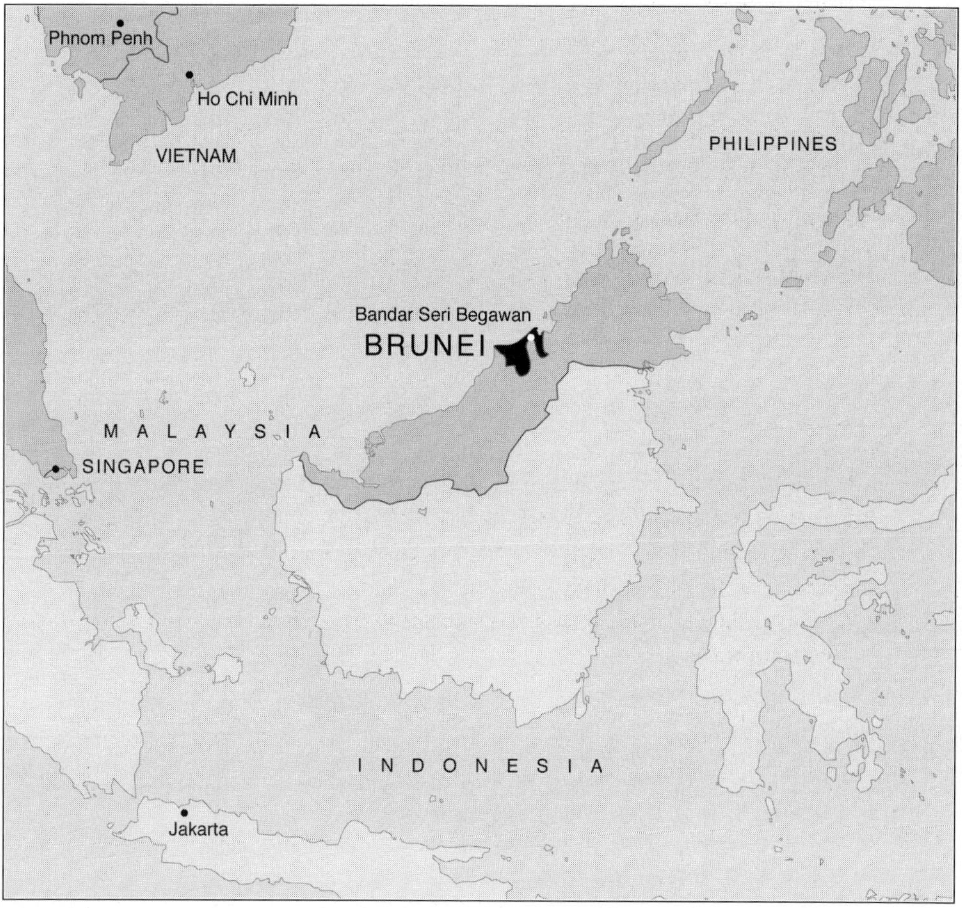

Abstract

Brunei Darussalam is a small state located on the north-west coast of Borneo, but its size belies its status as one of the world's richest nations. Among the geographically close countries that form the Association of South-East Asian Nations (ASEAN), Brunei Darussalam is exceptional in many ways, including its size, history, and economic growth and development patterns. Brunei is a modern, oil-rich welfare state. A monarchy dominated by Islam, it is cautiously opening up to the modern world in its efforts to ensure a prosperous long-term future. In this chapter an attempt is made to provide a brief introduction to marketing and consumer behavior in this little-known South-East Asian nation.

Introduction

"Languid" is a word frequently used to describe Brunei Darussalam. Weaver (1991, p. 65) provides details:

> What to do is a constant theme in Bruneian life; although the country is only 2 hours by plane from Singapore, it is amazingly isolated and remote. It has impressive museums, but no serious bookstores. It has no galleries, no concert halls, no political parties, no human-rights organizations, no discos. Most of its citizens are well educated, but it has no painters or poets of any note. It has no think tanks, no debating societies, and no parliament. It has no night clubs, no bars—no alcohol. All it has, really, is the second-highest per-capita gross national product in the world. Its two little parcels of petroleum-rich jungle are awash with oil and natural gas, and its 250 000 men, women, and children enjoy, according to official estimates, a per-capita GNP of some US$25 500[1] a year, second only to the per-capita GNP of Switzerland. (In the USA, each citizen's share of the GNP is US$21 737 per year.) Moreover, Brunei has substantial foreign investments, and, for the last six years, income from these investments has been greater than revenues from the export of gas and oil.[2]

Some things in Brunei have changed since Weaver's words were written; many have not. This brief portion of a much longer article describes a place that offers little excitement, but at the same time is compelling, puzzling, and relatively unique in the world. Among the geographically close countries that form ASEAN, Brunei Darussalam continues to be exceptional in many ways, including its size, history, and economic growth and development patterns. Often described as being more similar to Kuwait than its Asian neighbors, Brunei today is a modern, oil-rich welfare state. Not unexpectedly, Brunei's unusual and somewhat anachronistic qualities extend to demographic, economic, and sociocultural patterns. Of course, all of these factors have some bearing on the behavior of consumers in the country. Although these consumers are few, their purchasing power is impressive. And, as a market, they provide some clear—as well as some not-so-clear—opportunities and challenges.

The demographic environment

Located on the north-west coast of Borneo, Brunei Darussalam shares that island with the Malaysian states of Sabah and Sarawak and the Indonesian province of Kalimantan. Formerly an empire that controlled all of Borneo, Brunei is now the island's smallest independent territory, surrounded by the South China Sea and Sarawak. The country has a total area of only 5765 km^2, slightly larger than the US state of Delaware. However, Delaware's population is about 2.5 times that of Brunei's estimated 1995 population of 294 000 (World Book 1996). Official census population figures reported in 1991 were 260 482, an increase of 35% over the 192 832 figure listed in 1981 (see Table 2.1). About 67% of the population are Malay, 16% are Chinese, 6% are in other indigenous groups, and the remaining 11% make up other groups, mostly foreign residents. Approximately 53% are male (Economic Planning Unit (EPU) 1993).

Table 2.1 Population in census years, 1960–1991

Census year	*Population total*	*Average annual growth rate (%) between census years*	*Racial groups*			
			Malays	*Other indigenous*	*Chinese*	*Others*
1960	83 877	5.73	45 135 (54%)	14 068 (17%)	21 795 (26%)	2 879 (3%)
1971	136 256	4.51	89 268 (66%)	8 552 (6%)	31 925 (23%)	6 511 (5%)
1981	192 832	3.53	125 717 (65%)	15 175 (8%)	39 461 (20%)	12 469 (7%)
1991	260 482	3.05	174 319 (67%)	15 665 (6%)	40 621 (16%)	29 877 (11%)

Note:
In 1971, 1981, and 1991, the definition of "Malays" was changed to "Indigenous population of the Malay race," which consisted of Malays, Dusuns, Muruts, Kedayans, and Bisayas, the last four of which were included in the "Other indigenous" category in previous censuses.

Source: Adapted from Economic Planning Unit, Ministry of Finance, Brunei Darussalam (1993), *Brunei Darussalam Statistical Yearbook 1992*, EPU, Bandar Seri Begawan.

Well over half of the population (66%) lives in the Brunei/Muara District, the smallest of the four administrative districts in the area, which includes Bandar Seri Begawan, the capital city. The other three districts are Belait, with 20% of the population, Tutong, with 11%, and Temburong, with 3%. Household distribution is similar, with 63% of the households in Brunei/Muara, 24% in Belait, 11% in Tutong, and 3% in Temburong. The average number living in a household is 6. The population is primarily young (43% were under 20 years and 63% were under 30 years in 1992) and urban (67%) (EPU 1993).

Long-standing Bruneian ideology was declared the official national ideology at the time of independence in 1984. This is an integrated concept known as Melayu Islam Beraja (MIB), or Malay Islamic Monarchy. The three tenets of MIB are Malay language and culture, the Islamic religion, and the monarchy. These are an integral part of the education of all children and are expected to be respected, even if not practiced, by all citizens. Criticism of the sultan is forbidden, as is criticism of MIB.

Islam, the dominant religion in Brunei, is visible in many ways, not the least of which is the huge Omar Ali Saifuddin Mosque in Bandar Seri

Begawan. It dominates the skyline, and is frequently used as a symbol of the nation state. Deep religious beliefs are also reflected in the conservatism and orthodoxy of the population, as well as in the increase in the proportion of Muslims from 62.1% in 1971 to 67.2% in 1991 (EPU 1993). In accord with trends in Malaysia and Indonesia, the sultan has devoted increased attention to religious obligations since the late 1980s. The consequences for state policy have been apparent. For example, the sale and public consumption of alcohol was banned in 1991, and the celebration of Christmas was forbidden. In 1992, an edict decreed that all pig farms had to be phased out by early 1993 (Mani 1993). While alcohol can be consumed under strict conditions and pork can be imported for non-Muslims, these exceptions are not visible. In addition, increased funding lines to build mosques and upgrade religious education have been put into the national budget.

Brunei's government and political environment

Brunei's form of government has been described in different ways—as a constitutional sultanate, a government sultanate, and an absolute monarchy. Its strategic location on a primary China–Indonesia trade route led to the first direct reference to Brunei in 1365. The country became an independent sultanate around the mid-15th century, and the royal family line has been continuous since that time (Turnbull 1995). Though never formally colonized, Brunei was made a British protectorate in 1888, and, with the exception of the period when it was occupied by Japan (1941–1945), the British Resident was the effective ruler of Brunei until 1959. During this time of protection, however, the sultan typically played an active and visible role in government. In 1959, a constitution was finalized, and at that time internal affairs became the responsibility of Sultan Omar Ali Saifuddin III; England retained responsibility for defense and foreign relations.

It was just a few years after this shift, in 1962, that a short-lived rebellion occurred—the first and only in Brunei's modern history. It was stimulated by calls for internal democratic reforms by Brunei's first political party, the Partai Rakyat Brunei (PRB, or Brunei's People's Party). The result was the declaration of a state of emergency; this state of emergency, along with the laws it engendered, has never been lifted. In 1967 the sultan abdicated in favor of his son, the current sultan, HM Paduka Seri Baginda Sultan Haji Hassanal Bolkiah Mu'izzaddin Waddaulah (Hassanal Bolkiah), and in 1984 Brunei became fully independent from the UK (Turnbull 1995).

Calls for increased democracy have continued from time to time, but thus far have been resisted by the sultan in spite of some movement toward increased tolerance of political participation (Case 1996). In 1989, the sultan said he would establish more liberal institutions, and reintroduce elections and a legislature (elections of the Legislative Council last occurred in 1962) only "when I can see evidence of a genuine interest in politics on the part of a responsible majority of Bruneians" (US Dept of State 1991).

In 1992, the sultan marked his Silver Jubilee celebration by reaffirming the dominant role of the monarchy in Malay Islamic Brunei. Practical reaffirmation for this tenet of the MIB can be found in the structure of the government, where members of the royal family serve in a number of top government positions. The sultan, assisted by his five appointed councils, also is prime minister of the country and minister of defence, and has full executive authority. The remainder of the executive branch consists of an 11-member cabinet, called the Council of Cabinet Ministers. The Cabinet is composed largely of members of the royal family, two of whom (the ministers of foreign affairs and finance) are brothers of the sultan. The legislative branch is the unicameral Legislative Council. Although discussion of constitutional reforms has included consideration of an elected Legislative Council, such changes do not appear imminent (Weaver 1991; US National Foreign Assessment Center 1994; Case 1996). Until very recently, only one political party existed in Brunei: the Parti Perpaduan Kebangsaan Brunei (the Brunei National United Party); it only sporadically shows any signs of activity, but the fact that the sultan allowed a long-banned party (the Brunei Solidarity Party) to reorganize in 1996 has generated a modicum of speculation regarding Brunei's political future (Case 1996).

Brunei's primary legal system, adopted from the UK, is similar to that of Singapore and Malaysia. It is based on common law, with (in principle) an independent judiciary. Laws themselves are relatively brief and general. Judicial power is held by the Supreme Court, the Intermediate Court, and the Subordinate Courts. All major judicial posts are filled by appointees of the sultan (EIU 1995c). Legal matters pertaining to the Islamic faith are dealt with by Islamic courts, and laws are based on Islamic law ("Business Guide" 1995). The lower courts, those that try most cases, are both local magistrate's courts and religious courts.

The economic environment

In a region in which most countries are experiencing close to double-digit economic growth, Brunei's economy has been stagnant, and by some measures shrinking. However, this relatively closed economy may be opening gradually. A signal of potential change came in 1995, when Brunei applied for membership to the world's two leading financial institutions, the World Bank and the International Monetary Fund (IMF); membership was granted in October 1995. That Brunei had not done this earlier is noteworthy, especially in light of the fact that the only other Asian country that shared this non-member status with Brunei was North Korea. Brunei certainly did not make the move in haste; applications for membership were made a full 11 years after it joined ASEAN.

After Brunei became a member of ASEAN, a number of observers expected further change to occur relatively rapidly. The reasons this did not happen have not been explained directly by the Brunei government, but the 11-year delay is probably attributable to two or three important considerations. It may have been based partially on the complacency of some of Brunei's elite about the relative economic freedom the country has enjoyed. It may have had something to do with the fact that Brunei has been able to keep its financial affairs largely out of public knowledge, and even, to a surprising extent, out of public attention. Financial and economic data from Brunei are difficult to obtain, if obtainable at all, and are not timely when they are acquired. A complaint frequently heard from those whose attention has been captured by Brunei's financial situation is that it is not clear where the sultan's enormous personal wealth ends and Brunei's (also enormous) public funds begin. Membership in the IMF and World Bank may prove extremely helpful to Brunei's leaders as they try to inject vigor and diversity into the economy, but, for the first time, Brunei's financial dealings will be open to world scrutiny (Holloway 1995).

Income and GDP

Brunei's inhabitants enjoy one of the world's highest levels of per-capita income from an economy that is heavily dependent on crude oil, natural gas, and, to a lesser extent, petroleum products. (These and other basic economic indicators are listed in Table 2.2.) In 1990, the oil sector contributed 62.9% to GDP, while the non-oil government sector contributed 20.6% and the non-oil private sector 16.5% (EIU 1993–1994). A more recent estimate is that the gas and oil sector is now contributing less than 50% to GDP (Hiebert 1995). However, the generally heavy dependence on oil has led the government to enact policies that would move the economy toward increased internal diversification; though progress in this direction has been made, results in general have been limited and disappointingly slow.

Some observers have concluded that government efforts toward economic diversification inside the country lack impetus because of two things. First, the country enjoys substantial earnings (which surpass gas and oil revenues) from the country's huge foreign investments, which were reported to be US$36.5 billion in 1993 (Holloway 1995). Needless to say, this external diversification provides quite a comfortable cushion. Second, Brunei's oil supply is not running low (although this possibility certainly looms in the minds of forward-thinking government officials). Known oil reserves are expected to continue to power the economy for at least the near future—30 years is one estimate—and new discoveries seem to be a fairly regular occurrence ("A piece of royal fortune" 1992; Hiebert 1995).

Table 2.2 Economic indicators, 1974, 1981–1995

Indicator	*1974*	*1981*	*1982*	*1983*	*1984*	*1985*	*1986*	*1987*
GDP, current prices, B$ million	2 616.3	9 224.7	9 125.5	8 163.9	8 068.5	7 752.3	5 135.6	5 800.9
GDP, constant prices, B$ million, 1974 = 100	2 616.3	3 414.5	3 549.5	3 567.4	3 588.9	3 535.3	3 439.6	3 508.4
GDP per capita, B$	17 333	47 795	45 628	39 247	37 354	34 920	22 852	25 004
Real GDP growth, %								0.9[2]
Consumer price inflation, %		9.1	6.4	1.2	3.1	2.3	1.8	1.3
Consumer price index, average all commodities		1977 = 100 129.0	137.2	138.8	143.1	146.4	149.0	150.9
Population, '000		193	200	208	216	222	226	234
GDP, current prices, US$ million		4 499.9[4]	4 304.5[4]	3 814.9[4]	3 684.2[4]	3 656.7[4]	2 345.0[4]	2 886.0[4]
GDP per capita, current prices, US$		23 315[4]	21 523[4]	18 340	17 057[4]	16 472[4]	10 422[4]	12 440[4]
Exchange rate, B$: US$		2.05	2.12	2.14	2.19	2.12	2.19	2.01

Indicator	*1988*	*1989*	*1990*	*1991*	*1992*	*1993*	*1994*	*1995*
GDP, current prices, B$ million	5 414.8	5 845.0	6 508.6	6 604.3*	6 372.0*			
GDP, constant prices, B$ million, 1974 = 100	3 546.9	3 508.8	3 605.1	3 736.4	3 698.1			
GDP per capita, B$	22 656	23 760	25 424	25 401	23 865			23 400[1]
Real GDP growth, %	2.4[2]	2.5[2]	5.0[2]	1.0[2]				
Consumer price inflation, %	1.2	1.3	2.1	1.6	1.3	2.0*[3]	3.0*[3]	
Consumer price index, average all commodities			1990 = 100					
	152.7	154.7	158.0					
			100	101.6	102.9			
Population, '000	241	249	256	261	268	271	277*	285*
GDP, current prices, US$ million	2 762.7[4]	3 060.2[4]	3 636.1[4]	4 027.0[4]	3 861.8[4]			
GDP per capita, current prices, US$	11 559[4]	12 440[4]	14 203[4]	15 488[4]	14 464[4]			17 857[5]
Exchange rate, B$: US$	1.96	1.91	1.79	1.64	1.65	1.65	1.60	1.42

Notes:

* = estimates.

1 "Brunei Darussalam: Quick Facts" (1995), Brunei Press Sdn Bhd, Kuala Belait, Available: Netscape, URL http://sunsite.nus.sg/SEAlinks/brunei-info-html.
2 Economist Intelligence Unit (various), *Country Report: Malaysia, Brunei*, The Economist Intelligence Unit Ltd, London.
3 Economist Intelligence Unit (1995), *Country Report: Malaysia, Brunei*, The Economist Intelligence Unit Ltd, London, 3rd quarter.
4 Calculated using average annual exchange rates from the Brunei Association of Banks, Economic Planning Unit, Ministry of Finance, Brunei Darussalam (1993), *Brunei Darussalam Statistical Yearbook 1992*, EPU, Bandar Seri Begawan.
5 Kieran Cooke (1995), "Sultans Swing to Reform", *The Financial Times*, August 4, p. 18.

Source: Unless otherwise cited, all data are from the Economic Planning Unit, Ministry of Finance, Brunei Darussalam (1993), *Brunei Darussalam Statistical Yearbook 1992*, EPU, Bandar Seri Begawan.

In 1992, the non-oil economic sectors that were increasing their shares of GDP (current prices) were:

1 community, social and personal services (27.54%, which includes the substantial government expenditures for health and education)
2 wholesale trade (6.66%)
3 construction (4.89%)
4 transport, storage, and communication (4.86%)
5 retail trade (4.37%)
6 banking and finance (3.86%) (see Table 2.3)

Table 2.3 Shifts in industrial origin sectoral shares of GDP, 1982–1992

Kind of economic activity	*GDP shares (%) at current price*		*GDP shares (%) at constant price*	
	1982	*1992*	*1982*	*1992*
1. Agriculture & hunting	0.58	2.29	0.76	1.31
2. Forestry & logging	0.17	0.25	0.24	0.14
3. Fishing	0.10	0.47	0.12	0.26
4. Mining, quarrying, & manufacturing	76.60	41.66	72.98	56.03
5. Electricity, gas, & water	0.81	1.01	0.28	0.87
6. Construction	2.90	4.89	3.76	2.79
7. Wholesale	8.23	6.66	6.06	5.82
8. Retail trade	2.04	4.37	3.51	3.14
9. Restaurants & hotels	0.42	1.25	0.52	0.91
10. Transport, storage, & communication	1.46	4.86	1.64	3.36
11. Banking & finance	1.35	3.86	2.16	2.57
12. Insurance	0.06	1.18	0.1	0.78
13. Real estate & business services	1.09	1.10	1.75	0.74
14. Ownership of dwellings	1.29	1.08	0.45	0.58
15. Community, social, & personal services	5.83	27.54	8.81	23.27
16. Less: bank charges	-1.30	-2.46	-3.14	-2.57

Source: Derived from data, Economic Planning Unit, Ministry of Finance, Brunei Darussalam (1993), *Brunei Darussalam Statistical Yearbook*, EPU, Bandar Seri Begawan.

At constant prices, however, there have been declines in wholesale trade, construction, and retail trade.

The contribution of agriculture and livestock to GDP grew from 0.76% in 1982 to 1.31% in 1992 (constant prices). But, in general, the agricultural sector has moved especially slowly, in spite of the government's great desire to acquire self-sufficiency in food production. Agriculture, forestry, and fishing together contributed only 1.71% to GDP in 1992, which is quite low, and was up only slightly from the level of 1.12% recorded in 1982.

In its 6th National Development Plan (1991–1995), which lays out government spending proposals, the Brunei government allocated US$166.2 million for industrial development. Outside experts were employed to study ways Brunei might become more competitive in the global market and to construct a new industrial development program that could be implemented as part of the 7th National Development Plan (not yet available). The government has also enacted measures to encourage growth in its small private sector. Initiative in this direction depends largely on state funding of infrastructural development.

Primary industries

Brunei's primary industries are garment manufacturing and food and beverage processing. Very little of this output is exported, although in 1992 two textile factories did export garments worth US$9.7 million to Europe and the USA (EIU 1993–1994). A third, Perkasa-Hualey Garments, reportedly had a US$1 million per month US market in 1995 for knitted sport shirts (Hiebert 1995).

While the government has targeted furniture, pottery and glass, cement, chemicals, and plywood and perhaps even a downstream petrochemical industry for future development, Brunei's entrepreneurs face several obstacles. First, there is the fact that skilled labor is scarce, and production costs are driven up rapidly by the need to hire workers from the Philippines and other countries in the region; additional hindrances come in the form of bureaucratic delays and high freight and telecommunications charges. Also, some Bruneians are of the opinion that entrepreneurial spirit is hampered by the country's generous social welfare system (Hiebert 1995). If this is true, the minimal efforts the government has made to overcome such problems, such as a seminar series on privatization, will do little to encourage change.

The future

More recent ideas are that the government could provide incentives to Brunei's growing financial sector with the objective of eventually making it a regional center for financial activities. The potential success of such a direction may be questioned, given Singapore's proximity and well-proven track record in the same area. Another idea is to develop Brunei as a regional telecommunications hub. And a third direction that could gain momentum is ecotourism. This is a concept that:

> connotes a type of tourism which lends particular emphasis to a sustainable utilization of natural ecosystems and environmental resources whereby visitors would be encouraged to explore the rich and diverse ecosystems that exist in the natural tropical rain forests of the country (Borhan 1995).

Employment

In 1991, the government reported that 106 746 people were employed in Brunei, 46% of whom were employed in the public sector and 54% in the private sector (see Table 2.4). The heaviest concentration of employment is in the sector designated as community, social and personal services (49%, most in the public sector); followed by wholesale and retail trade, restaurants, and hotels (14%, most in the private sector); and construction (13%, most in the private sector). It is difficult to separate out employment numbers for the gas and oil sector, which employs persons in both the public and private sectors and has a spill-over effect on other sectors. However, in general, employment in that sector is relatively low because of its capital-intensive nature. Brunei Shell Petroleum, a joint venture owned equally by the government of Brunei and Royal Dutch Shell, employed about 3500 people in 1991 (Doshi 1995).

Over one-third of all people employed in Brunei are expatriates; foreigners seem to be needed in both the skilled and unskilled sectors. A training program has been established by the government to help alleviate the shortage of skilled labor (*Far Eastern Economic Review* 1996); its effects are not yet noticeable. And there continues to be a consistent shortage of manual laborers in Brunei. But, at the same time, there is a growing unemployment problem, particularly noticeable among young people. This situation is causing some attention and concern, perhaps particularly because it is seen as a source of potential social problems, but also because of the questions it raises for the economy in the long term (Cooke 1995; Doshi 1995).

A second employment issue that may have serious effects on Brunei's future is the fact that jobs are correlated with ethnicity, as they are in some other South-East Asian countries, perhaps especially Malaysia. Most Brunei Malays ('bumiputera') have a preference for working in government service. Employment there is relatively secure, and benefits are excellent.

In the past, when the overall percentage of public-sector jobs was higher, educated Malays felt almost assured of a government job. Now, however, as the government attempts to diversify the economy, it is cutting back on its still over-large public sector and people are being encouraged to find employment in the private sector. However, if well-educated bumiputera are

Table 2.4 Employment by economic sector and sex, 1991

	Total			*Public sector*			*Private sector*		
Sector	*Persons*	*Male*	*Female*	*Persons*	*Male*	*Female*	*Persons*	*Male*	*Female*
Agriculture, forestry & fishing	2 162	1 600	562	803	410	393	1 359	1 190	169
Mining, quarrying & manufacturing	9 397	7 268	2 129	305	175	130	9 092	7 093	1 999
Electricity, gas & water	2 223	1 912	311	1 985	1 698	287	238	214	24
Construction	14 145	13 534	611	1 651	1 529	122	12 494	12 005	489
Wholesale & retail trade, restaurants & hotels	15 404	10 284	5 120	462	362	100	14 942	9 922	5 020
Transport, storage & communication	5 392	4 203	1 189	1 692	1 289	403	3 700	2 914	786
Finance, insurance, real estate & business services	5 807	3 924	1 883	826	595	231	4 981	3 329	1 652
Community, social & personal services	52 121	29 535	22 586	41 256	27 080	14 176	10 865	2 455	8 410
Unknown	95	78	17	18	15	3	77	63	14
Total	**106 746**	**72 338**	**34 408**	**48 998**	**33 153**	**15 845**	**57 748**	**39 185**	**18 563**

Source: Economic Planning Unit, Ministry of Finance, Brunei Darussalam (1993), *Brunei Darussalam Statistical Yearbook 1992*, EPU, Bandar Seri Begawan, p. 42.

going to take a private sector job, they prefer employment considered prestigious–for example, jobs in banking and finance, or with Brunei Shell Petroleum or Royal Brunei Airlines. Increasing unemployment among the Brunei Malays has led the government to implement a policy ('Bruneization') giving Malays job preference.

So, for the Malays, jobs are there, but they are increasingly in the private sector and they are mid-level positions. Jobs for unskilled workers are also overabundant for the country's small (and educated) population, explaining the high number of immigrants who currently hold them. The result is an unemployment rate that is creeping upward; in 1991, it was 4.7% (EPU 1993) as compared with 3.6% in 1981, a year in which Brunei's unemployment problem already had been identified primarily as one not of a small population, but rather of mismatch (Arief 1986). The employment/ethnicity problem for the Chinese is slightly different; many have successful jobs in the private commercial sector, but they are feeling increasingly pressured by Bruneization.

Trade

Brunei's consistently positive trade balance in recent years is shown in Table 2.5. Between 1974 and 1984, Brunei's total exports consisted mainly of crude oil, natural gas, and petroleum products, and Japan was by far the largest recipient of these exports (Arief 1987). Since then, the situation has changed incrementally, but positively–away from excessive reliance on one sector and one market (see tables 2.6 and 2.7). However, oil and natural gas continue to account for almost all exports; in 1991, crude petroleum exports were 49% of estimated total exports, while natural gas contributed 46% (Doshi 1995). Japan's share of these exports has declined from 71% to 61% and 58% in 1980, 1985, and 1990 respectively (see Table 2.7). Export ratios of total exports to GDP also reflect this heavy but declining dependence on exports. These ranged from 93%, 84%, and 62% in 1980, 1985, and 1990 respectively. Some of the decline after 1981 is due to a fall in crude oil prices and production.

Brunei's trade surplus declined during the 1980s (see Table 2.5), not only because of lower oil prices but also because of industrialization and better living standards. Import shares of machinery and transport equipment and chemicals have been declining, while imports of manufactured goods classified chiefly by materials and miscellaneous manufactured products have been on the incline (see Table 2.6). During the period 1980–1990, Singapore, the USA, and Japan continued to be Brunei's largest importers, with imports from all three totaling between 63% (1980) and 56% (1990) of all imports (see Table 2.7).

Because Brunei manufactures relatively few consumer products, its imports in this category are high, and continue to rise rapidly. As per-capita income rises, ownership of goods typically increases dramatically, often in sales of major labor-saving tools and motor vehicles. The value of private

Table 2.5 Foreign trade (B$ million)

	1981	*1982*	*1983*	*1984*	*1985*	*1986*
Exports (including re-exports)	8 592	8 153	7 171	6 814	6 533	3 990
Imports	1 265	1 572	1 542	1 331	1 348	1 457
Balance	7 327	6 581	5 629	5 483	5 185	2 533
	1987	*1988*	*1989*	*1990*	*1991*	*1992*
Exports (including re-exports)	4 006	3 436	3 673	4 010	4 292*	3 863*
Imports	1 350	1 497	1 497	1 813	1 875*	1 917*
Balance	2 656	1 939	1 998	2 197	2 417	1 946

Note:
* = estimate.

Source: Economic Planning Unit, Ministry of Finance, Brunei Darussalam (1993), *Brunei Darussalam Statistical Yearbook 1992*, EPU, Bandar Seri Begawan, p. 75.

motor vehicles imported into Brunei between 1981 and 1989 increased from 6% of total imports to 8% (United Nations (UN) various years), while the number of registered private vehicles (all imported) doubled in the same period and had increased by 2.5 in 1992 (EPU 1993).

Over 90% of tariff lines enter Brunei duty free (US Department of Commerce 1995), so the country easily complies with the free-trade objectives of the General Agreement on Tariffs and Trade (GATT), of which it was a member until that body became the World Trade Organization (WTO) in 1995; now Brunei is a member of the WTO. It joined the original five ASEAN members (Indonesia, Malaysia, the Philippines, Singapore, and Thailand) in 1984, and now is also a member of the ASEAN Free Trade Association (AFTA) and the Asian-Pacific Economic Conference (APEC). In 1994, a sub-regional co-operation group, the East ASEAN Growth Area (EAGA) was formally established, consisting of Brunei, Sarawak and Sabah (East Malaysia), Mindanao (southern Philippines), and Kalimantan, Sulawesi, and Maluku (Indonesia). Brunei is well-located geographically in this grouping, and eager to take advantage of the opportunities it should offer.

Social and cultural environment

Human development

While it can be misleading to attempt to quantify human behavior, the United Nations human development index (HDI), developed in 1990, is a useful place to start when investigating people and cultures. The index averages three basic indicators, life expectancy at birth, educational attainment,

Table 2.6 Composition of trade by produce (B$million, %)

Commodity	*Exports*			*Commodity*	*Imports*		
	1980	*1985*	*1990*		*1980*	*1985*	*1990*
Minerals, fuels, lubricants & related material	9 714.34 (98.6%)	6 435.62 (98.5%)	3 871.05 (96.5%)	Machinery & transport equipment	497.52 (40.4%)	456.30 (33.8%)	624.32 (34.4%)
Miscellaneous manufactured products	46.82 (0.5%)	10.86 (0.17%)	30.46 (0.76%)	Manufactured goods classified chiefly by materials	298.14 (24.2%)	289.88 (21.5%)	489.38 (27.0%)
Machinery & transport equipment	44.93 (0.5%)	55.31 (0.85%)	54.63 (1.4%)	Food & live animals	146.75 (11.9%)	196.12 (14.5%)	277.10 (15.3%)
Manufactured goods classified chiefly by materials	31.09 (0.3%)	10.77 (0.16%)	20.38 (0.5%)	Chemicals	102.30 (8.3%)	95.09 (7.1%)	122.07 (6.7%)
Food & live animals	4.45 (0.04%)	10.04 (0.15%)	25.37 (0.6%)	Miscellaneous manufactured products	85.02 (6.9%)	165.28 (10.8%)	184.87 (10.2%)
Other	11.31 (0.11%)	10.29 (0.16%)	8.26 (0.2%)	Other	100.88 (8.2%)	165.72 (12.30%)	115.43 (6.4%)
Total (B$ m)	**9 852.94 (100%)**	**6 532.89 (100%)**	**4 010.15 (100%)**	**Total (B$ m)**	**1 230.60 (100%)**	**1 348.39 (100%)**	**1 813.16 (100%)**

Source: Adapted from Economic Planning Unit, Ministry of Finance, Brunei Darussalam (1993), *Brunei Darussalam Statistical Yearbook 1992*, EPU, Bandar Seri Begawan.

Table 2.7 Composition of trade by country (% of total value)

Exports						Imports					
Country	*1980*	*Country*	*1985*	*Country*	*1990*	*Country*	*1980*	*Country*	*1985*	*Country*	*1990*
Japan	70.9%	Japan	61.2%	Japan	58.1%	Japan	23.7%	Singapore	24.4%	Singapore	25.9%
USA	8.6%	Thailand	11.0%	Korea	12.4%	USA	20.0%	Japan	19.8%	USA	15.3%
Singapore	6.5%	Singapore	8.7%	Thailand	7.7%	Singapore	19.0%	USA	15.6%	Japan	14.6%
South Africa	4.9%	USA	7.3%	Singapore	7.1%	United Kingdom	9.8%	United Kingdom	9.2%	Malaysia	10.3%
Thailand	4.1%	Korea	7.0%	Philippines	4.9%	Malaysia	4.1%	Malaysia	5.2%	United Kingdom	6.5%
Taiwan	1.6%	Taiwan	3.5%	USA	3.4%	Germany	2.9%	Germany	3.8%	Germany	3.9%
Philippines	1.1%	Malaysia	0.6%	Taiwan	3.4%	Netherlands	2.9%	Thailand	3.1%	Thailand	3.7%
Malaysia	1.0%	Philippines	0.5%	Australia	1.3%	Thailand	2.5%	Taiwan	2.9%	China	2.7%
Australia	0.8%	Indonesia	0.3%	Malaysia	1.2%	China	2.2%	Australia	2.7%	Australia	2.6%
New Zealand	0.5%	United Kingdom	0.04%	China	0.1%	Australia	2.2%	China	2.0%	Italy	2.1%
Other	0.05%	Other	0.1%	Other	14.47%	Other	10.6%	Other	11.2%	Other	12.4%
Total (B$)	**9 852.94** (100%)	**Total**	**6 532.89** (100%)	**Total**	**4 010.15** (100%)	**Total**	**1 230.60** (100%)	**Total**	**1 348.39** (100%)	**Total**	**1 813.16** (100%)

Source: Derived from Economic Planning Unit, Ministry of Finance, Brunei Darussalam (1993), *Brunei Darussalam Statistical Yearbook 1992*, EPU, Bandar Seri Begawan.

and income, and provides a comparative indicator of human development (United Nations Development Program (UNDP) 1995, p. 1). Brunei was recently placed in the "high" category, with an HDI score of 0.868 out of 1.000, and a ranking of 41st of 174 (UNDP 1995).

Lifestyle extremes exist in Brunei: from the shopping complexes, government buildings, and variety of homes in Bandar Seri Begawan and its suburbs to farmers' timber-sided and tin-roofed houses on stilts in the Temburong District, to Iban longhouses in the Belait District. But state support of human welfare is extremely high throughout the country. In addition to education, the state provides food subsidies, a home-ownership scheme, and care of the elderly and needy. A strong commitment to family values exists. This, in conjunction with the level of government funding for children's welfare, affords children who grow up in Brunei a nurturing environment. Further nurturing comes through Brunei's health-care system, provided not only to children, but also to everyone else–at no charge (only foreigners must pay a minimal fee). Moreover, the quality of care provided is considered to be among the highest in Asia. There are 10 hospitals in the country, including general hospitals in Bandar Seri Begawan and Kuala Belait, and one hospital owned by Brunei Shell, plus numerous health-care units, and a Flying Doctor Service that reaches outlying areas (especially necessary when 75–80% of the country is tropical jungle and rain forest). Those who require specialized care are sent abroad; for citizens, the government bears expenses ("The Benevolent State" 1995).

Women in Brunei fare somewhat less well in general than children. Still, in a UN gender-related development index (GRDI) (supplemental to the HDI in that it measures the same basic capabilities, but also factors in inequality in achievement between women and men), Brunei received an even higher ranking than the 41st spot on the HDI. It came in 31st out of 174 countries. Given Brunei's status as a conservative, orthodox Muslim nation, this ranking also is notable.

Muslim women are strongly encouraged, but apparently not coerced, to wear the traditional *tudong* to cover their heads. With Koranic precepts as a basis, Muslim women in Brunei are denied equal status with men regarding divorce, inheritance, custody of children, and employment. In terms of the last, many women have recently entered the workforce, and are employed in a variety of capacities, including jobs in government and the military. There are no separate pay scales for women, but women who do not have university degrees are, unlike men, ineligible for permanent government employment. Rather, they are hired on a month-to-month basis.

Recent changes have improved certain of these inequities, however, as indicated by the fact that in 1993 a woman served as an intermediate court judge, the highest judicial position held by Bruneians (US Dept of State

1994). This is relatively recent and it seems to be exceptional; in 1991, Brunei's minister of education said:

> A woman can rise to every level, except a few . . . [S]he can't become a Sultan, of course, or a judge, or a Cabinet minister. In fact, the rule is really quite simple here–if the position is one in which the final decision is made, it cannot be held by a woman (Weaver 1991, p 82).

And, although there are some well-qualified candidates, since independence no woman yet has been appointed to ministerial rank.

The status of other minority groups varies. One negative for most minorities, however, is the official promotion of the state ideology, MIB. In particular, the inclusion of MIB in the educational system, especially its religious emphasis, has made some uncomfortable. Most indigenous people, as well as the Chinese, are non-Muslim. The Chinese, however, have to some extent avoided having their children receive Muslim religious indoctrination in the schools by establishing a school system of their own. And many indigenous people seem to be willing to live with the situation in return for the benefits gained from having good educations provided to their children by the state. In fact, some, for example Ibans from neighboring Sarawak, evidently immigrate solely to take advantage of the Bruneian school system.

The largest of the minority groups (16% of the population) is the Bruneian Chinese who, since 1985, have been classified as non-citizens:

> Those (Chinese) having no claims to other nationalities were "British-protected persons" prior to independence, and are now stateless and either permanent or temporary residents. Non-citizens may not own land but may hold property through long-term leases. The process of obtaining citizenship in Brunei is long and difficult. Many aspirants complain that the Malay-language test required for citizenship is administered so rigorously that it is almost impossible for a non-native speaker to pass (US Dept of State 1994, p. 6).

This, as well as the fact that Malay citizens are favored when it comes to government employment and university access, is causing some Chinese to leave Brunei for good. This is occurring in spite of the fact that here, as in many other countries, the Chinese in general have been able to prosper through their successful business activities.

Education

Education, which may begin in preschools, is provided free of charge by the government of Brunei, and is compulsory for 9 years. Schools are differentiated by language (with three official languages of instruction–Malay, English, and Chinese) and by type of administration. After 4 years of the total of 6 provided in Malay primary schools, students are examined to determine the type of secondary-school preparation they will receive; they may be directed into an English-language school, a Malay-language school or a religious school. All Malay schools are state-administered, while some of the English-language schools are state administered and some independent. Chinese schools, both primary and secondary, are privately administered, and not provided with government assistance ("Directory" 1995).

In general, schools are co-educational (EPU 1995). And, while the literacy level has climbed rapidly from 48% reported literate in the 1960 census to 89% in the 1991 census, the literacy rate for females has climbed even more rapidly. Between 1971 and 1981, the population literacy rate grew by 69%, while the female literacy rate grew by 83%. Comparable numbers for the 1981 to 1991 years were 56% and 65% (EPU 1993).

Bruneians who wish to go on to higher education and who are qualified to do so may continue their studies, either in Brunei or abroad, at government expense. Many have chosen to go abroad because facilities for higher education are still limited in Brunei. England is the preferred choice unless a student wishes to study religion, in which case the preferred location is often Cairo. There are 3 primary institutes of higher education within the country as well as 5 other technical/vocational centers. The University of Brunei Darussalam (UBD) opened in 1985, and in 1992 had an enrollment of 1065 students, most of whom had chosen to study education (EPU 1993).

Consumers in a unique marketplace

Imports of consumer goods

One factor that contributes to the unique aspect of Brunei's marketplace is the fact that the country imports 80% of its total food needs as well as most of its manufactured products ("Brunei Darussalam" 1995). In 1989 (the latest year for which disaggregated imports by SITC codes and broad economic categories were available for Brunei), 90% of imported food was for household consumption rather than for industry (UN 1988–1992).

Brunei is self-sufficient in egg production, nearly self-sufficient in poultry, and over 50% self-sufficient in vegetable production; however, only about 20% of its rice needs are supplied domestically, and almost all of its beef, fruit, and even fish are imported ("Great Strides" 1995).

Of the total manufactured products that Brunei imports, it is unclear exactly what percentage goes to industry and what to consumer goods. But, assuming that most of the passenger motor vehicles that are imported are purchased by consumers,[3] and adding in the food category and "other consumer goods" category, almost 40% of Brunei's total imports are consumer goods. Of these imported consumer goods, food represented 44.8% in 1981 and 40.1% in 1989 (see fig. 2.1).

Comparisons of Brunei's imports of selected consumer goods from 1981 to 1994 (the most recent to date) yield several interesting findings. First, they have increased significantly. During this 13-year period, while the population grew by about 52%, imports (by value) of perfume and cosmetics increased 170%; furniture and parts by 317%; clothing, accessories and shoes by 261%; and toys and sporting goods by 431% (see fig. 2.2; these figures have been derived from UN data, various years). Television and radio data do not appear in Figure 2.1 because of lack of SITC correspondence in the 1980s; however, Bruneians have both television and radio in their homes, and the numbers of each per household continue to rise. During the 1980s, the number of radios per household increased from 1.4 to 2.3, and the number of color television sets per household increased from 0.9 to 1.6 in the same period (EPU 1993).

Inflation accounts for part of the increase in imports in value terms, but another interesting aspect of Brunei's dependency on other countries for its consumer goods is the extent to which its consumer prices are determined by the economies in the countries from which it imports. Brunei's consumer price index for all commodities rose 20% between 1981 and 1989. For food

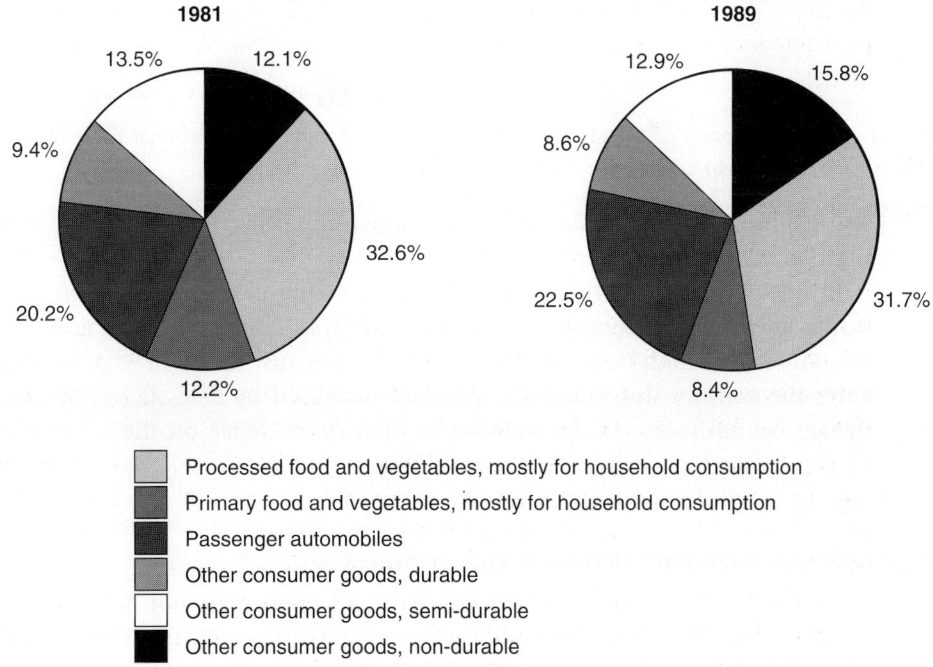

Fig. 2.1 Brunei's imports of consumer goods by broad economic category, 1981 and 1989: Percentage of estimated total consumer goods

Source: Adapted from United Nations data (various years), "Brunei Darussalam" in *Foreign Trade Statistics of Asia and the Pacific*, UN, New York.

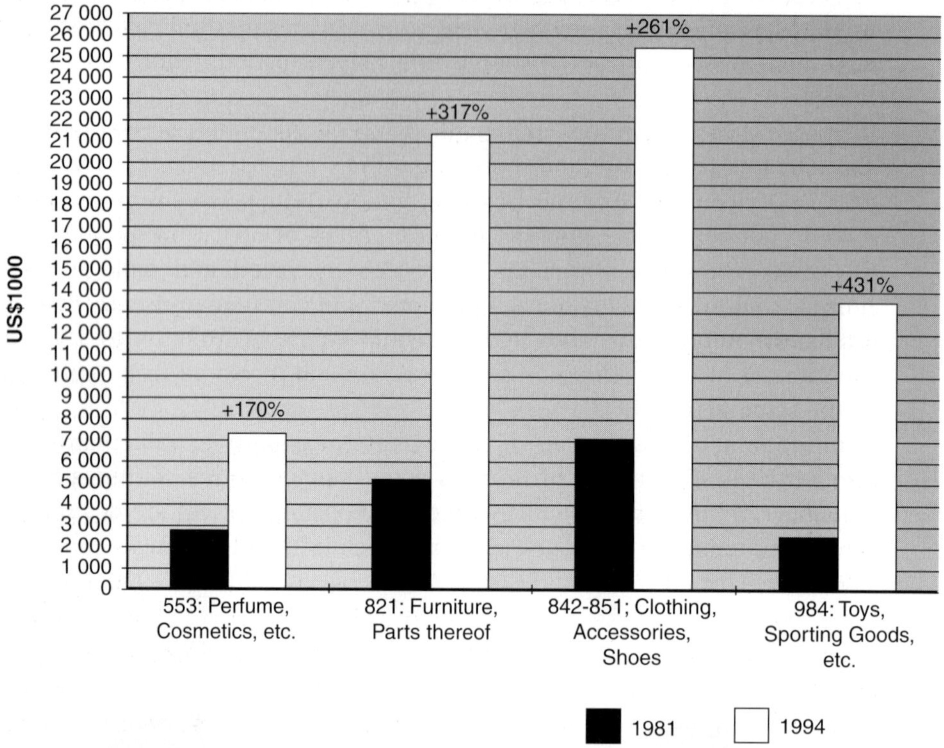

Fig. 2.2 Brunei's imports of selected consumer goods by standard international trade classification, 1981 and 1994

and clothing, the index showed an average annual percentage change during that time of 3.4% and 3.5% respectively.

Bruneians have grown fairly accustomed to the prices of imported consumer goods, prices that many tourists find high. The prices paid, however, are not usually high because of import duties, because about 90% of imports enter the country duty-free, nor are they increased by sales taxes, because Brunei has no sales tax. In addition to their dependence on the economies of the producing world and the world economy, however, consumers are paying distribution costs and retail markups.[4]

Similarities in consumer behavior and attitudes

Although it might at first appear that Brunei's consumers not only exist in a unique marketplace but are also extremely diverse and difficult to target, the population may usefully be divided into two groups. One group, approximately one-third of the population, is composed of those who live in the small villages and rural areas of Brunei, and consume relatively few of the manufactured consumer goods that are imported into the country. The imports they do consume, out of necessity, consist largely of food. The urban dwellers, who form the bulk of the population and live primarily in the Brunei/Muara district, purchase, on a regular basis, both domestic and imported goods. In addition to imported food, these consumers purchase a variety of other goods that come from abroad.

However, even these two seemingly different groups share a remarkable number of similarities: both are predominantly young (53% and 52% of the urban and rural groups respectively are under 25), and evenly split in gender (52% and 54% of the urban and rural groups respectively are male) (UN 1994). While it cannot be said that each group shares equally the country's high GNP per capita, both enjoy a high standard of well-being (as measured by education, health, longevity, etc.). It is, however, the wealthier, urban population that consumes the bulk of imported consumer goods and enjoys a wider variety of consumer goods than does the rural population. Still, the fragmentation and differences that exist in Brunei, noticeable especially in terms of ethnic groups and occupations, are arguably not true in terms of consumer behavior. In Brunei, consumer behavior is surprisingly homogeneous.

The urban areas also, of course, provide a greater choice among types of retail outlets. In the last 15 years, retailers have increased in number and variety, primarily in Bandar Seri Begawan, and consumers select from local markets, shophouses, supermarkets, emporiums, and department stores. Brunei's largest is the upscale Japan-based department store Yaohan, which has two locations, both in Bandar Seri Begawan. Other department stores, as well as smaller specialty shops, offer a wide selection of branded imported merchandise, often with traditional Bruneian handicrafts added to the mix. And of course shoppers continue to crowd Brunei's open markets; these markets, not location specific, are stocked with a variety of vegetables, flowers, and handicrafts, as well as clothing, accessories, household items, tapes, compact disks, and "stall food."

Consumer spending has increased right along with the increasing number of retail outlets, going from US$40 million in 1980 to US$65.6 million in 1990 (EIU 1993–1994). Additional impetus to consumer spending has been provided by improved access to both loans and credit. Such increased expenditures have been accompanied by increased consumer debt, and, while the correlation between these two may be shrugged off by some observers as part of a rather typical consumer pattern, others might find it unexpected in an Islamic country. Court records indicate that civil cases involving debt in Brunei in 1992 climbed to a level almost three times that of 1991, with the biggest jump in credit-card debt and motor vehicle repossession cases (Cleary & Francis 1994).

Other factors that contribute in some degree to similarities in consumer behavior are the mass media and other types of information to which Bruneians are exposed. As the numbers above indicate, radios and televisions are abundant. And one daily newspaper, published in two languages, is circulated countrywide. Still it is true that most Bruneians are exposed to limited media alternatives and therefore most have shared media experiences. To the extent that an increased variety of alternatives is available–alternatives that offer more breadth of information, ideas and increased stimulation–they are available primarily to urban consumers.

Radio Brunei has been broadcasting on two networks for almost 40 years. One of the networks is Malay, the other multilingual. There is only one national television network, and it is government owned. It features programs produced both locally and abroad, news broadcasts in Malay and English, and several international news services. A number of viewers appear to share the sentiment that, while this programming is "uninspired" (EIU 1995–1996), access to Malaysian television, which includes daily Cable News Network programming, provides relief in the form of breadth of views and variety of programs. However, even more variety, as well as entertainment, is provided by television sets if their owners have video cassette recorders and reasonably convenient access to video rental stores.

The independently-owned *Borneo Bulletin* is the only local daily newspaper, and the only commercial newspaper.[5] It began publishing on a daily basis in 1990, and is circulated throughout the country. In 1995 it went on-line; news stories about Brunei as well as country information are available. Again, media variety is provided to those who have access to the shops, bookstores, and hotels that carry foreign newspapers and magazines.

There are no laws prohibiting freedom of speech and freedom of the press, but government censorship of international periodicals and newspapers continues. Articles that are subject to such censorship are those that are potentially embarrassing to the sultan or other members of the royal family, critical of the sultan or the government, or simply judged to be in some way improper by the censors (US Dept of State 1994). Such articles may be removed or blacked out. The local newspaper avoids problems by practicing self-censorship.

Increasing use of fax machines and the Internet is making censorship increasingly difficult, if not impossible. There has been almost total absence of criticism or opposing views in past years (US Department of State 1994), but electronic media may cause governmental tolerance of political criticism to be tested before much longer. In the meantime, those who have access to computers and fax machines have much broader media alternatives than those who do not.

The monarchy and the consumer

Despite the fact that so many consumer goods are imported rather than produced in the country, the marketplaces of Brunei and the behavior and attitudes of its consumers clearly reflect the influence of Sultan Hassanal Bolkiah. One manifestation of this appears to be, not surprisingly, emulation of the sultan and the royal family. Among all countries of the world, only in Brunei does the head of state possess a private collection of some 150 Rolls Royces and do inhabitants possess almost three private cars per household (EPU 1993). However, the influence of this single person is far more pervasive than simple emulation. Such influence has become most apparent in the sultan's strong espousal of the national ideology, the MIB–Malay culture, Islamic religion, and monarchy. The word "monarchy" is weighted with meaning in Brunei. The sultan is the hereditary sovereign (following 28 predecessors), and ". . . a modern monarch, head of government, head of state, and a Malay Muslim Monarch" (Chalfont 1989). 'Beraja,' in combination with 'Malayu' and 'Islam' in MIB, is usually taken to refer directly to the state's political philosophy. All three tenets of the MIB are intricately blended, and seem to complement each other in the way they affect consumers and markets.

Islamic values, especially since the religious resurgence encouraged by the sultan since the late 1980s, affect the way people dress and what they eat. Islamic policies affect imports (such as alcohol and pork) and are seen as a force to counteract undesirable behavior (including rising debt and credit-card usage). Islamic and Malay values affect the media and advertising, education, the national budget, the institutions of the country, and the lifestyle of the people.

Certainly this is true to some degree in every country in the world. What makes it particularly notable in Brunei stems from its history, its location and physical size, the size of its population, its economic situation, and its continuing aura of isolation, even though it is only 2 hours by plane from Singapore. Consider again the contradictions of a population that is largely educated and relatively wealthy, but has:

> no serious bookstores . . . no galleries, no concert halls, no political parties, no human-rights organizations, no discos . . . no painters or poets of any note . . . no think tanks, no debating societies . . . no parliament . . . no night clubs, no bars–no alcohol (Weaver 1991, p. 65).

Brunei is not in fact an isolated country. Rather, it is contemporary, oriented toward the future, and located in a region that recently has been enjoying the highest economic growth in the world. Yet of its citizens (who have been described as restless and bored), only a few have turned their time to creative and/or entrepreneurial endeavors. Why? There seems to be no easy answer, but it probably lies in a combination of the same factors mentioned in the preceding paragraph–history, location, economic circumstances, etc.

Will this situation continue, or is Brunei on the brink of significant transformation? It is difficult to imagine that the country will remain unchanged much longer. Harbingers of change are increasingly visible. One is that Brunei is stepping up its global activities. It is opening more diplomatic missions (e.g. in Vietnam, Myanmar, Laos) and is not only a member of a great number of world organizations, but also increasingly visible in some of these. ASEAN ties are of particular importance, and these are burgeoning, with potential opportunities from the addition of Vietnam as a member, and the expected additions of Laos, Cambodia, and Myanmar. In July 1995, Brunei hosted a meeting for ASEAN foreign ministers, and then the second meeting of the ASEAN Regional Forum (ARF). In October (the same month IMF membership was approved) Brunei invited senior officials of the EAGA to meet in Bandar Seri Begawan. And in November it welcomed an unexpectedly large number of visitors to an extremely successful first international trade exhibition to promote EAGA and Brunei's other subregional grouping with Indonesia, Malaysia and the Philippines (BIMP). Brunei has been leaning hard on EAGA members to start implementing planned projects, including a maritime transport network, air links, direct telecommunications link-ups, and harmonization of customs and immigration rules (EIU 1995–1996, 1st quarter 1996).

Closer to home, a new process was effected in 1993: village leaders were elected locally (Mani 1993). In 1995 a committee was formed to investigate and make recommendations on the advisability of resuming limited national elections. In 1996, the Brunei Solidarity Party was allowed to hold an inaugural assembly, elect officers, recruit members, and hold additional meetings when requested (see Case 1996, who also reports on other moves toward political participation).

The ideas that have surfaced on economic development indicate concern that progress in the area of internal economic diversification, in spite of much rhetoric, has been largely disappointing. However, certain of these thrusts (e.g. to make Brunei a regional financial or communications center, the hub of a maritime transport and/or telecommunications network, or host to tourists and scientists interested in ecology and the environment) are likely to yield desired results.

All of these indications of change, taken together, foretell:

1 that the Brunei leadership will show a greater interest in and trust regarding international affairs and organizations
2 a willingness to establish more democratic processes
3 a continued and perhaps more highly prioritized focus on economic diversification

Brunei's industries and markets will be affected by each one of these three; changes in all three are likely to have substantial effects. And when these come, Brunei's restless and bored consumers will undoubtedly respond.

References

"A piece of royal fortune" (1992), *The Economist,* October 10, pp. 40–1.

Arief, Sritua (1987), *The Brunei Economy,* Rosecon for The South-East Asia Research and Development Institute, New South Wales.

Borhan bin Mohamad (1995), "Eco-tourism in Brunei Darussalam", Brunei Press Sdn Bhd, Kuala Belait. Available: Netscape, URL http://sunsite.nus.sg/SEAlinks/brunei-info.html.

"Business Guide" (1995), *Borneo Bulletin Brunei Yearbook 1996,* Brunei Press Sdn Bhd, Kuala Belait. Available: Netscape, URL http://sunsite.nus.sg/SEAlinks/brunei-info.html.

"Brunei Darussalam: Quick Facts" (1995), Brunei Press Sdn Bhd, Kuala Belait. Available: Netscape, URL http://sunsite.nus.sg/SEAlinks/brunei-info.html.

Case, William (1996), "Brunei Darussalam in 1995: New Party Politics and Diplomatic Presence", *Asian Survey,* vol. 23 no. 2, February, pp. 130–4.

Chalfont, Lord (1989), *By God's Will: A Portrait of the Sultan of Brunei,* Weidenfeld & Nicolson, London. As quoted in Mani, A. (1993), "Negara Brunei Darussalam in 1991: Celebrating the Silver Jubilee", *Southeast Asian Affairs 1993,* Institute for Southeast Asian Studies, Singapore, p. 96.

Cleary, Mark & Francis, Simon (1994), "Brunei: The Search for a Sustainable Economy", *Southeast Asian Affairs 1994,* Institute of Southeast Asian Affairs, Singapore, pp. 59–75.

Cooke, Kieran (1995), "Sultan's Swing to Reform", *The Financial Times,* London, June, p. 18.

"Directory" (1995), *The Far East and Australasia 1995,* 26th edn, Europa Publications Limited, London, pp. 168–71.

Doshi, Tilak (1995), "Brunei: Economy", *The Far East and Australasia 1995,* 26th edn, Europa Publications Limited, London, pp. 162–7.

Economic Development Board (EDB), Ministry of Finance, Brunei Darussalam, *Explore Brunei: A Visitor's Guide,* 2nd edn, EDB, Bandar Seri Begawan, Brunei.

Economic Planning Unit (EPU), Ministry of Finance, Brunei Darussalam (1993), *Brunei Darussalam Statistical Yearbook 1992,* EPU, Bandar Seri Begawan, Brunei.

— (1995), "Brunei: Statistical Survey", *The Far East and Australasia 1995,* 26th edn, Europa Publications Limited, London.

Economist Intelligence Unit (EIU) (1993–1994), *Country Profile: Malaysia, Brunei,* The Economist Intelligence Unit Ltd, London.

— (1995–1996), *Country Profile: Malaysia, Brunei,* The Economist Intelligence Unit Ltd, London.

— (various years), *Country Report: Malaysia, Brunei,* The Economist Intelligence Unit Ltd, London.

Far Eastern Economic Review (1996), *Asia 1996 Yearbook,* Review Publishing Company Ltd, Hong Kong.

"Great Strides in Agriculture" (1995), Brunei Press Sdn Bhd, Kuala Belait. Available: Netscape, URL http://sunsite.nus.sg/SEAlinks/brunei-info.html.

Hiebert, Murray (1995), "Do Not Disturb", *Far Eastern Economic Review,* August 25, p. 50.

Holloway, Nigel (1995), "Poor Little Rich Country", *Far Eastern Economic Review,* June 15, p. 80.

Mani, A. (1993), "Negara Brunei Darussalam in 1991: Celebrating the Silver Jubilee", *Southeast Asian Affairs 1993,* Institute for Southeast Asian Studies, Singapore, pp. 95–109.

"The Benevolent State" (1995), Brunei Press Sdn Bhd, Kuala Belait. Available: Netscape, URL http://sunsite.nus.sg/SEAlinks/brunei-info.html.

Turnbull, C. Mary (1995), "Brunei: History", *The Far East and Australasia 1995,* 26th edn, Europa Publications Limited, London, pp. 158–61.

United Nations (UN) (1994), *1993 Demographic Yearbook,* UN, New York.

— (various years), Economic and Social Commission for Asia and the Pacific, *Foreign Trade Statistics of Asia and the Pacific,* UN, New York.

United Nations Development Programme (UNDP) (1995), *Human Development Report 1995,* United Nations Development Programme, New York.

US Department of Commerce (1995), "ASEAN Big Emerging Markets: Brunei", Washington, DC, pp. 1-4. Available: Netscape URL http://www.ita.gov/region/asia/pacific/brunei.html.

US Department of State (1994), "Brunei Human Rights Practices, 1993", (Jan 31) pp. 1–8, Available: Netscape URL... c.th70/00/AsiaInfo/CountryInfo/Brunei/Human%20Rights%20in%20Brunei.

— (1991), "Brunei Background Notes", Bureau of Public Affairs, Washington, DC, July, pp. 1–7. Available: Netscape URL 70/00/AsiaInfo/ CountryInfo/Brunei Background%20Notes%20for%20Brunei.

US National Foreign Assessment Center (1994), "Brunei", *The World Factbook 1995.* Available: Netscape URL http://www.ic.gov/95fact/country/38.html.

Weaver, Mary Anne (1991), "In the Sultan's Palace", *The New Yorker,* October 7, pp. 56–93.

World Book (1996), "Facts in Brief on Asian Countries", *The 1996 World Book Year Book*, World Book, Inc., Chicago, p. 62.

World Development Report 1995 (1995), "Workers in an Integrating World", Oxford University Press, London, pp. 162–3, 248–9.

Notes

1 Dollar values in this chapter are given as US$ unless otherwise stated.

2 Brunei's actual GNP per capita is difficult to pin down. The World Development Report 1995 lists Brunei as being one of about 40 countries in the "high-income" bracket, but Brunei's exact GNP per capita does not appear on that publication's list of basic indicators. However, to provide some perspective, in 1993 over half the world's population lived in countries with an average per-capita income of only US$352. The average of the per-capita income in the 24 countries listed (World Development Report's Basic Indicators table, pp. 162–3) in the "high-income" bracket was US$21 170. Weaver's information notwithstanding (her source unknown), Brunei's Ministry of Finance (EPU 1993) estimates that Brunei's per capita income in 1992 was US$14 500 and, using data from Brunei Press Sdn. Bhd., in 1995 was US$16 500 (using average annual exchange rates to convert Brunei dollars to US dollars). In Asia, only Singapore and Hong Kong appear to have GNP per capita higher than that of Brunei.

3 Of course, the entirety of passenger motor-vehicle imports is not sold to consumers for private use. However, private ownership of automobiles has been encouraged not only by limited public transportation, but also by interest-free government loans for civil servants and subsidized motor fuel (Cleary & Francis 1994). And perhaps some balance in the estimation is achieved by not counting (as consumer goods) any of the other "transport equipment" categories as consumer goods. These include an "other" listing divided into "other industrial" and "other non-industrial," as well as a "parts and accessories" category. The other "non-industrial" category includes buses, trucks, motor cycles, motor scooters, and bicycles, at least some of which are owned by consumers, as is true of parts and accessories.

4 Tourism comprises a largely undeveloped, but potentially good, consumer market. However, tourists coming from countries that export manufactured goods to Brunei may find the prices, increased by distribution costs and retail mark-ups, extremely high. In contrast, tourists that come from a country that itself imports from, say, Japan or the USA, might find Brunei's imports from those countries more reasonably priced than in their own country, since they enter Brunei duty-free. Brunei's handicrafts (hand-carved silver, forged brass, and kain songket, for example) will, in general, be appealing to most tourists, though less so to those from neighboring countries that offer similar assortments.

5 There is one weekly newspaper, *Pelita Brunei,* published by the government, which features news of government activities, policies, and participants. A monthly paper, *Salam,* is published by Shell Oil Company.

CHAPTER 3

Cambodia

Transition, and the consequences for future consumption and marketing

CLIFFORD J. SHULTZ, II & NARANHKIRI TITH

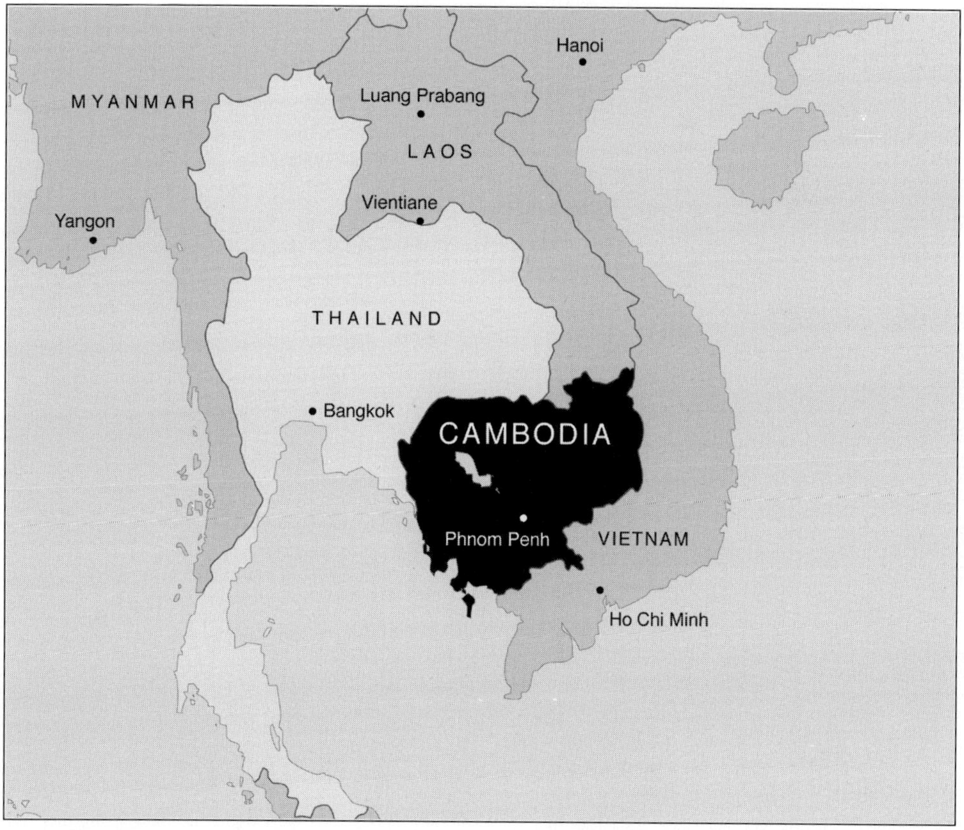

Abstract

Cambodia is a country struggling to rise from the ashes of genocide and profound economic mismanagement. Many marketers and investors have consequently overlooked it as a market opportunity. Yet, despite the atrocities of the killing fields and ongoing political discord and instability, both the consumers of Cambodia and the newly implemented government policies intend to transform this nation into a market economy, and are proving that Cambodia is a nation of promise. Goods and services from global marketers as well as an emerging consumer culture are now common in Cambodia's urban areas. In this chapter we discuss the historic developments and the current economic, social and political conditions that affect consumers and marketers, provide an overview of the macromarketing mix, and conclude with the authors' prognoses for Cambodian consumers, markets and marketing management.

Introduction

Since 1970, Cambodia's economic, political and social structures have undergone fundamental changes, changes of cataclysmic proportion. These have irreversibly and profoundly affected, and continue to affect, the behavior of all domestic economic agents, consumers, and the perception of the country by foreigners as a place in which to engage in marketing activities. The pace and success of Cambodia's emergence from "Year Zero" (i.e. 1975—see Ponchaud 1977) and the killing fields will coincide with several factors, including the government's economic and social policies, foreign investment, and the extent to which policy assures development and a stable consumer society emerges (Muscat 1989; United Nations 1991; World Bank 1992; Asian Development Bank 1994).

This last factor is particularly salient to Cambodia (or *Kampuchea,* as the Cambodians refer to their land), and at the outset it is important to mention that, despite the availability of cultivable land and natural resources, including oil and gas, and a relatively low population-to-land ratio, Cambodia is one of the poorest countries in the world. It is an economy in transition, and continues to demonstrate signs of political unrest. Moreover, unlike other countries in transition from a centrally planned to a market system, Cambodia is confronted with two other kinds of transition: the country must also transform from a less developed to a more developed country, and from a wartime to a peacetime economy.

The combination of these three forms of transition makes the task of managing the Cambodian economy particularly challenging. Understanding the dynamic interactions of consumers, marketers and extant environmental conditions, as well as the evolution of the interaction process, is equally challenging, particularly given both the absence of data, and the inaccuracy of the data that are available. Fundamental economic, market and social indicators for Cambodia are difficult to come by, or are often little more than educated guesses or extrapolations from 25-year-old statistics (Chandler 1992, p. 6).

Even compared to its Indochinese neighbors, such as Laos and Vietnam, which also are recovering from war decimation and are moving toward market economies, Cambodia is a difficult study because it remains volatile. And, while some observers believe Cambodia is again destined to disintegrate, a market economy with near double-digit growth rates has emerged in the last 2 years. Whether this trend can continue remains to be seen, but, only one generation since the carnage of the killing fields, many Cambodians have begun to embrace consumer culture, and marketers have begun to penetrate successfully this uncertain market. In this chapter, we discuss the recent historical events that created the present market conditions, and the relevant marketing and consumer-behavior issues that firms should understand before entering the market.

A period of systemic change after Independence

Since Independence from France in 1953, Cambodia has gone through a variety of political and economic regimes:

1 an autocratic monarchy (Sihanouk's national socialism, 1953–1970)
2 a republic (Lon Nol Republic, 1970–1975)
3 a primitive communist system based on the early Soviet Union's War Communism ('Democratic Kampuchea', better known as the Khmer Rouge, 1975–1978)
4 a foreign-imposed communist system (the People's Republic of Kampuchea of Hun Sen/Heng Samrin/Chea Sim, 1978–1991)
5 a mandate under the United Nations Transitional Authority (1991–1993)
6 a constitutional monarchy (1993 to the present)

During the 25-year period that commenced in 1970, Cambodia was engulfed in a long, bitter, and protracted civil war, a devastating holocaust, and a costly foreign invasion and occupation. These major upheavals have led to the loss of an estimated one-quarter of the population, and a near-total destruction of the country's social and physical infrastructure (United Nations 1991; Asian Development Bank 1991; World Bank 1992). It is important to review the changes during these periods, and their impact on consumer behavior.

Sihanouk's monarchy

The early period of Sihanouk's era (1953–1963), was peaceful; Cambodia managed to record modest rates of growth, and was self-sufficient in essential foods, and a net exporter of rice (Steinberg 1959; Prud'Homme 1969; Osborne 1979). Although agriculture dominated the economy as a source of both income and employment, a small but budding middle class started to take hold, especially in the capital city of Phnom Penh and some provincial capitals such as Battambang, Kompong Cham, and the port of Sihanoukville.

However, from 1963 to 1969, economic growth slowed considerably to around 3%, hardly enough to compensate for the increase in the population. At the same time, export surplus dwindled to a trickle, while the tax base was substantially eroded. One of the major factors behind this economic decline was Sihanouk's decision to phase out US assistance, and to increase the role of the state in the economy in an effort to minimize the spillover effects of the Vietnam War.

The economic and social infrastructure, although inadequate, had been developing and spreading slowly throughout the country, but Cambodia's neutralist foreign policy ultimately led to the termination of US economic, financial, and military assistance, and the Cambodian government began to manage the economy. The banking and foreign-trade sectors were nationalized, and the state set up a number of enterprises in the industrial and service sectors. This in turn led to the discontent of those businessmen and politicians whose interests were adversely affected by the loss of US assistance, especially the military. The increase in the role of the state in the economy led to increases in rent-seeking activities, and inefficiency. The combination of these two problems resulted in mounting dissatisfaction among those who were most affected by the rejection of US assistance and by the curtailment of the private sector. These internal factors, together with the US decision to withdraw its armed forces from Vietnam, provided the Cambodian military, led by General Lon Nol, an opportunity to stage a successful coup d'etat against Sihanouk in March 1970.

The Khmer Republic

After toppling Sihanouk, Lon Nol installed a republican regime known as the Khmer Republic, and attempted to return to the more liberal economic policies of the 1960s. However, the escalation of the civil war and pervasive corruption in his government quashed all hopes of an economic revival. The intensification of bombing and the takeover of much of the countryside by the Khmer Rouge led to the collapse of the Khmer Republic. During this period (1970–1975), all production indicators fell, and soon nearly half the population was living in beleaguered cities, having to rely on airlifted food and medical supplies. Throughout the entire Lon Nol period, the government was wholly dependent on support from the USA, since its spending had far outstripped possible tax revenue (Chantrabot 1993; Corfield 1994).

The Khmer Rouge and Democratic Kampuchea

Under the circumstances, Pol Pot's Khmer Rouge forces had few problems overcoming the American-supported Lon Nol forces, and marched into Phnom Penh on April 17 1975. From this capitulation emerged Democratic Kampuchea, a regime based on the system of "War Communism" installed in the Soviet Union at the beginning of the Bolshevik revolution. The Khmer Rouge immediately and brutally proceeded to transform the Cambodian economy into Pol Pot's extreme interpretation of a communist utopia (Chandler, Kiernan & Boua 1988; Twining 1989).

The country was sealed off, and then the cities were emptied as the entire urban population was sent to the countryside. Everyone was obliged to live and to work on a communal basis. Much of the traditional social and economic infrastructure was dismantled; the central government was destroyed; the currency was abolished. Private property was confiscated, all economic activities became part of the state apparatus, and markets ceased to exist. Many urban dwellers, citizens associated with the previous regime ("Old

People"), and the educated individuals in general, were executed or fled the country. More than a million Cambodians died from execution, exhaustion or starvation. Cities were emptied on short notice and their population was forcibly moved into slave-labor camps scattered throughout the countryside of Cambodia.

These slave laborers were mainly assigned to work on building the irrigation network known as the Pol Pot canal system. Work conditions were extremely inhuman. Collective manual labor for up to 18 hours a day, with the provision of starvation food rations only, became a widespread practice.

In addition, the Khmer Rouge abolished the traditional family structure, and cut communication with the outside world. In their efforts to create a new society, the Khmer Rouge ruthlessly suppressed religion by destroying Buddhist temples, which were the center of village life in pre-revolutionary Cambodia. Buddhists were killed or forced to break their vows, and ritual activities were forbidden. In place of religion, tradition, and family, the Khmer Rouge instituted a political ideology that stressed new values and codes of conduct. The Khmer Rouge demanded strict adherence to these codes and new values; those who dared to challenge them were harshly and swiftly punished. Agriculture was to be the cornerstone of the economy, while industry was given only secondary attention.

In virtually every area in which productivity could be measured, the quantity and quality of output were severely constrained by the highly labor-intensive methods and the implementation of ineffective administrative policies and radical production techniques. Foreign trade reverted to barter with those few countries that maintained economic relations with the Khmer Rouge.

The People's Republic of Kampuchea

On December 25 1978, the armed forces of the Socialist Republic of Vietnam invaded Cambodia, and drove the Khmer Rouge back along the border with Thailand (Leepson 1985). In January 1979, Vietnam installed a new government, headed by Heng Samrin, a former Khmer Rouge general, and the regime was renamed the People's Republic of Kampuchea (PRK). Cambodia's population by this time was on the brink of starvation. The whole economy had collapsed, and there was massive movement of Cambodians throughout the country (Boua 1983).

Under the PRK, the Cambodian economy was reorganized according to the more classical type of socialist system, based on a hierarchical centrally planned organization. The new regime initially made considerable headway in rebuilding economic infrastructure and institutions, including social institutions. Families, for example, were allowed to reunite, and to return to their places of origin. A central administration was re-established, the banking system was reopened, the national currency–the riel, or CR–was reintroduced, and some factories were also reassembled.

Other policies of the PRK allowed the cities to re-populate. This urbanization scheme was to introduce a new group of people who until then had never lived in urban areas, and were basically subsistence farmers with limited skill and experience. They were simply referred to as "New People." The original city dwellers, who were government officials, merchants, professionals, craftsmen, and laborers–the mercantile and intellectual core of the country–had either been killed during the Khmer Rouge era, or had escaped to settle as refugees in many parts of the world–the USA, Canada, France, Australia, and Thailand. Some estimates suggest that over 2 million Cambodians were murdered or fled the country.

The reconstruction efforts of the PRK were facilitated by the inflow of assistance from the former bloc of East European countries and the former Soviet Union. However, many of the central planning policies ultimately had to be abandoned because they were rejected by the population (Vickery 1990).

UNTAC and constitutional monarchy

The successful conclusion of the second Paris Conference in October 1991 led to the establishment of the United Nations Transitional Authorities in Cambodia (UNTAC), under whose mandate an election was organized and carried out in May 1993. The result of the election gave a clear majority to the non-communist parties of FUNCINPEC (Front Uni National pour un Cambodge Independent Neutre Pacific et Cooperative), led by Prince Norodom Ranariddh with 58 representatives, BLD (Buddhist Liberal Democratic) led by former Prime Minister Son Sann with 10 representatives, and Moulinaka (Mouvement de Liberation Nationale du Kampuchea), led by Mr Ros Roeun with 1 representative. In contrast, there were 51 representatives for the Cambodian People's Party (CPP), led by Hun Sen and Chea Sim, both former Khmer Rouge senior officials. The elected representatives established a Constitutional National Assembly, which in turn promulgated a new constitution. A new Royal Cambodian Government (RCG) was formed in September 1993 to take over all aspects of governance.

The RCG is a tenuous coalition, with two Prime Ministers and two Ministers of Defence and Interior, one from CPP and one from FUNCINPEC. Political infighting continues, both within and among the parties in the government. Corruption is widespread, and, combined with the present extremely low capacity of the government to manage, is increasing the threat of destabilization.

This has allowed the Khmer Rouge to continue to challenge the government's authority, especially in the countryside. This situation has also created widespread insecurity, thereby causing a delay in the badly needed reconstruction and rehabilitation of the country's economy, a delay that exists despite the availability of a sizeable amount of financial and technical assistance from the international community.

Hence, since the UN-sponsored election of May 1993, Cambodia has remained economically and politically unstable. After a short period of progress, the economic, social and political situations started to deteriorate very quickly.

The current situation is both precarious and promising, but certainly the potential for instability should be factored into any marketing strategy.

Economic environment

From 1953 to 1970, the Cambodian economy grew, in real terms, on average about 5% per year while the population grew about 2.5% per year–this meant an average real growth, for per-capita income, of 2.5% per year. During the Lon Nol period, the Cambodian economy registered negative rates of growth, while inflation rates reached triple digits. This period witnessed the beginning of a succession of upheavals in Cambodian society both in terms of its structure and behavior–upheavals that were to reign during the next two and a half decades. Economic indicators from 1975 to 1980 were virtually nil as the Khmer Rouge obliterated the economy.

More recently, Cambodia's economy has passed through several phases of slump and recovery. Both a reduction in aid from the former Soviet Union and unfavorable weather resulted in slow growth (about 2%) in 1989–1990. Until October 1991, economic recovery was severely hampered by ongoing civil war, the collapse of the socialist economies in Europe, and the lack of other sources of international support. However, output recovered strongly to an estimated 7% in 1991–1992 as economic activities were boosted by the return of good weather, increased demand associated with UNTAC personnel, and higher foreign-exchange receipts. Since 1993 the Royal Government has been "operating under the slogan 'Le Cambodge s'aide lui-meme' or 'Cambodia will help itself'" (St John 1995, p. 266), and has implemented a series of programs designed to rehabilitate the economy. To date, these programs have produced mixed results (see Table 3.1).

Foreign aid and assistance remain an indispensable component of the economy. Most assistance is now focused on the implementation of the National Plan to Rehabilitate and Develop Cambodia (NPRD), which is intended to transform the economic system into that of a viable market economy. Successful implementation of the NPRD will be difficult to achieve, however, given the many constraints of the current economic environment.

Table 3.1 Main economic indicators, and their rates of change, 1991–1994

Economic indicator	*1991*	*1992*	*1993*	*1994*
Real GDP	7.6	7.0	3.9	5.2
Domestic liquidity	28.6	17.3	20.3	16
Net credit to the government	35.3	200.8	19.6	6.2
Exports of goods	104.6	-23.8	-26.5	360
Imports of goods (retained)	-9.8	37.8	61.8	92
Ratio of GDP				
Budget revenue	4.4	6.2	5.2	8.2
Budget expenditure	7.8	9.8	11	14.7
Current expenditure	7.4	9.5	6.7	10
Capital expenditure	0.4	0.3	4.2	4.7
Current budget deficit	-1.2	-4.3	-1.5	-1.8
Over budget deficit	-3.4	-3.6	-5.7	-6.5
Domestic investment	9.4	9.8	14.2	19.2
Government investment	0.4	0.3	4.2	4.7
Non-government investment	0.9	9.5	10	14.5
Financing of investment	9.4	9.8	14.2	19.2
National savings	7.9	7.3	8.1	7.4
Foreign savings	1.5	2.5	6.1	11.8
BOP current-account deficit	-1.5	-2.5	-6.1	-11.8
Gross international reserve	N/A	1.0	2.0	2.1
GDP (billion riels)	1 336	2 508	5 546	6 048
Gross international reserve (US$ million)	0.3	29.9	70.7	110.5

Note:

1 Area: 181 000 km^2

2 Per-capita income (1993): US$200

Sources: Cambodian authorities; International Monetary Fund (1994), "Cambodia Emerges from Isolation as Economic Reforms Take Hold", September 26, IMF Survey, Washington, DC; World Bank (1992), *Cambodia: Agenda for Rehabilitation and Reconstruction,* The World Bank, Washington, DC.

Inflation and other pressures

The rate of inflation (as measured by the CPI) soared from about 90% during 1989 to over 150% in 1990, slowed down to 88% in 1991, and rose again to 177% in 1992. The exchange rate in the parallel market declined broadly in line with the underlying inflationary pressures. Strong inflationary expectations weakened the public's confidence in the domestic currency, contributing to widespread currency substitution. The main cause behind the inflationary pressures and exchange-rate devaluation was the monetary expansion, which in turn was the result of fiscal deterioration. Public finances deteriorated severely during this period. While the government responded to fiscal pressures by cutting its public-investment program, the overall budget deficit nevertheless widened and, in the absence of foreign financing, was covered by currency issued by the central bank, the National Bank of Cambodia.

By 1992 most employees in the industrial sector found it almost impossible to support households, while inflation preserved wide gaps between the living standards enjoyed by high-income earners and property owners and those without secure sources of income. Entrepreneurs and other private-sector businesspersons who have had good fortune with both legal activities (e.g. scooter-taxis and food vendors) and illegal activities (e.g. prostitution and smuggling) have also fared well, while soldiers and civil servants have seen their earning power erode, or even disappear. Such wage discrepancies and inflation are considered to be primary factors in rising crime rates and general civil unrest (Economist Intelligence Unit 1994).

In 1993, the unsettled security and political situation up to the time of the election slowed growth in the first half of the year. Improved domestic and external confidence contributed to a rebound in the second half of the year, with growth for the year as a whole estimated at 4%. Private consumption accounted for an estimated 85% during 1991–1993, and total investment is estimated to be rising from 9.5% in 1991 to 15.3% in 1993. The rise in investment resulted from a surge in public investment as official foreign aid began to flow after the successful conclusion of the Paris Agreements. There has also been an increase in private investment related to inflows of foreign direct investment. National savings increased only very modestly, from 7.3% of GDP in 1991 to 8.7% in 1993. Inflationary pressures improved dramatically in 1993 (an increase of 31%).

In 1994, the security environment deteriorated, and the resurgence of the Khmer Rouge adversely affected confidence and economic activity (Showcross 1994). The political environment has also been fragile and, in July 1994, the Government squelched an attempted coup. In an October 1994 Cabinet reshuffle, Mr Sam Rainsy of FUNCINPEC was replaced by Mr Keat Chhon of CPP. Another coup was "successfully" instigated in July 1997, and major economic ministries and the National Bank are now headed by CPP officials. Cambodia's full membership in ASEAN has been delayed.

Economic development was also affected by weather conditions. Severe flooding was followed by drought when the monsoon rains ended prematurely. As a result, output growth in 1994 was estimated at 5%. The low growth in production in the agricultural sector was the main cause behind this lower than expected growth. Consequently, Cambodia is again faced with shortages in rice production when it attempts to meet the consumption need for the population. However, growth in activities in other sectors has been stronger, especially in construction and logging.

Inflationary pressures as measured by the CPI in 1994 declined to around 30%. This, in turn, helped to stabilize the exchange rate of the riel. The balance of payments of Cambodia continued to record large deficits and to be extremely vulnerable to domestic and external shocks. Foreign financing, especially official financing, continued to be the main source of Cambodia's financing of the overall deficit of its budget and the current account of the balance of payments. A synopsis of inflation trends is presented in Table 3.2.

Table 3.2 Inflation as measured by Consumer Price Index

Year	*1991*	*1992*	*1993*	*1994*
CPI	87.9	176.8	31	30.1

Structure of the economy

Cambodia's economy continues to be predominantly agricultural, with farming accounting for about 50% of output, 85% of employment, and more than 90% of exports during the 1990–1993 period. Agriculture was mainly of a subsistence nature, with very little surplus for exchange with the rest of the economy, excepting for rice. Industry contributed to about some 17% of GDP. Construction represented a sizeable share of that sector, or about 9%. The manufacturing sector comprised only a small share of GDP, or about 7%, and consisted mainly of repair shops and small-scale family-owned enterprises. The services sector was made up of government services, wholesale, retail trade, restaurants, hotels, transports, energy, water supply, and communications. During this period, services benefited from increased tourism and the presence of UNTAC.

The strong economic performance during the last few years might lead to the conclusion that the conditions for output expansion are reasonably good. However, such a view could be misleading. Fundamentally, the performance of the economy remains unbalanced, its overall impact shallow and its benefits not spread evenly throughout the society. Much of this growth has been concentrated in the capital city (only 12% of the total population), and the Cambodian economy continues to suffer from the legacy of decades of war, foreign invasion, and internal strife. Nevertheless, the economic indicators are positive, and the RCG's current overriding objective is to "achieve a fair, just and peaceful society, and through accelerating the rate of economic growth, to raise the living standards of all Cambodians" (Asian Development Bank 1994, p. 79). Fundamental to this objective are new laws and policies that will nurture the private sector and promote direct foreign investment. Observers contend that Cambodia has some of the most favorable investment laws in Asia, including, for example, full repatriation of profits and a corporate tax rate (9%), regarded to be among the lowest in Asia (*Business Times* 1994).

Furthermore, the World Bank has supported a restructuring of Cambodia's financial system along free-market lines, and has also supported the reorganization of the National Bank of Cambodia. However, Cambodians retain a mistrust of banks and local currency, the currency remains dollar-centered and, in our assessment, despite some gains, the economy and the underlying economic institutions remain fragile.

Geographic and cultural influences

Cambodia is generally circular in shape, covers a landmass of 181 000 km^2, and borders Thailand, Laos and Vietnam. It also has over 200 km of coastline on the Gulf of Siam. Unlike other countries on mainland South-East Asia, Cambodia has no major north–south mountain ranges that have acted as natural barriers to invaders and traders. This physical feature, as well as its proximity to navigable waterways, has meant that Cambodia has always been influenced by other cultures and nations—most notably Thailand and Vietnam, but also India, China, the Mongols, Japan (for a brief period during the Second World War) and of course France. The Mekong River, the extensive canal system and the Tonle Sap—the last is the largest body of freshwater in South-East Asia—are also significant topographical influences on culture and commerce.

The country is fertile, has rich fisheries, mineral and timber wealth, and is strategically placed within the greater Mekong basin. Indeed, Cambodia's location near the dynamic economies in East and South-East Asia could work very much to its favor. It also has a wealth of historical and cultural treasures, most notably Angkor Wat, and other tourist sites, including beach resorts. The climate is tropical. Monsoons are biannual—

with the accompanying rainy season, they dictate many commercial and cultural activities. As Cambodia is a primarily agrarian economy, weather patterns strongly influence the country's economic output and welfare (Chandler 1992, pp. xvi, 7).

Perhaps as many as 90% of Cambodians are Khmer—some people use the terms "Cambodian" and "Khmer" interchangeably (Culturgram 1995). This makes Cambodia one of the most homogeneous countries in South-East Asia. The Chinese and Vietnamese are the largest minorities; they have traditionally been associated, respectively, with the general commercial sector and fishing industries. Both groups have also been persecuted—the Chinese community less so, however, and it is re-emerging as a significant commercial force. The remaining Cambodians are Cham Muslims (they number approximately 200 000) and various tribal groups (fewer than 100 000), typically found in Cambodia's mountainous regions.

Theravada Buddhism is the dominant religion, and influences much of Cambodian culture. The group or community is considered more important than the individual, as are rulers and ancestors. Although Western clothing is common in Phnom Penh, most Cambodians still opt for traditional clothing, such as the checked, rectangular cloth that is wrapped around the hips or worn like a kilt down to the ankles (*sampot* and *sarong* for women; *sarong soet* for men). A large multipurpose scarf/satchel/hat called a *krama* is also common.

Khmer is the national language. It is alphabetic and non-tonal; most Westerners find it relatively difficult to master. French was once commonly spoken, but English is clearly becoming the favored second language.

Societal structure and demographics

The social structure and demographic profile of Cambodia reflect the legacy of major social upheavals and warfare. Its HDI of 0.186 ranks it near the bottom of the list of all countries (Culturgram 1995).

There exist in Cambodia, therefore, unique conditions that could negatively impact on the future growth and development of marketing activity. One such condition is the phenomenon of internal refugees, or, more accurately, displaced persons. Of these, as many as 200 000 wander from area to area because they were displaced from their homes during fighting, while at least 300 000 additional refugees live in camps on the Thai border.

A second condition is the composition of the population by age group and sex. Cambodia has a very high dependency ratio—in 1993 the figure was 0.65 (i.e. only 35 out of 100 people were economically productive), and over half the population is currently under the age of 15. The sex ratio of the population has been dramatically skewed by the selective emigration of men, and by wars and executions, which took a disproportionate toll among the male population. In 1990, about 57% of the adult population, and 35% of heads of households, were women. The latter figure is the highest percentage in the world (see Table 3.3). The family as a unit, though discouraged by the Khmer Rouge and ravaged by war, is very important to Cambodians, and multiple generations tend to live in one family unit or in close proximity.

Table 3.3 Population by age group and sex (1990)

Age group	*% in total population*	*% females in total pop.*
All ages	100.00	53.70
Over 15	53.10	57.30
6 to 15	30.30	49.70
1 to 5	12.40	49.60
Under 1	4.20	49.80

The total population of Cambodia was estimated to be about 9.5 million in 1993, and present trends indicate it will increase at 2.7–3.3% per year. Phnom Penh is the largest city, with approximately 1 million residents, followed by Battambang and Kompong Som, with approximately 100 000 and 65 000 residents respectively. As with other statistics in the Cambodian context, however, the population measures are very unreliable. The figures given here are mere projections from the last population census that took place in 1962, but clearly the number and demographic profile of the people is radically different from "what might have been," and from typical growth patterns seen elsewhere in the region. The essence of the problem has been expressed well by Ebihara, Mortland and Ledgerwood (1994, pp. 14–15):

> Population statistics are one indicator of the tragedy that swept Cambodia. Cambodia's population was estimated at over 7 million in 1970 . . . It has been observed that, rather than the 11.5 million that would normally have been expected in 1989 from an annual growth rate of 2.7%, Cambodia's 1989 population was only 8.4 million, the difference resulting from the effects of war for over two decades.

Migration to urban centers seems to be a trend, but only an estimated 10–15% of Cambodia's population resides in towns and cities. With about 50 inhabitants per square kilometer, Cambodia still has a favorable labor-to-land ratio. There is practically no agrarian problem as most farmers own their land,

and there is no known tenancy or rural-debt problem. However, access to arable land and employment as a farm laborer has its drawbacks: Cambodia has more embedded land mines, and more embedded land mines per capita, than any other country in history. Not coincidentally, Cambodia also has the highest ratios of amputees and orphans per capita in the world, and even though many of these casualties are the result of injuries sustained over decades of war, death and dismemberment from contact with leftover explosive ordnance is still common. These unique conditions will inevitably influence future marketing and development strategies in Cambodia.

Furthermore, recent reports about increases in corruption, abuses of human rights, and curtailment of press freedom by the RCG have led some major donor countries to consider curtailing economic and financial assistance. The legacies of war communism and brutality in Cambodia are still so pervasive and visible that many objective and independent observers of Cambodian affairs have come to the sad conclusion that Cambodia can never again succeed as a fully independent nation. In this context, Shenon (1995) noted:

> Many of the people left to run the Government are corrupt and uneducated, their credentials consisting of their willingness to use violence unsparingly. Many of Cambodia's senior leaders are Khmer Rouge defectors who, while they may have renounced the ideology of Pol Pot, still make use of his savage tactics.

The air of repression and violence that permeates Cambodia is not only damaging to Cambodia's image as a potential investment market–it also harms the fragile social confidence needed if Cambodia is to move forward. Indeed, the country's future is contingent upon safeguards that ensure societal trust, optimism, and the collective belief that the future can provide better outcomes for a majority of Cambodians. To those ends, in addition to co-ordinated and sound economic development policies and political openness, a nation's commitment to education and health are foundations to individual, economic and societal development, and as such are integral to an assessment of Cambodia's will to move forward. Accordingly, we briefly address education and public health in Cambodia below.

Education

The education system was destroyed by the Khmer Rouge, and the RCG is trying to rebuild it. Although literacy rates are among the lowest in Asia, literacy is increasing, if at a modest rate. Still, despite literacy programs, almost 80% of women are unable to read and to write. And, while school enrollment percentages are increasing (especially for women–rectifying the gender imbalances in education is a government priority), the percentage of public expenditure that is dedicated to education is less than adequate. Another troubling trend is the situation that degrees at the tertiary education level can be bought rather than earned. Hence, as with so many measures in Cambodia, education statistics evoke both hope and despair.

Public health

Public health is another daunting challenge; the statistics present an appalling set of conditions. Life expectancy continues to hover around 50 years of age. Maternal, infant, and under-5 mortality rates remain unacceptably high. Only a small minority of the population has access to sanitation; malnutrition is still a problem for many Cambodians; access to fundamental health services is also problematic. Multilateral aid efforts have markedly improved conditions in recent years, providing a glimmer of hope for the future.

Implications for marketing and consumer behavior

Given the fragile economic, ecological, military, political, and social situation in Cambodia, it is reasonable to conclude that the performance of the economy will be erratic, and that the opportunities for marketers may be fleeting. The combination of the three types of transition discussed earlier—from a centrally planned to a market system, from a less developed to a more developed country, and from a wartime to a peacetime economy—make the task of finding the solution to the multifaceted problems in Cambodia very difficult. Any sustainable solution to the complex problem of economic development and growth is predicated on the normalization of the political situation. In-country observations, and a series of interviews by the authors over the last few years, indicate such normalization is possible, if not assured. Nevertheless, our observations also indicate that market-driven commerce is increasingly obvious, especially in Phnom Penh, Sihanoukville and other relatively urban sites. Indeed, the depth and breadth of marketing and consumption activity in Phnom Penh, for example, is almost startling, and seems to symbolize the resolve of the Cambodian people to enter the global economy despite extraordinary handicaps.

Therefore we submit that, pending political stability, marketing opportunities are promising. Others have also been cautiously optimistic (International Monetary Fund 1994; Lanchner & Shepherd 1994; Thayer 1994a). The remainder of this chapter provides a brief profile of the Cambodian consumer, and examines macromarketing-mix issues, the impact of commerce and change, and a look into the future.

Changes in consumer behavior: Segments and consumer values

The information already supplied in this chapter provides a crude indication of factors that will broadly affect consumption. But it does not really answer the question, "Who is the Cambodian consumer?" Or, perhaps more importantly, "How has consumer behavior changed, and what consumption patterns and consumer tendencies may marketers need to be cognizant of if they hope to succeed in this market?" The trends and economic and demographic indicators discussed earlier might suggest that the Cambodian consumer would not be worth the bother. Indeed, most Cambodians struggle simply to survive–but it would be short-sighted to conclude this market is not tenable.

Recent observations by the first author in Cambodian markets and consumption venues (e.g. cafés, homes and sites where consumers purchase and use goods and services) indicate that Cambodian consumers are many different types of people: rural and urban, young and old, male and female, traditional and more modern, poor and with some disposable income. In other words, in many instances consumers do live in abject poverty, but a class of consumers that values the goods and services found throughout South-East Asia is also emerging. These opinion leaders are typically urban, younger, and brand aware, and, while perhaps poor by Western standards, have aspirations not unlike more well-to-do opinion leaders in places such as Bangkok, Singapore or the USA. For them, the standard package (Keyfitz 1982) includes, for example, a motor scooter, a CD player and Western clothing, preferably a chic brand such as Levi's or Polo, or, more likely, a pirated version of them.

So the Cambodian market can be segmented several ways; marketers could consider as prime targets the urban, relatively young consumers who are starting to become affluent. Women, if for no other reason than they are a disproportionately large percentage of the population, are also a significant target, especially for marketers of household goods.

Another set of consumers, particularly in Phnom Penh, includes a large number of NGO personnel and the growing population of foreign investors. Although these consumers are present throughout South-East Asia they are especially significant to Cambodia and Phnom Penh because half the money in circulation in Phnom Penh alone is "artificial"–that is, Phnom Penh's economy is kept afloat by money infusions from the UN and other sources. This money is helping to restore infrastructure and stability generally, but it is also helping to maintain a Mercedes-Benz dealership, hotels and restaurants, the cellular phone market and other markets for products and services beyond the purchasing power of most Cambodians. The long-run repercussions for this artificial infusion of cash (preferably in the form of US dollars), goods and services include the rapid exposure to, and awareness and diffusion of products in Cambodian life. This diffusion process has not by-passed opinion leaders. The net result is that urban Cambodian consumers are much more "aware" of and receptive to new products and promotion mechanisms than we might initially surmise.

Changes in the macromarketing mix

The objective of this section is to present trends among the elements of the marketing mix at the national or aggregate level—that is, the macromarketing mix (Leeflang & van Raaij 1993, p. 353). This discussion includes elements of the classic marketing mix, such as product, price, distribution, and promotion; we also include a brief discussion on market research.

Products

Cambodia's liberalized economy has changed consumer behavior and the product offerings to consumers. For most consumers, products that clothe, feed and provide shelter are the highest priority; because of both poverty and scarcity, most products are recycled and lateral cycled (Belk 1988). This "waste-not" attitude has positive outcomes for consumers, because products, or frequently, product containers, are used time and again and for multiple purposes. (We should add that marketers would perhaps be surprised to learn how their products and containers are used: discarded liter-sized bottles of Pepsi and Mirinda, for example, are used for selling gasoline.)

Yet, despite poverty and the need to recycle, new-to-the-Cambodian-market products and brands that have been successful in other South-East Asian countries, particularly Thailand, are being diffused into the consciousness of Cambodian consumers, especially consumers in Phnom Penh; their consumption is generally increasing. For opinion leaders, as mentioned briefly above, products of favor include goods associated with popular culture and electronics technology—for example, hedonic or "fun" products such as Sony Walkman-type personal stereos and computer games. Other relatively inexpensive hedonic goods include tobacco products, soft drinks and alcoholic beverages; tobacco and liquor companies have been among the first to penetrate the Cambodian market successfully. Electronics companies have also quickly penetrated the urban markets. Brand images and loyalties are now emerging for the first time for many products, but, in essence, products that add immediate utilitarian value, such as bicycle parts, pumps and inexpensive shoes, are well received in the market. More hedonic goods, and venues for their consumption—such as cafés, and television cafés in which consumers can enjoy soft drinks, coffee or beer and watch television or listen to music—are also becoming increasingly popular. Even a national lottery has been established (*Phnom Penh Post* 1995).

It should be noted that Cambodia is also a large market for multilateral aid projects. Construction and infrastructure materials for roads, bridges, telecommunications and buildings are sold in large quantities. These products enhance life quality and enable the more efficient distribution of products, and, hence, greater access to consumers. Many goods and services target this "investor market." The Cambodiana Hotel, for example, and the casino ship moored in front of the Cambodiana, are specifically targeted to foreign investors, particularly Chinese from Hong Kong and Singapore.

Distribution

Not surprisingly, distribution in Cambodia is generally slow and inefficient. Poor roads and railways—and the presence of bandits in many parts of the country—make the transportation of goods difficult. Sihanoukville, on the gulf of Siam, is the primary port, although small container vessels can unload shipments at Phnom Penh. What Cambodia lacks in infrastructure that could facilitate transportation, it makes up for in the grit of its people. Bicycles, motor scooters, other small vehicles and ox carts transport many items. Larger vehicles supplied by the UN and other NGOs also lend support. There is also large-scale smuggling, especially along the Thai border. Huge amounts of timber and precious stones are smuggled across the border from Cambodia to Thailand—and, somewhat ironically, larger and better trucks are often used in this region to abet the illicit activities. Smuggling on the Thai border has been especially troublesome because it tends to be administered in part by the Khmer Rouge; there has been speculation that the Cambodian army is also involved (Thayer 1994b).

The increase in new products and the transportation of products to markets requires wholesale and retail outlets. Similarly to other South-East Asian countries, Cambodia tends to have central markets as the hubs of commerce. In Phnom Penh, for example, this market is referred to as the "New" market, and houses small stalls with everything from traditional Khmer textiles to televisions and computer games. New and smaller retail establishments—typically storefronts, kiosks or shacks—are proliferating, seemingly everywhere consumers tend to congregate. Indeed, an entire community of restaurants, cafés and other shops has emerged across the Tonle River from Phnom Penh since the "Japanese Bridge" (so named because of the benefactors) was completed.

Retailers generally range from very modest street cafés and run-down hotels to electronics stores and a Mercedes-Benz dealership. Again, the likes of prestige-brand car dealerships are predominantly intended to serve expatriates and foreign investors, but Cambodians are increasingly visiting and purchasing from small retailers throughout Phnom Penh and other larger communities. An–albeit fragile–"disposable-income" class is emerging that will be able to afford such "high-ticket" items.

Promotion

Promotion has become critical to the success of marketers in Cambodia. Message, medium and overall management of the marketing communications mix must be given careful thought. Furthermore, as is the case with other elements of the marketing mix, promotional strategy is partly dictated by whether a company is targeting Cambodians or expatriates and members of the multilateral aid market. If the latter group is being targeted, print advertisements in the English-language newspapers, such as the *Cambodia Times* and the *Phnom Penh Post,* are almost a requirement. Outdoor advertising is also important if a company is targeting this group: brewers, airlines, telecommunications companies, oil companies, electronics firms and tobacco companies are leaders in this medium. Personal selling and the hotel/restaurant lobby network is also important. The importance of this person-to-person contact in Cambodia should not be underestimated. Various hotel restaurants in Phnom Penh, for example, are known as "power breakfast" meeting places. The Cambodiana hotel–Cambodia's only "five-star" hotel–is also recognized as a site where "things get done." We would expect the previously mentioned floating casino and the Naga Casino Resorts casino, off the coast of Sihanoukville, to provide other personal-selling, networking and entertainment functions. Electronic media will become more significant, but at this juncture they are secondary elements of the communications mix–especially for this targeted group. Strategically placed flyers and promotional materials in hotels, restaurants and other consumption venues of the expatriate market will also be helpful.

If a company is targeting Cambodians, certain rudimentary factors must be addressed. Firstly, because of the relatively low literacy rate, outdoor advertising that displays easily interpreted symbols and images is a favored promotional tactic. Billboards with bold images and slice-of-life scenes tend to be effective. Products and brands in completely unfamiliar product classes will require advertising copy that simply demonstrates utilitarian or hedonic value.

It should also be noted that the lines demarcating promotion and distribution are frequently difficult to distinguish in Cambodia. Philip Morris, for example, recently opened a "Marlboro store" that sells nothing but Marlboro cigarettes. The store's facade provides outdoor advertising and point-of-purchase reminders. On the sidewalk in front of the store, attractive young ladies–dressed in red and white Marlboro jumpsuits and standing beside their red and white Marlboro scooters, parked under red and white Marlboro umbrellas–have helped to reaffirm the Marlboro image recognized around the globe.

Tobacco and liquor companies have generally been leaders in developing promotional strategies targeted at Cambodian consumers. The lessons learned from them are valuable, because brand loyalties have in many cases not yet been established, and, in the case of brewers, for example, the end product, beer, has not been historically popular. Annual beer consumption per capita in Cambodia is fairly low: 2 liters. Comparatively, consumers in Thailand and Japan drink 20 and 100 liters respectively. But brewers see this low consumption as an indicator of market potential, and not as a bad outlook for other goods and services in Cambodia. The almost uniformly tried strategy to increase consumption is as follows:

> Just about any night at the Hang Neak restaurant . . . pretty young women dressed in the multicolored uniforms of several major beer companies hurry through the crowds to greet each new table of customers. At the tables, the "beer girls" from Carlsberg, Tiger Beer, Angkor Beer or San Miguel hail customers with the same question: Would you like a beer? (Postelwaite 1995, p. 12).

As one of the beer girls noted,

> Most people don't know what they want . . . so they'll order from whatever girl arrives. On a good day, I can sell four to six cases (Postelwaite 1995, p. 12).

In addition to aggressive promotion and selling at the point of purchase, brewers, and other purveyors of consumer goods, are using park benches, the airwaves and billboards to promote their goods. Bottle-cap lotteries and other games popular in the USA and other countries a generation ago are very well liked by Cambodian consumers.

The optimal marketing communications mix varies broadly as a function of the target market, which may be either the expatriate/multilateral aid market or local Cambodians. Cambodian consumers will become more promotion-savvy, but in the foreseeable future, simple outdoor and print advertising, coupled with sponsorship and, for inexpensive consumer goods, sampling opportunities that create brand awareness, are likely to be the most effective.

Prices

The transformation to a market economy means, by definition, that market forces determine prices. Although consumers were buffeted by steep price increases in the early 1990s, thanks to economic policies to control inflation and good fortune with agricultural production, prices have been fairly stable. It should be noted that inflation control is a high government priority for the foreseeable future; however, further reforms are needed to assure long-term price stabilization. Most consumers still tend to have little confidence in the riel and, similarly to consumers in other parts of Indochina, they tend to save by hoarding dollars, gold or other tangible goods that will hold their value over time. And, as many consumers are destitute, function outside the economy or reside in rural areas, barter is a very common mechanism of exchange.

Market research

Market research tends to be fairly basic and qualitative. Most consumer-goods companies have been inclined to categorize the Cambodian market generally as a developing South-East Asian economy, and have tried to replicate strategies used successfully in other parts of the region while also attending to specific cultural sensibilities. This strategy has been reasonably successful, but as the market evolves firms are finding it necessary to collect more Cambodia-specific data.

Data can be collected by placing personnel in-country or by employing the services of market research firms and advertising firms that are now focusing on Cambodia. Whether companies outsource market research or use their own staff, data collection usually tends to be site-specific, person-to-person and/or labor intensive, as consumers are not familiar with questionnaires and are uncomfortable with the data-collection process—or, perhaps more accurately, are mistrustful of the process. In addition to being labor intensive (and costly), collecting accurate and representative data often can be dangerous as well, as researchers may need to gather information in parts of the country where security remains questionable. A recent fact-finding excursion into some remote north-west areas near Battambang by Australian Telecom employees illustrates the need for good judgment (or good luck):

> We were trying to determine the feasibility of building a relay station so my supervisor and I needed to visit the proposed site. We could only get there by helicopter . . . The pilot insisted on flying at 10 000 feet because that would keep us out of range of any snipers. Once we approached the site we made a military-style descent—fast, spinning round and round. By the time we hit the ground we literally couldn't walk straight because we were so dizzy. Anyway, a truck was waiting for us and we drove along this dirt road about 20 minutes or so until we were forced to the side by some gunmen who demanded all our money. My supervisor—it was his first time in Cambodia, I think—was pretty scared and asked me what we should do. I told him, "I reckon we ought to give it to 'em . . ." (Rourke 1994).

Although this scenario is not what one would expect to encounter in Phnom Penh or Sihanoukville—and many observers argue that one would not now encounter that kind of harassment even in the north-west provinces—it is important for researchers to keep in the back of their minds the fact that the situation can deteriorate quickly if they are asking the wrong questions, or collecting data in the wrong place at the wrong time.

Given the potential problems associated with the data-collection process, how do we gain an operable understanding of the Cambodian market? It has been suggested that the Indochinese situation requires that companies place multiskilled employees in-country to collect primary data relevant to company-specific needs and objectives (Shultz 1994). Cambodia, as illustrated by the Telecom excursion, is not an exception. Determining which products will sell is important, but determining where to sell them, how to transport, promote and price them is equally important. Thorough in-country assessments by investing firms that have examined arcane country conditions have led to successful product introductions that target the consumer and multilateral aid markets.

In summary, basic observational and qualitative market research can provide insights that will enable firms to be profitable in the Cambodian consumer market. Thorough site research, that goes beyond an examination of economic indicators, can pinpoint trends and future opportunities. Some international market research and advertising firms have begun to measure consumer attitudes toward products and brands, and to establish consumer profiles and segmentation schemes. These measures will become increasingly important if Cambodia can sustain its commercial renaissance. Furthermore, given the emphasis on donor assistance, multilateral aid projects and Cambodian restoration, many firms have been able to profit from understanding infrastructure needs and the construction boom by selling materials and machinery.

Future trends and expectations: Whither Cambodia?

Recent negative political and security developments do not augur well for the future growth and development of Cambodia. Yet, for all its troubles, commerce is alive and well. The relatively strong economic performance during the last few years, stable exchange rates, relatively low inflation, the country's new "observer status" in ASEAN, pending Most Favored Nation (MFN) status from the USA, continued foreign investment, and the government's efforts to promote Cambodia as a regional hub have inspired many observers to conclude that the conditions for further growth and development are reasonably good. Such conclusions, however, could be premature. Fundamentally, the performance of the Cambodian economy remains unbalanced. Its overall impact is shallow, and its benefits are not spread evenly throughout the society. Much of the growth has been concentrated in metro Phnom Penh (which has only 12% of the total population), and is partially explained by the artificial or support economy. One wonders whether these less than optimal outcomes are an evolutionary phase through which

Cambodia must pass before the fruits of reform reach all Cambodians, or whether these outcomes portend greater disequilibrium and another chapter in the Cambodian epic of war, foreign invasion, and internal strife (Prasso 1994).

Leaders of the RCG and foreign investors seem to be leaning toward more optimistic scenarios. Indeed, the RCG is literally banking on them, and the government's longer term vision has been interpreted as 5 primary goals (Asian Development Bank 1994, p. 79):

1 to double the present level of GDP by 2004 in real terms, and to place heightened emphasis on harnessing Cambodia's agricultural, industrial and tourism potentials
2 to extend health, education and social services to the entire population in order to ensure, within a decade, a peaceful way of life and a substantial standard of living
3 to improve rural living by promoting rural development as a central feature of development policies
4 to ensure that the pattern of development is sustainable politically, fiscally, and environmentally
5 to strengthen domestic self-reliance and thus reduce the current dependence of external financial and technical assistance

Again, economic indicators suggest some of these goals are tenable, but recent activities evoke a measure of skepticism. The political climate remains infected with a pall of corruption, incompetence and perniciousness. Corruption, particularly, is a corrosive factor that is not likely to subside soon. Some government officials and the Khmer Rouge, for example, continue to make shady deals in logging with foreign companies, leading to the rapacious and unrestrained exploitation of Cambodia's forest and other natural resources (*Economist* 1995a). Statistics provided by Thai customs authorities indicate that in 1993 the amount of timber imported by Thailand alone was greater than the total amount authorized to be exported by Cambodian authorities (St John 1995), and findings from recent field work by the first author paint an ominous picture. By many accounts the forest cover in Cambodia has been reduced by 50% since 1974, leaving only about 30–35% coverage in 1998. Most of the devastation has occurred within the last 8 years. If the current trend continues, the forests could be entirely depleted within this decade. Deforestation is particularly insidious because it damages other ecosystems, disrupts irrigation, causes flooding and drought, and ultimately threatens food supplies.

Part of this type of problem can be blamed on "favorable" foreign investment laws that virtually render Cambodian land and other resources "for sale." Malaysian interests, for example, which have pledged US$1.6 billion in investment aid, have purchased 12% of the Cambodian forests and 4% of the land mass (*Economist* 1995b); despite newly drafted laws intended to preserve natural resources, there is little evidence that environmentalism or resource replenishment are significant parts of the agendas for foreign investors or Cambodia policy makers. Not surprisingly, many development agreements have come under attack by environmentalists (Fitzgerald 1995), and much better resource-management and conservation practices are needed if Cambodia hopes to sustain development, improve life quality for the majority of the citizenry and enable Cambodians to participate in an enduring consumer society. The situation may be so dire as to require implementation of radical proposals such as the idea of turning Cambodia into a world national park that constitutes a development policy "based on nature-based and cultural tourism supplemented by a limited number of environmentally friendly resource-based industries" (*Economist* 1995c, p. 34).

Indeed, there is a feeling among many who know the Cambodian situation closely that, while the country is a nice outlet for consumer goods such as liquor, tobacco, soap, soft drinks, etc., few companies have the confidence to establish manufacturing sites or sustainable development projects. As one Western attorney, working in Phnom Penh, remarked:

> It [Cambodia] is a great market, look around–it's obvious people want all kinds of goods–but most foreign investors are afraid to actually build factories here because they don't think the situation is stable enough. They [potential investors] would rather bring the stuff in from Thailand or wherever–take their chances that way–than sink a lot of capital in a factory only to see it disappear if the situation deteriorates. It's sad, but you can understand why foreign companies feel that way (Shultz 1995).

Personal observation has substantiated this viewpoint to a large degree, but not everyone agrees that capital investments in factories and other long-term investments are too risky. The Angkor Brewery[1] is one example of a manufacturing facility being built with the support of foreign investment, and of course the donor assistance for infrastructure helps to instill confidence and to stabilize, but Angkor Brewery is the exception rather than the rule. If skepticism reaches the multilateral aid market–if donor countries find the Cambodian situation to be unacceptable–the consequences for Cambodia's renaissance would be devastating (Thayer 1995). Therefore, we believe that further reforms are necessary if the government wishes to see its ambitious goals bear fruit. These reforms must occur in both political and economic institutions, and should include:

- greater tolerance for freedom of expression and open discourse
- education investment to increase literacy and technical skills
- improvements in revenue collection
- changes to streamline bureaucracy
- a greater shift toward privatization
- revamped legal and accounting systems to match global standards
- sustainable development programs to assure long-term prosperity and environment protection
- tighter controls over government expenditure, which would reduce budget-deficit financing from the central bank

Marketing in Cambodia: Go vs no-go decision making

We reiterate that, despite instability and substantial difficulties, Cambodia is a viable market, with urban consumers keen to participate in the consumer culture. Whether marketers choose to establish manufacturing facilities in-country or to export to Cambodia should be predicated on an investor's risk/reward assessment of the country. Most country-risk-assessment formulae would indicate that Cambodia is truly a high risk country, and cynics (realists?) have tended to see the Cambodian market as untenable, or as an export market only. While we are not overly optimistic, we do believe that Cambodia provides marketing opportunities, and therefore we consider Cambodia to be a "go" market, given the following considerations.

Those who have successfully entered this market have learned that the situation requires an understanding of what makes Cambodia different from other markets, and how these differences affect management of the traditional 4 Ps. In Cambodia, however, there are 4 other Ps that are equally important: *predictability, prudence, patience,* and *perseverance.*

In one sense, the social, economic and political turmoil make Cambodia very unpredictable. In another sense, marketers have learned that, while they need to take into account unique Cambodian customs, habits and some demographic constraints, the Cambodian market does replicate the early stages of other more established markets in the region. Therefore, with a modest understanding of the Cambodian condition, including the inherent risks, it can be predicted with a fairly high degree of certainty that consumers will respond positively to marketing mix manipulations used in other emerging South-East Asian countries. Prudence and forethought, however, are required at every step. It could be argued that this recommendation is warranted for any marketing endeavor, but in Cambodia poor judgment and carelessness may not only cripple the marketer's plan(s), but may also result in political controversy, harassment and personal injury.

Marketing management in one of the world's poorest countries requires patience. Poor infrastructure, a poorly trained workforce without the skills required to succeed in today's competitive global market, bureaucracy and other challenges that define the Cambodian market will try the patience of the most serene manager. All of these factors indicate that perseverance is also required.

In conclusion, those deciding whether to enter this challenging market should know that, despite the obstacles, several firms have begun projects in Cambodia that are functional, have attracted customers keen to purchase the goods and services they offer, and in some instances are already profitable.

References

Asian Development Bank (1991), *Cambodia: An Economic Report,* The Asian Development Bank, Manila.

Asian Development Bank (1994), *Cambodia: Economic Review and Bank Operations,* The Asian Development Bank, Manila.

Belk, Russell W. (1988), "Third World Consumer Culture", in eds Erdogan Kumcu and A. Fuat Firat, *Marketing and Development: Toward Broader Dimensions,* JAI Press, Greenwich, CT, pp. 103–27.

Boua, Chanthou (1983), "Observations of the Heng Samrin Government 1980–1982", in eds David P. Chandler and Ben Kiernan, *Revolution and Its Aftermath in Kampuchea,* Yale University South-East Asian Studies, New Haven, CT.

Business Times (1994), "Cambodia Eyes $800 M in Investment", October 28, p. 2.

Chandler, David P. (1992), *A History of Cambodia,* Westview Press, Boulder, CO.

Chandler, David P., Kiernan, Ben & Chanthou, Boua (1988), *Pol Pot Plans the Future,* South-East Asian Studies, Yale University, New Haven, CT.

Chantrabot, Ros (1993), *La Republique Khmere (1970–1975),* Editions L'Harmattan, Paris.

Corfield, Justin (1994), *Khmers Stand Up!,* Monash University Centre of South-East Asian Studies, Clayton, Vic.

Culturgram (1995), "State of Cambodia", Brigham Young University, Provo, UT.

Ebihara, May M., Mortland, Carol A. & Ledgerwood, Judy (1994), *Cambodian Culture since 1975: Homeland and Exile,* Cornell University Press, Ithaca, NY.

Economist (1995a), "Cambodia's Wood-Fired War", June 17, pp. 35–6.

— (1995b), "Royal Flush", February 11, pp. 34–5.

— (1995c), "Stop the Clock", September 2, pp. 32–3.

Economist Intelligence Unit (1994), *EIU Country Profile: Cambodia.*

Fitzgerald, Tricia (1995), "New Logging Contracts Dwarf Samling's Deal", *Phnom Penh Post,* August 25–September 7.

International Monetary Fund (1994), "Cambodia Emerges from Isolation as Economic Reforms Take Hold", IMF Survey, September 26, Washington, DC.

Keyfitz, Nathan (1982), "Development and the Elimination of Poverty", *Economic Development and Cultural Change,* vol. 30 no. 6, pp. 346–55.

Lanchner, David & Shepherd, William (1994), "In Embryo Markets, Being First Counts", *Global Finance* , vol. 8, October, pp. 53–8.

Leeflang, Peter & van Raaij, Fred (1993), "The Changing Consumer in the Netherlands", *International Journal of Research in Marketing,* vol. 10, pp. 345–63.

Leepson, Marc (1985), "Cambodia: A Nation in Turmoil", *Editorial Resarch Reports, Congressional Quarterly,* Washington, DC.

Muscat, Robert J. (1989), *Cambodia: Post-Settlement Reconstruction and Development,* Columbia University, New York.

Osborne, Milton (1979), *Before Kampuchea: Preludes to Tragedy,* Allen & Unwin, London.

Phnom Penh Post (1995), May 5–8.

Ponchaud, Francois (1977), *Cambodia: Year Zero,* Holt, Rinehart & Winston, New York.

Postelwaite, Susan (1995), "Beer Brands Battle for Market Share", *Phnom Penh Post,* May 5–18, p.12.

Prasso, Sheri (1994), "Cambodia: A Heritage of Violence", *World Policy Journal,* vol. 11 (Fall), pp. 71–7.

Prud'Homme, Remy (1969), *L'Economie du Cambodge,* Presses Universitaires de France, Paris.

Rourke, Dennis (1994), Australian Telecom Field Representative, personal interview, January 9, Hanoi.

St John, Ronald Bruce (1995), "The Political Economy of the Royal Government of Cambodia", *Contemporary South-East Asia,* vol. 17 (December), pp. 265–81.

Shenon, Philip (1995), "Cambodia Can't Shake The Legacy of Madness", *The New York Times,* March 12.

Showcross, William (1994), "Cambodia's New Deal", Contemporary Issues Papers No. 1, Carnegie Endowment Publication, Washington, DC.

Shultz, Clifford J., II, (1995), May 12 field notes, Phnom Penh.

— (1994), "Balancing Policy Consumer Desire and Corporate Interests: Considerations for Market Entry in Vietnam", *Columbia Journal of World Business*, vol. 29, Winter, pp. 42–53.

Steinberg, David J. (1959), *Cambodia*, HRAF, New Haven, CT.

Thayer, Nate (1994a), "Golden Opportunities", *Far Eastern Economic Review*, May 19, p. 20.

— (1994b), "Log Jam", *Far Eastern Economic Review*, August 4, p. 55.

— (1995), "Compassion Fatigue", *Far Eastern Economic Review*, February 16, p. 19.

Twining, Charles H. (1989), "The Economy", in ed. Karl D. Jackson, *Cambodia 1975–1978*, Princeton University Press, Princeton, NJ.

United Nations (1991), *Cambodia's Rehabilitation Needs*, November 11, UN Development Programme, New York.

Vickery, Michael (1990), "Notes on the Political Economy of the People's Republic of Kampuchea", *Journal of Contemporary Asia*, vol. 20, no. 4, pp. 435–65.

World Bank (1992), *Cambodia: Agenda for Rehabilitation and Reconstruction*, The World Bank, Washington, DC.

Notes

1 This brewery is a source of considerable national pride to Cambodians, and the company's tagline, seen on billboards throughout Phom Penh, reinforces this pride: "Angkor–My Country, My Beer."

CHAPTER 4[1]

China

The changing consumer: Economic, demographic and social trends and their marketing implications

LAUREN SWANSON

Abstract

An overview is presented of consumer developments in what is potentially the world's largest economy. A brief introduction traces the rich history of China, with its varied traditions that form the backdrop for modern events. The statistical, economic and demographic situations are described, and future trends are evaluated. The continuing liberalization of Chinese economic and social life is expected to influence strongly the shape of the future as China joins the more developed nations and becomes a major, perhaps even a dominant, player on the world stage.

Introduction

History

With a claim of 5000 years of history, and a recorded chronicle of nearly 4000 years, Chinese civilization is one of the oldest in the world. The rise of modern China began in the 16th century with the arrival of seafaring explorers in South China, followed by traders, missionaries and the Russians via Siberia in the mid-17th century. With the 19th-century arrival of Europeans, China's age-old isolation was thoroughly broken, and the country was well on the way to engagement with the West.

By 1912, the imperial dynasty had been abolished—for the first time in 4000 years—and a Western-style republic was established. Subsequent years saw efforts to combat lingering corruption and warlordism, and attempts to create an effective political system. Two main philosophies competed, with the Marxist, revolutionary view eventually winning out over the Nationalist, evolutionary approach. The People's Republic of China (PRC) was established on October 1 1949 by the Chinese Communist Party.

Geography

China, one of the largest countries in the world, is relatively isolated by its geography. Not having ever developed a seafaring tradition, China has historically been cut off from the rest of the world by the sea in the east, the treacherous Tibetan plateau in the west, and deserts in the north.

The country consists of 5000 islands, with considerable climatic variation, from the bitter cold of the north and the western mountains to the unbearably hot desert and southern coastal regions. Its arable, cultivated land has been estimated at between 10 and 15% of the total landmass. This small percentage is a source of concern, as rich farmland is being converted to industrial purposes. This is making China a leading grain importer (second only to Japan) and a net grain importer for the first time in years.

From Beijing (Peking), the capital, the government manages 31 "administrative divisions," consisting of 23 provinces, 5 "autonomous regions," and the 3 municipalities of Beijing, Tianjin, and Shanghai. These all report directly to the central government. In addition, there are five Special Economic Zones (SEZs), all in southern China, which have been granted special powers to offer concessionary terms to encourage foreign enterprises, individuals, and overseas Chinese to invest or establish joint-venture enterprises.

Population

The largest population in the world resides in China—1223.89 million people (*China Statistical Yearbook* 1997, p. 70). About 95% of the population are Han Chinese, with the remainder consisting of about 55 minority nationalities, including Mongols, Tibetans, and Turkish-descended Muslim Uygurs of the north-west region. Most of these minority peoples reside in sensitive border regions. In the area of religion, the Chinese have been influenced by Taoism, Confucianism, Buddhism, and Christianity. The worship of ancestors and a host of gods and spirits is also strongly rooted in Chinese tradition.

Language

The official language of the People's Republic is the Northern Mandarin/ Beijing dialect of the Mandarin sublanguage. About 30% of the population are native speakers of this dialect, usually referred to as "Mandarin" in the west, and as *putonghua* or "common speech" in China. However, the 95% Han Chinese speak one of 9 major Sinitic sublanguages. These are divided into 23 major dialects, which are, in turn, divided into many distinctive subdialects. The Chinese share a common written language. However, Chinese characters used on the mainland (PRC) are simplified forms of the traditional characters used in Taiwan, Hong Kong, and Macau. This simplification reflects government efforts to increase the rate of literacy in the country.

Economy

Accompanying the political changes over the years have been fundamental transformations in the Chinese economy and society. In the recent past, following decisions made at the end of 1978, central control was relaxed and state-controlled enterprises were forced to set their own targets and given more latitude with buying, selling, hiring, and firing. A three-tier system currently exists:

1. the state controls supply and prices for industrial and raw materials and consumer staples
2. for many other products, prices vary, but the price range is within the limits set by the state
3. a third, "free-market" system allows prices to be established by buyers and sellers.

Generally, urban consumers earn about US$37 per month, and rural consumers on average about US$19. As a result of government subsidies for housing, staple foods, education, and health care, a large proportion of the average income is spent on food and discretionary consumer goods. Recent years have seen an enormous growth in the market for consumer goods.

An overview

Since the start of economic reform in China in 1978, the economy has been expanding at an average annual rate of 9% in real terms (State Statistical Bureau of The People's Republic of China 1994, p. 17). In economic terms, China is growing faster than any other country in South-East Asia (see Table 4.1) and, indeed, faster than most countries the world over. As a result, the consumer market has been expanding rapidly during the past decade, with retail sales for consumer durables growing by 18% and 26% in 1992 and 1993 respectively (Hong Kong Trade Development Council 1994a, p. 2). In 1993, total retail sales of consumer goods in China was about US$213 billion (Hong Kong Trade Development Council 1994a, p. 499).

Table 4.1 Asian economic growth—A comparison (US$)

Country/region	*Per-capita GDP (PPP)*	*GDP (PPP, US$b)*	*GDP growth %*
Greater China			
mainland	**2 428**	**2 855.0**	**11.4**
Hong Kong	21 670	130.0	5.5
Macau	16 840	6.4	5.0
Taiwan	12 315	257.0	6.5
Singapore	20 470	61.0	10.2
Japan	21 090	2 633.0	0.6
S. Korea	9 810	432.0	8.4
USA	24 750	6 387.0	4.6
Germany	20 165	1 619.0	2.8

Notes:
1 Gross Domestic Product (GDP) is the value of all goods and services produced in one year.
2 Purchasing Power Parity (PPP) takes into account price differences between countries to provide a more accurate picture of national wealth.
3 GDP Growth is adjusted for inflation.

Source: Asiaweek (1995), "The Bottom Line", April 7, the *South China Morning Post,* Hong Kong, pp. 49, 50.

In this chapter we describe developments in the various environments of commerce in China, and trace their marketing implications. We start with an overview of the general population and their daily consumption habits, followed by a look at the "real" consumer population. Having set the context, we then proceed with an environmental analysis, of the economic, demographic, and cultural domains respectively. The section following these analyses examines changes in consumer behavior. Then important developments in the composition of thc "macromarketing mix" are described: the aggregate trends in product, price, distribution, and promotion (aggregated at the national level). The final section deals with future trends, and what to expect in Chinese commerce in the 21st century.

Population

China has about 1.2 billion consumers. There are over 30 cities with urban populations exceeding 1 million, and 267 cities with a population greater than 300 000 (Hong Kong Trade Development Council 1994a, p. 2). By comparison, there are about 10 US cities with an urban population of over 1 million, and about 50 cities with a population of over 300 000 (*Information Please Almanac* 1995). Furthermore, with continued urban migration, Chinese cities will have to absorb many more millions (Kennedy 1995).

In addition to these urban population figures, to get a better picture of the enormous population of China it may also be helpful to consider its regions in relation to other nations of the world. China has 31 "administrative regions" (states), the largest of which is Sichuan Province, with a population of 108 million people. There are only 8 countries in the world with 100 million people or more! In southern China, the cities/territories of Hong Kong and Macau may be considered, economically, culturally, and geographically, a part of Guangdong Province, whose capital is Canton. Along with the 4 provinces contiguous to Guangdong Province, they have a total population of about 236 million people—this is comparable to the population size of the USA. In the north, the cities of Beijing and Tianjin (both surrounded by Hebei Province), along with the 5 provinces contiguous to the Province, have a combined population of about 343 million people. If this figure were the population of a country, that country would be the world's third largest, behind the rest of China, and India.

Daily consumption

The size of the population is in itself an important factor when considering consumption and marketing in China. The sheer size of China results in consumption numbers that are unimaginable for many who are used to dealing with amounts in smaller countries. For example, on an average single day, the Chinese people consume 52 000 tons of pork and buy 76 000 bicycles, along with 111 000 watches, 53 000 television sets, 12 000 refrigerators, and 25 000 household washing machines. On the same single day, freight traffic amounts to over 30 million tons, and the value of imports and exports is US$536 million; almost 6.5 million magazines and 53 million newspapers would be issued, 58 000 babies are born, and there are 25 000 marriages (State Statistical Bureau of The People's Republic of China 1997, p. 24). With an estimated 90% urban television penetration and a wide reach in rural areas, on any day about 600 million people may watch the evening news on China Central Television, and as many as 5 million copies of the newspaper the *People's Daily* may be circulated. China has 20 daily newspapers with circulations of more than a million. Hence China claims the world's largest TV audience and the largest daily newspaper circulation (Brooks 1994).

"Real" consumers

McKinsey & Company report that there are over 60 million people in China with an annual income in excess of US$1000–this number of consumers is greater than that for the whole of Thailand and Malaysia (Shaw & Woetzel 1992). There are also over a million people earning over US$200 000 a year—millionaires in Chinese Yuan (Hong Kong Trade Development Council 1994, p. 1). McKinsey & Company believe that the "real" consumer market consists of those whose annual incomes are US$1000 or more, because this represents the level required, in China, for people to begin to make significant purchases of durable and non-durable consumer goods as well as premium and luxury items. At current growth rates it is projected that there will be a population of 260 million people in this consumer category in the year 2000. "This increase would make China a larger market in 2000 for durable consumer goods, both in terms of purchasing power and population, than most of the East and South-East Asian countries [offer] today" (Shaw & Woetzel 1992, p. 8).

In addition to these changes, China has become increasingly urbanized. The national urban/rural population ratio, 39:61 in 1993 (State Statistical Bureau of The People's Republic of China 1994, p. 45) is expected to stabilize at 36:64 by the year 2000 (Hong Kong Trade Development Council 1994, p. 2). Despite marketization and the removal of some subsidies, buying power for consumer goods has been increasing, owing partly to people paying token, subsidized amounts for housing, clothing, transportation, taxes, staple foods, and medical care, thus enabling hundreds of millions of Chinese consumers to treat over 80% of their income as disposable (Yan 1994). There is high female participation in the labor force, and families have become smaller as a result of the policy of limiting them to one child. These factors, as well as an expanding economy, a growing consumer market with increasing buying power, urbanization, and the enormous size of China, combine to create a dynamic consumer market with great appeal to businesses seeking growth opportunities.

The economic environment

Table 4.2 shows the recent development of major economic variables—wage income, employment, consumer price index, and import/export figures. In brief, the Chinese have experienced dramatic rises both in workers' incomes and the rate of unemployment. At the same time, more people are employed in the market economy, and enormous growth has been achieved in China's import and export activity.

Income

While urban incomes had risen almost 40%, rural incomes had risen about 10%. However, these official figures do not reflect the concurrent rise in unreported incomes from second and additional jobs, which are easier to come by in urban areas. There is, therefore, a trend of population migration

Table 4.2 Developments with some economic variables, 1982–1993

Year	*1982*	*1985*	*1986*	*1987*	*1988*	*1989*	*1990*	*1991*	*1992*	*1993*
Per-capita annual income (US$)										
Urban	–	254	–	–	–	373	323	322	369	449
Rural	–	185	–	–	–	–	210	196	210	232
Employment (million persons)										
Urban										
State-owned	–	90	93	97	100	101	103	107	109	109
Collective	–	33	34	35	35	35	35	36	36	34
Joint-owned	–	0.38	0.43	0.50	0.63	0.82	0.96	0.49	0.56	0.66
Joint-stock	–	–	–	–	–	–	–	–	–	1.64
Foreign investment	–	0.06	0.12	0.20	0.29	0.43	0.62	0.96	1.38	1.33
Hong Kong, Macau, Taiwan investment	–	0.01	0.01	0.02	0.04	0.04	0.69	0.83	1.55	–
Private enterprise	–	–	–	–	–	–	0.57	0.68	0.98	1.86
Individual	–	4.50	4.83	5.69	6.59	6.48	6.14	6.92	7.40	9.30
Total	**–**	**128**	**133**	**138**	**143**	**144**	**147**	**153**	**156**	**160**
Rural										
Township enterprise	70	79	88	95	94	93	96	106	123	–
Private enterprise	–	–	–	–	–	–	1.13	1.16	1.34	1.87
Individual	–	–	–	–	–	–	14.91	16.16	17.28	20.10
Total	**–**	**371**	**380**	**390**	**401**	**409**	**420**	**431**	**438**	**443**

Unemployment (million persons age 16+)										
Employed	–	–	–	–	–	–	647	–	–	–
Unemployed	–	–	–	–	–	–	170	–	–	–
Unemployment rate (%)	–	–	–	–	–	–	21	–	–	–
Consumer Price Index (preceding year = 100)										
Urban	–	119.1	107.0	108.8	120.7	116.3	101.3	105.1	108.6	116.1
Rural	–	107.6	106.1	106.2	117.5	119.3	104.5	102.3	104.7	113.7
Imports & exports (US$ billion)										
Imports	–	42.25	–	–	–	–	53.35	–	80.59	103.95
Exports	–	27.35	–	–	–	–	62.09	–	84.94	91.76
Export/import ratio	–	64.73	–	–	–	–	116.38	–	105.40	88.27

Source: Based on State Statistical Bureau of The People's Republic of China (1994), *China Statistical Yearbook*, China Statistical Information and Consultancy Service Center, Beijing.

from the rural to urban centers; there is also great concern among government authorities about the potential of unrest among the inland's majority peasant population, who have not shared as much in the benefits of recent economic reform. There is also growing anxiety that prosperity and industrialization, major factors that gave impetus to higher demands on the food supply, have led to a decline in cultivated lands. The effect has been to make China a net food importer and the world's second largest grain importer, next to Japan; this has been driving domestic and international food prices higher (Brown 1995).

Employment

Growth in employment numbers among urban dwellers has been due largely to dramatic increases in the numbers working in China's market economy—that is, in the newly formed joint-stock companies, foreign and Greater China investment corporations, and private individual enterprises. Rural people have seen the most marked growth in the numbers of individual enterprises, which rose from none in 1985 to over 20 million people employed as individuals in 1993 (a number which is almost 30% of the number employed in township enterprises in 1985).

To understand these employment figures better, some explanation is in order regarding enterprise-ownership categories (see Table 4.2). The term "state-owned" refers primarily to large-scale industrial enterprises, as well as government agencies. "Collective" units are smaller scale co-operatives. "Joint-ownership" units are of 4 types: state and collectives, state and individuals, collectives and individuals, and Chinese (domestic) and foreign investors. "Joint-stock" units are joint-owned units that issue stocks traded on the stockmarket. "Foreign-investment" units are joint ventures comprising both domestic and foreign owners. "Hong Kong, Macau, and Taiwan investments" may be joint- or wholly owned ventures on the mainland. "Private enterprises" are distinguished from individual enterprises, in that the latter typically consist of individual laborers, as opposed to private firms of a more "blue-collar" nature. "Township enterprises" are rural, town-based co-operatives.

Unemployment

Among those over the age of 16 classified by the government as "unemployed," there was an increase from 15% to 21% between 1982 and 1990. This represents a very alarming 40% increase in the rate of unemployment in 8 years. Also, given the fact that many employed are only nominally employed, the 21% figure may be considered a very conservative, understated figure. The increase in unemployment can be attributed to economic reform initiatives which are aimed at making state-run enterprises more efficient. This problem of simultaneously re-engineering state-run enterprises and preserving social stability by either growth in the private sector or other means of social security is perhaps the most challenging, and at the same time urgent, of the dilemmas facing Chinese government leaders today.

Consumer price index

Overall, the consumer price index has remained relatively stable since 1985. This is a result, primarily, of state control of prices for housing, medical care, transportation, staple foods, and the rate of government taxation.

Imports and exports

Since 1985 there has been an almost 41% increase in imports, coupled with about 30% more in exports, with a combined effect for 1993 of almost US$196 billion in international trade. This figure is only US$17 billion short of the US$213 billion in total retail sales of consumer goods in China in 1993. China's trade deficit in 1993 was about 12%.

The demographic environment

Demographic changes have created dynamic new environmental conditions, to which Chinese and foreign-business strategists must adapt. This section will focus on the changes in population growth, age distribution, number of households, household size, and the aggregate "family life cycle." China's large population (especially its population of male children) is growing; at the same time, it is urbanizing and ageing, and its family structure is changing fundamentally. The effects of these factors on consumption are profound, and range from the development of larger markets to the emergence of niche markets consisting of the urban affluent and elderly.

Population size and growth

In the 8 years from 1985 to 1993, China's ratio of urban-to-rural population moved from 28:72 to 39:61. This represents a dramatic and very significant population shift–a decrease of over 44 million people in the rural population, coupled with an increase in the number of urban dwellers of over 82 million people in the same period (this means a 6% rural drop, and a 25% urban increase in population). In addition, some estimate that about 70 million additional Chinese live outside their home of registration, moving illegally to cities to try their luck. Worldwatch Institute in Washington, D.C. estimates that, in recent years:

> About 100 million Chinese workers have left the countryside to seek jobs in cities. Since each factory in the private sector (on average) employs just over 100 workers, creating the 100 million jobs needed to absorb this flow of migrants requires roughly one million factories–

factories that have to be sited where the people are . . . along the coast where much of the best cropland is (Brown 1995).

Thus we see that demand for food, and resulting food price increases, are due not only to rising affluence and an expanding population, but also to industrialization. These trends toward industrialization and urban immigration are also accompanied by factory expansion and an emphasis on car manufacturing and the building of highway infrastructure, along with increasing urban consumer and industrial consumption of water. All of these factors combine to force the remaining farmers to return to less productive rain-fed farming on a decreasing amount of cultivated arable land. Additionally, increased urbanization increases the already great need for housing, power, transportation, and waste treatment systems, to name only a few.

At the same time that the population has become more urbanized, the growth rate of the total population has declined, from 14.26 in 1985 to 11.45 in 1993. This is due to government enforcement of the 'one child per family' policy. Together, rapidly rising incomes in urban areas, rising unemployment, a declining rural population, and urban immigration pose daunting problems for the government, and offer unprecedented opportunities for solutions-minded marketers, urban planners, and development agencies.

Table 4.3 Population growth in China (million persons)

Year	*Total population*	*Residence*[a]		*Growth rate (birth rate/ death rate)*
		Urban	*Rural*	
1985	1 058.51	250.94	762.9	14.26
1986	1 075.07	263.66	754.8	15.57
1987	1 093.00	276.74	746.8	16.61
1988	1 110.26	286.61	741.9	15.73
1989	1 127.04	295.40	737.9	15.04
1990	1 143.33	301.91	735.9	14.39
1991	1 158.23	305.43	736.3	12.98
1992	1 171.71	323.72	723.7	11.60
1993	1 185.17	333.51	718.6	11.45
2000[b]	1 300.00	468.00	832.0	–

Notes:

[a] Urban plus rural populations approximate, but are a little less than, the total.

[b] *China's Consumer Market*, p. 2.

Source: State Statistical Bureau of The People's Republic of China (1994), *China Statistical Yearbook*, China Statistical Information and Consultancy Service Center, Beijing, p. 45.

Age distribution

Table 4.4 illustrates the fact that there has been a rather consistent decrease in the 0–6-year-old population percentage in China, and a general increase in the population percentage of retired persons since 1953. Since 1982 there has been a significant decline in the percentage of the population in the 0–15-year-old age range (a drop of 7.2%), coupled with a 5.1% increase of working-age people, and a 1% increase in the number of retirees. This may be cause for alarm when the likely increase in demands for old age social security benefits is considered, particularly as reliance on younger family members for support of the old will have to be reduced.

The child-bearing population as a percentage of the total population has grown by 4.2 percentage points from 1953 to 1990, resulting in a real increase of over 173 million women of child-bearing age. This puts a lot of pressure on those charged with controlling the population; at the same time, it is a great opportunity for those meeting the needs of first-time parents.

Table 4.4 Age distribution of the population (million persons)

Year	*1953*	*1964*	*1982*	*1990*
Total population	582.60	691.22	1 003.91	1 130.51
Population by age				
0–6	117.00 (20.1%)	135.42 (19.6%)	134.56 (13.4%)	155.48 (13.8%)
7–14	88.84 (15.2%)	145.25 (21.0%)	202.69 (20.2%)	157.52 (13.9%)
15	25.23 (4.3%)	14.99 (2.2%)	22.75 (2.2%)	21.64 (1.9%)
"working age" 16–59 for men 16–54 for women	299.83 (51.5%)	341.49 (49.4%)	550.87 (54.9%)	679.03 (60.0%)
Male age 60+ Female age 55+	51.70 (8.9%)	54.07 (7.8%)	93.04 (9.3%)	116.84 (10.3%)
Women at child-bearing age (15-49)	133.14 (22.9%)	151.61 (21.9%)	248.29 (24.8%)	306.35 (27.1%)
Gender				
Male	310.79	354.79	515.28	581.82
Female	280.81	336.43	488.63	548.69

Source: State Statistical Bureau of The People's Republic of China (1994), *China Statistical Yearbook*, China Statistical Information and Consultancy Service Center, Beijing, p. 47.

Households

The total number of households in China has increased by almost 150% since 1953, and by over 100 million since 1982 (see Table 4.5). Upon closer examination (see Table 4.6), we see that rural households are typically larger than their urban counterparts, but both urban and rural household sizes have decreased since 1985. However, the decreasing size of the family unit, due to the one-child policy, may be more revealing than household size, since the extended family size and income is quite different from that of a mere household, and the extended family, including aunts, uncles, cousins, and grandparents, traditionally forms a strong social and economic support group in China.

Table 4.5 Total households: 1953–1993 (million)

	1953	*1964*	*1982*	*1990*	*1993*
Total households	134.11	156.71	221.15	278.62	330.69

Source: State Statistical Bureau of The People's Republic of China (1994), *China Statistical Yearbook*, China Statistical Information and Consultancy Service Center, Beijing, p. 47.

Table 4.6 Urban and rural household size: 1985–1993

	1985	*1989*	*1990*	*1991*	*1992*	*1993*
Average household size (persons)						
Urban	3.89	3.55	3.50	3.43	3.37	3.31
Rural	5.12	–	4.80	4.71	4.67	4.59

Source: State Statistical Bureau of The People's Republic of China (1994), *China Statistical Yearbook*, China Statistical Information and Consultancy Service Center, Beijing, pp. 247, 267.

Family life cycle

The typical model of the family life cycle that appears in standard Western marketing texts may not exist in China. This is due to two main factors. First, it is not uncommon to have several generations of the family living under one roof; second, the influence of the extended family members who may or may not be living in the same house is much more significant in China than in most Western nations. However, having expressed such caveat, we can derive from the demographic data certain information that resembles the traditional cycle of family growth and development. For example, we know that 25% of the population over the age of 14 is unmarried—75% is married (State Statistical Bureau of The People's Republic of China 1994, p. 47). We also know that the average age at which women marry is 22, and that 63% of all first-born children are born to women aged between 20 and 24, and another 30% of all first children are born to women aged 25 to 29 (State Statistical Bureau of The People's Republic of China 1994, pp. 60, 61). Therefore 93% of first babies are born to women between 20 and 29. Bearing in mind the government one-child policy, it is likely that for most women the first child born will also be the last.

Looking at Table 4.7, we see that 5.8% of the total households in China in 1993 were single-person households. Such households may contain young, single unmarried people, married people who are living apart due to job assignments that separate them, or even older people living alone. It is also possible that the person living alone may not only be married and living separated from his or her spouse due to job assignment, but may also have a child living with a grandparent or relative. Odd as this may seem to a Westerner, this situation is not so odd in China.

In total, 11.2% of households consist of 2 persons. Most likely these are couples married without children, or older couples whose children have moved away (the "empty nest"). This leaves 83% of households with 3 or more persons living in them. The third person is likely to be either a child, or an elderly relative living with a married couple. Those homes with more than 3 persons in residence may consist of any of a number of relatives from the extended family. However, in the future, as extended families become smaller owing to the effects of the government one-child policy, household sizes can be expected to shrink, and the nature of family influence on consumption fundamentally changed.

Finally, we know that, in 1993, 20% of all households included persons aged 65 years or older (State Statistical Bureau of The People's Republic of China 1994, p. 63). Increasingly, these elderly can expect to receive less care from their children, especially if they have only one child. In cases where the only child is female, the elderly parent may eventually receive no care from a child at all; care will come solely from the state.

Table 4.7 Households by household size, 1993

	Household size (no. of persons)							
Number of households (million)	*1*	*2*	*3*	*4*	*5*	*6*	*7*	*8+*
330.69	19.45	37.12	86.69	85.16	54.31	25.76	12.04	10.17

Source: State Statistical Bureau of The People's Republic of China (1994), *China Statistical Yearbook*, China Statistical Information and Consultancy Service Center, Beijing, p. 62.

Cultural environment

Cultural changes in the level of literacy and education, in health care, as well as changes in people's economic expectations, also affect every aspect of the marketing task. In the discussion that follows, we will attempt to present a reasoned evaluation of the nature and the impact of these changes in China.

Education, literacy, and gender

Since 1964, the percentage of the population that is illiterate has been cut by over two-thirds. However, over one-fifth of the people still cannot read or write at all, or at a level equivalent to primary-school competency. Of these, women are almost 3 times more likely to be illiterate as men. Two-thirds of the population are either illiterate or have no more than a primary-school education, and 90% have not proceeded beyond the eighth grade (junior middle school in the USA). Just over one-quarter have a junior middle school education, with a 60:40 ratio of men to women. The high percentage of illiterate and modestly literate people, coupled with the enormous number of households with television, are certainly factors that influence the overwhelming preference of marketers for television as an advertising medium.

Although the population has become more educated, only 7% graduates from senior middle school (high school), and the rarity of a university education (just over 0.5% of the population) has remained relatively constant since 1964. Of the university graduates, there are over twice as many males as females. If one meets a graduate of a Chinese university, one has met a rare person indeed, especially if it this person is a woman.

In general, the population is becoming more literate, and consumers are becoming more discriminating as shoppers. Labor is becoming more skilled, incomes are increasing, and concerns are rising about getting the most value for money in purchases. The need to produce better quality goods and services is becoming acute as consumer expectations increase.

Table 4.8 Level of education of the population (%)

	1964	*1982*	*1990*
Population aged 6 and over			
by education level (million persons)	555.42	889.79	994.09
Illiterate & semi-illiterate	57%	32%	21%
Primary school	35	40	42
Junior middle school	6	20	27
Senior middle school	2	8	7
Technical secondary school	–	–	1.7
Junior college	–	7	1
University	5	–	0.6

Education level by gender (1990)			
(persons aged 15 and over)	% of total population	% male	% female
Illiterate & semi-illiterate	22	13	32
Primary school	35	35	34
Junior middle school	30	36	24
Senior middle school	9	11	7
Technical secondary school	2	2	2
Junior college	1	2	1
University	0.8	1	0.4

Source: State Statistical Bureau of The People's Republic of China (1994), *China Statistical Yearbook*, China Statistical Information and Consultancy Service Center, Beijing, pp. 5, 47.

Health

Using the indicators listed in Table 4.9, we can see that the level of health of the Chinese is among the lowest in Pacific Asia. While the ratio of people per doctor in China is better than that in Hong Kong, Taiwan, and South Korea, the average daily calorie intake in China is lower than that in all the countries listed except for Macau, and life expectancy is the lowest and infant mortality rates are the highest. The need for nutritious foods and a higher quality of medical care in China is apparent. A focus on health, personal appearance, and environmental concerns is increasing (Laurent 1995); these factors are likely to continue to grow in importance among Chinese consumers in the future. We can therefore anticipate a growing demand for simple but effective health care and for personal hygiene products as well as medicines and medical equipment. A concern for the environment and the consequent demand for environmentally friendly products is still in its infancy in China, but should not be ignored by forward-thinking manufacturers or retailers with niche interests.

Table 4.9 Comparisons of level of health

	Average daily calorie intake	*People per doctor*	*Life expectancy*	*Infant mortality*[a]
Greater China				
mainland	2 703	809	71	31
Hong Kong	2 857	866	78	5
Macau	2 162	758	73	9
Taiwan	3 036	910	75	5
Singapore	3 198	711	76	5
Japan	2 956	566	79	5
S. Korea	2 852	855	72	8
USA	3 671	420	77	9
Germany	3 522	333	76	6

[a] Number of babies per 1000 live births who die before reaching 1 year of age

Source: Asiaweek (1995), "The Bottom Line", the *South China Morning Post*, April 7, Hong Kong.

Economic expectations

Rising consumer incomes, high savings levels, and consumer expectations will affect spending levels. Inflation in China was 14.7% in 1993, and in April 1995 had risen to 22.4%, as compared to 10.1% in Hong Kong, 6.2% in Macau, 4.3% in Taiwan, 3.4% in Singapore, 0.7% in Japan, 4.9% in South Korea, 2.9% in the USA, and 2.4% in Germany (*Asiaweek* 1995). Along with reforming state-run enterprises, and dealing with urban immigration, reining in inflation is a major problem for the Chinese. However, World Bank president James Wolfensohn recently stated that China had reined inflation back to 15%, and expressed confidence that it should be able to maintain a healthy growth rate of 8–10% over the next 5 years. This was confirmed in the first quarter of 1996, when inflation was about 8%.

A survey of the opinions of businessmen in China, conducted by the magazine *Asian Business*, found that 82% believe inflation will remain at about 15% or accelerate (38% believe it will accelerate) (Linn 1994). In spite of this, there is general optimism among businesspeople. As far as the general economic climate is concerned, 59% felt more optimistic about the national economy than they did 6 months prior to the survey, and 21% felt the same level of confidence. The same survey, conducted in 1995, found that 71% felt more optimistic, while 18% had the same level of confidence (Linn 1995). When asked to project the next 12 months, the businesspeople surveyed rated economic performance at 7.74 on a 10-point scale, with 1 meaning "very poor" and 10 meaning "very good" economic prospects. The survey also indicated that businesspeople believed the highest priorities of the government should be increasing political stability and ending corruption. Almost 60% felt that the pace of economic reform was "just right."

Changes in consumer behavior

China's economy is dramatically transforming itself into what may make China the largest economic power in the world by 2010. Dramatic demographical and cultural changes characterize China as it moves into the 21st century. Consumer spending power is increasing, with emphasis on the purchase of greater amounts of more sophisticated goods and services. However, the population is still hesitant to spend, as the impressive savings figures show.

Savings

Chinese savings as a percentage of GDP—36%—are among the highest in Asia, surpassed only by Singapore (48%). We can rightly conclude that there is a significant amount of pent-up purchasing power among the Chinese, especially when we consider that there is undoubtedly a large pool of savings not held in banks, and therefore unrecorded in official government figures on consumer savings, along with unrecorded incomes from second jobs. As high as the 36% savings rate is, it is likely to be an underestimate in China.

Chinese consumers do not necessarily lack money to spend; rather, they lack products worthy of their spending. In fact, in the case of many consumer products, such as bicycles, there is no lack of products to buy, but

Table 4.10 A comparison of savings levels (% of GDP)

Country/region	*Savings as % of GDP*
Greater China	
mainland	36
Hong Kong	30
Macau	28
Taiwan	27
Singapore	48
Japan	34
S. Korea	35
USA	15
Germany	28

Source: Asiaweek (1995), "The Bottom Line", *South China Morning Post*, April 7, Hong Kong.

instead a paucity of products of sufficient quality to move people to part with their precious money (Associated Press 1991). However, this situation is changing, as enterprises change from producing to meet state set quotas to producing to meet market demands. The indications are that the propensity to spend is increasing, and the propensity to save may begin to decline soon, perhaps rapidly, from the present (1995) level of 20% of household income (Laurent 1995). The increased propensity to spend is driven by a combination of factors, including the following:

- increased confidence about the future of China, and therefore a lesser need to put money away for security
- increased orientation toward enjoyment and gratification *now*
- increased availability of quality consumer products

In 1993, the total level of savings deposits was almost 5 times the level of 1985, totalling US$264 billion. While rural household deposits have increased more slowly than their urban counterparts, in 1993 they were still 3 times the level they had been in 1985. By comparison, in 1985 urban households had almost twice as much money in the bank as their rural counterparts, but by 1993 urban homes had well over 3 times as much money on deposit in banks as rural homes. In 1993 the average urban home had US$2000 on deposit, while rural homes had an average US$395 in the bank. This US$2000 figure is twice as much as the median financial assets of the average US family (US$1000), and almost 4 times as much the figure for the average US home, whose head is between 33 and 44 years of age (US$600) (*Asian Wall Street Journal* 1995).[2] Stated otherwise, Chinese urban per-capita bank deposits were US$604, while rural per-capita deposits were

US$86.[3] It is no wonder that non-coastal provincial leaders, and the leadership in Beijing, are concerned about the threat to social stability arising from the fact that rural peasants have largely missed out on the country's economic boom, and unemployment in the countryside is rising as peasants quit their farms to seek work in cities throughout China (Yang 1995).

Table 4.11 Household savings deposit balance (US$ billion)

		Urban households			*Rural households*		
Year	*Total*	*Subtotal*	*Fixed deposits*	*Current deposits*	*Subtotal*	*Fixed deposits*	*Current deposits*
1985	55	36	28	7	19	13	6
1986	66	43	35	8	23	16	7
1987	82	56	44	11	27	19	8
1988	102	71	55	16	31	21	10
1989	138	100	83	17	38	29	9
1990	149	110	93	17	39	31	8
1991	171	127	107	20	44	34	10
1992	210	158	128	30	52	41	11
1993	264	202	159	43	62	50	12

Source: State Statistical Bureau of The People's Republic of China (1994), *China Statistical Yearbook*, China Statistical Information and Consultancy Service Center, Beijing, p. 247.

Household consumption

The proportion of the urban household budget spent on food, clothing, and household goods has remained noticeably constant since 1985, with food demanding the lion's share at about half of the living expenditure. Clothing and household goods follow at 14% and 12% of the budget respectively. By comparison, the rural household spends almost 60% of its income on food, and exactly half as much as its urban counterpart on clothing, household goods, and transportation and communication. However, rural households spend almost 3 times as much as urban households on education and recreation and almost 5 times as much on their place of residence. This phenomenon is due to the fact that rural homes are largely privately owned, while urban homes are largely state-subsidized, public residences.

Household possession of durables

Soon after modern economic reform began in 1979, the desires and status symbols of typical PRC consumers evolved from the 3 *da jian*, or 3 "big things" (bicycles, sewing machines, and wristwatches), to an extended list of

Table 4.12 Household annual living expenditure per capita (% of total)

Year	*1985*		*1990*		*1991*		*1992*		*1993*	
	Urban	*Rural*	*Urban*	*Rural*	*Urban*	*Rural*	*Urban*	*Rural*	*Urban*	*Rural*
Total living expenditure by category of goods (US$)	$228	$107	$271	$124	$273	$116	$304	$120	$367	$134
Food	119	62	147	73	147	67	161	69	184	78
	52%	58%	54%	59%	54%	58%	53%	58%	50%	58%
Clothing	33	11	15	10	38	10	44	10	52	10
	15%	10%	13%	8%	14%	8%	14%	8%	14%	7%
Household goods[a]	24	5	28	7	26	7	29	7	43	8
	11%	5%	10%	5%	10%	6%	10%	6%	12%	6%
Medicines		3		4		4		4		5
		3%		3%		4%		4%		4%
Transportation & communication		2		2		2		2	14	3
		2%		1%		2%		2%	4%	2%
Education & recreation	18	4	14	7	13	7	13	8	12	10
	8%	4%	5%	5%	5%	6%	4%	7%	3%	8%
Residence	4	20	7	21	7	19	9	19	12	19
	2%	18%	3%	17%	3%	17%	3%	16%	3%	14%

Note:
[a] Urban figures include medicines.

Source: State Statistical Bureau of The People's Republic of China (1994), *China Statistical Yearbook*, China Statistical Information and Consultancy Service Center, Beijing, pp. 248, 271.

"3 bigs," which added refrigerators, washing machines, and TVs to the list; next, the list changed to the 8 *xin jian* ("new things"), specifying color TV sets and adding cameras and video recorders (Tse et al. 1989). Hot items on the purchasing list in 1993 included gold jewellery, air conditioners, VCRs, and other household electric appliances (Hong Kong Trade Development Council 1994, p. 6).

Table 4.13 shows that virtually every urban household today is a 2-bicycle home, and every rural household has at least 1 bicycle. Almost every urban home has 2 sofas, while only half of all rural homes have one. Also, urban dwellers are twice as likely to have an electric fan, and 3 times as likely to have a tape recorder as their rural counterparts. Almost every urban home has a wardrobe and writing desk, over 3 out of 4 homes have a color TV set, electric washing machine and tape recorder, and well over half have an electric refrigerator. By comparison, it is still quite rare for a rural home to have a refrigerator–just 3% own one. The move toward more consumption of higher consumption products among urban dwellers is evident, in that 15% of households own computer games, and 12% have video recorders. Also, ownership of motorcycles is becoming more popular among the urban population.

Table 4.13 Household possession of major durable consumer goods (per 100 households)

	1985		*1990*		*1991*		*1992*		*1993*	
Item	*Urban*	*Rural*	*Urban*	*Rural*	*Urban*	*Rural*	*Urban*	*Rural*	*Urban*	*Rural*
Bicycles	152	81	189	118	159	122	190	126	197	133
Sewing machines	70	43	70	55	66	56	66	57	67	61
Electric fans	74	10	135	41	143	53	146	60	152	72
Washing machines	48	2	78	9	81	11	83	12	86	14
Refrigerators	7	0.06	42	1	49	2	51	2	57	3
Motorcycles	–	–	–	1	–	1	3	1	4	2
Sofas	131	13	157	37	159	43	179	47	190	55
Wardrobes	102	53	100	76	95	78	93	81	93	82
Writing desks	80	38	87	56	87	63	89	64	90	74
Radios	*	54	*	45	*	32	*	32	*	32
Black & white TVs	67	10	52	40	44	48	38	52	36	58
Color TVs	17	1	59	5	68	6	75	8	79	11
Tape recorders	41	4	70	18	70	20	74	21	76	24
Cameras	9	–	19	1	21	1	24	1	26	1
Computer games	–	–	–	–	–	–	–	–	15	–
Video recorders	–	–	–	–	–	–	–	–	12	–
Air conditioners	–	–	–	–	–	–	–	–	3	–
Vacuum cleaners	–	–	–	–	–	–	–	–	7	–

Note:
* No information available

Source: State Statistical Bureau of The People's Republic of China (1994), *China Statistical Yearbook*, China Statistical Information and Consultancy Service Center, Beijing, pp. 251, 278.

Comparing urban and rural households, we see an urban decline and a rural increase in the ownership of black-and-white TV sets. The urban decrease is offset by an increase in ownership of color TVs, as urban dwellers trade up in the product class. Since 1991, it has become more likely for a rural household to have a TV set than a radio, and in 1993 the ratio was almost 2 TV sets to 1 radio per household. Clearly, television viewing is becoming an increasingly popular pastime in China, and the increase is most dramatic in the countryside, while the level of penetration is still higher in urban areas.

Changes in the macromarketing mix

In this section, some trends in the marketing mix are described at the national, aggregate level. Trends in product, price, distribution, and promotion practices are discussed. Finally, some developments in marketing research are mentioned.

Products and price reaction

Yan (1994, p. 195) describes the new Chinese attitude to consumption as the following:

> For the Chinese, consumption is a novel pleasure. Having had very few choices for 4 decades, Chinese consumers are eager to see what is in the stores. They are especially curious about foreign goods, which are more widely available now. Consumers' limited experience with modern marketing leads them to depend on reputable brands.

Reputable brands are attractive because they afford security for the Chinese consumer. At the same time that consumption is "a novel pleasure," shopping is elevated in China to both an "art," and a necessary skill. The Chinese are persistent comparison shoppers who insist on the best quality at the lowest price–that is, value for money. In fact, some would say, only half-jestingly, that shopping is "sport" in China–one loses when one pays too much, that is, when one finds that less could have been paid for the same product. Shopping is a social "game" where people compare their wins and try to conceal their losses. It is common for Chinese to enquire of one another where something was bought and how much was paid, whereas in much of the West such an enquiry is commonly considered an unwelcome intrusion of privacy.

Brands

A recent study by a major Hong Kong advertising agency indicates a trend toward foreign brands, which are replacing Chinese products as brand leaders in practically every category surveyed, from powdered milk and baby foods to cars and computers (Brooks 1994, p. 6). Another study by a major Hong Kong consultancy found that, for a wide range of goods, brands accounted for one-third to one-half of all consumer expressions of intent to purchase (Yan 1994, p. 72). Chinese consumers are generally weary of the low quality of many of the products from which they have to choose, and are uncommonly preoccupied with where products are made. Imported products are generally most highly regarded, followed by joint-venture products, with domestic products the least highly regarded (Brooks 1994, p. 7). "High-end branded refrigerators, washing machines, and vacuum cleaners are finding buyers at 30% to 50% premiums over popular brands" (Yan 1994, p. 68). In one of China's largest department stores, in Guangzhou, the ratio of premium-product to popular/local-product sales has shifted in 2 years from 30:70 to 50:50. In Shenzhen, an SEZ across the border from Hong Kong, the proportion is now 60:40 (Yan 1994). Also, an estimated one-half of the premium goods bought are for the only child, colloquially termed the "emperor" of the family.

Though imported goods may cost 2 to 3 times as much as domestic competitors' products, many Chinese consumers are willing to pay more. Yan (1994, p. 195) summarizes this position as follows:

> Locally brewed Carlsberg beer and imported Carlsberg are sold side by side, but the import commands a 20% to 50% premium. Moreover, many Chinese brands that once carried premium prices are fast losing market share to locally made foreign brands. Even so, surveys show that consumers may end up rejecting a [foreign brand] that is made in China if its packaging does not look the same as, or at least closely resembles, the packaging used in international markets.

As we might expect, the popularity of branded durable and non-durable consumer products has given rise to a thriving industry for the manufacture and sale of counterfeit products. Concern is high among brand manufacturers that intellectual property in patents, trademarks, and copyrights should be protected by the rigorous enforcement of the law. The problem persists in China, though authorities are showing increasing concern.

Market segments

Although foreign brands are highly admired, preferred by many, and often thought to be better, there is no certainty that this preference will continue as consumers learn to make better, more objective product comparisons and domestic manufacturers make quality improvements. In fact, this predisposition may be fading fast, if the results of a very recent survey are any indication (Laurent 1995). The survey involved consumers in Beijing, Tianjin, Shanghai, Guangzhou, and Chengdu. Findings indicate that imported products are not necessarily guaranteed success. Well over half of those surveyed (58%) believed that locally made product quality matches that of the imported goods. Home-branded products are often preferred if there is a local alternative of acceptable quality at a competitive price.

An important fact that also goes unheeded very often is that there is no one "China market." The Laurent survey (1995) found that there are substantial differences in consumption behavior between cities and between regions. For example, in the area of cosmetics, Guangzhou shoppers are much more willing to try a foreign import than are their Shanghai counterpart. In addition, various consumer segments exist, as they do in all countries, with distinct value and product usage profiles. Laurent (1995) identified 8 such segments—the young individualists, older traditionalist, conventional modernists, self-sacrificers, indifferents, doubters, self-centered, and strict moralists. "The foreign company looking to (sell) an expensive product aimed at the mass market will need to think again" (Laurent 1995).

Another peculiarity of Chinese shoppers is that they have plenty of time to shop and compare products. In fact, there is a Chinese saying that one should "Never make a purchase until you have compared three shops" (Yan 1994, p. 69). Chinese consumers also prefer propitious-sounding brand names, especially those that evoke powerful images. Foreign importers to China need to pay keen attention to this fact when making a translation of their product and company name into Chinese.

Finally, as both Yan (1994) and Laurent (1995) note, the Chinese consumer is normally practical, and places a strong emphasis on products that are simple and functional, and deliver value. This is evident in that, whereas some consumers may feel that a product that performs more functions means better value, many feel that better is not achieved if the added functions are not needed; their reason is that superfluous functions add unnecessarily to product cost. Similarly, product communications strategies need to be simple and functional, and deliver value. Messages must deliver information concerning what the product is, what it is called, what it can do, where it can be bought, and how much it costs. Simple, direct approaches work best (Yan 1994, p. 71). Relatively speaking, Chinese consumers are more dependent on practical advertisements for helpful information than are their Western counterparts.

Distribution

Most consumer markets in China are very fragmented because of the lingering central-planning philosophy, which emphasizes self-sufficiency at a local level for all products (Yan 1994, p. 74). As a consequence, there exists a relatively undeveloped and inefficient national transportation infrastructure. In response to the need, some foreign and domestic manufacturers are working to develop transportation and channel networks to accommodate the products they hope to sell in China. In fact, some durable goods manufacturers in Hong Kong intend to make a business of selling channel access to non-competitors, who may benefit from using the same distribution network they are developing in China for their own purposes.

As for channel characteristics, Table 4.14 shows that, in 1993, the state still owned 79% of the country's wholesale and retail outlets. The proportion is even more lopsided in favor of the state when we include collectives, and other forms of joint ownership in which the government has a share. This amounts to almost 99% of all wholesale and retail outlets, and these outlets employ roughly 90% of all retail and wholesale employees. However, only 9% of the country's total workforce is engaged in wholesale and retail employment. The remainder of employees work in areas such as agriculture (56%), manufacturing, and construction and mining (see Table 4.16).

Table 4.14 Number of wholesale and retail outlets (1993)

Type of ownership	*No.*	*%*
State owned	56 461	79
Collective owned	13 709	19
Private owned	304	0.42
Joint owned	531	0.74
Joint stock system	27	0.04
Foreign owned	7	–
Hong Kong, Macau, Taiwan owned	19	0.03
Total	71 058	100 (approx.)

Source: State Statistical Bureau of The People's Republic of China (1994), *China Statistical Yearbook*, China Statistical Information and Consultancy Service Center, Beijing, p. 506.

In terms of the total value of retail sales, state units have been stable since 1985; the proportion of their contribution to total retail sales is 44% of the total sales volume. Here the oft-claimed inefficiency of state-run enterprises is evident: state-owned wholesale and retail firms, 79% of the total, contribute only 44% of total sales volume. At the same time, the relative contribution of collectives to retail sales has been steadily declining since 1985.

Total retail sales have grown by almost two-thirds since 1985 to a total of US$211 billion in 1993. This growth in retail sales has been largely due to growth in sales by private retailers. Private retail sales have steadily increased; by 1993, 25% of all retail sales were private. This remarkable growth has occurred in spite of persistent preference being given to state firms in terms of access to bank credit and other resources (Lam 1995). Also, a new order has been issued by the Organization Department of the Communist Party Central Committee, barring "red capitalists," or the bosses of private companies, from gaining Party membership (Lam 1995).

The 25 largest retail department stores in China, located in 13 major cities, accounted for a total turnover of US$4.139 billion in 1993. This was the result of an average increase of 67% on 1992 turnover figures. Over two-thirds of these stores are in the 6 cities of Beijing, Guangzhou (Canton), Shanghai, Tianjin, Nanjing, and Wuhan. Eight of the 25 stores are in the

Table 4.15 Number of employees by type of ownership (million persons)

Year	*Subtotal*	*State-owned*		*Collective-owned*		*Urban Joint-owned*		*Joint stock*		*Foreign-owned*	
		No.	*%*	*No.*	*%*	*No.*	*%*	*No.*	*%*	*No.*	*%*
1985	128.0	90.0	70.0	33.0	26.0	0.38	0.3	–	–	0.06	–
1986	133.0	93.0	70.0	34.0	26.0	0.43	0.3	–	–	0.12	–
1987	138.0	97.0	70.0	35.0	25.0	0.50	0.4	–	–	0.20	0.1
1988	143.0	100.0	70.0	35.0	24.0	0.63	0.4	–	–	0.29	0.2
1989	144.0	101.0	70.0	35.0	24.0	0.82	0.6	–	–	0.43	0.3
1990	147.0	103.0	70.0	35.0	24.0	0.96	0.7	–	–	0.62	0.4
1991	153.0	107.0	70.0	36.0	24.0	0.49	0.3	–	–	0.96	0.6
1992	156.0	109.0	70.0	36.0	23.0	0.56	0.4	–	–	1.38	0.9
1993	160.0	109.0	68.0	34.0	21.0	0.66	0.4	2.0	1.0	1.33	0.8

Year	*Urban Hong Kong, Macau, Taiwan owned*		*Private-owned*		*Subtotal*	*Rural Enterprises*		*Private*	
	No.	*%*	*No.*	*%*		*No.*	*%*	*No.*	*%*
1985	–	–	5.0	4.0	371.0	70.0	19.0	–	–
1986	0.01	–	5.0	4.0	380.0	79.0	21.0	–	–
1987	0.01	–	6.0	4.0	390.0	88.0	23.0	–	–
1988	0.02	–	7.0	5.0	401.0	95.0	24.0	–	–
1989	0.04	–	6.0	4.0	409.0	94.0	23.0	–	–
1990	0.04	–	7.0	5.0	420.0	93.0	22.0	16.0	4.0
1991	0.69	0.5	8.0	5.0	431.0	96.0	22.0	17.0	4.0
1992	0.83	0.5	8.0	5.0	438.0	106.0	24.0	19.0	4.0
1993	1.55	1.0	11.0	7.0	443.0	123.0	28.0	22.0	5.0

Source: State Statistical Bureau of The People's Republic of China (1994), *China Statistical Yearbook*, China Statistical Information and Consultancy Service Center, Beijing, p. 65.

cities Beijing and Guangzhou (4 stores each). And, by 1997, authorities in Beijing had established many new chain stores, hoping to tap foreign capital and modern management techniques in developing the city's retail sector

(Hong Kong Trade Development Council 1994, p. 8). This is an example of the ambitious plans of major municipalities to enhance the state-run retailing infrastructure. In fact, the Hong Kong Trade Development Council is involved in helping develop this infrastructure, as are several Hong Kong property developers.

Another significant trend in retailing in China is that "free markets"—where enterprises are given permission to buy and sell surplus goods freely—are becoming increasingly popular. The number of urban free markets more than doubled in the 12 years since 1985. This represents an average annual increase in the number of free markets of nearly 11%. In rural areas the average annual increase in free markets over the same period was nearly 3%, with an almost 25% increase in the total number of free markets in 8 years. As free markets and private retailers grow, consumers grow also in their experiential knowledge of how the market works and what benefits accrue from it. In time, we can expect even state-run firms to become more market oriented in order to compete—and survive.

Advertising

Spending on advertising in China increased by a phenomenal 43% from 1992 to 1993, to US$1.9 billion. This is 5 times the level of spending in 1989 (US$380 million), and well over 16 times the amount spent on advertising in 1985. Moreover, some predict at least a 30% annual growth rate up to the year 1998 (Brooks 1994, p. 12). By volume of advertisements, China ranks among the top 2 or 3 advertising markets in the world.

Table 4.16 Number of employees by sector (million persons)

Year	*Total*	*Services*		*Wholesale & Retail*		*Agriculture*		*Manufacturing*	
		no.	*%*	*no.*	*%*	*no.*	*%*	*no.*	*%*
1985	499	10	2	36	7	311	62	74	15
1986	513	11	2	38	7	313	61	80	16
1987	528	12	2	40	8	317	60	84	16
1988	543	13	2	43	8	322	59	87	16
1989	553	13	2	43	8	332	60	85	15
1990	567	14	3	44	8	341	60	86	15
1991	584	14	2	46	8	350	60	88	15
1992	594	15	3	49	8	348	59	91	15
1993	602	13	2	51	9	340	56	93	15

Source: State Statistical Bureau of The People's Republic of China (1994), *China Statistical Yearbook*, China Statistical Information and Consultancy Service Center, Beijing, p. 68.

Table 4.17 Total value of retail sales by ownership of selling agents, 1985–1993 (US$ billion)

Year	*State ownership*		*Collective ownership*		*Joint ownership*		*Private ownership*		*Total*
	$	*%*	*$*	*%*	*$*	*%*	*$*	*%*	*$*
1985	59	43	54	40	0.339	0.25	22	16	136
1986	57	43	53	39	0.587	0.44	23	18	134
1987	60	42	56	39	0.537	0.37	27	19	144
1988	79	43	69	37	0.806	0.44	35	19	184
1989	85	43	72	36	1.000	0.54	41	20	199
1990	70	44	56	35	0.847	0.53	33	21	159
1991	71	44	53	33	0.939	0.59	35	22	160
1992	82	46	56	31	1.000	0.81	41	22	180
1993	94	44	62	29	2.000	0.98	53	25	211

Source: State Statistical Bureau of The People's Republic of China (1994), *China Statistical Yearbook*, China Statistical Information and Consultancy Service Center, Beijing, p. 499.

Because advertising rates in China are low by international standards, advertisers can have a large impact without spending a lot. Comparison with per-capita advertising expenditures in some other countries may be helpful for understanding the Chinese situation. For example:

> in the US, advertisers spend US$500 per head of population annually; in Hong Kong, US$200 per person; in China, about US$1.61 per head (1993 figures). Even if advertising expenditure in China reaches US$5 billion by the turn of the century, as official forecasts predict, advertisers will still be spending less than US$5 per person (Brooks 1994, pp. 6–7).

Looking at the amount of media budget spent on the various media in China, we notice that in 1993 television accounted for the largest percentage of media spending, with a share of 35%. This represents an almost threefold increase since 1985 (12%), and is expected to continue to increase. TV is the dominant advertising medium for both foreign and domestic enterprises, owing to its image of prestige and its relatively low cost (because of its remarkable reach). Urban estimates are 90% penetration; 95% of Beijing, Guangzhou, and Shanghai households own a TV set (Yan 1994, p. 73). The Chinese national network, China Central Television, claims 600 million viewers for its evening news (Brooks 1994, p. 9). Among foreign-venture media budgets, it is not uncommon to see between 75% and 95% devoted to television. Outdoor advertising accounts for the next largest share, at 30%

Table 4.18 Turnover: China's 25 largest department stores (US$ million)

Ranking	*Name of department store*	*1992*	*1993*	*% increase*
1	Shanghai No. 1 Department Store	245	340	45
2	Tianjin Leader International Co.	138	264	100
3	Beijing Xidan Shopping Arcade	157	238	59
4	Shanghai Hualian Commercial Building	188	212	18
5	Beijing Wangfujing Department Store	141	192	41
6	Zhongzing-Shenyang Commercial Building	125	180	51
7	Wuhan Shopping Arcade	113	175	62
8	Nanjing Xinjiekou Department Store	113	167	54
9	Guangzhou Nanfang Building Department Store	125	167	40
10	Shanghai Yuyuan Shopping Center	113	164	51
11	Shenyang Commercial City	109	160	54
12	Beijing Urban-Rural Trading Center	75	152	111
13	Tianjin Hualian Commercial Building	118	151	34
14	Hangzhou Jiefang Lu Department Store	74	147	107
15	Dalian Shopping Arcade	91	142	62
16	Guangzhou Department Store	81	141	83
17	Hangzhou Department Store	69	141	114
18	Wuhan Zhongnan Commercial Building	83	140	76
19	Guangzhou Friendship Store	85	136	68
20	Chengdu People's Department Store	95	130	44
21	Changsha Zhongshan Commercial Building	70	124	86
22	Wuxi Commercial Building	88	122	44
23	Guangzhou Xindaxin Company	69	120	81
24	Beijing Lufthansa Center You Yi Shopping Center	57	117	116
25	Nanjing People's Department Store	75	117	62

Hong Kong Trade Development Council (1994), *Retail and Wholesale Distribution of Consumer Goods in China*, Research Department, Hong Kong Trade Development Council, Hong Kong.

of the media budget, with newspapers a close third at 27%. Outdoor media, whose largest components are billboards (39% of the total media budget in 1989) and newspapers have lost a significant share to TV since 1985. This trend is expected to continue.

Table 4.19 Number of free markets in urban and rural areas

Year	*1985*	*1990*		*1991*		*1992*		*1993*	
	No.	*No.*	*% increase*	*No.*	*% increase*	*No.*	*% increase*	*No.*	*% increase*
Urban	8 013	13 106	64	13 891	6	14 510	4	16 450	13
Rural	53 324	59 473	12	60 784	2	64 678	6	66 551	3
Total	**61 337**	**72 579**		**74 675**		**79 188**		**83 001**	

State Statistical Bureau of The People's Republic of China (1994), *China Statistical Yearbook*, China Statistical Information and Consultancy Service Center, Beijing, p. 505.

Table 4.20 Advertising expenditure

Year	*Advertising expenditure (US$ million)*	*Percentage increase (%)*	*Advertising expenditure per capita (US$)*
1985	115	–	0.11
1986	160	39	0.15
1987	211	32	0.19
1988	305	45	0.27
1989	380	25	0.34
1990	566[a]	49[a]	0.50[a]
1991	843[a]	49[a]	0.73[a]
1992	1 325	57[a]	1.13
1993	1 900	43	1.61
2000	5 000[a]	38[a]	5.00[a]

[a] estimate

Sources: Based on "1990 Yearbook of China Advertising Association" (internal document), Beijing, China; Janet Rae Brooks (1994), "Advertising: Reaching China's Billion Consumers", *International Market News*, Hong Kong Trade Development Council, Hong Kong, pp. 4–12.

The cost of advertising in China has a three-tiered media rate structure, with domestic advertisers paying a base rate, joint-venture companies paying about twice as much, and foreign companies being charged up to 5 times as much as their domestic counterparts (Brooks 1994, p. 7).

Although foreign companies advertising in China must now compete for scarce space and conform to sometimes arbitrary rules and regulations, they can look forward to a more open market by the year 2000. By then the growth of the country's media network will have changed the advertising business from a sellers' to a buyers' market (Brooks 1994, p. 12).

Table 4.21 Media shares of total advertising expenditures (%)

Year	*TV*	*Newspapers*	*Outdoor*[a] *& billboards*	*Magazines*	*Radio*
1985	12	36	43	5	4
1986	14	31	47	4	4
1987	15	32	45	4	4
1988	17	33	41	5	4
1989	18	32	42	4	4
1990	*	*	*	*	*
1991	*	*	*	*	4
1992	*	*	*	*	*
1993	35	27	30	5	3

Notes:
* data unavailable
[a] outdoor (neon signs, light boxes, etc.)

Source: Based on "1990 Yearbook of China Advertising Association" (internal document), Beijing, China; Janet Rae Brooks (1994), "Advertising: Reaching China's Billion Consumers", *International Market News*, Hong Kong Trade Development Council, Hong Kong, pp. 4–12.

Marketing research

A lack of reliable media viewing, listening, and readership data as well as other marketing statistics has hindered foreign as well as domestic companies from planning effective advertising campaigns and marketing strategies (Brooks 1994, p. 7). As we would expect, the government operates an enormous apparatus, which collects and analyzes information for central planning purposes, but the information is difficult to extract because it is scattered among various agencies, and the "right" person to dispense the data in a particular agency may be either unidentifiable or unco-operative (Yan 1994, p. 74). Several private research companies, however, have tried to fill this void. Among them, Survey Research Group China (SRG), based in Hong Kong, has launched market research services in 25 Chinese cities to monitor mass media use in Guangzhou, Shanghai, and Beijing, to follow advertising expenditures in various product categories in the three cities, and to track brand sales of consumer goods through retail outlets across China. Another company, Procter & Gamble, adopted the approach of acquiring a market research firm in Guangzhou. And recently, a consortium of research consultancies in the Asian region, headed by Asia Studies Ltd. in Hong Kong, conducted a broad-based market survey of consumer habits and preferences in Beijing, Tianjin, Shanghai, Guangzhou, and Chengdu. The full report of their findings was subsequently offered for sale to businesses interested in Chinese consumer markets. This kind of research service is becoming increasingly prevalent, and is popular among businesses seeking to succeed in the Chinese consumer market.

Trends and Chinese commerce—into the 21st century

In the years to come, China can be expected to undergo no less than a metamorphosis. Shaw and Woetzel (1992) note many of the most significant trends, which are summarized below. Among the most important developments are that consumer income can be expected to grow at an average annual rate of about 8% (after adjustments for subsidies and savings), and the population should increase at an annual rate of 2% as we enter the 21st century. There will be more and more people with more and more to spend.

Markets

The population of "real consumers" (those who earn at least US$1000 annually) should increase to about 260 million people by the year 2000. Those cities projected to have the largest numbers of these "real consumers" in the year 2000, while still primarily coastal, are likely to be more geographically diverse in the future, and will include, in rank order, Shenzhen, Shanghai, Guangzhou, Beijing, Tianjin, Hangzhou, Nanjing, Shenyang, Harbin, Wuhan, Haikou, Xining, Urumqi, Taiyuan, Changchun, and Xiamen. At the same time that this undoubtedly significant rich consumer niche grows, segments within it will become more pronounced in their purchasing habits, as will segments in the majority population that do not earn US$1000 or more annually. Researchers and marketers must—and will—become more sophisticated in their definition and targeting of distinct segments within the general population.

Transportation

Channel infrastructure will continue to make rather dramatic improvements. For example, foreign joint ventures and enterprises can now establish proprietary distribution and sales channels, thus allowing direct access to consumers, and bypassing the largely state-controlled wholesaling system. Chinese transportation infrastructure will also see dramatic change. Faster through trains from Hong Kong to Guangzhou are being rapidly developed.

This is already one of the most profitable rail sections in China for the Ministry of Railways. Also, another direct train link is being developed between Hong Kong and Beijing—the 2381 km Jingjiu railway—with priority to be given to freight traffic.

A Wuhan inland port is planned to serve as a mega-container port for transhipment by improved rail to Hong Kong. Wuhan is at the confluence of the east–west running Yangtze River and the north–south main rail trunk. Express highways are also being built. For example, the Hong Kong-to-Shenzhen-to-Guangzhou superhighway is now open. There is also a superhighway planned from Guangzhou to Yueyang on the Yangtze River which would allow highway freight to reach Hong Kong in 10 hours.

Economic sectors

By the year 2000, private enterprises will account for 25% of China's total economic output. Largely local township or neighborhood "collective" enterprises with increasingly "off-plan" commercial objectives will account for almost half of the total output. Thus the real private sector will play an increasingly larger role in the Chinese economy. Unprofitable state-run firms will gradually go by the wayside (go bankrupt or be absorbed by other state firms), and the remaining firms will gradually become more efficient and competitive.

Foreign investment liberalization

The Chinese government is expanding the number of geographic areas and industry sectors open to foreign participation. These include the inland provinces of Anhui, Jiangxi, Hunan, Hubei, and Sichuan. This appeasement is a response to the tension that exists between inland provinces and their relatively prosperous coastal counterparts, and reflects the desire of the inland peoples to share in both the opportunities offered by and the fruits of economic development. The resulting concern among coastal region officials, especially those from the five SEZs in the south, is that the central leadership may want to recentralize powers delegated to them in the past few years and revoke privileges such as lower import tariffs and tax breaks for foreign investors (Kwan 1995). Liberalization of foreign involvement may also be expected to continue in an increasing number of industries such as banking, tourism, real estate, shipping, civil aviation, and retailing—areas that have largely been off-limits to foreigners in the past.

Structural shifts in the economy

The Chinese economy will undergo a number of major structural shifts in the future. Among the most important, we will see an increasing regionalization of wealth, with concentrations in the coastal regions and around the traditional 3 centers of economic activity—Beijing/Tianjin, the Shanghai/Yangtze River delta, and the Canton/Hong Kong/Pearl River delta region. However, while these increasingly rich regions are tending to go their own way, Beijing is fighting to preserve its political authority and economic control (Kaye 1995), and President and Chinese Communist Party chief Jiang Zemin is becoming more vocal in urging provincial leaders to remember that "common prosperity" is the cardinal principle for China (Kwan 1995).

There are also plans for massive development of natural resources in the remote north-west region of China (Kwan 1995). Greater level of delegation of negotiating authority to regional/local governments is expected, with an increased liberalization of the business charters of ministries and government-affiliated companies, and a growth in the professionalization and profit orientation of government-affiliated companies.

Economic expansion and the new China

There will be continued economic expansion, which will turn more cities into attractive markets; distribution networks in secondary cities and between cities will continue to be modernized; as consumer wealth grows in general, the premium segments will grow; and foreign marketers will improve their cost positions by continuing to invest in local manufacturing (Yan 1994, p. 74). Finally, the resumption of Chinese sovereignty of the territories of Hong Kong and Macau (the latter due in 1999) is no small matter in terms of the effects on the Chinese economy. In fact, Hong Kong (now a Special Administrative Region of the PRC) and China are each other's largest trading partners, and are becoming increasingly interdependent. And Hong Kong and Macau are becoming increasingly dependent on the China market. These territories border prosperous mainland SEZs (Hong Kong borders Shenzhen and Macau Zhuhai), and the argument could be presented that economic integration has already occurred.

This integration has taken the form of import, export, re-export, manufacturing, and labor trade. For example, China accounts for 38% of Hong Kong's imports (the largest source), and is the largest market for Hong Kong's exports, 28% of the total (Census and Statistics Department 1994).

China is also the largest market for and supplier of Hong Kong's re-exports–88% of all goods re-exported through Hong Kong (55% is destined to China; 33% originates from China–Census and Statistics Department 1994). The 33% of re-exports originating from China means that Hong Kong is the conduit for one-third of China's total trade with the world. The value of re-exports destined to China through Hong Kong increased more than 29% in 1993 over the 1992 figures, reflecting Hong Kong's continued and growing importance as an entrepôt for China.

In the area of exports, China's State Planning Commission has divided the country into 10 major economic zones, with each designated for a specific purpose in economic development. Hong Kong is part of the Southern Coastal Economic Zone, which also comprises the provinces of Fujian, Guangdong,

Guangxi, and Hainan. This particular zone is the only one that focuses on the development of export-oriented industries and acts as an export base for China, with Hong Kong serving as a crucial conduit (Woo 1992).

As for industry, in the 1980s many Hong Kong manufacturers moved their production to China. Today it is estimated that in Guangdong Province alone there are more than 3 million PRC people working for Hong Kong companies. There are also an estimated 600 000 Hong Kong people (about 10% of the territory's total population) either stationed in China or travelling regularly in the country for their work–this reflects the increasing number of businesses expanding operations to incorporate a China component. As the Hong Kong, Macau, and mainland business and consumer cultures increasingly intermingle, the products and ways of the West that exist in these territories will increasingly penetrate China, and the merchandise and ways of China will in turn penetrate Hong Kong and Macau.

Future research on marketing in China

The scope of this chapter has been largely confined to macro-level analysis, with the major distinction being made between urban and rural areas. This has been done because the Chinese normally collect data in this manner. While Hong Kong and Macau data could be integrated with Chinese urban figures, each "city" certainly has its own peculiarities. As mentioned earlier, China is not one market. It consists of many markets (Swanson 1989). The substantial differences in economies, demographic composition and trends, and consumption behavior that exists between specific cities and between regions must be explored thoroughly if marketers are to adapt products and strategies to local conditions and successfully tap Chinese markets. While the nature and the specific direction of the future can not be exactly predicted, there is little doubt that China will play a large part in the events of the 21st century.

References

"1990 Yearbook of China Advertising Association" (internal document), Beijing, China.

Asian Wall Street Journal (1995), "Boomers Save Less", June 6, p. 9.

Asiaweek (1995), "The Bottom Line", April 7, *South China Morning Post,* Hong Kong, pp. 49, 50.

Associated Press (1991), "China Weighted Down With Unsold Goods", *South China Morning Post,* June 13, Hong Kong.

Brooks, Janet Rae (1994), "Advertising: Reaching China's Billion Consumers", *International Market News,* Hong Kong Trade Development Council, Hong Kong, pp. 4–12.

Brown, Lester (1995), "China's Growing Food Crisis", *South China Morning Post,* Hong Kong, p. F9.

Census and Statistics Department (1994), *Hong Kong 1994*, Hong Kong Government, Hong Kong, p. 54.

Hong Kong Trade Development Council (1994a), *China's Consumer Market*, Hong Kong Trade Development Council, Research Department, Hong Kong.

— (1994b), *Retail and Wholesale Distribution of Consumer Goods in China* (1994), Research Department, Hong Kong Trade Development Council, Hong Kong.

Information Please Almanac: Atlas & Yearbook 1995 (1995), 48th edn, Houghton Mifflin Co., New York.

Kaye, Lincoln (1995), "China: The Grip Slips", *Far Eastern Economic Review*, pp. 18–20.

Kennedy, Sean (1995), "Rail Traffic to Soar after 1997", *South China Morning Post*, April 26, p. B2.

Kwan, Daniel (1995), "Jiang Warning to Rich Regions", *South China Morning Post*, October 9, Hong Kong, p. 8.

Lam, Willy Wo-Lap (1995), "Jiang's Act Runs into Problems", *South China Morning Post*, October 11, Hong Kong, p. 19.

Laurent, Clint (1995), *China Scan*, Asia Studies Ltd, Hong Kong.

Linn, Gene (1994), "China: Stability is Priority", *Asian Business*, August, pp. 26–34.

— (1995), "Caution Tinged With Optimism", *Asian Business*, August, p. 33.

Shaw, Stephen M. & Woetzel, Jonathan R. (1992), "A Fresh Look at China", *The McKinsey Quarterly*, No. 3, pp. 3–17.

State Statistical Bureau of The People's Republic of China (1994), *China Statistical Yearbook*, China Statistical Information and Consultancy Service Center, Beijing.

— (1997), *China Statistical Year Book*, China Statistical Information and Consultancy Service Center, Beijing.

Swanson, Lauren A. (1989), "The Twelve 'Nations' of China", *Journal of International Consumer Marketing*, vol. 2, no. 1, pp. 83–105.

Tse, David K., Belk, Russell W. & Zhou, Nan (1989), "Becoming A Consumer Society: A Longitudinal and Cross-Cultural Content Analysis of Print Ads from Hong Kong, the People's Republic of China, and Taiwan", *Journal of Consumer Research*, vol. 15, March, pp. 457–72.

Woo, Peter K.C. (1992), "The China-Hong Kong Economic Partnership", speech delivered in Melbourne, Australia at the Asia 2010 Conference, July 20.

Yan, Rick (1994), "To Reach China's Consumers, Adapt to Guo Qing", *Harvard Business Review*, September–October, pp. 66–74.

Yang, Xiao (1995), "The Necessity for Growth", *Newsweek*, May 22, p. 56.

Notes

1 This chapter is based on Lauren Swanson, "Demography, Culture, and the Marketing Environment in the People's Republic of China", Working Paper, the Chinese University of Hong Kong. © Lauren Swanson 1995, reprinted with permission.

2 Merrill Lynch & Co. (*Asian Wall Street Journal* 1995) reports that median net financial assets of US families by age of family head are as follows: age 33–44 = $600; 45–54 = $2400; 55–64 = $$6600; 65–74 = $9600; 75+ = $8400; all families = $1000.

3 Table 4.3, which gives urban and rural populations, and Table 4.6, which lists urban and rural persons per household, are used to calculate the number of urban and rural households. With Table 4.11, which gives figures for total savings deposits for all rural and urban households, urban and rural deposits per household and per-capita deposits were used in the calculations.

CHAPTER 5

China, Part II

Markets within the market

PIA POLSA & BAI CHANG HONG[1]

Abstract

An overview of the market of the People's Republic of China (PRC) is presented, followed by the marketing implications for the diverse Chinese market. A huge country such as the PRC offers an interesting mixture of subcultures and submarkets within its national borders. The transition from a planned to a socialistic market economy adds a dimension to the diversity. In order to comprehend the consumer behavior of the Mainland Chinese, it is necessary to understand the diversity of cultures, geography and economic development and the changing purchasing power of citizens in different parts of the country. To provide this understanding, the following issues are covered: geography and climate, the economic history of the PRC, the current socio-economic environment, the demographic environment, culture and some changes in the culture, and employment and consumer income, as well as consumption patterns. Finally, macromarketing issues, involving branding, price, distribution, word of mouth, advertising, and marketing research, are presented. This chapter concludes with some ideas on the future directions of change.

Introduction

China, or more accurately, the People's Republic of China (PRC), is a socialistic republic, which was established on October 1 1949. An overview of this large country may give the impression that it is a single unified and homogenous market of the largest population of the world. However, a closer look at the PRC reveals the diversity of climate, history, culture, population and administration in different areas. Naturally, this diversity affects the consumer behavior of Mainland Chinese people, and consequently makes marketing strategies more complex than we could assume at the first glance.

In order to provide an understanding of the consumer behavior of PRC citizens, we first present the geography and climate of the nation. The variety in climate and geography has affected Chinese history and created subcultures inside the area that is currently the PRC. Therefore, knowledge of the geography and climate forms a base for an understanding of the emergence of cultural and historical differences within the PRC.

A brief look at Chinese economic history gives a further understanding of the heterogeneity of this country as well as the presentation of the current socio-economic environment. The current reform policies have had an uneven effect on economic development, thus deepening the gap between the purchasing power of the eastern and western populations. However, some attempts have been made to decrease the gap as well as to diminish the income difference between urban and rural residents.

The exposition of the demographic environment explains the current differences in urban and rural areas, and western and eastern regions. The country not only consists of the Han Chinese[2] (the majority of the population), but also of 56 different minorities with their different dialects and languages. Even the Han Chinese population may be divided into different cultures and levels of economic development. Demographic differences are crucial in understanding the market of the PRC. Due to periods of isolation during Chinese history, the culture of the PRC has some special characteristics. These basic cultural issues are discussed, together with the current level of education, and topics on gender and health. Some implications of these issues on marketing planning are presented at the end of the section.

The next section provides more detail on purchasing power by focusing on consumer income and employment issues, with an enumeration of segmentation possibilities. Based on these demographic, cultural and employment environments, the consumption patterns of the Chinese population are discussed next. Specifically, saving, single-child families, housing, household goods, eating habits, and leisure activities are discussed in detail. At the end of the section, the marketing implications are presented. The final sections take up the marketing topics of branding, pricing, distribution, word of mouth, advertising, and market research, and conclude with a description of likely future developments.

A brief introduction to geography and climate

China is located in the eastern part of Asia. The current PRC is approximately 9.6 million km^2 of territory, bordered by mountains and deserts in the west and north, the Yellow Sea in the east, and the South China Sea in the south. China occupies one-fifth of the world's land area, and one-quarter of Asia. It has borders with Mongolia and Russia in the north; Vietnam, Laos, Bhutan, Nepal, and Sikkim in the south; Afghanistan, Pakistan, India and Myanmar in the west, and Korea in the east (Shunwu 1992, p. 1).

China is characterized by contrasts in geography and climate. There are 3 high regions, starting from the west and approaching the eastern coast. The western part is Qinghai-Tibet Plateau, "the roof of the world." The height of this massive mountain area is typically between 4000 and 5000 m above sea level. The second part is composed of the Junggar, Tarim and Sichuan basins in addition to the Inner Mongolia, Loess and Yunnan-Guizhou plateaus. The average height of this part of the country is about 1000 to 2000 m above sea level. The most eastern part of the country drops to less than 500 m above sea level (Shunwu 1992, pp. 2–3). These variations in altitude partly explain the concentration of the population in the eastern parts of the PRC; these provide the most suitable living conditions, but occupy only about one-third of the area.

This difference in living conditions between the east and the west is further accentuated by variations in humidity. The moist regions in the east cover about 30% of the land. Semi-moist and semi-arid areas in the central parts of the country cover about 35%, leaving as much as about one-third of the country dry. The mountainous and arid western regions have always been sparsely populated. The country can be divided from south to north into 6 zones in terms of variations in climate. Differences are as drastic as differences in altitude, because the warmest climate in the south is equatorial and the coldest climate may drop to -24°C during the winter period. In between the south and the north of China the climate can vary from subtropical and intermediate-temperature, to warm-temperature areas (Shunwu 1992, pp. 4–5).

While its terrain divides China into 3 east-west staircases, rivers divide China into north-south regions. The PRC is crisscrossed with 50 000 rivers, scattered across the western desert and mountain areas and flowing to the oceans. The most important are the 3 famous rivers: the Yangtze (Changjiang), the Yellow River (Huanghe), and the Pearl River (Zhujiang). The Yangtze has provided fertile land for cultivation throughout history for many nations and dynasties because it is located in the subtropical monsoon climate. The Yellow River further north was the base for the birth of ancient Chinese civilization and culture, and even today provides a living for approximately 100 million people. The third river, the Pearl, is famous for the recent economic development of its delta area in the Guangdong province (Shunwu 1992, pp. 5–7). These large rivers have all been bases for different Chinese subcultures throughout history.

A brief introduction to the economic history of China

The economic history of the People's Republic can be divided into 3 stages, according to the shifts in economic policy: centrally planned economy (1953–78)[3], planned commodity economy (1979–92)[4] and socialist market economy (1993–)[5]. Table 5.1 summarizes the general stages of economic development during the last 40 years.

The political orientation since 1979 can also be called an "Opening Policy," as foreign investment was allowed at the end of 1978 and the planned economy restrictions were removed. Since the end of the 1970s there have been changes not only in the applied economic policy, but also in the economic ideology. The old planned economy system was never totally abandoned, but rather, parallel new ideas were cultivated. The objective of the reforms is to develop a socialism that is suitable to the conditions in China. According to Chinese scholars, socialism has not failed, but rather, China has failed to interpret socialism in a proper way (Hsu 1991, p. 171). Understanding of these changes in the economic philosophy or ideology is essential for the full comprehension of the current situation. It is necessary to emphasize that the old system and ideology have not been abandoned, and that the new system has to operate within the constraints of the old structures.

Development of consumer behavior since the Opening Policy has been rapid. The reforms have led to an increase in the range of products available, and an increase in people's incomes. There has also been a growth in inflation and a change in consumer attitudes, which will be discussed in more detail later in the chapter.

Current government structure and the political situation

The government of the PRC after Liberation in 1949 consisted of 3 components: the Chinese Communist Party (CCP), the formal governmental structure and the Army (Spence 1990, p. 519). Administrative power is in the hands of the CCP, whose highest organ is the National Party Congress. It meets every 5 years, and functions as the Central Committee with executive tasks. The Central Committee elects the Politburo of 22 members, and the Standing Committee of the Politburo. The National People's Congress (NCP) is elected every 5 years and represents a kind of parliament of the People's Republic, with a Standing Committee. The State Council of the NCP is headed by the Prime Minister and is composed of 5 Vice Premiers, 9 State Councillors and the Secretary General. A number of commissions, ministries, offices, agencies, institutions, and all the banks are directly under the State Council. The administration of the People's Liberation Army (PLA) is divided

Table 5.1 Different stages in the economic development of the PRC

Economic stage		*Characteristics*	
	Centrally planned economy (1953–78)	*Planned commodity economy (1979–92)*	*Socialist market economy (1993–)*
Government intervention	Direct administrative control	Diminished direct control	Indirect control
Orientation of business	Production oriented, plan fulfilment	Operation oriented, profitability, sales	Market oriented, profitability
Ownership	State, collective	State, collective, emergence of private and foreign	State (still dominant in some fields of industry), collective, private (high growth), foreign
Product policy	State plan	Limited freedom, meeting plan first	Autonomy
Price	Fixed	Fixed, floating, black market	Free market price (except raw material)
Advertising	Prohibited	Allowed	Allowed

Source: Adapted from Ying Fan (1994), *Blending East and West, How Can Western Management Know-how be Transferred to China's Socialist Market Economy?*, Durham University Business School, Durham.

into 6 regions: north-west, north, north-east, south-west, east and central-south China bureaus. The administrative structure of these units follows the hierarchical structure of the CCP and NCP.

At the local level, the PRC is divided into 31 provincial administrative divisions that are directly under the Central Government. These divisions are 3 municipalities (Beijing, Tianjin and Shanghai), 23 provinces, and 5 autonomous regions (Inner Mongolia, Guangxi, Tibet, Ningxia and Xingjiang). These divisions are further divided into 335 prefectures, 2142 counties, and 666 cities (Shunwu 1992, p. 2; *China Statistical Yearbook* 1997, p. 3). The administrative hierarchical structure of these local units follows the form of the Central Governmental structure. Usually, there are provincial- and city-level bureaus for each National Ministry. For example, Commercial Bureau executes the national economic laws and even controls local-city-level rules for local business conditions.[6] The dual reporting system to the local government, and to the higher level national ministries, creates confusing situations for lower level authorities. For instance, national economic policies or even laws are not implemented consistently all over the country at the local levels. Indirectly, this affects, for instance, the distribution of goods, as some health and quality inspections are locally defined.

The socio-economic environment

The average annual growth rate of the Chinese GDP has been high since the Opening Policy. In 1993 it was 13.5%, in 1994 it was 12.6%, and in 1995 it was 10.5%; the preliminary figure for 1996 is 9.7% (*China Statistical Yearbook* 1995, p. 765; *China Statistical Yearbook* 1997, p. 835). Naturally, the rapid development has had its effect on inflation. In 1994 the overall consumer price index was 287 and the food price index as much as 373[7] (*China Statistical Yearbook* 1995, p. 787). Chinese government actions since 1994 have not significantly slowed inflation. The most recent inflation figures are for 1996 (base year 1991): general index is 197, and food price index 222 (*China Statistical Yearbook* 1997, p. 842). A closer look at the figures per region shows tremendous differences between the areas in the PRC.

The economic environment can be roughly divided into 3 areas according to economic development and administrative differences: Special Economic Zones (SEZs), larger cities such as Beijing, Tianjin, Guangzhou, Shanghai, and western parts of the PRC. Special Economic Zones are cities and areas that were the first parts of the PRC to be open for foreign trade after the start of the reform policy in the early 1980s. The purpose of these zones was to stimulate the economy and simultaneously attract foreign investment. The areas were given preferential economic and political treatment and administration as well as preference in terms of investment policies. Consequently, these areas developed rapidly, prospered in all areas of commercial life, and significantly increased the living standard of their people. The first four SEZs were Shenzhen, Xiamen, Zhuhai, and Shantou. Later the status of an SEZ was given to the island of Hainan. Even today the SEZs are the richest parts of the country, and their prosperity has spread out to neighbouring areas. Table 5.2 shows some of the economic indicators of SEZs, 14 Open Coastal Cities[8] and average normal cities. However, we should not see the SEZ as the only lucrative market of China. Major cities, such as Beijing, Tianjin, Shanghai and Guangzhou, are also well developed, and there exists future market potential for the less advanced parts of the PRC.

In order to grasp this huge market, equal attention must be given to the lesser known parts of China. The provincial divisions are combined to provide larger entities in the coastal parts of China that include all the SEZs, central parts of China and finally inland parts of the country.[9]

These divisions give an idea of the differences of economic development in the different parts of the country, and describe the varying purchasing power of the consumers and market potential in the area. The divisions are neither official policy, nor are they exclusive; they are used in an attempt to clarify a wide-ranging topic.

Table 5.3 shows the provincial-level divisions, grouped as coastal, central and inland areas. The number of prefectures, counties and cities gives an

Table 5.2 Some economic indicators for Cities, Open Coastal Cities and Special Economic Zones (1995)

Economic indicator per city	*Cities (684)*	*Open Coastal Cities (14)*	*Special Economic Zones (4)*
Cross output value of industry (100 000 000 yuan)	116	1 390	686
Total number of telephones (10 000)	8	97	54
Total value of consumer goods (100 000 000 yuan)	27	308	169
Total wages of staff and workers (100 000 000)	10	106	62

Note:
* 8.45 yuan = $1 (US).

Source: China Statistical Yearbook (1997), China Statistical Publishing House, Beijing.

idea of the urbanization of these areas. Both the coastal and the central areas include more than 200 cities, while the inland part of the country has only 123 cities. However, the number of rural counties and prefectures is about the same in the inland and central parts of the PRC, leaving the coastal area as the most urbanized and the inland area as the most rural. Two-thirds of the population is concentrated in the coastal and central parts of the country, whereas only 22.9% of Chinese people live in the western provinces, which constitute 50% of the PRC. Similarly, the GDP is concentrated in the developed coastal provinces. The average GDP per capita is 9553 yuan in coastal areas, in contrast to the rest of the country, where the average GDP per capita is 4008 yuan–less than half of the GDP of the coastal provinces. The growth rates for the average per-capita GDP figure between 1994 and 1996 reveal a possible future convergence between economic development in the coastal and central parts of the country, as the growth rates are 90% for coastal areas and 106% for rural areas.

Table 5.4 tells a similar story. Total Gross Domestic Expenditure in the coastal regions is 3 times more than in the inland areas of the country and twice more than in the central areas. The ratio of investment to consumption is approximately equal in the eastern part of the country, while both in the central and the western regions consumption counts for more than investments. The rich areas export more than they import, whereas the inland areas do not produce for export but are dependent on imported goods. As a consequence, the per-capita consumption in coastal areas is 63% higher than in the central areas, and even as much as 98% higher than in

Table 5.3 Administrative divisions in the PRC (1996)

Provinces, municipalities, and autonomous regions	*Number of prefectures*	*Number of counties*	*Number of cities*	*Per-capita GDP (yuan)*
National	**335**	**2142**	**666**	
Coastal areas				
Beijing	0	8	1	15 044
Tianjin	0	5	1	12 270
Hebei	11	138	34	5 345
Liaoning	14	44	31	7 730
Shanghai	0	6	1	22 275
Jiangsu	13	64	39	8 447
Zhejiang	11	64	35	9 455
Fujian	9	61	23	8 136
Shangdong	17	95	48	6 834
Guangdong	21	79	54	9 513
Hainan	2	17	8	5 500
Guangxi	15	81	18	4 081
Total	**113**	**662**	**298**	average: 9 553
Central areas				
Inner Mongolia	12	85	20	4 259
Shanxi	11	101	22	4 220
Jilin	9	41	28	5 163
Heilongjiang	13	67	31	6 468
Anhui	16	67	21	3 881
Jiangxi	11	84	21	3 715
Henan	17	116	38	4 032
Hubei	12	68	35	5 122
Hunan	14	90	29	4 130
Total	**115**	**719**	**245**	average: 4 554
Inland areas				
Sichuan	23	174	35	3 763
Guizhou	9	80	11	2 093
Yunnan	17	123	15	3 715
Tibet	7	77	2	2 732
Shaanxi	10	92	13	3 313
Gansu	14	75	13	2 901
Qinghai	8	39	3	3 748
Ningxia	4	18	4	3 731
Xinjiang	15	85	17	5 167
Total	**107**	**763**	**113**	average: 3 463

Source: China Statistical Yearbook (1997), China Statistical Publishing House, Beijing, p. 3, pp. 44–5.

Table 5.4 Gross domestic expenditure by region, and per-capita consumption (1996)

Provinces, municipalities, and autonomous regions	*Total expenditure (100 million yuan)*	*Total consumption*	*Total investment*	*Net export*	*Per-capita consumption*
Coastal areas					
Beijing	1 694.89	506.58	1 256.28	-67.97	3 519
Tianjin	920.11	386.99	524.77	8.35	3 380
Hebei	2 849.52	1 348.75	1 226.07	274.70	1 686
Liaoning	2 793.38	1 501.84	1 046.61	244.93	2 900
Shanghai	2 462.57	1 085.33	1 551.20	-173.96	6 712
Jiangsu	5 119.17	2 250.66	2 479.30	389.21	2 557
Zhejiang	3 569.15	1 495.24	1 786.79	287.12	2 831
Fujian	2 160.52	1 160.68	996.17	3.67	2 944
Shangdong	4 895.26	2 479.05	2 247.58	168.63	1 943
Guangdong	5 733.97	3 189.84	2 381.31	162.82	3 832
Hainan	364.17	188.50	219.21	-43.54	2 197
Guangxi	1 606.15	1 041.93	632.47	-68.25	1 664
Total	**34 168.86**	**16 635.39**	**16 347.76**	**1 185.71**	Average: 3 014
Central parts of the country					
Inner Mongolia	815.82	505.84	372.98	-63	1 729
Shanxi	1 090.29	627.23	412.42	50.64	1 589
Jilin	1 139.40	703.38	474.32	-38.30	2 292
Heilongjiang	2 006.48	1 201.53	724.46	80.49	2 649
Anhui	2 003.58	1 174.65	824.61	4.32	1 669
Jiangxi	1 217.13	790.36	444.93	-18.16	1 559
Henan	3 002.74	1 595.23	1 244.31	163.20	1 382
Hubei	2 435.04	1 333.82	987.03	114.19	1 954
Hunan	2 195.70	1 396.88	800.50	-1.68	1 752
Total	**15 906.18**	**9 328.92**	**6 285.56**	**291.7**	Average: 1 842
Inland parts of the country					
Sichuan	3 534.00	2 193.23	1 346.15	-5.38	1 624
Guizhou	628.98	513.46	235.94	-120.42	1 258
Yunnan	1 206.68	689.39	492.77	24.52	1 484
Tibet	69.65	37.14	32.56	-0.05	1 202
Shaanxi	1 000.03	673.42	480.48	-153.87	1 431
Gansu	553.35	376.81	222.57	-46.03	1 172
Qinghai	165.81	112.24	77.67	-24.10	1 689
Ningxia	169.75	113.31	82.45	-26.01	1 643
Xingjiang	825.11	495.56	473.70	-144.15	2 146
Total	**8 153.36**	**5 204.56**	**3 444.29**	**-495.49**	Average: 1 517

Source: China Statistical Yearbook (1997), China Statistical Publishing House, Beijing, pp. 48, 292.

the western parts of the country. These figures give a general view of the uneven distribution of wealth between the eastern and western parts of the PRC.

China's geographical economic development since 1979 can be further explained by the central government's economic development preference policy, which was implemented in 3 stages from south to north. The first stage of economic development was the creation of SEZs in South China around the Pearl River delta, in the provinces of Guangdong and Fujian. The second development stage started from the end of the 1980s. Its focus has been on the area of the Yangtze River delta around Shanghai-Putong, and consequently had an effect on, for example, Zhejiang and Jiangsu. The third development stage has occurred further north. This development has concentrated on the shore of the Bohai Sea in the Liaoning and Shangdong Peninsulas. The capital of the PRC, Beijing, will be affected by these investments, and the other large city, Tianjin, will be the essential port. The reunification of Hong Kong in 1997 and Macao in 1999 with Mainland China gives further economic importance to the southern parts of the country. Guangdong, Guangxi, Hainan, Macao, and Hong Kong will form a significant economic area for both domestic and foreign trade.

The three preferential policy stages have widened the economic development gap between east and west. However, the current Chinese government has made efforts to decrease this gap. Two current investment projects emphasize this. The first one is the huge investment in the Jingjiou railway from Beijing to Kowloon, Hong Kong. The regions around this transportation line benefited from the economic development the railway brought, and it also had effects on the central parts of the country. Provinces such as Hebei, Hunan, Shangdong, Anhui, Jiangxi, Hubei, Fujian, and Guangdong have benefited from the railway. The other large investment project will bring the development further west. It is the Changjing-Sanxia project, which is reconstructing the Yangtze River so that vessels from Shanghai will be able to sail all the way up to Yibin city in Sichuan province. This Golden Water Channel will bring east and west together, and provide higher income possibilities for the people living around the area.

The structure of the economy has also changed during the years of the People's Republic, following the normal trend in any developing country. Table 5.5 shows that, while primary industry occupied as much as 84% of the total employment in 1952, its share in 1996 was only 51%. The share of secondary industry has increased during the 40 years of the socialist regime, but seems to have been stable at around 20–23% during the last 15 years. Tertiary industry is still increasing its share, and in 1996 employed more than 25% of the workforce.

To overcome the economic gap between the rural and urban areas, and the problem of the decreasing importance of primary industry, the government

Table 5.5 Employment by type of industry

Year	*Primary industry*	*Secondary industry*	*Tertiary industry*
1952	84%	7%	9%
1962	82%	8%	10%
1970	81%	10%	9%
1980	69%	18%	13%
1985	62%	21%	17%
1987	60%	22%	18%
1990	60%	21%	19%
1991	60%	21%	19%
1992	58%	22%	20%
1993	56%	23%	21%
1994	54%	23%	23%
1995	52%	24%	26%
1996	51%	24%	26%

Source: China Statistical Yearbook (1995) p. 83, China Statistical Publishing House, Beijing; *China Statistical Yearbook* (1997), China Statistical Publishing House, Beijing, p. 94.

has tried to improve economic conditions in rural areas. The reform policy of the late 1970s started in the countryside when the government eased control, and the farmers were allowed to sell part of their production on the free market. Later, land reform allowed farmers to rent out their piece of land if they did not wish to work it, although it was still owned by the government. The establishment of township and village enterprises was one way to stimulate the economy in the rural areas and create employment (Rana 1993, p. 9). The introduction of township and village enterprises was closely related to the effort to industrialize the countryside. To improve living standards in rural areas, the government sought to facilitate the distribution of commodities while providing subsidies for agricultural products.

The demographic environment–population: Size and distribution

With a total population of 1223.89 million persons by the end of 1996, and with a natural growth rate of 1.04%, China is the most populous country in the world. Mainly due to the strict one-child policy, the growth rate has decreased, from an average 1.4% in the period 1981 to 1992, to the current

1.1% (*China Statistical Yearbook* 1995, p. 59; *China Statistical Yearbook* 1997, p. 70). The natural growth rate has decreased (1.055% in 1995) (*Guangming Daily* 1996). The population of the PRC includes 56 nationalities. The majority, 94%, are Han Chinese, and 55 ethnic groups make up 6% of the population. Despite the small percentage of minorities, their population is still important. For example, Zhuang, the largest minority, has a population of 10 million people, which exceeds the population of many European countries. The population of the rest of the minorities ranges from 5 million to 15 million.

Geographic distribution

Two-thirds of the Chinese population is in the eastern and central parts of the country. For geographical and climatic reasons, these parts of the country have been the most advantageous places for agriculture and commerce. Table 5.6 shows that the coastal provinces of the country cover only 13% of the land, making the average population density highest in the eastern parts.

China is a country of extremes. The population density of Shanghai is as high as 2365 persons per square kilometer, but in Tibet there are only 2 persons per square kilometer. Consequently, the most lucrative market for consumer goods is the coastal and central provinces, given that economic development is also the highest in these areas.

Urban versus rural population

In 1992, 27.6% of the population lived in urban areas, while 72.4% lived in rural areas (*China Statistical Yearbook* 1995, p. 760). In 1996, urban residents totaled 29.4% of the total population (*China Statistical Yearbook* 1997, p. 69). The division between urban and rural is more complicated than it was in the past. Nowadays there is a large population of rural people called an urban “floating” population (Wiemer 1992, p. 172). These people are the ones who immigrate to cities, work there temporarily in less wanted jobs, and occasionally return to their home towns. Formally, they are still registered in their countryside residences. They form bridges between the rural and urban population, which otherwise differ in culture and habit.

The impact of the consumption habits of the “floating people” is twofold. First, urban immigrants send their salaries home, hence affecting the purchasing power of rural residents. Second, these immigrant people affect the social structures of the society, sometimes creating problems such as crime. However, “floating” people are the potentially powerful future consumers because they earn more than average and represent the rural majority of the population.

Age distribution

As in other developing countries, the majority of the population in the PRC is young. One-third of the population is under 20 years old, and only 7% of

Table 5.6 Population distribution in the coastal, central, and inland areas

Provinces, municipalities, and autonomous regions	*% of total population (end 1996)*	*Area (10 000 km²)*	*Population (10 000 persons– end 1996)*	*Population density (10 000 per km²)*
National	1 223 890 000[10]	967.8		
Coastal areas				
Beijing	1.0	1.7	1 259	741
Tianjin	0.8	1.1	948	862
Hebei	5.3	18	6 484	360
Liaoning	3.4	15	4 116	274
Shanghai	1.2	0.6	1 419	2 365
Jiangsu	5.9	10	7 110	711
Zhejiang	3.6	10	4 343	434
Fujian	2.7	12	3 261	272
Shangdong	7.2	15	8 738	583
Guangdong	5.7	18	6 961	387
Hainan	0.6	3.4	734	216
Guangxi	3.8	23	4 589	200
Total	**41.2**	**127.8**	**49 962**	**391**
Central areas				
Inner Mongolia	1.9	128	2 307	18
Shanxi	2.6	16	3 109	194
Jilin	2.2	18	2 610	145
Heilongjiang	3.1	47	3 728	79
Anhui	5.0	13	6 070	467
Jiangxi	3.4	17	4 105	241
Henan	7.6	17	9 172	540
Hubei	4.8	18	5 825	324
Hunan	5.3	20	6 428	321
Total	**35.9**	**303**	**43 354**	**143**
Inland areas				
Sichuan	9.4	57	11 430	201
Guizhou	2.9	17	3 555	209
Yunnan	3.3	39	4 042	104
Tibet	0.2	120	244	2
Shaanxi	2.9	20	3 543	177
Gansu	2.0	45	2 467	55
Qinghai	0.4	72	488	7
Ningxia	0.4	7	521	74
Xinjiang	1.4	160	1 689	11
Total	**22.9**	**537**	**27 979**	**52**

Source: China Statistical Yearbook (1997), China Statistical Publishing House, Beijing, p. 70; Zhou Shunwu (1992), *China Provincial Geography*, Foreign Languages Press, Beijing.

the population is over 65 years (see Table 5.7). Population distribution is changing because of increasing living standards, the one-child policy, and higher life expectancy.

Table 5.7 Age distribution (sample survey, 1996)

Age	*Total per age group ('000)*	*% of population*
0–14	322 330	26%
15–64	837 470	67%
65+	86 443	7%
Total	**1 246 243**	**100%**

Source: China Statistical Yearbook (1997), China Statistical Publishing House, Beijing, p. 76.

The Chinese household

During the last decade, the average size of households has constantly decreased in both the urban and rural areas, as shown in Table 5.8. In the urban regions, the one-child policy has already had its effect on the size of households. This tendency will continue as the one-child policy continues to be in effect. The latest statistics show that the average number of persons per common Chinese household was 3.8 in 1996 (*Guangming Daily* 1996).

Table 5.8 Average number of persons per household, 1985–1996

Year	*1985*	*1990*	*1992*	*1993*	*1994*	*1995*	*1996*
Urban households	3.89	3.50	3.37	3.31	3.28	3.23	3.20
Rural households	5.12	4.80	4.67	4.59	4.54	4.48	4.42

Source: China Statistical Yearbook (1995), China Statistical Publishing House, Beijing, pp. 262, 268; *China Statistical Yearbook* (1997), China Statistical Publishing House, Beijing, pp. 294, 312.

Table 5.9 gives an idea of the typical Chinese household. The most typical is a household of 2 generations, but even today about one-fifth of the households consist of more than 2 generations. Household size has been influenced by the government population policy. During the early 1960s to 1970s, the large size of the national population was believed to be the power of a nation. There were no restrictions on family size, and hence households from that period often included as many as 5 or 6 children (Spence 1990, p. 685). Children born during the 1960s and 1970s are now adults, and in their turn building families. Due to the one-child policy, the size of their households is only 3 persons, unless the grandparents are living in the household. In modern urban households it is not unusual to have no children, and 10% of married-couple households in Beijing fall into this category. However, this often does not hold in rural homes, where children are still considered a resource, and where, despite the one-child policy, families may have more than 1 child—and not divulge this information for official statistics.

Table 5.9 Type of household, in terms of percentage of total households, at October 1 1994

Region	*Households–total no.*	*Single*	*Married couple*	*Two generations*	*More than two generations*	*One generation and other*	*More than one generation and other*
National	329 088	6%	8%	64%	18%	1%	3%
Beijing	22 354	8%	10%	60%	18%	1%	3%
Guangdong	9 709	9%	5%	54%	26%	1%	5%
Henan	12 488	5%	6%	67%	18%	1%	3%
Sichuan	14 946	7%	7%	61%	21%	1%	3%

Source: China Statistical Yearbook (1995), China Statistical Publishing House, Beijing, p. 65.

Marriage is still an important factor in Chinese society despite some attempts to discourage it to prevent overpopulation (Spence 1990, pp. 686–7). One of these attempts has involved the revision of the legal marriage age to 22 for males and 20 for females (Spence 1990, p. 685). It is even higher than this in some local working units. Nevertheless, only 28% of the population over 15 years of age was single in 1982, and this figure decreased to 25% in 1990 (*China Statistical Yearbook* 1995, p. 61). In the latest sample survey on population (1996), 20% of the respondents were unmarried (*China Statistical Yearbook* 1997, p. 80). Practical considerations encourage marriage despite official efforts to discourage it. In many government units such as universities, better housing is provided for married couples than for single persons. For instance, in Guangxi Teacher's College, unmarried persons share a room with 1 other adult teacher. However, a married couple is given a larger room. Furthermore, many young people buy their first household durable goods only after the wedding, rather than investing in their comfort as single persons. During their single life they save in order to be able to provide a good material start for their marital life.

These marketing implications may be deduced from Chinese demography:

- Because of purchasing power and population concentration, the most lucrative markets of the PRC are the coastal areas, but in the future the developing central regions will be increasingly important.
- The market of young consumers is significant in the current China.
- The decreasing size of the household will affect household consumption needs.

- A good target market for promotion of household durables is provided by young couples of marriageable age rather than single persons.

Culture and cultural change

With its origins over 5000 years ago, Chinese culture is one of the rare ancient civilizations that has survived and is still vital. Because China has always been, in one way or another, isolated from the other parts of the world, some features of its culture have developed independently. Naturally, many features of Chinese culture are also common to other cultures, especially in Asia, but there still exist some unique characteristics. Chinese culture is based on Confucian philosophy as well as ideas from Buddhism and Taoism. The establishment of the PRC has had a great impact on the culture of Mainland China, adding a third ideology, Marxism, to the factors affecting the culture. For example, the view of the woman's role has become more liberated due to the ideas of Mao Zhedong, and this, along with the current one-child policy, has affected the traditional role of family. In the course of the last 20 years, the Open Door Policy has changed the values of the Mainland Chinese despite the intention to focus only on economic development. This policy, while bringing back some old traditions, such as women staying at home, has also mixed the original Chinese values with western ways (e.g. changing eating habits). Only the future will show how deeply rooted the socialist ideas of equality have been, and to what extent the Chinese culture will absorb Western ideas.

Basic features of Chinese culture

Culture is of critical relevance to marketers, because successful strategies cannot be developed without taking into account the specific features of Chinese culture. The issues associated with culture are so important that some writers even call for a special marketing theory for Chinese culture (Ambler, Lee & Yau, cited in Schütte 1995). Chinese cultural values are based very much on interpersonal relationships and social orientation. Compared with Western cultures, Chinese culture is more collective (Hofstede 1994, pp. 49–78). Individuals are seen as existing in relationships, and some of these relationships are of special importance. Confucius defined the Cardinal Relations as those between sovereign and subject, father and son, elder brother and younger brother, husband and wife, and friend and friend. These relationships also have hierarchical patterns: a senior member is superior to a junior one. Social order is based on everyone respecting these hierarchical relationships (Bond & Hwang 1987, pp. 215–16).

Guanxi,[11] based on personal connections, is an important factor of Chinese culture; it is not the same as the commonly used concept of relationships in Western cultures, but is an implication of the above-mentioned collectivism.

First, good *Guanxi* in certain situations, for instance between 2 countries during the Second World War, can affect other situations such as business connections. As Wei-Ping Wu states: "Good exchange within a *Guanxi* Network can be anything as long as it is of value to parties concerned, be it legal or illegal, corruptive or non-corruptive" (Wu 1994, p. 3). Hence, *Guanxi* cannot be limited to only some aspect of a relationship, but in any situation can affect all other situations. Second, Guanxi involves reciprocal obligations (Leung et al. 1993, p. 1). If a person has received a favor, he or she knows that he or she is obliged to return a favor when requested. Buying back favors or services can even mean a personal sacrifice. With favors you can also strengthen your *Guanxi*. While giving favors, one should consider the cost of the favor, the effective component, the probability of reciprocation of the favor from the receiver, and reaction from the social network of the persons involved (Bond & Hwang 1987, pp. 224–5). These 4 factors are important in order to reach the goal with the favor, and also in order to save the face of the receiver. Third, *Guanxi* not only involves favors between 2 persons, but also extends obligations to entire *Guanxi* networks (Leung et al. 1993, p. 1). If I do you a favor, you can pay it back by doing a favor for any one of the members of my social network if I order so.[12] Figure 5.1 illustrates the boundaries of obligation in A's *Guanxi* network. Through B, A is obliged to give to and also get favors from C and his *Guanxi* network, even if the networks of A and C do not overlap.

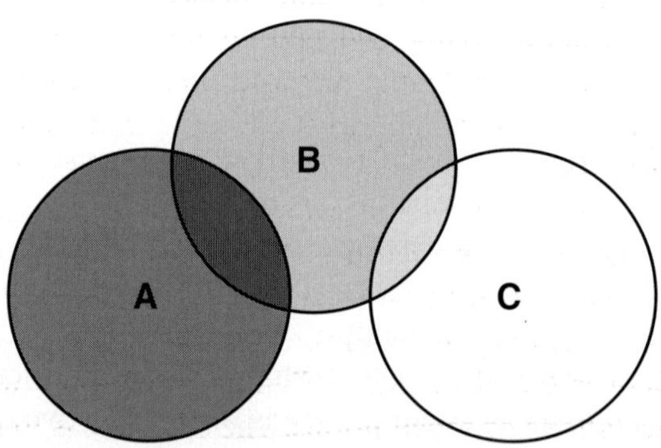

Fig. 5.1 *Guanxi* network boundaries

The fourth difference between *Guanxi* and relationships in the West involves the formation of *Guanxi*. Building up *Guanxi* includes building immediate trust through common connexions (i.e. friends, relatives and classmates). Thus, mutual trust in a *Guanxi* relationship can be established immediately through common connections without any exchanges between the actors, and the exchanges do not have to be institutionalized in order to gain trust in a relationship. This differs from a normal relationship because it exists between 2 parties without any episode between these parties. *Guanxi* exists in a latent form within one's own Guanxi network, and between the *Guanxi* networks of members of one's *Guanxi* network. Hence, *Guanxi* is a social resource.

Another way of strengthening *Guanxi* is through what is known as "face-work." The Chinese language and culture distinguishes two kinds of face: *lian* and *mianzi*. A person with *lian* has a good moral character. The *lian* face is more ascribed than achieved, while the *mianzi* face can be achieved by building up a personal reputation by the person's own efforts. Thus the *mianzi* face is more achieved than ascribed (Redding & Ng 1983, pp. 95–102; Harris & Yau 1994, p. 13). Building *Guanxi* at any level of human behavior involves both *lian* and *mianzi*. Face-work is an important way of asking and giving favors. They must be requested and rejected in a way that allows both partners to save face (Bond & Hwang 1987, pp. 225–6). For this reason a negative answer from a person in Chinese culture is less direct than a negative answer in a Western context. Face-work includes enhancing one's own face, enhancing the other's face, losing one's own face, hurting the other's face, saving one's own face and saving the other's face (Bond & Hwang 1987, pp. 245–9). The habit of giving gifts is connected to favors, and has its root in the history of tributes to the imperial court. By receiving a gift one becomes in debt to the donor of the gift, and similarly one can give a gift, so placing the receiver in debt. Gift-giving traditions are different in China than in Western countries (Hill & Romm 1994, pp. 68–86), and as a consequence have implications for consumer behavior.

Face-work through giving and getting favors in a *Guanxi* relationship does not need immediate "equal reciprocation" from the partners involved. A weaker member, for example, with a lower hierarchical status in Cardinal Relations in the *Guanxi* network, can pull *Guanxi* by, for instance, giving gifts to the stronger member. The stronger member is obliged to do the asked favor if he or she has accepted the gift. Both parties have gained benefits: the weaker the favor, and the stronger the *mianzi* face through the achieved reputation in the *Guanxi* network (Harris & Yau 1994, p. 12). Behavior in Chinese society is based on the individual's tendency to act according to external expectations or social norms. The objective is to maintain harmony in a group and maintain face. In Western culture a person's behavior is based more on individual, personal, and inner values (Bond & Hwang 1987, p. 231). This difference in behavior affects not only management and decision making in organizations, but also consumer behavior, as purchasing decisions are made with social acceptance in mind. However, it should be noted that collectivism does not mean a homogeneous society. Collectivism works within small social contexts like family, clan or *danwei*,[13] and the nation is constituted from these smaller units. The collective units of social harmony have traditionally been the family and clan, but society is changing, and collective groups are forming outside the family. Differences between the units or regions are large, and form a complicated society of regional heterogeneity. This heterogeneity is further reinforced by the extreme linguistic differences between the regions.

The national language: Putonghua

The official language of the PRC is Putonghua (also called Mandarin or standard Chinese), the dialect spoken in the northern parts of the country, mainly in Beijing. The written language is the same all over the PRC, but Mainland Chinese use simplified characters, while the traditional characters are used in Taiwan, Hong Kong and Macao. Most of the people in the PRC understand Putonghua because television and radio use it, but in many cases locals are not able to speak the language. Dialects are spoken, and these often do not cross ethnic boundaries–for example, Cantonese spoken in the Guangdong province may not be understood in the neighboring province, Guangxi. The dialect spoken in Tianjin, about 200 km from Beijing, is barely understood in Beijing. Shanghai has a language of its own.

Languages allow access to inner circles of regional societies. Depending on the dialect, you may be regarded as a local or an outsider. Even when Putonghua is understood, the local dialect is an advantage in marketing operations.

These cultural features, which form the underlying fabric of the society, are being modified by Marxist ideologies and the current rise of consumer culture.

Education

Traditionally, education has been highly appreciated in Chinese society. Illiteracy/semi-illiteracy decreased from over 3 million in 1964 to about 2 million in 1990 (*China Statistical Yearbook* 1995, p. 61). The latest illiteracy–semi-illiteracy figure, from the sample survey of 1996, is 18% of the population over 15 years of age (*China Statistical Yearbook* 1997, p. 77).

Nevertheless, the educational level is relatively low. One of the reasons is the turbulent time of the Great Cultural Revolution during the late 1960s and the 1970s, when some of the schools and universities were closed, and foreign-language education was abandoned. This has deprived a generation of education, and is handicapping the next generation, because of the lack of availability of skills such as foreign-language teaching.

Table 5.10 shows that the number of university students per 10 000 persons has increased every year since 1978, indicating improvement in higher educational levels. In 1995, 207 per 10 000 people had higher education, compared with 142 people per 10 000 in 1990 (*Guangming Daily* 1996). However, the student-teacher ratio–7.1–shows that there are more students per mentor in higher educational institutions. Nonetheless, this ratio is still low when compared to the same rate for the USA in 1990 (17:1) (*China*

Statistical Yearbook 1995, p. 805). Interestingly, primary and secondary schools have maintained and even improved their student–teacher ratio. The educational system is also changing as a part of the general reform movement, and tuition fees are increasing; for example, primary school fees per year may be as high as 10 000 yuan (about the annual salary of a university professor). Also, a number of private schools are flourishing in the well-developed cities such as Beijing, Shanghai and Guangzhou. Consequently, much of current household expenditure goes to educate children.

Table 5.10 Level of education, and related issues

Year	*University students per 10 000 persons*	*Student/teacher ratio–higher education*	*Student/teacher ratio–secondary school*	*Student/teacher ratio–primary school*
1978	8.90	–	–	–
1980	11.59	4.6	17.9	26.6
1985	16.09	5.0	17.2	24.9
1990	18.04	5.2	14.6	21.9
1993	21.4	6.5	14.7	22.4
1994	23.4	7.1	15.2	22.9
1995	24.0	7.2	15.2	22.9
1996	24.7	7.5	16.4	23.7

Source: China Statistical Yearbook (1995), China Statistical Publishing House, Beijing, p. 596; *China Statistical Yearbook* (1997), China Statistical Publishing House, Beijing, p. 646.

Gender issues

Table 5.11 shows the differences in gender ratios for the different age groups. There has been an abnormal increase in the number of males born, and if this trend continues it will have a significant impact on the gender ratio. This increase suggests the persistence of traditional values among the population. Sons are respected and regarded as social security for the parents. Even today most parents live in the households of their sons. However, the role and status of women are in flux. The image of the "ideal female" during the early years of Liberation was that of the austerely dressed socialist hero who played her equal part in the development of the New China: this is in stark contrast to the soft-skinned, fashionably dressed beauty in a well-furnished home currently appearing in printed advertisements (Hooper 1994, pp. 160–7). The freedom to express female beauty and femininity again has in some cases led well-off women to revert to the traditional roles of housewife and mistress, but there is also a strong emergence of professional women (*Marketing Guide Magazine* 1995). The percentage of female students at tertiary institutions has increased steadily, from 24% in 1978 to more than 36% in 1996 (*China Statistical Yearbook* 1997, p. 647). The same trend exists at the lower educational levels.

Table 5.11 Sex ratio by age group

Age	*Sex ratio (female = 100)*
0–14	111.15
15–19	105.71
20–24	100.95
25–34	101.51
35–49	104.64
50–64	104.13
65+	51.21
Total	**103.99**

Source: China Statistical Yearbook (1995), China Statistical Publishing House, Beijing, p. 62.

Health

Life expectancy is higher in China (68 years for males and 71 years for females)[14] than the average world figure. This shows that the general level of health is better on average than that for other countries in the world. Life expectancy is higher in China than life expectancy in Indonesia, the Philippines and Vietnam, about the same as in Thailand, and lower than in Malaysia and Singapore (*China Statistical Yearbook* 1995, p. 759). Health care has normally been handled at the work-unit level. For example, universities have their own pharmacies and health centers and even hospitals. Similarly, former state-owned factories have taken care of the health of their employees.

But this situation is undergoing change. The reforms of state-owned sectors have made state-owned units responsible for producing profit, and as a consequence many benefits, such as health care, have been cut. Further change in the consumption of health care products is expected in the future. Currently, health care comprises only 3% of consumption expenditure (see Table 5.16, below).

Here are some marketing implications of the contemporary Chinese culture:

- Face-work, through giving and receiving favors, has an impact on consumer behavior. A gift given in order to build up a relationship has to fit with the status of the person to whom the gift is given as well as to save the face of the donor. Hence, classy, expensive and prestigious gifts are exchanged among Chinese. Furthermore, clothing and choice of restaurant are considered to enhance one's status. Conspicuous consumption is a way to show off one's position in the network of one's social circle (Schütte & Vanier 1995, pp. 18–20). Reciprocal obligation implies that the receiver responds with a gift of the same monetary value.

- Despite the need for status, pragmatism and situation orientation have led Chinese consumers to search for practical, utility products (Schütte & Vanier 1995, p. 21). In Mainland China, the most popular gifts are the ones that can be eaten or drunk, contrary to the Western preference for a gift that leaves a memory of its giver. The combination of the need for utility and status explains the popularity of XO cognac as a gift in PRC, where its sales are the largest in the world.
- The collective nature of the society affects the degree of involvement in purchasing situations, particularly for products, like gifts, that are for social purposes and for which the degree of involvement is much higher. A product bought for social purposes is important because it signals the factors that give face for both receiver and giver. Such factors are price, brand name, prestige, and packaging (Schütte & Vanier 1995, pp. 22–3). The degree of involvement for products purchased for private use is low.
- Purchasing decisions are made by one social group (i.e. the family); most purchasing decisions are jointly made. Other reference groups that influence the decision are relatives, friends and colleagues (*Marketing Guide Magazine* 1995).
- The Chinese desire for harmony leads to two patterns in consumer behavior. First, Chinese are likely to be brand loyal, and second, they have a lower tendency toward risk taking than their Western counterparts (Schütte & Vanier 1995, pp. 31–4).
- *Guanxi* that is based on long-lasting relationships has a great impact on marketing efforts. Schütte points out three main implications (Schütte & Vanier 1995, p. 43). First, promotions need to be done at the retailer level in order to gain trust among customers. The concept of trust is a well-understood marketing tool among retailers in China (Polsa 1996, pp. 99–124). Second, the major information source among Chinese consumers is most probably the word-of-mouth channel. Third, trusting the salesperson is considered important, and this requires the selection of trustworthy and well-connected personnel.
- A good example of the drastic change in consumer habits that are dependent on political and ideological changes in Mainland China is the consumption of cosmetics. The production of cosmetics has a 2000-year history in China, and production of cosmetics in modern China started as early as the 1830s (*China Market* 1992, p. 11). However, during the period

of liberation (the 1950s and 1960s), cosmetics were considered "a remnant of capitalism" (Li 1992, p. 12). Despite the abandonment of cosmetics for almost 30 years, recent production has increased, from 200 million yuan in 1982 to 3 billion yuan in 1991 (Li 1992, p. 13).

- Among modern Chinese women, both the traditionalist and the independent professional, the demand for high-quality clothing and cosmetics is increasing. Similarly, convenient home commodities such as fast food, kitchen appliances, and electronic goods are in demand (*Marketing Guide Magazine* 1995).
- As the cost of education and health care increase, the larger portion of household income will go to these expenses, at the same time creating a market for education and health services.

Employment and consumer income

Table 5.12 shows that rural units other than enterprises provided a livelihood for most of the people until the reform policies were implemented in the late 1970s. In the rural areas the only possible employment before reforms were in state-owned and collective units. Since the 1980s there have been more alternatives for enterprise employment, because of ownership reform.

The first economic reforms started in rural areas, where township and village enterprises were established. Their share of the total employment has increased constantly. The other new forms of companies, both in rural and urban areas, have also increased their share in the employment market–but not significantly. Hence, we can argue that ownership reform has not yet been a solution for employment problems other than in the case of township and village enterprises. The reason for allowing the establishment of private and individual companies has been the desire to stimulate the economy and to provide self-created employment for the unemployed population (Xie 1991, pp. 459–87; Xiao 1993a, 1993b; Private Business Association 1993, pp. 2–6).

As the state-owned sector still plays a major role in urban employment, the government has made a plan to reinforce government business by focusing its policies on the improvement of state-owned companies. This 5-year plan was put into effect in 1995, and will mainly benefit the 1000 largest state companies that hold the majority of state capital. Their management systems will be improved, and operations changed to meet the needs of the market and the market economy.

The small state-owned companies are allowed to go bankrupt, and in case of malfunction the government will allow mergers and acquisitions. The slogan is: "Grasp the biggest, release the small." This policy has had an effect on the retailing and wholesaling business, because the small state-owned companies control this area, and also provide the largest portion of employment (see Table 5.12).

Table 5.12 Employment by (a) urban and (b) rural enterprises and state-owned units

(a)

Year	*Total*	*Urban state-owned units*	*Urban collective units*	*Urban foreign-funded units*	*Urban: other ownership*[a]	*Urban: private*[b]	*Urban: individual*
1952	20 729	8%	< 1%	0	0	0	4%
1962	25 910	13%	4%	0	0	0	1%
1970	34 432	14%	4%	0	0	0	< 1%
1980	42 361	19%	6%	0	0	0	< 1%
1985	49 873	18%	7%	< 1%	< 1%	0	1%
1987	52 783	18%	7%	< 1%	< 1%	0	1%
1990	56 740	18%	6%	< 1%	< 1%	< 1%	1%
1991	58 360	18%	6%	< 1%	< 1%	< 1%	1%
1992	59 432	18%	6%	< 1%	< 1%	< 1%	1%
1993	60 220	18%	6%	< 1%	< 1%	< 1%	1%
1994	61 470	18%	5%	1%	< 1%	< 1%	2%
1995	67 947	17%	5%	1%	1%	1%	2%
1996	68 850	16%	4%	1%	1%	1%	2%

(b)

Year	*Total*	*Rural: Township and village enterprises*	*Rural private*	*Rural individual*	*Rural other*
1952	20 729	0	0	0	88%
1962	25 910	0	0	0	82%
1970	34 432	0	0	0	82%
1980	42 361	7%	0	0	68%
1985	49 873	14%	0	0	60%
1987	52 783	17%	0	0	57%
1990	56 740	16%	< 1%	< 1%	55%
1991	58 360	16%	< 1%	< 1%	54%
1992	59 432	18%	< 1%	< 1%	53%
1993	60 220	20%	< 1%	< 1%	49%
1994	61 470	20%	< 1%	< 1%	48%
1995	67 947	26%	1%	6%	48%
1996	68 850	28%	1%	7%	46%

Notes:
[a] Includes joint-owned and shareholding economic units.
[b] The difference between private and individual entrepreneurship is in the number of employees. If the total number of employed personnel is less than 8 persons, the company is an individual enterprise; if there are more than 8 outside personnel, the company is called "private" (Xie 1991, pp. 456–9).

Source: China Statistical Yearbook (1995), China Statistical Publishing House, Beijing, pp. 84–5; *China Statistical Yearbook* (1997), China Statistical Publishing House, Beijing, pp. 96–7.

Furthermore, comparison of the average income in different enterprises shows that total average annual salary per worker is higher in other ownership groups than in the traditional state-owned and collective units (see Table 5.13). In addition, the annual salary index has increased over time. This shows that, although the government sector employs the majority of the population, non-government employees have higher purchasing power. As the share of the non-government sector is increasing, it is this population, employed by the non-government enterprises, that will, in the future, consist of the most powerful consumers.

Not shown in the official statistics are the material benefits, other than salary, offered by state-owned enterprises. Such benefits can be holidays, clothes, and dinners. Despite the increasing purchasing power of non-government employees, the employees and managers of the state enterprises are also still an important segment for marketing.

Even if the statistics for rural collectives shows the lowest general income in Table 5.13, their importance as consumers should not be underestimated. Some rural villages are extremely rich, partly because ownership reform started in the countryside. Many farmers make their living in production or other kinds of businesses. The possibility of making money through other sources than cultivating land has given the rural population an opportunity to become a prosperous consumer group.

Unemployment

Table 5.14 shows the number of officially registered unemployed persons in the labor force. Although the rate of unemployment is around 5%, the developed parts of the country have a lower level of unemployment than inland provinces, where average unemployment is 6.7%. Highly developed areas such as Beijing, Shanghai, and Guangdong, as well as the moderately developed central province Jingxi, have severe unemployment problems. These figures lead us to conclude that unemployment is an urban problem, and that it is associated with economic development. Future unemployment figures will be further affected by the reforms of state-owned enterprises, when the bankruptcy of smaller unprofitable units may be allowed. Statistics do not tell the whole story of the unemployment situation, because there is a large population of unregistered persons, some of who establish businesses or make their living in other entrepreneurial ways.

Socio-economic classes

In a country like Mainland China, with an economy and ideology in transition and living standards changing rapidly, it is difficult, even impossible, to make an accurate socio-economic classification of the population. The rural and urban populations differ in their purchasing power and consumption habits. Throughout history there has been a huge contrast between the

Table 5.13 (a) Total wage indices for staff and workers, and (b) average annual salary per worker

(a)

Year	*Total average annual salary per worker (yuan)*	*State-owned units*	*Urban collective units*	*Other ownership units*
1952	–	–	–	–
1962	–	–	–	–
1970	615[a]	644	506	–
1980	762	803	623	–
1985	1 148	1 213	967	1 436
1987	1 459	1 546	1 207	1 879
1990	2 140	2 284	1 681	2 987
1991	2 340	2 477	1 866	3 468
1992	2 711	2 878	2 109	3 966
1993	3 371	3 532	2 592	4 966
1994	4 538	4 797	3 245	6 303
1995	5 500	5 625	3 931	7 463
1996	6 210	6 280	4 302	8 261

Note:
[a] Year: 1978.

(b)

Year	*Total–Index (preceding year = 100)*	*State-owned units*	*Urban collective units*	*Other ownership units*
1952	120.3	114.6	155.7	–
1962	90.6	87.5	111.2	–
1970	103.6	105.5	95.3	–
1980	119.4	118.6	123.3	–
1985	122.0	121.6	123.0	164.1
1987	113.3	113.3	112.8	149.7
1990	112.7	113.4	108.7	135.8
1991	112.6	111.7	113.4	153.1
1992	118.5	119.1	112.8	149.9
1993	124.8	123.4	114.4	240.2
1994	135.4	135.8	120.4	179.7
1995	121.7	117.4	N/A	N/A
1996	112.1	111.7	N/A	N/A

Source: China Statistical Yearbook (1995), China Statistical Publishing House, Beijing, pp. 109, 113; *China Statistical Yearbook* (1997), China Statistical Publishing House, Beijing, pp. 121, 123.

Table 5.14 Unemployment figures for 1994

Provinces, municipalities, and autonomous regions	*Total registered (10 000 persons)*	*Unemployed (10 000 persons)*	*% unemployed in relation to total registered persons*
National	**5 929.2**	**318.3**	**5.3**
Coastal areas			
Beijing	2.8	7.9	282.1
Tianjin	153.2	7.3	4.8
Hebei	379.4	9.4	2.5
Liaoning	1 245.1	38.7	3.1
Shanghai	31.0	6.2	20.0
Jiangsu	356.8	16.3	4.6
Zhejiang	192.0	7.6	4.0
Fujian	132.9	8.3	6.2
Shangdong	447.2	13.2	2.9
Guangdong	264.3	51.4	19.4
Hainan	34.3	2.5	7.3
Guangxi	71.4	5.1	7.1
Total	**3 310.4**	**173.9**	**5.3**
Central areas			
Inner Mongolia	68.6	5.9	8.6
Shanxi	184.4	9.9	5.4
Jilin	270.3	9.8	3.6
Heilongjiang	409.1	33.2	8.1
Anhui	174.1	6.0	3.4
Jiangxi	40.0	6.2	15.5
Henan	514.6	13.7	2.7
Hubei	203.7	9.3	4.6
Hunan	82.4	5.8	7.0
Total	**1 947.2**	**99.8**	**5.1**
Inland areas			
Sichuan	289.7	21.4	7.4
Guizhou	19.8	1.8	9.1
Yunnan	68.3	5.0	7.3
Tibet[a]	–	–	–
Shaanxi	101.1	5.0	4.9
Gansu	47.8	1.9	4.0
Qinghai	26.0	1.5	5.8
Ningxia	9.2	0.3	3.3
Xinjiang	109.9	8.1	7.4
Total	**671.8**	**45**	**6.7**

Note:
[a] No data available

Source: China Statistical Yearbook (1995), China Statistical Publishing House, Beijing, p. 128.

peasants and the city population, to the extent that some of the dynasties have risen and fallen when farmers rebelled against wealthy urban residents. According to nationwide research with 3400 respondents, conducted by Gallup China Ltd, the rural and urban segments also differ in their consumption behavior. For instance, rural consumers buy more domestic products and have less trust in advertising than their urban counterparts (Li & Gallup 1995, p. 20). Table 5.15 shows the recent average annual income differences between the urban and rural populations. Currently, the expected annual growth rate of rural income is 5%, and for urban income the figure is 8%, hence the income difference will persist (*Marketing Guide Magazine* 1995).

For the purposes of economic classification, China can be divided into rural and urban segments. Both classes can be further divided into smaller groups according to their income in different geographical areas and different occupations. For example, in Guangdong rural people are much richer than urban citizens. However, at the moment large numbers of rural people work and make their living in urban areas while bringing their income to their villages. This bridge between urban and rural population reflects both urban tastes and rural consumer habits.

Table 5.15 Annual per-capita net income in rural and urban areas (yuan)

Area	*1978*	*1980*	*1985*	*1990*	*1993*	*1994*	*1995*	*1996*
Rural	133.6	191.3	397.6	686.3	921.6	1 221.0	1 577.7	1 926.1
Urban	316	439	685	1 387	2 337	3 179	3 893	4 377

Source: China Statistical Yearbook (1995), China Statistical Publishing House, Beijing, p. 257; *China Statistical Yearbook* (1997), China Statistical Publishing House, Beijing, p. 291.

The new economic class that has appeared in the PRC since the early 1980s is the "new rich." This class began to emerge when private and individual businesses were first allowed. Deng Xiaoping's policies allowed some people and some areas to become rich ahead of the others, and consequently a group of "new rich" was born (Wentao 1994, pp. 4–6; Li & Gallup 1995, p. 21).

Today members of this group are located mainly in the coastal areas of the country, and are not only urban dwellers. Many of the "new rich" are private entrepreneurs, both in the countryside and in the cities. Most of these rich people have minimum education, some of them being the youth of the Great Cultural Revolution, a period of some 10 years during which schools and universities were either closed or in turmoil.[15] Nevertheless, their purchasing power is strong.

The other class of people based more on social classification than on economic specification is the "white-collar" class. Its members live in metropolitan areas, have higher incomes, are young, and obtain higher education.

They are often affected by foreign influences, having been educated abroad and/or working in enterprises funded by foreign investment. In many cases they are government and military leaders and/or their offspring.

The nature of the socio-economic structure of China has several marketing implications:

- The "new rich" spend freely. To them money does not matter, and they like to display their wealth with visible goods such as clothing, motor vehicles, and personal adornments (Hooper 1994, p. 165). Also, they have the habit of spending enormous amounts of money on restaurants and karaoke entertainment.
- The consumption of the "white-collar" class is influenced by Western tastes. As with the "new rich," money does not matter for this group. These young people accept foreign fashion and prefer imported goods, being less traditional in their consumption habits than the "new rich." High-grade fashion clothes, new-style electronic products, famous-brand cosmetics, and leisure and sports goods are a significant component of their purchases. (*Marketing Guide Magazine* 1995).
- Another important group of customers for consumer goods is that of the managers charged with decisions concerning material incentives other than money for the workers of state-owned companies.

Consumption patterns

Currently, the majority of expenditure is still allocated to the daily necessities, as Table 5.16 shows. The amount of household income spent on food in the most developed cities in China, Beijing, Shanghai, Guangzhou, and Shenzhen (SEZs), has gone down to 40%, and even to 32% in Shenzhen, while it is still as high as 50% in smaller cities. Clothing, health care, leisure activities, education, and housing expenses require about the same amount of the total household income in the 4 developed metropolitan areas as in the other parts of the PRC. Transportation and communications, however, are either more expensive or important in urban than in rural areas. If other living expenditures and household facilities are combined, as in Table 5.16, they equal almost the same portion of income expenditure as other necessities for living in the 4 developed cities. We can conclude that the 10% lower proportion on food expenditure in Beijing, Shanghai, Guangzhou and Shenzhen equals the amount that is spent on personal consumption in these cities (see Table 5.17). This indicates not only higher income in these cities, but also changing consumption habits. The traditional importance of eating in Chinese culture may be declining, while other areas may be gaining popularity–examples are karaoke bars, cosmetics, traveling, pets, and movies in the cities that are more exposed to outside influences.

Table 5.16 Proportion of living expenditure on different goods, 1994 and 1996 (yuan)

Goods	*Urban households*		*Rural households*	
	1994	*1996*	*1994*	*1996*
Total	**2 851.34**	**3 919.47**	**1 016.81**	**1 572.08**
Food	50%	49%	59%	56%
Clothing	14%	13%	7%	
Household facilities	9%	8%	5%	5%
Health care	3%	4%	3%	4%
Transportation and communications	5%	5%	2%	3%
Leisure time, Education	9%	10%	7%	8%
Residence	7%	8%	14%	14%
Other	3%	3%	3%	3%

Source: China Statistical Yearbook (1995), China Statistical Publishing House, Beijing, pp. 267–76, 283; *China Statistical Yearbook* (1997), China Statistical Publishing House, Beijing, pp. 267–76, 301–7, 317.

Table 5.17 Proportion of living expenditure on different goods in Beijing, Shanghai, Guangzhou and Shenzhen, 1995

Goods	*Beijing*	*Shanghai*	*Guangzhou*	*Shenzhen*
Total monthly income (yuan)	1 548	1 873	2 113	3 679
Food	43%	40%	40%	32%
Clothing	10%	7%	7%	8%
Health care, Leisure, Education	9%	9%	10%	10%
Transportation and communications	5%	6%	6%	7%
Residence	8%	9%	13%	12%
Other living necessities	12%	12%	12%	13%
Personal consumption	13%	17%	12%	18%

Source: China Business (1996), "How about Chinese Life? A Survey Report of Family Consumption in Beijing, Shanghai, Guangzhou and Shenzhen", 1 February (in Chinese).

Savings

Income figures and household expenditures do not give a complete view of the purchasing power of Chinese people: according to Asian Development Bank (1996) statistics, the saving ratio of Mainland Chinese is the highest in the world. Thirty-five per cent of Chinese household income goes into savings. At the same time, consumption on credit is very low, so that the potential for the credit-card market is also very low (*Marketing Guide Magazine* 1995). Table 5.18 shows that savings have increased dramatically since the

.arly 1980s. Urban households are saving almost 60 times as much, and rural households over 40 times as much. Per-capita savings-deposit balances show a similar increase. That means that the increase in income has not diminished the savings ratio.

Table 5.18 Savings-deposit balance in urban and rural households

Year	*Savings-deposit balance per capita (yuan)*	*Urban households (100 000 000 yuan)*	*Rural households (100 000 000 yuan)*
1952	–	8.6	–
1962	–	31.4	9.7
1978	22	154.9	55.7
1980	40	282.5	117.0
1985	153	1 057.8	564.8
1990	615	5 192.6	1 841.6
1991	–	6 790.9	2 319.4
1992	–	8 678.1	2 867.3
1993	1 283	11 627.3	3 576.2
1994	1 795	16 702.8	4 816.0
1995	2 449	23 446.7	6 195.6
1996	3 164	30 850.2	7 670.7

Source: China Statistical Yearbook (1995), China Statistical Publishing House, Beijing, pp. 257, 259; *China Statistical Yearbook* (1997), China Statistical Publishing House, Beijing, pp. 291, 293.

The single-child market

The one-child policy has many implications for consumer habits in Mainland China. The possibility of having only one child makes that child a very special treasure for the family. He or she becomes the "Little Emperor." Parents are willing and able to spend a great portion of their income on the child's material welfare. The investment is put into the child's nutrition, health, education, and leisure activities (*Marketing Guide Magazine* 1995). Toy-industry data emphasize this trend:

- sales of toys are growing at 20% per year
- spending on toys will remain a priority in household budgets
- Taiwanese and Hong Kong investors plan to build a "toy kingdom" in Fujian province. One investor is setting up a 6000 m^2 toy store in Guangzhou, and Hong Kong Toys Center has plans to double the number of its retail outlets to 42 (Ling 1994, p. 19).

Housing

In the past, housing was provided by government–that is, by the working unit a person belonged to. The establishment of private enterprises and foreign-funded companies has changed this tradition, and the need has emerged for types of housing facilities other than those provided by the government. Furthermore, the housing reform of 1994 encouraged residents to purchase apartments that used to be part of the property of the working unit. Statistics in Table 5.19 for the 4 main cities, Beijing, Shanghai, Guangzhou and Shenzhen, show that the majority of the houses are still provided by the working unit. In all cities except Shenzhen, one-fifth of all houses are rented. The housing reform has been best executed in Shenzhen, where as many as 40% of the houses have been purchased from the unit.

Table 5.19 Origin of house ownership in Beijing, Shanghai, Guangzhou and Shenzhen, 1995

City	*Allocation by working unit*	*Rent*	*Commercial houses*	*Buying from the working unit*	*Heritage from ancestors*	*Other*
Beijing	55%	20%	3%	6%	5%	11%
Shanghai	37%	26%	4%	5%	11%	17%
Guangzhou	36%	22%	3%	15%	12%	12%
Shenzhen	34%	5%	10%	40%	2%	9%

Source: China Business Times (1996), "Income From South to North, A Survey Comparing Family Income in Beijing, Shanghai, Guangzhou and Shenzhen", 8 February (in Chinese).

Per-capita living space in rural areas is more than double that for the urban areas. Table 5.20 shows that there has been no significant change over time in this ratio, but the size of both urban and rural houses has increased. This tendency is confirmed when the unit used is numbers of rooms per household. In rural areas there are more rooms, as well as more people per household, than in the major cities (see Table 5.21). Nevertheless, the average number of rooms per person is still higher in rural areas than it is in the most developed cities.

Table 5.20 Per-capita living floor space in rural and urban houses

Area	*1978 (m^2)*	*1980 (m^2)*	*1985 (m^2)*	*1990 (m^2)*	*1993 (m^2)*	*1994 (m^2)*	*1995 (m^2)*	*1996 (m^2)*
Rural	8.1	9.4	14.7	17.8	20.7	20.2	21.0	21.7
Urban	3.6	3.9	5.2	6.7	7.5	7.8	8.1	8.5

Source: China Statistical Yearbook (1995), China Statistical Publishing House, Beijing, p. 257; *China Statistical Yearbook* (1995), China Statistical Publishing House, Beijing, p. 291.

Table 5.21 Average number of rooms in a household

City/area	*Average number of permanent residents in a household*	*Average number of rooms*	*Average number of rooms per person*
Beijing	3.41	2.27	0.67
Shanghai	3.28	1.89	0.58
Guangzhou	3.56	2.39	0.67
Shenzhen	3.51	2.89	0.82
Rural areas	4.54	5.91	1.30

Sources: China Statistical Yearbook (1995), China Statistical Publishing House, Beijing; *China Business* (1996), "How about Chinese Life? A Survey Report of Family Consumption in Beijing, Shanghai, Guangzhou and Shenzhen", February 1 (in Chinese).

The household's bundle of goods

The level of household equipment varies between rural and urban households, as shown in Table 5.22. There is still potential to sell such necessities as washing machines and refrigerators to rural residents, as well as leisure goods such as color televisions and cameras. In the future there will be high demand by urban households for goods such as air conditioners, stereos, motor cycles, telephones, and cameras (*Marketing Guide Magazine* 1995). As shown in Table 5.22, there is an increasing demand for microwave ovens and stereos in highly developed cities such as Beijing and Shenzhen. Fourteen per cent of households in Beijing and Shenzhen intend to buy a personal computer within 1 or 2 years (*China Business* 1996).

Table 5.22 Coverage rate of some household durables in urban and rural households

Consumer durable	*Coverage rate in urban household (%)*	*Coverage rate in rural household (%)*	*Coverage rate in Beijing (%)*	*Coverage rate in Shenzhen (%)*
Washing machine	86.36	13.82	93	92
Refrigerator	56.68	3.05	97	94
Color TV	79.46	10.86	99	97
Camera	26.48	0.99	–	–

Source: China Business (1996), "How about Chinese Life? A Survey Report of Family Consumption in Beijing, Shanghai, Guangzhou and Shenzhen", 1 February (in Chinese).

There are some unique aspects in the consumption habits of rural consumers. Although there is a potential market for household goods such as TV sets, motor cycles and washing machines, it is important to note that only one brand will gain popular acceptance. Villagers are extremely consistent in their habits, and tend to purchase the same product with the same brand as their neighbors. This kind of behavior is typical for rural areas, and is in keeping with the collective culture and people's desire to be socially accepted.

Nutrition and eating habits

Eating is an important happening in Chinese culture. A common greeting is, "Have you eaten?", and popular gifts are edible ones. Over the years eating habits have changed, and vegetables are a smaller part of the diet today. Table 5.23 shows the change during the last 10 years. Consumption of grain and fresh vegetables has decreased in both urban and rural areas. The diet of rural residents contains more grain but less meat than the diet of urban people.

Table 5.23 Per-capita consumption of food in urban and rural households (kg)

Item	*1985 (kg)*	*1990 (kg)*	*1991 (kg)*	*1992 (kg)*	*1993 (kg)*	*1994 (kg)*	*1995 (kg)*	*1996 (kg)*
Urban								
Grain	135	131	128	111	98	102	97	95
Fresh vegetables	144	139	132	125	121	121	116	119
Meat	19	22	22	21	21	20	19	20
Poultry	3	3	4	5	4	4	4	4
Fish	7	8	8	8	8	9	9	9
Sugar	3	2	2	2	2	2	2	2
Rural								
Grain	257	262		250	266	261	259	259
Fresh vegetables	131	134		129	107	108	105	106
Meat	11	11		12	12	11	11	13
Poultry	1	1		1	2	2	2	2
Fish	2	2		2	2	3	3	3
Sugar	1	1		2	1	1	1	1

Source: China Statistical Yearbook (1995), China Statistical Publishing House, Beijing, pp. 263, 287; *China Statistical Yearbook* (1997), China Statistical Publishing House, Beijing, pp. 295, 321.

Leisure activities

The leisure time of Mainland Chinese has increased steadily. Some years ago it was not unusual for Chinese to work 7 days per week. As expected, urban residents have more leisure time than farmers, who are dependent on their fields. Since May 1 1995, a 5-day working week has been implemented in the PRC. This reform will gradually affect leisure activities and, consequently, consumption patterns.

Until recently the difficulty of traveling has led affluent people to spend their income on leisure activities other than tourism. Expenditure in restaurants increased by 34% during the first 3 quarters of 1994 (*China Business Times* 1996). Karaoke bars and discos (for the younger population) are popular activities, as is window shopping. During the weekends, shoppers crowd the marketplaces and shopping centers. It is therefore important to create a pleasant atmosphere for socialization in shopping places, and the possibility for interaction between potential consumers and salespersons (Schütte & Vanier 1995, p. 45). This is the time when relations between customers, retailers, and sales representatives can be built and strengthened in a culturally acceptable way.

Though traveling abroad is not yet a common activity, internal travel is popular. Some working units sponsor holiday travel or have it as a bonus for good workers. Similarly, companies have common traveling activities during the holidays for all their employees. However, travel within China is difficult because most of the time it involves long-distance trains and buses rather than the convenience of airlines. Nonetheless, tourism and travel both within China and externally, and related consumer goods, have a huge market potential, particularly as living standards increase and latent demand is released.

Here are the marketing implications, based on the analysis of consumption patterns:

- The high savings ratio creates a market for consumer investment and banking
- Expenditure on child-care goods is increasing in the Chinese household.
- Rural households are larger compared with even the most developed cities when both number of persons and space are considered. Consequently, the requirements of rural households differ from those of urban households.
- Eating is still an important event in a Chinese family. More Western dishes and restaurants (e.g. McDonald's and Kentucky Fried Chicken) have entered the Chinese markets, and are modifying eating habits.
- Eating out is one of the most popular leisure activities.
- The increase in leisure time has increased the market potential of services such as golf courses, skating areas and skiing resorts.
- Travel and tourism provide immense opportunities. Far-sighted tourist-seeking nations should enter the market now to build awareness and image, and to be ready to seize the market when latent demand is released.
- Future high-demand markets are likely to be in the consumer durables field. As many affluent households already have TV sets, videos, washing machines and air conditioning, the high demand has turned to computers, automobiles and cellular phones.
- In future, Chinese consumers will invest in real estate, particularly as liberalization continues.
- Demand for automobiles will decrease in urban areas while increasing in rural areas. In many larger cities in China, the traffic is almost impossible to negotiate, and hence motor vehicles are a less attractive means of transportation. In the rural areas, however, vehicles are more or less a necessity for transportation and work.

The macromarketing mix

Branding

The consumer goods market in the PRC can be divided into three main areas: imported luxury brands, imported middle-class brands and locally made brands (*Economist* 1994, pp. 63–4). Foreign brands have a natural competitive advantage because foreign products are highly appreciated and seen as good quality (Hooper 1994, p. 169; d'Astous et al. 1995, pp. 33–8). This belief is so strong that some consumers do not buy products manufactured by Sino-foreign joint ventures, but prefer the equivalent more expensive imported products.[16] This preference for foreign products is typical of many economies with a similar level of development to the PRC (Ger 1995, pp. 11–17). We could predict that, in the context of Chinese culture (the history of isolation, high respect for its own capacity and ethnocentrism), the change to preference for domestic products may be more rapid than in other developing economies. Foreign companies are already using China and Chinese cultural heritage in their promotion. An example is the Chinese brand name for Revlon, which is linked to a famous Chinese poem of love between a Tang Dynasty king and one of the most beautiful women in Chinese history (Schütte & Vanier 1995, p. 29). Similarly, Procter & Gamble and Unilever use local detergent brand names to build up their position (*Economist* 1994).

In the Chinese context, corporate image is as important as brand development. Company image, however, is not based on the same criteria as in the West. *Asian Business* annually selects a company of the year using the following criteria: quality of management, quality of products/services, contribution to the economy, size and type of charitable donations and establishment of educational foundations, concern shown for the environment, the image projected of being honest, ethical and a considerate employer, and potential for growth (Schütte & Vanier 1995, pp. 30–1). It is not only the increased wealth of shareholders that is important, but also the extent of social activity and responsibility. Similar attitudes are seen in Mainland China. For example, a private businessperson concerned about the educational level of private entrepreneurs used a part of the profits of his company in supporting teachers to develop training programs for private businesses. This may be explained by *Guanxi,* which requires good relations in any social interaction to be shared and transferred for the benefit of other social relationships.

Packaging

Packaging is a very important signal of the product quality for Chinese consumers. In addition to price and quality, packaging was found to be one of the key criteria for choice of products among retailers (Polsa 1996, pp. 96–8). Not until very recently have Mainland Chinese consumers started to trust the quality of products, and the habit of opening packages in supermarkets has diminished. However, even today Chinese consumers have, when purchasing consumer durables, a tendency to open the package and test the product in the shop. This is a common habit even if a warranty is provided for the product.

According to Yan (1994, pp. 66–74), Chinese consumers like to have complete information about a product and through this information understanding and a feeling of security are gained. This desire is based on the importance in Chinese culture of the maintenance of harmony, and the need to avoid fake and low-quality products (Chengguang 1994). The search for harmony creates post-purchase behavior that is characterized by conflict avoidance and reluctance to express dissatisfaction (Schütte & Vanier 1995, pp. 46–50). Chinese consumers test the product carefully beforehand rather than coming afterwards to claim their rights. Despite this, in the PRC the number of complaints to the China Consumer Association increased by 41% between 1993 and 1994 (Zhiping 1994).

Price

Pricing is a new form of marketing strategy in the PRC among domestic producers. For example, in the field of food production pricing was released from state control in 1992. Traditionally, Chinese consumers are price sensitive, and used to bargaining while they shop. In the open marketplaces for food and vegetables, and in the more recently established clothing markets, bargaining is a common habit, a way of shopping. A smart consumer gets the price to a suitable level, and his or her bargaining is even appreciated by the seller. However, in the state-owned shops the prices have always been fixed, and no bargaining is possible. Currently, consumers assume that state-owned stores are cheaper than the private ones. This assumption is true, because many private sellers allow a margin for bargaining in their prices.

Where consumer durables and branded products are concerned, price is not an important issue any more. The segment that can afford these products is not price sensitive, but spends more money on good-quality brands rather than less conspicuous products, although there is some evidence that discount brands are having an impact in these more affluent markets (*China Economic Review* 1994, p. 16).

Distribution

The Chinese distribution system is characterized by its fragmented structure. In contrast to the former planned-economy system, there are now, at least in principle, no restrictions concerning how a product is distributed. Since the early 1980s, a large number of retailers and wholesalers have emerged in the distribution market. At the moment private business is encouraged by the government, and is growing rapidly. However, the planned distribution system has not been abolished, but remains as a base structure for the entire distribution system.

Wholesaling and retailing outlets can be categorized according to their ownership and function as:

- state-owned retailers and wholesalers
- collective retailers and wholesalers
- private retailers and wholesalers

This classification helps to divide the players into different groups, and distinguish their relative differences, strengths and weaknesses. Table 5.24 shows the importance of the respective subnetworks of state-owned, collective, and private wholesalers and retailers. The number of outlets at both the retailer and wholesaler levels are largest in the private sector, even though that sector covers only a fraction of the total sales volume of domestic trade. Hence, private outlets are small, and function as convenient stalls for the nearby residents. The state-owned sector forms the most important part of the retailing and wholesaling sector.

Table 5.24 State-owned, collective, and private retailers and wholesalers, 1994, 1996

	State-owned		*Collective*		*Private*		*Foreign funded*		*Other*	
Business type	*1994*	*1996*	*1994*	*1996*	*1994*	*1996*	*1994*	*1996*	*1994*	*1996*
Wholesalers										
Number of outlets—% of total	25%	20%	27%	23%	47%	55%	< 1%	< 1%	1%	1%
Retailers										
Number of outlets—% of total	2%	2%	6%	5%	91%	93%	< 1%	< 1%	1%	< 1%
Value of retailer sales—% of total	32%	27%	21%	19%	28%	32%	–	–	19%	22%
Value of wholesaler and retailer sales—% of total	67%	64%	28%	27%	0.5%	2%	0.5%	1%	4%	7%

Source: China Statistical Yearbook (1995), China Statistical Publishing House, Beijing, pp. 511, 522, 594; *China Statistical Yearbook* (1997), China Statistical Publishing House, Beijing, pp. 556, 565, 569.

Private retailers are small in size, compared to collective and state-owned retailers. Usually they are family businesses, and can be grouped as individual businesses because they do not employ more than 8 persons. The number of private retailers and wholesalers is great, but their importance is less than the number of outlets would indicate, since their size is small. State-owned retailers are large outlets or department stores. They tend to be competitive because of their resources and location. Collective retailers and wholesalers are medium in size, compared with the small private and the large state-owned retailers. The largest and most powerful wholesalers are the former second-level state-owned wholesalers.

The retailers argue that private retailers and private businesses in general are more flexible in their way of doing business and in reacting to fashion and consumer tastes. State-owned retailers, in contrast, have the reputation of being trustworthy, but bureaucratic and inflexible. Some complain about the bureaucratic system of the state-owned companies' contracts and plans, but at the same time appreciate their reliability. It is natural that the newcomers in the market (those established after the 1979 reform policies), who are mainly private businesses, cannot gain the trust of consumers as easily as the old ones that have a long history. As the state-owned enterprises learn the new system of market forces they will probably change their policy to become more flexible and provide a wider choice of products.

The old state-owned businesses have a better knowledge of business and the market. However, the market is changing, and the old rules do not apply. The *Guanxi* of the state-owned businesses is a major asset. Old friends from production units, transportation and government offices provide valuable resources to state-owned retailers and wholesalers. Private businesspeople usually need to build up their relations from scratch. However, some government officials have established private businesses, and consequently enjoy the relations from their former working places.

Private companies tend to differ from state enterprises in terms of the education of employees and owners of the company. Traditionally, private businesspeople were formerly unemployed people, or farmers with no education. This also is changing as many university students, despite their opportunities for secure government employment, are starting private businesses. Nonetheless, in general, the most educated people in retailing business are employed by the state-owned outlets.

As a result of the issues discussed above, the state-owned distribution channels seem to be the most powerful at present. This is particularly the case in the rural interior. In the lucrative markets such as Guangdong, Shanghai and Beijing, state-owned firms have taken over a significant part of the distribution. Collectives have taken over markets, and some, managed by Hong Kong mother companies, have been successfully established in the PRC. At present it might be wise to use the well-established powerful state-owned channels, but we should also recognize the potential of the growing private and collective businesses in retailing and wholesaling. Resources that currently secure power for state-owned businesses could also be available for other businesses in the near future. For example, access to transportation and financing is currently a problem for new businesses, but in the future they may also develop relations with these institutions and gain resources.

Transportation is a problem in most parts of the PRC. The central government policy has been favorable for establishing infrastructure in the eastern parts of the country, specially in the SEZs. Those parts of the country that do not receive special treatment struggle with inadequate transportation and telecommunications. This situation increases the state owned businesses' power, because their *Guanxi* gives them access to scarce infrastructure. To overcome these difficulties of transportation and warehousing, enterprises use railroads for long-distance transportation and trucks for local transportation, or establish their own transportation systems. They also use distributors that have traditionally taken care of that type of product line, in order to minimize risks with storage (Reinganum & Helsell 1994). This favors state-owned distribution networks because of their relationship with transportation officials, and their knowledge of traditional distribution and warehousing.

Retailing

In China today, the following retailing outlets exist:

1 *Grocery stores:* these are located in residential areas, and sell packaged food products and other household supplies (Zhou 1993).
2 *Department stores:* these have a food stuff department selling packaged food products, and are officially called "General Retail Enterprises" (Hong 1990, p. 376).
3 *Chain stores:* this means several outlets under the same organization. They have standardized management, and suppliers sell packaged food products and household supplies (*China Daily* 1993; Zhou 1993).
4 *Supermarkets:* the first opened in 1981 in Guangzhou and Beijing (Ho & Lo 1987, p. 34).
5 *Open marketplaces:* individuals (farmers) selling fresh food products (Vernon-Wortzel & Wortzel 1987, pp. 56–63).
6 *Speciality stores for one brand:* for example, Li-Ning stores.

Large grocery stores, department stores, chain stores and supermarkets are mainly either government owned or foreign investments. The reform in the former second-level wholesaler units emphasized building up a chain-store system at the retailer level. The network of former third-level wholesaling outlets in city districts provides good infrastructure for this. Some of the collective wholesaling and retailing organizations function very much like a chain store system, but do not officially carry this status. Supermarkets are a popular new retailing form in the PRC. Even small private sellers have built up small, self-service outlets that they call supermarkets. In general, all private outlets are small neighborhood convenience stores.

One popular way of distributing consumer goods is through a franchising agreement, as exemplified by Li-Ning sportswear (Bai 1996), as well as some foreign products (Ho & Leigh 1994). Distribution in any market is never static, but in a market like the PRC the change is even more evident, as a result of the changing economic policies and the growing economy. Actors emerge and disappear, new rules transform the functions of distribution, the buying power of consumers changes, and the value system of the reforming economy affects trade.

These are the implications for distribution management:

- A general rule in the distribution of consumer goods is to maintain contacts at all levels of the distribution channel. Mars candies and Canpotex fertilizers (de Keijzer 1992), and Hewlett-Packard computers (*Business China* 1984) have been successful because they have fostered relations with government units and state-run enterprises while at the same time regularly visiting retailers, trialing sale products through private channels, and upholding intense contacts with end users.
- Currently the state-owned, collective and private sub-networks, at least at the retailing level, fulfill complementary functions so that they provide different benefits for a distributor.
- Sales teams' regular visits are important to keep displays and inventory in order. M&M's success in distribution is based partly on an effective well-trained salesforce (de Keijzer 1992, pp. 71–2), and a detergent producer is building up its offices and salesforce teams on the premises of the most important wholesalers.[17]
- HP and Canpotex have established service centres or information counters at the retailing level (de Keijzer 1992, pp. 77–9; *Business China* 1984, pp. 169–70)
- To overcome distribution problems, foreign companies have used the following 4 strategies: establishing retail outlets of manufacturing joint ventures; franchising; distribution agreements with Chinese companies; sale of the company name to an existing retailer, and then managing operations under a long-term management contract. For example, foreign firms may rent space in a large department store or in a shopping mall (Ho & Leigh 1994, pp. 22–8).

Word of mouth

In China, one of the main factors affecting consumer behavior is the influence of friends, relatives and colleagues, as the experience and knowledge of these people is respected (*Marketing Guide Magazine* 1995). The collective culture and emphasis on social relations provide fertile soil for word-of-mouth marketing strategies in China. *Guanxi* networks are effective tools for spreading information. Even though families are smaller these days, and consequently networks of relatives are less widespread, the contemporary society provides new kinds of networks, such as working units.

A successful way of encouraging word-of-mouth marketing is sales promotions at retailer level (Schütte & Vanier 1995). Supermarket cosmetics are widely promoted this way. Further, hierarchical relations in these networks make possible the use of opinion leaders. The elderly are naturally respected in all age groups and social classes. Also, salespersons are consulted and trusted (Schütte & Vanier 1995). It is also argued that word-of-mouth communication would be an important source of information among educated consumers (Schmitt 1997, p. 194).

The collective society, group orientation and hierarchical relations characteristic of China have been successfully used by a Canadian fertilizer manufacturer. Its marketing consists of 4 main elements: demonstrations, farmer meetings, field inspections for leaders, and harvest field days. Provincial soil and fertilizer institutions run demonstrations for farmers, and farmer meetings and harvest field days gather the farmer communities together. Harvest field days offer leisure activities such as Chinese opera and cultural shows. Furthermore, the company has a long-term orientation of at least 10–15 years, and this has surprised even the Chinese (de Keijzer 1992).

Advertising

There has been a steady increase in the advertising industry in the PRC since the early 1980s. The turnover of the advertising industry has grown rapidly, and, naturally, so has expenditure on advertising. Part of the growth is the result of an increase in the cost of advertising, 20–30% for newspaper advertising and about 70% for television advertising during the Opening Policy (Guo et al. 1995).

Despite the increase in price, the cost of advertising in the PRC is still relatively low, making it a cost-efficient tool of marketing. For example, a unit of 30 seconds of prime-time advertising on national television costs about 25 000 RMB, compared with the same spot in Hong Kong, which costs 97 000 RMB. There are 220 million TV sets and a population of one billion in Mainland China, compared with a population of 6 million and 10 million TV sets in Hong Kong (Guo et al. 1995).

In the PRC, television is the medium that consumers are most exposed to, as Table 5.25 shows. "Still something of a novelty, the ads are regarded by many viewers as the best feature of the medium rather than providing space for a teas or coffee break," notes one observer (Hooper 1994, p. 167).

After television, consumers are most exposed to printed advertisements, followed by radio and outdoor advertisements. The effect of TV advertising is further strengthened by the fact that TV advertisements are the ones that are most accurately memorized by the audience. Table 5.26 shows that consumers remember radio advertisements better than printed advertising. Outdoor advertising has a less long-lasting effect on the audience. When the actual purchasing decision is made, the effect of TV advertising is still strong, but does indeed vary for different product groups.

The other forms of mass-media promotion are not as important as information from the network of friends: the effect of friends' opinions is the next most influential agent after TV advertising for all product groups (see Table 5.27). This proves that traditional cultural influences on social relations still persist. In addition to this, the importance of exhibitions as a motivation for apparel purchase reinforces the principle that Chinese consumers want to investigate consumer durables before they purchase, rather than using the possibility of after-sales service or warranty.

Table 5.25 Audience exposure to advertising media

Frequency of exposure	*Daily*	*Often*	*Rarely*	*Never*
TV ads	60.7%	25.0%	6.6%	7.7%
Radio ads	14.0%	36.0%	41.4%	8.5%
Printed ads	17.7%	50.9%	15.0%	16.4%
Outdoor ads	10.5%	40.0%	23.6%	26.0%

Source: Q.G. Guo, F. Tong, H. Niu & L.S.C. Yip (1995), "Firms' Media Strategy in the Advertising Industry of China", in eds K. Basu, A. Joy & Z. Hansheng, *Proceedings of the Fifth International Conference of Marketing and Development*, June 22–25, Beijing, p. 405.

Table 5.26 Advertising medium, and audience memory of advertisement

Imprint on memory	*TV ad*	*Radio ad*	*Print ad*	*Outdoor ad*
Strong	49.9%	9.3%	8.2%	2.5%
Weak	48.1%	64.1%	53.4%	37.0%
Nil effect	2.0%	26.6%	38.4%	60.5%

Source: Q.G. Guo, F. Tong, H. Niu & L.S.C. Yip (1995), "Firms' Media Strategy in the Advertising Industry of China", in eds K. Basu, A. Joy & Z. Hansheng, *Proceedings of the Fifth International Conference of Marketing and Development*, June 22–25, Beijing, p. 405.

Table 5.27 Product type and promotional media

Product type	*TV ads*	*Radio ads*	*Print ads*	*Outdoor ads*	*Friends*	*Exhibition*
Household electronics	52.4%	3.7%	2.8%	1.2%	23.0%	2.7%
Daily necessities	37.7%	9.5%	4.1%	2.1%	14.8%	3.0%
Food	37.2%	6.0%	3.3%	2.4%	13.1%	3.8%
Apparel	29.2%	7.2%	7.9%	2.1%	12.6%	1.3%
Drugs	37.1%	7.2%	7.9%	2.1%	12.6%	1.3%
Health care	34.2%	5.0%	6.1%	1.4%	8.5%	1.9%

Source: Q.G. Guo, F. Tong, H. Niu & L.S.C. Yip (1995), "Firms' Media Strategy in the Advertising Industry of China", in eds K. Basu, A. Joy & Z. Hansheng, *Proceedings of the Fifth International Conference of Marketing and Development*, June 22–25, Beijing, p. 405.

If the selection of media seems to be fairly clear, the selection of advertising agency is more complex. The different possibilities are:

- state-owned advertising agencies
- in-house media advertising agencies
- private advertising agencies
- foreign-funded advertising agencies, which are new players (Luk et al. 1995).

The advertising agencies connected with the government units are the ones with a close relationship with government-owned media. Private and foreign agencies are new, and do not yet have a wide network of contacts with the necessary media and research institutions. It is also argued that many agencies engage in creating advertising, but cannot provide a full range of marketing services (Guo et al. 1995). However, Luk et al. (1995) point out that relationship management, a crucial marketing function in the Chinese cultural context, can be provided by many agencies (Luk et al. 1995, p. 4). Because media firms are in "a superior political position to advertising agencies," in many cases they decide with whom they will deal and what kinds of advertising they will accept. Therefore, in-house media agencies provide good connections to media, but most of the time are unable to provide other marketing services (Luk et al. 1995). Many multinational advertising agencies operate in China, serving mainly foreign-funded or joint-venture companies (Cheng & Frith 1996, pp. 34–41). They provide internationally skilled marketing services, but consider as their main problem connexions to media organizations. For example, media rates vary according to how 'foreign' the advertised product is (Cheng & Frith 1996, p. 37).

The first comprehensive advertising law became effective at the beginning of 1995. The advertising regulations include prohibition of claims that play on superstition, and directions that the content of the advertising has to fit the national culture, and consumer tastes (Luk et al. 1995). The following ideas could be taken into consideration when planning advertising content in the PRC:

- Identify the influential authority figures in the PRC, and use them in advertising. In the Chinese cultural context, opinion leaders are older people, political leaders, family elders and authoritarian types (Schütte & Vanier 1995, p. 37).
- Use dialects in local advertising on local TV and in local newspapers.
- Use objective, functional, straightforward advertising, and explicit conclusions rather than symbolism (Guo et al. 1995; Schütte & Vanier 1995).
- "Products for social usage should be advertised in a more emotive way while those for private usage would benefit from an advertisement that reinforces habit" (Schütte & Vanier 1995, pp. 22–3).

Market research

Conducting marketing research in the PRC is difficult. The country is huge, and consists of tremendously different submarkets. China may be viewed not only in terms of coastal, central and inland areas, but also in terms of rural and urban areas. The size of one submarket in China is larger than the size of an entire national market in many other countries. For example, the population of Beijing is 11 million, twice as much as the population of Finland. To overcome these problems, one needs to rely more on sample surveys than on general statistics for the PRC. According to some experts, it is almost impossible to rely on the results of consumer research in China. Chinese tend to give answers that they assume the researcher wants to get, hence causing biases. One way to do marketing research is simply to trial products within a limited market, for example, starting with some cities, and slowly widening the sales area.[18] For instance, Lu Biscuits sells packets of biscuits that include samples of most of its brands. This way consumers taste even those biscuits that they would not otherwise pick up from the shelf, and the producer gains market information.

A number of market research agencies and consultants exist in China despite these difficulties. For example, Gallup China Ltd has conducted consumer-behavior research since 1994 (Li & Gallup 1995). The China Statistical Bureau provides general statistics for the PRC—although their veracity has been questioned. China is a country with huge variations and rapid changes, therefore sample investigations of well-defined submarkets may lead to more accurate information.

Expected changes in the macromarketing mix

The behavior of Chinese consumers in the future is very much dependent on official government policies. Execution of these policies varies at the local level, as do the implications of these policies, although the national policy provides the framework for the change in economic environment, and, consequently, consumer behavior. The start of the Ninth 5-year Plan (1996–2000) by the 14th Party Central Committee in October 1995 indicates the continuation of the current policies on "building up socialism with Chinese characteristics" (*China Daily* 1995a, 1995b). Therefore we can conclude that the present trends are likely to continue as follows:

- diminishing population growth, a male-dominated sex ratio, and smaller households
- continuing economic growth and higher consumption power (Weiling 1995)
- conspicuous consumption with a material preference
- differences in economic change consistent with the east–west and rural–urban divide, but less obvious than before

- continuing urbanization of the population (*China Daily* 1995a, 1995b)
- increasing unemployment, which will create small businesses
- greater leisure time, and changing leisure activities, with a wider range of possibilities
- further "opening wider to the outside world" (*China Daily* 1995a, 1995b), affecting consumer tastes and habits
- increasing reversion to the underlying traditional Chinese culture as Marxist ideologies continue to have a decreasing effect on consumer behavior. The following issues will be affected: value of the family and social circle, role of women, education, sex ratio, and consumption patterns based on desire for social acceptance–that is, the demand for high-class products
- greater government control in some areas, such as the media
- further steps toward modern marketing strategies, but under the basic cultural constraints

References

Asian Development Bank (1996), *Key Indicators of Development in an Asia-Pacific Context XXVII*, Oxford University Press, London.

Bai, C.H. (1996), Li-Ning Stride to World, unpublished working paper, Nankai University, Nankai, PRC.

Bandyopadhyay, S. & Dong, G. (1995), "Beyond Country-of-Origin Effect: Introducing the Concept of Place-of Origin", in eds Basu K., Joy A. & Hansheng Z., *Proceedings of the Fifth International Conference of Marketing and Development*, June 22–25, Beijing, pp. 39–43.

Bond, M.H. & Hwang, Kwang-Kuo (1987), "The Social Psychology of Chinese People", in ed. Michael Harris Bond,*The Psychology of the Chinese People*, Oxford University Press, Oxford, pp. 213–66.

Business China (1984), "HP's JV in the PRC is Second Stride in Two-Step Strategy", November 28.

Cheng, H. & Frith, K.T. (1996), "Foreign Advertising Agencies in China", *Media Asia, an Asian Mass Communication Quarterly*, vol. 23, no. 1, pp. 34–41.

Chengguang, Ma (1994), "Fake Goods the Result of Slack Inspections", *China Daily*, December 28, vol. 14, no. 4320.

China Business (1996), "How about Chinese Life? A Survey Report of Family Consumption in Beijing, Shanghai, Guangzhou and Shenzhen", 1 February (in Chinese).

China Business Times (1996), "Income From South to North, A Survey Comparing Family Income in Beijing, Shanghai, Guangzhou and Shenzhen", 8 February (in Chinese).

China Daily (1993), "Challenge for Chain Stores", vol. 13, no. 3937, December 6.

— (1995a), "Principles on Modernization Drive", October.

— (1995b), "Process of Urbanization Speeds Up", October.

China Economic Review (1994), "Brand Ambitions", March, pp. 15–16.

China Market (1992), "Fast Developing Cosmetics Production", no. 4, pp. 11–12.

China Statistical Yearbook (1995), China Statistical Publishing House, Beijing.

— (1997), China Statistical Publishing House, Beijing.

d'Astous A., Ahmed, S.A. & Wang, Y.H. (1995), "A Study of Country-of-Origin Effect in the People's Republic of China", in eds K. Basu, A. Joy & Z. Hansheng, *Proceedings of the Fifth International Conference of Marketing and Development*, June 22–25, Beijing, pp. 33–8.

de Keijzer, A.J. (1992), *China: Business Strategies for the '90s*, Pacific View Press, Berkeley, CA.

Economist (1994), "How not to Sell 1.2 Billion Tubes of Toothpaste", December 3, pp. 63–4.

Fan, Ying (1994), *Blending East and West, How Can Western Management Know-how be Transferred to China's Socialist Market Economy?*, Durham University Business School, Durham, England.

Ger, G. (1995), "Consumer Culture and Development Contexts", in eds Basu K., Joy A. & Hansheng Z., *Proceedings of the Fifth International Conference of Marketing and Development*, June 22–25, Beijing, pp. 403–5.

Guangming Daily (1996), "China National Statistic Bureau, Main Publication Data of National Population", February 15 (in Chinese).

Guo, Q.G., Tong, F., Niu, H. & Yip, L.S.C. (1995), "Firms' Media Strategy in the Advertising Industry of China", in eds K. Basu, A. Joy & Z. Hansheng, *Proceedings of the Fifth International Conference of Marketing and Development*, June 22–25, Beijing.

Harris, P. & Yau, Kwok K. (1994), Understanding Chinese Buying Behavior—A Cross-cultural Interaction Model, paper presented at the International Conference on Management Issues for China in the 1990s, Cambridge, March 23–25.

Hill, C. & Romm, C.T. (1994), "Gift-Giving Family Styles: A Cross-cultural Study with Consumer Socialization Implications", *Australian Journal of Chinese Affairs*, no. 14, vol. 7, p. 8.

Ho, D. & Leigh, N. (1994), "A Retail Revolution", *The China Business Review*, January–February, pp. 22–8.

Ho, Suk-ching & Lo, Wing-chun (1987), "The Service Industry in China, Problems and Prospects", *Business Horizons*, July-August, vol. 30, no. 4, pp. 29–37.

Hofstede, G. (1994), *Cultures and Organizations; Intercultural Co-operation and Its Importance for Survival,* HarperCollins Publishers, New York.

Hong, Ma (1990), *Modern China's Economy and Management,* Foreign Languages Press, Beijing.

Hooper, B. (1994), "From Mao to Madonna: Sources on Contemporary Chinese Culture", *Southeast Asian Journal of Social Science,* vol. 22, pp. 161–9.

Hsu, R.C. (1991), *Economic Theories in China, 1979–1988,* Cambridge University Press, Cambridge.

Leung, Thomas, Wong, Syson & Wong, Y.H. (1993), Hong Kong Businessmen's Perceptions of Guanxi in the People's Republic of China, paper delivered at the Academy of International Business Conference, Hong Kong, June 23–25.

Li, Zhang (1992), "Regrets of the Cosmetics Market", *China Market,* no. 4, pp. 13–17.

Li, D. & Gallup, A.M. (1995), "In Search of the Chinese Consumer", *The China Business Review,* vol. 22, no. 5, pp. 19–22.

Ling, D. (1994), Selling to the Little Emperors, *China Economic Review,* March.

Luk, S.T.K., Li, H.Y., Guo, Q.G. & Yip, L.S.C. (1995), The Strategic Roles of Advertising Agencies in Chinas's Domestic Market, unpublished working paper, Hong Kong Polytechnic University, Hong Kong.

Marketing Guide Magazine (1995), "Features and Trends, Characteristics and Prospects of Consumption Market in China", February (in Chinese)

Polsa, P. (1996), Distribution of consumer goods in the People's Republic of China, An empirical study of packaged food products, Swedish School of Economics and Business Administration, licentiate thesis (forthcoming), Finland.

Private Business Association (1993), A paper concerning the encouragement of the private business, Guilin, Guangxi.

Rana, P.B. (1993), *Reforms in the Transitional Economies of Asia,* Asian Development Bank, Oxford University Press, London.

Redding, S.B. & Hg, M.(1983), "The Role of 'Face' in the Organizational Perceptions of Chinese Managers", *International Studies of Management & Organization,* vol. 13, no. 3, pp. 92–123.

Reinganum, J. & Helsell, T. (1994), "To Market, To Market", *The China Business Review,* January–February, pp. 30–4.

Schmidt, B. (1997), "Who is the Chinese Consumer? Segmentation in the People's Republic of China", *European Management Journal,* vol. 15, no. 2, pp. 191–4.

Schütte, H. & Vanier, V. (1995), *Consumer Behavior in Asia,* Euro-Asia Centre Research Series, INSEAD Euro-Asia Centre, Fontainebleau.

Shunwu, Zhou (1992), *China Provincial Geography,* Foreign Languages Press, Beijing.

Spence, J.D. (1990), *The Search for Modern China,* W.W. Norton & Company, New York.

Vernon-Wortzel, H. & Wortzel, H.L. (1987), "The Emergence of Free Market Retailing in the People's Republic of China: Promises and Consequences", *Californian Management Review,* vol. 29, no. 3, Spring, pp. 59–76.

Weilng, L. (1995), "Problems Solved Gradually Through Fiscal Reform—Vice Minister, Revenue to Grow 14%", *China Daily,* vol. 15, no. 4591, October.

Wentao, X. (1994), "Social Effects of Emerging 'Nouveaux Riches'", *Shanghai Shehui* (Shanghai Society), no. 110, March; English translation in JPRS-CAR, April 27.

Wiemer, C. (1992), "Price Reform and Structural Change, Distributional Impediments to Allocative Gains", *Modern China,* vol. 18, no. 2, April, pp. 171–96.

Wu, Wei-Ping (1994), Guanxi and its Managerial Implications for Western Firms in China—A Case Study, paper presented at the International Conference on Management Issues for China in the 1990s, Cambridge, March 23–25.

Xiao, Chen (1993a), "Private Business Taps Advantages of State Firms", *China Daily,* vol. 12, no. 3722, May 5.

— (1993b), "Production Comes First in Big Ownership Debate", *China Daily,* vol. 13, no. 3912, November 11.

Xie, Bai-san (1991), *China's Economic Policies, Theories and Reforms Since 1949,* Fudan University Press, Shanghai.

Yan, R. (1994), "To Reach China Consumers, Adapt to Guo Qing", *Harvard Business Review,* September–October.

Zhiping, Ma (1994), "Consumer Beefs Focus on Quality", *China Daily,* October 28.

Zhou, Yuan (1993), "Food Chain Altering the Face of Beijing Shopping", *China Daily/Business* Weekly, vol.13, no. 3761/28, June 13–19.

Notes

1 The authors would like to thank Bai Chen Xi for her great assistance.

2 The people who comprise the majority of the people are called Han Chinese.

3 The First Five-Year Plan was drawn up for the years 1953–1957. Before that the economic policies of the People's Republic were called "the task of rehabilitating the national economy" (Hong 1990, pp. 11–15). Hence the Centrally Planned Economy has its origin in 1953.

4 The Third Plenary Session of the 11th Central Committee of the Communist Party of China at the end of 1978 made a decision to change the Chinese economy to "socialist modernization" (Hong 1990, p. 27).

5 The economic policies and changes could be divided according to Five-Year Plans, but the main political changes concerning the economy happened in 1979 and after 1993.

6 Interview with the director of the Commercial Bureau of Guilin, January 3 1996, in Guilin, Guangxi.

7 The base year is 1980.

8 The 14 Coastal Cities are Dalian, Qinghuangdao, Tianjin, Yantai, Qingdao, Lianyungang, Nangtong, Shanghai, Ningbo, Wenzhou, Fuzhou, Guangzhou, Zhangiang and Beihai.

9 The same division is used by the *China Statistical Yearbook*, 1995.

10 Military personnel included to the national total population, but excluded from the provincial figures. The provincial figures add up to 1 212 950 000.

11 In this study, the words "relations," "connexions," and *Guanxi* are used as synonyms.

12 Cf. Use of "back door" (Bond & Hwang 1987, p. 225).

13 Means working unit such as a hospital, state-owned enterprise or university.

14 The average world figures were 64/68 in 1992. The Chinese figures are from 1990.

15 For example, 2 respondents in a sample of 32 (Polsa 1996).

16 Some studies have, though, found opposite attitudes. For instance, male consumers do not distinguish between sino-Japanese joint-venture and imported Japanese TV sets (Bandyopadhyay & Dong, 1995, p. 41).

17 Interview with representative of detergent joint venture in Guilin, Guangxi, January 5 1996.

18 Interview with a British consultant in Hong Kong, September 3 1993.

CHAPTER 6

Hong Kong

The consumer market in the 1990s

MARK W. SPEECE & STELLA L.M. SO

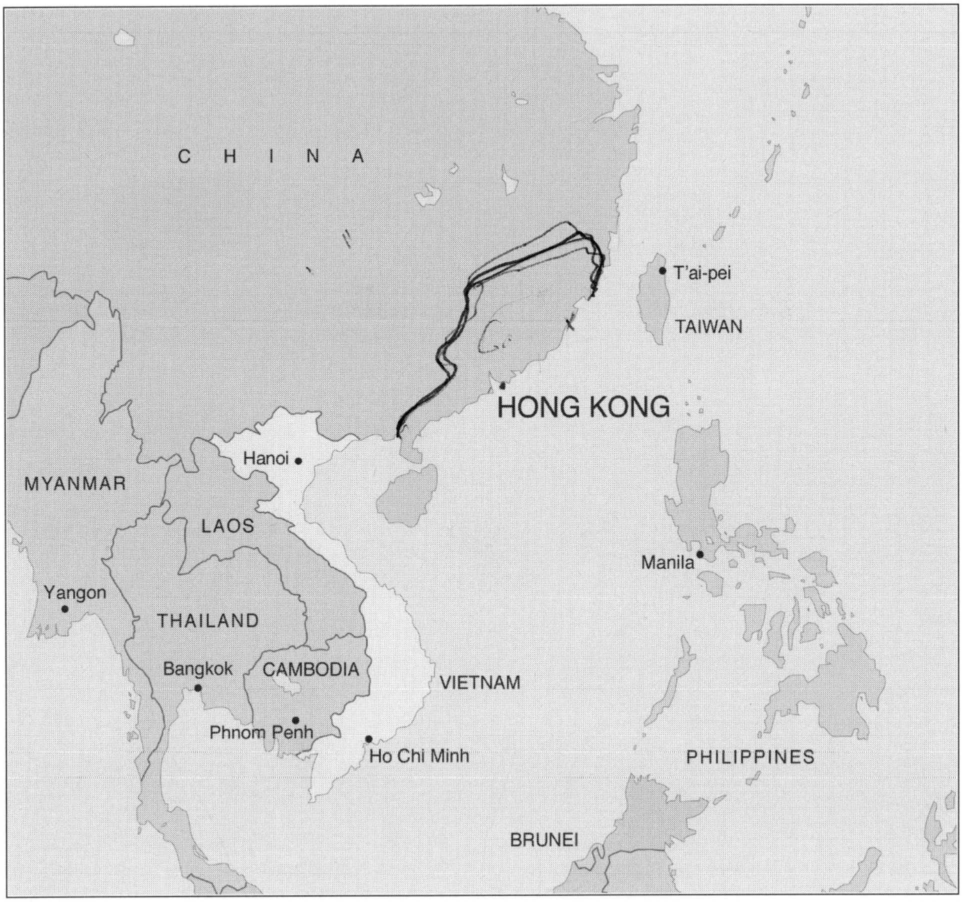

Abstract

The Chinese take-over has been effected, and the territory of Hong Kong is beset with uncertainty about its future. While it is certain that changes will come and that the transition period will be unsettling, no-one is confident about the final outcome of the process. Within the community both optimism and pessimism exist. The bases for these differing views are explained in this chapter, which provides an overview of the historical development of Hong Kong and future trends from a marketing perspective.

Introduction

Hong Kong, now officially a part of China, was formerly called a "Territory." It was a British Crown Colony, located on the coast of southern China. Hong Kong was returned to China on July 1 1997. The Territory consists of Hong Kong Island (about 7.5% of total land area), Kowloon (about 4% of land area), many outlying islands (about 15%), and the New Territories. Lantau, to the west of Hong Kong island and Kowloon, is the largest island, and it contains the site of the new airport currently under construction. (However, most of the site will be developed through land reclamation along Lantau's north coast.) All other islands are much smaller than Hong Kong Island. Lamma, just to the south-west of Hong Kong Island, is the only one of any local importance.

Hong Kong's climate is subtropical, with a hot humid tropical monsoon season and a temperate, cooler season. Winter monsoons blow from the north-east, bringing relatively cool and dry weather from September to April. Mean daily temperature is usually lowest in January and February, at about 15.7°C. From April to September south-west monsoons prevail, bringing very hot and humid weather. The hottest months are usually July and August, which average nearly 29°C. May to September is typhoon season, and, in an average year, 5 to 7 tropical cyclones can be expected. Occasionally one of these hits the territory with hurricane force. Of about 2215 mm of annual rainfall, two-thirds falls in the period June to September.

The Territory has an area of about 1078 km^2, which represents a slight increase over the past decade because of land reclamation. Although most people think of Hong Kong as a densely populated urban area, much of the Territory's topography is quite rugged. Most of the undeveloped areas are not really useable for anything, but approximately 7.5% of total land area is classified as suitable for agriculture. Only about half of this is actually used for agriculture now, because opportunities in other economic sectors have become substantially better in the past decade.

Only about 20% of the Territory's land area is built-up land. Over 98% of the population lives on this "built-up land," that is, in urban areas. These areas include the north coast of Hong Kong Island, scattered areas of the south coast, Kowloon, and several New Towns in the New Territories. Shatin, about one-third of the way between the tip of Kowloon and the "border" with China, is the largest of the New Town urban areas (HKCSD 1994, 1995b; HKGIS 1995).

Structure of the economy

Hong Kong achieved one of the world's most rapidly growing economies over the 1970s and 1980s. During most of the 1980s, economic growth rates ranged between 6% and 10% annually (in constant prices), but reached 14.5%

in 1987 (see Table 6.1). The economy slowed down substantially after 1989, though it soon recovered somewhat, and Hong Kong still posted impressive growth by world standards during the global recession in the early 1990s. The Tiananmen Square crackdown in China ushered in slower growth. It was followed by austerity programs in China to slow the overheated economy, and a depression in the West and Japan, which are key markets.

Table 6.1 Gross Domestic Product (expenditure-based)*

	Current market prices				*Constant 1990 prices*	
Year	*Total (HK$ mil)*	*Change (%)*	*Per capita (HK$)*	*Change (%)*	*Total (HK$ mil)*	*Change (%)*
1984	256 493	20.6	47 517	19.4	404 872	10.0
1985	–	–	–	–	–	–
1986	312 561	15.1	56 576	13.6	450 411	10.7
1987	384 488	23.0	68 898	21.8	508 763	13.0
1988	455 022	18.3	80 855	17.4	549 302	8.0
1989	523 861	15.1	92 128	13.9	563 368	2.6
1990	582 549	11.2	102 121	10.8	582 549	3.4
1991	668 512	14.8	116 166	13.8	612 016	5.1
1992	779 335	16.6	134 102	15.4	650 347	6.3
1993	900 153	15.5	152 079	13.4	692 167	6.4
1994	1 022 733	13.6	168 729	10.9	729 432	5.4
1995**	762 075	4.5				
1996***	788 711	3.5				
1997***	802 036	1.7				

Notes:
* $1(US) = HK$7.73
** figures for 1995 are an estimate
*** figures for 1996, 1997 are forecasts by Economist Intelligence Unit (1996), *Country Report: Hong Kong and Macau, 1st Quarter 1996*, EIU, London.

Sources: Hong Kong Census and Statistics Department (1994), *Hong Kong Annual Digest of Statistics*, 1994 edn, Government Printing Department, Hong Kong; Hong Kong Census and Statistics Department (1995), *Hong Kong Social and Economic Trends*, 1995 edn, Government Printing Department, Hong Kong.

Although the territory is unlikely to return to the growth rates of the 1980s, it benefited from the global recovery, with an increase in GDP of 6.4% in 1993, and 5.4% in 1994. (Note that some estimates are slightly lower than official figures.) Through the end of the 1990s, however, most observers expect the economy to slow further as the economy shifts into a mature, service-oriented phase. Estimates for 1995 ranged from 4.5 to 5.0% (*FEER* 1995; *BP* April 9 1996; EIU 1996). Most recent estimates (*AsiaWeek* 1996c) indicate a current annual growth rate of 4.2%. Some forecasts expect growth to continue to drop off to a rate of 1.7% by 1997 (EIU 1996). Official forecasts are somewhat more optimistic, but they have not been met recently (*AWSJ* 1996b, 1996d).

The economy of Hong Kong was traditionally based on trade and low-cost manufacturing. In the 1980s, it also developed into a very important financial and services center for East Asia. Manufacturing remains important, but in recent years has slowly declined relative to other sectors. In 1994, it accounted for only 11% of GDP, down from nearly one-quarter just a decade earlier (see Table 6.2). Hong Kong has been slower than other East Asian competitors to move toward technology, capital, and/or skill-intensive industries. However, it is no longer very competitive in the labor-intensive industries which fueled the rapid growth of the 1970s and early 1980s.

Table 6.2 Gross Domestic Product by share of economic activity

Economic activity	*1984*	*1989*	*1994*
Agriculture & Fishing	0.5	0.3	0.2
Mining & Quarrying	0.1	0.0	0.0
Manufacturing	24.3	19.3	11.1
Electricity, Gas, & Water	2.4	2.2	2.1
Construction	5.4	5.2	5.2
Wholesale, Retail, Trade, Hotel & Restaurant	23.1	25.0	27.0
Transport, Storage, & Communication	7.8	8.9	9.5
Finance, Insurance, Real estate, Services	15.6	19.5	25.8
Community, Social, & Personal services	15.4	14.1	15.7
Ownership of premises	10.2	10.3	11.0
(Finance service charge)	-4.9	-4.8	-7.6
	100.0	100.0	100.0

Source: Hong Kong Census and Statistics Department (1995), *Hong Kong Social and Economic Trends*, 1995 edn, Government Printing Department, Hong Kong.

Hong Kong companies remain heavily involved in relatively low-tech and labor-intensive industry, but much of it has moved across the border into

China to keep labor costs, and prices, low. More than 16 000 companies involving Hong Kong interests are registered in neighboring Guangdong province, and Hong Kong-owned factories provide an estimated 3 million jobs in Guangdong. Hong Kong's cumulative realized investment of US$68 billion accounts for about 60% of all realized foreign investment in China. About US$25 billion of Hong Kong's investment is in Guangdong, about 70% of the total in that province (Chang 1995; *FEER* 1995; Lam & Liu 1995; *Bangkok Post* 1996).

The government's philosophy of minimal direct involvement in the economy while maintaining a stable and relatively corruption-free regulatory environment has made Hong Kong a favorite regional center for financial and other business services. By 1994, finance, insurance, real estate, and other business services accounted for nearly 26% of GDP, up from 15.6% in 1984 (see Table 6.2). Most major banks with any international presence are represented in Hong Kong. The Hong Kong stock exchange has become one of the largest outside the USA, UK, and Japan, and a large number of multinationals have made the Territory the headquarters for regional operations (*FEER* 1995; Gaeta 1995; Howe 1995; Li 1995).

Hong Kong is also one of the primary trade centers of East Asia. Traditionally, it served regional trade. However, a decade ago domestic exports were still much larger than re-exports. Since then, trading has increased to dwarf domestic exports (see Table 6.3). Also, once China began to open after 1979, Hong Kong increasingly became the trade link between China and the outside world. In 1994, China received over 27% of Hong Kong's domestic exports, and over one-third of re-exports. It also accounts for nearly 38% of Hong Kong's imports (HKCSD 1995b). In 1994, 27% of China's total exports moved through Hong Kong (CSY 1995). In the first 8 months of 1995, 88% of Hong Kong's re-exports either went to or came from China (*Bangkok Post* 1996). For the next decade, Hong Kong will undoubtedly continue to dominate China's trade, because it is so closely linked with Guangdong, the fastest growing part of China. In the long term, its relative importance will decline somewhat as other parts of China catch up and other Chinese ports, especially Shanghai, develop (for transportation infrastructure development in China, see e.g. Speece & Kawahara 1995; Speece 1996).

Hong Kong is likely to continue its rapid economic progress for at least several more years. However, the future after 1997, under Chinese sovereignty, seems uncertain to many people. Some are quite optimistic, but many are worried that tight control by Beijing and/or large-scale Chinese style corruption may damage Hong Kong's prosperity (see e.g. Lee 1995; Fong & Wilson 1995). If this does happen, however, it is likely to be a slow process. Hong Kong will undoubtedly remain a very affluent market throughout the 1990s and into the next century.

Table 6.3 Trade and top trade partners

Year	*1984*	*1989*	*1994*
Domestic exports to	(%)	(%)	(%)
USA	44.5	32.2	27.7
China	8.2	19.3	27.5
Germany	7.0	7.0	5.8
Singapore	1.9	2.6	5.5
Japan	3.7	5.8	4.7
UK	7.6	6.5	4.6
Total domestic exports (HK$ billion)	**137.9**	**224.1**	**222.1**
Re-exports to	(%)	(%)	(%)
China	33.6	29.9	34.1
USA	14.5	20.8	22.2
Japan	5.5	6.4	5.8
Germany	1.3	3.9	4.4
UK	1.2	2.6	2.9
Taiwan	5.8	4.8	2.4
Total re-exports (HK$ billion)	**83.5**	**346.4**	**947.9**
Imports from	(%)	(%)	(%)
China	25.0	34.9	37.6
Japan	23.6	16.6	15.6
Taiwan	7.8	9.2	8.6
USA	10.9	8.2	7.1
Singapore	5.5	4.0	5.0
South Korea	3.3	4.5	4.6
Total imports (HK$ billion)	**223.4**	**562.8**	**1 072.6**

Source: Hong Kong Census and Statistics Department (1995), *Hong Kong Social and Economic Trends*, 1995 edn, Government Printing Department, Hong Kong.

Another possible problem is that Hong Kong is increasingly being integrated into the Southern China economy. Beijing has not yet worked out how to maintain smooth, sustainable growth. Strong boom–bust cycles have been characteristic of the period since reform began in 1979, and many observers expect this to continue as China continues to develop. In the past, this did not affect Hong Kong very severely, but future economic performance may fluctuate more erratically as Hong Kong's economy merges more completely with southern China's.

Demographics

Hong Kong's estimated population in mid-1995 was about 6.189 million, with about 50.8% male (HKCSD 1995a), reflecting labor immigration, which is mostly male. These figures are estimates. The last full census was in 1991, which showed the population was 5 522 281, or slightly more if Vietnamese refugees and residents away from Hong Kong during the census enumeration are counted. In practice, the government hopes that the Vietnamese will soon be gone, and many absent residents have probably emigrated permanently.

Table 6.4 Hong Kong population by (a) age and (b) area

(a)			
Year	*1984*	*1989*	*1994*
Age group	%	%	%
Under 15	23.8	21.8	19.4
15–34	39.7	37.6	34.6
35–64	29.3	32.3	36.6
Over 65	7.2	8.3	9.4
Total	**100.0**	**100.0**	**100.0**
Median age (years)	27.7	30.4	33.1

(b)			
Area	%	%	%
Hong Kong Island	21.9	22.0	21.8
Kowloon & New Kowloon	42.8	35.8	32.8
New Territories	34.7	41.9	45.1
Marine	0.7	0.3	0.3
Total	**100.0**	**100.0**	**100.0**
Total population	5 397 990	5 686 200	6 061 000

Source: Hong Kong Census and Statistics Department (1995), *Hong Kong Social and Economic Trends*, 1995 edn, Government Printing Department, Hong Kong.

The population is concentrated in urban areas on Hong Kong Island, in Kowloon, and in the New Territories. The New Territories is the only region with rapid growth, which mostly represents a population shift out of Kowloon. Although the New Territories is a large region, most of its population is concentrated in the New Towns, and very few Hong Kong residents in any area could be classified as rural. The vast majority of residents are Chinese (mostly Cantonese), and only about 3.2% claim a non-Chinese language as their mother tongue (HKCSD 1991a, 1994, 1995b).

Population growth has been slow, just 2.34% since 1986, and did not exceed an annual rate of 1.0% in any year from the early 1980s to 1992. The rate has increased to 1.8% and 2.4% in 1993 and 1994 respectively (HKCSD 1991a, 1994, 1995b). In part, this slow growth is due to the fact that the increasingly affluent population is following the common trend in industrial countries toward small families. Average household size has slowly declined—for example, from about 3.7 in 1984 to 3.4 in 1994 (HKCSD 1995b; *AA&M* 1996c estimates 3.37 in 1995). The percentage of families classified as unextended nuclear family grew from 54% in the 1981 census to nearly 62% in the 1991 census. The large extended family of traditional Chinese society is fast disappearing in Hong Kong (HKCSD 1991a, 1994, 1995b).

Growth is low partly because emigration in recent years has been high, reaching a peak level of 66 000 in 1992. This figure fell back to about 53 000 in 1993. By mid-1997, those who find it easiest to gain foreign passports or visas have already acquired them. However, an estimated 700 000 residents have foreign passports or visas, so potential emigration is huge, should people lose confidence in Hong Kong during the transition to Chinese rule (Kwong 1990; Skeldon 1991; Farh, Leung, & Tse 1995; HKCSD 1995b; Lam & Liu 1995; EIU 1996).

Immigration from China is likely to grow, and this accounts for some of the recent increase in growth rates. Prior to 1980, official policy was to grant right of abode to anyone from China who could reach Hong Kong. However, as China opened up in the late 1970s, the trickle turned into a massive flow, and nearly half a million immigrants came in the few years before 1981. Hong Kong started sending back illegal immigrants then, allowing only about 27 000 to come legally each year. This rose to 38 200 by 1994, with priority (and most places) going for family reunification. Illegal immigration has sometimes been estimated to be about equal to legal, but by the mid-1990s it was probably much higher. In the past few years, the Hong Kong government has begun to allow more legal entries because of labor shortages (HKGIS 1994, 1995; Lam & Liu 1995).

Many observers worry that immigration from China may become a flood again after 1997. However, this is a sensitive political issue, which all sides prefer to ignore politely. Unpublished statistics cited in Skeldon (1991) show arrests and deportations fluctuating widely between about 5 000 to over 22 000 annually from 1981 to 1990. Over 37 000 were arrested in 1993, but this figure fell to under 32 000 in 1994 (HKGIS 1995). Estimates for how many evaded capture are pure guesses—the figure for 1990 was over 18 000, about twice as many as were caught. Therefore, reliable figures on the magnitude of illegal immigration into Hong Kong from China are not readily available, and it is difficult to arrive at realistic estimates on what may happen after 1997.

Hong Kong's population is gradually ageing, also following patterns in industrial countries. The median age rose from 27.7 in 1984 to 33.1 in 1994 (see Table 6.4; HKCSD 1994). The percentage of people over 65 increased from 7.2% to 9.3% during that time, and the rate for those under 15 years declined from 23.7% to 19.4%. Median age at first marriage is also increasing, reflecting the trend toward working longer before marriage. In 1984 it was 27.5% and 24.7% for men and women respectively. By 1994, median age at first marriage was up to 29.6% and 26.5% respectively (HKCSD 1994, 1995b; *AA&M* 1996c).

Tourism also contributes substantially to consumption in Hong Kong. In 1994 there were over 9.3 million tourist arrivals, up from 3.3 million in 1984. The vast majority of visitors are from East Asia, with China accounting for 21% of tourists in 1994. Taiwanese and Japanese accounted for another 18% and 15% respectively, followed closely by visitors from South-East Asia and then Europe. Together, the top 4 Asian groups accounted for about two-thirds of visitors in the same year. These trends are quite different from those a decade earlier. While tourism from most major countries has increased, Taiwan and China have contributed by far the most to this increase (see Table 6.5).

Table 6.5 Visitor arrivals in Hong Kong

Year	*1984*		*1989*		*1994*	
Arrivals from	*No. ('000)*	*%*	*No. ('000)*	*%*	*No. ('000)*	*%*
China	215	6.5	730	12.2	1944	20.8
Taiwan	167	5.0	1133	18.9	1665	17.8
Japan	584	17.7	1176	19.7	1441	15.4
South-East Asia	665	20.1	710	11.9	1197	12.8
West Europe	437	13.2	713	11.9	1126	12.1
USA	563	17.0	624	10.4	776	8.3
Australia/New Zealand	305	9.2	302	5.0	316	3.4
Canada	94	2.9	151	2.5	185	2.0
Other	275	8.3	445	7.4	681	7.3
Total	**3 304**		**5 985**		**9 331**	

Source: Hong Kong Census and Statistics Department (1995), *Hong Kong Social and Economic Trends*, 1995 edn, Government Printing Department, Hong Kong.

Employment, income, and housing

Hong Kong's labor force stood at about 2.97 million in 1994, an increase of 367 000 over a decade (see Table 6.6). However, the labor-force participation rate among those aged 15 and over declined slightly, reaching 78% for men and 47% for women in 1994. These slight declines are due almost entirely to the increasing tendency for younger men and women to stay in school longer to improve job prospects, and for people to retire earlier as living standards increase (Farh, Leung, & Tse 1995). Employment in the manufacturing sector has declined to less than half the levels of 1984, but services-sector jobs have expanded rapidly. However, unemployment had risen to 3.5% by 1995, after remaining between 1% and 2% from the late 1980s until 1994. In the fourth quarter of 1995, estimates indicated that manufacturing employment had dropped further to about 386 100, but the government mainly blamed declines in the restaurant industry for the rise. Other observers cited the increased import of low-skill labor. By late 1995, the government promised to reduce the numbers of non-professional workers entering the Territory (HKCSD 1994, 1995b; Farh, Leung, & Tse 1995; Lam & Liu 1995; EIU 1996).

Table 6.6 Labor-force indicators

Year	*1984*	*1990*	*1992*	*1994*
Population over 15 ('000)	3 979	4 346	4 484	4 757
Labor force ('000)	2 606	2 748	2 793	2 973
Men	1 647	1 748	1 766	1 861
Women	960	1 000	1 027	1 111
Participation rate (%)	65.5	63.2	62.3	62.5
Men	81.3	79.1	78.0	77.6
Women	49.1	46.8	46.2	47.1
Unemployment rate (%)	3.9	1.3	2.0	1.9
Industry sector ('000)				
Manufacturing	898.9	715.6	565.1	423.0
Wholesale retail restaurants hotels	573.8	829.6	914.8	1021.9
Finance insurance real estate	169.5	276.6	314.5	369.6

Source: Hong Kong Census and Statistics Department (1995), *Hong Kong Social and Economic Trends*, 1995 edn, Government Printing Department, Hong Kong.

About one-quarter of the male workforce is in managerial or professional level jobs (see Table 6.7). Craft-type jobs are still common among workers in Hong Kong, and account for nearly 21% of employment among men. About one-fifth of women are in managerial or professional occupations, but they are somewhat less likely than men to be among the higher level managers, and more likely to be at the lower levels of professional occupations. The largest single category for women is clerks, 29% (HKCSD 1994, 1995b). Compared to many other Asian countries, Hong Kong offers women relatively good opportunities to work and to advance, but there is still some inequality. Women still earn only about 71% of what men earn, on average, even after adjustments are made for experience and occupation. However, the gap declines for higher education levels, and seems to be declining also for younger women (Siu & Chu 1994; Suen 1995).

Table 6.7 Working population by occupation and sex, 1991

Work sector	*Male*	*(%)*	*Female*	*(%)*
Managers & administrators	198 857	11.8	50 390	4.9
Professionals	68 516	4.1	30 815	3.0
Associate professionals	164 121	9.7	115 788	11.3
Clerks	135 665	8.0	295 986	28.8
Service & sales	230 823	13.7	128 496	12.5
Agricultural & fishery	13 688	0.8	6 767	0.7
Craft & related	352 264	20.9	45 728	4.4
Plant & machine operators	234 929	13.9	130 897	7.8
Elementary occupations	280 434	16.6	223 398	21.7
Armed forces or unclassified	7 069	0.4	472	0.0
Total	1 686 366		1 028 737	

Sources Hong Kong Census and Statistics Department (1994), *Hong Kong Annual Digest of Statistics*, 1994 edn, Government Printing Department, Hong Kong.

Hong Kong's remarkable economic performance has resulted in living standards comparable to those in the advanced countries of the West and Japan. Living standards are high and have been rising rapidly. Per-capita GDP was over HK$168 000 in 1994. The Hong Kong dollar is currently pegged to the US dollar, and fluctuates in a narrow band around 7.8 HK$/US$. During the 1990s the rate has usually been closer to 7.73 to 7.75 (EIU 1996; HKCSD 1995a, 1995b). Current estimates place Hong Kong among the top in the world in terms of per-capita income at purchasing power parity, similar to countries such as Japan, Switzerland, or the USA (*AsiaWeek* 1996b). Many households benefit from dual incomes, since nearly half of all women work, and this results in very high household incomes. From 1986 to 1995, the proportion of Hong Kong households earning HK$10 000 or more per month (just over US$ 15 000 annually) increased from only 18% to 78% (see Table 6.8). The proportion earning over HK$20 000 monthly (US$31 000 annually) increased from under 5% to 42% over the past decade. About 13% of households earn over US$61 000 annually. Households also benefit from a low personal-tax rate (15.5%; no taxes for lower income levels), so that people enjoy high take-home pay and households have considerable purchasing power. Hong Kong residents enjoy disposable incomes that may be the highest in the world.

Table 6.8 Percentage of domestic households, by monthly household income

Monthly income (HK$)	*1986 (%)*	*1991 (%)*	*1995 (%)*
under 2 000	9.7	4.8	
2 000–3 999	25.4	7.3	
under 4 999			8
4 000–5 999	23.5	12.8	
6 000–7 999	14.4	13.8	
5 000–7 499			6
8 000–9 999	8.6	11.5	
7 500–9 999			8
10 000–14 999	10.1	19.9	20
15 000–19 999	3.7	11.1	15
20 000–24 999	1.8	6.3	12
25 000–29 999	0.9	3.6	8
30 000–34 999	0.6	2.4	
35 000–39 999	0.3	1.4	
30 000-39999			9
over 40 000	1.0	5.1	
40 000–49 999			5
over 50 000			8
Total	**100.0**	**100.0**	**99***
Over 10 000	18.4	49.8	78
over 20 000	4.6	18.8	42
Total households	1 452 576	1 582 215	1 795 000

Note:
*1995 figures inexact due to rounding.

Sources: Hong Kong Census and Statistics Department (1991), *Hong Kong 1991 Population Census: Summary Results*, Government Printing Department, Hong Kong; *Asian Advertising & Marketing* (1996), "Profile of Hong Kong", March 8, p. 10.

Hong Kong has acquired a reputation for very expensive housing, but these high costs are more characteristic of upper middle to upper-class housing than of accommodation for the population as a whole. The government subsidizes housing for much of the population, and this public-sector competition keeps costs from going too high in the lower to middle part of the housing market. Of the 806 100 residential flats built between 1984 and 1994, about 60% were public housing. The government has been especially active in building the New Towns, to encourage dispersal of population to the New Territories (HKGIS 1994, 1995; HKCSD 1995b). Approximately 45% of households resided in public and subsidized rental housing blocks in 1994. (Another almost 2% resided in government housing, which was supplied as a job benefit.) Ownership of the flat in which the household lives increased from 31% to 45% over the decade to 1994. Home purchase can be either from the private sector, or through the Housing Authority Home Ownership Scheme, which allows the purchase of public housing flats. About 10% of households were in this scheme in 1994. Median rentals in public housing and median payments under the home ownership scheme represented just under 8% of household income in 1991, the date of the most recent detailed expenditure survey (Wong 1990; Lau 1991; HKGIS 1994, 1995; HKCSD 1995b).

Although the private sector does construct some lower- and middle-income housing, much private sector building has concentrated on the higher end of the market, where prices and rents did become exorbitant by the early 1990s. Rentals of upper-middle-class housing in private estates (such as stand alone houses) had median rentals/payments of HK$3558 in 1991, which represented nearly one-quarter of household income. In the following few years, prices soared for middle- to upper-class housing, and the middle class began to criticize the government for failing to help the so-called "sandwich class." These families had incomes too high to qualify for many government subsidies in rent or purchase of flats, but they were not rich enough to keep up with soaring prices if they wanted to buy.

In 1994 and 1995, the government did take some measures to cool the property market. For example, it began releasing some government land for development. Laws have been enacted to discourage speculation, such as requiring at least 10% initial down payment, and prohibiting the resale of unfinished flats (HKGIS 1995). Property prices have fallen back somewhat, though, mainly as a result of slack demand as the economy slows and because of growing uncertainty over 1997.

Some critics of the government point out the crowded conditions in many public housing estates, which are usually constructed in clusters of high-rise buildings. Safety and security are occasionally somewhat less than might be desired, though the government usually moves quickly to improve conditions in estates where this becomes an issue. There is certainly room for some improvement in housing conditions, but, in general, Hong Kong has made remarkable progress at providing affordable basic housing to a very densely packed population. The situation may not be perfect, but, compared with other major urban areas in Asia, the housing situation seems quite good.

Cultural environment

In this section, we will briefly discuss several issues that have brought changes in consumer behavior over the past 2 decades. Education levels are very high in Hong Kong, with the result that consumers have become quite sophisticated and discriminating. Women have been integrated into the workforce and are beginning to achieve top-level positions, although there is still much progress to be made before women gain status equal to men in Hong Kong society. Concern about the environment is no longer regarded as a luxury, but a key issue in improving the quality of life. Finally, because of uncertainty over 1997, expectations have gradually been changing. This has had a major impact on consumption.

Education

Educational levels are quite high, with 9 years of schooling free and compulsory. By 1994, nearly 64% of the population over the age of 15 had at least a secondary education (see Table 6.9). The seemingly high proportion of people without formal education (10.8% in 1994), or only primary education (25.4%), reflects, in part, immigration from China, especially illegal immigration. These immigrants generally have low educational levels.

There is little difference in educational level by sex, except for the category of people without formal education. Women are 2 to 3 times more likely to lack formal education (for issues relating to education, see Luk 1990; Cheng 1991; HKCSD 1994, 1995b; HKGIS 1994, 1995).

Enrollment ratios at primary and lower secondary levels slightly exceeded 100% of the corresponding age level, due to adult education and to a few children in classes who were not the usual age for the level. At the upper secondary level, which is not compulsory, enrollment ratios rose from 85% in 1984 to 91% in 1994 (HKCSD 1995b). Nearly 18% of the population over age 15 in 1994 had some post-secondary education, and this included 7.3% with university degrees. These figures are somewhat depressed because Hong Kong has been losing many highly educated people through emigration.

Because of this "brain drain," the government vastly increased university intakes in the mid-1990s. This is reflected in the enrollment ratio in the 6th and 7th forms for 1994. These 2 forms are largely regarded as preparation for college, and usually it is only students seriously considering college or university who follow these courses.

Women

Women have made substantial progress in the past several decades. In the 1960s, only about 36% of adult women worked (Chow 1995). As noted above, by 1994 nearly half of adult women participated in the labor force, and they represented over one-third of the total labor force. For the most part, women achieve similar educational levels to males. The percentage of women with very low education is larger than among men, but this is mainly due to recent immigration, and is characteristic of Mainland Chinese society, not of Hong Kong society. The proportion of women who receive higher education, though slightly less than that for men, is rapidly catching up.

Table 6.9 Education indicators for Hong Kong—(a) education levels, (b) enrollment ratios

(a)
Education levels of population over age 15

Level	*1984*	*1989*	*1994*
No formal schooling	14.3	12.4	10.8
Primary	31.8	28.8	25.4
Secondary	41.9	44.3	25.4
Matriculation	9.2	3.7	4.1
Post-secondary	incl. above	6.0	6.3
Degree course	2.8	4.8	7.3
Total	**100.0**	**100.0**	**100.0**

(b)

Enrollment ratios (%)	*1984*	*1989*	*1994*
Kindergarten	90	85	82
Primary	105	104	102
Lower secondary	97	103	102
Upper secondary	85	84	91
Sixth and seventh forms	19	19	33

Source: Hong Kong Census and Statistics Department (1995), *Hong Kong Social and Economic Trends*, 1995 edn, Government Printing Department, Hong Kong.

Women generally have good prospects in the workforce relative to most Asian countries, and even to many Western ones. Like career women everywhere, they must balance the conflicting demands of work and home, and find this somewhat more stressful than do their male counterparts. There is still some discrimination, and segregation of some jobs by sex. Women tend to enter service industries, such as advertising, public relations, publishing, media, tourism, catering, accommodation, social services, and personnel. Despite the fact that they perform quite well in some male-dominated industries, such as banking or engineering, women are not perceived to be good managers (Siu & Chu 1994; Ng 1995).

In law and politics, Hong Kong women face the problem that much of the population is still tradition bound. Women account for only 13% of members of the Legislative Council, Hong Kong's highest law-making body. On lower level district boards, they account for only the slightly higher rate of 20% of members. Many of the more outspoken women law makers attribute the low levels of women in politics to traditional thinking among both men and women (*FEER* 1995b). Traditional thinking often seems to be reinforced in the media, which tend to present women in relatively traditional roles. Many mass circulation general interest periodicals usually portray women's place in the family. The majority of women's radio programs are devoted to family matters such as child care and housekeeping. Glossy, full-color, lavishly photographed magazines targeted at younger women have become very successful in the 1990s, but the editorial content of these magazines is not very deep. The focus is mainly beauty or fashion (So & Speece 1991; Bernas 1996b).

Some local magazines have recently emerged, as well as local and regional editions of international magazines, which have upgraded the intellectual level of the content. By Asian standards, these Hong Kong magazines are sometimes quite progressive about dealing with personal issues such as women's sexuality. However, the content of most Hong Kong magazines and editions is not as risqué as many Western women's magazines (So & Speece 1991; Bernas 1996b).

Environment

As do most major Asian cities, Hong Kong faces some serious pollution problems. In 1994, the annual average total suspended particulates in the air was 153 micrograms per m^3, and 67 for respirable suspended particulates, figures well above government standards. An estimated 98% of air pollution downtown comes from vehicle emissions. Enforcement of air-pollution controls on vehicles is lax, with resistance from parts of the business community to stricter enforcement or tougher laws, such as banning leaded petrol. In outlying areas, the government has been more active in forcing factories to cut air pollution. For example, high-sulfur fuel oil was banned in 1990, leading to immediate improvements in air quality in industrial areas (Chau 1990; Siddall 1991; HKGIS 1995; *AsiaWeek* 1996c).

Locally, some air pollution also comes from dust raised by construction. Throughout 1994, many of Hong Kong's 7 pollution reporting stations reported dust levels exceeding government standards, even at rooftop level, where the stations are located. In 1995 Hong Kong introduced air-quality alerts, which would warn people of conditions under which those with respiratory or heart problems were advised to stay indoors. This is a critical problem for many people; respiratory problems led to 600 deaths in 1995, and asthma kills about 90 people per year, one-third of them under 35 years of age. Such alerts have only actually been issued a few times since, but their institution points out the serious nature of the problem, which is likely to become worse. Some observers expect air quality to deteriorate further, by up to 50% by the year 2000 (*AsiaWeek* 1996c).

Water quality has been poor in several of Hong Kong's harbors for the past decade. Again, the government has taken some action, sometimes more forcefully than with air-pollution problems. The first stage of the East Kowloon sewerage improvement scheme, which was substantially completed in 1994, is supposed to reduce organic pollution entering the typhoon shelter (part of the harbor) by 30 tons per day. In industrial areas, some progress has been made in halting the large-scale dumping of chemical waste into the sewage system or local waters. However, there are still many areas that are highly polluted (Chau 1990; Kwong 1990; Siddall 1991; HKGIS 1995).

Many Hong Kong people are becoming quite concerned about pollution. As early as 1989, a general survey found that pollution ranked as the 4th most important concern, after the stationing of PLA troops in Hong Kong after 1997, the hand-over in 1997, and the "brain drain" because of the coming hand-over (Chau 1990). A survey in 1990 had nearly 20% responding that pollution was a "very serious" social problem, and a further 54% said it was "serious." This survey did not include 1997 issues in its answers. "Vietnamese boat people" was the only answer that substantially out-polled pollution (Wan 1991).

A survey in 1993 showed that, among a list of environmental issues, people were most concerned with air and water pollution, but the level of concern was only moderate, not strong. People who have developed more environmental awareness are beginning to worry more about recycling, reducing waste, and reusing some materials. Younger and more educated people are beginning to change consumption behavior, for example, by purchasing recycled or recyclable products. However, this is not yet a very strong trend (Chan 1994).

Expectations

In 1985, several surveys showed that, on a 5-point scale, about three-quarters of Hong Kong residents were either "satisfied" or "very satisfied" with Hong Kong society and with their own lives. Half of them stated that their lives had improved over the past 5 years, while only one-fifth felt that life was getting worse. About one-third expected further improvement in the future, but only 11% actually expected things to get worse. Nearly everyone (88%) agreed that Hong Kong was a place of opportunity, where individual effort largely determined whether one could get ahead. The cultural heroes and models were successful entrepreneurs who started with next to nothing and became rich (Lau & Kuan 1988).

However, even in the mid-1980s, there were signs that, despite some optimism, people were not totally confident. For example, a similar survey in 1986 showed that only 64% of people were either "very satisfied" or "satisfied" with their lives. Much of the pessimism lurking underneath related to the return of Hong Kong to China in 1997. In the 1986 survey, half of the respondents believed that living standards would stagnate, or drop after

1997. Only 17% believed that Hong Kong people could enjoy a happy and blissful life after 1997 (Lau & Kuan 1988). This underlying worry about 1997 has been an (often unspoken) issue in people's lives since the early 1980s when the treaty was signed to return Hong Kong.

In a 1990 survey, the number of people who said they were "satisfied" or "very satisfied" with overall life declined to 56.9%. On the specific question of financial situation, only slightly more than one-third indicated some level of satisfaction. People were still quite worried about 1997. However, they did have confidence that the economy and their own lives would improve in the immediate future (i.e. the next few years). Trust in government fell off substantially over the 1980s. In 1986, two-thirds of respondents said they were either "trustful" or "very trustful." By 1990 this had declined to 42% (Wan 1991). Generally, confidence in the long-term future has remained at relatively low levels. Surveys in 1995, for example, showed that 60% of respondents had little or no faith in post-1997 leaders, and that 38% of younger people would emigrate if possible (EIU 1996).

A survey in early 1996 showed that 49% of Hong Kong Chinese identify themselves as "Hongkongers," not as Chinese. Only 36% identified themselves specifically as Chinese. Over one-third feel that places such as Tibet, Taiwan, and Hong Kong should have self-determination. Nearly two-thirds rate freedom and human rights as more important than the state. Such views are clearly going to generate some conflict with Chinese authorities after 1997. In this survey, 40% said they would consider leaving Hong Kong (*AWSJ* 1996c).

Prices and expenditure

The Hong Kong government computes several price indices designed to summarize changes in prices for baskets of goods and services typical of different income levels. In the late 1980s and early 1990s, Hong Kong recorded inflation rates at around 10–11%, and the different CPIs did not diverge much from each other. By 1994, overall inflation had been slowed somewhat, so that the composite inflation rate (whole population) was about 8.8% according to government figures (HKCSD 1995b; Table 6.10), or slightly lower by some other estimates (8.1%–EIU 1996). However, government figures showed that in September 1995, prices were up by about 9.2% over the previous September (HKCSD 1995a). The Economist Intelligence Unit (1996) also expected prices to be up by 8.7% in 1995, but then forecasted declining inflation of 7.0% and 6.5% for 1996 and 1997 respectively.

Since the early 1990s, inflation has diverged slightly in the different indices calculated by the government. Prices went up somewhat more strongly for many goods purchased by higher income households. In particular, prices for higher income housing rose even more quickly than for other housing, at a rate of 14.6% in 1994 (HKCSD 1995b; see Table 6.10). In

Table 6.10 (a) Prices, (b) Percentage change in prices over previous year, 1989–1994

(a) Prices

Consumer Price Index	*1984*	*1989*	*1990*	*1991*	*1992*	*1993*	*1994*
CPI(A)	70.6	93.5	102.6	114.5	125.2	135.9	146.9
CPI(B)	70.6	93.5	102.5	114.1	125.1	136.0	147.7
CPI (Hang Seng)	66.2	92.5	102.8	114.0	125.1	137.0	150.7

Note: October 1989–September 1990 = 100

(b) Percentage change in prices over previous year, 1989–1994

Index	*1989*	*1990*	*1991*	*1992*	*1993*	*1994*
CPI(A)	10.1	9.8	12.2	9.4	8.5	8.1
food	12.3	9.9	11.4	8.8	7.2	6.4
housing	7.0	8.8	12.6	13.0	12.6	11.2
misc. services	11.4	13.0	14.1	11.8	9.5	11.8
CPI(B)	9.7	9.7	11.6	9.6	8.7	8.6
food	12.6	10.4	11.7	9.0	7.5	6.6
housing	5.5	8.6	12.2	13.6	13.0	12.1
misc. services	11.6	12.6	13.2	11.0	8.8	10.8
CPI (Hang Seng)	11.0	11.2	11.1	9.8	9.5	10.0
food	12.5	9.6	10.4	9.3	8.3	8.3
housing	11.5	14.9	13.7	12.0	13.7	14.6
misc. services	12.1	12.0	10.8	9.6	7.6	9.2

Note:
CPI(A) represents consumption patterns of the lowest 50% of households. CPI(B) and Hang Seng represent the next 30% and 10% respectively.

Source: Hong Kong Census and Statistics Department (1995), *Hong Kong Social and Economic Trends*, 1995 edn, Government Printing Department, Hong Kong.

September 1995, the index for upper income housing stood at 202.3, prices having more than doubled from the base year (1989–1990 = 100). It was at 190.0 in the CPI(A), which represents spending patterns among the lower half of household income (HKCSD 1995b).

Prices for food, clothing and footwear, and durable goods of the type purchased by upper income households, also rose more rapidly than in the 2 CPIs computed for lower- and middle-income spending patterns. For clothing the difference was dramatic. The September 1995 index stood at 146.8 in CPI(A), but at 162.4 in the Hang Seng CPI (HKCSD 1995a, 1995b). Rates noted in the CPI(B), characteristic of middle-income purchasing patterns, remained between the other two, generally somewhat closer to CPI(A).

Despite relatively high inflation and worry about the 1997 issue, (or perhaps because of these things), consumer spending soared during the 1980s and early 1990s, and Hong Kong became a major East Asian market for a host of foreign products. In the last extensive household expenditure survey in 1990, average monthly spending was about US$1 360 per household. Of course, the range of expenditure was large, from under US$500 for lower-income families to over US$6 500 in spending per month for the most well-off families (HKCSD 1991b). Since 1990, estimates are that increases in expenditure have outpaced the increase in GDP.

Food and housing account for about 60% of household expenditure overall in Hong Kong, but this varies somewhat by expenditure level (which is closely correlated with household income). Lower-income households spend up to half of their money on food. At about the 35th percentile in expenditure, the figure is 45% (see Table 6.11), with about 20% spent on housing. Spending on food increases with expenditure level, but declines as a percentage of budget. However, the percentage spent on housing increases substantially, so even top-income households still spend about half on these two categories.

Table 6.11 Percentage of expenditures on various categories, by selected average bi-weekly household expenditure level (HK$)

	Bi-weekly expenditure level (%)			
Product category	*2 310–3 459**	*5 770–6 919**	*over 17 310**	*All*
Foodstuffs	45.37	35.98	14.75	34.21
Housing	20.53	24.68	36.49	25.58
Fuel & Light	3.48	2.51	1.09	2.40
Alcoholic drinks & Tobacco	2.05	1.09	0.65	1.35
Clothing & Footwear	4.50	7.70	8.85	7.52
Durable goods	2.26	4.42	5.52	3.83
Misc. goods	6.24	6.66	6.22	6.70
Transport & Vehicles	6.78	6.47	13.15	7.60
Services	8.78	10.49	13.58	10.81
Total	**100.0**	**100.0**	**100.00**	**100.00**
Average expenditure (HK$)	2 913	6 329	25 391	5 250

Note:
* These three levels correspond, approximately, to the 35th, 75th, and 99th percentiles in household expenditure.

Sources: Hong Kong Census and Statistics Department (1991), *Hong Kong 1991 Population Census: Summary Results*, Government Printing Department, Hong Kong; Hong Kong Census and Statistics Department (1991), *1989/90 Household Expenditure Survey and the Rebasing of the Consumer Price Indexes*, Government Printing Department, Hong Kong.

One indication of Hong Kong's prosperity is the ownership of consumer electronics products. In 1995, an estimated 98% of households owned at least 1 television set, and 34% owned 2 or more. Three-quarters of households also owned a videocassette recorder, while 38% owned the more expensive laser disk player for watching movies at home (*AA&M* 1996c).

However, in 1995 spending fell off sharply as consumers began holding onto their money. Median monthly household income rose about 13% on GDP growth of about 4.8% in 1995; inflation was about 8.5%. However private-consumption expenditure rose only 1%, after outpacing GDP growth strongly in most of the previous years of the past decade. Even food sales at supermarkets and other shops fell. Durables were especially hard hit. After years of replacing items such as TV sets or stereos every 3 or 4 years, consumers started holding onto them longer. Sales of consumer durables dropped 15% in the first 11 months of 1995, and motor-vehicle sales were down 35% for the year. About the only product categories that continued to show some growth were the types that tourists purchased (*AWSJ* 1996a; Bernas 1996c; EIU 1996).

Though some observers try to make light of these retail slumps, and predict upturns soon, most attribute slow spending to growing worry about 1997. This issue is not going to go away. In fact, in the first quarter of 1996, automobile sales remained 39% down from the first quarter of 1995. There has been some renewed interest in houses after the housing market declined substantially over 1995 and 1996. Prices are now lower than they have been for years, and houses represent a certain amount of security in uncertain times (*AWSJ* 1996a; Bernas 1996c; *Bangkok Post* 1996; EIU 1996).

Consumers and health care

General levels of health in Hong Kong approach the standards for most advanced industrial countries. Even critics agree that the quality of basic medical and health services is high. But some criticize the government for not providing some services, and for its low efficiency in delivery, crowded conditions, waiting time, and impersonal service. Some also point out that there is no clear policy for dealing with the shift toward health needs characteristic of an ageing population in a developed economy (This discussion is from the following sources: Ng 1990; WPPHC 1990; HKCSD 1991b; Huang 1991; Wong 1991; Hay 1992; HKGIS 1994, 1995).

Government policy stipulates that everyone should have access to adequate medical treatment, regardless of means. Patients are free to choose between private medical care, for which they pay themselves, or public care, which has only nominal costs. The basic care in public institutions is good, but they do suffer from the criticisms noted above. It is mainly the elderly and lower-income people who go to public clinics. Most patients in the middle class or above prefer private doctors. As a result, the private sector provides about 70% of primary care, and nearly 60% of registered doctors work in the private sector.

Medical care funding comes from the government, insurance, and out-of-pocket payments. The insurance industry has traditionally been weak in health care in Hong Kong. Growth is now being stimulated because comprehensive health-care insurance is becoming an important incentive companies use to attract and keep employees.

Health insurance was growing at about 40% annually in the early 1990s. However, in 1990 the majority of private expenditure was probably still out-of-pocket expenses, rather than insurance.

Consumer spending on medicines in 1989–1990 ranged from just a few Hong Kong dollars biweekly to almost HK$130 biweekly for households with the highest levels of expenditure. Typical middle-class families spent from HK$40 to HK$60. Spending on medical treatment was similarly very low for the lowest income families, but was over HK$250 to HK$300 for about 8% of households with the highest expenditure levels. These patterns reflect the public vs private sector choices. Lower-income people almost always go to government hospitals and/or clinics. The proportion of those seeking private medical help, and paying private-sector prices, increases as income increases.

High living standards and educational levels bring some awareness of health issues, as do cultural and social influences. For example, smoking, especially among women, is quite low in incidence compared to figures for the West and many Asian countries, so that diseases and birth complications associated with smoking are less common. Chinese family structure is strong, and the birth rate among young, unmarried women is very low. Drug use is quite low. The Chinese diet leads to far less obesity and associated health problems than the Western diet. In other words, many things that contribute to mortality in the West are much less prevalent in Hong Kong.

However, surveys suggest that most consumers are not very active in self-promotion of health. Most still believe in traditional explanations of illness, especially the "hotness" and "coldness" of traditional Chinese medicine. Although most still use them, very few regard traditional Chinese medicine practitioners or remedies as their primary health care. Nearly half change doctors frequently, even during the same illness. Partly this is because they seek quick relief from symptoms, and feel the doctor has failed if they do not get this; partly it is because, with minimal information available to consumers, they want to get an idea of the methods used by different doctors. Doctor "shopping" is most common among younger people from 20–29 years.

Consumers generally have low expectations when they visit a doctor or clinic, but they do expect the doctor to give them medicine. Surveys show that around 80% want this, and they also show that the vast majority have used over-the-counter (OTC) medication before visiting a clinic. A survey of doctors showed that 42% believe medication should be given for every consultation. Another survey of clinic patients found that doctors issue an average of over

3 different medicines per visit. But 70% in this survey left clinics without learning their diagnosis.

This is a major source of dissatisfaction. Consumers would like more complete information, but the health-care culture is not very open about giving information. As a result, people want to provide their own treatment if it is relatively simple. The OTC market is expanding as many pharmaceuticals shift from prescription drugs, available only through doctors, to OTC medicines. This shift has already occurred with many products, for example, cimetidine, topical antifungal preparations, and anti-diarrheal medicines. Large pharmaceutical companies such as Abbott, Pfizer, and Roche are rapidly expanding into this OTC market. Cheaper generics may become important in the lower end of the market, but the large, affluent middle class mainly demands branded products which they can trust to be effective.

Food-consumption patterns

Average biweekly household food expenditure in Hong Kong was nearly HK$1800 in 1990, the time of the most recent detailed survey on expenditure. This represents an average of about one-third of household expenditure (see Table 6.11), and about half of the expenditure, on average, is made in restaurants. Households with less money spend up to half of disposable income on foodstuffs. However, Cantonese truly love eating. As their incomes rise, they spend much more on food than needed simply to improve their diet somewhat. The 100 000 households with highest expenditure levels spend US$1000 or more per month on food (discussion drawn from Speece 1994, numerous consulting projects on food products conducted by Speece & So, and additional sources as noted).

Diet in Hong Kong is still thoroughly oriented toward Chinese, and especially Cantonese, cuisine. Western food, though, is becoming increasingly popular, especially in restaurants and fast-food outlets. Higher income consumers are most likely to visit Western restaurants. However, fast-food restaurants are popular among all income levels. All types of restaurant have enjoyed strong growth, but fast-food restaurants have far outpaced other types.

As they become more affluent, many Chinese start eating at home some foods that one would expect in the West, even though the style of preparation may remain Chinese. For example, pork, chicken, and seafood are the traditional meats in the Chinese diet, but beef sales have been expanding dramatically in the past decade. Lower income households mostly eat pork, usually imported from China. Higher income families eat more meat, including beef, imported from Western countries and Latin America. Fresh vegetables are traditional, but the use of Western vegetables such as bell peppers or broccoli has been increasing. Rice makes up a higher proportion of expenditure in less affluent families. Higher income families shift toward grains and processed products common in Western diets, such as bread, cakes, and biscuits.

More affluent consumers are demanding more variety in food products, and younger people actively seek new products. Many people are becoming more concerned about hygiene, which affects the type of restaurants and retail stores they visit. They are paying more attention to the ingredients in food, and are beginning to demand complete information on package labels. Freshness, always important in Chinese cooking, has become more critical to many consumers, leading to stagnant sales of many processed products, such as canned food (Chan & Yu 1992; Brabant 1995).

The high labor-force participation rate among women has also led to increasing demands for convenience. This is partly reflected in the very large share of total food expenditure which is allocated to restaurants. In part, the need for convenience translates into the use of convenience foods in home cooking. Microwave ownership has expanded at about 45% per year in recent years, and was at about 16% of households in 1989 (*AgExporter* 1991). Convenience is also behind the increasing popularity of precut and/or preseasoned packaged fresh meat and vegetables.

Health issues are also becoming important in food choice. For example, some stores now carry Hong Kong-grown organic vegetables, which are well accepted by consumers, even though prices are generally 15–30% higher than for other produce. In a small random sample (n = 93) of lower-middle to middle-class residents, over one-fifth said they were likely to choose organically grown vegetables. Similarly, canned/packaged foods without MSG and beverages without artificial additives were each preferred by about 15%. One-quarter of respondents said they were very likely, and another third somewhat likely, to switch brands if they saw a new brand advertised that stressed such characteristics (Tong 1991).

The impact on marketing of this increasing health consciousness is illustrated by a recent example. In December 1995, consumers began complaining about a sour smell and taste in some packages of Vitasoy soy milk. It turned out that, while the contaminating bacteria made the milk smell and taste sour, there was no actual health hazard. Nevertheless, consumer perceptions about the hygiene of the product had been damaged. In January, Vitasoy recalled all paper packaged drinks and stopped production at all plants until it could determine the source of contamination, at a total estimated cost of between HK$120 and HK$155 million (Silverman 1996). Anything else would probably have damaged severely the long-term prospects of the product. Hong Kong consumers are well aware of their rights to demand hygienic food products, and will simply stop buying products from manufacturers whom they perceive do not care about health safety.

Price has become unimportant in buying decisions for the majority of consumers. Surveys on a wide variety of products show that less than 25%

of the market is typically very price oriented. The Hong Kong consumer is invariably looking for better quality, based on whatever criteria he or she considers important—freshness, nutrition, taste, hygiene, or many others. Consumers trust and prefer popular brands, usually from the West, though in recent years many local brands have also become strong (Chan & Leung 1992; Chan & Yu 1992; Kawahara & Speece 1994; Speece, Kawahara & So 1994; Speece, So, Kawahara & Milner 1994).

Retailing

During the 1980s, department stores and large chains became increasingly popular, and by the 1990s they had established a dominant position in retailing. However, in the 1990s, smaller modern specialty stores also grew rapidly. They did not usually take much market share from the large stores, although growth of the large stores slowed. Rather, growth of these specialty stores came mostly at the expense of smaller, more traditional stores.

The popularity of larger stores is demonstrated by the concentration of sales. In the 1992 survey of wholesale and retail trade (the latest available), over 60 000 non-restaurant retail stores were recorded (see Table 6.12). Nearly 97% of these stores engaged fewer than 10 persons (in small stores, many of the people engaged are not employees, but family members). However, these small stores accounted for only 37% of sales revenue. Over 35% of sales were concentrated in the 141 stores (0.2% of all stores) with over 100 employees. (In the larger stores, persons engaged are employees.) These proportions were hardly changed at all from 1988, although nearly 9000 new stores had been added since the 1988 survey of wholesale and retail trade. In 1992, the 8 largest stores averaged over HK$3 billion in sales revenue each (HKCSD 1991c; HKCSD 1994).

These largest stores are mostly department stores. Department stores, especially the Japanese stores, have become key retail outlets in Hong Kong, setting the pace for many other retailers. Generally, younger consumers and those who consider themselves more modern and more concerned about their appearance tend to favor Japanese stores. They believe that the Japanese stores carry higher quality goods than local stores, and offer a better atmosphere and better service. These consumers are not put off by the perceived higher prices in the Japanese stores. By the early 1990s, 11 major Japanese department stores were present in Hong Kong, some with multiple stores, and they had captured over 40% of department-store sales (McGoldrick 1992; Phillips, Sternquist & Mui 1992; Kawahara & Speece 1994).

Consumers generally perceive the local Chinese department stores to be low- to middle-market retailers (see Table 6.13). Several Japanese stores, such as Yaohan or Jusco, also compete quite successfully in this part of the mass market. The middle part of the market is dominated by Japanese and

Table 6.12 Indicators of retail performance by store size, 1992

Number of persons engaged	*Number of stores*	*Sales revenue (HK$ mil)*	*Sales per store (HK$1000)*	*Sales per person engaged (HK$1000)*	*Sales per m² (HK$1000)*
< 5	53 557	50 722	947	490	37.9
5–9	5 250	30 165	5 746	942	82.4
10–19	1 199	24 346	20 305	1 671	111.7
20–49	412	19 259	46 745	1 657	70.8
50–99	146	15 982	109 466	1 771	85.9
100–199	56	9 896	176 714	1 349	45.6
200–499	57	21 312	373 895	1 171	47.6
500–999	20	21 176	1 058 800	1 551	66.2
1000 & over	8	24 371	3 046 375	1 420	41.1
Total	**60 705**	**217 229**	**3 578**	**957**	**54.9**

Note:
Number of persons engaged exceeds employees. Some people working in stores (e.g. family members) are not employees.

Sources Hong Kong Census and Statistics Department (1994), *Hong Kong Annual Digest of Statistics*, 1994 edn, Government Printing Department, Hong Kong.

Western stores, though a few Chinese stores still compete in this part of the market. Mitsukoshi represents this strategy in Table 6.13, but most other Japanese stores, such as Sogo, Daimaru, or Tokyu, compete similarly. The main up-market department stores are Seibu and Lane Crawford (Lum 1990; Kong & Wong 1991; Kawahara & Speece 1994).

In the tighter retail market of the mid-1990s, all types of stores are suffering. Many small stores that lack much modern management expertise are already losing sales, and only ones that adopted more modern planning and management have continued to be competitive. The rapid growth of specialty stores, such as fashion boutiques and jewelry/watch stores, has slowed to almost nothing (Table 6.14). Even department stores, which had already achieved their dominant position by the 1990s, still posted slow growth in the early 1990s—but volume declined slightly in 1995. The difficult market, combined with very high rents and uncertainty over 1997, have led some Japanese stores to close or reduce the size of their operations in 1994 and 1995 (Phillips & Calantone 1994; EIU 1996).

Food retailing

Food retailing shows similar patterns, except that several local chains, not connected to the local department stores, have become very strong. There are

Table 6.13 Consumer perception of department-store target markets

	% of respondents who think the target is:			
Store	*Up-market*	*Mid-market*	*Lower-end*	*(Don't know)*
Yaohan	3	41	55	1
Jusco	5	50	41	3
Wing On	3	41	56	–
Sincere	4	47	49	–
Mitsukoshi	23	70	10	1
Shui Hing	29	50	18	3
Marks & Spencer	30	51	16	3
Lane Crawford	86	11	2	1
Seibu	52	22	1	25

Note:
Seibu had opened less than a year before the survey, and some respondents were not familiar with it.

Source: C.H. Kong & W.S.Wong (1991), An Opportunity Study for an American Department Store in Hong Kong, unpublished MBA thesis, Chinese University of Hong Kong, cited in Yukiko Kawahara & Mark W. Speece (1994), "Strategies of Japanese Supermarkets in Hong Kong", *International Journal of Retail and Distribution Management*, vol. 22, no. 8, pp. 3–12.

still some traditional outlets remaining in modern Hong Kong, including small neighborhood stores and wet markets (fish and other produce). Most customers at small stores tend now to be older, less educated, and have a low income. However, even many "modernized" Chinese shop for some foods in wet markets, primarily because they believe that many kinds of food are fresher in these markets. The vast majority of fresh fruits and vegetables sold in Hong Kong probably move through wet markets (Choy 1991; Speece 1994).

Many middle-class people are showing a preference for shopping in supermarkets. This has led to the rapid evolution of food retailing in Hong Kong during the past 15 years, with an increasing concentration of sales in supermarkets. There were nearly 23 000 food retailing outlets in Hong Kong in 1986, but fewer than 21 000 by 1992. It is estimated that more than one-half of all food sales now go through supermarkets. Over 36% of sales moved through just 14 stores in 1989, and the trend toward concentration has continued. Both volume and value of sales through supermarkets have expanded more rapidly than sales through other kinds of food retail outlets (see Table 6.14; Kawahara & Speece 1994; Speece 1994; HKCSD 1994, 1995b).

Supermarkets were first introduced into Hong Kong over 20 years ago. There were only about 100 by 1975, and 200 by 1980. But by 1990 there were well over 800 supermarkets, and the major chains were still growing rapidly. By 1990, the two largest chains were Park'N Shop and Wellcome,

Table 6.14 (a) Retail sales, and (b) indices of sales—value and volume—by product category

(a)

Year	*Sales revenues (HK$ million)*	*Year*	*Sales revenues (HK$ million)*	*Year*	*Sales revenues (HK$ million)*
1984	66 107.6	1988	101 895.7	1992	159 497.6
1985	67 901.0	1989	107 523.6	1993	179 782.7
1986	71 996.3	1990	115 365.0	1994	201 149.7
1987	84 003.1	1991	135 388.5	1995*	208 122.3

(b)

Indices of sales (value, volume)

Year	*1984*	*1990*	*1991*	*1992*	*1993*	*1994*	*1995**
Food/drinks/tobacco	73.9	102.5	114.7	119.0	126.9	135.7	139.8
volume	92.9	101.2	102.3	99.5	100.6	103.2	101.7
Supermarkets	45.8	102.3	116.3	127.9	140.6	155.9	163.9
volume	63.2	99.9	103.0	104.7	107.6	111.5	111.5
Clothing/footwear	49.5	100.8	124.6	156.4	204.5	257.8	280.3
volume	76.9	98.8	113.8	130.0	157.2	182.0	185.2
Motor vehicles/parts	27.4	101.7	128.2	191.8	193.9	186.0	154.3
volume	44.4	99.9	114.8	162.1	151.4	134.8	105.1
Other durables	83.7	104.5	123.9	140.8	164.5	179.9	179.8
volume	101.3	103.6	119.2	133.8	153.5	164.1	160.0
Department stores	41.7	103.6	115.6	131.8	144.5	155.0	159.4
volume	61.5	101.7	106.4	111.7	114.3	114.6	111.2
Jewelry/watches	59.7	98.2	116.3	137.4	152.0	171.2	176.7
volume	75.4	97.2	116.0	142.3	153.1	162.7	165.8
All retail outlets	58.7	102.4	120.1	141.5	159.5	178.5	184.4
volume	77.4	100.5	110.9	124.3	132.9	140.6	139.4

Notes:
* 1995 covers the period September 1994 to August 1995.
October 1989–September 1990 = 100.

Sources Hong Kong Census and Statistics Department (1994), *Hong Kong Annual Digest of Statistics*, 1994 edn, Government Printing Department, Hong Kong; Hong Kong Census and Statistics Department (1995), *Hong Kong Monthly Digest of Statistics*, Government Printing Department, Hong Kong, November.

whose parent companies are two of the largest importers of food items in Hong Kong. These chains have extensive penetration throughout all areas of Hong Kong, and in 1990 controlled, respectively, an estimated 24% and 34%

of packaged food sales in Hong Kong. Although some stores serve up-market customers, most focus on the broad middle- and lower-middle-class market (Kawahara & Speece 1994).

Many of the major non-local supermarkets are Japanese, located in Japanese department stores. One set of Japanese stores focuses on the broad market among middle- to upper-middle-class local Chinese, and defines the two major local chains as their main competition. Typical examples of these stores would be Yaohan or Jusco. The majority of the product assortment in these stores is oriented toward Chinese customers, but the stores do have small sections for Japanese and Western foods, because many such items have been adopted as normal parts of the diet. This category of Japanese stores does not compete on price very much, and often sets trends in the introduction of new products and new merchandising techniques (Kawahara & Speece 1994).

Other Japanese supermarkets are more like specialty niche marketers. They stock a high percentage of Japanese products, and target Japanese expatriates and local people who want a good selection of Japanese foods. There are also several small up-market chains (such as Lucullus and Oliver's) which cater mainly to Western expatriates and locals who have a taste for Western food products. These stores are located in major middle- to upper-class shopping districts rather than in the main residential areas. Both these Japanese and Western-style supermarkets usually set premium prices and aim for up-market customers (Speece, Kawahara, & So 1993; Kawahara & Speece 1994).

Warehouse stores are another type that should be mentioned, with Wal-Mart Value Clubs a typical representative. They are situated in residential areas, and target price-conscious households. However, shoppers are not visiting Value Clubs as often or spending as much as managers would probably like. Most Hong Kong people place a premium on convenience, service, and atmosphere. The warehouse format does not appeal to them much. Furthermore, few Hong Kong consumers buy in bulk, both because they prefer fresh food and because they have little extra storage space in their homes (this is especially the case for lower-income consumers). Furthermore, the Value Clubs tend to stock about 70% imported products, and only 30% local, but Hong Kong consumers are very traditional in what they eat at home, especially lower-income families (Herndon 1994, 1995). Only somewhat less than 25% of the market is truly price conscious, but these people do not buy in bulk, nor are they very interested in Western food products, no matter how cheap.

Restaurants must also be mentioned. Eating out is very popular among Hong Kong Chinese, and about half of the total food budget is spent in restaurants. All income levels frequent Chinese restaurants extensively. Fast-food restaurants also have widespread appeal, including Western chains such as McDonald's, but some local chains serving Chinese fast food are also popular. However, the retail slowdown has even hit Chinese restaurants.

Sales have been slipping since 1994 (Silverman 1995). Chinese restaurants now employ fewer people, the lucrative banquet business is slow, and many traditionally managed restaurants are suffering badly.

Advertising

Total spending on advertising (adspend) grew 6.6% in 1995 to reach US$1.95 billion, but this represents no real growth after inflation. Television was the favorite medium, accounting for over US$960 million, nearly half of total adspend (*AA&M* 1996e; Bernas 1996a; see also Table 6.15). Television has very extensive penetration in Hong Kong, giving very wide reach to advertisers. Nearly 99% of households own at least one set, while 34% of households own 2 or more (*AA&M* 1996c). In the first half of 1995, Hong Kong residents spent an average of 19.79 hours per week watching TV. Most of this was on weekday nights, with only a few hours devoted to TV during weekdays or on the weekend (*AA&M* 1995b).

Table 6.15 Advertising indicators: Advertising spending by media, 1995

Media	*Million US$ per year*	*Growth (%)*	*Share (%)*
Television	960.61	19	49.2
Newspapers	565.53	–12	29.0
Magazines	232.06	9	11.9
Radio	126.35	20	6.5
Mass Transit Railway	50.76	14	2.6
Movies	6.13	–24	0.3
Other	11.79	10	0.6
Total	**1 953.24**	**7**	**100.0**

Source: Asian Advertising & Marketing (1996), "Top Ten: A Regional Ranking of Adspend and Agency Billings in 1995", April 19, pp. 12–14.

There are two main local broadcast companies, each with a Chinese-language channel and an English language channel, as well as a Chinese channel that can easily be received in Hong Kong. In addition, there are numerous cable and satellite channels. Only about 6% of households had cable by mid-1995, but it is likely (though unmeasured) that more have satellite reception. TVB Jade, a local Chinese-language channel, dominates the ratings. This channel held all of the top 10 positions in the 4th quarter of 1995, and each of the 10 shows had ratings of 30 to 33 (*AA&M* 1996c).

Newspapers' share of total adspend fell to 29% in 1995. Total adspend for China properties, which was the highest overall spender in 1994, fell 70%.

This resulted in declining revenues for newspapers, which had taken the majority of revenue from such ads. Local property adspend in newspapers, however, was up slightly. Property companies have shifted their strategy somewhat, with strong cost-cutting measures in advertising. This has caused some shifting of accounts away from major agencies, and some observers note lower quality advertisements (Bernas 1996a, 1996c; see Table 6.16).

Table 6.16 Top 10 product categories, total advertising spending, 1995, and media share for the top five

	Adspend (US$ million)	*Annual Growth (%)*	*TV (%)*	*Radio (%)*	*Share Newspaper (%)*	*Magazine (%)*
Communication equipment & services	78.25	32.0	43.1	16.1	33.6	4.7
Residential estates—sales/rental	76.68	35.0	16.5	3.0	78.4	1.1
Travel/accommodation—overseas	63.29	3.0	40.7	6.8	42.6	6.4
Newspapers/books/magazines/radio/TV	62.22	–2.0	33.4	6.0	44.7	14.2
Watches	53.23	–3.0	54.9	1.1	11.6	27.9
Movies/entertainment	52.69	12.0				
Credit cards	52.55	47.0				
Restaurants/clubs	46.56	21				
Mainland China properties	43.75	–70.0				
Records and tapes	41.35	30.0				

Sources: Asian Advertising & Marketing (1996), "Profile ofHong Kong", March 8, p. 10 (media breakdown for top five); *Asian Advertising & Marketing* (1996) "Top Ten: A Regional Ranking of Adspend and Agency Billings in 1995", April 19, pp. 12-14 (overall figures).

Newspapers have also attracted new attention recently because of a fierce price war. The *Apple Daily*, a new Chinese language newspaper, at HK$4 undercut the HK$5-per-copy price that has been standard in the industry for several years. It rapidly gained the number 2 spot in circulation (but mainly because of its pro-Hong Kong editorial stance relative to China). Other major newspapers cut their prices to retaliate, and some went as low as HK$2 per copy. Advertising placement has increased dramatically in the newspapers that are winning the circulation wars, as advertisers hope to take advantage of increased circulation for not much additional cost. However, the losers saw their advertising revenue decline.

Several newspapers could not sustain the war, and closed, prompting some to complain that the price war would hurt press freedom after 1997 because there would be fewer independent papers. By March 1996, however, several major papers were slowly raising prices again, especially after seeing that the *Apple Daily* had not really suffered much. It had triggered the war, but never lowered prices beyond the original HK$4. Most of the gains for the winners came at the expense of the smaller competitors (*AA&M* 1996d; Hille 1996a, 1996b).

Magazine and radio advertising account for smaller shares of adspend. Magazines are a key medium for several product categories, such as leisure, retail, personal items, toiletries, clothing, and watches (see Table 6.17). Radio is a minor medium for most important product categories. However, in certain segments, especially for younger consumers, radio is becoming important. Among these consumers listenership has increased in recent years, spurred by the increasing popularity of Walkman-type radios with small earphones. Pop singers and popular DJs have increased the appeal, and many observers expect future growth in advertising on radio to reflect this trend (*AA&M* 1995a, 1996a; *AsiaWeek* 1996a).

There is also some outdoor advertising, though this part of the industry is small compared to some Asian countries, such as Japan or Korea. Although the garish neon lights are conspicuous in Hong Kong's night-time skyline, most outdoor adspend is actually on the MTR (Mass Transit Railway). Most advertising on the MTR is for young adult fashion and consumer electronics. A few products also make good use of tram and bus-shelter advertising (*AA&M* 1995a, 1996b; *AsiaWeek* 1996a).

Advertisements in Hong Kong are among the most sophisticated in the world in terms of technological and artistic competence, though not every supplier meets the high standards. For example, advanced digital techniques are now common, and the Hong Kong industry picks up advances rapidly, particularly if they come from North America or Japan. Most major advertising agencies from these countries have a strong presence in Hong Kong. Local consumers expect high quality advertising, and they rarely respond well to those that are not up to high standards (Bernas 1995).

Creative appeals are shifting from hard sell to a softer approach that incorporates emotional appeal. This is more in line with local culture, and may reflect the growing influence of locals in the multinational agencies. Relative to Western advertisements, humor seems to be less frequent. Many advertisements now reflect Chinese family values and human concern for those close to the viewer. People seem to appreciate advertisements that demonstrate warm feelings, a "people" orientation, the natural environment, and even a rural setting to provide a contrast with hectic daily life.

Consumer worry and caution in 1995, which caused a slump in retail sales and slowed spending in advertising, did provide opportunities for some

Table 6.17 Top 5 product categories in adspend by media

Top five categories advertised on TV (US$ million)

Category	*Jan–June 1995*	*Jan–June 1994*	*Change (%)*
Haircare and conditioner	18.02	12.29	46.7
Credit cards	17.22	10.94	57.4
Watches	12.97	13.31	-2.6
Various media	12.95	16.45	-21.3
Communication equipment/services	12.23	8.97	36.3

Source: Asian Advertising & Marketing (1995), "Television Roundup: Top Five Advertisers and Categories", December 1, pp. 10–11.

Top five categories advertised in newspapers (US$ million)

Category	*Dec 1994–Jan 1995*	*Dec 1993–Jan 1994*	*Change (%)*
Residential estates—sales/rental	27.73	25.77	7.6
Mainland China properties	20.24	52.81	-61.7
Travel/accommodation—overseas	13.23	16.06	-17.6
Newspapers/books/magazines/radio/TV	11.97	9.99	19.8
Movies/entertainment	11.61	11.55	0.5

Source: Asian Advertising & Marketing (1995), "Top Five Newspapers in Asian Countries", September 22, pp. 6–7.

Top five product categories in magazines, January to June 1995

Category	*Value (US$ million)*
Leisure	15.716
Retail	12.746
Personal items	12.302
Toiletries	11.943
Clothing	10.910

Source: Asian Advertising & Marketing, (1996), "Top Magazines in Asian Countries", January 12, pp. 8-9.

industries. Banking and financial products expanded their services and stressed messages focused on security and ensuring future family prosperity. The top 10 advertised brands in 1995 were banks (including credit cards), which also showed some of the highest increases in adspend for 1995 (Bernas 1996a). Adspend for telecommunications equipment grew by 30% as the industry was deregulated and new competition entered the market.

Computer adspend grew 27% in recognition of the increasing enthusiasm for multimedia and Internet/online services (Bernas 1996c).

Many other product categories increased adspend to try to counter declining consumer sentiment. Liquor increased adspend by 31%, records/tapes 30%, toiletries 22%, and retailing 14%. Top advertised brands in 1995 included Kao (a Japanese consumer-products company), Hong Kong Bank, Marlboro, Hutchinson Communication Equipment (a local telecommunications company), McDonald's, ATV (a Hong Kong TV station), National/Panasonic/Technics (from a Japanese consumer-electronics company), Standard Chartered Bank, Hang Seng Bank, and American Express. Among these, growth in spending by Marlboro, McDonald's, and National/Panasonic/Technics barely kept pace with inflation (*AA&M* 1996e; Bernas 1996c).

Due to the retail-sales slowdown in 1995, many advertisers have become more oriented toward short-term sales promotions, especially price-offs and sales. Consumers are not expecting large bonuses or much improvement in salaries, so sentiment is not likely to change rapidly, and consumers will continue to respond to deals. Some advertising reflects this, concentrating on the deals, not the product characteristics and image as was done in the past. Such trends are visible for real estate, automobiles, consumer electronics, computers, and even jewelry (Bernas 1996c).

Future trends

Over the past several decades, Hong Kong consumers have become used to ever-increasing incomes and spending power. As a result, they have been on a huge spending spree until quite recently. These decades saw a wholesale shift away from pure price consciousness toward a greater value and quality orientation. Many local businesses did not keep up with changing consumption habits, and continued to believe that local consumers were all price conscious. This gave foreign products easy entry into Hong Kong. Much of the local middle class became very brand conscious, favoring, especially, foreign brands and retailers.

Most forecasts see the economy slowing during the last years of the 1990s. Under Chinese rule, it is unlikely that Hong Kong will again see the high growth rates characteristic of the 1970s and 1980s. The particular advantages that helped fuel rapid growth will be diluted, including Hong Kong's unique position as a gateway to China. Hong Kong is hustling to remain China's most important warehouse and distribution center, port, and financial center, and there is no doubt that it will retain an important role into the foreseeable future (Pinkerton 1995). However, relatively tight Chinese control will tend to dampen growth, since the advanced, internationally oriented service economy requires free movement of capital, information, and people.

In the long run, Hong Kong is likely to become a services center for the Guangdong economy, with increasing economic integration into South China. This in itself is not a small role. Hong Kong will be an important Chinese city, certainly, and part of the vibrant economy of South China. But it will start to look more like a Chinese city, and gradually lose its character as an advanced international city with very high living standards. Sinization is likely to occur throughout all spheres, including the cultural and economic spheres, and consumer behavior.

This is not necessarily bad for Hong Kong. The "Greater China" economic region (usually Guangdong, Fujian, Taiwan, and Hong Kong) looks set to continue its economic growth, and Hong Kong will be a key part of the region. This southern China–Taiwan–Hong Kong triangle is becoming increasingly integrated economically, and already has an aggregate economy which ranks it among the top trading powers in the world (Hamilin 1994; Chang 1995). Hong Kong will therefore remain a key commercial center within a very dynamic regional economy, but that does not mean that it will remain unchanged.

There may well be changes in Chinese policy within a few years, since part of the reason for hard-line policies in many areas is uncertainty over succession. However, unless there are substantial changes in policy toward Hong Kong relatively soon, it seems likely that a large part of the middle class will emigrate. Buying power will decline. Hong Kong consumers are beginning to adjust to lowered expectations. In 1994 the first signs came that spending would slow down, and in 1995 spending fell across many product categories.

Hong Kong consumers have developed a very high level of brand consciousness, and up-scale brands (usually foreign) have done very well. However, a strong shift toward value oriented brands is beginning. The brands may still be expensive, but not as much as luxury brands. Consumers perceive many in-house brands from retailers such as Giordano (clothing), Marks & Spencer (department store), and Park 'N Shop (supermarket) as offering better value for the money. These tend to be mid-market brands (Bernas 1996c). Prospects for such local value brands are very good.

Many local companies have patiently built up their position over the past decade, and the payoff is likely to come with this new consumer sentiment. There is also increasing competition from Chinese brands as Chinese companies upgrade their product quality and their marketing expertise to move into value markets. Very strong foreign brands will continue to find a market, especially if they are international and not too oriented toward the pure luxury market. However, there will almost certainly be a sharp decline in the strong sales of everything Western or Japanese at high prices simply because these goods were foreign. Many luxury brands are likely to decline most rapidly.

The market will probably not be able to support such a high concentration of large foreign stores in the upper parts of the market through the end of the 1990s. Some of them will either reduce their scope of operations, or withdraw. However, the local chains will continue to expand, and small traditional stores will continue to decline. Discount and wholesale/warehouse-type stores will begin to enter the market more strongly. There are already some Chinese chains present, but they appeal mainly to price-oriented segments. Chinese retailing has not yet been quite as fast to modernize as some other sectors, so the Chinese stores are likely to be slow at moving into value segments to compete strongly against local stores.

Advertising will probably begin to shift to appeal more strongly to Chinese tastes, as Westernized Chinese either leave or shed their Westernization. Creative appeals are already beginning to shift away from hard sell, more typical of the West, to a soft-sell approach that uses emotional appeal more in tune with local culture. Thus advertising reflects the trends that will probably prevail throughout Hong Kong society: localization toward becoming more Chinese and less obviously Western. Hong Kong is good at adapting, and will eventually redefine for itself a prominent role.

Conclusion

To date, it is clear that any changes in Hong Kong will be gradual. Among other things, current trends indicate that there will probably be a gradual erosion of democratic rights, and a creeping shift in the business culture to match the PRC more closely. These should have little immediate impact on consumption patterns. Some dire predictions have not yet materialized. For example, Beijing has been quite strict in controlling immigration into Hong Kong, even to the extent that tourist arrivals from the PRC are down sharply. Similarly, middle-class residents are not yet leaving at a higher rate than they were immediately before the hand-over.

Most worrying for marketing is continued slow economic growth, and the continuation of the retail slump. Growth for fiscal 1996 and 1997 was estimated at 4.7% and 5.5% respectively (*FEER* 1997). There was a short-term upturn in economic growth, consumer spending, and retail sales in the run-up to the hand-over, but, as of December 1997, all have slowed down again.

Part of the problem for retail revenues is the sharp drop in tourist arrivals. The economic crisis in much of East and South-East Asia has hit many of Hong Kong's tourist markets. The return to China makes it less exotic, in the perception of many tourists, and more like many other Chinese cities. When Hong Kong's high prices are added in, the city seems much less competitive relative to many other Asian cities, especially for shopping (BD 1997; IHT 1997).

However, local spending is also down. Consumers are worried about the economy, which has suffered fallout from the general economic downturn in most neighboring countries. The stockmarket fell sharply during

November, there was a (so far unsuccessful) speculative attack on the Hong Kong dollar, and there have been runs on banks and retail stores. In addition, spending power has been eroded somewhat by higher mortgage rates, because property prices have risen rapidly until recent months, and because interest rates have been raised in an attempt to curb speculation (*AWSJ* 1997a; *AW* 1997; *BP* 1997a; *Nation* 1997).

Yaohan, a major Japanese department-store chain, closed in late November, and a number of retailers in which Yaohan held shares have suffered a loss of confidence. However, its problems are more a reflection of difficulties in Japan and over-ambitious expansion than of Hong Kong's economic fundamentals (*AW* 1997; *AWSJ* 1997b; *BP* 1997b). Hong Kong's current slowdown is simply a continuation of trends evident before China took over. It mainly reflects the transition to a mature economy, rather than the serious structural problems evident in several neighboring countries, or any reaction to Chinese rule.

References

AgExporter (1991), "Snack Food Exporters Can Make (Micro) Waves in Hong Kong", June, pp. 9–11.

Asian Advertising & Marketing (*AA&M*) (1995a), "Top Five Newspapers in Asian Countries", September 22, pp. 6–7.

— (1995b), "Television Roundup: Top Five Advertisers and Categories", December 1, pp. 10–11.

— (1996a), "Top Magazines in Asian Countries", January 12, pp. 8–9.

— (1996b), "Lure of the Bright Lights Dims (Special Focus: Outdoor)", January 26, pp. 12–13.

— (1996c), "Profile of Hong Kong", March 8, p. 10.

— (1996d), "End to HK Price War in Sight", March 22, p. 6.

— (1996e), "Top Ten: A Regional Ranking of Adspend and Agency Billings in 1995", April 19, pp. 12–14.

Asian Wall Street Journal (*AWSJ*) (1996a), "Car Sales Fell 39% in Quarter in Hong Kong", April 24, pp. 1, 6.

— (1996b), "Hong Kong Residents Say they are more 'Hongkongers' Than Chinese", May 31–June 1, p. 3.

— (1996c), "Hong Kong's Growth Expected to Undershoot Official Forecast", May 31–June 1, p. 3.

— (1996d), "Hong Kong Keeps GDP Outlook for Year After Quarter's Results", June 3, p. 50.

— (1997a), "Hong Kong Housing Sector Defies Sell-Off Scenario", November 25, pp. 1, 5.

— (1997b), "Hong Kong Shoppers Are Reaping Bargains Sowed by Stores' Setbacks", December 1, p. 1.

AsiaWeek (1996a), "Rattling All the Way to the Bank: For Advertisers, Hong Kong's Trams are on the Right Track", March 22, p. 44.

— (1996b), "The Bottom Line", April 12, p. 55.

— (1996c), "The Price of Pollution", April 26, pp. 34–9.

— (1997), "Consumers on the Run", December 12, p. 31.

Bangkok Post (BP) (1996), *Hong Kong: the Financial Times Survey, Exclusive to the Bangkok Post* (articles on business environment, economy, trade, manufacturing, property, new airport, airlines, port, telecommunications), April 9, pp. 21–4.

— (1997a), "HK 'to Survive Speculative Attacks'"; "HK Investors Watch Market Wipe Out Their Dreams", October 29, p. B4.

— (1997b), "Yaohan Shuts HK Stores Amid Liquidation Threat", November 22, p. B2.

Bernas, Miguel (1995), "Digital Technology Weaves TVC Magic", *Asian Advertising & Marketing*, November 17, pp. 13–14.

— (1996a), "Move Over, Darling", *Asian Advertising & Marketing*, January 12, pp. 10–11.

— (1996b), "You've Lost That Spending Feeling", *Asian Advertising & Marketing*, March 8, pp. 12–13.

— (1996c), "Asian Advertising Review: Hong Kong", *Asian Advertising & Marketing*, April 19, p. 19.

Brabant, LaVerne E. (1995), "Tiny Hong Kong Offers Huge Market for Consumer Products", *AgExporter*, August, pp. 14–15.

Business Day (Bangkok) (BD) (1997), "Santa Unlikely to Bring Asian Retailers Much Cheer", December 5–6, p. 2.

Chan, Hing Lin (1995), "Chinese Investment in Hong Kong: Issues and Problems", *Asian Survey*, vol. 35, no. 10, pp. 941–54.

Chan, Kenneth Kin Nin & Leung, Elisa Wai Man (1992), A Market Research Study on Hong Kong People's Attitude Towards Breakfast and Breakfast Cereals, unpublished MBA Thesis, Chinese University of Hong Kong, Hong Kong.

Chan, Mei Yao Wendy & Yu, Jammy Yim Sheung (1992), A Study on Customer Profile of the Canned Fruits Market of Hong Kong, unpublished MBA Thesis, Chinese University of Hong Kong, Hong Kong.

Chan, T.S. (1994), "Environmental Consciousness and Consumer Purchase Preferences: A Hong Kong Study", *Capitalizing the Potentials of Globalisation: Proceedings of the Third Annual World Business Congress, June 1994, Penang, Malaysia*, Universiti Sains Malaysia, Penang, pp. 208–14.

Chang, Maria Hsia (1995), "Greater China and the Chinese 'Global Tribe'", *Asian Survey*, vol. 35, no. 10, pp. 955–67.

Chau, Simon S.C. (1990), "The Environment", in eds Richard Y.C. Wong & Joseph Y.S. Cheng, *The Other Hong Kong Report 1990*, Chinese University Press, Hong Kong, pp. 491–505.

Cheng, Kai Ming (1991), "Education", in eds Sung Yun Wing & Lee Ming Kwan, *The Other Hong Kong Report 1991*, Chinese University Press, Hong Kong, pp. 275–310.

China Statistical Yearbook (1995), China Statistical Publishing House, Beijing.

Chow, I.H.S. (1995), "Career Aspirations, Attitudes, and Experiences of Female Managers in Hong Kong", *Women in Management Review*, vol. 10, no. 1, pp. 28–32.

Choy, Nam Wo (1991), Wholesale Vegetable Marketing in Hong Kong: A Perspective on Marketing Channels, unpublished MBA Thesis, Chinese University of Hong Kong, Hong Kong.

Economist Intelligence Unit (EIU) (1996), *Country Report: Hong Kong and Macau, 1st Quarter 1996*, EIU, London.

Far Eastern Economic Review (*FEER*) (1995a), "Hong Kong. Asia 1996", pp. 122–6.

— (1995b), "A Woman's Place: For Three, It's in Hong Kong's Legislature—Making Waves", January 12, pp. 60–1.

— (1997), "Economic Indicators, Selected Asian Countries", December 11, pp. 72–3.

Farh, Jiing Lih, Leung, Kwok & Tse, David K. (1995), "Managing Human Resources in Hong Kong: 1997 and Beyond", *Columbia Journal of World Business*, vol. 30, no. 2, pp. 52–9.

Fong, Alex & Wilson, Barry W. (1995), "Executive Opinions on Hong Kong: Point and Counterpoint", *Columbia Journal of World Business*, vol. 30, no. 2, pp. 60–4.

Gaeta, Gordian (1995), "Hong Kong's Financial Industry in Transition", *Columbia Journal of World Business*, vol. 30, no. 2, pp. 42–50.

Hamilin, Kelvin (1994), "Greater China", *International Business*, vol. 7, no. 2, February, pp. 66–76.

Hay, Joel W. (1992), *Health Care in Hong Kong: An Economic Policy Assessment*, Chinese University Press, Hong Kong.

Herndon, Neil (1994), "Wal-Mart Goes to Hong Kong, Looks at China (Value Clubs)", *Marketing News*, November 21, p. 2.

— (1995), "Hong Kong Shoppers Cool to Wal-Mart's Value Club", *Marketing News,* November 20, p. 11.

Hille, Alfred (1996a), "No End in Sight for HK Newspaper Wars", *Media,* January 19.

— (1996b), "Apple Daily Eating Away at Readership of Rival Papers", *Media,* March 15.

Hong Kong Census and Statistics Department (HKCSD) (1991a), *Hong Kong 1991 Population Census: Summary Results,* Government Printing Department, Hong Kong.

— (1991b), *1989/90 Household Expenditure Survey and the Rebasing of the Consumer Price Indexes,* Government Printing Department, Hong Kong.

— (1991c), *Hong Kong Annual Digest of Statistics,* 1991 edn, Government Printing Department, Hong Kong.

— (1994), *Hong Kong Annual Digest of Statistics,* 1994 edn, Government Printing Department, Hong Kong.

— (1995a), *Hong Kong Monthly Digest of Statistics,* Government Printing Department, Hong Kong, November.

— (1995b), *Hong Kong Social and Economic Trends,* 1995 edn, Government Printing Department, Hong Kong.

Hong Kong Government Information Services (HKGIS) (1994), *Hong Kong 1994,* Government Printing Department, Hong Kong.

— (1995), *Hong Kong 1995,* Government Printing Department, Hong Kong.

Howe, Christopher (1995), "Hong Kong: Economy", *The Far East and Australasia 1995,* Europa, London, pp. 273–8.

Huang, Chen Ya (1991), "Medical and Health", in eds Sung Yun Wing & Lee Ming Kwan, *The Other Hong Kong Report 1991,* Chinese University Press, Hong Kong, pp. 311–28.

Internal Herald Tribune (IHT) (1997), "Once a Tourist Mecca, Hong Kong Loses Appeal as Passport Trophy", December 3, pp. 1, 10.

Kawahara, Yukiko & Speece, Mark W. (1994), "Strategies of Japanese Supermarkets in Hong Kong", *International Journal of Retail and Distribution Management,* vol. 22, no. 8, pp. 3–12.

Kong, C.H. & Wong, W.S. (1991), An Opportunity Study for an American Department Store in Hong Kong, unpublished MBA Thesis, Chinese University of Hong Kong, Hong Kong.

Kwong, Jo Ann (1990), *Market Environmentalism: Lessons for Hong Kong,* Chinese University Press, Hong Kong.

Kwong, Paul C.K (1990), "Emigration and Manpower Shortage", in eds Richard Y.C. Wong & Joseph Y.S. Cheng, *The Other Hong Kong Report 1990,* Chinese University Press, Hong Kong, pp. 297–337.

Lam, Kit Chun & Liu, Pak Wai (1995), "Labour Shortage in Hong Kong: Causes, Consequences and Policies", *Asian Economic Journal*, vol. 9, no. 1, pp. 71–87.

Lau, Kwok Yu (1991), "Housing", in eds Sung Yun Wing & Lee Ming Kwan,*The Other Hong Kong Report 1991,* Chinese University Press, Hong Kong, pp. 343–87.

Lau, Siu Kai & Chi, Kuan Hsin (1988), *The Ethos of the Hong Kong Chinese,* Chinese University Press, Hong Kong.

Lee, Martin Q.C. (1995), "Business and the Rule of Law in Hong Kong", *Columbia Journal of World Business,* vol. 30, no. 2, pp. 28–32.

Li, David K.P. (1995), "Enter the Dragon: Hong Kong's Growing Role in World Finance", *Columbia Journal of World Business,* vol. 30, no. 2, pp. 34–40.

Luk, Bernard H.K. (1990), "Education", in eds Richard Y.C. Wong & Joseph Y.S. Cheng, *The Other Hong Kong Report 1990,* Chinese University Press, Hong Kong, pp. 361–94.

Lum, Y.C. Richard (1990), Exploring the Reasons of Success of Japanese Department Stores in Hong Kong, unpublished MBA Thesis, Chinese University of Hong Kong, Hong Kong.

McGoldrick, P.J. (1992), "International Positioning: Japanese Department Stores in Hong Kong", *European Journal of Marketing,* vol. 26, no.8/9, pp. 61–73.

Nation (Bangkok) (1997), "HK-based Bank Admits 'Minor Run' On Deposits", November 11, p. B4.

Ng, Anthony (1990), "Medical and Health", in eds Richard Y.C. Wong & Joseph Y.S. Cheng, *The Other Hong Kong Report 1990,* Chinese University Press, Hong Kong, pp. 395–427.

Ng, Catherine W. (1995), "Hong Kong MBA Student's Attitudes Toward Women as Managers: An Empirical Study", *International Journal of Management,* vol. 12, no. 4, pp. 454–9.

Phillips, Lisa A. & Calantone, Roger (1994), "Hong Kong Retailers: The Relationship between Environment Hostility, Planning and Performance", *International Journal of Retail & Distribution Management,* vol. 22, no. 8, pp. 13–24.

Phillips, Lisa A., Sternquist, B.J., & Mui, S. (1992), Hong Kong Department Stores: Retailing in the 1990s, *International Journal of Retail & Distribution Management,* vol. 20, no. 1, pp. 16–24.

Pinkerston, Janet (1995), "Capitalism as Insurance", *Dealerscope Consumer Electronics Marketplace,* vol. 37, no. 12, December, pp. 13, 49.

Siddall, Linda (1991), "The Environment", in eds Sung Yun Wing & Lee Ming Kwan, *The Other Hong Kong Report 1991,* Chinese University Press, Hong Kong, pp. 403–19.

Silverman, Gary (1995), "Let Them Eat Linguini: Hong Kong's Chinese Restaurants Suffer a Slump", *Far Eastern Economic Review,* August 10, p. 68.

— (1996), "Say Sorry, Swiftly: Vitasoy Gives Hong Kong a PR Case Study", *Far Eastern Economic Review,* February 1, p. 45.

Siu, W.S. & Chu, P. (1994), "Female Entrepreneurs in Hong Kong: Problems and Solutions", *International Journal of Management,* vol. 11, no. 2, pp. 728–36.

Skeldon, Ronald (1991), "Emigration, Immigration and Fertility Decline: Demographic Integration or Disintegration", in eds Sung Yun Wing & Lee Ming Kwan,*The Other Hong Kong Report 1991,* Chinese University Press, Hong Kong, pp. 233–58.

So, Stella L.M. & Speece, Mark (1991), "Gender Stereotyping in the Mass Media: A Review of the Hong Kong Situation", Mass Media Awareness Seminar: Mass Media and Women in the 90s, Hong Kong, December 1990, pp. 177–82.

Speece, Mark W. (1994), "Wholesale Markets for Fresh Fruits and Vegetables in Hong Kong" (Technical Report No. 4), Regional Agribusiness Project, Bethesda, MD (USAID Contract AEP-0009-C- 00-3057-00).

— (1996), "Transportation Sector in China", *Asian Infrastructure: Opportunities for Cooperation,* Asian Institute of Technology, Bangkok [for Forum Engleberg, ESTA Strategy Project, Asian Challenge for Europe (European Commission)], pp. 146–66.

Speece, Mark W. & Kawahara, Yukiko (1995), "Transportation in China in the 1990s", *International Journal of Physical Distribution and Logistics,* vol. 25, no. 8, pp. 57–75.

Speece, Mark W., Kawahara, Yukiko, & So, Stella L.M. (1993), *Evaluation of U.S.FAS Market Development Activities in Hong Kong,* for U.S. Foreign Agriculture Service, Hong Kong.

— (1994), "Imported Beer in the Hong Kong Market", *British Food Journal,* vol. 96, no. 1, pp. 10–18.

Speece, Mark W., So, Stella L.M., Kawahara, Yukiko, & Milner, Laura M. (1994), "Beer Preference and Country-of-Origin in Hong Kong", *Journal of Food Products Marketing,* vol. 2, no. 2, pp. 43–64.

Suen, Wing (1995), "Gender Gap in Hong Kong: An Update", *Asian Economic Journal,* vol. 9, no. 3, pp. 311–19.

Tong, Edwin Ka Hung (1991), A Study of the Effect of the Green Movement on Consumers' Purchasing Behaviour Towards Non-Durable Goods, unpublished MBA Thesis, Chinese University of Hong Kong, Hong Kong.

Wan, Po San (1991), "The Quality of Life", in eds Sung Yun Wing & Lee Ming Kwan,

The Other Hong Kong Report 1991, Chinese University Press, Hong Kong, pp. 421–46.

Wong, Luke S.K. (1990), "Housing and the Residential Environment", in eds Richard Y.C. Wong & Joseph Y.S. Cheng, *The Other Hong Kong Report 1990,* Chinese University Press, Hong Kong, pp. 445–58.

Wong, K.H. Raymond (1991), "Pharmaceuticals", *American Chamber of Commerce in Hong Kong, Doing Business in Today's Hong Kong*, AmCham, Hong Kong, pp. 309–16.

Working Party on Primary Health Care (WPPHC) (1990), "Health for All: The Way Ahead, Report of the Working Party on Primary Health Care", Government Printing Department, Hong Kong.

CHAPTER 7

Indonesia

An emerging market with great potential

LAWRENCE H. WORTZEL & IGNAS G. SIDIK

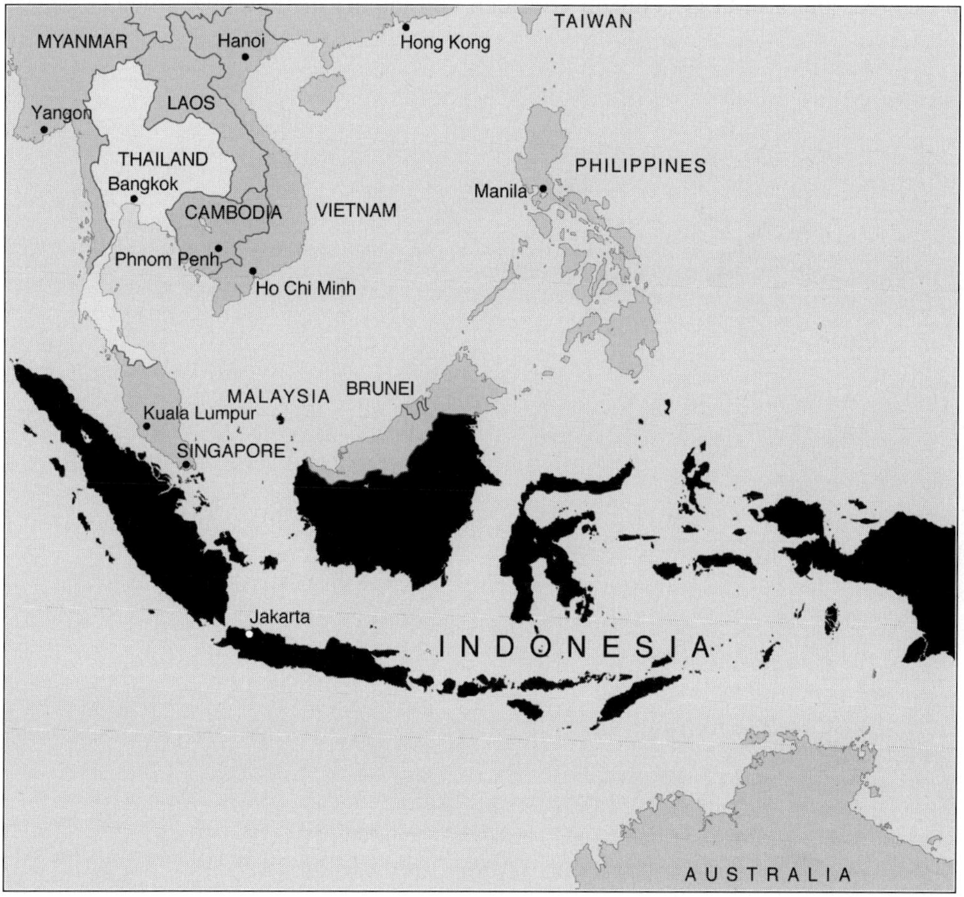

Abstract

An overview of the Indonesian market is presented, followed by a discussion of the most appropriate approaches to attaining access to its substantial potential. Indonesia is a complex country with considerable internal diversity in culture, geography and purchasing power. Because of its diversity, understanding Indonesia as a nation is a prerequisite for the comprehension of its marketing environment. To provide this understanding, the country's geography and climate is explained, followed by the demographic, economic, and cultural domains. Consumption patterns and some of the consumer motivations that drive consumption are then discussed, followed by an analysis of the traditional marketing mix variables and their use in Indonesia. Finally, predictions about the future of marketing in Indonesia and recommended marketing strategies are presented, and a brief conclusion considers the impact of the 1997 financial crisis.

Introduction

The Republic of Indonesia is one of the largest South–East Asian nations in area. In population it is the fourth largest in the world, and in 1997 it was home to more than 195 million people. The World Bank classifies Indonesia as a low-income country. Because of the country's large size and low per-capita income, a marketer could assume that its population would be primarily rural, thinly dispersed over an extremely large area. A thinly dispersed, low–income rural population, however large, does not make for an attractive business opportunity.

A closer inspection indicates that Indonesia's classification as a low-income country obscures significant present and near-term future opportunities. The country has been developing rapidly, and is in transition from a commodity-based economy to a higher value-added manufacturing economy. Indonesia has an established and fast growing middle class with significant purchasing power. The concentration of this purchasing power in a few urban markets allows for cost-effective market entry. For a wide variety of products, Indonesia is a market worth entering, and offers the prospect of sustained growth as more and more people enter the middle class.

In this chapter we present an overview of the Indonesian market, and discuss how to tap its substantial potential. Indonesia is a complex country with considerable internal diversity in culture, geography, and purchasing power. Because of its diversity, understanding Indonesia as a country is a prerequisite for the comprehension of its marketing environment. We therefore begin this chapter with an analysis of the Indonesian environment. The first aspect covered is the country's geography and climate, and we move then to the demographic, economic, and cultural domains. Next we discuss consumption patterns and some of the consumer motivations that drive consumption, and this is followed by an analysis of the traditional marketing-mix variables and their use in Indonesia. We close with predictions about the future of marketing in Indonesia, and recommend marketing strategies that are likely to lead to success in the country.

A brief introduction to Indonesia's geography and climate

Indonesia is an archipelago located in the Indian and Pacific oceans. It extends 5152 km from east to west and 1771 km from north to south, and consists of more than 13 000 islands. Its three largest islands, Sumatra, the Irian Jaya area of New Guinea, and the Kalimantan (approximately 75% of Borneo, the balance belonging to Malaysia and Brunei) account for about 75% of Indonesia's land area. Java, the Sulawesi (Celebes), and the Maluku (Molucca) Islands make up most of the remaining land area. The capital, Jakarta, is on Java. Indonesia is most famous, of course, for Bali, a small island off the southern coast of Java.

Marketers usually divide Indonesia geographically into 5 areas: Java and Bali; Sumatra; Kalimantan; Sulawesi; and East Indonesia, encompassing Maluku, Nusa Tenggara, and Irian Jaya. As we shall see, the country's population and its inhabitants' income are distributed unevenly across these marketing areas. To give a sense of perspective, the island of Java, encompassing 7% of Indonesia's land area, is as large as England. Sumatra, with 25% of the land area, is as large as France, and the Irian Jaya portion of New Guinea is about the size of Spain or California (*Euromoney* 1991).

Much of Indonesia has an equatorial monsoon climate, but the country exhibits substantial variation within this climate type. Around the equator, rain occurs more or less evenly throughout the year. The more northerly and southerly regions have a wet and a dry season. The north–east monsoon creates the wet season, which occurs from November to March; the south–west monsoon brings the dry season, extending from June to August or September. During the wet season rainfall is very heavy in most areas; during the dry season most areas become quite dry. The most easterly portions of Indonesia have a very dry season, which can extend for 7 months of the year. In most of the country, humidity is usually quite high, averaging between 70% and 90%. Temperatures range from 20–25°C in the evening to 28–34°C in the daytime, depending on the season and elevation from sea level.

The demographic environment–population: Size and distribution

As of 1997, Indonesia had almost 200 million inhabitants (Edwards, MacIntyre & Asra 1994), making it, next to China, by far the largest country in Asia. Its population is approximately 11 times that of Malaysia, 3 times that of the Philippines, and 4 times that of South Korea. It contains 58% of the total population of the ASEAN nations (Malaysia, Singapore, Philippines, Brunei, Thailand, and Indonesia). Due to a very successful nationwide family planning program, Indonesia held its population growth rate to 1.98% per year during the 1980–1990 period.

Geographic distribution

Table 7.1 shows the geographic distribution of the Indonesian population in 1990, and illustrates several important aspects of this distribution:

1 About 55% of Indonesia's population lives on the island of Java, which represents just 7% of Indonesia's landmass.

2 The Jakarta metropolitan area is extremely densely populated, holding almost 5% of the country's population and over 8% of Java's. By way of comparison, Kalimantan, with a population just 10% larger than Jakarta's, has a land area 810 times larger than Jakarta.

3 The population density of Java (755 people/square km) is more than 6 times that of the next-densest area, Nusa Tenggara.
4 Nusa Tenggara, however, because of its small size, is home to less than 6% of the Indonesian population.
5 Sumatra, with a much lower density than Java, holds 20% of the country's population.
6 The remaining 20% are scattered all over the archipelago; therefore most of Indonesia's land remains unoccupied.

Table 7.1 Population density of the major islands/groups of islands in Indonesia

Island/group of islands	*Area (1000 km²)*	*% of area total*	*Population as % of total 1971*	*1980*	*1990*	*Population (millions) 1990*	*Population per km² 1990*
Jakarta metropolitan area	0.7	0.03	3.8	4.4	4.6	8 228	12 500
Java (excluding Jakarta metropolitan area)	131.5	6.9	59.4	57.5	55.4	99 299	755
Nusa Tenggara (including Bali)	88.5	4.6	5.6	5.8	5.7	10 162	115
Sumatra	473.5	24.7	17.5	19.0	20.4	36 472	77
Sulawesi (Celebes)	189.2	9.9	7.2	7.1	7.0	12 510	66
Kalimantan (Borneo)	539.5	28.1	4.3	4.6	5.1	9 096	17
Maluku & West Irian	496.5	25.9	1.7	1.8	2.0	3 438	7
Total Indonesia	**1 919.3**	**100.0**	**100.0**	**100.0**	**100.0**	**179 248**	**93**

Source: Indonesian Central Bureau of Statistics (1993), Statistical Reports, Jl Dr Sutomo 68, Jakarta 10710.

Table 7.1 also points out some trends in the geographic distribution of the population since 1970. During the period 1970–1990, Jakarta's share of the Indonesian population increased as rural Javanese migrated there in search of jobs. During the same period, Java's share of population decreased, due, in part, to government policies that encouraged migration to other islands. Indonesia is a predominantly rural country in transition: on its way to becoming urbanized. In 1990, only 28% of Indonesian people were categorized as urban, and just 11% lived in urban aggregations having 1 million or more inhabitants (World Bank 1994b).

In actuality, contemporary Indonesia consists of 3 submarkets: rural, urban excluding major cities, and major-city urban. While there are hundreds of urban areas in Indonesia, there are only 27 that can be classified as major cities. Table 7.2 shows the development of Indonesia's 27 major cities from 1930 to 1980, ranked by 1980 size. While all grew during the period 1971–1980 (the last period for which figures are available), their growth rates ranged from 10.6% (Madiun) to 144.6% (Padang). This table understates Indonesia's urbanization, since most of these cities have suburbs that de facto belong to a particular city. Administratively they are not part of the city to which they actually belong, and therefore they are not counted in the figures.

Table 7.2 Development of Indonesia's 27 largest cities with more than 1 million in population, 1930–1980, ranked by 1980 population

No.	*City*	*Province*	*Number of population ('000)*				*Growth (%)*
			1930	*1961*	*1971*	*1980*	*1971–80*
1	Jakarta (5 cities)	Jakarta	533.0	2 971.1	4 576.0	6 503.4	42.1
2	Surabaya	Eastern Java	341.7	1 007.9	1 556.3	2 207.9	41.9
3	Bandung	Western Java	166.8	972.8	1 201.7	1 462.6	21.7
4	Medan	Sumatra	76.6	479.1	635.6	1 378.9	116.9
5	Semarang	Central Java	217.8	503.1	646.6	1 026.6	58.8
6	Palembang	Sumatra	108.1	474.9	582.9	787.1	35.0
7	Ujung Pandang	Sulawesi (Celebes)	84.9	384.2	434.8	709.0	63.1
8	Malang	Eastern Java	86.6	341.4	422.4	511.7	21.1
9	Padang	Sumatra	53.1	143.7	196.3	480.2	144.6
10	Solo (Surakarta)	Central Java	163.0	367.6	414.3	469.8	13.4
11	Yogyakarta	Yogyakarta	136.6	321.6	342.3	398.7	16.5
12	Banjarmasin	Kalimantan (Borneo)	65.7	214.0	281.7	381.2	35.3
13	Pontianak	Kalimantan (Borneo)	45.2	150.2	217.5	304.7	40.1
14	Tanjung Karang/ Teluk Betung	Sumatra	52.2	133.9	198.9	284.2	42.9
15	Balikpapan	Kalimantan (Borneo)	N/A	91.7	137.3	280.6	104.4
16	Samarinda	Kalimantan (Borneo)	N/A	69.7	137.5	264.7	92.5
17	Bogor	Western Java	N/A	154.1	195.9	247.4	26.3
18	Jambi	Sumatra	22.9	113.0	158.5	230.3	45.3
19	Cirebon	Western Java	N/A	158.3	178.5	223.7	25.3
20	Kediri	Eastern Java	48.5	158.9	178.9	221.8	24.0
21	Menado	Sulawesi (Celebes)	27.5	129.9	169.9	217.1	27.8
22	Pakan Baru	Sumatra	N/A	70.8	145.0	186.2	28.4
23	Madiun	Eastern Java	N/A	123.4	136.1	150.5	10.6
24	Pematang Siantar	Sumatra	15.5	114.9	129.2	150.3	16.3
25	Pekalongan	Central Java	N/A	102.4	111.5	132.5	18.8
26	Tegal	Central Java	N/A	89.0	105.7	131.7	24.6
27	Magelang	Central Java	N/A	96.4	110.3	123.4	11.9

Source: B.N. Marbun (1994), *Kota Indonesia Masa Depan: Masalah dan Prospek*, Airlangga, Jakarta.

The country's urban population has been growing at a high rate. From 1970 to 1992 the average urban annual growth was 5.1%, compared to a world urban growth rate of 2.7% (World Bank 1994a). By 1995, the urban population percentage had increased to 33%. The consensus prediction is that urbanization will continue to increase (see Table 7.3). One reliable source predicts that Java's urban population could reach 50 million by 2000 and 85 million, or 60% of the island's total population, by 2020 (World Bank 1994b).

Table 7.3 Urban and rural population, Indonesia, 1990–2020

Year	*1990*	*1995*	*2000*	*2005*	*2010*	*2015*	*2020*
Urban population (millions)	51.9	63.7	76.7	90.3	104.6	118.8	132.5
Rural population (millions)	128.5	132.1	133.6	132.8	130.5	126.6	121.2
Total population (millions)	180.4	195.8	210.3	223.2	235.1	245.4	253.7
Urbanization (%)	28.8	32.6	36.5	40.5	44.5	48.4	52.2

Source: Clive Edwards, Andrew MacIntyre, & Abuzar Asra (1994), "Peluang-peluang Baru untuk Saling Mengisi: Perubahan Demografis dan Permintaan terhadap Sekor Jasa", *Melebarkan Cakrawala: Australia dan Indonesia Menuju Abad ke 21,* Pustaka Sinar Harapan, Jakarta, pp. 27–60.

Age distribution

Table 7.4 confirms that Indonesia, in common with most other countries at its stage of development, is a country in which the young are in the majority. In 1995, one-third of the population (66.2 million) were 14 years of age or younger. Just 4% (8.6 million) were over 65. The high consumption age group (25 to 64) was 81 million, or 42% of the total.

Based on increasing life expectancy and the continuance of Indonesia's very successful family-planning program, its population is expected to grow by 29% over the next 20 years, adding some 57 million people. Children aged 14 or younger will decline slightly during this period, while the 25–64 age group will increase dramatically. In 2015, the number of 25–64-year-olds will increase by 62% to some 131 million, making up 51% of the population (World Bank 1994a).

The Indonesian household

In 1995, there were more than 45 million households in Indonesia. As Table 7.5 shows, the number of households has increased by nearly 50% since 1980, considerably outstripping population growth. From 1990 to 1995, the number of households increased by 13.8%, an average of 2.76% per year. These figures reflect the large number who became of marriageable age during this period.

The rate of household formation should mirror any changes in the population of marriageable age. A glance at Table 7.3 indicates that the 20–34

Table 7.4 Population by selected age groups, 1995–2015

Year	*1995*		*2000*		*2005*		*2010*		*2015*	
Age group	*million*	*%*	*million*	*%*	*million*	*%*	*million*	*%*	*million*	*%*
0–14 yrs	66.3	33.5	67.0	31.4	65.5	28.8	64.0	26.5	63.7	25.0
15–19 yrs	21.6	10.9	21.1	9.9	22.3	9.8	22.2	9.2	21.9	8.9
20–24 yrs	19.7	9.9	21.4	10.0	21.0	9.2	22.1	9.2	22.1	8.7
25–34 yrs	31.2	15.8	35.9	16.8	40.4	17.7	41.8	17.3	42.6	16.7
35–49 yrs	32.0	16.2	37.2	17.4	42.6	18.7	48.8	20.2	55.2	21.7
50–64 yrs	18.6	9.4	20.8	9.7	24.1	10.6	28.5	11.8	33.4	13.1
(20–64 yrs)	(101.4)	(51.2)	(115.3)	(54.0)	(128.1)	(56.2)	(141.2)	(58.5)	(153.3)	(60.1)
(60–64 yrs)	(5.0)	(4.9)	(5.7)	(4.9)	(6.4)	(5.0)	(7.2)	(5.1)	(8.7)	(5.7)
65+ yrs	8.6	4.3	10.2	4.8	12.0	5.3	13.9	5.8	16.1	6.3
Total	**197.9**	**100.0**	**213.6**	**100.0**	**227.8**	**100.0**	**241.4**	**100.0**	**254.9**	**100.0**

Source: Indonesian Central Bureau of Statistics (1993), Statistical Reports, Jl Dr Sutomo 68, Jakarta 10710.

age group should increase by 27% from 1995 to 2015, growing from 51 to 65 million. The number of households should therefore continue to grow substantially during the period 1995–2015, but at a somewhat slower rate than in the recent past. This somewhat more modest rate of increase results from the effectiveness of Indonesia's family-planning programs.

Table 7.5 Household by island/group of islands, 1980–1995 ('000 households)

	1980		*1990*		*1995*
Island/group of islands	*Households ('000)*	*Average size (persons)*	*Households ('000)*	*Average size (persons)*	*Households ('000)*
Java (excluding Jakarta)	18 459	4.6	23 168	4.3	27 725
Sumatra	5 375	5.2	7 474	4.9	8 899
Sulawesi (Celebes)	1 923	5.4	2 585	4.8	2 931
Kalimantan (Borneo)	1 323	5.1	1 942	4.7	2 430
Nusa Tenggara (including Bali)	1 684	5.0	2 136	4.8	2 422
Jakarta metropolitan area	1 164	5.6	1 740	4.7	2 054
Maluku & West Irian	444	5.8	677	5.2	861
Indonesia	**30 372**	**4.9**	**39 772**	**4.5**	**45 267**

Source: Indonesian Central Bureau of Statistics (1993), Statistical Reports, Jl Dr Sutomo 68, Jakarta 10710.

Average household size declined from 4.9 persons in 1980 to 4.5 in 1990. Most observers expect still further declines. Older families are typically of larger size than younger families. Prior to the 1960s, families with more than 10 children were not uncommon. As recently as 20 years ago, a family with 4 children was considered normal in size. Now such a family is considered large, even in rural areas. Family-size expectations have definitely changed. The majority of young Indonesian families intend to have 2 children at most.

Table 7.6 depicts the changing age composition of households. The proportion of children aged 0-4 years declined from 24.4% in 1980 to 16.8% in 1995, and is predicted to decline to 9.2% by 2010. In a period of sharp increase in the number of households, this prediction is in line with expectations that families with 2 children will be the norm. Since 1980, the Indonesian household has been moving from child dominated (48% from 0–9 years of age) toward teen and adult domination.

Table 7.6 Percentage of children in Indonesian households by age, 1980–2010

Age group	*1980*	*1985*	*1990*	*1995*	*2000*	*2005*	*2010*
0–4 yrs	24.4	21.4	19.3	16.8	14.3	11.7	9.2
5–9 yrs	24.0	22.7	22.8	22.2	21.6	20.9	20.3
10–14 yrs	21.4	21.6	21.5	21.6	21.7	21.7	21.0
15–19 yrs	16.6	17.7	17.5	17.9	18.4	18.9	19.0
20–24 yrs	8.5	10.1	10.8	11.9	13.1	14.2	15.0
25+ yrs	5.2	6.5	8.1	9.6	11.1	12.5	14.0
Total	**100.0**	**100.0**	**100.0**	**100.0**	**100.0**	**100.0**	**100.0**

Source: Clive Edwards, Andrew MacIntyre & Abuzar Asra (1994), "Peluang-peluang Baru untuk Saling Mengisi: Perubahan Demografis dan Permintaan terhadap Sekor Jasa", *Melebarkan Cakrawala: Australia dan Indonesia Menuju Abad ke 21*, Pustaka Sinar Harapan, Jakarta, pp. 27–60.

Growth in the proportion of urban households (see Table 7.7) also mirrors both population growth and the size differences between rural and urban households. As this table shows, the ratio of rural to urban households fell from 3.84 in 1980 to 1.96 in 1995. For the period 1995–2010, the prediction is that the number of rural households will stay almost constant; virtually all of the projected increase in the number of households will occur in urban areas.

Additional household residents

Children and their parents are not the only residents in a typical Indonesian household, especially in urban areas. Most families in urban areas have full time servants or "house assistants". In rural areas, only affluent families can afford servants. Currently, most urban families have at least 1 servant. The more

Table 7.7 Number of households, urban and rural, 1980–2010 (millions)

Household type	*1980*	*1985*	*1990*	*1995*	*2000*	*2005*	*2010*
Urban	6.3	8.7	11.6	15.1	18.8	23.2	27.0
Rural	24.2	26.4	28.0	29.6	30.6	31.1	31.0
Total	30.5	35.1	39.6	44.7	49.4	54.3	58.0

Source: Clive Edwards, Andrew MacIntyre & Abuzar Asra (1994), "Peluang-peluang Baru untuk Saling Mengisi: Perubahan Demografis dan Permintaan terhadap Sekor Jasa", *Melebarkan Cakrawala: Australia dan Indonesia Menuju Abad ke 21,* Pustaka Sinar Harapan, Jakarta, pp. 27–60.

affluent families usually hire more than 2 servants. In a typical upper-middle-class family there is likely to be a cook (usually female), 1 or 2 house assistants (either female or male), and 1 or 2 drivers (invariably male). It is also customary to hire a full-time babysitter (invariably female) when there are babies in the household. With the exception of drivers, most house assistants live in the family house. The home owner provides them with board and lodging.

In large cities like Jakarta, a driver's monthly salary in 1995 ranged from US$100 to US$300, and a good cook cost between US$30 and US$100, while a general house assistant cost between US$20 and US$50 per month. In smaller cities with a lower cost of living, salaries are approximately half of those in large cities. Salaries of household workers will inevitably increase substantially as the job market expands. With a high rate of industrialization, jobs as house assistants become less economically attractive than factory or office work.

In addition to house assistants, many households are home for an extended as well as a nuclear family. Parents, aunts, uncles, cousins, nephews, and nieces may be among those present in the household. This practice is more prevalent among urban families, especially among Javanese and Chinese. Other ethnic groups, such as the Sundanese, are less likely to host an extended family. Typically, members of the extended urban family are from rural areas. Many have come to the city for a variety of reasons, such as attending school or college, or hunting for a job. Others may, temporarily or permanently, have no other place to stay. In effect, the hosting family subsidizes its boarder-relatives. Space limitations in the cities, resulting from high demand for housing and the higher cost of living, may change this picture.

Marketing implications of Indonesian demography

Indonesia's projected demographic changes contribute to its market potential. For example:

1 Continued growth in the number of households will result in expanding markets for a wide range of consumer durables. Since incomes will also be increasing, these new households should be able to accumulate larger inventories of household goods.

2 Continued urbanization will increase the geographic concentration of consumer markets.
3 Expected higher costs of household servants should increase the demand for labor-saving household durables.
4 The trend toward fewer children suggests higher per-capita spending per child.
5 A continued pace of rural electrification will open new markets for small appliances such as lamps and electric fans.
6 If industry continues to spread geographically, the result would be a broadening of the market beyond urban areas.

The economic environment

Beginning in the 1970s, Indonesia has made a major transition from a poor, less developed country to a newly industrializing country. Its gross domestic product (GDP) in 1994, US$126 billion, reflects a country that has reduced the proportion of its people living in abject poverty from 60% in 1970 to 15% by 1990 (World Bank 1994a, p. xv). Table 7.8 shows that GDP has grown at over 6% per annum since 1990. During the period 1990–1994, total exports grew by 50%, while non-oil exports doubled, rising from 56% of total exports to over 75%. Growth in exports will provide both jobs and a significant portion of the funds required to expand industrial output.

Table 7.8 The economy in brief

Feature	*1990*	*1991*	*1992*	*1993*	*1994*
Growth rate of GDP (% p.a.)	7.4	6.6	6.2	6.6	6.9
Total exports (US$ billion)	26.8	29.6	33.8	36.8	38.5
Non-oil export (US$ billion)	14.9	18.2	23.3	27.4	29.3
Total imports (US$ billion)	21.4	24.8	26.8	28.1	30.2
Current account (US$ billion)	−3.2	−4.4	−3.1	−1.9	−3.5
Bank credit (Rp.* billion)	97 696	113 608	123 689	147 887	N/A
Bank savings (Rp. billion)	9 662	15 553	25 469	35 605	N/A
Inflation rate (% p.a.)	9.5	9.5	4.98	9.77	N/A
Average short-term credit (% p.a.)**	24–30	29.0	23.7	18.6	17.9

Notes:
* $1 (US) = R2 321.
** for private banks.

Source: Indonesian Commercial Newsletter (1995), "The Indonesian Economic Trends", Jakarta.

Indonesia's economic growth has been concentrated in its west (Seda & Watts 1994). Java and Bali contribute 57% of Indonesia's GDP, with Jakarta itself contributing 11%. Sumatra contributes another 27%. Together, Java, Bali, and Sumatra account for 84% of GDP. The remaining 16% comes from Kalimantan (9%) and East Indonesia (Sulawesi, Maluku, Nusa Tenggara, and Irian Jaya) (7%). These data reflect the concentration of manufacturing in the west, principally on Java.

The Indonesian government has been making efforts to foster economic development in the eastern provinces. These efforts include providing incentives for industry to locate in these provinces and encouraging the emigration of farmers as well as workers. If these efforts are successful, the result will be a more dispersed population and a more equal distribution of income across the archipelago.

One of the most important agenda items for Indonesia's government since the mid-1960s has been controlling inflation. The government's goal has been to hold inflation to single digits. Table 7.9 shows inflation rates for some major classes of goods during the period 1989–1993. With the exception of housing, inflation management has been successful. The high rate of migration to the cities, coupled with the inevitable lag in responding to housing demand, has fueled price increases in this sector. If inflation is to be contained in the future, it will be up to the government to take action whenever the economy starts to overheat. Given past experience and current policy, it is not unreasonable to expect that a single-digit inflation rate will continue over the next several years.

Table 7.9 Inflation rates in 27 major cities in Indonesia, calendar year (% per annum)

Type of inflation	*1989*	*1990*	*1991*	*1992*	*1993*
General price	6.0	9.5	9.5	4.9	9.8
Food	6.7	7.0	9.6	6.0	5.1
Housing	6.1	12.4	7.7	4.6	15.5
Clothing	4.7	4.8	5.2	7.2	8.0
Other goods & services	4.6	11.6	13.2	3.4	9.9

Source: Indonesian Central Bureau of Statistics (1994), "The Big Rise", *Fortune*, international edition, Indonesian Economic Report 1993, May 30, pp. 40–6.

Continued economic growth is imperative for the country. The projected increases in the working-age population (see Table 7.3) will add about 2.3 million people to the workforce each year. Absorbing them requires a sustained growth rate of 6–7% per year in the non-oil sector to maintain the country's rate of improvement in living standards. Consensus is that Indonesia will maintain annual growth at over 6% to the year 2000.

Achieving this growth rate will increase private consumption from approximately US$75 billion per year to US$100 billion by the year 2000. This achievement will substantially enlarge the market for goods and services.

Social welfare

Economic growth has enabled substantial improvements in social welfare (see Table 7.10). For example, the illiteracy rate among the population over 10 years of age halved between 1980 and 1993, dropping from 28.8% to 14.3%. In urban areas, the illiteracy rate for this age group was just 7.2% in 1993. Literacy, of course, is critical to the modern productive workforce Indonesia needs to meet its growth objectives.

Table 7.10 Selected welfare indicators of urban and rural areas, various years

Welfare indicators	*Illiteracy rate of population, 10 years+, %*			*Immunized babies, %*		*Houses with electricity, %*		
Year	*1980*	*1987*	*1993*	*1989*	*1993*	*1985*	*1989*	*1993*
Urban	14.5	9.0	7.2	81.3	86.2	72.8	83.9	90.0
Rural	33.2	22.7	17.9	65.1	72.0	15.9	28.3	38.8
Total	**28.8**	**18.9**	**14.3**	**60.3**	**76.3**	**30.5**	**47.0**	**55.3**

Sources: Indonesian Central Bureau of Statistics (1994), "The Big Rise", *Fortune*, international edition, Indonesian Economic Report 1993, May 30, pp. 40–6; Dumairy (1995), "Evaluasi Kebijakan Pemerintah Menanggulangi Masalah Kemiskinan dan Kesenjangan", in eds Awan Setya Dewanta et. al., *Kemiskinan dan Kesenjangan di Indonesia*, Aditya Media, Yogyakarta, pp. 75–90.

By 1993, the proportion of urban households with electricity had reached 90%. In rural Indonesia, however, households with electricity were in the minority; only 39% were electrified. Rural electrification has spread significantly since 1985, when only 16% of rural dwellings had electricity. Electrification projects have had to compete for funds with other infrastructure projects, limiting the speed with which electrification has proceeded. Opening up the power-generation sector to private investment could increase the rate in the future.

Health has also improved. The proportion of immunized babies from urban areas increased from 81.3% to 86.2% between 1989 and 1993. The proportion in rural areas is lower, but has been increasing at a faster rate than in urban areas. Not mentioned in Table 7.10 is another welfare indicator, the number of physicians. In 1970, there was 1 physician for every 26 820 inhabitants. By 1990, the ratio had decreased to 1 for every 7030 (World Bank 1994a).

The Indonesian sociopolitical environment

Indonesia began its life as a sovereign nation as an amalgam of some 300 ethnic groups speaking almost 600 different languages and dialects. There were several religions practiced, although one, Islam, predominated. During the period since independence, Indonesia has not experienced the degree of ethnic or religious strife evident in some of the other countries with highly diverse populations. The Indonesian nation has, in fact, become more united since its birth. Several factors have contributed to the nation's increasing unity:

- Indonesia's motto, *Bhinneka Tunggal Ika*, roughly "Unity in diversity," recognizes the fact of diversity as well as the need for unity, and has guided much government action.
- The concept of *Pancasila*, articulated by Indonesia's founding father and first president, Sukarno, has been strongly inculcated in the population. *Pancasila* rests on 5 principles: belief in the one supreme god, a just and civilized humanity, the unity of Indonesia, democracy guided by the inner wisdom of unanimity and social justice for all the people of Indonesia.
- There has been tolerance of religions other than the predominant religion, Islam. The government officially recognizes 4 religions: Islam, Hinduism, Christianity (including both the Catholic and Protestant groups), and Buddhism.
- Religious fundamentalism has been actively discouraged.
- A strong central government has moved, when necessary, to limit the influence of dissident groups.
- The country adopted a single national language, *Bahasa Indonesia*, which is the only language taught and used in government-run schools.

As is the case in most other countries, Indonesia is not without its dissidents. Small groups of Islamic fundamentalists, based primarily in Northern Sumatra, have agitated for a more traditional approach to religion. East Timorese, who are predominantly Catholic rather than Moslem, have strongly pressed for East Timor to be an independent state.

Government structure

Indonesia is a republic governed by a president who heads both the executive and legislative branches of government. There is a parliament, the House of People's Representatives (*Dewan Perwakilan Rakyat*, or *DPR*), consisting of 500 members. Of these, 400 are elected by the people, and the remaining 100 are appointed by various functional groups and political parties to represent a specific constituency. One party, the Golkar, has dominated Indonesian politics since the 1970s. Senior military officers have also been active participants in government, both in parliament and in the executive branch. The country is divided into 26 provinces, each headed by a governor, and further divided into second- and third-order divisions. Fifty-four of the largest cities are autonomous units. Power, though, resides principally with the federal government. Officials of the central government head all provincial and local governments. Observers comment that Indonesia's strong central government has contributed to the country's political stability.

The national language: Bahasa Indonesia

During their term as rulers of Indonesia, the Dutch did not make efforts to diffuse the Dutch language widely in the Indonesian population. Among Indonesians only the ruling upper class and government officers spoke fluent Dutch. In fact, at that time, the ability to speak Dutch was considered a sign of breeding.

Since the late 19th century, rank-and-file Indonesians have begun to adopt the Malay language in addition to their own dialects. Malay became widely accepted, and began its metamorphosis into the Bahasa Indonesia that became the national language after independence.

Diffusion of Bahasa Indonesia after independence was fast and thorough. The new, young group of government officials that came to prominence after independence had grown up speaking Bahasa rather than Dutch. Although some ethnic groups still maintain their own language or dialect, Bahasa Indonesia is the only official communication vehicle, and dominates the media.

The growing role of the English language

English has been a part of the formal school curriculum since the late 1960s for students with education beyond elementary school. It is taught at 7 grade levels, 3 during junior high school, 3 more in the high school, and at least the freshman year of college. Until the mid-1970s, however, few Indonesians spoke fluent English because there was little need or motivation to do so. The tourism boom, beginning in the late 1970s, revitalized efforts to study English because knowledge of English could lead to a good job. Furthermore, many high school graduates from the affluent upper and middle classes began to go abroad for university-level studies.

By the late 1980s, Indonesia had a cadre of English-trained graduates who had returned from the USA, Australia, and the UK. Additionally, English movies, books, and television programs had become widely available. The growth of direct foreign investment and joint ventures created demand for English speaking employees. English had become the worldwide *lingua franca* of business, and was permeating Indonesian life.

In the 1990s, there has been some government reaction to the proliferation of English usage. Many domestic companies started using English brand names. In the fast food industry, for example, indigenous enterprises began using names such as California Fried Chicken in order to imitate the US franchise Kentucky Fried Chicken. Most new property developments in large cities began to use names such as The Regency, or Lippo Village to emphasize their luxury or exclusivity. In early 1995 the government began to take action to limit the use of foreign names, considering this unpatriotic.

However, despite expressions of government displeasure, the use of English will keep increasing. English will not, however, supplant Bahasa as the country's established language. However, Indonesia's traditional tribal and ethnic languages and dialects are in danger of becoming extinct. In the younger generation of virtually every ethnic group, Bahasa Indonesia has replaced the traditional ethnic language as the mother tongue. We expect that the local dialects will become archaic over the next few decades.

English is well established as Indonesia's second language, most notably among the upper and upper-middle classes. English language advertising in newspapers, on television, and in direct mail is common. Most executives have a good working command of English, and are using it extensively in domestic commerce. It is doubtful that English will replace Bahasa as Indonesia's primary domestic business language; it will remain the second language of business. It is likely, though, to become even more widely used, especially in advertising and business documents such as product-information brochures. More and more product information will be presented bilingually—in all media.

Consumer income and socio-economic class

On a nationwide basis, the Indonesia of the mid-1990s is still classified as a poor country, with an average per-capita annual income of US$670. Its Gini ratio, which reflects income disparity, is low, as Table 7.11 shows. The low ratio suggests that the income disparity between rich and poor is relatively small. Furthermore, the Gini ratio for rural Indonesia (0.26) is lower than the urban area ratio (0.33). This suggests that income disparity is lower in rural areas. However, the Gini ratio tells only a small part of the story because it does not measure the magnitude of income. In reality, the urban population has much higher purchasing power than the majority of the population.

Table 7.11 Distribution of income (as % of population) and Gini ratio of urban and rural population, 1993, based on expenditure

Population sector	*Lowest 40%*	*Middle 40%*	*Highest 20%*	*Gini ratio*
Urban	20.5	37.3	42.2	0.33
Rural	25.1	38.4	36.5	0.26
Total	**20.3**	**36.9**	**42.8**	**0.34**

Source: Indonesian Central Bureau of Statistics (1994), "The Big Rise", *Fortune*, international edition, Indonesian Economic Report 1993, May 30, pp. 40–6.

Moreover, per-capita incomes can be misleading indicators of purchasing power, for reasons other than masking income distribution. Price levels also determine purchasing power, and the only safe route to understanding a group's purchasing power is to examine it in some detail. Since the consumption unit for many products is the household, the number of income earners per household also affects its purchasing power. In addition, the large proportion of low-income people and the high percentage of them who work in the informal sector may result in the understating of this group's income; they may earn more than the estimates.

Table 7.12 shows the prices in mid–1995 for a variety of consumer products. At the prevailing exchange rate (R2 321=US$1), the prices of most necessities are low by developed-country standards. A kilogram of rice, for example, cost US$0.44, and a packet of noodles just US$0.13. A simple street lunch could be had for under a dollar (US), and "Coca-Cola" to accompany it was only an additional US$0.22. A locally built Toyota Kijang cost US$12 600, which put it within reach of the middle class.

Economic class

Indonesia's population is usually grouped into 5 socio-economic (or, actually, economic) classes: A, B, C, D, and E. The definitions of the classes, however, are not universal. Table 7.13 presents two such classifications, one made by a marketing research firm, the other by The Demographic Institute. Both classifications are expenditure rather than income based, and show the expenditure range in each class in both rupiah and US dollars. The classes form the basis for social-class distinctions.

In a country such as Indonesia, an expenditure-based classification is likely to provide a more accurate picture than a classification based on income. For many reasons, income data for the Indonesian population are not highly reliable. In many cases, a household's expenditures may exceed the reported income of its breadwinners. Hiding sources of income is a common practice among all socio-economic classes.

Although Indonesia's officially calculated per-capita income is low, *Fortune* (1994) estimates that there are more than 15 million households in Indonesia that have annual purchasing power parity between US$10 000 and US$40 000. Other observers call the *Fortune* estimate too low and claim, with some justification, that the number of households with purchasing power parity between US$10 000 and US$40 000 was closer to 25 million in 1993. By any measure, a solid and growing middle class was in place by 1993.

Yet other observers are more cautious. One such observer (Tait 1995) reports estimates of the middle-income group at 7–8% of the population. She places the proportion of urban adults with the ability to spend over R600 000 per month (the upper half of the "B" class and above) at 1 in 6. She also notes, optimistically, that the number of A and B households in Indonesia's 4 largest cities may have increased by as much as 49% between 1990 and 1994. This would suggest an increase from 2.2 to 3.4 million households.

Table 7.12 Retail prices in Jakarta of some commonly purchased goods (mid-1995)

Product	*Price (in rupiah)*
Automobile—rent or mortgage payment (per month), for household with R600 000/month	
Kijang (locally made, bottom-of-the-range)	28.6 million
Toyota Corolla1600	82 million
Mercedes Benz E 320	273.2 million
Monthly rent or mortgage payment	
Household with monthly income of R600 000	200 000
Household with monthly income of R2 million	750 000
Color TV	
Sony (21")	980 000
Polytron (domestic 20")	910 000
Electric rice cooker (1 liter)	40 000
Electric fan (basic model)	14 000
Men's white dress shirt (basic)	15 000
Athletic shoes	
Nike (top quality)	80 000
Nike (seconds—from local manufacture)	20 000
Domestic brand	15 000
Colgate toothpaste (100 g)	1 600
Lux Soap (bar)	450
Gasoline (per liter)	700
Cigarettes	
Marlboro (pkt of 20)	1 600
Jarum (domestic brand, pkt of 12)	900
Instant noodles per 1-serving pkg.	300
Candy bar (domestic brand)	300
Rice (1 kg)	1 000
"Coca-Cola" (small bottle)	500
Beer (375–500 ml bottle, domestic brand)	2 000
Bottled water (1 liter)	1 000
Cooking oil (1 liter)	1 700
Fresh pineapple (1)	500–2 000
Bananas (1 bunch)	2 000–6 000
Lunch	
At a street stand (*warung*)	2 000–3 000
At McDonald's or equivalent	6 000–10 000

Table 7.13 Socio-economic classes, based on household expenditure (rupiah per month)

Market research firm		*$ **	*The Demographic Institute*		*$ **
A+	> 900 000	> 410	n/a	-	-
A	700 000–900 000	320–410	n/a		
B	500 000–700 000	230–320	A	> 500 000	> 230
C+	300 000–500 000	135–230	B	300 000–500 000	135–230
C-	150 000–300 000	70–135	C	150 000–300 000	70–135
D	< 150 000	< 70	D	< 150 000	< 70

Note:
* using the exchange rate for January 1995: $1(US) = Rp. 2 321

Source: Private research.

Rural incomes include incomes in rural areas adjacent to large cities. According to government statistics, in 1995 just 25% of the rural group had monthly expenditure greater than R100 000 per month. In urban areas, 47% spent between R100 000 and R300 000, and 44% spent more than R300 000 per month.

The Jakarta income bulge

Compared with other areas in Indonesia, Jakarta looks like a foreign country that was simply dropped into Indonesia. According to one source (*Republika* 1995), per-capita income in Jakarta in 1993 had reached almost US$2500, as compared with US$670 for the country as a whole. Another source estimated per-capita disposable income in Jakarta at between US$1776 and US$4000. *Asian Business* (1993) estimated that 25% of Jakarta's population belonged to the A and B income groups.

There is still poverty in Jakarta, however. In 1991, 57% (1.25 million) households in Jakarta spent at a rate of less than US$100 per month. These poorer households' spending represented only 26% of the total spending of households in Jakarta, while the top 24% represented 74% of total spending (*Republika* 1995). This finding suggests that income distribution in Jakarta may be more extreme than in other urban areas.

Social class

Definitions of social class, as used in Europe and the USA, are usually based on differences in several facets of human life, including education, wealth, taste, hereditary background ("breeding"), and political power (Fussel 1983). These definitions work best in a mature, stable society; they are somewhat more difficult to use in a rapidly developing and changing society such as Indonesia.

There are distinct upper and lower classes in Indonesia that meet many of the definitional parameters; many experts question, however, whether Indonesia has a true middle class using the above definition (Dick 1993). There is a lack of agreement as to whether certain groups are more appropriately included in the middle or upper class. For example, the "large tycoons" classified by Dick (1993) as upper–middle class are economically far better off than business owners in the layer immediately below. The basis for classifying the large tycoons as upper–middle class follows the argument that the only true upper class that has ever existed among Indonesians has been the Sultans and other nobility. If a European/US definition of class is used, this claim is probably right.

The consensus among Indonesian social scientists is that Indonesia's middle class is best described in terms of its "economic consumption behavior." Other aspects such as political goods, it is argued, are less or not relevant (Dick 1993, p. 68). For marketing purposes, especially in light of Indonesia's rapidly changing environment, we recommend extending this argument to other strata. Specifically, we propose a classification system based on consumption behavior, or ability to consume. We prefer to classify the population into economic consumption cohorts on a spectrum from upper to lower, based on the ability and desire to consume.

By the same reasoning, although top executives and intellectuals may have annual income in the order of hundreds of thousands to millions of dollars, they have far less net worth than the large tycoons, and we should therefore classify them separately, far apart from the top layer. For these reasons, it may be more accurate to upgrade Dick's "upper middle class" into "upper class," and then split it into two subclasses: upper class and lower upper class.

Not all scholars agree on this point, however. On Java, there was a traditional bureaucratic elite class, officials who served and reported to the Sultans. This bureaucratic elite was able to gain personally from the Sultans' wealth and influence while serving them (Koentjaraningrat 1985). It can be argued that these bureaucrats were the predecessors of the modern tycoons, whose paths to riches were made smoother by their access to the top levels of government.

The upper cohort

The upper cohort includes two subgroups, the upper and the lower upper. The principal difference between the two groups is net worth. Their incomes and occupations may be similar, but members of the upper cohort are at the very top, or most influential level, of their occupations.

Indonesia's really large tycoons may have personal wealth in the order of hundreds of million dollars. Using any relative measure, this group is part of Indonesia's upper class. Some members of the upper cohort own the big businesses in Indonesia. Others are or have been top-level government officials or top military officers. Since the Soeharto government began, there has been a tradition of close relationships between business and the government. It is not uncommon for government officials to be stockholders in Indonesian businesses.

The number of upper-cohort households is small, most likely numbering only in the thousands. Their money is new, at most 20 to 25 years old. The majority of this top layer sprouted up in the early 1970s when the Indonesian economy was in the critical stage of a structural reshaping. Most members are first-generation rich, having earned their fortunes themselves quite quickly during the 1970s and early 1980s. Upper-cohort members' incomes can only be described as astronomical. As a group, they act as *nouveau riches,* living quite cosmopolitan, "jet-set" lives. They exhibit a distinctive and quite visible lifestyle. Although small in size, this group's behavior has influenced structural changes in Indonesia's lifestyle. By and large this is a group that celebrates consumption, and the visibility of its activities serves as a model for other cohorts.

Most members of the Indonesian upper cohort enjoy luxurious living. They own large houses, luxury cars, and apartments in major world cities, and pursue expensive hobbies such as car and horse racing, and sailing (Lubis 1993). They may collect works of art such as paintings and antiques. The exceptions are those who have been rich for several generations (the "established" or "old rich"). This small group is less extroverted in its behavior and lifestyle. After the mid-1960s reform, some of the established rich slid down in status to the upper-middle class.

The lower layer of the upper cohort consists primarily of top professionals such as physicians and lawyers; top executives of large businesses who are not owners; owners of larger but not the largest businesses, and the next-to-the-top rank of government officials. Members of this lower upper cohort have, at the minimum, monthly incomes of around R20 million per month (approximately US$10 000). This layer has a potentially very strong influence on the behavior of the middle strata.

The middle cohorts

Dick (1993), along with his definition of an upper-middle class, defines the middle class as being divided into two groups. The "middle-middle" includes the intellectuals, the professionals, most high-level civil servants, and entrepreneurs in medium-sized businesses. The "lower-middle" class embraces a very broad spectrum of the population. In his definition, it includes, *inter alia,* entrepreneurs, proprietors and managers of small businesses, rural landlords with small holdings, middle-level civil servants, and factory supervisors.

Mackie (1993) recommends the term "middle-income population" to describe this diverse group. Zulkarnain, Siagian and Ida (1993, p. 13) propose, as a criterion for inclusion in the middle-income group, "a part of the society that has fulfilled their basic needs, as described by Abraham Maslow—that is, needs for foods, drinks, security." These authors' inclusion criterion means simply having enough resources to live above the subsistence level.

Indonesia's middle cohort is actually a diverse group of various clusters cutting across several income layers, each with its own peculiarities. Mahasin (1993) offers a potentially more useful classification. He divides the Indonesian middle class into three subclasses: upper-middle, middle-middle, and lower middle. This classification adds occupation to income as a classifying variable. It, too, requires some adjustment from the usual European/American definition.

The upper-middle cohort's income ranges from R10 million to R20 million (US$5000–US$10 000) per month. As we have noted, this cohort includes people whose societal positions have diminished as well as those who are in ascendancy. The ascendants, mostly professionals and entrepreneurs/owners of medium-sized businesses, aspire to the lifestyle of the upper class. Because their incomes limit their spending, they focus their discretionary consumption on products that are visible upper-class symbols. This cohort very much colors the urban lifestyle.

The middle group, composed mostly of intellectuals and middle managers, includes a higher proportion of people who seem to prefer a somewhat simpler life. This second subgroup is somewhat introverted in their consumption. This group may develop into the real upper-middle class in Indonesia's future. It is estimated to have a current range of income between R2 million and R10 million per month (US$1000 to US$5000) per month. These layers may turn out to be the true lower-upper and upper-middle classes in Indonesia's future. A spokesperson from the Bank of Bali suggests middle class "would probably imply private car ownership; enough income to eat out 3 to 4 times a week; and a shopping expedition to a supermarket (or department store) once a week and to a bookstore once a quarter" (Tait 1995).

The lower-middle cohort is the largest among middle-income cohorts. The income level for this group ranges between R0.5 million and R2 million (US$250–US$1 000) with a mode (most frequent value) of R600 000 (US$300) per month (Sarjadi 1994). There is hence a large gap in spending power between the lower-middle and the middle-middle class. The bottom of this group is barely over the line between poor and halfway comfortable living. Lower middles tend to be family oriented. They place great value on family development and family activities. They are very concerned about education for their children. By and large, this is a group with a firm hand on the lowest rung of the ladder. Many do not expect to climb very high on it, but they want their children to do so. While its per-household consumption may be low, this group is important both for its size and because it may be the model for new entrants to the middle class.

The lower cohort

The lower cohort is composed of the traditional farmers in rural areas and the poor inhabitants in urban areas. It is worthwhile to distinguish between the urban and rural groups. Most members of the urban group work in the informal sector, albeit sporadically, or at best on a day-to-day basis. Several household members may work. The urban cohort, however poor, are part of the monetary economy. Although any single household may have very low spending power, the cohort as a whole still represents a very large segment of the population. This urban cohort represents a distinct and valuable market for necessities, including food, clothing, and basic health and beauty aids. It is also a substantial market for basic household goods such as radios, cooking utensils and electric fans. The urban lower cohort has access to the same goods as its more affluent neighbors, and as some escape the lower class they are likely to emulate the behavior they see among the lower-middle cohort.

Most households in the rural lower cohort are subsistence farmers. Many have only minimal contact with the monetary economy. Their only source of income comes either from selling part of their crops or from finding work as laborers. They can buy little beyond the absolute necessities that they produce.

We should note, however, that not all farmers are members of the lower cohort. Some, including many rice farmers, grow cash crops and are forming a growing rural middle cohort.

Marketing implications

Given the above statistics, it is tempting to dismiss the Indonesian market as simply too small and underdeveloped to be worth the time and effort that could be required to establish a position in it. If a potential market entrant considers only present prospects, such a conclusion might be the result.

However, the cost of a delayed entry might well be greater than the cost of an early entry. There is abundant evidence that it is much more difficult to build a brand in an established, mature market than in a market that is in the early stages of growth. Many marketers already understand this, and are therefore willing to bear the costs of an early entry into a market perceived as too small to support product-launch and product-maintenance expenditures. The most important consideration in deciding to enter a market such as Indonesia's is not its present size, but rather the rate and direction of the market's projected growth. A rising tide floats not only all boats, but local equity issues as well.

Employment

Historically, agriculture has been the backbone of the Indonesian economy. During the Dutch occupation, most native Indonesians worked as farmers. There was very little manufacturing in the country. All trading activities were handled by non-native Chinese and Arabs. Trading activities were forbidden to native Indonesians, and non-natives were not allowed to work in agriculture. Table 7.14 shows the distribution of employment by sector and sex in 1971 and 1990, the most recent year for which data are available. During this period, the population grew about 50%, from 119 to 179 million, while the workforce grew by 80%, from 39 to 70 million. In common with many other industrializing countries, the workforce consists predominantly of males; the proportion of females in the workforce increased only slightly during the period, from 33% to 35%.

Table 7.14 Growth in employment, 1971–1990

Sector	*Share of employment (%)*			
	Males		*Females*	
	1971	*1990*	*1971*	*1990*
Agriculture	66	50	65	49
Manufacturing	6	10	11	15
Construction	3	6	–	–
Trade	9	12	5	20
Transport	3	6	–	–
Services	12	13	9	14
Other	1	3	4	5
No. ('000)	26 184	45 490	13 026	25 118

Source: Terence H. Hull & Galvin W. Jones (1994), "Demographic Perspectives", in ed. Hal Hill, *Indonesia's New Order*, University of Hawaii Press, Honolulu, p. 157.

In addition to industrialization, a key government goal, achieved during the period, has been to gain and maintain independence in food production. The country has achieved this objective, while the proportion of employed workers engaged in agriculture has decreased. Better methods of farming, coupled with improved varieties of staples such as rice, have led to productivity increases.

Despite the large increase in the output of manufactured goods between 1971 and 1990, workers in manufacturing remain a distinct minority in the workforce. In 1990, this sector employed just 10% of men and 15% of women. Employment in manufacturing accelerated, however, during the 1980s. It grew at a rate of 4.5% per year in the first half of the decade, to almost 7% during the latter half (Manning 1992). This higher growth rate has extended through the mid-1990s.

These data do not capture a most important part of the structural changes in workforce composition that have taken place over the last 20 years.

During this period, the number of managerial and professional workers has increased monumentally, especially in urban areas. And this number has been accelerating rapidly in the 1990s. As Hull and Jones (1994) point out, production has been shifting structurally toward industries that require a higher proportion of managers and professionals; within industries, the share of such employees has also increased.

A substantial proportion of employment in Indonesia is in the informal sector, indicating an economy in which there is a labor surplus. For example, most of the people employed in retail trade are street peddlers rather than clerks in large retail establishments. Such informal employees live day-to-day, in economic terms, and have virtually no safety nets. Much agriculture is basically subsistence farming, with some peddling of excess production. Table 7.15 compares the proportion of informal-sector employment in several occupational classifications in 1980 and 1990. Note that the proportion has decreased in every sector except manufacturing. Alongside the large, modern firms that have grown over the past 2 decades, a large and bewildering array of cottage producers has emerged, creating a wide variety of simple goods.

Table 7.15 Proportion of informal-sector employment in selected sectors, 1980–1990

Sector of employment	*% in informal sector*	
Year	*1980*	*1990*
Trade	88.7	85.1
Agriculture	83.2	82.3
Transport	48.7	43.2
Manufacturing	28.7	45.2
Construction	32.8	25.9
Other services	34.2	20.5
Mining	57.6	12.6
Electricity	21.2	10.5
Bank, Finance	10.1	3.7
Total	**69.1**	**63.4**

Source: Hans-Dieter Evers & Ozay Mehmet (1994), "The Management of Risk: Informal Trade in Indonesia", *World Development*, vol. 22, no. 1, pp. 1–9.

As industrialization proceeds, non-agricultural employment will continue to grow. This means more people will be buying their food rather than growing it. As a result, subsistence farming for profit will increase, while subsistence farming will decrease. Rural incomes will therefore increase, drawing more farmers into the monetary economy. The informal sector should continue to shrink, even in manufacturing, as both farms and businesses increase in size.

Gender issues

Prior to independence, women in many parts of Indonesia were treated as second-class citizens. One of the famous traditional Javanese sayings about wives is "*Surga nunut, neraka katut*" (if the man goes to heaven, she will go with him, but if the man goes to hell, she is to follow). In contrast, the Minang people of Southern Sumatra explicitly place women at the head of the family. The Minang espouse a matrilineal social system in which both wealth and family name flow from mother to daughter. The wife is clearly the head of the household.

Government policy has explicitly defined sex roles. In the government's view, economic development is primarily a male activity, and the female role should focus on the home and family; in most circumstances, women should not work (Guiness 1994). As we have noted, however, women do make up a substantial and—albeit slowly—increasing proportion of the workforce. For example, despite government policy, women's participation in the civil service has increased. In 1992, women comprised 33.1% of Indonesia's civil service employees (see Table 7.16). However, 88% were concentrated primarily at Rank II, the next-to-lowest classification. This may be an artefact of shorter length of service. Several women have served as ministers (the highest rank in the civil service), but the proportion of women in high-ranking positions is low; they represent only about 11% of Rank IV from a total of almost 4 million persons.

Table 7.16 Civil servants by rank and sex, 1992

Rank	*Male*	%	*Female*	%	*Total*
I (lowest)	531.8	87.0	79.4	13.0	611.2
II	1 611.5	60.6	1 049.4	39.4	2 660.9
III	465.0	72.7	174.8	27.3	639.8
IV (highest)	31.4	89.2	3.8	10.8	35.2
Non-state salary scale	2.5	92.9	0.3	7.1	2.8
Total	**2 642.3**	**66.9**	**1 307.9**	**33.1**	**3 950.1**

Source: Indonesian Central Bureau of Statistics (1993), Statistical Reports, Jl Dr Sutomo 68, Jakarta 10710.

Wives of male civil servants, though not official members of the government, do have the opportunity to affect women's roles. Each wife is required to be a member of *Drama Want*, a very powerful organization in Indonesia's bureaucracy. This organization concerns itself with identifying issues of importance to women and encouraging action on the issues they identify.

Although women's rate of participation in the manufacturing sector is low, it has been increasing, especially among young women aged 15–25 from poor households, rural as well as urban. Women in this age group have been shifting into factory work from domestic service, farming, and informal trade activities. As they make this shift, they enter the monetary economy and become potential customers for products such as clothes and cosmetics.

All is not rosy for these young women, however. Working conditions in the factories may be less than ideal, hours may be long, and the work exhausting. Health problems may appear.

Typically, women earn lower wages than men, and have substantially fewer opportunities for advancement. Moreover, as women move from the village to the urban factory, they lose the family and other support systems their former situations provided (Guiness 1994).

More urban women, primarily those from the upper-middle and upper cohorts, are engaging in business careers. This is especially true among the Chinese minority. A few women have reached top management. For example, the President and CEO of Bank Niaga, one of the largest indigenous private banks, is a woman, as is the COO of Bank Danamon. The CFO of the Astra Corporation, the largest public company in Indonesia, is also a woman. The number of women in middle-management positions has been increasing very rapidly, as has the number of women studying business administration in universities, both in Indonesia and abroad. The wide availability of household servants makes it somewhat easier for an Indonesian woman to pursue a managerial career and a family simultaneously than her counterparts in countries such as the USA or Australia.

Education

In a world in which the ability to use technology has become critical to economic development, educational attainment is an important indicator of a country's capacity for growth. Indonesia has made substantial progress in the education of its workers and managers. Between 1971 and 1990, the proportion of the population over 15 years with no schooling fell from 45% to 19%. Most of those with no education were from rural areas. During this period, the proportion of the population who had completed secondary school rose from 8% to 25%. By 1990, the literacy rate among those under 15 years of age approached 100%.

Education at all levels remains higher among males than females. In 1990, 29% of males, as compared with 21% of females, had completed secondary school; 25% of females, compared with only 12% of males, had no schooling (Jones 1994). In the future, the proportion of secondary-school graduates is likely to continue its steady increase, and the gender gap will narrow.

From 1980 to 1990, the education level of Indonesians occupying positions as professionals, managers, and supervisors also increased markedly (see Table 7.17). In 1980, for example, 31% of managers and supervisors had earned university degrees. By 1990, the proportion had risen to 47%. Educational attainment among these groups is also likely to continue increasing, as more students in Indonesia complete secondary school and increase the potential pool of university students. Many of the more affluent students attend universities abroad, principally in the USA.

Table 7.17 Indonesia's workforce by education level, %

Education level	*Professionals*			*Managerial & Supervisory*		
Year	*1980*	*1985*	*1990*	*1980*	*1985*	*1990*
Primary-school graduate	15.17	5.66	4.20	23.44	12.56	10.14
High-school graduate	73.81	75.63	66.60	44.92	52.48	42.46
University graduate	10.98	18.71	29.20	31.49	34.96	47.40
No response	0.04	–	–	0.15	–	–
Total	**100.00**	**100.00**	**100.00**	**100.00**	**100.00**	**100.00**

Source: Business News (1994).

Culture and cultural change

Traditional Indonesia is the antithesis of a monocultural society such as Japan. There are many ethnic groups, languages, and dialects in Indonesia, as well as 4 recognized religions, numerous variations of them, and some other religions as well. Indigenous groups predominate. The largest ethnic group is the Javanese, who number almost 100 million; more than 75% are Moslems. The Javanese, together with the Sundanese, Balinese, and Madurese, represent about two-thirds of the Indonesian population. In contrast, the smallest ethnic units may consist of only a few hundred people.

Javanese, especially Moslem Javanese, dominate the government bureaucracy. Almost all Balinese (90%) are Hindus. With the exception of Bali, the west is predominantly Moslem, while the east has a substantial concentration of Protestants on Flores and Catholics on Timor.

The predominant non-indigenous ethnic groups are the Chinese, the Indians, and the Arabs, each of which represents only a small minority. There are very few Africans and Caucasians in Indonesia. Among the non-indigenous groups, the Chinese are probably the most assimilated and, at the same time, the most visible. Most have roots in Indonesia going back several generations. Almost all have taken Indonesian names; some have become Moslem, others Catholic, and few, especially among the young, can speak Chinese. Chinese represent, at most, 5% of the population. The

Chinese population is concentrated in the urban areas of Java and Sumatra, where it is engaged in business, and in Western Kalimantan, where many of its members farm or fish for a living. Chinese own or manage a significant proportion of Indonesia's large business firms.

Indonesia is experiencing some of the cultural tension that inevitably accompanies economic development, as "modern" or "Western" (Euro-american) culture vies to supplement or even replace the traditional. On the one hand, people want to shed those vestiges of their traditional lives, both behaviors and symbols, that they believe conflict with the increased sense of entitlement that comes with their economic progress. They want to substitute new behaviors and symbols they perceive as more consonant with where they are going and less consonant with where they have been. On the other hand, during a time of rapid change, they do not want to cast themselves adrift without some anchors to a safer, though less promising, past.

The process of cultural change that has been accompanying economic development in Indonesia is particularly complex and, at times, paradoxical—therefore the effects of change can be difficult to understand. New behaviors and symbols people adopt may be less diverse across ethnic groups than the symbols and behaviors they replace. The diversity of traditional cultures, however, makes it quite difficult to predict just which behaviors and symbols different groups will retain. Clearly, ethnicity, religion, and their associated traditional customs all play a role in determining the new behaviors and symbols Indonesians will adopt, as well as those they will retain. At the same time, ethnic identity and religion are becoming less influential, especially among the younger generation, and most especially in the cities. As has been the case in some other countries, urbanization is breaking down cultural barriers and contributing toward similarities in consumer behavior as people of different backgrounds are thrown together in the workplace, the street and supermarket, and the neighborhood.

In the main, the direction of cultural change is toward consumption. Indonesia has become a society in which the acquisition and display of goods is an extremely important goal. Increasingly, affluence has become the most important symbol of achievement. This is not unusual for a growing economy. The acquisition and display of certain products is a major way of demonstrating affluence. Products that consumers perceive as symbols of affluence are therefore likely to be in great demand.

Government policy has been to encourage the growth of a capitalist economy. An outgrowth of this policy has been the burgeoning of an urban middle class of managers and professionals who have built their lifestyles around consumption. Consumption in this group focuses on the modern rather than the traditional, and is oriented toward the Euro-american pattern (Guiness 1994). Gaining affluence and demonstrating it through consumption is a particularly important goal among younger, urban Indonesians, which is not necessarily the case with the older generation. Not all young Indonesians, however, share this view. Some are still struggling for the necessities of life. Others, such as the devout or orthodox Moslems, deem practicing their religion a more important goal.

In a work of this size it would be impossible to capture the variety and richness of Indonesian cultural change and the symbols that accompany it. However, it is possible to present some examples.

Dress and food

"Traditional" dress is fast disappearing, replaced by Euro-american dress. For example, the Dayak tribes of Kalimantan have given up their traditional clothing in favor of t-shirts and jeans. The business-suit-and-tie combination is gradually replacing the safari suit among urban businessmen. A domestic designer fashion industry has grown up, using some traditional, local materials such as batik, but the material designs and the clothing styles are not traditional.

There are, however, some exceptions. Devout Moslem women wear modest long dresses and cover their heads and much of their faces and necks. In Banjarmasin, Indonesia's 12th largest city, a high proportion of men have made *Haj*, the pilgrimage to Mecca. Their everyday dress is a white robe, the symbol of their pilgrimage. Modern Javanese couples may get married in traditional Javanese dress. Franchises such as Pizza Hut and Kentucky Fried Chicken co-exist with traditional fast foods such as satay. Pork is much in evidence in Hindu Bali and in areas that are heavily Chinese or Christian, but is difficult to find in areas where Moslems predominate.

Ethnic origins

Transplanted urban dwellers do not forget their roots. Many still consider themselves members of their ethnic group of origin, and consider their birthplace their "real" home. The typical Indonesian speaks of his/her birthplace as "my *Kampung,*" a word that stands simultaneously for compound, village, or geographic area.

After the Moslem fasting month of Ramadan there is a massive exodus from the cities to people's home towns or villages of origin. Members of some ethnic groups prefer to stay in their homelands, while members of other groups tend to move into other areas. Typical quality-of-life measures are not good predictors of the tendency to migrate.

In most ethnic groups, individuals have distinctive names that reveal their ethnic identity.

Who are the innovators of cultural change in Indonesia?

In many instances, cultural innovators are groups well outside the mainstream of their society. They may even be poor. In Indonesia, the innovators are from the upper-middle and upper strata of the country. Among this group, the leaders are those from the younger generation who have gone abroad to study, especially those who have studied in the USA. This is the group that has brought Euro-american culture to Indonesia, and along with it the Hard Rock Cafe and Planet Hollywood.

Marketing implications of cultural change

Ethnic group and religion appear to be promising variables for consumer segmentation. Yet they must be used with a good degree of caution, and with the application of a sizeable portion of insight. In periods of rapid cultural change such as Indonesia is now undergoing, behavior is likely to be unstable. Many consumers, especially the newly affluent, are likely to be searching for new identities and ways of expressing them.

It is also critical to distinguish the difference between correlation and causality when interpreting consumer data or observing behavior. This is especially true for products that have the potential to convey symbolic value. It is important to recognize the products and brands that may have such potential. Unfortunately, at the time of writing, few, if any, studies have been conducted in Indonesia that might provide the insight or guidance.

Also of critical importance is gaining an understanding of the role of symbols in governing consumers' product choices. It is reasonable to expect that the most important symbols in a fast-growing economy such as Indonesia's would be those of affluence and modernity. An understanding of the process by which a particular product gains (and loses) its symbolic value can be a great asset for the marketer.

Consumption patterns

In the following discussion, we will attempt to describe the modal consumption patterns that are emerging in the country. Obviously, there are significant differences across income and certain ethnic groups, and between urban and rural households. Our focus will be the urban middle class, since this is the group that will be of principal interest to most marketers. Readers should understand, however, that the ability to consume is only a recent acquisition for a significant proportion of this group. Many are still learning what to buy and how to buy. Under such conditions, consumer behavior can change rapidly.

Housing

Prior to the mid-1990s, almost all Indonesians, whether center-city, suburban, or rural dwellers, lived in single houses. Housing prices vary significantly, and are based on location and size. In the larger metropolitan areas such as Jakarta, Bandung, and Surabaya, a small house typically stands on a lot of not more than 20–80 m². The house itself would range from 15–70 m² in size. Land costs for such houses range between US$50 and US$1 000 per square meter, and the house itself would cost from US$5 000 to US$15 000. The higher economic cohorts typically have larger, more spacious houses. Typically, these houses stand on lots of from 100–400 m². Houses built on such lots can range in cost from US$35 000 to US$300 000. The upper cohorts are likely to live in houses costing at least US$500 000. A top-of-the-line house in the most expensive cities such as Jakarta can cost between US$2 million and US$4 million.

In urban areas, it has been customary for owners of small businesses, especially retailers and craftsmen, to live on the same premises as their businesses. Buildings combining stores or offices and living premises are called *Ruko (rumah-toko* = house & store) or *Rukan* (*rumah-kantor* = house & office). They are the Indonesian version of the shophouse found throughout Asia. Such buildings are usually 2 to 4 storeys high, with land areas of between 50 m² and 100 m², and are located on main streets. The building takes up virtually all the land area, except for a sidewalk in front. Typically, the first floor houses business activities, while the upper floors are living areas. Because of their larger land and building size, shophouses are relatively expensive. For example, in 1995, in a new suburb 20 km from the east side of Jakarta, the smallest ruko (3 stories, with a land area of 90 m²) sold for US$150 000, while the top of the line, with 170 m² of land, cost US$400 000.

Beginning in about 1994, high-rise apartment buildings have been proliferating, especially in Jakarta. Apart from the unfamiliarity of living in small spaces in high rises, many Indonesian families find them unattractive because of their high prices. A good apartment in a prime Jakarta location would be priced at US$2 000 to US$3 000 per square meter. Hence a 2-bedroom apartment with a total area of 50 m² would cost at least US$100 000 to US$150 000. Escalating land costs in Jakarta are making this intrinsically less attractive option more of a necessary choice; the land cost for a single family dwelling in a good location is becoming out of reach.

Another recent urban trend is the development of high-rise apartment buildings for the poor. These developments are an attempt to solve two problems. One aim is to get rid of unsightly slums, some of which may be in prime residential or business areas. The other is to free the valuable land the slums occupy for other uses. Although these low-cost high rises were small in number in 1995, we believe such housing will become more important in the future.

In rural areas, land and houses are much cheaper than in the cities. Although poverty has been significantly reduced since the early 1970s, rural households are markedly different from urban households. Most rural families are farmers. Some have their own farms, but many work only as farmworkers, typically on a profit-sharing basis. Many houses in rural areas are not built with bricks and cement, as is the case with most urban dwellings. The rural poor are likely to live in houses made from materials they can forage for rather than buy. Typically, such houses have walls made from bamboo mats. The floors of these houses are, simply, earth. The proportion of houses with cement floors and brick walls, however, is increasing as more farmers enter the monetary economy. With continued economic development, the rural dwelling will become more like its urban counterpart.

The household's bundle of goods

Households can spend funds on acquiring goods once they have satisfied their food and housing needs. Table 7.18 shows the proportion of their monthly income that households at different income levels spend on food vs non-food expenditures. As can be seen from this table, in 1993 the proportion of household income spent on food fell below 50% as per-capita income reached R100 000. It is the group with incomes above this level that begin to be customers for durable goods.

Table 7.18 Percentage of average per-capita monthly expenditure in urban and rural areas by consumption item, 1993

		Socio-economic	*Urban*		*Rural*	
Per-capita	*Household**	*class***	*Food*	*Non-food*	*Food*	*Non-food*
< 59 999	270	C-; D	64.4	35.6	68.6	32.3
60 000–99 999	270–450	C+; B	50.5	49.5	55.4	44.6
100 000–149 999	450-675	B+; A	43.9	56.1	45.8	54.2
150 000–199 999	675–900	A	37.6	62.4	36.6	63.6
>200 000	> 900	A+	30.9	69.1	33.1	67.9

* average household size: 4.5 persons
** The Demographic Institute's classification

Source: Jakarta Statistical Office (1993), reports.

Indonesia is a market of substantial size for food products. The consumption value of food products also appears to be increasing significantly. Table 7.19 shows consumption in rupiah of a list of such products between 1991 and 1993. Note that the consumption of instant noodles increased almost fourfold in this period. Even cooking oil consumption increased by about 30%, and processed milk by over 33%.

Indonesian households have experienced major changes in their aspirations for household durable goods. This is a result of the increasing availability of consumer goods over the last decade, as well as increased purchasing power. Consumer durables such as stereos, refrigerators, air conditioners and

Table 7.19 Market value of selected consumer products, 1991 and 1993

Product category	*Market value (billion Rupiah)*		*Market value (million $*)*		*Market value per capita **($)*	
Year	*1991*	*1993*	*1991*	*1993*	*1991*	*1993*
Cooking oils	1 550.0	1 900	778.1	N/A	4.25	N/A
Processed milks	447.0	600	224.4	N/A	1.23	N/A
Soft drinks (including bottled water)	424.9	N/A	213.3	N/A	1.17	N/A
Instant noodles	278.7	1 200	140.0	N/A	0.77	N/A
Coffee	216.9	470	108.9	N/A	0.60	N/A
Beers	188.1	N/A	94.4	N/A	0.52	N/A
Snacks	168.7	N/A	84.7	N/A	0.46	N/A
Canned fish	154.3	N/A	77.5	N/A	0.42	N/A
Canned meat	95.8	N/A	48.1	N/A	0.26	N/A
Candy	62.2	400	31.2	N/A	0.17	N/A
Canned fruits	18.7	N/A	9.4	N/A	0.05	N/A
Total	**3 605.6**	**–**	**1 810.0**	**–**	**9.90**	**–**

*1$ (US) = R1 992 (1991 exchange rate).
** Population 1991 = 182.9 million

Sources Sembada Swa (1992), "Pertempuran di Jalur Distribusi", vol. 8, no. 4, July, pp. 14–19; Sembada Swa (1994), "Triliunan Rupiah di Bisnis F&B", vol. 9, no. 12, Maret, pp. 22–5.

television sets were considered luxuries just 10 to 20 years ago. By the mid-1990s these items had become common household possessions. Table 7.20 lists some of the durables typically owned by urban households in different income cohorts. As this table shows, even the lower-middle cohort is likely to have a respectable inventory of durable goods. Higher-income groups have both broader inventories and more expensive models of goods than those held by the lower middles. Differences between the durable-goods inventories of urban and rural households are much more likely to result from income differences than from differences in preferences or taste.

Table 7.21 gives a rough idea of what these consumption patterns have meant to Indonesian consumer-durables manufacturers. This table presents statistics on the production of TV sets for the 5 years between 1988 and 1992. Production may be used as a rough proxy for consumption. During this period, annual production almost doubled, from 675 000 units to over 1 200 000, and the production of color TV sets increased almost fourfold. Considering the number of households in Indonesia, there is much growth potential left.

Table 7.20 Durable-goods inventories and economic cohort

Socio-economic class	*Typical occupation*	*Household income level*	*Items*
Upper-middle	Top professionals, intellectuals, medium entrepreneurs	R10–20 million	2+ cars, medium house (300–800 m^2 building area); large TV (35" (88 cm)+, more than 1 TV in the house); large parabolic antennae; quality home theatre and sound system; vacation home; quality paintings/art collection; luxurious watches; upper-scale furniture
Middle-middle	Small entrepreneurs, upper-level government officials	R2–10 million	classy passenger car (up to 2 cars); small house (100-400 m^2 building area); larger refrigerator; larger TV (27"–31" (68–78 cm)); home entertainment; personal computer; air conditioner; excellent garden
Lower-middle	Supervisors, junior managers, middle civil servants, rich farmers, small rural landlords	R0.5–2 million	multipurpose/passenger car; small house (50-100 m^2 building area); inexpensive hi-fi & sound system; laser-disc player and home video; washing machine; electric fans; selected kitchen appliances

Source: Authors' estimates, based on several unpublished market research studies.

Table 7.21 Production of television sets in Indonesia, 1988–1992

Year	*1988*	*1989*	*1990*	*1991*	*1992*
Color	224 000	327 600	602 360	982 147	896 130
Black & White	451 038	469 000	480 000	369 279	344 504
Total	**675 038**	**796 600**	**1 082 360**	**1 351 426**	**1 240 634**

Source: Informasi (1993), "Kondisi Industri Televisi Indonesia", no. 10, p. 29.

The same is true for other durables. Table 7.22 shows ownership of selected durables in 1993 by households with access to electricity. Note that just 10% of such households had refrigerators, and fewer than 10% had electric rice cookers. Almost two-thirds were without an electric fan. Clearly, there is great growth potential in these markets as well.

Table 7.22 Ownership of selected consumer durables, 1993

Product	*% of households with electricity*
Electric fan	34.3
Electric iron	14.1
Refrigerator	9.9
Rice cooker	8.2
Electric well-water pump	7.9

Source: Bisnis Indonesia (1995), "Memacu konsumsi 'hair dryer' ...", Electronics Supplement, March 15, p. 3.

There are two aspects of Indonesian durable-goods consumption that are not apparent in Table 7.22. It is critical that marketers recognize both, in their choice of products and positioning for this market. The first is technological leapfrogging—that is, the desire to have the very latest technology. In consumer electronics, Indonesia is a late-adopter country, but with an inordinately high proportion of the most technologically advanced products of their type. Many Indonesian households will simply skip the older product, and select the very newest for their first adoption. There is little, and diminishing, interest in anything that smacks of "old technology." It is fair to say that the high level of Japanese penetration in the consumer electronics and other durables market has contributed to this phenomenon. Another contributor has been the lack of alternatives that are available in some other countries. For example:

- When choosing a means of showing movies at home, Indonesians are more likely to pick a laser-disc player than a VCR. There is an abundance of laser-disc rental shops in urban areas.
- Cordless telephones are very popular, perhaps more popular than the cord style.
- Every household that can possibly afford one has a satellite dish. The lack of a cable TV system, coupled with the limited programming choices available domestically, have encouraged the purchase of dishes.
- One-hour mechanized processing of color film is available virtually everywhere.

- Jakarta has a well-developed cellular-phone system. Its rapid growth has been in part driven by frustration with the hard-wired phone system, and by the amount of time people must spend in their cars because of traffic jams.
- Among refrigerator purchasers, fuzzy logic is very much in demand.
- There is an apparent preference for electronics over electrics; consumers would rather have cordless phones than electric rice cookers.

The second aspect of Indonesian durable-goods ownership is the somewhat more limited penetration of labor-saving devices and modern kitchen appliances than might be expected. Every household with electricity does have its electric rice cooker, but may have little else. There are still servants to do the household's laundry and to do the cutting, grinding, or mashing of food that may accompany the preparation of a meal. In addition, door-to-door vendors, as well as an abundance of take-away places, can supply the components of a meal at very low cost. It is likely that the expected diminishing availability of servants will increase demand for household labor-saving devices.

Health and fitness

In common with most of the world, Indonesians are generally more concerned about health than they were 20 years ago. From the early 1980s, fitness centers sprouted in many large urban areas. In the 1990s, they have become a visible part of urban life, especially for the younger generation. Stores featuring home exercise equipment are in every shopping mall. Aerobic exercise such as jogging and bicycling is very popular. In almost all urban areas, people gather in the city's parks and main streets to jog and to cycle. Because of the heat and humidity, these activities start very early, at about 4:30 a.m., and finish about 2 hours later, at around 6:30 a.m. Tennis and badminton are popular. The number of golf courses is increasing rapidly.

Cigarette smoking is still prevalent, but less so among younger people. A wide variety of vitamin and mineral supplements is much more visible, and much more widely available than in the early 1980s. Both the multinational and some domestic pharmaceutical companies are actively promoting the use of a broad range of nutritional supplements. The result has been steadily increasing demand, and growth of this market has been limited only by income.

Self-medication for a variety of real and imaginary ailments is very popular. For many ailments, modern and traditional treatments co-exist. The traditional treatment, *jamu*, consists of herbal remedies derived from the very wide variety of indigenous botanical substances available in the country. There are *jamu* for treating everything from colds to infertility. Vendors in street markets all over Indonesia sell prepackaged and labeled *jamu*. *Jamu* are inexpensive (R500–1500 per packet), and do not require a prescription.

Modern pharmaceuticals are also widely available. Virtually every multinational pharmaceutical company markets its products in Indonesia, and there are domestic marketers as well. Consumers can purchase both over-the-counter (OTC) and ethical (prescription-only) products without a physician's prescription. Ethical pharmaceuticals are distributed only through *Apotiks* (pharmacies), while even small neighborhood stands sell popular OTCs.

Nutrition and eating habits

The traditional Indonesian diet is a nutritional and health paradox. On the healthy side of the ledger, rice has always been the basic staple, supplemented by some vegetables and a bit of fish or meat. Soybeans in cake form (*tahu*) or fermented (*tempe*) have been a major source of protein. Tropical fruits are also abundant. On a less healthy note, the use of coconut milk or cream, heavy in saturated fat, is ubiquitous. *Padang* food, popular throughout the archipelago, combines coconut milk and organ meats. Frying is the preferred cooking method for *Padang* food. Of the 2 national dishes, *Nasi Goreng* (fried rice with accompaniments), and satay (little skewers of meat), the first is fried in coconut milk and the second is served with a sauce of coconut milk and ground peanuts. *Krupuk*, a wide variety of fried crackers, are also popular everywhere.

Echoing the heightened interest in fitness and nutritional supplements, Indonesians' food habits are changing also. There is much more awareness of the fat and cholesterol content of traditional foods, and there is increasing concern for limiting one's caloric intake. The discussion following will identify some of the changes taking place, and will suggest that these changes signal potential opportunities to introduce new food products.

Eating out (in this case eating outside) is common. Every city neighborhood and every tiny village has a collection of small stands with a few rude tables, stools, or benches in front that sell a variety of local dishes. In addition, there are traveling food vendors who go from house to house, each offering their particular specialty. Prices at the stands and from the vendors are so low that they compete with home-prepared food.

People typically eat 3 full meals per day: breakfast, lunch, and dinner. If taken at home, all 3 meals are served at the dining table. A typical Indonesian meal consists of rice and several accompanying foods, served family style. Each region has its own cuisine. The most notable are the previously mentioned *Padang* foods (spicy, coconut milk and chili based), *Sunda* food (fritters with fresh vegetable), *Yogya* and *Solo* food (spicy, sweet), and *Madura* (famous for satay). Many start the day with a breakfast of *nasi goreng* (fried rice), *nasi soto* (rice served with various other ingredients as a soup), or plain rice served with leftovers from the previous night's dinner. Older middle-cohort people who were raised under the Dutch culture may have a continental breakfast: white bread with butter and chocolate rice (*muisjes*) or jam.

Some breakfast habits are changing. A small survey conducted among middle-class residents of South Jakarta found that almost 30% of them usually skipped breakfast. Instant noodles are becoming increasingly popular as a breakfast food. (In 1994, total sales of instant noodles reached US$600 million.)

Marketers have introduced breakfast cereals, but with very little success. One reason may be that fresh milk is not a common item in the household inventory.

In some of the smaller cities, such as Solo or Semarang, it is still a common practice for people to have their breakfast in small restaurants, foodstores, or from streetside food sellers. In rural areas, it is customary for people to have a light breakfast such as steamed yams or bananas at home, or to buy their breakfast (rice based) from street peddlers. Poor farmers' families may skip breakfast and have brunch instead, taking only 2 meals a day.

In sum, there is a trend, especially in the large urban areas, toward faster, lighter breakfasts that include more and more non-traditional foods. This trend reflects both the heightened interest in nutrition and the time pressures in an urban work environment. We expect the trend to continue. With patience and sound marketing, we believe cereals, especially high-fiber cereals, will catch on also.

People spend more time at lunch than at breakfast, though not nearly as much as in the past. Factories and offices have lunch breaks. Some factories provide a subsidized lunch for their workers. In those factories where lunch is not provided, workers buy their lunch from nearby food peddlers. These peddlers appear wherever there is potential business to be had. Some offices provide lunch. Otherwise, office workers and managers usually go to nearby fast-food outlets, restaurants or fast-food courts in malls. It is uncommon for people to bring their own lunches to work.

In rural farming areas, wives may bring the meal and the children to wherever in the fields their husbands are working, and the family eats together.

As recently as 20 years ago, it was customary to have a siesta after lunch. Offices and stores closed, and people went home for lunch and a nap. Government offices closed for the day at 2 p.m.; stores reopened at 5 or 6 p.m. In some of the smaller cities, such as Solo, there are still some traces of this practice. Since school ends at 12:30 p.m., mothers who do not work wait for their children to return from school, and all have their lunch together.

Traditionally, dinner is an important family event. Most families always try to eat dinner together. The best foods are served during this meal. A typical dinner includes rice, 2 to 5 different accompanying foods, *krupuk*, drinks (usually iced tea, iced water, or orange juice), and dessert (most likely fresh fruits such as bananas, melons, or oranges). Families sometimes go out together to eat in restaurants.

However, family togetherness at dinner has become a less frequent event, especially among the more affluent. Long working hours and time spent on commuting make it more difficult for the breadwinner(s) to make it home in time. The children in the family are also busy with school-related group work, sport, and other activities. Therefore, real family dinners are tending to take place principally on weekends. The weekend may well include a shopping expedition or two; if so, the family will have its meal together on the way to or from shopping. The custom of 3 meals a day consumed at home by the whole family together is disappearing.

Eating out has changed the composition of meals. Foreign foods, particularly fast foods, have become part of the Indonesian diet, especially in urban areas among children. The USA, for example, has contributed, among others, McDonald's, Burger King, Kentucky Fried Chicken, Church's Fried Chicken, Dunkin' Donut, Wendy's, and Pizza Hut. Local entrepreneurs have also developed their own fast-food chains, based on US concepts. There is California Fried Chicken (100% Indonesian owned), Putri, and Nyonya Tanzil Fried Chicken. Indigenous restaurant chains featuring Indonesian food are also sprouting everywhere, such as Nyonya Suharti Fried Chicken, Handayani, and Bakmi Gajah Mada. A food revolution is well under way; it started in the large cities, and is spreading rapidly to the smaller cities and beyond.

Accompanying the fast-food revolution is a marked increase in the variety of processed foods available in the marketplace. There are, for example, several brands of ready-mixed seasoning packets for making the traditional Indonesian dishes. Condiments, traditionally made fresh, come in plastic squeeze bottles. Supermarket shelves display foreign foods, in processed form, both Asian and Western.

Leisure activities

Table 7.23, using 1991 data, shows that Indonesians participate in a wide variety of activities, but that their participation rates vary based on their geographic location. People living in Jakarta show the highest rates of participation in many of the activities listed in the table. Interestingly, they are less likely to attend cultural performances or become members of social organizations than are people who reside elsewhere. In general, the percentages for many activities show marked differences across islands or group of islands. These differences may be due to differing proportions of urban versus rural inhabitants. For example, inhabitants of Java, the most urbanized island, are the most active users of the media.

The low rates of newspaper reading outside Jakarta result from several factors:

- illiteracy is higher in rural areas
- newspapers are national and contain little local news

Table 7.23 Percentage of population aged 10 years and over involved in social & cultural activities, 1991

Island/groups of islands	*Listening to radio*	*Watching TV*	*Going to movies*	*Reading newspaper/ magazines*	*Sport activity*	*Attending cultural performances*	*Member of social organizations*	*Persons involved*	*Persons aged 10+yrs*	*% involved*
Sumatra	51.5	66.3	6.0	20.7	26.5	9.3	46.7	23.4	26.9	87.0
Java (including Jakarta)	72.1	69.8	7.4	24.5	26.2	8.6	45.3	76.4	84.1	90.8
Jakarta	82.8	93.5	20.0	64.6	42.0	5.9	30.0	6.5	6.6	98.5
Nusa Tenggara & Bali	43.2	44.0	2.8	10.9	20.1	8.9	44.3	5.5	7.6	72.3
Kalimantan (Borneo)	55.2	62.5	7.1	19.1	25.8	6.5	39.9	5.7	6.7	85.1
Sulawesi (Celebes)	55.1	56.6	5.5	19.9	27.0	6.1	37.6	7.9	9.6	82.3
Maluku & Irian Jaya	34.2	43.8	2.9	15.1	24.8	9.2	34.0	1.8	2.5	72.0
Total	**63.8**	**66.0**	**6.6**	**22.3**	**25.9**	**8.5**	**44.5**	**120.7**	**137.5**	**87.8**

Source: Jakarta Statistical Office (1991), Reports.

- print media are less widely available in rural areas
- newspapers are expensive for most lower-income people (approximately $8 per month)

This picture may change in the future, when the costs for newspapers may be lower and regional editions may be allowed.

Television is the most popular medium across all Indonesia. Changes since 1991 probably understate TV usage in 1995, the last date for which data were available. In 1991, only state-owned television could reach all parts of the country. Private TV stations existed only in the Jakarta and Surabaya areas, and there was only a private station in each area–RCTI in Jakarta and SCTV in Surabaya. By 1995, there were 3 additional private stations: Indosiar, ANTEVE, and TPI, making a total of 6 available stations. In addition, each province also provided its own regional programs.

By investing in a relatively low-cost parabolic antenna (US$250–500), a viewer can gain access to most programs from almost anywhere in Indonesia. PT Indosar's satellite makes this possible. More expensive parabolic antennas (costing US$1000–3000) enable viewers to access foreign broadcasts, ranging from those of neighboring countries to European stations. The very largest parabolic antennas can even access US stations.

Another survey conducted in Jakarta in 1993 (see Table 7.24) shows an increase over the 1991 survey results just discussed. Except for newspaper readership, the percentage of males and females using the media are similar. The difference in newspaper readership, however, is quite significant–70% for males, compared to 60% for females. These, and the previous findings, offer another example of technological leapfrogging. Television has developed faster than print in Indonesia. Print media did not have the opportunity to develop before its advent.

Table 7.24 Percentage of population in Jakarta over 10 years of age in terms of access to media, 1993

Type of media	*Male*	*Female*	*Total*
Television	91.6	92.6	91.9
Radio	80.6	78.1	79.3
Newspaper	69.8	56.9	63.3

Source: Jakarta Statistical Office (1993), reports.

Although it is not evident from this list, playing golf is a significant leisure/sport activity among the more affluent. To give a perspective, at the end of 1992 greater Jakarta had just 10 golf clubs, 4 of which were public courses. In 1993, another 6 courses opened (*Economist* 1993). In 1994 and

1995 more new golf clubs were under construction. Most other major cities also have at least one golf course.

Consumer credit and consumer banking

Credit cards have become part of the lifestyle for much of the middle class, especially in urban areas. In addition to global cards such as Visa, Mastercard, American Express, and Diners Club, national cards have also flourished. One of the most successful national cards is the BCA card issued by Bank Central Asia. In Jakarta only, the turnover of Visa cards in 1991 had already reached US$488 million. In this year, 40 000 Jakartans had American Express cards, a fourfold increase since 1986 (*Asian Business* 1993). These numbers have grown considerably since 1993.

The deregulation of the banking system that took place in the early 1990s, coupled with the more consumption-oriented lifestyle of the middle class, have also fostered the use of consumer loans. Many banks and other financial institutions now offer consumers financial products that simply did not exist 10 years ago. For example, mortgage-based home-equity loans have become quite popular in large cities. First introduced by Citibank Indonesia several years ago, this flexible loan is commonly offered by many banks. Some stores, like the indigenous supermarket chains Hero and Golden Truly, have even issued their own store cards.

Most Indonesians purchase automobiles and houses using consumer credit. Car loans are usually financed either by consumer banks or by automobile credit companies. Loans for household appliances are popular for the lower and lower-middle income groups. Stores selling consumer durables on credit have existed since the mid-1970s. In addition to banks and credit companies, Indonesian consumers can also finance their purchases by using credit facilities offered by employee co-operatives. In rural areas, there are many traveling entrepreneurs (one-man "stores") that sell household appliances on credit, collecting on each subsequent visit. The availability of consumer credit, coupled with consumers' evident willingness to make use of it, will accelerate the development of the consumer-durables markets at a rate faster than income increases alone would allow. In a society with a consumption-oriented lifestyle, consumers are more likely than not to use their expanded debt capacity. As a household's income increases, its perceived debt capacity will also increase.

The macromarketing mix

Branding

Typically, a consumer-goods market in Indonesia includes both domestic and multinationally owned brands. For example, the market shares for a range of both domestic and multinational brands in 2 toiletry product categories, astringents and hand-and-body lotion, is dominated by domestic brands. We should not assume, however, that for a domestic brand, a dominant position is a secure position. This is especially true if a broad income spectrum of consumers uses the generic product.

In many industrializing countries there is a 2-tiered market. In the top tier are the brands owned by multinational firms. They are typically more prestigious, more expensive, and perceived by consumers to be of higher quality than the lower-tier, domestically owned brands. In actuality, the tiers may offer identical performance; it may be perception rather than reality that guides consumers' judgments.

As consumers become more affluent, a phenomenon we call "brand shedding" appears. With affluence, consumers may shed the domestic brands they grew up with and adopt the more prestigious multinational brands. This may occur even if the domestic brand is every bit as good as the multinational; it's a matter of symbolism, not performance. In more and more product categories, indigenous brands have succeeded in replacing foreign-owned brands. A good example is the cosmetics industry. Indigenous brands dominate the astringents category, whereas, for hand-and-body lotion, foreign brands dominate, but some indigenous brands have pushed into the top 10 brands. This situation seems to call into question the notion of brand shedding.

The data, however, are not inconsistent with brand shedding. In a product category with a broad base of consumer use, extending across economic cohorts, the bulk of users may be from lower economic cohorts simply because the lower cohorts contain more people. Many of them may shed their present brands as their incomes increase. The future prospects of widely used brands may be less bright than their present market shares would suggest.

Price

Traditionally, Indonesians are price sensitive, and trained to bargain when they shop. The common practice for vendors is to set a price merely as a starting point for negotiation. Buyers then bargain until buyer and seller reach agreement. Most people are happy to get "discounts." Recently, however, more and more stores have been switching to fixed prices. In such stores there is absolutely no price negotiation. Examples are supermarkets, department stores, and stores located in upscale locations–in short, most modern retailers.

At the same time, however, there are still stores that openly invite price negotiation. There are evidently 2 price segments among consumers. Those seeking convenience are "price takers." They search for stores with an image of "dependable price setter" and shop happily in those establishments. Others, who are more price sensitive, or enjoy bargaining, go to "negotiable price stores."

This price segmentation applies to shopping for most consumer durables, garments, and even fresh produce. There are indications that urban people are behaving more as price takers, a trend that should become stronger in the future, especially among the young affluent urban population. However, negotiable-price practice is likely to continue for the next few decades, especially in rural and smaller urban areas.

Distribution

There are 2 merchandise classifications in Indonesia. The one that consists of items in short supply or susceptible to market rigging is heavily regulated. Some of the heavily regulated items are sugar, rice, cement, steel, wheat flour, and cloves (a key ingredient in Kretek cigarettes, which are very popular). Distribution of most other goods is not highly regulated. Foreign manufacturers, even if producing in Indonesia, cannot sell directly to retailers. They must use independent distributors. Foreign retailers must have domestic partners.

Traditional and modern distribution channels exist side by side. The modern system includes outlets such as large self-service supermarkets, convenience stores, department stores, and the like. Traditional outlets range from small, individually owned stores to little street stands. Although there is a shift occurring in many urban areas from traditional outlets to modern outlets, the traditional distribution system still accounts for the majority of sales in rural areas.

Interestingly, recent developments in modern distribution outlets in Indonesia are almost exact replications of outlets found in the USA and other advanced industrialized countries. It seems that, while the traditional distribution system is unchanged, the modern distribution system leapfrogs to include the most advanced forms in use anywhere. The modern outlets include non-store retailing, such as direct marketing, and telemarketing. These developments are expected to continue, at an increasing speed.

Packaged-goods distribution

Traditionally, packaged consumer goods are distributed through small stores. Indonesian traditional small stores are interesting enterprises. They can be shacks called *warung* with only 2 m^2 of floor area set up along the street pavement, or they can be real stores that sell many items, not unlike the Western general store of the 19th century. Most traditional stores are full-service rather than self-service based. Table 7.25 lists several types of small stores, and describes their physical form and the merchandise lines they carry. To give some idea of the breadth and number of outlets in Indonesia, Unilever, the acknowledged market leader, distributes either directly or indirectly to over 400 000 retail outlets.

There are two ways for a manufacturer to reach these traditional outlets. One is to go through a chain of distributors. The manufacturer sells to a national distributor, then the national distributor sells to a regional (provincial)

Table 7.25 Some types of traditional small stores

Local name	*Physical form*	*Product assortment*
warung rokok	A very small shack, usually 2 m^2 floor area, 2 m high	Cigarettes, limited range of over-the-counter products (cold tablets, shampoo, etc.), soft drinks, bottled water, snacks (100–300 items)
warung	Small store, usually 25–50 m^2, one story, sometimes built in front of residential houses, sometimes in "shopping areas/streets"	Similar to *warung rokok*, but with far greater range of product assortments (300–1000 items)
warung nasi	Traditional food stores	Food (usually ethnic); also serve soft drinks
toko kelontong	Larger than warung, mostly stand-alone units in "shopping areas/streets"	Similar to *warung*, plus some clothing, toys, canned foods; product assortments may vary from store to store
toko P&D	Size similar to *toko kelontong*	Specialize in food & beverages, including breads, cakes, and local fresh snacks
toko elektronik	Size similar to *toko kelontong*	Mostly electronic

distributor, who then sells to local distributors. The local distributor sells to local wholesalers, who finally sell to the ultimate outlets or the *warungs*. There are many firms that act as exclusive distributors at the national level for specific products such as PT Wicaksana, PT Tempo, and PT Borsumij Wehry. They then appoint regional or provincial distributors, which appoint lower layers of distributors.

The other way is through canvassing. In this system, the distribution company can be owned either by a manufacturer that sets up its own direct-distribution channel, or by a general wholesaler that sells directly to the final outlets. Typically, a canvassing firm has a fleet of small trucks. Each truck carries a driver, and a salesperson who also acts as a collector. The truck starts a canvassing trip by leaving the manufacturer's warehouse filled with inventory.

The salesperson determines the trip route, stopping at each *warung/toko* along the way. At each stop, the salesperson checks the outlet's inventory (not unlike the rack jobber in the USA), places new inventory, issues an invoice, and collects for outstanding past invoices. While the sale made at each outlet may be very small, the very close distance between outlets, coupled with the very low salaries paid to the salesperson and driver, make this system economically feasible. Whether or not it will be sustainable is open to some question.

Unilever is using a variant of this system, reminiscent of Good Humor marketing in the USA, to sell its Wall's Ice Cream in Jakarta. It has a fleet of tricycles, each equipped with an insulated plastic box, that sells icecream novelties direct to consumers. Prior to the introduction of this system, icecream for immediate consumption was not intensively distributed because the mostly small *warung* that would have been the natural outlet could not afford freezers. Once again, low rates make the Unilever/Wall system possible.

Fresh produce

Most fresh produce is distributed through the traditional system. Farmers have two alternatives for marketing their produce. They can sell directly to local (usually rural) markets, or they can sell to traders in fresh produce who bring the produce to urban areas. In every city there is a *pasar induk* (main market), where produce wholesalers bring their inventories to sell either to lower-level distributors or directly to final retailers.

Fruit is distributed somewhat differently. Some goes through the same system as fresh produce, while some goes to special areas that sell fruit in streetside shacks. These areas are usually quite specialized in the type of fruit they offer. A row of such shacks might sell, for example, only bananas. The very many varieties of bananas available in Indonesia make this level of specialization possible. Another recent development in urban areas are fruit shops that exclusively sell a specific variety of fruit.

Consumer durables

Channels for durables are typically shorter than for non-durable consumer products. Durables are sold in chain stores and stores dedicated to electronics, and even on market stalls. Many manufacturers appoint exclusive distributors. For imported products, parallel imports are a critical concern. For example, firm A may have the exclusive right to distribute imported products from manufacturer B. At the same time, an independent distributor may, on its own, import the same manufacturer's products from a distributor in Singapore or Hong Kong. Products from the two sources compete, with the parallel imports usually offered at lower prices.

Warranties and after-sales service are becoming more important to consumers. As they become more experienced, they become more demanding and more knowledgeable about their rights as consumers. In theory, this should work in favor of the appointed distributor; if Indonesia repeats the US experience it will not. Independent providers of after-sales service have blunted the competitive edge held by appointed distributors.

The emergence of a modern retailing sector

The 1990s have brought a boom in modern retailing, mostly in urban areas. Almost all types of modern retailing exist in Indonesia's urban areas.

Supermarkets and department stores are part of everyday urban life. Foreign-owned chains have entered the retail market, using local partners. Indonesian-owned chains have appeared everywhere. Table 7.26 presents a list of some of the major chains, classified by country of origin.

Table 7.26 Some new store types and their owners

Type of store	*Foreign-owned brands*	*Indigenous brands*
Megastore	Makro (The Netherlands)	Goro
Department store	Yaohan, Sogo (Japan), Metro (Singapore), JC Penney (USA), WalMart (USA)	Matahari, Pasaraya, Ramayana, Robinson, Golden Truly
Supermarket	N/A	Hero, Gelael
Restaurants	Pizza Huts, Tony Romas (USA)	Ayam Ny. Suharti, Handayani
Fast Foods	Kentucky Fried Chicken, McDonald's, Burger King, Wendy (USA)	Es Teler 77, Ny. Tanzil, California Fried Chicken
Specialty store	Shop In (USA)	Optik Melawai, Gramedia

The growth of chain stores is one of the most important trends in Indonesian retailing. Chain stores, of course, bring distribution efficiencies by shortening channels and increasing order sizes. They facilitate entry into the market by taking over some of the distribution and promotion functions manufacturers previously had to perform. They also facilitate a shift in channel power from manufacturer to retailer.

Another example of technological leapfrogging is the rapid development of ultra-modern shopping malls. In most urban areas they have been sprouting up like mushrooms after a rainstorm. By 1995 Indonesia had at least 90 shopping malls, with a total area of 2.4 million m^2. About 70% of this space was in Greater Jakarta and its surrounding cities (*Bisnis Indonesia* 1995a).

The Jakarta greater metropolitan area includes Jakarta itself and 3 surrounding smaller cities–Tangerang, Bogor, and Bekasi. Residential real-estate development has turned much of the metropolitan area into bedroom suburbs complete with shopping malls. Space devoted to malls increased from 145 052 m^2 in 1988 to 677 500 m^2 in December 1994, an increase of 367% in 6 years (*Republika* 1995). The construction of new malls is proceeding apace. Table 7.27 lists 9 new shopping malls that are scheduled for building between 1995 and 1997. These will be spread all over the metropolitan area and will add an additional 1 million m^2 of shopping space to the metropolitan area (*Bisnis Indonesia* 1995a).

Within Jakarta itself, the 10 largest shopping centers in 1994 occupied 538 000 m^2 (see Table 7.28). The city's shopping malls are distributed unevenly. South Jakarta, which is considered the most affluent residential

Table 7.27 New shopping-area development in Jakarta Greater Metropolitan area, 1995–1997

Building name	*Location*	*Area (m^2)*
BSD Mall	Serpong, Southern Jakarta	200 000
Lippo Supermall	Lippo Village, Tangerang	200 000
Pluit Mega Mall	Pluit, Northern Jakarta	142 000
Taman Anggrek Mall	Slipi, Western Jakarta	132 000
Citraland Golden	Karet, Central Jakarta	100 000
Senayan Square	Senayan, South Jakarta	80 000
BNI City Mall	Sudirman, South Jakarta	60 000
Puri Indah Mall	Puri Indah, West Jakarta	60 000
Chase Plaza Mall	Sudirman, South Jakarta	35 000
Total		**1 009 000**

Source: Bisnis Indonesia (1995), "Kendala dan prospek pusat perbelanjaan", Property Supplement, March 17, p. 1.

area in Indonesia, has 28.3% of Jakarta's shopping space. Central Jakarta, which is the historical trading center of Jakarta, has 26.9%. West Jakarta, which is mainly a middle-class, residential area, has 21.6%. North Jakarta and East Jakarta have 13.8% and 9.3% respectively.

Table 7.28 Jakarta's 10 largest shopping centers in 1994

Name	*Location*	*Area (m^2)*
Citraland	Grogol, West Jakarta	70 000
JITC	Mangga Dua, Central Jakarta	68 000
Plaza Indonesia	Sudirman, South Jakarta	60 000
Pasar Pagi	Mangga Dua, North Jakarta	60 000
Pasaraya	Blok M, South Jakarta	60 000
Gajah Mada Plaza	Gajah Mada, Central Jakarta	54 000
Blok M Plaza	Blok M, South Jakarta	43 500
Glodok Plaza	Glodok, Central Jakarta	42 500
Pondok Indah Mall	Pondok Indah, South Jakarta	40 000
Kelapa Gading Permai	Kelapa Gading, North Jakarta	40 000
Total		**538 000**

Source: Bisnis Indonesia (1995), "Kendala dan prospek pusat perbelanjaan", Property Supplement, March 17, p. 1.

Direct marketing and telemarketing

A somewhat unreliable and overburdened telephone system has limited the growth of telemarketing, Direct marketing using catalogs or TV commercials has been growing rapidly. Indonesians with satellite dishes have access to the offers presented on CNN, and Indonesia is included more frequently as one of the countries in which CNN advertisers offer to fulfil orders. The Indonesian Post Office has set up a special unit to assist direct marketers with order fulfillment.

Direct marketing may be an important channel for reaching rural consumers in the future. Because this population is so widely and thinly dispersed, in-store retailers may not be able to serve them adequately even when their incomes increase to the point where they are potentially attractive consumers.

Amway, together with a variety of indigenous multilevel marketers, is already in operation. Various indigenous firms market kitchenware, health and beauty aids, and myriad other product lines. Multilevel marketers appeal primarily to the lower-middle cohort. Incentive arrangements make it easy to recruit salespeople. Because many women in this population segment are housewives, salespeople can reach them with ease.

Advertising

In the earlier days of the Soeharto government, government regulations forbade advertising on TV. The government believed that advertising encouraged consumption, and that it was more important for people to save than to consume. This attitude has now changed completely.

The government now believes that the desire to consume is an important motivation for people to enter the workforce. It also believes that building a mass consumption society will help break down ethnic barriers and contribute to a united country.

When privately-owned TV stations came onto the scene, TV advertising was permitted, and TV has rapidly become the advertising medium of choice, followed by radio. Newspapers are a less important medium while magazines, because they can reach a specialized audience, are growing in importance for products that are targeted to specific consumer segments. Incidentally, the government prohibits cigarette advertising in newspapers, but allows it on TV.

Advertising has become the most important promotional tool. Both multinational and indigenous firms use it extensively. Table 7.29 presents a list of some of Indonesia's major advertisers, together with their expenditures in 1993. Unilever, with at least one leading brand in virtually every important consumer-packaged-goods product category, is far and away the heaviest spender. Indigenous marketers can compete with the multinationals, however.

Table 7.29 Advertisement spending for consumer products—printed media & TV, 1993

Company name	*1993 spending (R billion)*	*% of total 1993 spending*
Unilever	59	5.5
Indofood	14	1.3
Susu Bendera	10	0.9
ABC Group	8	0.7
Proctor & Gamble	7	0.6
Subtotal for top 5 companies	**98**	**9.2**
Others	972	92.8
Total	**1 070**	**100.0**

Source: Sembada Swa (1994b), "Raja Iklan", vol. 9, no. 12, pp. 32–3.

The leading spender among indigenous companies is Indofood. It has used TV and radio advertising very effectively to build its brand of instant noodles, Indomie, into the largest selling brand in the country by far. The Indomie name is synonymous with the instant-noodle category. Indofoods has used its position as an indigenous firm to advantage. It has adapted two lines of a popular patriotic song into a jingle, changing them from (translation) "Indonesia my homeland. From Timor to Talaud," to "Indonesia my homeland. Indomie my favorite" (*Economic and Business Review Indonesia* 1994).

Sales promotion

Sales promotion of consumer goods has been a common practice, especially in rural areas. Marketers participate in village fairs or appear at the weekly markets commonly held in these areas. A group of traveling players may perform a skit, which is a "live" commercial for the product. Sampling is common at such events. However, with the advent of satellite TV the live commercial has become less important

Sweepstakes and contests are popular, as are give-aways or premiums. A typical give-away is a dinner plate, or an item of glassware. Bundled goods—for example, bar of soap packaged as a give-away with a bottle of shampoo—are also common. Marketers have not used coupons in the media to the extent that they have done so in the USA. One reason is that, given the large number of very small stores, redemption costs could be very high. The advent of chain stores could significantly increase the use of couponing.

The growth of both malls and chain stores are facilitating the use of point-of-sale (POS) displays and in-store sampling. In many cases a young woman is present at a POS display to answer questions and to encourage purchase of the product. Sampling is a particularly effective way of introducing new products, especially food products. The trend toward fixed-price stores has increased the amount of price promotion. Periodic or seasonal sales are fast becoming the norm for chains, which can use the newspaper or TV to advertise these events. With increasing retail competition, the use of price promotion will inevitably continue to increase.

Market research

It is not easy to conduct market research using secondary data. The most reliable statistical data are published by Indonesia's Central Bureau of Statistics. Their annual statistics become available in the middle of the year following the year for which data are presented. The Bureau's reports can be had at relatively low prices. However, the information contained in these reports is designed for use in making policy, and economic and welfare evaluations. The data are usually presented at a high level of aggregation. The smallest unit of analysis is usually a province, and classification is only by rural or urban household. The Bureau's publications are really useful only as a starting point for analysis. The microdata usually needed for supporting firm-level or brand-level marketing strategies cannot be found in these reports. They leave a large vacuum.

With the advent of modern marketing in the early 1980s, market research firms began to fill the vacuum. There are 2 types of market research firms: independent firms, and those that are a part of an advertising agency. Among the independent firms, early comers such as Survey Research Indonesia (SRI) have been an important factor in the research market. Many of the leading consumer-goods firms, such as Konimex and Kalbe Farma for OTC products, are placing increasing emphasis on market research as the basis for their marketing strategies and marketing-mix decisions. Multinationals such as Unilever, P&G, and the like also rely heavily on market research. As the number of practitioners who have formal training in market research increases, use of marketing research should also increase.

In addition to firms dedicated to conducting consumer research, there are also firms that deal with broader subjects, such as collecting industry information (e.g. PDBI and Indoconsult), and doing economic forecasting. Most research firms are located in Jakarta, although their operations can be anywhere in Indonesia depending on clients' project requirements. Jakarta's 1995 *Yellow Pages,* for example, lists several firms in the market research category.

The fees charged for market research field projects vary, with approximately US$2500 at the low end per project, and several tens of thousands dollars at the high end, depending on number of respondents, sample coverage, and the complexity of the research questions. Interviews with executives of Jakarta-based market research firms reveal that advanced techniques have been utilized.

Focus-group discussions are popular, and are almost invariably followed by surveys. Usually, the survey is primarily descriptive. The most popular statistical method is cross-tabulation. Statistical information such as confidence levels, t-test scores, and the like are not usually reported. Advanced techniques such as multidimensional scaling and factor analysis have also been utilized. Market research trainers from firms such as the Burke Institute from the USA have also appeared in Jakarta on a periodic basis.

Mass market information is also increasingly available. For example, Surindo, a Jakarta-based market research firm, finished a survey of 5 major cities in 1995 and offered the reports for US$5000 each. Business Advisory Indonesia also offers such reports, at a price of US$3000. But marketers need to be careful when purchasing such reports. Higher prices do not necessarily have a linear correlation with information quality. Industry studies are also available.

In general, market research, although in its second decade in Indonesia, is still in the early stage of its lifecycle. We expect that, from the user's side, more market information will be sought as a result of increasing competition and the ever higher complexity of the marketplace. The emergence of mass retailers, some of whom are using scanners, coupled with the growing prominence of large consumer-packaged-goods firms, both multinational and locally owned, will spur demand for market research. The number of firms and the quality of market research are almost certain to increase, as a result of demand by larger, sophisticated research users. Among market research firms, higher quality work and more newcomers will be in evidence. All of these developments, we believe, will come quickly.

Expected changes in the macromarketing mix

Indonesia is beginning to experience many of the marketing-mix changes that accompany economic development. Clearly, for most goods and services, Indonesia is already–and firmly–a buyer's market. The market will become both more turbulent and more complex as consumers learn new roles and have more choices. As deregulation continues, making it easier for more foreign as well as domestic firms to enter the market, competition will increase still further. Change will be the only constant.

Here are some of the changes marketers must anticipate:

- The role of brands will increase still further in importance for a time as consumers use brands as guarantors of value. As consumers become more experienced and able to distinguish similarities and differences, the guarantor function brands serve will become less important to consumers.
- Opportunities to build new brands are now excellent because of the large numbers of households entering the middle class. These opportunities will

diminish, however, as the market grows and more brands become established. As any market matures, brand building becomes more and more difficult.
- Products and brands with symbolic value, especially those that are symbols of affluence, will continue to be very important; however, such products and brands will quickly lose their symbolic value if they are too widely adopted by consumers.
- In building a brand, especially a brand that has potential symbolic value, the quality of the brand's customers in the brand's formative stages is more important than their quantity.
- The consumer information environment will become much richer and broader. The use of satellite dishes makes product information from other countries, some presented as commercials, readily available to Indonesian consumers.
- The proliferation of both products and brands will persist until market growth slows. Domestic firms are introducing new products at a growing rate, multinational firms are expanding their offerings, and more multinational and other foreign firms are entering the market.
- The time lag between the introduction of a new product anywhere in the world and its first appearance in Indonesia will continue to shorten, and finally disappear. If the originator does not enter the market directly, an importer or imitator will.
- A modern retailing sector, composed of large chain units, malls, and strip centers, will continue to develop rapidly in the small cities and suburbs as well as in the largest.
- The continuing growth of chains will shift distribution-channel power from manufacturer to retailer.
- As long as factory wages remain low and unemployment remains significant, *warungs* and other forms of small retailing and peddling will persist. The *warung* will remain an important distribution channel for reaching both lower-income urban consumers and rural consumers.
- In new neighborhoods housing the emerging middle class, convenience stores such as those found in the industrialized countries will replace the *warung* as the neighborhood outlet for convenience goods, and will be a more central component of every marketing strategy.
- Consumers' desire for the very latest technology will persist, and high–tech consumer products will be in demand.

Conclusion

Our purpose has been to focus on the consumer behavior and marketing aspects of developments in Indonesia, and we have not spent much time analyzing the political aspects. We have emphasized the recent progress, and despite the problems we have presented an optimistic scenario. However, since mid-1997 Indonesia has been forced to endure a financial and economic crisis. The magnitude of the crisis can be appreciated by noting that the rupiah has declined in value vis-à-vis the US dollar by more than 50% since July 1 1997, and the current-account deficit has reached about US$8 billion. The nation's economic prospects are uncertain, and there is a serious danger of political instability. All sectors of the community have in some way been hurt by the depreciation of the currency and the credit squeeze mounted by the central bank. Growth has slowed, and signs of economic downturn are clearly visible–for example, panic buying, resulting from the currency drop, has cleared supermarket shelves.

Despite some reluctance, the government appears to be accepting the necessity for reforms, as demanded by the international community in return for assistance. In October 1997, Indonesia agreed (although there appears to be some backsliding) to implement radical reforms in return for a US$68.2 billion rescue package from the International Monetary Fund.

The immediate future is clearly problematical, and a pessimistic prognosis suggests that the business contraction will stretch through 1998, growth will drop to less than 3%, and as a result unemployment will rise. The optimistic projections predict a temporary slowing of growth to 5–6% as exports accelerate due to the devalued rupiah. It is our view that, although present events will strongly affect short-run consumer behavior and marketing, the direction for the long run has been set and the current situation presents a business opportunity. The material in this chapter should make it easier to take advantage of this opportunity.

References

Asian Business (1993), "Indonesia and China: The Retail of Two Cities", October, pp. 12–14.

Bisnis Indonesia (1995a), "Kendala dan prospek pusat perbelanjaan", Property Supplement, March 17, p. 1.

— (1995b), "Memacu konsumsi 'hair dryer' ...", Electronics Supplement, March 15, p. 3.

Business News (1994).

Dick, H.W. (1993), "Refleksi Lanjutan terhadap Kelas Menengah", in eds Richard Tanter & Kenneth Young, *Politik Kelas Menengah Indonesia*, LP3ES, Jakarta, pp. 67–76.

Dumairy (1995), "Evaluasi Kebijakan Pemerintah Menanggulangi Masalah Kemiskinan dan Kesenjangan", in eds Awan Setya Dewanta et. al., *Kemiskinan dan Kesenjangan di Indonesia*, Aditya Media, Yogyakarta, pp. 75–90.

Economic and Business Review Indonesia (1994), "What's in a name? Market Share", no. 132, October 22, pp. 38–9.

Economist, the (1993), "Among the Rich", February 6, pp. 42–3.

Edwards, Clive, MacIntyre, Andrew, & Asra, Abuzar (1994), "Peluang-peluang Baru untuk Saling Mengisi: Perubahan Demografis dan Permintaan terhadap Sekor Jasa", *Melebarkan Cakrawala: Australia dan Indonesia Menuju Abad ke 21*, Pustaka Sinar Harapan, Jakarta, pp. 27–60.

Euromoney (1991), *Indonesia in the 1990s*, Euromoney Publications, London.

Evers, Hans-Dieter & Mehmet, Ozay (1994), "The Management of Risk: Informal Trade in Indonesia", *World Development*, vol. 22, no. 1, pp. 1–9.

Fussel, Paul (1983), *Class*, Ballantine Books, New York.

Guiness, Patrick (1994), "Local Society and Culture", in ed. Hal Hill, *Indonesia's New Order*, University of Hawaii Press, Honolulu, pp. 267–304.

Hull, Terence H. & Jones, Galvin W. (1994), "Demographic Perspectives", in ed. Hal Hill, *Indonesia's New Order*, University of Hawaii Press, Honolulu, pp. 123–44.

Indonesian Central Bureau of Statistics (1993), Statistical Reports, Jl Dr Sutomo 68, Jakarta 10710.

— (1994), "The Big Rise", *Fortune*, international edition, Indonesian Economic Report 1993, May 30, pp. 40–6.

Indonesian Commercial Newsletter, "The Indonesian Economic Trends".

Informasi (1993), "Kondisi Industri Televisi Indonesia", no. 10, p. 29.

Jakarta Statistical Office (1993), reports.

Jones, G.W. & Manning, C. (1992), "Labor Force and Employment During the 1980s", in ed. A. Booth, *The Oil Boom and After: Indonesian Economic Policy and Performance in the Soeharto Era*, Oxford University Press, Singapore.

Koentjaraningrat (1985), *Javanese Culture*, Institute of South-East Asian Studies and Oxford University Press, Singapore.

Lubis, Mochtar (1993), "Kesemuan Kelas Menengah Indonesia", in eds Happy B. Zulkarnain, Faisal Siagian & Laode Ida, *Kelas Menengah Digugat*, Fikahati Aneska, Jakarta, pp. 107–25.

Mackie, James A. (1993), "Uang dan Kelas Menengah", in eds Richard Tanter & Kenneth Young, *Politik Kelas Menengah Indonesia*, LP3ES, Jakarta, pp. 105–35.

Mahasin, Aswab (1993), "Kelas Menengah Santri: Pandangan dari Dalam", in eds Richard Tanter & Kenneth Young, *Politik Kelas Menengah Indonesia*, LP3ES, Jakarta, pp. 151–9.

Manning, C.G. (1992), "Survey of Recent Developments", *BIES*, vol. 28, no. 1, pp. 3–38.

Marbun, B.N. (1994), *Kota Indonesia Masa Depan: Masalah dan Prospek,* Airlangga, Jakarta.

Republika (1995), "Berebut perhatian kaum remaja", vol. III, no. 01, January 4, p. 7.

Sarjadi, Soegeng (1994), *Kaum Pinggiran Kelas Menengah Quo Vadis?*, Gramedia Pustaka Utama, Jakarta.

Seda, Frans & Watts, Donald W. (1994), "Kerjasama Ekonomi Northeastern Territory/Indonesia Bagian Timur", *Melebarkan Cakrawala: Australia dan Indonesia Menuju Abad ke 21,* Pustaka Sinar Harapan, Jakarta, pp. 163–239.

Soemardjan, Selo & Breazeale, Kennon (1993), *Cultural Change in Rural Indonesia,* Sebelas Maret University Press, Solo.

Swa, Sembada (1992), "Pertempuran di Jalur Distribusi", vol. 8, no. 4, July, pp. 14–19.

— (1994a), "Triliunan Rupiah di Bisnis F&B", vol. 9, no. 12, Maret, pp. 22–5.

— (1994b), "Raja Iklan", vol. 9, no. 12, pp. 32–3.

Tait, Nikki (1995), "In Search of Big Spenders", *Financial Times Survey Indonesia, Financial Times,* June 9, p. VI.

World Bank (1994a), *Indonesia: Sustaining Development,* The World Bank, Washington, D.C.

— (1994b), *Indonesia Environment and Development: Challenges for the Future,* Report No. 12083-IND, The World Bank, Washington, D.C., p. 11.

Zulkarnain, Happy B., Siagian, Faisal, & Ida, Laode (1993), "Preface", in eds Happy B. Zulkarnain, Faisal Siagian, & Ida Laode, *Kelas Menengah Digugat,* Fikahati Aneska, Jakarta, pp. 9–26.

CHAPTER 8

Japan

High noon for the rising sun—new realities and forces of change in a mature consumer market[1]

TSUTOMU OKAHASHI, N. CLAY GARY &
STEVEN CORNISH-WARD

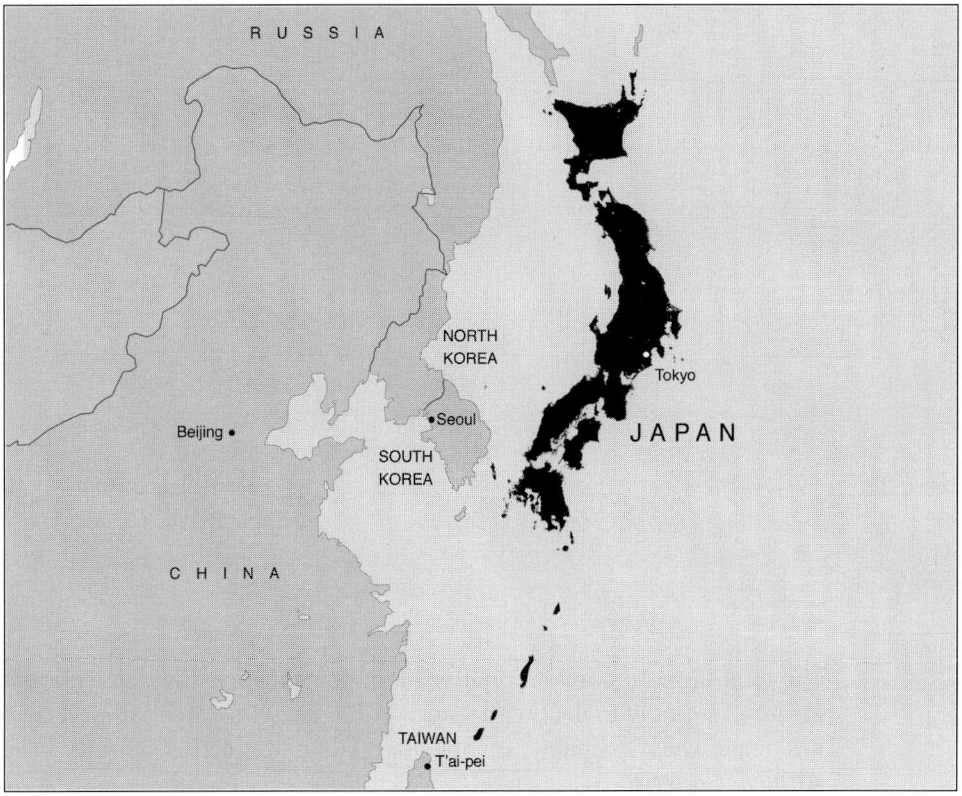

Abstract

Japan, often portrayed as the "invincible mercantilist juggernaut" poised to rule world markets, has began to show signs of economic strain. The realities suggest that after some years of recession the state of the economy is still problematical. The economic conditions have destroyed preconceptions and traditional perceptions of Japan. A reassessment of marketing and consumer behavior is not only timely, but also of critical relevance for future strategy development.

> The fatal blow to conventional wisdom comes when the conventional ideas fail signally to deal with some contingency to which obsolescence has made them palpably inapplicable (John Kenneth Galbraith, *The Affluent Society*).

Introduction

In the Japan of the 1990s, if the conventional wisdom has not yet received its knock-out punch, it is certainly on the ropes. Although indisputably a first-rate economic power with enduring traditions, Japan in this decade has economically, politically, and socially reached high noon. The country is undergoing a painful shift from the fast-growth, production-led "rising sun" of Asia to that of a slow-growth, consumption-led mature economy. So recently characterized by the West as "Japan Inc.," an invincible mercantilist juggernaut, poised to rule world markets, the Japanese economy is looking far less menacing to its growing ranks of competitors from every corner of the globe.

Consumer confidence, measured by a variety of surveys, has been befuddled by this new state of affairs, alternately rising and falling from one month to the next in response to media reports that seem to change with the weather. To blame are frequent contradictions between the official media statements and the actions of Japan's highly respected bureaucracies. A perfect example was chronicled in the *Asian Wall Street Journal* (October 28 1995) on the Bank of Japan's (BOJ) aggressive money-market intervention tactics. As the premium the country's bad-debt-saddled banks were required to pay to procure funds overseas rose, the message from the ever-steady BOJ was that everything was under control. The market was unimpressed. As one insider quipped, "[BOJ] started the week trying to tell everyone that the economy is recovering and the banking crisis is subsiding, but that was hard to digest as the Japan premium kept rising." Indeed, Japanese officialdom's propensity for optimism, consistently borne out by a post-war history of continuous economic growth and rising prosperity, was everywhere being cruelly betrayed by stark realities.

The realities about the economy in the fall of 1995 were simple. After what had already been 4 years of recession, the economy was still ailing. Daily, newspaper headlines chronicled new disclosures of the severity of bad debt problems in Japan's banking industry, a continuing bear market in the financial sector, and a renewed decline in real estate values. Worldwide demand for Japanese-made consumer durables, once expected to grow without limit, remained flat due to the high yen and the increasing quality and popularity of cheaper products from South Korea and elsewhere. Although 1995 saw many manufacturers reporting higher earnings, there was simultaneously a consensus that the lifetime employment system, the foundation of Japan's post-war "economic miracle," was giving way to a more fluid, merit-based employment market with far less job security.

Against this backdrop, the reform of Japan's post-war political system, long dominated by the Liberal Democratic Party, continued to lurch forward in fits and starts as a rough-hewn coalition government of diverse and conflicting interests struggled to reach consensus on a panoply of issues. On the foreign policy scene, everything from Japan's role in the UN to a reassessment of its close security ties with the USA was in transition, with no clear future in sight. In regional politics, the simultaneous ascension of two populist, anti-party former actors to the mayoral offices of Tokyo and Osaka underscored increasing public discontent with the machine politics that had ruled the nation for 5 decades.

On the social front, doubts were growing about the conventional wisdom that Japan would always be a safe, peaceful country with a level of social harmony championed as a triumph of Asian values. The Sarin gas attack on Tokyo's subway system by a religious cult provided a glimpse of tensions emerging in step with the disintegration of consensus on social and cultural mores. On another front, the government's relief efforts in response to the catastrophic earthquake in Kobe came under attack in the media for being slow and clumsy, highlighting a growing lack of confidence in the effectiveness of the country's paternalistic bureaucracies. In short, the recession is undermining conventional wisdom in every facet of Japanese life. In turn, the face of the consumer marketplace is changing in ways that make the conventional wisdom on the Japanese consumer palpably inapplicable. A reassessment of consumer behavior in Japan is therefore particularly timely now.

The Japanese consumer: The conventional wisdom

The conventional wisdom on Japan is that it is different: an island country with a history that reaches back to antiquity, and inhabitants with homogenous ethnic origins, a single common language, and unique culture and customs. When it comes to consumer markets, Japan is regarded as similarly unique, a place in which historical relationships and collective prosperity have taken precedence over individual financial gain. Japan's homogenous consumers are inscrutably complex, finicky and fickle in their tastes. Owing to the high quality of Japanese products, they are likely to prefer Japanese products to imports with the exception of import luxury goods or fashion designer brands not available in Japan.

All of this is undeniably accurate, but even as marketers worldwide were coming face-to-face with this conventional wisdom on the Japanese consumer, the seeds of change were already being sown. The so-called "Bubble Economy" of 1986–1990 did much to cultivate these seeds, revealing that Japanese consumers, when left to their own devices, can show the same propensity for greed and for desiring status and luxury as consumers in other markets. In the aftermath of the Bubble, consumers are showing similarly comprehensible growth into mature, marketing-wise value-seekers, not so easily duped by hype as once supposed.

The Bubble Economy

Japan's speculative Bubble Economy was the crowning moment in its ascension into the ranks of the world's economic elite. It was a heady time for

Japan. The growth rate of its traditionally high-growth economy, fuelled by a soaring yen, accelerated even further, in defiance of the laws of economic gravity. It has been noted that Japan grew by the equivalent of the GNP of Korea each year during the Bubble Economy, and by the end it was "one France larger" (Wood 1993, p. 181). This unprecedented growth brought with it the spotlight of worldwide attention. After 4 decades of Japanese businessmen travelling overseas to visit factories and learn from the West, during the 1980s it was Western managers and academic gurus who came to Japan to pay homage to and glean the secrets of Japan's "Economic Miracle."

The Bubble was a boon to Japanese consumers. The strong yen, the expansion of consumer credit, the repeal of an exorbitant luxury excise tax, and broad liberalization of import restrictions, gave the Japanese middle class access, for the first time, to every imaginable kind of luxury imported good, from bejewelled watches to expensive designer handbags. A nearly threefold increase in foreign travel, mostly a result of increased demand for holiday travel by young singles, rapidly expanded exposure to foreign cultures and ideas. Accordingly, the diversification of values and lifestyles was accelerated.

Yet Japan Inc. was, even during its economy's finest hour, accumulating a bad debt overhang owing to rampant speculation in securities markets and real estate. Meanwhile, a boom in Japanese auto and electronics industry investment in new production capacity unhappily coincided with the downturn of worldwide demand. When these problems came to a head with the crash of the Tokyo Stock Exchange in 1990, Japan Inc. went into a state of shocked denial that it is still coming to terms with. Wood (1993, p. 7) wryly notes this:

> Isaac Newton actually arrived in Japan in 1990. His presence did not prove a pretty sight in a country where too many people had concluded that the laws of gravity, when applied to their own [economy], had somehow been suspended.

Indeed, unwillingness to accept the laws of gravity meant that many of the changes most commentators believe are required for Japan to restore economic stability were still being postponed in 1995. And the consensus of most was that the longer they were postponed, the more prolonged and painful the adjustment process would be.

Does this mean the denouement of the Japanese economic juggernaut which terrorized the West during the 1980s? And more importantly, for our purposes, does it herald the end of the attractiveness of the Japanese consumer marketplace for foreign marketers? While admitting that it would be absurd to declare the Japanese economy finished, Wood (1993) asserts that the immediate future is far bleaker than most suppose, and that the process of clearing the wreckage will be painful, contractional and time-consuming, and will inevitably reduce the country's capacity for economic growth. This will inevitably impact negatively on consumer spending power, and it has, in fact, already done so, as we shall see.

But Wood and others also predict that recovery from the current recession will entail greater convergence with the international marketplace. For foreign marketers, this should mean a broad expansion of opportunities in Japan in the coming years as the strong yen, continued deregulation and reform of the distribution system, and diversification in consumer values clear the way for greater foreign-product participation in the consumer marketplace.

What follows is an attempt to present the conventional wisdom about the Japanese consumer side by side with powerful evidence that this wisdom is no longer applicable to current realities. The goal will be not to create a substitute conventional wisdom, but to understand where consumer behavior has been and to suggest the directions it will take during the years to come.

The economic environment

The economic environment has remained precarious and unpredictable. Forecasting is always complicated by the Japanese bureaucracies' ever-sanguine interpretations of their voluminous data on Japanese economic life. Having presided over Japan's economic miracle, the Economic Planning Agency (EPA), the BOJ, the Ministry of International Trade and Industry (MITI) and others are not accustomed to making pessimistic predictions. Indeed, during what in 1995 had become a 4-year slump, the EPA and the BOJ proclaimed several times that the recession was in fact over, only to watch the economy slide further.

Economic growth

The economic growth rate had slowed to 0.5% in 1994, and in 1995 there lay the specter of no growth—or even negative growth. No comment is necessary on the negative impact of such a result on consumer confidence. But such a result might also force the hand of a business establishment that up to the present day has tried to maintain its commitment to the covenant of lifetime employment, at least in principle.

Decline of lifetime employment

Most observers expect lifetime employment to come under increasingly direct pressure. A survey conducted by leading Japanese advertising agency Dentsu Inc. (1993a) in the fall of 1993 revealed that as many as 57% of all Japanese believe fewer people will work for only one company until retirement. Meanwhile, 90% responded that developing specialized skills and expertise would be important in the future. This reflects the growing belief that the future will call on employees to take the initiative in building and maintaining skills that make them viable as workers.

Current employment outlook

Due to corporate efforts to ease the shift to a more fluid employment structure, nominal unemployment remains low by Western standards. As Table 8.1 shows, Japanese consumer durables manufacturers are steadily moving production overseas, primarily to South-East Asian countries with cheap labor. In the midst of this seismic shift, retraining for intra-company transfer and outplacement programs in the manufacturing sector have helped minimize layoffs of blue-collar workers. Nevertheless, at nearly 3%, unemployment in 1995 was at a historical high for Japan (Ministry of Labor 1995). And this statistic hides the phenomenon of *shanai shitsugyo,* or intra-company unemployment, a fancy term for white-collar overstaffing.

Table 8.1 TV production—location

Year	*Domestic (%)*	*Overseas*
1984	58.2	41.8
1985	61.2	38.8
1986	52.8	47.2
1987	51.3	48.7
1988	45.3	54.7
1989	39.9	60.1
1990	37.2	62.8
1991	34.1	65.9
1992	28.1	71.9

Asahi Shimbunsha (1995), "Asahi ki wado 95–96" (Asahi Keywords), Tokyo, March.

Wood asserts that over-staffing is partly due to over-hiring in the 1980s and the acceptance of the "myth of the labor shortage," a favorite precept of the conventional wisdom of the day. Director and vice-president of Bain & Company, Japan, Shintaro Hori (1993) concurs with this analysis, asserting that Japan's services sector now "tolerates levels of employment that would be considered unusually high in other countries." Hori estimates that 5 to 6 million Japanese white-collar workers are in fact "redundant." If these jobs were eliminated outright, unemployment would soar to over 10%, although this would be highly unlikely owing to the tacit commitment to lifetime employment.

Rather than eliminate jobs outright through layoffs, Japanese firms have quietly used a variety of tactics to decrease their white-collar payrolls. The gradual rise of both voluntary and compulsory early retirement programs, transfers to lower-paying subsidiaries, merit-pay systems, and cutbacks in annual hiring of new college graduates are all evidence of these efforts. Meanwhile, government surveys reveal that Japanese worker attitudes toward employment are more liberal. In 1992, nearly 3 million full-time Japanese workers changed jobs, and the number who said they would like to change jobs stood at 6.2 million (Management and Co-ordination Agency 1994a). Although some job-changing may be due to corporate outplacement, Japanese workers who are disgruntled with pay and conditions in one job are showing greater willingness to look for greener pastures elsewhere.

The future

In spite of corporate attempts to reduce the pain of the changing employment structure, if estimates of the slack in white-collar employment are even half-right, and if the economy continues to be sluggish over the near to mid-term, greater dislocation is undoubtedly in store. The brunt of it would be borne by Japan's young people. This was foreshadowed as early as 1994, when a record 150 000 new university graduates were not hired by any company to which they applied. Many had offers withdrawn by companies who belatedly realized they could not afford to make lifetime commitments. In Japanese society, a society that tacitly assumes universal employment, these young people are stigmatized. Should expectations of universal lifetime employment be betrayed, resulting in higher structural unemployment, there would be a potential for the emergence of a Japanese "Generation X," an economically disenfranchised generation of young people, raised in affluence but with significantly dimmer financial prospects than their elders.

Income

As shown in Table 8.2, Japan has the most equitable distribution of wealth of all the advanced industrial countries. An average increase in base salary of 4.3% for industrial workers in 1995 pointed to increased income in most countries. However, real net income actually declined by 1.1% in 1994 (Table 8.3). In 1995, a thinktank annual survey cited in the *Nihon Kogyo Shimbun* reports a 5.6% drop in year-on-year average gross household income. Corporate ceilings on overtime hours, a significant component of gross white-collar income, were a key factor in income decline. Monthly spending was also down slightly, due to both low confidence in the economy and a deflationary trend in consumer prices, which will be discussed later. Also, although the Japanese household savings rate remains the highest among the advanced countries, consumer debt is on the rise (see Table 8.4).

In a positive sign for income prospects, in June 1995 semi-annual bonuses rose for the first time in 3 years by an average 1.7%, according to the *Nihon*

Table 8.2 Income distribution (% share of GDP, 1990)

Lowest 20%	*Second 20%*	*Third 20%*	*Fourth 20%*	*Top 20%*	*Top 10%*
8.8	13.2	17.4	23.1	37.5	22.4

Source: Genzberger et al. (1994), *Japan Business: The Portable Encylopedia for Doing Business with Japan*, World Trade Press, San Rafael, California, p. 172.

Table 8.3 Average monthly salary of nationwide non-agricultural households

Year	*Net income (yen)*	*Net expense (yen)*	*Net income change after inflation (%)*
1975	236 152	186 676	2.7
1980	349 686	282 263	–0.6
1985	444 846	360 642	2.7
1990	521 757	412 813	2.0
1991	548 769	430 380	1.8
1992	563 855	442 937	1.1
1993	570 545	447 666	0.1
1994	567 174	439 112	–1.1

Source: Management and Co-ordination Agency (1995), "Annual Report on the Family Income and Expenditure Survey, 1994", Tokyo.

Table 8.4 Outstanding non-housing consumer debt

Year	*Debt*
1984	25.1
1985	27.4
1986	31.0
1987	35.7
1988	43.0
1989	52.9
1990	63.1
1991	68.4
1992	71.5
1993	74.1

Note:
All values in trillions of yen (1994: Y100=$1(US)).

Source: Japan Consumer Credit Industry Association (1995), "The Origin and Development of Consumer Credit in Japan", Tokyo.

Keizai Shimbun (1995a). Since bonuses in Japan have traditionally been linked to total corporate performance rather than individual performance the rise suggests that the worst of the recession may be over for Japan's manufacturing sector, which engaged in aggressive restructuring activities between 1991 and 1994. Nevertheless, as the white-collar employment situation suggests, future prospects for nominal income growth are not good. Certainly, the increased fluidity of the labor market and the decline of seniority-based compensation will mean greater opportunities for talented employees. Yet current hiring moves by major corporations hint at downward pressure on the corporate salary structures. Japan Airlines, having suspended its hiring of flight attendants under the lifetime employee system after 1992, has shifted to ad-hoc hiring of contract flight attendants. First-year contract employees are paid an hourly wage, not a salary, and can expect to make roughly half of what first-year flight attendants made in 1992. Contract employees have fewer benefits, and may be released at the expiration of their contracts.

Inflation

As Table 8.5 shows, inflation has declined dramatically since the bursting of the Bubble. Continued price destruction and the looming threat of debt deflation, described earlier, could even result in deflation in the near term. This is underscored by the EPA's near-zero forecasts for 1995 and 1996.

Table 8.5 Inflation rate

Year	*Inflation (%)*
1971	6.4
1980	7.8
1990	3.1
1991	3.3
1992	1.7
1993	1.3
1994	0.7
1995*	0.3
1996*	0.2

* Projected

Source: Economic and Planning Agency (1994), "Degree of Satisfaction with Living Situation", Tokyo.

The demographic environment

That Japan is an ethnically homogeneous country is generally well known. As of 1990, 99.3% of the country's population held Japanese citizenship. Nevertheless, the rising number of legal and illegal residents is contributing to greater ethnic diversity in urban areas. People from other Asian countries are frequently brought to Japan on labor contracts with small industrial firms to do the so-called Three-K jobs: *kitanai* (dirty), *kitsui* (hard), and *kiken* (dangerous). Demand for such foreign laborers is expected to increase as Japan shifts increasingly to a service-oriented economy and younger Japanese are less willing to take these kinds of jobs. Meanwhile, little population growth is expected due to a persistently low birth rate, to be discussed in detail below (see Table 8.6).

Table 8.6 Population growth in Japan

Year	*Average annual growth rate (%)*
1971–1980	1.3
1981–1990	0.5
1991–2000*	0.3
2001–2010*	0.2
2011–2020*	–0.2

* Projected

Source: Ministry of Health and Welfare (1992), "Population Projections for Japan 1991–2090", Tokyo.

Age distribution

In 1987, 10.9% of Japan's total population was 65 years of age or older. This figure is low in comparison with such Western countries as Sweden, where the ratio is nearly 20%, and the United Kingdom, where the ratio is over 15%. However, with average life expectancies in Japan the highest in the world at 81 years for women and 75 years for men, the ratio of senior citizens is increasing sharply, and is expected to reach 23.6% by 2020. Also, with a birth rate of less than 1.5 per couple, the population 15 years old and under is expected to decline to 15.2% by 2000 (see Table 8.7).

The "Dankai" Generations

An important feature to note in Japanese demographic composition is the existence of two huge baby-boom generations (see Table 8.8). They are commonly known to marketers as the Dankai Generation and their children, the Dankai Junior Generation. Although each represents only a 4- or 5-year period, and is therefore not a full generation in the strict sense, these two

Table 8.7 Projected age distribution of the population

Age	*1995*	*2000*	*2010*	*2020*
0–14	16.0	15.2	16.4	15.5
15–64	69.4	67.8	62.4	59.0
>65	14.5	17.0	21.3	25.5

Source: Ministry of Health and Welfare (1992), "Population Projections for Japan 1991–2090", Tokyo.

groups are considered opinion leaders for broad segments of the population, and are tracked closely by marketers for clues to changes in consumer behavior.

Table 8.8 Birth rate

Year	*Rate (%)*
1960	2.0
1970	2.13
1980	1.75
1990	1.54
1995*	1.50
2000*	1.60
2010*	1.78
2020*	1.80
2025*	1.80

* Projected

Source: Ministry of Health and Welfare (1992), "Population Projections for Japan 1991-2090", Tokyo; Ministry of Health and Welfare (1995), "Vital Statistics", Tokyo.

The "Dankai" Generation are the children of Japan's post-Second World War baby boom. Some 9 million strong, they are currently in their mid-to late forties. This means they are beginning to enter the upper echelons of corporate Japan. The Dankai were the driving force behind Japan's student protest movement in the late 1960s and early 1970s. They challenged authority on a variety of issues, including the country's support of the US war effort in Vietnam. Although they eventually settled down into jobs within the Japanese establishment, the Dankai have remained proud of their self-styled maverick image. They perceive themselves as having made constructive changes in Japanese society by actively supporting government and corporate policies to encourage more individuality, greater internationalism and shorter working hours. As Kawakami (1993) notes, while they have, on the surface, been able to adapt to the corporate establishment, because Dankai distrust the establishment they have a strong belief that "work is not everything," and their strongest loyalties are to their families, not the company.

Although the leisure boom is a relatively new consumer trend, it has been argued that the "all work no play" philosophy of the Japanese workforce actually began to change in the early 1970s when the Dankai generation entered the workforce. Dentsu Inc.'s Teizo Tsutsumi (Tsutsumi et al. 1986, p. 17) has argued that the Dankai led the revolutionary shift in Japanese worker behavior from "ant-like" to "grasshopper-like," taking his metaphor from an Aesop's Fable. Whereas the ant works himself to the point of death to gather food for tomorrow, the grasshopper prefers to enjoy today and lets tomorrow take care of itself. Table 8.9 shows the steady decline in average annual working hours by Japanese workers since the Dankai entered the workforce in the early 1970s. From a consumer-behavior perspective, it is interesting to note that Honda and Sony, innovative mavericks of the Japanese corporate establishment, are brands that are closely associated with and favored by the Dankai Generation.

Table 8.9 Monthly working hours in the manufacturing sector (hours)

Year	*1970*	*1975*	*1980*	*1985*	*1990*	*1994*
Regular	169.5	160.7	161.3	160.2	157.1	148.7
Overtime	18.1	10.6	14.1	15.5	14.7	10.3
Total	187.6	171.3	175.4	175.7	171.8	159.0

Source: Ministry of Labor (1995), "Monthly Labor Survey", Tokyo.

The Dankai Junior Generation are the children of the Dankai Generation. Born between 1970 and 1973, Dankai Juniors number more than 8 million. Now entering their adult years, they are entering the workforce and beginning to exert their adult spending power on the marketplace. Their consumer behavior will be discussed in more detail later.

Cultural environment

Education

The education system is divided into 5 stages:

1 kindergarten (1 to 3 years of schooling)
2 elementary school (6 years)
3 middle school (3 years)
4 high school (3 years)
5 university (generally 4 years)

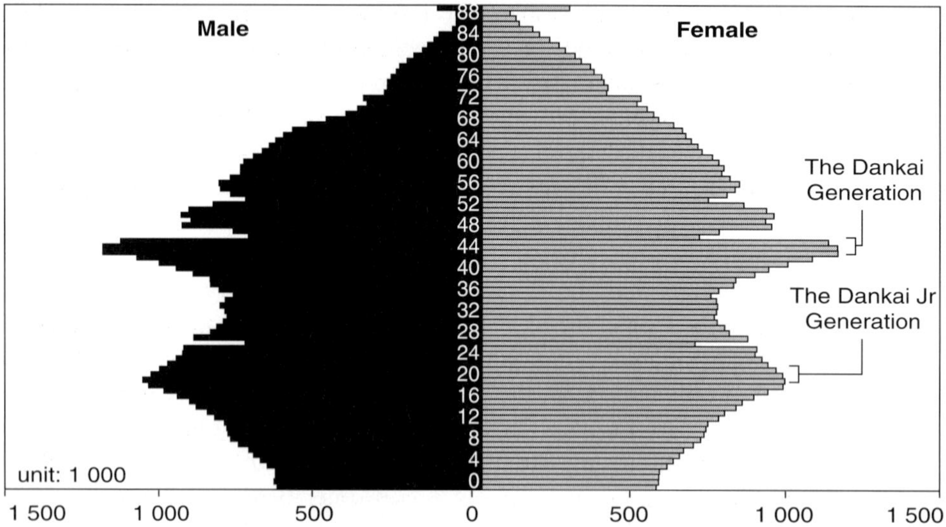

Fig. 8.1 Age distribution in Japan (1993)

Source: Ministry of Health and Welfare (1992a), *Population Projections for Japan 1991–2090.*

There are also junior colleges offering courses of study of 2 or 3 years in duration; these are predominantly for women. In addition, many universities provide postgraduate courses for advanced studies. Primary and middle school education is free and compulsory. In 1994, 97% of all students entered high school, a ratio similar to that of the USA, indicating that high school is in fact an essential part of a child's education. Of all high school students, 36% continued on to 2-year women's colleges or 4-year universities. This is a smaller ratio than that of the USA, where nearly half of all students enter university, but more than that of western European countries, where averages range between 20% and 30%.

Private schools exist at all stages of the system. As of 1994, as many as 80% of children in kindergartens and 73% of students in universities were enrolled in private institutions, and 30% of all high school students were attending private schools.

Traditionally, educational background has been an important factor in Japan's lifetime employment system. In order to land a job in a top-ranking company, it is necessary to be graduated from a top-ranking university, a qualification that is dependent in turn upon graduation from a top high school and middle school. Hence students generally attend private entrance examination, or "cram," schools. These schools, which provide supplementary, after-school instruction to help students enter the school of their choice, exist at all levels, from nursery school through university.

Because even public high school education is not free, and because of the connection between educational background and employment, household educational expenses are uniformly high. A 1995 survey by Sanwa Bank (Nihon Keizai Ryutsu Service Shimbun 1995) indicates that the cost of sending one child to private schools from nursery school through university is approximately US$264 000. The typical cost for a child who attends only public institutions is US$114 000. These daunting costs, coupled with generally high child-rearing expenses, may be one factor in the declining birth rate, which will be discussed later.

Education reform

The post-Second World War education system was designed to produce an obedient workforce with uniform training, knowledge and values. This system has been credited with creating the efficient worker culture necessary to achieve Japan's "Economic Miracle." However, there is overwhelming consensus in favor of education reform. The fierce "examination hell" students go through to gain a place in the best schools has long been decried for placing undue stress on children at an early age. Also, the institutionally encouraged practice of bullying students judged by teachers to be "different" from others has come under attack. A 1995 independent report (Jiji Press, Naigai Kyoiku 1995) on the need for education reform states that 97% of Japanese agree that education needs reform. Top reasons cited include "intensity of entrance examination system" (60%), "increasing bullying" (37%), "problems with the quality or nature of instruction" (35%), and "too much emphasis placed on in-school education" (32%) (Hori 1993, pp. 170–1). Perhaps more importantly, it has been argued that the increasingly competitive international business environment demands a more diverse workforce with specialized skills and the intellectual flexibility to make quick decisions.

In the early 1990s, the Ministry of Education began to reform the education system to address these issues. Reforms include the de-emphasis of rote memorization of a uniform body of common knowledge, a new emphasis on out-of-classroom learning experiences, and greater tolerance for individual differences. As of 1995, school children have had two Saturdays off per month as the first step toward the implementation of a 5-day school week. The stated purpose of cutting school hours is to provide students with the opportunity to pursue extra-curricular activities, with a view to producing more well-rounded adults. In addition, since many companies implemented a 5-day work week during the 1980s, children can now spend more time with their families.

Liberalization

The traditional family

Before the Second World War, most Japanese lived in an extended family of 3 or more generations. In their adherence to Confucian traditions, which entered Japan via China and Korea, family relationships were governed by a rigid hierarchical system. The elderly members of the household held an honored position, and parental authority was strong. As the nominal head of the household, a father commanded special respect and obedience from his children and his wife. However, the de facto head of household affairs would be his mother, who would manage all household affairs, including the budget. Upon marriage, a new bride was expected to live with her husband's family and faithfully obey her parents-in-law, of whom she would also be the primary caretaker in their old age. The young housewife served what amounted to a Cinderella-like apprenticeship to an often strict and unforgiving mother-in-law. From her mother-in-law, the young housewife learned how to keep house, manage the family budget and cook. Typically, she could never do enough to please, especially if she failed to bear her mother-in-law a grandson. Indeed, strained relationships between young wives and mothers-in-law are still popular subject matter for television dramas today.

Changes in household composition

Rapid economic growth and urbanization have wrought major changes in the traditional family. There has been a sharp decline in the number of persons per household, which now stands at 2.99 people, down from 4.14 in 1960 (Table 8.10). Urbanization has resulted in a decrease in the number of extended families as children leave home to attend universities and take jobs in the cities. Extended families accounted for 36.5% of all households in 1955, but this ratio has declined steadily, dropping to 17.8% in 1990. In contrast, the number of one-person households has skyrocketed—from 3.4% in 1955 to 20.2% of households in 1990; according to one estimate, it rose further to 23.1% by 1995 (Suzuki & Krishima 1995). Meanwhile, the number of nuclear families, comprised of parents and children, which had gradually increased to 63.3% by 1980, had declined slightly to 61.8% by 1990. As women increasingly opt for full-time careers, the number of double-income-no-kids, or DINKs, households has begun to rise, as suggested by the relatively stable figure for earners per household (Table 8.11), in spite of the declining number of persons per household. Also, with the decline of the extended family, the number of elderly living alone is rising. The number of households in which the householder is over 65 years of age increased from 2.2% in 1955 to 13.2% in 1994 (Ministry of Health and Welfare 1995a).

Compounding changes in household size and composition is the declining birth rate. In 1930 women gave birth to an average of 4.7 children, but this had fallen to 1.5 by 1995. The aforementioned rise of one-person and DINKs households and the tendency to delay marriage are closely related to this trend. The high cost of child rearing and education, combined with the decreasing average size of housing, is discouraging some people from marrying, or even from having children. For working women, a lack of sufficient affordable childcare services is a major deterrent to childbearing.

Table 8.10 Persons per household

Year	*Average no.*
1960	4.14
1970	3.41
1975	3.28
1980	3.22
1985	3.14
1990	2.99

Source: Management and Co-ordination Agency (1992), "1990 Population Census of Japan", Tokyo.

Table 8.11 Earners per household

Year	*Average no.*
1970	1.64
1975	1.59
1980	1.55
1985	1.56
1990	1.60
1991	1.63
1992	1.62
1993	1.60

Source: Management and Co-ordination Agency (1995), "Annual Report on the Family Income and Expenditure Survey, 1994", Tokyo.

As a result of the decline of the extended family and the increasingly long life expectancy of the Japanese, the ratio of households consisting only of people aged 65 or older jumped from 2.2% in 1955 to 13.2% in 1994 (Ministry of Health and Welfare 1995a). In 3-generation households, grandparents enjoyed an honored role, and children and grandchildren were committed to taking care of parents and grandparents until death. However, younger Japanese are far less inclined to honor this commitment of taking care of their elders than were previous generations. Consideration of the problems that elderly people face when living on their own inspired a government campaign to promote the merits of extended-family units.

The dramatic shift toward one-person households has not yet been sufficiently reflected in official statistics on Japanese consumers. As two Sumitomo Life Insurance Research Institute researchers note in a recent article contributed to *Nihon Kogyo Shimbun,* one-person households are still not included in the government's "Annual Report on Family Income and

Expenditure Survey," the most widely used source of data on Japanese consumer behavior (Suzuki & Krishima 1995). The article points out that many one-person households are comprised of singles under 30 who, free of the burden of high child-rearing and educational expenses, have high disposable incomes to spend on advanced consumer durables such as personal computers and overseas travel. Major factors in the rise of one-person households are declining average living space per family and a growing preference for privacy and independence, which encourages many children to live on their own. The rising average age of first marriage, 28.4 years for men and 26.1 years for women in 1993, will contribute to a further increase in the number of one-person households.

Table 8.12 Type of family (%)

Year	*Nuclear family*	*Extended family*	*One-person household*
1920	55.3	38.2	6.0
1955	59.6	36.5	3.4
1960	60.2	34.7	4.7
1970	63.5	25.4	10.8
1980	63.3	20.7	15.8
1990	61.8	17.8	20.2

Source: Management and Co-ordination Agency (1992), "1990 Population Census of Japan", Tokyo.

Supporting the continued growth of one-person and DINKs households is the diffusion of modern household appliances, the expansion of the instant and frozen-food industries, and the proliferation of home delivery services for everything from mineral water and fresh vegetables to dry cleaning and pizza. These conveniences allow one-person households and DINKs to balance busy work schedules with their broad leisure interests. Meanwhile, in more traditional families, these conveniences have freed housewives to take part-time jobs, enrol in courses at community centres or continuing education programs at universities, or participate in volunteer activities.

Gender issues

The revision of the Civil Code in 1947, which gave women equal legal status with men in all aspects of life, was the first step toward abolishing the patriarchal character of the family. As in Western countries, an increasing number of women are now entering the workforce. In 1994, the number of women workers totaled 20.34 million, and accounted for 38.8% of the nation's workforce, up from 32% in 1975 (Management and Co-ordination Agency 1994b). The number of women committed to long-term employment continues to increase, as shown by the fall in the number of women who quit their jobs for reasons relating to childbirth or marriage. The figure is down from 22% in 1977 to 7% in 1992. Women in the workforce are more educated than their counterparts in the past, with the number with 2- and 4-year college degrees increasing to 22% in 1987, up 9% from 1977. Moreover, female graduates of 4-year universities comprised 31.3% of all 4-year graduates in 1994, up from 18.0% in 1970 (Management and Co-ordination Agency 1994a). Nevertheless, there is evidence that corporate freezes on new hires during the recession have hit women harder than men. Of female 4-year college graduates, 16.3% were unable to obtain lifetime employment in 1994, compared to 9.9% for males (Asahi Shimbusha 1995).

Back to the family

Although still low, the divorce rate is rising, reflecting the breakdown of the traditional family (see Table 8.13). One reason may be the long hours fathers typically spend away from the home, as a result of long working hours and work-related social commitments. During the recession, media reports have focused on the difficulty some fathers have in integrating themselves into family life now that overtime hours and time spent wining and dining customers have decreased. A spate of television advertisements depicted formerly "workaholic" fathers feeling out of place in the home or in family settings. Older men in particular, having spent little time at home during their work careers, have difficulty getting along with their wives upon retirement. Referred to as *sodai gomi*, or "oversized garbage," by their wives, such men have become strangers in their own homes by the end of their work careers.

Table 8.13 Divorce rates

Year	*Divorces (per 1000)*
1950	1.01
1960	0.74
1970	0.93
1980	1.22
1985	1.39
1990	1.28
1991	1.37
1992	1.45
1993	1.52

Source: Asahi Shimbunsha (1995), " Asahi ki wado 95-96 (Asahi Keywords)", March, Asahi Shimbun-sha, Tokyo.

Among younger generations of fathers, however, there is a stronger desire to balance work and family. Also, one positive side effect of the recession has been that fathers are spending more time at home and enjoying leisure activities with their families. As discussed earlier, the two extra holidays per month being given to school children are also supporting this trend. All of these factors have contributed to a renewed emphasis on family life among parents, from the Dankai Generation onward.

Materialism, the environment and health

It has been noted by many commentators that, if the Japanese government's mission after the Second World War was to catch up with the West economically, the dream for the average Japanese worker was to catch up to the lifestyle of the American middle class in terms of the ownership of durable goods. The US occupation forces gave Japan its first exposure to everything from "Coca-Cola" and instant coffee to Levi's, and the image of the USA as an affluent middle-class consumer culture had enormous appeal. While it has been noted that aspirations for the American lifestyle have declined since the late 1980s, trends from America and Europe still have a major influence on popular consumer culture in Japan, especially among the young (Dentsu Inc. 1994). It is worthwhile taking a look at changing attitudes toward material wealth during the past two decades.

During the 1970s, the so-called Three Cs, for "Car," "Cooler," and "Color TV," were the leading icons in the rush to achieve a "middle class" standard of living. Along with the cultural emphasis on conformity to the group, the obsession with the American middle class may be one of the reasons for Japan's oft-noted middle-class consciousness. As Japan has become more affluent, the government has sought to nurture the emergence of this consciousness, as well as relative equality in the standard of living. Hence it is not surprising that annual polls on the life of the nation conducted by the Prime Minister's Office since 1964 have consistently indicated that an overwhelming majority of the people feel that they belong to the middle class. And, as discussed earlier, Japan does indeed have the greatest equality of all the advanced countries in terms of the distribution of wealth. It will be interesting to see how this consciousness will be reconciled with potentially greater disparities in wealth as trends such as merit-based compensation (discussed earlier) progress.

Until the 1980s, even as affluence continued to increase, the realities of the declining size of the average home and the high cost of housing, coupled with the highest consumer prices in the world on daily goods, dictated a relatively austere lifestyle for the average Japanese. Ariga and Gary (1990), for example, cite a survey by the Japan Economic Research Center which showed that at this time 76% of Japanese believed they would never own their own home.

Table 8.14 Floor space per dwelling

Year built	*Area (m²)*
Prior to 1945	132.9
1945–1950	104.8
1951–1960	95.8
1961–1970	86.6
1971–1975	88.6
1976–1980	93.9
1981–1985	92.8
1986–1988	83.7
1989	85.0
1990	84.6
1991	85.7
1992	89.7
Jan–Sep. 1993	92.7

Source: Management and Co-ordination Agency (1995c), "1993 Housing Survey of Japan", June, Tokyo.

Then the strong yen, the deregulation of import and luxury goods markets, and the expansion of consumer credit during the Bubble Economy of the late 1980s gave many Japanese consumers the opportunity to enjoy their country's affluence for the first time. Having satisfied their material goals in terms of consumer durables, consumers moved on to designer brands, foreign travel and other luxury items previously beyond their reach.

The expansion in the range of choice during this period, owing to the influx of imports and the product diversification strategies of Japanese durables manufacturers (to be discussed later), created an emphasis on the differentiation of lifestyles through consumption. In addition, greater access to luxury goods created a boom in expensive lifestyle products with high-class images. This explains why studies in the 1980s indicated that Japanese consumers looked on consumption as a means of self-expression and self-realization. It has been noted that self-expression through consumption has allowed the average Japanese to build an independent identity in personal life while maintaining conformity with society in public or professional life. For both men and women, the choice of imported fashion brands became a primary means of creating an individual identity. This attitude meant that the latest styles from Europe and America quickly took hold.

Since the "bursting" of the Bubble Economy, however, consumer attitudes toward material goods have begun to change. For one thing, consumers are less conscious of images of status and luxury and, in turn, with high fashion per se. While consumption remains a key means of self-expression, consumers seem more comfortable with down-to-earth lifestyle goods. Moreover, rather than focusing on what a chosen brand will mean to others, they are basing decisions on which brands to buy based on whether or not a particular brand fits their own self-image. This is a subtle but important change, from the "me-too" consumption style to a more thoughtful, personal, and truly individual one (Oshashi 1989; Dentsu Inc. 1994). This change will be discussed further, in the section titled "Recent changes in consumer behavior."

As a result of their long working hours, Japanese workers traditionally had little free time for leisure. Moreover, the corporate work ethic dissuaded workers from taking their full allotment of paid vacation for fear of incurring the disapproval of both co-workers and superiors. However, since 1970, both regular working hours and overtime hours have declined steadily. Furthermore, from the Dankai Generation onward, Japanese workers have become more leisure-oriented and are willing to take holidays to enjoy the fruits of their labor. According to an annual survey by the Leisure Research and Development Center, the proportion of Japanese who say they stress leisure time more than their career increased from 27.1% in 1985 to 32.7% in 1994. The proportion of those who stress career over leisure time fell from 44.4% to 38.7% over the same period, while the figure for those who seek a balance between career and leisure rose slightly from 27.5% to 28.3%.

The strong yen has made overseas travel a particularly popular and attractive leisure pursuit. Peak demand for overseas travel tends to focus on three

Table 8.15 Working hours per person—National average

Year	*Average working hours (hrs/month)*
1960	202.7
1965	192.9
1970	186.6
1975	172.0
1980	175.0
1985	175.8
1990	171.0
1991	168.0
1992	164.3
1993	159.4

Source: Ministry of Labor (1995), "Monthly Labor Survey", Tokyo.

national holiday seasons, *O-shogatsu* (the New Year season), the "Golden Week Holidays" in May, and the *O-Bon* holiday week in August, indicating that workers are still somewhat reticent about taking long vacations during non-holiday seasons. Yet the rise of cost-consciousness among consumers has also produced higher demand for foreign travel during periods when airfares are lower, immediately before and after peak travel seasons.

Internationalism and materialism

Internationalization due to increased foreign travel, lower prices on imports due to the high yen and deregulation, and the increased pace of exchange of popular culture through the mass media, will accelerate the convergence of the Japanese consumer culture with the global consumer culture. Yet aspects of Western materialism are often adapted in unique ways to the Japanese lifestyle. In a nation where less than 1% of the population is Christian, Christmas has become an important festival. For many years, there has been a custom of fathers bringing home special "Christmas cakes" for their families. In some families, children can expect to receive Christmas gifts from their parents. For young singles, Christmas has strong romantic connotations, and having a date for Christmas night is a major concern. East Japan Railways' "Santa Claus Express" advertising in recent years dramatizes this trend. Promoting the Bullet train as a means for young lovers working or attending school in different cities to get together for Christmas, advertisements have depicted lovelorn couples enjoying an evening of bliss together. Couples often exchange expensive gifts, and may choose from a variety of "Christmas Date Courses" at major hotels. The courses usually include a formal Western-style meal, combined with entertainment and a night's accommodation. Typically, reservations must be made months in advance. In 1993, Christmas-related sales in Japan were down 5% on the previous year due to the recession, but still amounted to 5.85 billion yen (*Focus Japan* 1994).

In the future, Japanese youth are expected to lead the greater convergence with Western materialism. Kenichi Ohmae, former partner in McKinsey & Company's Tokyo office, believes that Japan's young people, whom he calls "Nintendo Kids," have a different way of perceiving the world from their elders—but that their world view is very similar to that of young people in other countries. Having grown up playing sophisticated video games, Nintendo Kids "have learned to revisit the basic rules of their world and even to reprogram them if necessary." Noting that this kind of thinking is "alien to Japanese culture," Ohmae predicts that Nintendo Kids will use technology to reach out to their multimedia peers in other countries (Ohmae 1995). It is certainly true that Japanese children in the 1990s often listen to the same music, watch the same American movies and TV shows, and have the same sports heroes as other Nintendo Kids throughout the world.

Environment

Despite the continuing influence of animistic religions such as Shinto and Buddhism, concern about the environment in Japan is much lower than in Western countries. According to a Gallup survey quoted by Simon (1992), only 40% of Japanese consumers avoided environmentally harmful products, compared to 57% in the USA, 81% in Germany and 75% in the UK. Only 4% of those surveyed were involved in environmental groups (see Table 8.16). The *Japan Times* (1995) cites a 1995 survey by the Environment Agency, in which 58% of Japanese in their twenties said they would change their lifestyles to help the environment. Willingness to change lifestyle for the environment was even higher for those in their seventies, at 88%. Yet none of those over 70, and only 18% in their twenties, said they would be willing to pay more for ecologically friendly products. Therefore, in spite of the relatively high level of stated willingness to change lifestyles for the environment, this and other surveys reveal that the Japanese are actually doing very little for the environment in practice. The report on a 1994 survey conducted by homebuilder Daiwa House (1994), for example, notes that the only thing more than 80% of Japanese actively do for the environment is separate their garbage according to material type for recycling (Daiwa House Industry Company Ltd 1994).

Nevertheless, there is a growing number of products on the market making environmental claims. Imported "environmental-chic" brands such as The Body Shop are also popular. The rapid growth of this category has prompted the Environment Agency to review its criteria for granting products its "Eco Mark" certification of environmental friendliness. The original 1989 writ, which created the mark, required a product merely to contain some environmentally friendly features in order to display the Eco Mark on its package. The Agency is now said to be considering the implementation of a "product life-cycle assessment method" which would evaluate every stage of product life from raw material procurement to disposal in determining eligibility for Eco Mark certification (Dentsu 1995b). Thus, although active involvement in protecting the environment and willingness to pay more for environmental goods remains low compared to other countries, the market for environmentally friendly products is expanding. Interest in the environment and nature among younger Japanese is also rising, according to a 1993 survey by Dentsu Inc. (1993a) on the Dankai Junior Generation. Therefore it is fair to assume that interest in and commitment to buying environmental products will continue to grow in the future.

Health

Westernization, urbanization, and increasing affluence have increased the stress of daily life and changed eating habits dramatically. These issues were discussed in a recent article (*Nihon Keizai Shimbun* 1995b), quoted in the

Table 8.16 Personal environmental commitment: Japan vs major Western countries (%)

Country	*Avoided environmentally harmful products (%)*	*Active in environmental group (%)*	*Voted/worked for pro-environment candidate (%)*
USA	57	11	19
Canada	77	12	15
Japan	40	4	14
Germany	81	10	18
United Kingdom	75	10	10
Netherlands	68	7	21
Denmark	65	10	18

Source: Simon, Francoise (1992), "Marketing Green Products in the Triad", *Colombia Journal of World Business*, vol. 27, no. 3(4), p. 273.

Japan Economic Journal (*Nikkan Kogyo Shimbun*), entitled "The Shadow of Ill-health Looms Over the World's Longest Life Expectancy." The article explains that, in spite of having the longest life expectancy in the world, Japanese are generally less healthy than they were 10 years ago. It blames increasingly Westernized eating habits for increasing high blood pressure and heart-disease rates. It notes that, according to a Ministry of Health survey (Ministry of Health and Welfare 1995a), the number of registered cancer patients had jumped to 200 000 in 1993 from 130 000 in 1983, and that the proportion of people in their forties who receive a clean bill of health at regular medical checkups declined to only 19% in 1994, whereas the figure was 31% 10 years earlier (*Nihon Keizai Shimbun* 1995b).

In spite of these ominous statistics, surveys show that Japanese are relatively ambivalent about their health, neither greatly concerned nor completely confident. In a 1994 survey by Sumitomo Life Social Welfare Services Foundation of working men and women 30 to 59 years of age, only 25.7% said they lacked confidence about their health, whereas 24% said they were confident about their health. Meanwhile, 51% were non-committal, claiming neither to have nor lack confidence. Women who said they lacked confidence made up 36% of the total, while men who lacked confidence totaled only 15%. When asked when they tended to worry about their health, 30% responded that this occurred upon the death of an associate. This response was highest for those in their fifties, at 37% (Sumitomo Life Social Welfare Services Foundation 1994). When asked what they were doing regularly to maintain their health, respondents provided a wide range of answers, with the most frequent response being "Watching what I eat" (18%). Meanwhile, 42% of men cited drinking and smoking as a means to fight stress, compared to 34% who cited sports activities. Women tended to fight stress through social activities such as chatting with friends (66%) and shopping (46%) (Sumitomo Life Social Welfare Services Foundation 1994).

Among young adults, however, the popularity of fitness clubs as a means to stay healthy is increasing. In 1988, a Ministry of Health and Welfare survey found that there were 711 sports clubs in Japan, and that 55% were planning to expand their facilities over the next 5 years. From this survey it was estimated that there had been an average of 45 new companies entering the fitness industry annually since 1981.

Despite concern over the health consequences of changes in the traditional diet, eating habits are becoming increasingly Westernized and convenience oriented. A survey by the Ministry of Health and Welfare in 1992 showed that the use of pre-cooked food in Japanese households was quite extensive. While only 2% of housewives used some kind of pre-cooked food as a main dish every day, 13% used some kind of pre-cooked food as a main menu item once or twice a week. Meanwhile, 15% used pre-cooked food every day as a side dish, and 30% use pre-cooked food as a side dish once or twice a week (Ministry of Health and Welfare 1992b).

At the same time, eating out of the home is on the rise over the long term, although the recession has seen a slight decline in spending on meals outside the home. Figures for use of convenience foods and eating out are significantly higher for DINKs and one-person households.

At this time, the anti-smoking movement is relatively weak in Japan, although an increasing number of companies are implementing restrictions on where and when employees may smoke. Also, restaurants are increasingly offering non-smoking sections, something which has been unheard of in the past. Cigarette advertising is permitted in public places and on late-night television. Smoking advertising is prohibited in magazines targeting women, although there are no such restrictions on TV advertising. The only other restriction is that advertising images may not target minors.

Expectations

As a result of the recession, nearly 40% of the readers of the magazine *Nihon Keizai Shimbun* surveyed in September 1995 (September 24 1995, p. 43) said they believed their standard of living would decline over the next 5 years. A monthly survey of consumer confidence by Dentsu Inc. (1995a) revealed that 81.3% of those surveyed in August 1995 perceived the economy's condition as "bad," as against 3% who perceived it as "good." Those who believed the economy would improve totaled 27%, as against 25% who felt the economy would worsen, and 48% who were undecided. Although the results do not show an overwhelming pessimism, these data reveal there is considerable uncertainty about the future of the economy. Also, as aforementioned, results of consumer confidence surveys vary radically from month to month, depending on the tone of media reports.

Several years into Japan's recession, the fact remains that wholesale layoffs have been avoided and employee salaries, although down slightly as a result of the lower overtime hours and lower bonuses discussed earlier, have remained largely unaffected by the downturn. The yen skyrocketed to a historical high, briefly exceeding the level of 80 yen to the US dollar over the summer of 1995, and badly pinching profits for exporters, but by fall 1995 it had eased, and stabilized at the level of 100 yen to the dollar. For the time being, a serious crisis had been avoided. However, the lack of a concrete plan for resolving the bad debt crisis in the banking industry, declining real-estate prices, and a stagnant stock market are dark clouds on the economic horizon. Nineteen ninety-eight is a crucial year in determining the direction consumer confidence will take in the mid-term. However, it is clear that consumer values have changed significantly since the recession took hold, and not all of these changes are merely a product of the tightening of purse-strings to weather the recession. Some of the changes are in fact due to the greater maturity and experience of Japanese consumers. These changes will be discussed in detail in the next section.

Changes in consumer behavior

During the early 1990s, consumers became far more conscious of price than they had been during the 1980s. So-called price destruction—deflationary pressure on retail prices due to reform of the distribution system (Tanzer 1992)—and cheaper import prices owing to trade liberalization and the high yen have given rise to greater price competition (Eisenstodt 1992). Consumers, in turn, have learned to take advantage of this trend by shopping around for a better price when making big-ticket purchases. This is a major change, because during the Bubble Economy high price was associated with prestige, and a high price tag was hence an important component of a brand's value. At the same time, diversification of consumer values is expected to create greater differences between the way individual consumers spend their money. A report by Dentsu Inc. (1993a) suggests that Japanese will become less conformist in their behavior in the future. The report says that individuals will develop their own unique "lifestyle fundamentals" by which they will determine their spending priorities. Expectations of products are also changing. Especially for consumer durables, the emphasis is increasingly on such factors as design and ease of use, rather than on high-tech "bells and whistles." These changes will be discussed further in the section "Changes in the macromarketing mix" below.

Consumer credit

In seeming contradiction to the trend toward greater consumption, Japanese maintain the highest savings rate among the advanced countries. In spite of greater spending on leisure and imported goods during the 1980s, the savings rate rose, as a result of dramatically increased income from overtime hours and bonuses during the economic boom. Another factor is that older, more conservative consumers, at the top of the seniority pyramid and hence with higher incomes, tend to lead far more austere lifestyles than younger Japanese. Since the recession began, savings as a percentage of income have continued to rise owing to the combined forces of lower retail prices and greater consumer price consciousness, which has curtailed consumer spending. In 1994, a tax rebate intended to stimulate consumer spending backfired as a result of low consumer confidence. Instead of greater consumption, the rebate resulted in increased savings, which rose to an average of 17.8% of net income, up from 17.0% in 1993 (see Table 8.17).

Table 8.17 Savings rates as a percentage of disposable income

Year	*% of total income*
1975	14.8
1980	13.0
1985	12.9
1990	16.9
1991	17.9
1992	18.2
1993	17.0
1994	17.8

Source: Management and Co-ordination Agency (1995), "Annual Report on the Family Income and Expenditure Survey, 1994", Tokyo.

Meanwhile, consumer debt has been on the rise, and this rise is led by younger consumers. As Table 8.4 reveals, non-housing-related consumer debt nearly tripled between 1984 and 1993. During the same period, the total number of credit cards issued annually increased from just under 87 million cards in 1984 to more than 220 million in 1994. It is mainly the younger Japanese with whom credit cards are popular. These consumers are often given cash loans in their university years of up to US$1600, and revolving credit (Holden 1992). They often use such credit to buy clothing, skis, and airplane tickets. Interest rates range from 10.8% to 27.8%.

In a related trend, there has been a proliferation of so-called prepaid debit cards. These machine-readable cards are generally issued in denominations ranging from 1000 to 10 000 yen. There are prepaid cards for public telephones, *pachinko* parlors, public transportation, and vending machines, and they are even issued by some major department stores in lieu of gift certificates. More than 989 million prepaid cards were issued in 1994, and 1.5 billion cards were forecast to be issued during 1995. By 2000, the total is expected to reach 2.6 billion cards (Fuji Kimera Research Institute Inc. 1995).

Consumption

The Japanese household has had substantial increases in real income over the past couple of decades, but, as previously mentioned, it has also faced a high cost of living. As can be seen in Table 8.18, the percentage of living expenses in relation to total income, for example, has declined, from 79.7% in 1970 to 75.3% in 1994. Japanese have been remarkably good at putting this additional disposable income into savings, and savings have increased from 13.0% in 1980 to 17.8% in 1990 (see Table 8.17). An important influence on mid-term consumption trends will be the manner in which these percentages respond to downward-pressure income, and the phenomenon of so-called price destruction.

Food still accounts for a large proportion of living expenses for the average Japanese household. It accounted for 23.1% of living expenses in 1995, down from 32.2% in 1970. The disproportionately high ratio is due to traditionally high distribution costs and price supports for Japan's heavily protected agricultural sector. However, food prices will decline further in the future, as a result of continued deregulation. And, in spite of the perception, pervasive throughout the 1980s, that the Japanese palate is too finicky to readily accept imported foodstuffs, there is clear evidence that the Japanese consumer is highly receptive to less expensive imported agricultural products.

Imported beef is an excellent example. Prior to the liberalization of beef imports in April 1991, Japanese consumers had a distinct prejudice against it. According to an EPA report, quoted in Fields (1990), only 15% of respondents found imported beef "tasty," as opposed to 36% who said it was "not tasty." Between 1988 and 1993, however, the percentage of imported beef as a component of total beef consumption nearly doubled, from 28% to 55%, 99% of which was imported from America and Australia. Aggressive trade marketing and consumer advertising campaigns by government-backed beef export organizations from both countries have supported the growth in demand. According to the 1993 edition of the Japan Meat and Poultry Association yearbook, the top three reasons for buying imported beef were its "inexpensive price" (88%), "wide availability in stores" (45%), and "good quality" (13%) (Japan Meat and Poultry Association 1994). It can therefore be rationalized that, in spite of the perceived superior quality of domestic beef, demand for imported beef has expanded because it is less expensive and perceived as "tasty enough." Also, in a variety of other formerly regulated product categories, cheaper imports can be expected to make similar inroads into the market shares of domestic products.

Table 8.18 Monthly income and expenses in yen (nationwide non-agricultural households)

Year	*1970*		*1980*		*1985*		*1990*		*1994*	
	Yen	*%*	*Yen*	*%*	*Yen*	*%*	*Yen*	*%*	*Yen*	*%*
Income	112 949		444 846		331 595		521 757		567 174	
Living expenses:	82 582	100	238 126	100	289 489	100	331 595	100	353 116	100
Food	26 606	32.2	66 245	27.8	74 369	25.7	79 993	24.1	81 513	23.1
Housing	4 364	5.3	11 297	4.7	13 748	4.7	16 475	5.0	22 446	6.4
Utilities	3 407	4.1	12 693	5.3	17 125	5.9	16 797	5.1	19 150	5.4
Clothing	7 653	9.3	17 914	7.5	20 176	7.0	13 103	4.0	13 239	3.7
Furniture	4 193	5.1	10 092	4.2	12 182	4.2	23 902	7.2	21 963	6.2
Medical care	2 141	2.6	5 771	2.4	6 814	2.4	8 670	2.6	9 474	2.7
Transport and communications	4 550	5.5	20 236	8.5	27 950	9.7	3 3499	10.1	37 301	10.6
Education	2 212	2.7	8 637	8.5	12 157	4.2	16 827	5.1	18 988	5.4
Recreation	7 619	9.2	20 135	8.5	25 269	8.7	31 761	9.6	34 549	9.8
Other	19 837	24.0	65 105	27.3	79 699	27.5	90 569	27.3	94 491	26.8
Net income	103 634		305 549		373 693		440 539		481 178	
Net savings	13 480		39 714		48 181		74 526		85 503	
Living expenses as % of net income		79.7		77.9		77.5		75.3		73.3

Source: Management and Co-ordination Agency (1995), "Annual Report on the Family Income and Expenditure Survey, 1994", Tokyo.

The increasing participation of women in the labor force may have contributed to the rise in expenditure on "eating out." This type of expenditure rose from 9.1% of leisure expenditure in 1965 to 16.9% in 1990, but the recession has had a braking effect on this trend, and expenditure remained relatively stable between 1990 and 1994. The other major increases in consumer expenditure over the last couple of decades were on transport and communications, which increased from 5.5% of living expenses in 1970 to 10.0% in 1991, and education, which increased from 2.7% in 1970 to 5.0% of living expenses by 1991. Education expenses can be expected to remain high, due to the increasingly competitive employment market. Indeed, Dentsu Inc.'s Consumption in the Heisei Era Survey (1994) reveals that 71% of Japanese between 18 and 59 of age intend to further their education with the objective of "self-improvement," which they see as a necessary hedge against increasing uncertainty.

Despite the long working hours faced by most Japanese workers, recreational expenditure as a percentage of living expenses has increased dramatically, from 17.4% of living expenses in 1965 to 24.4% of living expenses in 1990. As has been suggested previously, the largest increases in the share of the leisure yen is in the area of eating out, and self-improvement, or experiential consumption, such as "recreation" and "tours." Expenditure on "tours," which includes both domestic and overseas travel, has also increased dramatically–from 6.6% to 14.6% of leisure expenditure by 1990. Recreation expenditure increased from 15.0% to 20.9% of leisure expenditure over the same period. The large expenditure on "recreation" and "tours" may reflect the interest in the Japanese consumer for self-actualization rather than material benefit (Oshashi 1989). Expenditure on durable goods has, for example, remained constant at around 4–6% of total recreational expenditure over the last few decades.

Youth consumption trends, meanwhile, are naturally focused heavily on leisure. Many teens have part-time jobs, or *beito* (from the German "Arbeit"), which often earns them a fair amount of cash. Tully (1994) describes Naoshi Saito, a 17-year-old student whose *beito* with a moving company "riding around the streets of Tokyo with the drivers, reading complicated maps of the city's streets" pays him the equivalent of US$855 per month (Tully 1994). Because Japanese parents typically support their children until graduation from university, all of such income is disposable, and is used on clothes, CDs, and leisure activities. International sports such as soccer and basketball have been especially popular with youth in the 1990s. Japan's professional soccer league, the "J-League," markets heavily to teenagers, as do international sports shoe and apparel companies Nike and Reebok.

Overseas travel

The strong yen generally makes overseas travel more affordable than domestic travel. Ohmae (1995, p. 154) noted that "flying round-trip between Tokyo and Okinawa now costs more than flying between Tokyo and Chicago." Particularly alluring are lower prices for shopping, fine dining, and leisure activities such as golf and scuba diving, all popular Japanese pastimes which can be enjoyed more cheaply overseas than in Japan. This situation has prompted a recent advertising campaign by the Guam Visitors Bureau using the slogan "Rather than a distant Japan, come to nearby Guam." The campaign draws attention to the fact that, for less money and in about the same amount of time it takes to get to Okinawa, Japan's southernmost resort island, urban Japanese can travel to Guam. Nearly 14 million Japanese travelled overseas in 1994, more than 9 million for tourism, more than 1 million to visit relatives, and nearly 300 000 on honeymoon. The average overseas traveler spends 431 000 yen per trip, including 112 000 yen on shopping (Japanese Travel Bureau Overseas Travel Development 1995).

Changes in the macromarketing mix

The marketing mix is undergoing revolutionary changes which are making Japanese consumers more value conscious. Three main factors have conspired to cause this revolution in Japanese marketing. The first is greater choice in terms of price, cultivated largely by greater retail competition as a result of deregulation (De Rossario 1993; Holyoke & Glasgall 1994). Direct marketing is also becoming a more accepted means of distribution, because consumers are placing a lower priority on the kind of fawning and costly service traditionally provided by Japanese retailers (Nakanomyo 1990). A second factor has been the recent slowdown in the Japanese economy, which has made consumers more careful about how they spend their money (Miller 1992). A third has been the diversification of consumer values over the long term, which is making consumers more heterogeneous in their spending priorities (Oshashi 1989).

Products

Significant changes have occurred in consumer expectations about products during the last 10 years, particularly in regard to consumer durables. During the 1980s, consumer emphasis on lifestyle differentiation through consumption fueled the success of Japanese manufacturers' much-touted strategies of offering wide product ranges, high product variation, and rapid innovation through lightning-quick product cycles. New products were automatically perceived as superior, and the more leading-edge features a product boasted, the greater the premium it could command (Shephard, Helms & Rodney 1992; Yoshimori 1992).

March (1990, p. 8) quotes a senior Japanese businessman, Mr. Toshifumi Suzuki, chairman of the Japanese Franchise Association, who offers the following insight on this phenomenon:

> They say that today's consumer is individualistic, diverse in thinking and tastes. I say consumers have been more sheep-like in their attitudes. The reason their buying habits look diversified is the extremely short product lifecycle of most popular products. Makers put new versions on the market so quickly these days. They don't trust their own judgment. That's why they tend to buy brand-name products. From childhood, they've been dressed in uniforms and their individuality has been carefully killed off.

Yet, even as Mr Suzuki was making this comment, consumers had begun to realize that sheep-like behavior could lead to bad purchase decisions. Increasingly short product cycles also meant that, when a new model hit the market, there were bargains to be had on the previous model. Moreover, aside from minor changes or added functions, the basic performance specifications of air conditioners, for example, did not change significantly from model to model. These facts, coupled with increasing value consciousness, have made consumers far less willing to pay a premium for trivial product enhancements. This has been a boon to discounters, as well as to consumers who are willing to buy older models in exchange for savings; these can be spent on other lifestyle priorities, such as leisure.

Stalk and Webber (1993) argue that, because all Japanese companies followed the same strategy, differentiation became a commodity, not a persuasive value-added feature. Moreover, the authors argue that Japanese manufacturers in the 1980s:

> substituted a scattershot approach to production as a substitute for the hard work of real marketing . . . As long as the Bubble Economy in Japan made money cheap and consumer demand grow, it made little difference that manufacturing operations were unconnected to consumer needs.

During the 1990s, manufacturers have streamlined product line-ups and lengthened product cycles. Nissan received favorable publicity from the auto industry press when it launched its new sub-compact, the "March," with the declaration that there would be no model change for 8 years. Meanwhile, Toyota was "reducing [the] varieties of Corolla from 11 to 6." In the electronics industry, Sony ceased offering 27″ (68 cm) and 31″ (78 cm) television sets, and Matsushita began streamlining its ranges of 220 television and 62 VCR models, "recognizing that only 10% sold well" (Stalk & Webber 1993, p. 98).

Fast-moving consumer goods (FMCGs) giants Kao and Lion are also scaling back on their product line-ups. With FMCGs, one of the influences has been point-of-sale (POS) information systems which supply retail chains with up-to-the-minute data on what sells and what does not, giving them significant power to dictate to manufacturers what they will sell and what they will not. Another factor that will place limitations on the speed with which manufacturers can bring new products to the market over the long term will be the new, stricter product liability law implemented in 1995.

Dankai Juniors and the product mix

From the Dankai Juniors—born between 1970 and 1973—onward, Japan's youth have been more savvy, independent and confident consumers. The Dankai Juniors are the first generation to have grown up with their own color TV sets, CD players, and air conditioner in their own room. They, like Ohmae's younger "Nintendo Kids," help their parents to make many decisions about what products to buy. The recognition of this fact led to a Mercedes-Benz advertisement for its new value-for-money-oriented C-Class in 1993. It featured a stern, conservative father, next to his young, trendy son, declaring, "It was my son who recommended I buy the new C-Class." Affluent and lethargic, yes, but smart consumers through and through. The values of these consumers are the values of the current age. They are changing the kinds of products manufacturers offer.

Fashion has also changed as young consumers require less status recognition and focus more on comfort and value for money. Even university students in the 1980s aspired to ostentatious fashion brands such as Armani, Chanel, and Louis Vuitton. And even "casual-dress" standards were quite formal. In the 1990s, however, laid-back, outdoor-oriented brands such as L.L. Bean and Eddie Bauer have stolen the fashion show (Miller 1993). Table 8.19 shows that product values which appeal to young people in the 1990s tend toward the "simple," "natural" and "down-to-earth." In the 1980s, popular values with the young would have been "rich," "stimulating," "novel/original," and "luxurious." These values have plummeted to the bottom of the list in the 1990s. This change has not been lost on the domestic fashion industry, which now offers a number of "outdoor casual" fashion brands.

Consumer reactions to price

Price destruction is a term Japanese have coined to describe the breakdown of retailer margins and the manufacturer's recommended retail pricing system. The effects of cheaper imports and the rise of discount shops have led a shift toward "open pricing," wherein the retailer agrees to accept the risk for unsold products, formerly the manufacturer's responsibility. According to the conventional wisdom, consumers' respect for traditional relationships made them not only tolerant of exorbitant prices at their neighborhood electronics shops, but also decidedly scornful of the discount appliance stores. However, discount stores were rapidly multiplying even as the same wisdom predicted their doom. From 1990–1993, for example, the number of independent electrical retail chains in Japan trebled to 2000, and prices of consumer electronics fell by an average of 30–40% (Tanzer 1992).

Table 8.19 The Dankai Juniors' favored product values

Quality	*Value attributed*
Simple	68.8
Natural	44.4
Down to earth	43.2
Intelligent	31.6
Basic	29.3
Unique	29.3
Orthodox	23.7
Profound	19.9
Major	19.2
Rich	14.3
Stimulating	13.5
Genki	12.8
Novel	10.2
Luxurious	7.2
Minor	6.8

Source: Dentsu Inc. (1992), "ROMANJI-JAPANESE (Study of the Baby Boomer Jr. Generation)", Tokyo.

The changes in the attitudes of Japanese consumers to prices are best summarized by comments made by an ex-prime minister, Mr Kiichi Miyazawa, who noted: "What Japan has learned throughout this recession is cost-consciousness." Three major economic and political events have elevated the position of price on the Japanese consumer's priority list. First, the appreciation of the yen has lowered the prices of many imports. Second, there has been great pressure from major trading partners, particularly the USA, for the Japanese to open their markets. This has allowed greater product competition, which has further increased price competition. Retailers and manufacturers have had to reduce prices because of this, in order to revive consumer spending during the recession. Finally, changes in distribution resulting from deregulation and new information technology have increased competition among retailers, which has also contributed to lower prices (Holyoke & Glasgall 1994). Price falls in several major product categories between 1991 and 1994 are shown in Table 8.20. In some categories, such as consumer electronics, the falls can also be attributed to saturation. For example, the household penetration rate for television sets is virtually 100%.

Table 8.20 Retail price falls for selected products

Product	*1994 price (US$)*	*Net change (%)*
Tape recorder	161.06	−29.74
Women's coat	220.55	−26.62
Video-cassette recorder	552.20	−26.56
Men's coat	258.72	−25.01
TV set	768.47	−23.95
Egg	2.39	−22.90
Men's jacket	194.40	−20.75
Whisky	25.11	−19.05
Air conditioner	1387.22	−17.81
Beef	26.87	−17.09

Source: Management and Co-ordination Agency (1995), "Annual Report on the Family Income and Expenditure Survey, 1994", Tokyo.

Distribution

Perhaps one of the most important changes that has occurred over the last 10 years in Japan is the rationalization of Japan's notoriously Byzantine distribution system. This system is still often described as outmoded, confusing, economically inefficient and unfair to consumers (Nakanishi 1981; Lazar, Murata & Kosaka 1985), but major changes are evident. Below, we will outline some of the traditional features of the distribution system, along with recent changes.

The Japanese distribution system has been characterized by a profusion of tiny retail stores and vast, powerful wholesale trading houses. On a per-capita basis, Japan has more retail outlets than any other advanced country. In 1991, Japan had 14.3 retail outlets per 1000 people, compared to 8.4 in the UK and 6.7 in the USA (Ariga, Gary & Nishimaki 1991). Many of Japan's retail outlets are small stores, employing only one or two people. In 1988, for example, the total number of retail outlets in Japan was 1 620 000, with more than half employing one to two people (Nakanomyo 1990). Small neighborhood merchants traditionally enjoyed the loyal patronage of people in the local community. As Table 8.21 reveals, however, the total number of retail outlets has declined gradually since 1985.

As noted above, many changes in the retail scene have their origins in deregulation, which has given retailers more flexibility in responding to emerging consumer needs. For example, both urbanization and the growing number of women in the workforce have increased the need for longer store hours. Twenty-four-hour convenience stores have therefore increased rapidly in number with the roll-back of restrictions on store operating hours (see fig. 8.2). The growth in the number of supermarkets has been fueled by the revision of zoning regulations originally designed to protect neighborhood merchants. As the number of suburban supermarkets in large shopping complexes

Table 8.21 Number of retail shops, by type, 1985–1991

Year	*Department stores*	*General supermarkets*	*Special supermarkets*	*Other supermarkets*	*Convenience stores*
1985	438	1 634	5 873	56 643	29 236
1988	433	1 851	6 397	53 834	34 550
1991	455	1 924	7 130	67 473	41 847

Year	*Specialty stores*	*Traditional stores*	*Others*	*Total*
1985	1 004 883	524 885	2 052	1 628 644
1988	1 007 756	513 338	1 593	1 619 752
1991	1 000 166	470 289	1 939	1 591 223

Source: Ministry of International Trade and Industry (1992), "Census of Commerce, 1991", Tokyo.

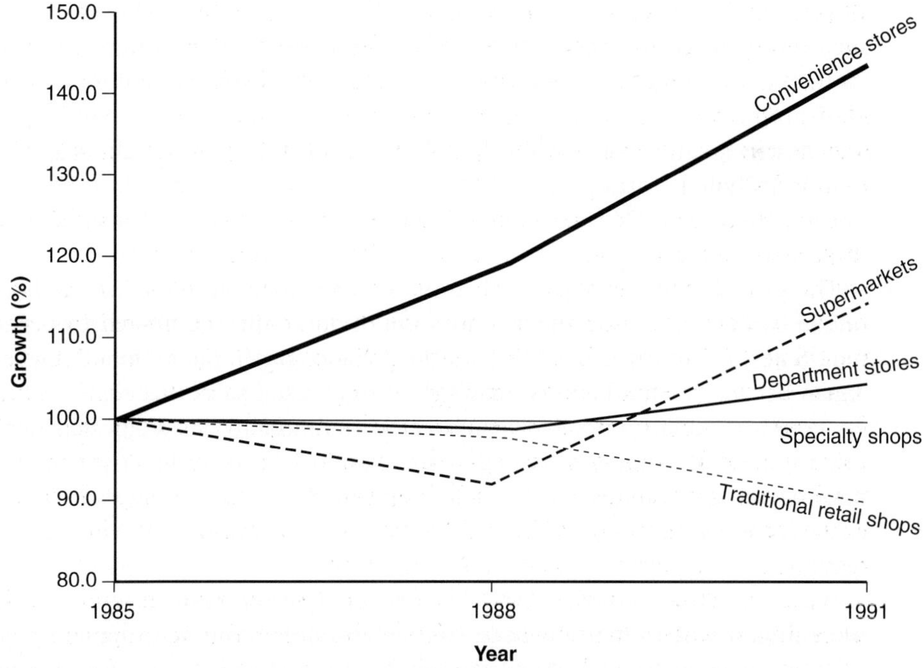

Fig. 8.2 Growth in retail stores, by category

Source: Ministry of International Trade and Industry (1992), *Census of Commerce, 1991*, Tokyo.

has multiplied, the higher prices, shorter business hours and limited product selection of neighborhood merchants has increasingly put them out of favor with busy, mobile urban consumers who have no strong neighborhood loyalties. Another factor has been that, whereas traditional Japanese housewives could make frequent trips by bicycle to the neighborhood store, working women cannot. Thus, supported by the widespread ownership of both large refrigerators and motor vehicles, Japanese consumer grocery shopping patterns are changing. Increasingly working women drive with their husbands to supermarkets in large suburban shopping centres to do their grocery shopping once a week, or less often. Meanwhile, consumers can rely on the growing number of convenience stores if they need to pick up odds and ends between major shopping trips (Ariga, Gary & Nishimaki 1991).

The traditional system was a pyramid, with large manufacturers on top, and, in descending order, "contract" wholesalers, and then second-tier wholesaler and neighborhood retailers at the bottom. A complex system of processing fees, margins and rebates resulted in 38 of every 100 consumer yen going toward distribution (Fuji Keizai Corporation 1994). For the small retailer, refusing to follow the manufacturer's suggested price in the absence of an agreement with a wholesaler for another manufacturer could be suicidal. On the other hand, there were many benefits to honoring the system. For example, retailers could expect a full refund for unsold stock from the manufacturer. For merchants who agreed to be exclusive manufacturer chain stores, there were even more benefits. For example, manufacturers would pay for the promotional expenses, provide additional sales staff and accept IOUs from chain-store retailers. For example, Shiseido, a Japanese cosmetics company, still makes 70% of its sales through its 25 000 tied or affiliated stores (Morris 1994). It is not surprising that these sorts of arrangements are often perceived by foreign manufacturers as a significant trade barrier.

The growth of huge supermarket and convenience-store chains has been one of two key factors in the deterioration of the traditional distribution system. Sales by large retailers such as Ito Yokado, Daiei, Seiyu, and 7-Eleven Japan became such a large component of total retail sales that manufacturers could no longer effectively enforce the manufacturer's suggested retail pricing system. Such chains began to insist on dealing directly with the manufacturer, cutting out the wholesaler and sharply reducing distribution cost. These savings were, in turn, passed on to consumers, who gladly accepted the opportunity to save money on their favorite products (Morris 1994). In addition, supermarkets now put pressure on manufacturers' prices by selling private or house brands, sourced through manufacturing contracts with companies in other Asian countries with cheaper labor costs. Import deregulation and the high yen have contributed to extremely competitive prices for private-brand products.

Technologies such as POS computer systems have also aided large retail supermarket chains such as Daiei Nakauchi, the largest retailer in Japan, in gaining the upper hand on manufacturers. By arming large retailers with up-to-the-minute data on product sales, POS systems give retailers significant leverage to dictate which product lines they will carry and at what price. This is a dramatic change from the days when a manufacturer with a top-selling product line in one category could force a small neighborhood grocer to carry its low-selling lines in other categories at the exclusion of other manufacturers' lines (Ariga, Gary & Nishimaki 1991).

The second key factor has been the rise of discount stores that liquidate manufacturers' excess inventories. During the 1980s, the inefficiencies of the traditional system contributed to price destruction, as manufacturer production levels outstripped demand, producing a glut of inventories. There was also a greater number of unsold products that manufacturers were required to buy back from retailers, under the traditional system described above. This inventory pinch coincided with the deregulation of retail zoning laws—and this spurred rapid growth in the number of large-scale discount stores specializing in electronics. Within 2 years of the deregulation of the retail industry in 1990, the number of independent electronics retail chains in Japan, for example, trebled to more than 2000, and prices of consumer electronics fell by an average of 30–40% (Tanzer 1992). Another recent phenomenon is illustrated by the case of the Aoyama Trading Company. Previously a small, regional men's clothing retail chain, Aoyama has become a national retail power through the practice of buying direct from the manufacturer and taking the risk on all inventory purchased, and through stocking a variety of domestic brands at low prices. As a result of all of these changes, Japanese consumers enjoy lower prices and a more competitive retail sector offering a greater degree of choice. For foreign marketers, these changes will mean greater access to the marketplace.

Vending machines

Although not new, automatic vending machines are another key distribution channel. Numbering 54 million, Japan's automatic vending machines are the most numerous in the world. An astounding variety of goods can be purchased through vending machines in Japan, including such common products as soft drinks and cigarettes, as well as less common ones such as beer, CDs and videocassettes, and even fresh flowers. The average Japanese buys US$400 worth of products from vending machines per year, and 50% of all alcoholic and non-alcoholic canned beverages are sold through automatic vending machines. The use of automatic vending machines was the key to the success of the "Coca-Cola" Japan Company, which, an exception in terms of foreign-affiliated companies in Japan, has long been one of the leading soft drink companies in Japan, and a feared competitor in the industry.

Direct marketing

Direct marketing is not yet as pervasive in Japan as in Germany, the UK and the USA, but it is growing rapidly. Catalog sales in 1985, for example, were 1% of retail sales in Japan, compared to 4.9, 3.4 and 3% for Germany, the UK and the USA respectively (Sanghavi 1988). Nevertheless, over the period 1983–1992, catalog sales grew from 830 billion to 2.23 trillion yen, and comprised 1.6% of retail sales (Itoh 1993). Other forms of non-store retailing are becoming more popular in Japan too. Door-to-door sales are becoming increasingly popular. Some Japanese *takyubin,* or home freight delivery firms, now provide sales as well as delivery services to Japanese households. In 1986, for example, during the New Year's gift-giving season, *takyubin* companies sold 400 000 salted salmon direct to consumers. Daiei, the largest retailer, sold 250 000, and Nichii, a medium-size retailer, sold 20 000 (Sanghavi 1988).

Large retail institutions in Japan have also been developing their own specialized forms of direct marketing. Matsuzakaya, a leading retail company, has set up a satellite link with a German department store and mail-order group, to provide an on-line catalogue. The Seibu department-store chain has set up a number of videotext catalogues and ordering systems in special kiosks throughout railway stations in Japan; in the future, these will possibly be available in the trains themselves (Sanghavi 1988).

The increasing popularity of direct marketing in Japan may be due to both demographic and technical factors. As has already been mentioned, more women are now entering the workforce, there is a greater willingness of young people to buy on trust and experiment, and there is an ageing population, which is becoming more interested in convenient ways of shopping (Sanghavi 1988). Technically, the introduction of toll-free phone numbers and credit cards has greatly facilitated the development of direct marketing in Japan. In future, media such as cable TV videotext and "smart cards," containing memory chips in which customer information can be stored, should greatly encourage the further development of direct-marketing services. Of course, the recent recession and government deregulation of the retail sector have greatly assisted this process by breaking down the manufacturer-led pricing system and increasing consumer price sensitivity.

Advertising

In 1993, for the first time since 1965, Japanese advertising spending fell by 4.5% to 4.2 trillion yen. This came as a shock to an industry that had been accustomed to seeing advertising expenditures growing at an annual rate of around 17% during the 1980s. Both the recession and manufacturers' focus on internal restructuring were the key factors in the decline. As shown in Table 8.21, in the latter half of this decade the split of advertising expenditure between the 4 major media of television, newspapers, radio and magazines has remained fixed, at around 30% for television, 25% for newspapers,

7% for radio and 4.3% for magazines. Collectively, advertising in these media accounted for around 67% of total promotional expenditure in Japan. There is a trend in Japan, as in other counties, to shift more marketing communications spending to sales promotion, event sponsorship and direct marketing. The trend toward "integrated marketing communications" (IMC) and relationship marketing has increasing influence in Japan as well.

Media planning

IMC-style media planning in Japan is somewhat hampered by some key differences from the US situation. For one thing, cable television has not yet taken off in Japan. Cable networks have tended to be small in terms of subscribers, and limited in geographic scope. Hence the highly segmented targeting of television audiences, possible in the USA, is not yet possible in Japan. Moreover, the largest television audience rating service in Japan can provide only household viewership, and not individual viewership, data. Therefore, clear segmentation of television audiences is still difficult, and commercials tend to target broad segments of the population. Nevertheless, television is the most popular medium for advertisers, and is extremely expensive—due to high viewership of Japan's 5 national commercial networks and, traditionally, high demand for commercial slots.

Newspapers are also a popular medium for advertisers. Their popularity stems from their high readership levels and the fact that most Japanese spend a long time commuting: since white-collar workers in Tokyo, for example, face an average commute of nearly 70 minutes each way between home and the office, they have ample time to read print media (Ariga & Gary 1990). The morning edition of the *Yomiuri Shinbun,* for example, has a national circulation of more than 9 million. Magazines allow greater segmentation, as many are able to target efficiently both demographic and psychographic reader segments. The magazine *25 Ans,* for example, targets marriage-minded young single women from affluent families who live with their parents and do not work. Radio is also important, and is considered good value for money. Outdoor and transit media are also important, and will be discussed in the context of the total campaign.

A typical Japanese advertising campaign targeting businesspeople could kick off with a commercial on one of the popular late-night news-analysis programs on network television. The next morning a full-page advertisement elaborating on the TV commercial could be run in *Nikkei* ("Japan Economic Journal"), read by many business people on their way to work. At the same time, advertisements would be placed on in-train advertising boards on key white-collar commuter rail lines. Later in the week, more advertisements would appear in weekly news and general-interest magazines commonly read by the business target. This exposure could be combined with an evening rush-hour promotional event in an outdoor square near one of the hub stations of the commuter rail system.

This kind of integrated, multilayered approach can be used to reach the target from many different angles during a single 24-hour period, increasing campaign reach, frequency and awareness percentages in an extremely short timeframe (Syedain 1993/1994).

Table 8.22 Advertising expenditure by medium, 1992, 1993, 1994

Media	*Advertising expenditure (in billions of yen)*			*Component percentage (%)*		
Year	*1992*	*1993*	*1994*	*1992*	*1993*	*1994*
Major media						
Newspapers	1 217.2	1 108.7	1 121.1	22.3	21.6	21.7
Magazines	369.2	341.7	347.3	6.7	6.7	6.7
Radio	235.0	211.3	202.9	4.3	4.1	3.9
Television	1 652.6	1 589.1	1 643.5	30.3	31.0	31.8
Subtotal	3 474.0	3 250.8	3 314.8	63.6	63.4	64.1
Sales promotion						
Direct mail	222.2	225.4	256.9	4.1	4.4	5.0
Flyers	323.2	330.6	363.3	5.9	6.5	7.0
Outdoor	375.4	330.9	324.6	6.9	6.5	6.3
Transit	267.2	247.2	238.1	4.9	4.8	4.6
POP	146.7	137.2	141.6	2.7	2.7	2.7
Telephone directories	160.0	171.5	173.2	2.9	3.3	3.4
Exhibitions/screen displays	481.0	421.8	343.2	8.8	8.2	6.6
Subtotal	1 975.7	1 864.6	1 840.9	36.2	36.4	35.6
New media	11.4	11.9	12.5	0.2	0.2	0.3
Total	**5 461.1**	**5 127.3**	**5 168.2**	**100.0**	**100.0**	**100.0**

Source: Dentsu Inc. (1995a), "Shohisha jikkan chosa (Dentsu Bi-Monthly Consumer Confidence Survey)", Tokyo.

Television advertising—content, tone and manner

Owing to the prevalence of 15-second spots in Japanese television formats, television advertising has traditionally focused on creating memorable images and evoking emotional responses in a short period of time. Mitsubishi, for example, ran a successful campaign featuring an Australian frill-necked lizard! Such memorable images are used to link and unify an advertising run simultaneously on TV, in national newspapers and magazines, and on metro-transit posters and outdoor signs. The role of print media is to provide detailed product specifications and information on price and sales outlets which cannot be provided in a 15-second TV spot (Syedain 1993/1994).

Hiroshi Tanaka of Dentsu Inc. also attributes the use of seemingly irrelevant imagery in TV commercials to differences in the way Japanese process messages. Citing a 1987 study on advertising messages in Japan, Tanaka argues that Japanese tend to process information top down instead of bottom up. Top-down processing means developing an overall impression of the target object first and evaluating it as good or bad before focusing on the details, whereas bottom-up processing refers to building a total impression from consideration of the parts. By extension, Japanese would seem to be less concerned about the logical reasoning of commercial messages than, say, Americans might be (Tanaka 1993).

For this reason, indirect, image-oriented advertising may be used more often in Japan than in other countries. Indeed, Tanaka cites a 1990 study showing that 73.3% of Japanese commercials can be classified as indirect, image-oriented, soft-sell commercials, as opposed to 50.9% for the USA. However, it is not necessarily true, as has been argued in the past, that Japanese reject direct, logic-oriented, or hard-sell commercial messages. Tanaka also notes a 1991 study by Matsui that found:

> no differences in the communicative effectiveness on brand awareness and purchase intention scores between direct and indirect expressions in Japan. This seems to contradict the conventional wisdom which states that indirect forms of advertising expression are preferred by consumers in Japan (Tanaka 1993).

Comparative advertising

Some argue that many advertising preferences attributed to Japanese consumer tastes are at best out-dated, and at worst the product of Japanese manufacturers' cartel-like competitive practices. George Fields, former Chairman of ASI-SRG Japan, charges that for too long Japanese corporations have assumed that their own values are shared by the consumer. While no law exists against comparative advertising, there has been a tacit agreement among advertisers to avoid direct competition for the consumer's allegiance through comparison of product benefits. This agreement has been veiled under the claim that "the overt knocking of a competitor goes against Japanese cultural values, and wouldn't be tolerated by the consumer" (Fields 1993). Fields notes that, contrary to the "consumer-values" argument against it, comparative advertising campaigns by Pepsi and General Motors have been implemented without obvious damage to those companies' reputations with consumers. Yet, while Japanese computer maker NEC ran a campaign demonstrating its PC's superiority to the IBM PC in processing Japanese text, there have been as yet no major examples of Japanese–Japanese comparative campaigns (Fields 1993).

Price in advertising

Another interesting development of note in advertising is that price is playing an increasingly important role in advertising expression, in line with the increased price consciousness of consumers. The conventional wisdom says that prominent references to price in advertising is a "hard-sell" tactic which would be an insult to consumer sensibilities. Nevertheless, auto importers made major inroads into a slumping auto market in 1994 primarily by means of aggressive price-oriented campaigns. Fast-food giant McDonald's, which pioneered the industry in Japan as in the rest of the world, has also leveraged its price advantage–a result of cheap materials sourced overseas–to make price a central part of its marketing mix, offering "value meals," which include a hamburger, fried potatoes and a soft drink at a low price; it has even advertised "100 Hamburgers," the lowest price in the industry. McDonald's competitors have been forced to respond with value campaigns of their own.

Corporate branding

Strong corporate branding is another traditionally important feature of Japanese advertising that is undergoing change. Rather than spending time and marketing resources to build stand-alone product brands, Japanese advertisers have tended to focus on maintaining the consistency of the advertising tone and manner across their entire product portfolio. Brand equity is therefore measured on the corporate level, not at the product level, and the corporate logo plays a prominent role in many product ads.

As Tanaka (1993) notes, there are two important reasons for the focus on corporate branding. First, it reflects the cultural emphasis on relationships. Familiarity, trust and reciprocity between consumers and those who provide the products they use in their homes have traditionally been an important cultural pact. In a former age, Japanese consumers preferred to buy goods from a neighborhood merchant–who would be likely to reciprocate the patronage–rather than from an unfamiliar merchant in another neighborhood. Similarly, today, Japanese working for a major bank with business ties to a particular brewer are likely to be loyal drinkers of the brewer's product, and the brewers' employees are likely to deposit their salaries with the bank. Thus, unlike in Western countries, the product maker in Japan has had greater importance than the values the product stands for. A second important aspect of corporate branding is that it has facilitated what Stalk and Webber (1993) refer to as "scattershot marketing." Tanaka (1993) notes that, when the corporate-branding approach is used instead of stand-alone branding, the quick scrapping and building of product brands is possible at a minimum marketing cost.

Nevertheless, even large traditional marketers are beginning to reconsider their devotion to this time-honored practice. For example, Kao, which formerly marketed everything from shampoo to floppy disks under its corporate name, has moved toward stand-alone brand strategies through the gradual de-emphasis of the corporate name in advertising and packaging for its Sofina skin care line (Okahashi 1995).

Sales promotion

As shown in Table 8.22, sales-promotion expenditure from 1992 to 1994 made up around 36% of total media expenditure in Japan. Share of expenditure across a range of media for this type of promotion expenditure remained constant over this same period. In 1994, 5.0% of the total promotional budget was spent on direct mail, 7.0% on newspaper and magazine flyers, 6.3% on outdoor advertising, 4.6% on transit, 2.7% on POP, 3.4% on telephone directories and around 6.6% on exhibitions and trade displays. Given that the long commuting times of the Japanese consumer are likely to continue, the popularity of transit and flyers as means of sales promotion are likely to continue. The greater level of price discounting and competition in the retail sector should lead to an increase in POP and direct-mail expenditure.

Market research

In 1991 there were 69 market research organizations in Japan, employing, on average, 42 people. Historically, market research has not been considered an important adjunct to the marketing strategy of Japanese companies (Nisihikawa 1989). However, as Table 8.23 shows, the number of market research organizations, the total number of employees in the field and the average number of employees per firm has risen steadily since 1987. This reflects an increasing emphasis on market research in light of the changing competitive environment, with a focus on product strategies, value consciousness among consumers, and the diversification of consumer values as a whole.

Table 8.23 Number of marketing research companies & employees

Year	*No. of companies*	*No. of employees*	*Average no. of employees*
1987	50	1958	39.2
1988	53	2087	39.4
1989	61	2380	39.0
1990	69	2894	41.9
1991	69	2885	41.8

Source: Japan Marketing Association (1993), "White Paper 1993", Tokyo.

Future trends and expectations

Economic trends

The near to midterm future of consumer behavior is inexorably linked to the speed with which Japan's current bad debt crisis can be remedied and the real estate price slide halted. If further delay occurs, there are great risks to political and social stability, as the 1995 Sarin gassing of Japan's subways attests—however indirectly. Certainly, all evidence points to the need for Japan Inc. to swallow bravely the bitter pill on which it has been choking in recent years.

If Wood's (1993) warning of the threat that the economy could enter a depression-like debt-deflation spiral seemed merely the alarmist assessment of an ill-informed foreigner, a few years later there were many Japanese who could assent to his view. *Tokyo Business Today*'s November 1995 issue quotes a real-estate industry insider as follows:

> The government's delay in solving the bad debt problem, along with the increasing deflationary trend, has sowed the seeds of widespread pessimism and sent land prices into a downward spiral. The situation looks so much like [the Great Depression] that I don't want to think about it (Kudo 1995).

Indeed, there is a growing feeling that reforms to date in government and industry have only just scratched the surface of what must be done to complete the transition to the post-Bubble Era. The following analysis by Wood in 1992 of the problem with the financial industry remains an accurate assessment of the current situation in many sectors of the Japanese establishment:

> Instead of responding to adversity, meeting the challenge, and moving on, senior managers in Japan's leading financial institutions are more like frightened rabbits caught at night in a car's headlight. Confronted by the unfamiliar and used to being told what to do by the overweening Ministry of Finance, they are frozen into inaction. Not knowing how to respond, they have decided to do nothing, hanging on in the forlorn hope that the problem will go away.

This echoes a comment made by former MITI vice minister, Amaya, that Japanese bureaucrats were like racing greyhounds who had chased the rabbit of economic development with great speed and grace ever since the end of the Second World War. Now, having crossed the finish line, and finding no more rabbits in sight, the bureaucrats do not know which way to turn. Ultimately, the restructuring of Japanese banking, finance and manufacturing in response to the bursting of the Bubble Economy, along with a continued strong yen, and *gaiatsu,* or foreign pressure, for deregulation and the reform of trading practices, should greatly encourage the transformation of Japan from a producer to a consumer economy. But, in the near term, it is likely that consumer confidence will remain low, especially in view of the rough waters ahead for personal income.

Demographic trends

The key demographic issues are the ageing of the population and the deterioration of its health, which will place unprecedented stresses on the nation's workforce, and the social welfare and health infrastructure. The *Nikkei* (1995) article discussed earlier notes that the health of the elderly is already declining. A recent Reuters (1995) article adds that, while Japan enjoys the highest life expectancy in the world, it also has the "lowest survival rates among the very old." This is further evidenced by the fact that the amount spent on health care per person over 65 years of age rose from US$3500 to US$6800, while the number of invalid senior citizens rose from 4.6% to 5.3% between 1986 and 1993 (*Nihon Keizai Shimbun* 1995b). How to care for a growing and increasingly infirm elderly population remains a central concern. Clearly, there will be major market opportunities for goods and services designed to meet the needs of the elderly.

Another important demographic trend to watch will be the increasing education and workforce-participation levels of women. As discussed earlier, women workers have fared worse than men during the recession. Whether or not women make real gains in terms of salary and opportunities for promotion will be a telling indicator of the degree of change in gender roles in Japan's traditionally male-oriented work culture. It will also determine the degree to which expenditures are made on services by Japanese households, and such things as growth in the use of convenience food products.

Cultural trends

The desire for social harmony and the belief in the collectivist spirit are rapidly being replaced by a greater degree of individualism. How the balance can be struck between these competing forces will be a critical issue at every level of society. Yet it is clear that, for individuals, the demise of the lifetime employment system, the reduced working hours and the gradual withdrawal of corporate funding for employee leisure facilities and other benefits will undoubtedly change the way leisure time and money are spent. The number of Japanese traveling abroad has quadrupled since 1975, which means a greater exposure to the products, services and lifestyles of other countries. Coupled with the increased penetration of Japanese markets by foreign products as a result of the high value of the yen and trade liberalization, this will mean greater diversification of tastes and preferences, as well as an expansion in the range of consumption choices available to the average consumer. Also, now that the Japanese people's goals in terms of consumer durables have largely been satisfied, consumers will continue to shift their priorities toward lifestyle goods and services and leisure pursuits.

Consumption

As mentioned, the proportion of expenditure on food is expected to fall, as a result of the high value of the yen, the continued liberalization of trade and the reform of the distribution system. Recreational expenditure is likely to increase as a result of reduced working hours. Expenditure on eating out is expected to continue to rise as the labor-force participation of women increases.

Consumer credit is clearly also a permanent part of the Japanese consumer scene. Constraints imposed on bonuses and overtime payments by many Japanese corporations may provide an added incentive for the use of credit.

Potentially lower real-estate prices over the mid-term may mean that the younger Japanese, to whom owning a home of their own once seemed a pipe dream, may become increasingly thrifty in order to buy homes at an earlier age. Cheaper imported building materials are already making inroads into a once jealously protected housing market. It has also been argued that reforming the archaic zoning regulations, which, among other things, reserve 65% of the land within a 50-km radius of Tokyo for agriculture, would allow the average family to "be able to afford 120 to 150 square meters of living space, instead of today's 55 to 78" (Ohmae 1995, p. 158). Such a dramatic change in the size of housing consumers can afford would have broad implications on consumption habits.

Marketing management in the 1990s

Internationalization

Greater purchasing-power parity, due to the high yen and trade liberalization, should encourage greater internationalization of the Japanese economy. It has been noted that, as foreign products in all categories become more accessible, Japanese consumers show increasing willingness to shrug off traditional prejudices against non-Japanese products. Meanwhile, unprotected by trade restrictions and spurred on by the intensifying global competitive environment, Japanese manufacturers' products will increasingly be made to world-market specifications, not to specifications that please an insular and unique domestic consumer. This trend should be continued through deregulation and greater competition in the retail sector, lower prices for consumers and continued emphasis on value for money.

But not all observers are sure this is the right direction. For example, Ohmae (1995, p. 161) gripes, "Japan's leaders are trying to hold back a future that has already arrived . . . and the Japanese consumers will continue to pay for their obstructionism." Where to strike the balance between Japan's traditional insularity and the need for industry to continue to internationalize will be an important issue in the years to come.

Packaging

Packaging is likely to remain an important consideration of product strategy in Japan, as Sherry and Camargo (1987, p. 174) note:

> Packaging, or wrapping (*tsumi*), has a venerable history in Japan. It has been an art for 10 centuries. Not only does it play a central role in a

range of spiritual and cultural aspects of Japanese life, but it has become an end in itself in so far as the symbolic and monetary value of the package often exceeds that of its contents.

It is likely, therefore, that packaging will remain an important product attribute for many consumers, despite the effect that economic factors and greater foreign imports may have in reducing costs. Moreover, Japanese manufacturers' excellence in aesthetic areas such as packaging represent a crucial competitive edge with which foreign marketers will have to contend.

Price consciousness

As mentioned earlier, price destruction, fueled by the high yen, trade liberalization and greater retail competition, should continue to have a marked downward effect on prices in many product categories. In spite of recent price declines, Tokyo consumer prices remain the highest in the world, and there will be considerable downward pressure on prices in the near to mid-term, particularly in view of similar downward pressure on household incomes. This will mean that consumers in Japan will remain cost conscious, intent on obtaining the best value for their money in the foreseeable future.

Distribution

Japan is currently experiencing a retail revolution. A greater use is expected of specialist discounters by Japanese consumers—as well as an increase in the popularity of Western chain stores, such as Toys "R" Us. Changes in the Large-scale Retail Store Law, formerly designed to protect small stores, will encourage the shift toward large-scale retail stores. Direct marketing will continue to grow, given the high level of development of technology and the widespread use of credit cards. Further impetus will come from changes in demographics, such as the rising numbers of invalid senior citizens and working women; these factors will make shopping by catalog and television shopping programs (becoming increasingly popular) as necessary as they are convenient.

Advertising and the media

Although some would argue that marketing communications campaigns have long been executed in the integrated manner described earlier in this chapter, the diversification of consumer lifestyles and changes in macro-marketing factors are putting pressure on Japanese brand managers and their advertising agencies to achieve the kind of total integration, pinpoint targeting, and cost performance promised by the IMC revolution currently being imported from the USA. Mr Mori, a managing director for corporate communications of cosmetics at giant Shiseido, underscores many of the changes afoot in the advertising industry. In a December 1994 interview with the trade magazine *Advertising Monthly* (Gekkan Advertising 1994), he notes, "In this era when price destruction is a continuing concern, when consumers have become more sophisticated . . . there is pressure on marketing to justify itself in terms of cost performance."

Mr Mori also notes that major advertisers such as Shiseido will, in turn, put greater pressure on advertising agencies to provide new and better consumer targeting data as justifications for their media plans. The evolution of the cable television industry will undoubtedly play an important role in the way campaigns are designed and targeted.

Conclusion

In spite of the temptation to write Japan off, there are no grounds for arguing that Japan's economic prosperity is over. In 1995, reports of improved corporate performance due to restructuring were already beginning to filter in. The bad-debt problem will inevitably be resolved, albeit not without suffering. And Japan's new consumer-led marketplace will undoubtedly be vibrant. *Newsweek* observed this during the summer of 1995 (Ernsberger & Takayama 1995):

> When America was at a comparable point [to Japan] in its own restructuring, around 1990, there was much talk (not least in Japan) of America's descent. Five years later, the United States is rejuvenated economically, technologically ascendant and politically the sole superpower. It will take Japan longer, but Ueno Park's cherry-blossom seasons in the 21st century should be pretty joyous times.

The day of reckoning has arrived, and eyes are opening to new economic, political, and social realities. These realities demand a broad revision of the conventional wisdom about Japanese consumers. Deregulation has catalyzed changes in retailing and distribution which have closed the gap between manufacturers and the marketplace. Increasingly, it is the consumer who has the power to determine the winners and losers at the storefront. This right to choose comes at the price of greater uncertainty. Increased competition is already eroding the safety net of lifetime employment, and will also mean greater access to the Japanese market for foreign marketers. Internationalization of the marketplace is urging on what Wood (1993) describes as a "greater convergence" with the global economy. This convergence will create new opportunities in Japan. Even as new markets in China, South-East Asia, and India beckon, Japan, for its part, will be a more accessible and inviting consumer marketplace than it was in the past. For the Japanese consumer, the sun is no longer rising, nor is it setting. Rather, it has reached midday, with the prospects of blue skies ahead.

References

Agency for Cultural Affairs (1995), "Syukyo Nenkan 1994", March, Gyosei, Tokyo.

Amagai, Jiro (1987), "Japan's Distribution Industry: Short and Long Term Prospects", *Business Japan*, July, pp. 75–9.

Amaya, Naohiro (1989), "Time to end the greyhound era", *Shizuoka Shimbun*, November 11, Tokyo, p. 2.

Ariga, Masru & Gary, Clary (1990), "Seven Crucial Viewpoints to Understand the Japanese Consumer", Marketing Planning Department, Dentsu, Inc., Tokyo.

Ariga, Masru, Gary, Clary & Nishimaki, K. (1991), "Mass Retailing to the Japanese Consumer", Marketing Planning Department, Dentsu, Inc., Tokyo.

Asahi Shimbunsha (1995), "Asahi ki wado 95-96 (Asahi Keywords)", March, Asahi Shimbun-sha, Tokyo.

Asian Wall Street Journal (1995), October 28.

Bolwijin, P.T. & Brinkman, S. (1987), "Japanese Manufacturing: Strategy and Practice", *Long Range Planning*, vol. 20, No. 1, pp. 25–34.

Bownas, Geoffrey (1988), "Japan Goes For The Good Life", *The Director*, December, pp. 113–15.

Bureau of Citizens and Cultural Affairs (1987), "Trend of Family Eating Out", Tokyo Metropolitan Government.

Chain Store Executive (1991), "Retailing in Japan", January, pp. 103–10.

Daiwa House Industry Company Ltd. (1994), "Erkoroij to seikatsu (Ecology and lifestyle survey report)", Dentsu Inc., Tokyo.

De Rossario, Louise (1993), "Retailing: Sell 'em cheap: The Japanese Discover No-frills Electrical Goods", *Far Eastern Economic Review*, February 4, pp. 44–5.

Dentsu Inc. (1990), *Dentsu Japan Marketing/Advertising Yearbook*, Tokyo.

— (1992), "Romanji-Japanese (Study of the Baby Boomer Jr. Generation)", Tokyo.

— (1993a) "Hesei shohi tenbo (No life No Consumption: Consumption in the Heisei Era)", Tokyo.

— (1993b), "Iruka no sedi (The Dolphin Generation)", Tokyo.

— (1994), "Hesi shohi tenbo Rasen shijo no haken (Consumption in the Heisei Era: Discovering the Spiral Lifestyle Market)", March, Tokyo.

— (1995a), "Shohisha jikkan chosa (Dentsu Bi-Monthly Consumer Confidence Survey)", Tokyo.

— (1995b), "Haya giki saki dori karenda (You heard it here first)", Tokyo.

— (1995c), "Advertising Expenditures in Japan", Tokyo.

Di Bendetto, C.A., Tanate, M. & Chandran, R. (1992), "Developing creative advertising strategy for the Japanese marketplace", *Journal of Advertising Research*, January/February, pp. 39–48.

Economic and Planning Agency (1994), "Degree of Satisfaction with Living Situation", Tokyo.

Economist (1993), "The Enigma of Japanese advertising", August 14, pp. 59–60.

Eisenstodt, Gale (1992), "Value for Yen", *Forbes*, April 27, pp. 78–9.

Ernsberger, Richard Jr. & Takayama, Hideko (1995), "Behind the Mask. Believe it or Not, Japan Really is Changing", *Newsweek*, July 3, pp. 15–16.

Fields, George (1990), "Buy Domestic or Buy Foreign? What's the Story in Japan?", *Tokyo Business Today*, July, p. 11.

— (1993), "Can it be? Comparative Advertising Sprouting in Japan?", *Tokyo Business Today*, April, p. 41.

Focus Japan (1994a) "The Best and Worst Times for the Japanese Consumer", December, pp. 1–2.

— (1994b), "Christmas in Japan", December, p. 4.

Fuji Keizai Corporation (1994), "Ryutsu Shin Jidai no genjo to shorai tenbo (New age for distribution: Current realities and future prospects)", Tokyo.

Fuji Kimera Research Institute Inc. (1995), "Kado sijou marketingu youran (Card market report)", Tokyo, p. 4.

Gekkan Advertising (1994), "Kei ei senryaku kara mita IMC (IMC from the point of view of management strategy)", *IMC toku shu* (Special Edition on IMC), Dentsu Inc, Tokyo, December, pp. 8–12.

Genzberger, Christine A. (ed.) (1994), *Japan Business: The Portable Encylopedia for Doing Business with Japan*, World Trade Press, San Rafael, CA.

Hanna, Nessim, Gordon, Geoffrey & Ridnour, Rick E. (1994), "The Use of Humor in Japanese Advertising", *Journal of International Consumer Marketing*, vol. 7, no. 1, pp. 85–106.

Holden, Ted (1992), "The Japanese Discover the Perils of Plastic", *Business Week*, February 10, p. 42.

Holyoke, Larry & Glasgall, William (1994), "A Bargain Basement Called Japan", *Business Week*, June 27, pp. 14–15.

Hori, Shintaro (1993), "Fixing Japan's White Collar Economy: A Personal View", *Harvard Business Review*, November–December, pp. 157–72.

Institute of Population Problems, Ministry of Health and Welfare (1992), "September 1992 Population Projections for Japan: 1991–2090", Tokyo.

Itoh, Kimio (1993), "Catalog Sales: Major Firms and Current Business Data", Manufacturing Markets Research Institute Publications Department, Tokyo.

Japan Consumer Credit Industry Association (1995), "The Origin and Development of Consumer Credit in Japan", Tokyo.

Japan Electrical Manufactures' Association (1987), "Electric Appliance Needs Across Three Age Brackets".

Japan Marketing Association (1993), "White Paper 1993", Tokyo.

Japan Meat and Poultry Association (1994), "Yearbook of Meat and Poultry '95", Tokyo.

Japan Times (1995), "Elderly Will Alter Lives to Aid the Earth", November 8, p. 4.

Japan Travel Bureau Overseas Travel Department (1995), "JTB Report 95. All about Japanese overseas travelers", Tokyo.

Kawakami Seiji (1993), "Tamesareru dankai no sedai no tsuyosa to yowasa (Strengths and Weaknesses of The Dankai Generation: The Test Lies Ahead)", ZAIKAI Special Spring Edition, Zaikai Research Insititute Ltd, January 19, pp. 72–5.

Kishii, T. (1983), "Message versus Mood—a Look at some of the Differences between Japanese and Western Television Commercials", *Japan Marketing and Advertising Yearbook 1988,* Dentsu Inc., Tokyo, pp. 51–7.

Kudo, Yasushi (1995), "No Bottom in Sight", *Tokyo Business Today,* November, pp. 10–15.

Lazar, W., Murata, S. & Kosaka, H. (1985), "Japanese Marketing: Towards a Better Understanding", *Journal of Marketing,* vol. 49, pp. 69–81.

Mallaby, Sebastian (1994), "Japan: Death of a Role Model", *The Economist,* July 9, pp. 1–18.

Management and Co-ordination Agency (1992), "1990 Population Census of Japan", Tokyo.

— (1994a), "Employment Structure of Japan, 1992", Tokyo.

— (1994b), "Annual Report on Labor Force Survey, 1994", Tokyo.

— (1995a), "Annual Report on the Family Income and Expenditure Survey, 1994", Tokyo.

— (1995b), "Annual Report on the Consumer Price Index", Tokyo.

— (1995c), "1993 Housing Survey of Japan", June, Tokyo.

March, Robert, M. (1990), *The Honourable Consumer: Marketing and Selling to the Japanese in the 1990s,* Longman Professional, Adelaide, Australia.

Miller, Karen Lowry (1992), "How Can You Call This a Recession?", *Business Week,* April 27, p. 58.

— (1993) "You Just Can't Talk To These Kids", *Business Week,* April 19, pp. 104–6.

Ministry of Finance (1994a), "Annual Report on the National Accounts", April, Tokyo.

— (1994b), "Labor Statistics, 1994", Tokyo.

Ministry of Health and Welfare (1986), "National Nutrition Survey", Tokyo.

— (1988), "Questionnaire Survey of Companies Operating Fitness Facilities", Tokyo.

— (1992a), "Population Projections for Japan 1991–2090", Tokyo.

— (1992b), "Food and Processed Food Survey", Tokyo.

— (1995a), "Report on Comprehensive Survey of Living Conditions", Tokyo.

— (1995b), "Vital Statistics", Tokyo.

Ministry of International Trade and Industry (1992), *Census of Commerce, 1991,* Tokyo.

Ministry of Labor (1987), "White Paper on Women Workers", Tokyo.

— (1995), "Monthly Labor Survey", Tokyo.

Morris, Kathleen (1994), "Adam Smith in Tokyo", *Financial World,* January 4, pp. 22–4.

Mueller, B. (1987), "Reflections on Culture: An Analysis of Japanese and American Advertising Appeals", *Journal of Advertising Research,* June/July, pp. 51–9.

— (1992), "Standardization versus Specialization: An Examination of Westernization in Japanese Advertising", *Journal of Advertising Research,* January/February, pp. 51–9.

Nakanishi, M. (1981), "Marketing Developments in Japan", *Journal of Marketing,* vol. 45, pp. 206–8.

Nakanomyo, Takashi (1990), "Distribution System Faces Changed Environment", *Business Japan,* August, pp. 89–93.

Nihon Keizai Ryutsu Service Shimbun (1995), "Atama itai kyoiku hi. Oru shiritsu de 264 man (Education fees headache. 26.42 million for all private education)", Nikkan Shimbun Company Ltd., Ryutsu Service Shimbun, Tokyo.

Nihon Keizai Shimbun (1995a), "Bonasu konnatsu 1.7%, zo sannen buri purasu (Summer bonuses up by 1.7%)", Nikkan Kogyo Shimbun Company Ltd., Tokyo, July 7.

— (1995b), "Chouiji sekai-ichi ni kenkou huan no kage (The Shadow of Ill Health Looms Over the World's Longest Life Expectancy)", September 22, p. 17.

— (1995c), "Nen-go no seikatsi 'kurushi naru 4 wari (Standard of Living will decline, 40% believe)", September 24.

— (1995d), "Koukou kara daigaku made, heikin de 932 man en (From high school to university an average of 9.32 million yen)", October 25, p. 3.

Nikkei (1995), Monday September 24.

Nisihikawa, Toru (1989), "New Product Planning at Hitachi", *Long Range Planning*, vol. 22, no. 4, pp. 20–4.

Ohmae Kenichi (1995), "The Triad World View", *Journal of Business Strategy*, vol. 7, no. 4, pp. 8–18.

Okahashi, Tsutomu (1995), "Relationship Marketing in Japan is a Tradition or a New Trend?", ESMOR TRIAD 2000, June 13, New York.

Oshashi, Terue (1989), "Marketing in Japan in the 1990s: Homing in on the Holonic Consumer", *Marketing and Research Today*, November, pp. 220–9.

Ramaprasad, J. & Hasegawa, K. (1992), "Creative Strategies in American and Japanese TV Commercials: A Comparison", *Journal of Advertising Research*, January/February, pp. 59–67.

Reuters News Service (1995), "Americans over 80 Years Old Found to Outlive the Elderly of other Nations", *Japan Times*, November 3, p. 3.

Sanghavi, Nitin (1988), "The Japanese Yen for Non-Store Retailing", *Direct Marketing*, April, pp. 24–8.

Shephard, David C., Helms, Marilyn M. & Tilloston, Rodney C. (1992), "Japanese Marketing: A Review", *Marketing Intelligence and Planning*, vol. 10, no. 10, pp. 35–40.

Sherry, John F. & Carmargo, Eduardo G. (1987), "May Your Life Be Marvellous. English Language Labeling and the Semiotics of Japanese Promotion", *Journal of Consumer Research*, vol. 14, September, pp. 174–87.

Simon, Francoise (1992), "Marketing Green Products in the Triad", *Colombia Journal of World Business*, vol. 27, no. 3(4), pp. 268–85.

Smith, R.J, (1983), *Japanese Society: Tradition, Self and Social Order*, Cambridge University Press, Cambridge.

Stalk, George Jr. & Webber, Alan M. (1993), "Japan's Dark Side of Time", *Harvard Business Review*, July–August, pp. 93–102.

Sumitomo Life Social Welfare Services Foundation (1994), "Health Survey of Middle Aged People", October.

Sumitomo Bank (1988), "Salaried Men's Health and Stress", Sumitomo Bank, Tokyo.

Suzuki, Toshi & Kirishima Kazutaka (1995), "Shinku tanku no me. Kakudai suru wakamono shohi shijio (From the eyes of a think tank. The expanding youth consumption market)", *Nihon Kogyo Shimbun*, Tokyo, March 7, p. 20.

Syedain, Hashi (1993/1994), "Understanding the Inscrutable", *Marketing Director International*, Winter, pp. 19–21.

Tanaka, Hiroshi (1993), "Branding in Japan", in eds David A. Aaker & Alexander L. Biel, *Brand Equity and Advertising. Advertising's Role in Building Strong Brands*, Lawrence Erlbaum, Hillsdale, N.J.

Tanzer, Andrew (1992), "A Message from Akihabara", *Forbes*, June 8, pp. 42–3.

The Leisure Research and Development Center Foundation (1995), "Leisure White Paper", Tokyo.

Tsutsumi, Tezio et al. (1986), "Ari gata ningen. Atarashi seikatsu wo tsukame (Ant-like People and Grasshopper-like People: Understanding the New Tokyo)", *Dentsu Marketing Study Group Report*, Yosensha Publishing Inc., Tokyo.

Tully, Shaun (1994), "Teens. The Most Global Market of them all", *Fortune International*, May 16, pp. 24–9.

van Wolferen, Karel (1990), *The Enigma of Japanese Power*, Vintage Books, New York.

Wilk, Robert J. (1991), "The New Rich: A Psychographic Approach to Marketing to the Wealthy Japanese Consumer", *Marketing and Research Today*, February, pp. 62–8.

Wood, Christopher (1993), "The Bubble Economy: The Japanese Economic Collapse", Charles E. Tuttle Company, Tokyo.

Yano Research Institute Ltd. (1993), "Leisure Industry White Paper", Yana Research Institute Ltd, Tokyo.

Yoshimori, Masaru (1992), "Sources of Japanese Competitiveness: Part II", *Management Japan*, vol. 25, no. 2, Autumn, pp. 31–6.

Notes

1 The authors of this chapter wish to express their deepest appreciation to Wakako Takahashi and Keith N.J. Kotval. Wakako's cheerful, tireless efforts to manage the data and create the charts smoothed the process. Keith was indispensable for his incisive comments on the text, keen eye for detail, and witty companionship during the many dark hours before dawn in which this paper was largely completed. It would have been impossible without you both. Thanks also to our colleagues in Planning Department 5 for graciously accommodating our unreasonable demands for computer time, and especially to Koichi Yamamoto and Cauitie Ocada for their help with the technical side and to Mano-san for everything else.

CHAPTER 9

Korea

Changing consumer trends and implications for marketers[1]

JAMES W. GENTRY, SUNKYU JUN, GYUNGTAI KO & HEESUK KANG

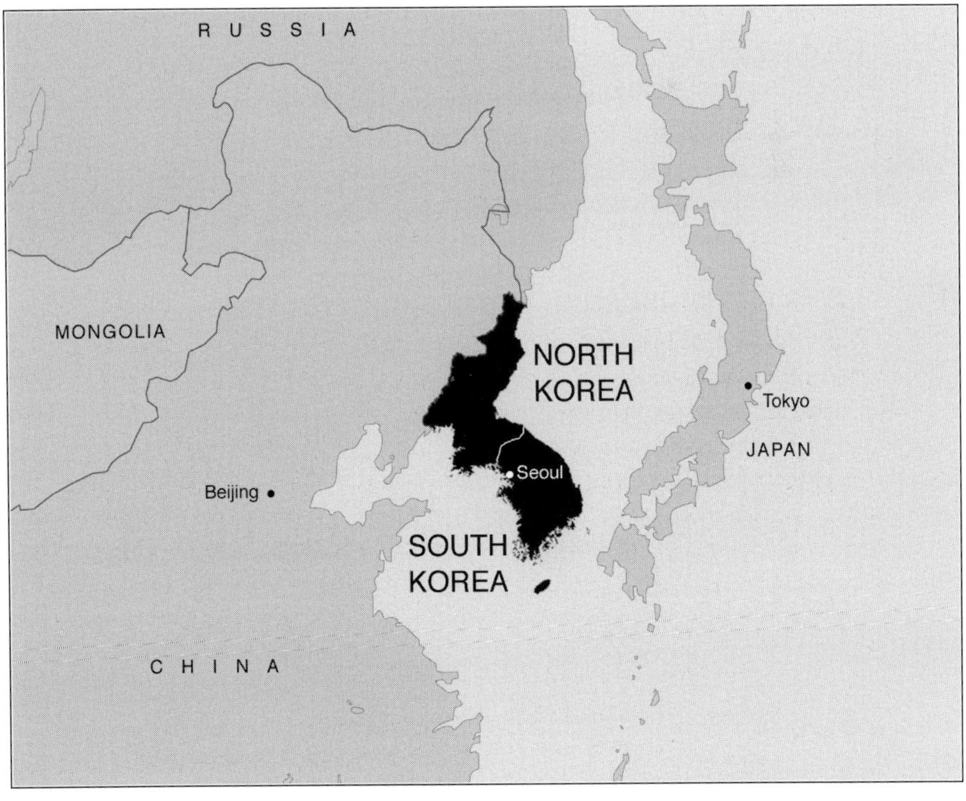

Abstract

South Korea has experienced nearly unprecedented economic growth in the last 3 decades, while North Korea lost its economic lead over South Korea in the 1950s and has become isolated both politically and economically. Yet the two Koreas share an old, unique culture, and the likelihood of reunification is great. In this chapter the changing consumer environments in the two Koreas will be discussed, with coverage of the historical, cultural, economic, and political forces that underlie those changes.

Introduction

Korea is an enigma. On the one hand, there is tremendous appreciation for tradition. Its history is a long one: Koreans refer to "Five thousand years of Korean civilization" (Hoare & Pares 1988). On the other hand, Korea has changed enormously in the past decade. It is split into two halves which would seem, at first sight, to be radically different North Korea (or, officially, the Democratic People's Republic of Korea) is one of the few surviving communist nations. The loss of support from the USSR and, to some extent, China, has turned it into an even more isolationist extension of the "Hermit Kingdom," the name applied to the Korean Peninsula due to its policy of exclusionism during the Yi Dynasty (1392–1910). In contrast, South Korea (or, officially, the Republic of Korea) has blossomed into one of the major players in the global economy. From 1960 to 1990, South Korea was the second fastest growing economy (International Strategies, Inc. 1994). At the same time, the two Koreas remain one of the most unified areas in the world—probably only the Japanese are as homogeneous in term of racial origin and national identity as the inhabitants of the two Koreas (Clifford 1994).

Further, despite its global pressure, South Korea also demonstrates remnants of its Hermit Kingdom roots; for example, Templeman and Nakarmi (1994, p. 6) stated, "Korea's market is so hermetically sealed that it makes Japan's market look positively open." While even Singapore let superstar Michael Jackson perform in late 1993 as a part of his world tour, Korea alone in all of Asia refused to let the singer tour there (Clifford 1994).

A brief historical perspective

Korea's long history has seen it dominated by several foreign powers, especially during the 20th century. Pressure to open Korea came from Western powers in the 1860s; at this stage both China and Japan had been opened for trade (in the 1840s and in 1854 respectively). Japan opened Korea by force in 1876, and later occupied the peninsula in the first decade of the 20th century with the tacit agreement of the USA and the UK, who feared further Russian expansion into East Asia (Hwang 1993).

From 1910 to 1945, Japan dominated Korea. During the colonial era, Korean trade was almost solely with Japan: 85% of exports went to Japan, and 73% of imports came from there. After the attack on Pearl Harbor, Koreans became wartime resources for the Japanese, as both men and women were forced to work 11-hour days and 7-day weeks supporting the war effort. In 1943, Koreans were prohibited from using their own language, and instead forced to read only Japanese newspapers, books, and magazines. They were even compelled to change their family names into Japanese (Hwang 1993). There is good reason for the antipathy and even hostility of many Koreans toward the Japanese.

Korea was split by the Western powers (Russia and the USA) as a temporary expedient, determined by the occupying forces. However, the idea of dividing the Korean peninsula had originated as early as 1593, at the time of a Japanese invasion. China and Japan discussed splitting the 8 Korean provinces, with the northern 4 being ruled by the King of Korea and the remaining 4 being ceded to Japan. The negotiations failed, and the war continued. The Japanese–Russian conflict at the turn of this century also involved negotiations concerning the division of Korea, with Russia attempting to select the 39th parallel as the dividing line between the spheres of influence of the two nations. Again, no agreement was reached, and the war was continued (Kim 1992).

The Korean War devastated both parts of the country. Some 3 million Koreans, nearly 1 of every 10 people, were killed, and over 40% of all industrial installations were heavily damaged. The North's economy rebounded faster than that of the South, despite the fact that post-war aid was at least 7 times greater for the South (Kim 1992). The American military government's attempt to impose a full market economy in the South did not work well in a Confucian culture. While Western powers established the two Korean states, Eastern powers played a more decisive role in shaping the courses of development selected. South Korea dropped the US model of development in the 1960s in exchange for the Japanese model, adopting the principle, "Do what the Japanese have done, but do it cheaper and faster." The choice of the Japanese model over the American model may have been due in part to the fact that Park Chung Hee, the military strongman who commanded South Korea from 1961 until his assassination in 1979, was educated in Japanese military academies and was said to be more comfortable speaking Japanese than Korean (Mallaby 1995). Similarly, North Korea modeled itself after the Stalinist model during the late 1940s and 1950s, but has since been influenced more by the Chinese Communist model (Kim 1992).

Political environment

Though the emphasis of this chapter is on economics, it would be fruitless to discuss the two Koreas without confronting political issues. We only need to consider the role of defense spending in the two nations to realize the strong interface between politics and economics. The combined countries have the world's fifth largest number of military personnel, and are thirteenth in military spending (Kim 1992). Military spending in the South is US$10 590 million (3.8% of its GNP), while the North spends US$5 130 million, or 22.4% of its GVSP (Gross Value of Social Production) (North Korea Research Institute 1993). South Korea continues to seek a self-reliant defense capability, but North Korea still maintains its numerical superiority over the South in military forces. North Korea has the ability to conduct limited guerilla warfare, mobilize the entire population rapidly in an emergency, and wage an all-out war effort with little notice (Whang 1991). One of the few reliable export industries in the North has been its arms industry.

The Korean War and the nearly constant state of tension between the two countries since then are indicants of their focus on one another in terms of most policy decisions. However, there are indicators that situations are changing in both countries. The South has become more democratic since the 1987 elections, and especially since the 1993 elections. In fact, Chalmers Johnson (cited in Clifford 1994, p. 330) states, "[South] Korea is without doubt the most democratic country in Asia right now." By and large, South Koreans are free to say and write what they think. Eight years ago they were not (*Economist* 1990a). Barriers to wage constraints were eased in the late 1980s, and the military/business interface has been under overt political attack since then.

The political situation in North Korea is changing as well, due in part to the death of its long-time leader Kim Il Sung–Bracken (1995) notes that his son Kim Jung Il lacks his father's widespread support in the regime and also in the larger society as a whole–but more to the changing political environment globally. Though the *Chuche* ("self-reliant") ideology of autonomy was adopted by Kim Il Sung as early as 1955, North Korea has relied heavily on the former Soviet Union and the PRC for both political and economic support. The Soviet transformation has forced North Korea to rethink its political future. Even before the fragmentation of the USSR took place, South Korean leader Roh Tae Woo met with Gorbachev in San Francisco in 1990, an event which the *Economist* (1990a) called the "most significant event in Korean diplomacy since the Korean War." By meeting with the South, Gorbachev gave the clear signal that the USSR would no longer support (either financially or militarily) the North's aggressive stance against the South. Further, despite all of the ideological ties between the North and China, as early as 1990 China had 6 times the level of trade with the South as it did with the North (*Economist* 1990a). President Roh created a second historic meeting in September 1992, when he visited Beijing (Nakarmi, Brady & Curry 1992). Hence, on the surface at least, it would appear that both countries are moving in directions more amenable to reunification.

While the South Korean economy continues to grow rapidly, the North's economy is thought to have shrunk by 25% between 1990 and 1994 (Mallaby 1995). The closed environment in Pyongyang makes it very difficult to get an accurate reading of what is transpiring. Breen (1990, p. 44) quotes a Western intelligence source in Seoul as acknowledging, "Different observers see it differently." The political divisions between countries run deep, and the rhetoric observed in the world press offers only rare glimpses of conciliatory statements. It would appear that the North Korean economy is in such a poor state that the North cannot continue long on its own.

Whether it will react violently with another invasion into the South or whether it will move slowly toward reunification remains to be seen; Bracken (1995, p. 63) phrases this question as whether "the end for Pyongyang [the capital of North Korea] comes with a bang or a whimper." Certainly the changing global relations are providing impetus for change. Understanding the political environment in the two Koreas clearly provides us with greater appreciation for the delicacy of the agreement reached on August 13 1994 about nuclear issues. North Korea removed its US trade ban as a part of the August agreement. The South, too, has made conciliatory gestures; for example, the *Economist* (1994a, p. 32) quotes South Korean President Kim Young Sam: "The problems of the North are our own problems. We must always be prepared to co-operate with our brethren." On November 7 1994, President Kim announced a partial lifting of the ban on trade with the North, but with strong limitations. Progress toward normalization is evident, but also evident is the increasing military capability of the North (Bracken 1995).

The political situation in the Koreas has served to raise even more questions than usually exist about the validity of economic statistics reported by developing countries. Such statistics are often called into question in many parts of the world, but this may be especially true with the Koreas given their continuing battle for prestige in the world community. As Hwang (1993) notes, there is a serious lack of published data for North Korea, while there is a wealth of published data and statistics from South Korea. Chung (1986) asserted that withdrawing information has been one of North Korea's main means of concealing unfavorable developments. For this reason, our discussion of the South's economy will be far richer in detail. But even here we should be quite careful. Hwang (1993, p. 100) notes that economic data with political implications (income distributions, credit rationing, etc.) must be handled with care. Similarly, Halladay (1989) notes that official Pyongyang claims are often exaggerated, but that Western and Seoul downgradings of the North are also usually inaccurate.

A case in point is the reporting of North Korean agricultural output. In early 1995 the South Korean state-run Rural Development Administration estimated that the North's grain harvest was one-third below the level needed to prevent food shortages. The estimates were compiled from studying crop yields in border areas and weather patterns. Similar South Korea reports from earlier years have been common; in contrast, the North Korean-controlled media annually boast bumper crops. Hwang (1993) and Merrill (1989) have found the North's agricultural achievements to be impressive, especially given its unfavorable climate and terrain. Therefore, we will attempt to provide an objective evaluation of the marketing systems in the two countries, but will have to acknowledge that some of our "facts" may well be misrepresentations of the actual circumstances.

The economies of the Koreas

Comparing the economies of the North and the South is a complex task and, as will be indicated, there is little consensus on the pertinent numbers. It is clear, though, that the South is doing much better now, and that those performances were reversed in the 1960s. One problem with comparing the economies is that the countries use different measures. The South uses GNP data, which included both productive and non-productive (service) sectors in its measurement. The North uses GVSP data, which includes intermediate material inputs except for goods consumed within the same enterprise, but does not include non-productive sectors. To complicate matters, since the North Korean currency is not convertible, there are multiple exchange rates to use in the analyses. Hwang (1993) found that the North led the South in per-capita GNP until 1985 if the official exchange rate is used, but only until 1974 if the trade exchange rate (which is more than twice the official rate) is used. Meanwhile, Seoul claims that it overtook the North in 1969, while the US CIA claims this happened in 1976 (Hwang 1993).

South Korea's "miracle economy" started showing signs of trouble in 1996, when banks first reported large losses on loans to chaebols. The South-East Asian currency problems in October 1997 added to the uncertainty in the South Korean financial markets, and the exchange rate for the won fell over 20% against the US dollar within a month. Some official sources estimated that South Korea urgently needed to borrow US$60 billion in November to avoid bankruptcy (*Economist* 1997c).

Income

Kim (1992, p. 95) summarizes the income distributions in the two countries in Table 9.1. It appears that the poor (the lowest 10%) in the South may have less than the poor in the North; however, 90% of the South are above the median income in the North and 70% of the South have incomes comparable to the top 20% in the North. Again, it should be noted that data from both Koreas may need to be viewed with skepticism. Breen (1990) notes that, officially, Pyongyang claimed its annual per-capita income to be US$2500, but one UN official said the figure was around the US$1000 mark, and a diplomat from Beijing who had been assigned to the North said that its per-capita income was "definitely" below China's figure of US$450.

Confucianism (plus Communism in the North) has worked to reduce the disparity of incomes in both Koreas. In 1970, by one measure South Korea had a more equal income distribution than Japan or the USA (*Economist* 1990b). Clifford (1994) also notes this strong egalitarian tradition, and acknowledges that the division between rich and poor is not that great. He also notes that there is great reliance by government on the use of slogans and symbols calling for sacrifice; frugality sometimes resembles a religion.

Table 9.1 Per-capita income distribution in 1988

Percentage of Population Below	*Income Level*	
	South Korea	*North Korea*
0–10	648	720
10–20	1 264	900
20–30	1 684	1 000
30–40	2 010	1 100
40–50	2 349	1 200
50–60	2 755	1 300
60–70	3 211	1 400
70–80	3 818	1 500
80–90	4 850	2 000
90–100	8 897	4 200

Source: Kim, Byoung-Lo Philo (1992), *Two Koreas in Development,* Transaction Publishers, New Brunswick, NJ.

For instance, President Kim eats noodles and shuns golf. Kim Woo Choong, founder of the Daewoo conglomerate, who regards a dinner jacket as an extravagance even for a billionaire like himself and who once sacked an employee because his wife wore a mink coat, was voted South Korea's most respected businessman in 1993 (*Economist* 1995a). At the same time, Seoul probably has more chauffeured cars than any other city in the world. Government ministries and large corporations have private elevators reserved for executives, while other elevators in the same building may be taken out of service as part of a governmental energy-saving campaign (Clifford 1994).

Both countries have somewhat inflexible class structures. In South Korea, as in the USA, blue-collar workers rarely move into management, as the hierarchical system is generally accepted (Clifford 1994). In North Korea, every individual in North Korea is classified into one of 51 categories according to his/her *sungboon*–the family's class background. The highest group includes anti-Japanese guerrilla fighters and their families; orphans of parents killed in anti-Japanese activities or in the Korean War; and the families of party members, government officials, and military officers. The elite receive preferential treatment in the acquisition of food and other consumer goods. Those at the bottom of the ladder include descendants of landlords, capitalists, rich peasants, collaborators with the Japanese, and members of religious groups as well as the families of persons who fled to South Korea. Persons with a good *sungboon* find their entry into the best schools and their rise in the bureaucracy facilitated. Those with a bad *sungboon* have little chance of a good education or a good job. Because family background is passed on from parents to children, stratification seems to be hardening, and opportunities for those at the bottom of the ladder seem to be declining (Kim 1992).

Employment

Employment levels in both countries have traditionally been high, in part because of the close interface between business and the government. In the North, a "paradise on Earth" was built: no taxes, no crime, no beggars, no unemployment, no corruption. The price for this paradise was no television, no refrigerators, and a lack of decent clothing and comfortable housing (Kim 1992). Urban workers usually work 6 days a week, with 15 days' paid vacation a year. Rural farmers have every first, eleventh, and twenty-first day of the month off. Most white-collar workers (with the exception of those in the teaching profession) must engage in some sort of manual labor, such as digging ditches, every Friday. Saturday is "education day" (indoctrination day) for all people (Chung 1986).

Prior to the mid-1980s, wage rates in the South were quite low, helping exports to be price competitive in global markets. Trade unions lacked power, as union membership included only a small percentage of the workers (about 7% in 1985). Many firms do not accept trade unions. In the 1980s, holidays were limited to a weekly rest day and public holidays, and employers sometimes obligated employees to put in extra hours in order to meet production peaks (Hoare & Pares 1988). South Korean employees retired at the age of 55, receiving a lump-sum retirement allowance. Promotion was based primarily on seniority, and not on performance. The incentive systems usually included seasonal bonuses, which were uniform and not tied to performance (Yoo & Lee 1987).

In 1985 there was a political liberalization, which resulted in workers demanding higher wages. This brought an end to the relatively cheap, high quality, co-operative Korean labor force. The heaviest losers were key export markets such as electronic equipment, textile fabrics, iron and steel, miscellaneous manufacturing, and non-metallic metals (Clifford 1994). Steel, one of Korea's success stories, is a typical case. Production costs of cold-rolled steel products were only three-quarters of the Japanese levels in 1988, but by 1993 had risen to nearly 90% of Japan's. Rising wages have priced the shoe manufacturers of South Korea out of world markets. Largely as a result, unemployment in the industrial port city of Pusan has risen to 4.3%, well above the national average of 3.3% (Clifford 1994).

The government's reaction to the downturn in the early 1990s was a campaign launched in 1991 urging citizens to work more (an extra 30 minutes a day), save more (another 10% of income), export more, produce more, and live a more frugal life. The so-called "Five Mores" campaign was launched by all major business organizations with the backing of government (Clifford 1994, p. 8). In late December 1996, President Kim's government pushed through new labor laws that made it easier to lay off employees, and resulted in numerous strikes and riots (*Economist* 1997a).

Prices and credit policy

In North Korea, a commodity's price is determined not by the demand and supply mechanism, but arbitrarily, by the central planners who seek to control the demand for and supply of commodities. Therefore, in many cases the price of a commodity is not relevant to the actual value of that commodity. Based on so-called "socially needed labor time," which represents the average quantity of labor put into the production of the good, the price is determined so as to raise labor productivity, increase cost effectiveness, and reflect savings in the use of raw materials and consumers' living standards (Hwang 1993). In general, all prices in the North are controlled by the government except for those for agricultural products in the farmer's market (flea market) on the 1st, 11th, and 21st days of the month.

Pricing in the South is more market oriented. A World Bank study in 1983 showed that South Korea had one of the least price-distorting regimes in the world. With the increase in wages after the mid-1980s, prices rose, especially as increasing attention was paid to domestic demand as opposed to exporting. The government's rice-buying prices rose 30% between 1988 and 1990 (*Economist* 1990a). Inflation rose as high as 12% following the wage increases (Nakarmi 1991), but was brought down to 4.5% by 1992 (International Strategies, Inc. 1994).

The South Korean government has long rationed the flow of credit (Hoare & Pares 1988), making funds available for business expansion but restricting credit access in consumer markets, especially the supply of credit for house buying. Mortgages are scarce, and it is difficult to get one for more than 20% of the value of a house or apartment (*Economist* 1990c). In early 1995, in order to cool down the economy, the government dictated that banks could no longer issue credit cards to people under 20, university students, or workers during their first year on the job. This was seen largely as a symbolic gesture, as this segment does not spend nearly as much as older population segments. Most people reacted positively to the policy, as there was fear that the free-wheeling youth market would undermine the social order (*Economist* 1995a).

Government/business interface

In the North, a controlled economy exists; business activities are government run. In the North Korean command economy, the priorities of production are ranked from public goods, producers' goods and light-industry goods down to consumer goods, so that consumer preferences on the micro level are neglected for the sake of the macro-level targets of the planners (Hwang 1993). In the South, there is also a strong history of government playing a dominant role in business. Park Chung Hee decided in the early 1960s that the correct path for development was to favor a few companies (now known as *chaebols*) with carefully channeled credit and subsidies. In return for these favors, the firms had to meet the government's expectations (*Economist* 1990c).

Business exists at the pleasure of government, and is expected to put national development ahead of private desires (Clifford 1994). As a result, the economic power in the South is quite concentrated; 10 of the country's firms are responsible for more than half of its exports (*Economist* 1990c). The concentration of the workforce is indicated by the very low ratio of companies to population in South Korea: 0.7%, compared to 4.4% in the US, 5% in Japan, 4.1% in the UK, and 2.5% in Taiwan (Park 1994). The authorized *Handbook of Korea* (1987 edition) states, "The national economy can be divided into two parts: the government sector and the private sector functioning under the government's policy" (Hoare & Pares 1988).

There are similarities between the Korean *chaebols* and the Japanese *zaibatsus;* for example, both names are derived from the same Chinese characters and both are loosely translated as "conglomerates" (Chang 1988). But the close government/business relationship in Korea ("Korea Inc.") differs from that of "Japan Inc.," which reflects a consensus of equals. Traditionally, Korea Inc. has seen more government leadership, due largely to the Korean government's strong control over access to credit, whereas the large Japanese *zaibatsus* often have their own banks from which they can obtain credit (Yoo & Lee 1987).

Chang (1988) uses the acronym FARS (Family, Alumni, Regional, State relationships) to explain the intricate nature of *chaebols.* Unlike the *zaibatsus,* most *chaebols* (with the possible exception of Daewoo) are dominated by the founding families, and appear to be able to continue to do so. There is a strong preference for employees who have attended the right schools (Kyunggi High School and Seoul National University). For example, 7 of the 9 inner-circle executives at Daewoo in the 1980s were graduates of Kyunggi High School. Chang (1988) noted that 62% of the top executives of the 7 largest *chaebols* were graduates of Seoul National University. Similarly, most top executives of the *chaebols* come from the same geographic region of Korea as the founders.

The political influence of the *chaebols* has diminished with the election of non-military leaders. President Kim's lifting of sanctions on trade with North Korea was intended to allow small and medium-sized South Korean companies, rather than the *chaebols,* to venture North. Unfortunately, the *chaebols* are probably more likely to have the funds and the willingness to take the risks needed to establish large-scale trade (*Economist* 1994f). However, public resentment toward the *chaebols* and the rich families that control them makes it politically expedient to push them around (*Economist* 1990b). There is indication that the government pressure on the *chaebols* is changing the nature of business, as the percentage of sales in more competitive markets (i.e. markets where the top 3 firms had a market share less than 50%) increased from 26% in 1981 to 37% in 1992.

The most evident split between the *chaebols* and the government occurred when Hyundai's founder Ju Yung Chung stood in the presidential elections. He was the first to break the unwritten rule by being a political opponent of the government. He had irritated the government by being the first prominent businessperson to visit the North in 1990, and in October of that year Hyundai was singled out for tax evasion. In 1992 Ju Yung Chung attempted to make public the collusion that exists between *chaebols* and government by providing details of millions in payments to Korean politicians, including Roh Tae Woo's government. Roh admitted receiving the money, but said that it was spent on the "needy" (Nakarmi 1992).

In the early fall of 1996, former presidents Chun Doo Hwan and Roh Tae Woo were imprisoned for their roles in a 1979 military coup and the 1980 massacre of pro-democracy demonstrators in Kwangju. Further, the heads of 8 *chaebols* were given prison terms for bribing Roh, and 4 of these prison terms were subsequently suspended (Lee 1996). The government/*chaebol* interface became even more complex in late 1996 with the collapse of Hanbo Steel and the subsequent charges made against President Kim's son for his role in that failure (*Economist* 1997b).

Barriers to trade

The North Korean market has been closed to much of the world since its inception. In 1987 North Korea began to let Western tourists visit, and in 1989 reported that 25 000 tourists had visited from Western Europe, Australia, Canada, and Hong Kong (Breen 1990). The facilities for tourism are in place, as Pyongyang is a clean city with wide streets and a new streetcar system, and has several modern hotels, monuments, museums, and scenic parks. However, tourism revenues dropped drastically with the disintegration of the Russian economy. Pyongyang's finest hotel, the Koryo, has 500 rooms, but a visitor in 1991 found only 35 of them occupied. Similarly, the Hyangsan Hotel, situated in the north-western hills of Pyongyang, was found not to have a single overnight guest one summer night in 1991 (Gluckman 1991). It appears that, while North Korea would like to have the revenues generated by tourism, it is still scared of the possible cultural contamination tourism might bring.

Since 1988, Seoul has allowed indirect trade with the North, with each *chaebol* permitted to buy a little under US$200 million per year of gold, zinc, fish, and rice liquor, shipping their goods via China or Hong Kong (*Economist* 1994d). Once the US trade ban was removed in January 1995, firms such as "Coca-Cola" and AT&T made immediate plans to send representatives to the North (Nakarmi 1995a).

One obvious problem is the lack of a hard currency; as South Korean firms have noted (*Economist* 1994d), how much zinc and rice liquor does one need? Further, North Korean quality standards have been found to be below those of the South. For example, Breen (1990) reports an instance where an entire shipment of coal from the North was of a significantly lower grade than specified, and was returned. For the North, importing does not present quality problems, but rather image problems. Electronics imported from the South were stripped of their brand name by authorities in Pyongyang in order to prevent its citizens from perceiving that the South was capable of producing more sophisticated products (Breen 1990).

Though its trade with the West has been very limited, the North has borrowed US$1.2 billion, which it has shown absolutely no intention of paying back (*Economist* 1994d). Eisenstodt (1990) notes that Japan's trading companies have knocked at the North's door over the years, though they have generally been "burned" whenever the door was opened. In 1975, Japan's Ministry of International Trade and Industry (MITI) stopped providing export insurance for Japanese trade with North Korea, as Pyongyang had run up debts of over US$500 million in the early 1970s, and these were still unpaid.

Remnants of the Hermit Kingdom legacy are also evident in the South. Its export-driven economic policies reduced its attraction as a consumer economy, though the liberalization in the 1980s changed matters somewhat. In order to manage trade deficits, the South's government has used a variety of tariff and non-tariff barriers. While tariffs have been falling in general (from 12.7% in 1989 to 7.9% in 1993), duties remain very high on high-value and value-added agricultural and fisheries products (International Strategies Inc. 1994). During the high inflation in the early 1990s, the South placed limitations on the number of "luxury" goods (Kraft & Chung 1992).

Non-tariff barriers pose greater problems. Frustration has been encountered as a result of the complicated licensing requirements, the inspection of industrial goods, and "special laws" that give line ministries broad powers to "stabilize" markets by controlling imports (International Strategies Inc. 1994). In 1990, Korean importers were slapped with strict new guidelines that raised the price of foreign goods to extraordinary levels; for example, a General Electric refrigerator selling for about US$1600 in the US cost US$4200 in Korea. The government went so far as to send its tax inspectors to dig into the records of Koreans who had bought imported cars, and even of those who had been salmon fishing in Alaska or golfing in Hawaii (Nakarmi 1991). The tax audits of people buying imported cars stopped in 1993, though more subtle forms of intimidation still exist. As a consequence, only about 2000 imported cars were sold in 1993 in a market of about 1 million cars (Templeman & Nakarmi 1994).

In March 1990, the Korean government announced that retailers must display two prices on certain retail products. The first price is the ex-factory price for domestic goods, or the customs-clearance price for imported goods; the second is the retail price. Because of the difference in the composition of the ex-factory and the customs-clearance price, the markup on imported goods appears higher, making them less attractive to Korean customers (International Strategies Inc. 1994).

The government of South Korea has made progress with gradually opening its market to foreign investment. About 98% of the industrial areas and 62% of the service areas are now open to foreign investment. Foreign businesses operating in South Korea may now purchase land and housing for their staff without obtaining government approval. In recent years, Korea has received a relatively small amount of Foreign Direct Investment (FDI) compared with other developing countries in the region. During the period 1988–1992, Korea received US$5.5 billion in FDI compared with US$87.6 billion for China, US$30.4 billion for Thailand, US$24.7 billion for Malaysia, and US$9.1 billion for Taiwan (International Strategies Inc. 1994).

Citibank's early experience has reduced interest in South Korea on the part of other US financial institutions. Authorities insisted that its cash machines could operate only during normal banking hours, that it could not join a national payment network, and that each branch had to be capitalized and operated as if it were a separate bank, with separate reporting and operating structures (Clifford 1994).

In 1992, authorities detained a shipment of US$250 000 worth of Snickers and Skittles candy bars at the port of Pusan. The imported candy lacked a quarantine certificate testifying that the sweets adhered to new "internal guidelines," although these candies had already been imported for several years with no problems. The guidelines were never made public (Clifford 1994).

The existence of bureaucratic barriers has continued into the Kim Young Sam administration. In June 1993, just 4 months after Kim took office, prosecutors arrested 7 executives from Amway and Sunrider International. Sunrider's top executive in Korea was jailed for operating a multilevel, or pyramid, sales network, which special prosecutor Kwak Young Chul said could lead to "serious social disorder" (Clifford 1994). Nevertheless, President Kim has initiated many changes aimed at attracting foreign investment. In July 1994, the Ministry of Finance announced a special corporate-profit tax exemption for a period of 5 years for new high-technology businesses created by foreign corporations in Korea.

The government plans to foster a one-stop service system to handle applications for and the approval of the establishment of companies or factories. Financial market accessibility has been improved, and, by August 1994, 74 foreign banks, 39 foreign securities firms, and 28 foreign insurance companies had entered South Korea and been accorded full national treatment. Foreign banks have enjoyed high profitability in recent years, recording an average return on assets over 3 times that of Korean banks (*Korea Business World* 1994).

Further, Holstein and Nakarmi (1995, p. 63) note that the return of many US-trained PhDs is "tilting the balance away from an inward-looking, relatively closed nation toward one that is eager to play a larger international role." The liberalization process is a gradual one. For example, the won will become convertible, and foreigners will soon be allowed to buy as much as 25% of a company's equity, but limits will be placed on capital outflow, and foreign majority control of Korean companies will not be allowed. Holstein and Nakarmi (1995) expect that Korea will open its markets more widely to the USA and Europe in order to reduce its dependence on the Japanese for capital goods and components.

Korean–Japanese trade relations

Despite the ill will still lingering from the colonial period, both Koreas are more dependent on Japan than on any other country (Kim 1992). In May 1955, leftist Koreans in Japan formed an organization named *Choch'ungnyon,* and this organization was soon brought under the direct control of North Korea. The organization was designed to capture the leadership of all Korean residents in Japan (some 600 000 in total). Gradually relations with Japan deteriorated in the 1960s as Japan's economic ties with South Korea improved. In 1972 Japan sent a goodwill mission to Pyongyang, which marked a new stage in bilateral agreements. Kim Il Sung indicated that the normalization of relations between Japan and North Korea would not be hampered by the existing relationship between Japan and South Korea. Japan's official policy is to continue to pursue a "two-Koreas" policy (Eisenstodt 1990).

In 1989, Japanese/North Korean trade came to almost US$500 million and involved more than 40 joint ventures, yet this was a mere trickle compared with Japanese/South Korean trade (US$30 billion at that time). Still, the Japanese trade was of immense importance to North Korea. Much of the trade involves small firms owned by Koreans in Japan (Eisenstodt 1990). In 1989 the volume of North Korean trade with Japan was second only to its trade with the USSR, and larger than that with China (Kim 1992). More recently, China has become the North's major trading partner, but it is now reluctant to provide oil and foodstuffs to the North at "friendship prices" (Bridges 1995). Japan remains the North's major link to the developed world.

In contrast to the appearance of South Korean dependency on the USA, the South's trade volume with Japan is 1.7 times larger than that with the USA. With the yen up 13% against the South Korean won in 1993 and 1994, Seoul was able to boost exports by 7.3%, helping to cut its overall trade deficit by nearly 70%, to US$1.5 billion. But, as Korea is heavily dependent on Japan for capital goods and components of its exports, Japan's trade surplus with Korea (US$4.7 billion through May 1994) is widening (*Business Week* 1994b).

The demographic and social environments

Population

Koreans are changing. For example, they are getting bigger: 14-year-old (South) Korean boys in 1990 were 5 inches taller than 14-year-olds in 1965 (*Economist* 1990c). In 1910 the population of Korea was said to be over 13 million, while in the early 1920s it was just over 17 million. A census in 1949 gave the population of South Korea as just over 20 million, compared to the level of 45 million in 1995.

Estimates in 1995 put the population of the North at about 22 million. In 1962, the Korean government introduced the national family planning program, which successfully reduced the annual population growth rate (from 3.0% in the 1950s, it dropped to 1.6% in the 1970s). This rate will decline further, nearing the 1% level by the year 2000. Yet, despite such efforts, the population of South Korea is projected to reach 50 million by the year 2000. This growth will significantly increase a population density that is already the world's third highest, following Bangladesh and Taiwan (Whang 1991). Today many towns have "population clocks" that, by regularly showing the rate of population increase, are supposed to help slow it down (Hoare & Pares 1988). Traffic in the average Korean city is heavier than in Western cities, even though more people may walk or ride bicycles in order to have greater flexibility of movement (Choe & Pitman 1993).

The school-age population is expected to decrease from 38% of the population in 1980 to 28% in 2000, reversing the growth trend of the past 2 decades. The aged population is estimated to grow at an annual rate of about 3.7%, with those over 65 reaching 6.2% of the population by 2000 (Whang 1991). Life expectancy at birth improved from 53 years in 1960 to 69 and 68 years in South and North Korea respectively (Kim 1992). The total fertility rate for the South is recorded as 4.2 in 1970 and 2.1 in 1988, while for the North it is 5.4 and 3.5 for the corresponding years (Hwang 1993).

Table 9.2 Population (millions)

Year	*South Korea*	*North Korea*
1945	16.0	9.9
1946	19.4	9.3
1953	21.6	8.5
1989	43.1	21.0
1992	43.7	22.3

Source: Kim, Byoung-Lo Philo (1992), *Two Koreas in Development*, Transaction Publishers, New Brunswick, NJ.

Immigrants

There are almost no ethnic groups in South Korea, other than about 20 000 Chinese. Since the late 19th century, there has been a small Chinese minority, mainly concentrated in Seoul. Even this Chinese minority is dwindling, due in part to bureaucratic barriers such as nationalization, the requirement that Koreans need to sponsor migrating Chinese, a good job, and over US$60 000 in cash. The stores in the "Chinatown" area of Seoul (Myongdong) are now run by Koreans (*Economist* 1996). Other than the diminishing Chinese minority, Korea is inhabited by people who display few regional differences, either physical or cultural. Only in Cheju are speech patterns and cultural practices noticeably different from those elsewhere, and even these differences are minimal (International Strategies, Inc. 1994).

Education

The adult literacy rates in both Koreas reached over 98% in 1988. North Korea spends more time on the ideological education of students (Kim 1992). Over 37% of South Koreans and 23% of North Koreans get at least some higher education (compared to 60% of Americans, 45% of Taiwanese, and only 22% of Britons–*Economist* 1990b). Education has played an important role in South Korea's post-war modernization, primarily because of the almost blind faith in the value of educational attainment among Korean people (Whang 1991). Students in South Korea attend class 222 days a year, compared to 180 in the USA and 188 in Canada (International Strategies, Inc. 1994). This reverence for education (and the equating of education with the ability to pass standardized tests) is a holdover from Confucianism. In mathematics tests administered by the Educational Testing Service to 13-year-old students from a variety of countries, including the USA, Koreans ranked first in each of the 5 categories of problems (Clifford 1994). However, densely-populated South Korea cannot afford free government education for every child at all levels. Six years of free schooling were provided in the 1980s, and the number of years has been extended to the middle-school level. At this level, scholarships provide for some of the able poor (Hyde 1988).

Health care

North Korea claims to spend far more effort and money on health and to have a much higher ratio of doctors to population than the South (24 per 10 000 people, compared to 10 per 10 000 people). But the North's definition of "doctor" does not always make it clear whether he or she is a licensed doctor who has received a regular education at medical school (Hwang 1993). The South has 32 hospital beds per 10 000 people (*Asian Business* 1992). South Korea is able to provide all Korean citizens with comprehensive health protection, and gives a pension to those who were hired in the firms with the size of 5 or more employees, and public support to those with low incomes (Pae 1992).

Family relations

Two-generation families are common in South Korea, while 3-generation families are as common in North Korea. In South Korea, the nuclear family is increasing as the dominant type of family. During the 1975–1980 period the numbers of 1- and 2-generation families increased by 47.2% and 19.1% respectively. However, the number of 3-generation families increased only 2.7% during the same period (Hwang 1993). The proportion of households with grandparents dropped from 19% of households in 1970 to 9.5% in 1990. In the North, families are organized into groups of 5, sharing a bathroom, eating together, and spying on each other. Disloyalty to the government results in time in labor camps, while loyalty may be rewarded with party membership, which can lead to material benefits (Mallaby 1995). In South Korea, men marry around the age of 27, while women are married at about 24. Love matches are quite common today, with parents giving their approval for such marriages (Hwang 1993).

Traditional family values still are very prominent. The family has an essential role as the forum of worship of the ancestors and guarantor of the ancestral lineage. Perpetuation of the male line is a duty of each new generation, as is the proper observance of mourning rites for deceased parents. Traditionally, a woman's chief function has been to produce a male heir for her husband's family. The husband's family and its needs still take social precedence over the wife's. Headship of a family still passes to the eldest son, and it is his duty to look after a widowed mother and any unmarried siblings. Divorce is now legally permissible and is becoming more frequent, though socially it is still viewed askance (Hoare & Pares 1988).

The socialization of children is a primary concern among Koreans. Koreans have a great respect for learning, and their children are under tremendous pressure for high academic achievement. In fact, Hupp, Lam, and Jaeger (1992) report a study finding that 24% of Korean parents migrating to the USA listed the most important reason for their immigration as the desire to give their children a better education. Hupp et al. (1992), in a study comparing play activities of 1-year-olds in Anglo- and Korean-American families, found that Korean parents intervened significantly more during the play sessions than did the American parents. The Korean parents perceived that their children had a desire for more adult guidance, and wanted to be less independent than did the American parents. Independent exploration was appreciated far more by Anglo parents.

In 1990, a Korean court decided to allow divorced women access to their children. Recently, a divorcee whose husband had died won custody of her children despite the fact that she was an adulteress. Previously, it was always assumed that the dead husband's parents had a prior claim. Adulterous women have also gained the right to receive alimony, after they have completed their prison terms for breaking their marriage vows. One out of every

7 South Korean marriages now falls apart, a threefold increase since 1972 (*Economist* 1994b).

Gender relations

Females, in accordance with Confucian ideals, are given family-centered, informal instruction in the virtues of diligence, frugality, and chastity. A woman's existence is meaningful only in terms of her relationships with men: she is a man's daughter, a man's wife, and finally, if she is lucky, a man's mother (Hyde 1988).

Legally, women are equivalent to men, as there is universal suffrage at 20 years of age (International Strategies, Inc. 1994). The constitution of 1948 introduced a Family Law, which sought to impose a measure of legality on customary family relations (Hoare & Pares 1988). Still, gender norms have been slow to change. For example, wives do not often accompany their husbands to parties, and frequently they are not included in business entertainment (Choe & Pitman 1993).

In both North and South Korea, men occupy most top jobs in the civilian economy. This is particularly true in top jobs in government and industry. Women make up about 48% of the North Korean total workforce, and about 45.5% of the industrial workforce in South Korea (Hwang 1993). The female workforce is still quiescent, and a considerable discrepancy exists between average wages for men and for women. Women's problems stem partly from negative attitudes among both men and women toward female participation in work outside the home (a non-working wife is interpreted by some as a sign of a man's good financial standing). Their poor status is reflected in their relatively low earnings, and in their general absence from managerial and decision-making grades (Hoare & Pares 1988). Females in South Korea work longer hours than their sisters elsewhere in the world, but they earn only 54% as much as men (*Economist* 1994b).

But times are changing. During the summer of 1994, the hottest in Korea since the turn of the century, there was a fad among young South Korea women for wearing cropped t-shirts that leave the midriff exposed. A policeman in Kwangju arrested two 20-somethings for flaunting their navels in the street. What did come as a surprise was that a judge threw the case out, ruling that the flashing of a female navel was not indecent. An Equal Opportunities Law was passed in 1987, but the maximum penalty inflicted on firms that openly recruit only men for any post more responsible than tea-serving has been a modest one million won (US$1250). Bosses can get 2 years in prison for paying different wages for the same work, but none has yet done so. In April 1994, a professor at Seoul National University was ordered to pay 30 million won (US$37 500) in damages to a female assistant who claimed she had been fired for resisting his advances. This was Korea's first successful sexual-harassment suit.

Crime

The rate of violent crime in South Korea is relatively low: 1.4 murders per 100 000 population per year. This level has been virtually unchanged since 1960. In the USA the rate is 9.4, and in France 4.5. But the South's government is concerned about growing violence, and recently 15 convicted killers who happened to be on death row at the wrong time—a time that the appeal process was being handled more quickly—were hanged (*Economist* 1994c).

The cultural environment

Religion

The North Korean culture is characterized by the absence of any significant religion, a major contrast to the situation in South Korea. Instead, Kim-worship (the reverence for Kim Il Sung) took on a religious fervor, and in some homes his picture stands on the altar where tablets of ancestors once stood (Kim 1992). Lee (1995) reported that this reverence for the North's leader is especially strong among the less educated, but that even the more educated never fail to respect their leader. North Koreans wear Kim badges on their lapels in the same way that Catholics wear crucifixes (Mallaby 1995). Two Christian churches opened in 1988 and one in 1989, and these are presently the only churches in the North. The estimates on the number of Christians in North Korea have varied widely from some 770 to 10 000. It is reported that there are only 7 theology students in North Korea (Kim 1992).

In South Korea, the religious adherents are estimated as 48.6% Christian, 47.4% Buddhist, and 3% Confucianist, as well as small numbers following pervasive folk religion (Shamanism) and *Chondogyo* ("religion of the heavenly way") (International Strategies, Inc. 1994). A second source (Kim 1992) lists South Korea as being 24% Christian and 27% Buddhist. These numbers are hard for Westerners to reconcile, but many Koreans adopt the philosophy that "if one religion is good, all religions are good," making religious data somewhat unreliable.

Many Koreans, old and young, still cling to the age-old belief in spirit possession and destinies written in the stars. There are no statistics on how many share this faith. But one telling sign is that churches and wedding halls were booked solidly months in advance for October 23 1994, which fortune tellers touted as one of the luckiest dates for a wedding. Though most of the population is Buddhist or Christian, many hedge their bets, seeking help from other spiritual advisors too. The Reverend Chun Ji-Seok of the Christian Academy estimates that 3 of 10 Christians turn to shamans and fortune tellers in times of need (*Lincoln Journal Star* 1994).

One difference in the economic history of the two Koreas has been the growth of Christianity in the South and the development of more assertive and ambitious mindsets among its adherents. Numbering only 1.2 million in 1957, Christians now are very similar in numbers to Buddhists. In Japan, Christian missionaries have failed to convert more than a trifling 1% of the people. The popular explanation is that Koreans turn to the gospels because they have suffered so much. As an indication of the increasing role of Christianity, President Kim Young Sam is a Presbyterian (*Economist* 1994g).

Confucianism

The economic rise of East Asia has brought Confucianism much attention in the recent past. Some academics have looked to culture for an explanation of economic success, and concluded that "Confucian ethics," stressing the claims of the community over the individual, are the key. Part religion, part ethical code, part social ritual, and part political philosophy, Confucianism remains an elusive concept. It has become a codeword for a set of "Asian" values: commitment to education and family loyalty, and a quiescent attitude to authoritarian rule, where the government assumes the role of the father in a family. One reason for the reassertion of Confucian values is that people often turn back to old beliefs in times of rapid change. As divorce rates and delinquency rise in Asia, as voters become less acquiescent, so fathers and rulers insist that the old, obedient ways are best (*Economist* 1995c).

The Confucian ethic is evident in the people's general attitudes. However, the generalization of Koreans as typical Asians may be a gross oversimplification. For example, Alston (1989), Dubinsky et al. (1991), Hupp, Lam, and Jaeger (1992), and West (1989) note that Asian countries such as Japan and South Korea should not be viewed as single homogeneous entities with respect to business conduct.

The Confucian culture has been credited as being a major part of the remarkable success of South Korean development. One wonders how the same Confucian culture that is practiced in both Koreas can yield such different results. Confucianism as a religion is not actively practiced in either Korea today, but one of its important aspects as an ideology is the emphasis placed on effort. Working hard is valued immensely, which means that the actual process of being industrious is as important as the result.

The same Confucian value system held by the two Koreas has produced two fundamentally different outlooks toward development. For example, Korea has historically emphasized the importance of the Confucian belief in scholarship as more significant than commerce and material things. Traditional Confucian ideology disdains commercial activities; this tradition was therefore easily sustained in North Korea, where Communism disdained commercial and service activities. People were mobilized not by material incentives but by moral exhortation. In South Korea, pluralistic values help explain the extraordinary commercial bustle, the materialism, and the conspicuous consumption of the people. Christians are somewhat over-represented in the entrepreneurial population in South Korea, and this has introduced the notion that commercial activities can lead to one's personal salvation (Kim 1992).

Korea and Japan: Cultural similarities and differences

Westerners tend to lump Japanese and Koreans together. Both cultures share Confucian traditions. For instance, like the Japanese, Koreans say of their society that "the nail that sticks out gets hammered down" (Clifford 1994). But, compared to the Japanese, Koreans are much franker and do not have the same degree of outward politeness. Koreans are more emotional, more openly distrustful, and more willing to act on that distrust (Clifford 1994).

Despite many outward similarities in business culture, Korea is not a second Japan. Korean companies are much more confrontational in their dealing with each other and with the government than their Japanese counterparts. Korean employees are also less loyal to their firms than the American image of Japanese workers. It is not unusual for Korean middle managers to work in several companies over the course of their careers (International Strategies Inc. 1994). This mobility may be due in part to the rapid growth of the Korean economy, which has created competition for middle-management personnel.

Further, business decision-making processes differ from those in Japanese firms. Unlike their Japanese counterparts, Korean companies are still young enough to be led firmly from the top. The Japanese system of *nemawashi* (coming to a decision by a sort of collective consent) is unknown (*Economist* 1990c). For example, Lee (1989) asserts that Korean workers tend to work within a top-down authoritarian structure, and require a higher level of definition in their job structure to avoid suffering from role conflict than do Japanese workers.

Comparisons using Hofstede's cultural dimensions

Hofstede (1984) compared work attitudes of IBM employees across 53 countries, uncovering 4 underlying dimensions: uncertainty avoidance, masculinity/femininity, individualism/collectivism, and power distance. As can be seen in Table 9.3, Korea and Japan are quite similar in terms of power distance and uncertainty avoidance and have higher levels than does the US. On the other hand, Korea is much more collective than Japan, which is itself much more collective than the USA. Japan was found to be the most masculine country in the world, whereas Korea is relatively feminine, with the USA falling in between. ("Masculinity," in the Hofstede schema, relates to an emphasis on work goals and work-related assertiveness, as opposed to personal goals and nurturance.)

Interpersonal interactions

In Korea, there are many rituals of courtesy, formality in behavior, and customs regulating social interactions. Hard work and piety are valued

Table 9.3 Hofstede's findings for Korea, Japan, and the USA

	Ranking of countries[a]		
Dimension	*Korea*	*Japan*	*USA*
Power distance	27/28	33	38
Uncertainty avoidance	16/17	7	43
Individualism	43	22/23	1
Masculinity	41	1	15

[a] The numbers in this table represent the rankings of countries in the original Hofstede (1984) study, with no. 1 being the highest ranking. For example, Japan was found to be the most masculine of the countries studied.

Source: Hofstede, Geert (1984), *Culture's Consequences: International Differences in Work-Related Values,* Sage Publications, Beverly Hills, CA.

characteristics. Compliments and honors are graciously denied. Friendship is valued and respected. The Korean method of social intercourse consists of pretending to like something though it is bad, and pretending to dislike something though it is good (Kim 1975). Many decisions of Korean consumers are made under heavy influence from the group with which they are interacting, such as the extended family, neighbors, friends, co-workers, and even people in the overall society. For example, it is not unusual to find that many Korean people living in the same area (e.g. an apartment building) use the same brand of detergent (Lee & Green 1991).

Respect for age

It is not a coincidence that the majority of Koreans like the fall best, while most Americans prefer spring. Philosophically speaking, spring is the time of youth, and autumn is the time of old age. Americans generally consider youth the best time of life, and accept old age with reluctance (Kim 1975). But reaching the age of 60 has long been a triumphant moment in a Korean's life. Respect and a large measure of personal freedom become one's due at this point, whether one is male or female. This used to be the age when women may start to smoke in public. The sense of pride was especially strong in earlier days when average life expectancy was lower. Now, with life expectancy about 70, the sixtieth birthday is no longer so remarkable, but is still seen as a time for congratulation.

Financial support of the elderly has been traditionally left to families, but will increasingly be met now by a network of pension systems. Not all old people will be cared for by families, and day centers and residential homes are starting to appear (Hoare & Pares 1988).

Relationship with nature

Western people look for the beauty discovered in humanity, while nature is the background for humanity. Koreans have the opposite perspective. While most Western magazine covers show human beings, most Korean magazine covers show nature without a human being in the background (Kim 1975). Despite this profound respect for nature, air and water, pollution is a problem in South Korea, especially in the densely populated cities. Over 80% of the people live in cities (Hyde 1988).

Changes in the macromarketing mix

Comparison of the two Koreas

In North Korea, heavy industry is in the domain of the central government, which also manages large factories producing consumer goods—textile mills are an example. However, most consumer-goods and food-processing industries are run by local governments. For the two Koreas, the production of television sets, refrigerators, wristwatches, clothes, and other consumer goods such as toothpaste show remarkable contrasts. South Korea by far surpasses North Korea in the production of such consumer goods (Kim 1992).

The January 1995 issue of *Shin Dong-A* presented the comparisons of the two economies; these are shown in Table 9.4. Marketing in North Korea occurs in accordance with the state plan. The types of marketing are classified according to different ownership types, with differing price systems applying to each. For example, different wholesale-price structures exist for transactions between two state-run enterprises, and between a state-run enterprise and a co-operative organization. Markets are divided into state-run markets, co-operative markets, and farmers' markets. In the state-run market, wholesale trade of industrial products dominates, with occasional retail transactions also occurring. The co-operative market includes the farmers' co-operative market, the producers' co-operative market, and the marine products co-operative market, as well as such entities as barbershops and public bathhouses (Hwang 1993).

To some extent, North Korea's opening of markets has resembled China's. But the Chinese have policies designed to activate the domestic economy by expanding the market-price system. Only recently has Pyongyang taken steps to reform its domestic economy, which comprise:

- the expansion of farmers' markets
- the introduction of direct-sales stores
- recently granted permission for working people to buy goods at the Nakwon ("Paradise") stores in urban areas
- the introduction of a productivity-linked payment system in the production of consumer goods

Table 9.4 Comparison of the two Korean economies in 1992

Item	*Unit*	*North Korea*	*South Korea*
Oil imports	10 000 tons	152	6 930
Crops produced	10 000 tons	427	621
Rice	10 000 tons	153	533
Fish	10 000 tons	114	329
Steel	10 000 tons	179	2 865
Cement	10 000 tons	475	4 265
Fertilizer	10 000 tons	139	399
Cars	10 000	1.04	172.5
Telephone lines	10 000	40	1 529
International airlines	Number	4	51

Source: Shin Dong-A (1995), *Kim Jung Il and North Korean Encyclopedia*, Dong-A Il Bo, Seoul, January.

- an autonomous business management system in factories
- a material incentives system (Hwang 1993)

Basic consumption in the two Koreas

The lack of data on North Korea often results in the reliance upon defectors for a portrayal (possibly biased) of conditions there. Kim (1992, p. 92) provides a rare exception: the summary of consumption patterns in the two countries shown in Table 9.5. Lee (1995) reports that flea markets operate every 10 days (the 1st, 11th, and 21st of each month); here farmers are allowed to barter their possessions. However, products of greater value are likely to be traded in the black market, which is run largely by the small Korean Chinese minority.

For the South, statistics are more abundant. Table 9.6 shows how expenditure patterns have changed between 1973 and 1992. (Obviously discrepancies exist between the figures reported by Kim (1992) and those reported by the Korean Statistical Office, especially for housing.) Penetration of consumer durables from a nationwide survey in January 1994 was: colour TV sets 99.5%, audio systems 81%, refrigerators 99.3%, VCRs 75%, washing machines 92%, air conditioners 14%, personal computers 33%, and cars 45%.

Food

In 1985, the World Bank estimated that North Korea's food intake was slightly higher–that is, 130% of the daily calorie requirement per capita, compared with 125% for the South. In the North, food is either rationed by

Table 9.5 Composition of household consumption expenditures

Item	*South Korea (%)*	*North Korea (%)*
Food & drink	36.0	44.0
Clothing & footwear	7.6	33.0
Housing	20.0	0.7
Fuel and power	6.5	4.0
Household equipment	4.2	2.4
Health, education, etc.	25.7	15.9

Source: Source: Kim, Byoung-Lo Philo (1992), *Two Koreas in Development*, Transaction Publishers, New Brunswick, NJ, p. 99.

Table 9.6 Trends in household consumption in South Korea, 1973–1992

Item	*1973 (%)*	*1992 (%)*
Food & drink	48.7	30.4
Clothing & footwear	10.1	8.0
Housing	2.7	4.2
Utilities	6.4	4.1
Furniture/home appliances	2.1	5.5
Medical care	2.9	5.4
Education/entertainment	10.9	13.3
Transportation/communication	5.0	9.2
Other	11.1	20.1

Source: Korean Statistical Office (1992), December.

the government or distributed in rural areas according to each member's work contribution (Hwang 1993). In the South, 66% of households had eaten at fast-food restaurants, though there was strong variance across age groups (36% of those in their 50s, versus 87% of those in their 20s). KFC was the most likely to have been experienced (56%), followed by Pizza Hut (40%) and McDonald's (38%). Most adult Korean males smoke cigarettes (Choe & Pitman 1993).

Housing

All housing in the North is either state-owned or co-operatively owned (Hwang 1993). The quality of houses in North Korea is far lower than that of South Korea. According to a video-tape report, the 2-bedroom apartment of one upper-middle-class family was strikingly small, and 8 family members, including 4 relatives, lived there (Kim 1992).

Most dwellings in the North are either flats or (rented) terraced houses. The living space per general worker family is 26.4 m^2 (8 *pyong*), and this is equivalent to 5.3 m^2 (1.6 *pyong*) per individual. Housing space levels (in m^2) have been the following for South Korea: 35.9 in 1970; 41.4 in 1975; 45.8 in 1980; 45.3 in 1985. The living space per capita was 6.8, 8.2, 10.1, and 11.1 m^2 per individual respectively for the same periods (Hwang 1993).

A journalist's view of North Korea

In December 1994, Lee Chan-sam, managing editor of the *Joongang Daily News* and a US citizen originally from Seoul, used a forged Chinese passport to visit North Korea. Hiring a Chinese woman to act as his wife in order to attract less attention, he visited both Pyongyang and outlying areas. Lee described the North Korean situation as "beyond description." He found residents hungry and unable to afford even 2 meals a day. The children were small and malnourished, with bloated stomachs and skinny arms and legs. Many people lacked shoes, having wrapped their feet with pieces of old cloth. Travelers often carried their own food supplies, with sacks of corn, grain, acorns, and other goods kept close at all times to avoid theft. Government permits were needed to travel out of their city or county. People told Lee that the elderly and children were falling down from starvation nearly everywhere. Recent defectors from the North have also said that conditions border on famine, with food distribution stopped altogether in many regions (Thurber 1995).

Advertising

The remainder of our discussion of the macromarketing mix will deal only with South Korea. The basic media for advertising in the South are, in order of importance, newspapers, TV, radio, magazines, and movies. Total advertising expenditures in 1992 were 2868 billion won (1.3% of the GNP). Newspapers' share was 44%, and TV 28%, with magazines and radio having 5% each. Advertising expenditures vary by industry, with TV being the dominant medium for advertising food and beverages, drugs, clothing, and cosmetics and detergents; services, entertainment, and electronics spend more on newspaper advertising (Han & Chang 1994).

Among the more than 100 advertising agencies approved by the Korea Broadcasting Advertising Corporation (KOBACO), over 30 agencies are in-house (affiliates of local business conglomerates or parent companies), and half of the top 30 agencies in terms of billing amount are in-house agencies of the *chaebols*. Over 20 agencies have foreign-investment or technical co-operation, and 6 of these are locally established multinational agencies in joint-venture arrangements. The broadcasting of advertising is wholly controlled by the KOBACO, which designates official broadcasting advertising agencies every year and pays agency commissions, which it determines. For

1992, 95 agencies were selected as official KOBACO agencies, including 14 newcomers (International Strategies Inc. 1994).

The Korea Newspaper Advertising Association approves official advertising agencies for newspapers every year. As of December 31 1991, the number of designated agencies was 46. About 60 newspapers and 2200 magazines are available in the local market. Han and Shavitt (1994) performed a content analysis of two magazines in Korea (*Wolgan Chosun* and *Yosong Donga*) and comparable US magazines (*Newsweek* and *Redbook*). The US advertisements were rated significantly higher in terms of individualism, while the Korean advertisements were rated higher in collectivism. In an experiment, US subjects were more persuaded when the advertisements presented individualistic rather than collectivistic appeals, whereas Koreans were more persuaded overall when the advertisements presented collectivistic rather than individualistic appeals. However, Wilcox et al. (1995) failed to replicate this finding.

Keown, Jacobs, and Ghymn (1993) performed a systematic content analysis of Korean, US, Japanese, and Chinese mass-media advertising. Korean television advertising was more likely to promote non-durables than was the advertising for the other countries. Korean radio advertising was also more likely to promote non-durables than was US or Chinese radio advertising, but advertising levels were very similar to those employed by the Japanese. Korean newspaper advertising was more than twice as likely as newspaper advertising in the other countries to promote consumer services.

Both Japanese and Korean television advertisements were about 20 seconds long, compared to 30-second advertisements in the USA; Chinese advertisements ranged between 20 and 60 seconds. The nature of Korean television advertisements differed from that for the other 3 countries; Korean advertisements informed the viewer of attributes and functions, whereas the advertisements in the other countries informed of the existence of the product, and its attributes. Like Japanese television advertisements, demonstration formats were very common in Korean television advertisements. Testimonials were used less frequently in Korean television advertisements than in Japanese and US advertisements.

Nearly all Korean television advertisements showed or named the product, and the logo was shown in 84% of advertisements. Voice-overs were used in most advertisements, with the voice being male in two-thirds of cases. The product was more likely to be shown in Korean advertisements (97% of the time) than in the other 3 countries, and the product was shown in use in 50% of cases. People were used in commercials 60% of the time, with either only males in the advertisements or a mixture of males and females (female-alone presentations occurred only 7% of the time). Price was mentioned more (63% of the time), but slogans were used less often than in Japanese and US television advertisements. Korean advertising had about half the informational cues of US commercials (Keown, Jacobs, & Ghymn 1993).

Context in advertising

Gudykunst, Yoon and Nishida (1987), Hall (1976), and Kim (1985) indicate that Korean language and communication is "high context," meaning that indirect and ambiguous messages tend to be utilized. Taylor, Wilson, and Miracle (1995) found that low-context brand-differentiating messages were present in only about 3% of the commercials coded. They found that Korean students liked brand-differentiating messages as well as more high-context messages, but it may be that the students concerned were attracted by the novelty of the approach.

Use of humor

Alden, Hoyer, and Lee (1993) found that Korean television advertisements had a lower percentage of humor (57%) than did those from Germany (92%), Thailand (82%), and the USA (69%)—humor was defined as incongruent contrasts. The two nations high on Hofstede's collectivism dimension (Korea and Thailand) had a substantial number of humorous advertisements with 3 or more central characters, whereas the 2 that were low context (the USA and Germany) had substantially fewer advertisements with 3 or more characters. Further, the cultures high on power distance (Korea and Thailand) had more advertisements with characters of unequal status than countries low on this dimension (Germany and the USA).

Distribution

Retail distribution in South Korea is complicated, as the majority of outlets are small one-family stores, stalls in markets, or street vendors. However, there are many middle-sized department stores in Seoul and Pusan, and the chain-store and supermarket concept is developing rapidly. There are approximately 12 000 supermarkets throughout the country, including 2400 in Seoul; however, none of the supermarkets is truly large by common US standards. Foreign participation is prohibited in 7 service sectors, including the retailing of tobacco, antiques, arts, and publicly-consumed alcoholic beverages (International Strategies, Inc. 1994). Wholesalers tend to dominate the distribution channels, and often dictate terms to manufacturers. It is common for the wholesaler to obtain considerably longer credit terms from the manufacturer than are extended to the retailer, and this sometimes allows the wholesaler to earn substantial interest on the difference (International Strategies, Inc. 1994). The distribution industry represents 14.4% of South Korea's GNP, and 27.8% of employment as of December 1992. However, the industry is still in its infancy, as it has been regarded as a non-productive industry for a long time. Actually, 91% of retail businesses employ fewer than 2 persons, and 78% of the businesses operated have a floor-space smaller than 10 pyong (about 33 m^2) (International Strategies Inc. 1994).

Table 9.7 Size of distribution entities in South Korea

Entity	*No. with 2 employees or fewer*	*Sales revenue per store*
Retail	91%	US $74 000
Wholesale	32%	US $668 300

Source: International Strategies, Inc. (1994), "Republic of Korea", Export Hotline, Boston, MA.

The dominant retail type in the South is the department store, with total sales 5 times greater than the amount for convenience stores, and almost 100 times greater than the amount for supermarkets. Of department store sales, 45% is from clothing, 19% from food and beverage, and 8% from electronics (*Korea Chamber Weekly* 1994).

New types of businesses, such as discount stores, general-merchandise stores or hypermarkets, are being introduced. For example, Price Club and other foreign discount stores have opened recently in Seoul (Nakarmi 1995b). However, expensive land prices and the unique environment of the local distribution industry may be negative factors for foreign companies planning to start any large-scale operations in Korea. The Korean government deregulated restrictions on land acquisition in July 1993. In terms of construction, the restrictions on the construction of sales facilities which are larger than 40 000 m^2 were removed in the first part of 1994 under the "Metropolitan Area Maintenance Plan Law" (International Strategies Inc. 1994).

Liberalization of investment in wholesale/retail business may prevent further trade distortions caused by the distribution network. Some major Korean department stores are linked to *chaebols,* which are often also manufacturers of consumer goods carried in the stores. Consequently, these stores are interested primarily in selling imported goods that complement their own product lines. Other manufacturers have set up franchised distributors. There are almost no mid-sized independent retailers in South Korea (International Strategies Inc. 1994).

Changing trends

Intellectual property protection

One of the most serious problems for US business in South Korea has been the protection of intellectual property rights (IPR). In 1992, South Korea was placed on the priority watchlist for its lax protection of intellectual property, and enforcement still remains a problem in several important areas, including copyright, three-dimensional characters, and the confidentiality of required government documentation. The US government has pressured the Korean government to recognize the need for better protection of intellectual property and, as a result, several taskforces have been formed to root out the piracy of software and trademarks, and other IPR infringements (International Strategies, Inc. 1994).

Changing technology

One of the South's assets for building future growth is its engineering population. As the Korea Institute for Industrial Economics & Trade (KIET) points out, there are almost 80 engineers per 100 000 Koreans, compared to 72 in Japan and 41 in the USA (*Business Week* 1994b). Signs of technological progress are common. Huge machines are eating through the hills south of Seoul to make way for a track that will carry Europe's famous *trains à grande vitesse*. The trains will link Seoul with Pusan, 450 km south, at a projected cost of US$13.4 billion. Additional new technology in the works include a US$5 billion new Seoul airport at Inchon, 30 new power plants, including several nuclear ones (total investment of US$50 billion), and a US$1.2 billion mobile telecommunications network (Holstein 1994).

Some of the rush to new technology is confronting Koreans with cultural problems. Cable television has come to Seoul, providing access to movies, sports, home shopping, and news 24 hours a day. Satellite dishes are also becoming common, bringing Japan's NHK and Hong Kong's STAR-TV into homes. The government is attempting to limit culture shock by requiring that cable channels have at least 70% domestically-produced programming while sports and documentary channels have a 50% quota (*Lincoln Journal Star* 1995).

Consumer issues

Our discussion of consumer issues tends to focus on differences rather than similarities. To some extent, there is value in this approach as it may reduce tendencies on the part of Western marketers to be ethnocentric. However, similarities have been reported as well. Hafstrom, Chae, and Chung (1992) found that several consumer decision-making styles used by young US consumers are similar to those used by young Korean consumers. Lee and Green (1991) found that US and Korean students identified the same set of six salient attributes with regard to their purchase of sneakers: price, style, comfort, brand, durability, and color.

Information search

Whang and Min (1978) found that consumers in the market for refrigerators considered very few brands, visited few stores, and relied heavily on neighbors and family for information. On the surface, this would indicate lower levels of consumer search by Koreans. However, Olshavsky, Moore, and Lim (1988) note the role that structural forces play:

- only 4 brands of refrigerators are available in Seoul, and few brands are imported
- some types of in-store information (i.e. point-of-purchase materials and catalogs that systematically display the available brands, models, and product characteristics), available in the USA, are not available in Korea
- the average household size is far greater in Korea than in the USA
- exclusive dealership for refrigerators is more common in Korea, making the distance to stores greater
- there is little price variation across such dealerships
- there is far greater reliance on mass transportation and less family car ownership in Korea

Innovativeness

In a study of college-aged consumers in 5 countries (Korea, the USA, Senegal, India, and Thailand), Tansuhaj et al. (1991) found Koreans more willing to adopt new technological products, but less willing to adopt new media products, entertainment offerings, and fashion products. Similarly, Koreans indicated that they were less likely to buy new products, less likely to seek advice about new products, and less likely to give advice about new products. Characteristics offered as explanations for these findings were that, among the 5 cultures, Koreans have relatively high levels of fatalism, traditionalism, and religious commitment.

Gift giving

Koreans' strong motivation not to "lose face" is reflected in their consumption behavior. They exhibit a strong tendency to purchase a product whose price, brand, and package match their social position and reputation, in order not to lose face. For example, when giving gifts, Koreans usually purchase as gifts products that are expensive enough to match their income or the receiver's status, so that the gifts can maintain the face of the receiver, and that the giver does not lose face at the same time (Lee & Green 1991). Teachers receive gifts from children and parents, who feel indebted to them. The hierarchical gift-giving practices in Japan can also be found in Korea. In contrast, Americans tend to exchange gifts with only close family members and friends, and do not usually give gifts to their superiors (Green & Alden 1988).

Howe (1988) observes that Koreans usually entertain guests more lavishly than they can really afford, in order to save the host's face as well as the guest's. Gifts are usually not opened in the presence of the giver, and should always be wrapped, especially if the gift is money. Gifts are given only as a sign of good manners, nothing more, and require no more than spoken thanks. If one is bringing a real gift, something that has required some time and thought to buy, it is good manners to apologize for its insignificance, whatever its value. This is intended to relieve the recipient from feeling indebted. One of the most distinctive differences between US and Korean practices is that Koreans use cash gifts much more often. For example, it is conventional, in Korea, to give a cash gift for weddings and funerals. Also, it is common for Korean adults, when they visit the home of people with whom they have a very close relationship, to give some money to children or very old family members. The gesture is perceived as an expression of kindness and thoughtfulness. It is a Korean custom to give some money to children on New Year's Day, as children make a deep bow and the New Year's blessing words to their parents, and relatives and to other adults close to them (Howe 1988).

Social role

Lee and Green (1991), in a study of sneaker purchases, found that US and Korean respondents identified friends and family as two of the most influential referent individuals or groups in the purchase of sneakers. But the third influential referent for Koreans was the store salesperson, while it was the boyfriend or girlfriend for the US respondents. The social atmosphere in Korea discourages students from having extensive interaction with the opposite sex during the college period.

Lee and Green (1991) also found that social norms are more important than attitude in the determination of behavioral intentions for Koreans, while Americans use attitude as the primary determinant (as in the purchase of sneakers).

The future

Reunification

The overriding concern of all Koreans about the future is the reunification of the two Koreas. Reunification, whatever its timing and however it occurs, will come. Whether it comes with a bang or a whimper, it will change the country profoundly (Clifford 1994). As noted earlier, both the North and the South have made some conciliatory gestures. Lucky Goldstar has recently been asked to take over the North's largest steelworks, as North Korea needs the trade and investment. It already has an SEZ designed for foreigners, although, observers note, this is in the far north, well away from big centers of population.

The biggest obstacle to more trade and investment may be opinion in Seoul. Conservatives argue that the embargo is prudent; the North's malodorous regime should not be propped up by South Korean companies, and technology transferred to Pyongyang could be used to guide missiles more accurately onto Seoul (*Economist* 1994d). For its part, the North continues to rattle sabers. For example, on February 20 1995, its defense ministry announced that the North had produced and deployed along the border a new kind of tank and some new artillery, and that it was building submarines and high-speed hovercraft.

There is evidence that the South is still very tense. In 1994, after the death of Kim Il Sung, some southern students built altars to him. While most in the South saw this as harmless folly, the government incarcerated the altar builders (*Economist* 1995d).

However, the South has paid careful attention to the economic problems associated with the German reunification, and is apparently far less interested in driving the North's economy to ruin (Hwang 1993). In order to create the North's economic dependence on the South, there has been an effort to create a "Greater Korea" that also includes neighboring regions of China and Russia, where 3 million ethnic Koreans live. Already, signs in China's Shandong Peninsula, directly across the Yellow Sea from the Korean Peninsula, are written in Korean as the number of Korean companies there increases. This so-called "Nordpolitik strategy" is merging technology and capital from the South with the rich natural resources of North-East Asia. The inclusion of the North in the concept of Greater Korea is evidenced in such dealings as the plan to lay a gas pipeline from Yakutsk in eastern Russia to South Korea, through North Korea. Daewoo's Kim Woo Chung was able to persuade Russian President Boris Yeltsin, South Korean President Roh Tae Woo, and North Korea's leader Kim Il Sung to agree to the transaction (Nakarmi, Brady & Curry 1992). The dynamics of the two Koreas' relationship continues to be increasingly complex; in 1996, the North had to acknowledge the sending of spies via submarine to the South, and then saw one of its highest officials, Hwang Jang Yop, defect to the South via Beijing (*Economist* 1997).

Despite subtle preparation economically for reunification, there is recognition that the process in Korea is likely to be much more complex than it was in Germany. There were at least 4 West Germans to share the economic burden of each East German, but South Korean has only 2 people for every North Korean. A study conducted at Korea University puts the cost of moving the North's economy to the South's level at US$1.2 trillion, 4 times South Korea's GNP (Mallaby 1995). "The Germans argue that they will need at least a generation to alleviate the problem. Our situation is much, much worse than Germany's" (Dae-jung 1994, p. 91).

There is much economic incentive for reunification, as the two Koreas have always offered each other what is needed. Before the division of Korea, northern Korea had 75% of the heavy industry, while southern Korea had almost 75% of the light industry. Today, the specific problems faced by each state are "complementary"; that is, the states have the potential to be each other's best markets. For example, in trade, South Korea could probably become more efficient by importing North Korean fishing and mining products, while the

North could import capital and technology from the South. The North could probably become more efficient by reducing its agricultural population. Capitalist South Korea could do so by relocating some of its wasteful service population (Kim 1992).

As a unified nation, Korea would be the world's 12th most abundant country in labor force, and the world's 20th-wealthiest country in terms of size of the economy. The wasteful military defense burdens could be diverted to the construction of a powerful economy. As noted in the German unification, many North Koreans may face unemployment for the first time ever.

Korea's role in a global economy

Even if the reunification goes smoothly, Korea's adaptation to the global economy may create problems, given its Hermit Kingdom heritage still evident in both states. Whang (1991) discusses the arising conflict caused by Korea's need to preserve its national and cultural identity during the process of internationalizing the economy: the integration of the Korean economy into the rest of the world will likely cause an identity crisis for Korea, unless its unique national spirit is reflected consistently in both its internal societal management and its external relations.

Clifford (1994) asserts that Koreans will not easily dispense with their xenophobia and their sense of being a unique people. Ingrained nationalism and a rigid sense of hierarchy (a hypersensitivity to title, status, and educational background) are evident in both states. South Korea has been virtually alone among developing nations in its ability to chart a high-growth trajectory while strictly limiting foreign control of the economy. "But what was a point of national pride now threatens to shut Korea out of an increasingly integrated world economy" (p. 334).

There is evidence (Nakarmi 1995b) that the *chaebols* are restructuring in order to be more competitive in world markets. The Hyundai group is considering divesting; Samsung is trying to increase sales internationally to 30% of the total up from 20%, and Daewoo is concentrating on developing markets. President Kim Young Sam is pressing for changes in the ownership structure of the *chaebols*. The founding families own about 10% of the group's total capital, and control more than 40%. The government is making it harder for *chaebols* with more concentrated ownership to raise funds and to pursue new businesses (Nakarmi 1995b).

As Korea has opened itself to the world, it has paid a price in terms of facing change in traditions. For example, hosting the Olympic Games in 1988 has resulted in an increase in tourism ever since (Berry 1989). As a partial result of sponsoring the games, Visa-Card holdership has more than doubled in South Korea since the Games. The exposure helped Visa tack 4% onto an already commanding 57% share against its prime competitors (Berry 1989).

However, despite opposition to changes in culture, since early 1994 there have been many signs that Korea is proceeding with plans to bring its foreign-investment laws, trade codes, and capital markets in line with international standards of openness by 1998 (Engardio 1995). Another tangible sign is that Michael Jackson is no longer banned, as he was permitted to perform in Seoul in June, 1995.

At the root of present chaos in the housing market and in labor-management relations is the desire for a higher standard of living. Koreans want to spend more on cars, on houses, on telephones and washing machines, and all the other baubles their counterparts in Europe and America spend their time working for. This has been evident in the form of feverish crowds in department stores, and the clogging up of Seoul's roads with the new cars that middle-class people are beginning to be able to afford (*Economist* August 18, 1990). While consumer desires are being stifled in the South, this situation is still far superior to that being experienced in the North.

Conclusion

South Korean economic progress, which has been hailed as an "economic miracle," suffered a major setback in mid-1997 when the currency dropped by over 26%, the stockmarket also declined by 35.5%, and consumer prices rose by 4.2%. The current-account deficit for 1997 appears likely to exceed US$19 billion. This has been a major shock, as until that time South Korea was cited as an example of the unique Asian approach to economic development.

Modeling itself on Japan, South Korea has grown by an average of 9% since 1992, leading to an arrogance and lack of discipline that, accompanied by corruption and cronyism, were bound to lead to problems. The decline of exports has placed pressure on heavily indebted companies. This, as well as a flight of foreign capital, has led to the collapse of a number of major corporations, including the Hanbo Steel Company. As a result, the South Korean government has been forced to appeal to the IMF and the international community for help. While this help appears to be forthcoming, it will have strings attached, and the government will have to implement economic restructuring policies. The future in the short term is therefore clouded with uncertainty, and, while difficult times are ahead for Korean consumers and marketers, they will not easily accept a reversal of the progressive trends that the country's economic achievements have set in motion.

References

Ahn, Shin-Ho, Lee, Seung-Hye & Kwon, Oh-Seek (1994), "The Structure of Emotion: Analyses of Korean Affect Terms", *Korean Social Science Journal*, vol. 20, pp. 7–27.

Alden, Dana L., Hoyer, Wayne D. & Lee, Chol (1993), "Identifying Global and Culture-Specific Dimensions of Humor in Advertising: A Multinational Analysis", *Journal of Marketing,* vol. 57, April, pp. 64–75.

Alston, Jon P. (1989), "'Wa,' 'Ganxi,' and 'Inhwa': Managerial Principles in Japan, China, and Korea", *Business Horizons,* vol. 32, pp. 26–31.

Asian Business (1992), "South Korea: Statistics", vol. 28, June, pp. 43–4.

Asian Wall Street Journal (1995), October 28, p. 5.

Berry, Jon (1989), "Asia Minors", *Adweek's Marketing Week,* July 17, pp. 32–40.

Bracken, Paul (1995), "Risks and Promises in the Two Koreas", *A Journal of World Affairs,* vol. 39, no. 1, pp. 55–64.

Breen, Mike (1990), "Pyongyang Opens the Door a Crack", *Asian Business,* vol. 24, June, pp. 44–6.

Bridges, Brian (1995), "North Korean after Kim Il-Sung", *World Today,* vol. 51, June, pp. 103–7.

Business Week (1994a), "Korea's Export Boom Is Hurting—and Helping—Japan", August 8, p. 6.

— (1994b), "South Korea: The New Titan of Technology", Advertising Supplement, November 28.

Chang, Chan Sup (1988), "*Chaebol:* The South Korean Conglomerates", *Business Horizons,* March–April, pp. 51–7.

Choe, Sang T. & Pitman, Glenn A. (1993), "Conducting Business with Koreans", *Marketing Intelligence & Planning,* vol. 11, no. 2, pp. 44–6.

Choi, Toon Hong (1993), "KOTRA's Role in High-Tech Age", *Trade & Culture,* Fall, pp. 44–5.

Chung, Joseph S. (1986), "Foreign Trade of North Korea: Performance, Policy, and Prospects", in eds Robert A. Scalapino & Hongkoo Lee, *North Korea in a Regional and Global Context,* Center for Korean Studies, Berkeley, CA, pp. 78–114.

Clifford, Mark L. (1994), *Troubled Tiger: Businessmen, Bureaucrats, and Generals in South Korea,* M.E. Sharpe, Armonk, NY.

Crane, Paul S. (1978), *Korean Patterns,* The Royal Asiatic Society, Korea Branch, by Kwangjin Publishing Co., Seoul.

Dae-jung, Kim (1994), "The Impact of the US–North Korean Agreement on Korean Reunification", *Korean Journal of Defense Analysis,* vol. 6, Winter, pp. 85–100.

Dubinsky, Alan J., Jolson, Marvin A., Kotabe, Masaaki & Lim, Chae Un (1991), "A Cross-National Investigation of Industrial Salespeople's Ethical Perceptions", *Journal of International Business Studies,* vol. 22, pp. 651–70.

Economist, the (1990a), "When Democracy Hits the Purse", March 10, p. 36.

— (1990b), "Two Paths to Prosperity", July 14, pp. 19–20, 22.

— (1990c), "A Survey of South Korea", August 18, pp. 1–20.

— (1990d), "The Last Communist Recluse Puts His Nose Out of Doors", September 29, pp. 35–6.

— (1992), "Korea's Virtuous Trade", July 11, p. 69.

— (1994a) "The Koreas: Up to a Point", August 20, p. 32.

— (1994b), "The Battle of the Belly Button", September 24, p. 39.

— (1994c) "Shop till You Drop", October 15, p. 44.

— (1994d) "Cousins Less Removed", October 22, pp. 38–9.

— (1994e), "Seoul's Big Splash", November 5, pp. 63–4.

— (1994f), "Into the Hermit Kingdom", November 12, p. 81.

— (1994g), "Blessed Are the Rich", December 10, p. 35.

— (1995a), "Down with Youth", January 14, p. 35.

— (1995b), "North Korea Takes the Money", January 14, p. 36.

— (1995c), "Confucianism: New Fashion for Old Wisdom", January 21, pp. 38–9.

— (1995d) "Infection from the North", February 25, p. 34.

— (1996), "The Vanishing of Chinatown", August 3, p. 34.

— (1997a), "The Trouble with South Korea", January 18, pp. 35–7.

— (1997b), "Korea's Twin Crises", February 22, pp. 42, 45.

— (1997c), "A Fatal Resolve not to Budge", November 22, pp. 83–4, 87.

Eisenstodt, Gale (1990), "Hold the Applause", *Forbes*, October 1, pp. 182–3.

Engardio, Pete (1995), "Can Korea Pull the Thorn from Its Foot?", *Business Week*, January 16, p. 15.

Gluckman, Ron (1991), "Profit versus Paranoia", *Asian Business*, vol. 27, November, pp. 23–4.

Green, Robert T. & Alden, Dana L. (1988), "Functional Equivalence in Cross-Cultural Consumer Behavior: Gift Giving in Japan and the United States", *Psychology and Marketing*, vol. 5, no. 2, pp. 155–68.

Gudykunst, William B., Yoon, Young-Chul & Nishida, Tsukasa (1987), "The Influence of Individualism/Collectivism on Perceptions of Ingroup and Outgroup Relationships", *Communication Monographs*, vol. 54, September, pp. 295–306.

Hafstrom, Jeanne L., Chae, Jung Sook & Chung, Young Sook (1992), "Consumer Decision-Making Styles: Comparison between United States and Korean Young Consumers", *The Journal of Consumer Affairs*, vol. 26, no. 1, pp. 146–58.

Hall, Edward T. (1976), *Beyond Culture*, Anchor Press/Doubleday, Garden City, NY.

Halladay, Jon (1989), "The Economies of North and South Korea", in eds John Sullivan & Robert Foss, *Two Koreas—One Future?*, University Press of America, Lanham, MD.

Han, Min Hee & Chang, Dae Ryun (1994), *Advertising Management*, Hak Hyun Sa, Seoul.

Han, Sang-Pil & Shavitt, Sharon (1994), "Persuasion and Culture: Advertising Appeals in Individualistic and Collectivistic Societies", *Journal of Experimental Social Psychology*, vol. 30, pp. 326–50.

Hoare, James & Pares, Susan (1988), *Korea: An Introduction*, Kegan Paul International, London.

Hoecklin, Lisa (1995), *Managing Cultural Differences: Strategies for Competitive Advantage*, Addison-Wesley Publishing Company, Wokingham, England.

Hofstede, Geert (1984), *Culture's Consequences: International Differences in Work-Related Values*, Sage Publications, Beverly Hills, CA.

Holstein, William J. (1994), "Building the New Asia", *Business Week*, November 28, pp. 62–8.

Holstein, William J. & Nakarmi, Laxmi (1995), "Korea", *Business Week*, July 31, pp. 56–63.

Hong, Yoo-soo (1993), "Korea's Economic Prospects: The Next Five Years", *Korea's Economy*, pp. 7–8.

Howe, Russell Warren (1988), *The Koreans: Passion and Grace*, Harcourt Brace Jovanovich, New York.

Hupp, Susan C., Lam, Shui Fong & Jaeger, Janice (1992), "Differences in Exploration of Toys by One-Year-Old Children: A Korean and American Comparison", *Behavior Science Research*, vol. 26, nos 1–4, pp. 123–35.

Hwang, Eui-Gak (1993), *The Korean Economies: A Comparison of North & South*, Clarendon Press, Oxford.

Hyde, Georgie D.M. (1988), *South Korea: Education, Culture and Economy*, New York: Macmillan Press.

International Strategies, Inc. (1994), "Republic of Korea", Export Hotline, Boston, MA.

Jacobs, Laurence, Keown, Charles, Worthley, Reginald, & Ghymn, Kyung-Il (1991), "Cross-Cultural Color Comparisons: Global Marketers Beware!", *International Marketing Review*, vol. 8, no. 3, pp. 21–30.

Keown, Charles F., Jacobs, Laurence W., & Ghymn, Kyung-Il (1993), "Content Analysis of Major Mass Media Advertising in the United States, Japan, South Korea and China", *Asian Journal of Marketing,* December, pp. 31-43.

Kim, Byoung-Lo Philo (1992), *Two Koreas in Development,* Transaction Publishers, New Brunswick, NJ.

Kim, C.I. Eugene (1986), "In the Shadow of Chuch'e: North Korea's Relations with Japan", in eds Robert A. Scalapino & Hongkoo Lee, *North Korea in a Regional and Global Context,* Center for Korean Studies, Berkeley, CA, pp. 263–83.

Kim, E.H. (1985), *Korea: Beyond the Hills,* Seoul and Samwha Printing Co., Seoul.

Kim, Ki-hong (1975), "Cross-Cultural Differences between Americans and Koreans in Nonverbal Communication", East-West Culture, Vol. 8, Kye-Myung University: East-West Culture Institute, pp. 39–53.

Korea Chamber Weekly (1994), July 25.

Korea Business World (1994), "An Improving Environment", August, pp. 18–20.

Korean Statistical Office (1992), December.

Kraft, Frederic B. & Chung, Kae H. (1992), "Korean Importer Perceptions of US and Japanese Industrial Goods Exporters", *International Marketing Review,* vol. 9, no. 2, pp. 59–73.

Kuznets, Paul W. (1994), *Korean Economic Development: An Interpretive Model,* Praeger, Westport, CT.

Lee, Catherine Keumhyun (1996), "Unfinished Business: Kim Sends the Chaebol a Message", *Business Week,* September 9, pp. 56–7.

Lee, Chan-sam (1995), "Ohk-Wha Comrede, Don't Wait for Me", *Sung Ang Daily Newspaper,* January 10, p. 1.

Lee, Chol & Green, Robert T. (1991), "Cross-Cultural Examination of the Fishbein Behavioral Intentions Model", *Journal of International Business Studies,* September, pp. 289–305.

Lee, Hak Chong (1989), "Managerial Characteristics of Korea Firms", in eds K.H. Chung & H.C. Lee, *Korean Managerial Dynamics,* Praeger, New York, pp. 147–62.

Lee, Kyu Tae (1983), *Patterns of Korean Way of Thinking,* Shinwon Publishing, Seoul.

Lim, Chae Un, Kotabe, Masaaki & Dubinsky, Alan J. (1991), "Relationship Between Self-Monitoring and Salesperson Performance: A Cross-Cultural Investigation", *Proceedings of the Society for Consumer Psychology,* pp. 116–17.

Lincoln Journal Star (1994), "South Koreans Hedge Their Bets on the Occult", November 18, p. 20.

— (1995), "Cable TV Wires in S. Korea", March 2, p. 5.

Mallaby, Sebastian (1995), "The House That Park Built: A Survey of South Korea", *The Economist*, June 3, pp. 1–18.

Merrill, John (1989), "North Korea's Halting Efforts at Economic Reform", Paper presented to the Fourth Conference on North Korea, Seoul, August.

Nakarmi, Laxmi (1991), "Korea Throws Open Its Doors", *Business Week*, July 29, p. 46.

— (1992), "A *Chaebol* Plays Hardball and Roh Wae Too", *Business Week*, February 24, p. 50.

— (1995a), "A Coke with Kimchi?", *Business Week*, February 6, p. 4.

— (1995b), "A Flying Leap toward the 21st Century?", *Business Week*, March 20, pp. 78–80.

Nakarmi, Laxmi, Brady, Rose & Curry, Lynne (1992), "Can Korea Unite and Conquer?", *Business Week*, November 16, pp. 52–4.

"North Korean Scriptwriter Defects" (1995), Associated Press, January 6.

North Korea Research Institute (1993), *Handbook of North Korea: 1983–1993*, Pyongyang.

Olshavsky, Richard W., Moore, David J. & Lim, Jeen-Su (1988), "An Information Processing Interpretation of Cross-National Consumer Characteristics", *Journal of Global Marketing*, vol. 1, Summer, pp. 25–40.

Pae, Sung Moon (1992), *Korea Leading Developing Nations: Economy, Democracy, and Welfare*, University Press of America, Lanham.

Park, Untae (1994), *Korea's Economic Development*, Kyung Yeon Publishing Inc., Seoul.

Shin Dong-A (1995), *Kim Jung Il and North Korean Encyclopedia*, Dong-A Il Bo, Seoul, January.

Shin, Jung Hyun (1986), "North Korea's Relations with Japan: The Possibilities for Bilateral Reconciliation", in Robert A. Scalapino & Hongkoo Lee (Eds.), *North Korea in a Regional and Global Context*, Center for Korean Studies, Berkeley, CA, pp. 240–62.

Statistical Footprints of Korea (1992), Bureau of Statistics, Seoul.

Sung, Cho (1992), "The Advertising Services Market in Korea", paper prepared for American Embassy, Seoul.

Tansuhaj, Patriya, Gentry, James W., Joby, John, Manzer, L. Lee & Cho, Bong Jin (1991), "A Cross-national Examination of Innovation Resistance", *International Marketing Review*, vol. 8, no. 3, pp. 7–20.

Taylor, Charles R. & Omura, Glenn S. (1995), "Analyzing Economic Development in the Republic of Korea: An Evaluation of Alternative Paradigms of Marketing and Economic Development, Part II", *Journal of Macromarketing*, 15, Fall, pp. 66–90.

Taylor, Charles R., Wilson, R. Dale & Miracle, Gordon E. (1995), "The Impact of Brand Differentiating Messages on Effectiveness in Korean Advertising", *Journal of International Marketing,* vol. 3, no. 1.

Templeman, John & Nakarmi, Laxmi (1994), "For Korea, A Taste of Its Won Medicine", *Business Week,* April 4, p. 6.

Thurber, David (1995), "Disguised Reporter Travels North Korea", *Lincoln Journal Star,* January 17, p. 3.

West, Philip (1989), "Cross-Cultural Literacy and the Pacific Rim", *Business Horizons,* vol. 32, pp. 3–17.

Whang, Eui R. & Buyng, M. Min (1978), "A Study of Brand Choice Behavior", *Research Bulletin,* Korean Institute for Research in the Behavioral Sciences, March, p. 11.

Whang, In Joung (1991), "The Korean Economy Toward the Year 2000", in eds Gerald E. Caiden & Bun Woong Kim, *A Dragon's Progress: Development Administration in Korea,* Kumarian Press, West Hartford, CT.

Yoo, Sangjin & Lee, Sang M. (1987). "Management Style and Practice of Korean Chaebols", *California Management Review,* vol. 29, Summer, pp. 95–110.

Yoon, Suk Bum (1986), "Macroeconomic Interaction between Domestic and Foreign Sectors in the North Korean Economy: A Schematic Interpretation", in eds Robert A. Scalapino & Hongkoo Lee, *North Korea in a Regional and Global Context,* Center for Korean Studies, Berkeley, CA, pp. 55–77.

Notes

1 The authors wish to thank Ju Young Park for his comments on an earlier draft of this chapter.

CHAPTER 10

Laos

From Marx to market–marketing and consumer behavior in the heart of the golden quadrangle[1]

WILLIAM J. ARDREY IV, CLIFFORD J. SHULTZ, II &
PHONESAVANH CHANTHAVILAY

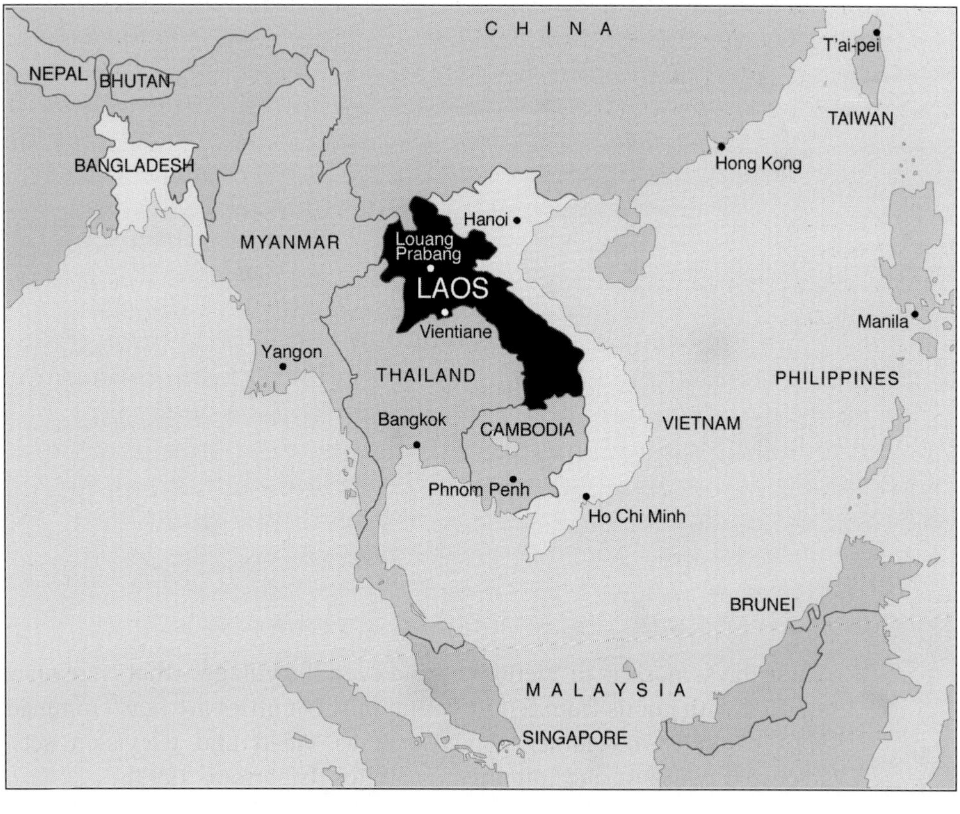

Abstract

Laos, one of the least developed countries in South-East Asia, is struggling to catch up with both the high-growth economies of Asia, and its reforming socialist neighbors. The Laotian economy in 1998 is similar to Vietnam's 5 years ago, and China's economy a decade ago. The transformation was initiated by rural reform, and followed by a gradual opening to foreign investment and goods, and the development of a basic service economy. Growing incomes and reduced state controls over the economy and private life, and Laos' strategic position at the heart of the Golden Quadrangle, are determining a new marketing environment. The transformation has important implications for consumers and companies interested in establishing businesses in or penetrating the Laotian market. In this chapter, the authors discuss the changing political, social and economic environment, and the impact these changes have and will continue to have on consumers and marketers.

> These days, markets in Vientiane—and even the villages—that were once stocked with goods from fellow communist countries are now crammed with capitalist consumer goods such as video and television sets, imported whiskey, and imported cigarettes (Ismartono 1993).

Introduction

Laos, officially the Lao People's Democratic Republic (LPDR), is a landlocked and least-developed country (LDC). It has been a late but steady participant in the market-reform process initiated in 1986. Official per-capita income remains among the world's lowest, and Laos has not developed extensive trading links with the more developed nations. Indeed, basic economic indicators suggest Laos is one of the region's development laggards, but legal and market reforms have progressed steadily. The regulatory environment has been stable, without the constantly changing regulations and other pitfalls faced by companies doing business in neighboring socialist market economies such as Vietnam. The net result is that firms are beginning to have modest successes in the Laotian market.

Laotian consumers are still primarily focused on obtaining basic necessities. Poverty, underdevelopment and inadequate infrastructure have made it difficult for much of the population to benefit fully from the process of the market economy. Its integration into the world economy, as well as its own consumer revolution, continue to lag behind those for other South-East Asian nations. Trends in consumer behavior starting to appear today are:

- gradual economic prosperity
- a move away from dependence on government for salaries and goods, which is stimulating a small but growing middle class
- market segmentation
- the evolution of a subsistence economic culture into a developing consumer culture

To elucidate the marketing, development, and consumer trends, this chapter addresses the effects of political and economic reforms on consumption patterns of the 3 main consumer cultures of Laos. These are the peasant culture, the upland tribal culture, and the more sophisticated trading and urban[2] cultures. There is, in the cities, a newly wealthy class of Laotian international traders, involved in the trading and marketing of consumer goods throughout South-East Asia. Part of this focus includes a general examination of the effects of the New Economic Mechanism (NEM) reforms and the special role landlocked Laos plays in distribution throughout the Greater Mekong Sub-Region and the Golden Quadrangle. The intent, therefore, is to expand the literature on marketing in South-East Asia by illuminating marketing trends and resultant consumption patterns in one of South-East Asia's most provincial transforming socialist nations.

The economic environment

Similarly to other socialist countries transforming from Marx to market, Laos has undertaken major economic reforms, commencing with the NEM, which was introduced in 1986. The NEM represented a radical shift in economic policy by the government, led by the Lao People's Revolutionary Party. Implementation of the NEM resulted in the transition from central planning to decentralized economic decision making, the removal of price controls and subsidies, and a drive to improve the country's dismal economic performance.

Initial basic reforms were followed by a push to reduce inflation, establish a modern foreign investment code by 1988, permit foreign ownership of enterprises in Laos, and reform banking by 1989. A more serious drive–to promote export growth, privatize state industries, build import-substituting industries, and attract foreign investment–began in 1990, and continues today. Total foreign investment in Laos has reached US$7.5 billion since 1989, and cuts in corporate taxes (from 45% to 20%), tax holidays, and other incentives (especially in hydropower and mining) are being used to attract further investment (Clifford Chance 1997).

Recent socio-economic indicators are provided in Tables 10.1 and 10.2. These statistics indicate that, despite economic reforms, Laos remains one of the world's poorest countries. Nevertheless, a 6.5% per-annum growth rate is promising, and Laos's geographic location and natural resources make it an attractive market as well as an important conduit to other markets in the region. At the present time, the government of Laos is working actively to carry out, under market mechanisms, a development strategy to improve the Laotian economy by the year 2000. This development strategy has 8 priority programs:

1 food production
2 the elimination of slash-and-burn agriculture
3 commodity production
4 infrastructure development
5 rural development
6 wider economic co-operation
7 human resource development
8 the building of a services sector

The emergence of modern Laos

Laos is considered to be one of the most enigmatic countries in Asia. Mountainous, landlocked, with a large area-to-population ratio, ethnically mixed, gripped by monsoons for long periods, and one of the most heavily bombed countries in history, it has been divided and conquered numerous times over the centuries.

The Lao people have had to struggle for independence since the 18th century, because Laos was administered by outside powers until after the Second World War. The most recent power to dominate Laos, France, withdrew from

Table 10.1 Overview of socio-economic indicators 1992–1994

Year	*1992*	*1993*	*1994*
Real GDP growth	7.0	5.9	8.1
Inflation rate	9.9	6.3	6.0
Foreign investment			
Approved (in US$ million)	130.1	1 537.7	2 597.4
International reserves (in US$ million)	81.2	150.9	159
Per-capita GDP (US$)	250	290	335

Source: Laos United Nations Mission (1995), "Basic Data and Economic Indicators", Permanent Mission of LPDR to the United Nations and Vientiane, the Statistical Center of the Lao PDR, New York; Clifford Chance (1997), *Asian Financial Services Newsletter*, vol. 1, Clifford Chance, London.

Table 10.2 Other social-welfare statistics

Item	*Statistic*
Per-capita income	US$232
Literacy rate	83%
Calorie intake	2 630
Infant mortality	91/1000
Crude birth rate	41.6/1000
Population growth	2.4%
Population density (per person, per km^2)	18.4
Population density, Vientiane Municipality	12.5
Labor force as % of total population	71%

Source: Laos United Nations Mission (1996), "Basic Data and Economic Indicators", Permanent Mission of LPDR to the United Nations and Vientiane, the Statistical Center of the Lao PDR, New York.

Laos in 1953, but left the country with many political and economic challenges to overcome. By 1975, national liberation was completed. A Congress of People's Representatives met in Vientiane, accepted the abdication of the king, and proclaimed the Lao People's Democratic Republic. In the years after 1975, the government introduced a centrally planned economic system, but faced many economic difficulties. Western aid and assistance ceased, the value of the kip (the national currency) plummeted, and contact with the international economy was minimal. An estimated 10% of the population, including the educated and technically trained specialists, left the country.

In the international arena, the Lao Government will continue to apply its consistent policy of peace, friendship and co-operation with all countries. The government created a special department in the Foreign Affairs Ministry to assist in meeting ASEAN criteria (Lengsavad 1995). This involves improving English proficiency within Laos, and encouraging other friendly countries and international organizations to provide assistance for these efforts.

In the late 1980s, and coinciding with the disintegration of the former Soviet Union, the political system changed to one of "softened authoritarianism" (Ljunggren 1992, p. 11). Reforms to bring about a market economy followed. At the same time, Laos began diplomatic efforts to improve relations with its neighbors. These efforts resulted in exchanges of senior diplomatic visits, and the signing of "Treaties of Friendship and Co-operation" with Thailand (1991), Cambodia (1992), China (1994), Myanmar (1994), and stronger ties with Vietnam (a similar treaty was signed with Vietnam back in 1977). In the case of Thailand, the treaty in 1991 resulted in diplomatic exchanges, including the visit of the Thai crown prince in 1992 and the Thai king in April 1994 to open the Australian-financed "Friendship Bridge" (*Bangkok Post* 1994).

Improving external political relations has become important to Laos in the late 1990s. Before joining ASEAN in 1997, Laos used its "observer" status in the organization to improve ties with member states, and saw the benefits of strong bonds with ASEAN as the organization came to represent a growing share of the world's economic wealth. With full ASEAN membership, Laos committed itself to the organization's goals of creating a relatively free trading area by 2003, reducing customs taxes, and participating in regional economic and political forums. Relations with Singapore, Malaysia and other regional countries remain a priority. Laos is also seeking, independently and through ASEAN, additional foreign investment, co-operative economic integration, and better political relations with South Asian countries and Western nations (Kittikhoun 1996; Tilleke & Gibbins 1997).

Laos has used its diplomatic initiatives effectively to increase trading links in the region. The recent opening of the "Friendship Bridge" between Laos and Thailand is one such illustration. Warming relations with China, and greater involvement in commercial and developmental activities during the same year, are other illustrations. And, since Laos continues to import most of its consumer goods from abroad, this co-operative trend has resulted in more goods coming into Laos, and more opportunities to export agricultural and simple manufactured goods.

Laos, through the NEM, has followed China's and then Vietnam's lead to develop market socialism, a market economy under the aegis of single-party authoritarian rule (cf. Shultz 1994). Laos' interpretation of market socialism has led to product and retail proliferation, and a rapid increase in the choices available to consumers. Where only a few years ago the population struggled to overcome economic difficulties, Laos is transforming both socially and economically, and new classes of consumers are emerging. The needs and wants of these consumers and private business are beginning to encourage government policies to move toward more rapid reforms. The present situation suggests government authorities have realized that, in order to keep their central position in the reform process and to lead the country into the next millennium, they need to improve policy co-ordination, continue economic reforms and—literally—deliver the goods.

Today, the Lao economy is expanding, and the government has sent clear signals that it is moving away from import-substitution policies and toward economic openness. The effects of reforms are being felt in many sectors, and the previously cited economic growth rate of almost 7% is testimony to this expansion. The current growth, as well as the development environment, have encouraged foreign investment in Laos by multinational corporations and medium-sized firms from, among others, Japan, Thailand, and Hong Kong.

The government has been satisfied with the economic reforms and the market mechanism in Laos. Since 1994, the National Assembly has improved the Law on the Promotion and Management of Foreign Investment in Laos. Laos enjoys "political and economic stability, and social order with an economic growth rate of 7%. These indicators give confidence to foreign and local business people, increasingly, to invest in Laos" (Lenosavad 1995). Like its neighbors in Vietnam and China, Laos has fought inflation and courted foreign investors, and continues to improve economic conditions in the country.

Income and employment

Wage rates have increased since the NEM was first implemented. However, the Laotian workforce has very little disposable income, and only low levels of domestic savings. This condition is partly explained by employment patterns: almost 80% of the workforce is engaged in agriculture, which contributes approximately 55% of GDP (Frontier Funds Management Company 1997).

Historically, the agricultural workforce has been underemployed, working only a few hours a day for months at a time, and unable to obtain the resources to build handicrafts or other tradeable non-agricultural items. Fortunately for Laos, traditional agricultural practices—based on slash-and-burn cultivation, barter and state-enforced collectivization—are responding to market forces; the country is becoming a money-based agricultural economy. The extension of the money economy, in turn, increases the demand for cash incomes from marketable crops (Asian Development Bank 1993, p. 3). The government has responded to the development of a modern, cash-based economy by licensing 11 banks (4 are state-owned, 5 are Thai-Lao joint ventures, and 2 are joint ventures with other foreign investors). Banks are regulated, but free to take deposits from, or lend to, state companies, private firms, or individuals. Commercial banks can issue bonds to raise capital, and current finance laws work to improve financial infrastructure and permit securities issuance (Frontier Funds Management Company 1997).

Cash, rather than barter or government-issued ration coupons, is increasingly the measure of income and mechanism for commercial exchange. Income trends for various sectors are presented in Table 10.3. Although most countries see the greatest real-income growth in manufacturing and urban development, the opposite will be the case in Laos for the near future. Agricultural production continues to increase at a rate of over 8.3% and accounts for over half of all production, with industrial growth increasing by 7.5%; agricultural growth will become less volatile with improved irrigation and government-sponsored crop diversification for export purposes (Frontier Funds Management Company 1997). Thus agriculture and agribusiness are fueling economic growth for the present, and participants in this boom will see their incomes rise (United Nations 1995). Conversely, state employees and collective agricultural workers will see little if any real wage growth. As part of economic reform, civil servants and employees of state-owned enterprises (SOEs) left after the recent drastic staff reductions have seen their wage increases capped at 1.7% (Asian Development Bank 1993, p. 3; Frontier Funds Management Company 1997, p. C-3). In real terms, many workers will see their incomes reduced in the near term as a result of government cutbacks, but workers in smaller factories, or joint ventures with Thai or other foreign partners, will see real wages rise.

Table 10.3 Income and wage rates

	Average monthly salaries (kip)					
Year	*1986*	*1987*	*1988*	*1989*	*1990*	*1991*
Productive sector	4 020	3 900	4 800	12 250	15 000	20 000
% increase	21.8	−2.9	2.30	155.0	22.4	33.0
Non-productive sector	3 022	2 917	3 375	9 546	13 911	15 019
% increase	65.3	−3.4	15.7	183.1	45.7	8.0
Education	3 100	2 900	3 510	10 200	14 801	15 043
Health	3 097	2 800	3 400	10 200	12 371	14 193
Administration	3 005	3 000	3 300	8 500	14 235	15 419
Other	2 555	2 680	2 860	8 300	14 235	15 419

Average wage increases 1991–1997 have been estimated at 5%.

Source: Asian Development Bank (1992), *LPDR: Economic Review and Bank Operations*, ADB, Manila, p. 54.

So, while official figures point to underdevelopment and low per-capita income, money is flowing into Laos for several reasons. First, Laos receives almost US$150 million annually in aid from many of the world's developed economies and international organizations. Second, and more importantly, direct foreign investment is rapidly increasing. Thailand, for example, invested almost US$300 million through official channels in 1995. Third, electricity and timber exports for hard currency are growing and trade, generally, is booming along the Thai border. Fourth, service industries are expanding in Vientiane and other major cities at an annual rate of over 15% (LPDR Foreign Investment Management Committee 1995, p. 14), with new hotels and tourist-based services paying increased wages. Fifth, this robust activity, coupled with Laos's geographic location, provides significant opportunities for Laos to serve as a "middleman" between Thailand, China, Vietnam and Myanmar, and, therefore, for Laotians to earn incomes through facilitative transportation activities.

As previously mentioned employment is declining in the state sector; staff reductions are affecting almost all areas of government, especially in Vientiane and other urban areas–most notably Luang Prabang. The private sector has been able to absorb many displaced urban workers, but often the worker's initial remuneration will be lower than his or her previous wages, and without benefits.

> As the number of civil servants has been reduced at the same time as SOEs have been slated for privatization and likely payroll cuts, urban dwellers have been left to find alternative employment. Many of them have done so by moving into the informal sector. It is reported informally that high proportions of women are among this group. But . . . these lower-income groups are self-employed or working in small establishments that do not provide non-wage benefits (Asian Development Bank 1993, p. 4).

Basic labor-force indicators are provided in Table 10.4, but employment trends and worker location/migration are perhaps more noteworthy. Approximately 16% of the population lives and works in cities (where, it is important to note, urban dwellers may continue to be involved in family farming near or in the cities). Average unemployment is approximately 17%, although towns on the Thai border–which have benefited most from growing trade–have far less unemployment and pay higher wages. Between 1986 and 1991, agricultural employment fell by over 30%, as both the younger generation and displaced agricultural workers looked to commerce and industry for employment. By 1995 the workforce was greater than 1.9 million. This was partly because there has been a constant increase in the labor force since 1990 (a rate of 3%) as a result of the migration of women workers from the rural areas into the city to work in the garment and textiles as well as the service industries (Frontier Funds Management Company 1997).

Although the economy is still agrarian, and responsible for initial growth measures and very modest personal wealth, implicit in these trends is greater population migration to more prosperous and urban centers (Xinhua 1991). Excess agricultural workers will, over time, migrate toward towns and cities, with hopes of finding jobs as vendors or unskilled laborers. However, because transportation in Laos is poor, and many villages are isolated and maintain traditional cultures that could discourage relocation, this migration will be gradual, and a large part of the populace will remain employed in the countryside. The pace of migration is also partly explained by the under-development of urban centers, which also have not grown sufficiently to cause rural dwellers to migrate. Moreover, until 1996, the government required citizens to receive permission to change residences (Kittikhoun 1996).

Table 10.4 Employment in various sectors in Laos

Year *Sector*	*1986* *Employees ('000)*	*1990* *Employees ('000)*
Agriculture	1 364.1	1 545.0
Industry	27.2	37.3
Construction	10.2	15.6
Transportation	10.2	15.6
Trade	39.2	48.9
Civil servants/public employees	254.1	293.4
Total	**1 705.0**	**1 955.8**

Source: LPDR (1995), "World Summit for Social Development, National Report", LPDR, Vientiane.

Significant staff reductions have taken effect in this sector during the period 1990–1995. Like the neighboring transition economies of China and Vietnam, Lao state industries are under pressure to become more efficient. Staff reductions were enacted in state industries and government industries during the period 1990–1995. City dwellers were, in many cases, able to secure other employment in private business, construction, or with joint-venture or foreign companies, because the Lao economy has continued to grow through 1997. Residents of the countryside who work for the state or for state companies have found it more difficult to replace or supplement state wages.

The Laotian economy is gradually entering the modern global economy. Non-farm employment has grown from less than 10% in 1985 to almost one-quarter of the workforce. Foreign direct investment, especially in the garment industry, has created over 10 000 new, and in some cases better-paying, jobs. Almost half of the new private-sector jobs will be in the services sector. And the services and garment-manufacturing sectors will be employing increasing numbers of Laotian women.

These income and employment trends have several implications for consumers and marketers. First, purchasing power will remain modest, but it will grow. The consumer culture sweeping through South-East Asia, while not yet entrenched in Laos, and lagging behind even Vietnam and Cambodia, is imminent. Second, firms that wish to establish production sites or that intend to employ Laotians in service enterprises will need to appreciate that, while one could expect to pay minimal wages for Laotian labor, one could also expect to encounter a shortage of skilled labor for some time. Indeed, employee training will be paramount, regardless of the non-agrarian commercial sector in which Laotians are employed.

Inflation

Inflation rose dramatically during the initial phase of economic reforms, climbing from 6% in 1986 to 76% in 1989. Tighter money supply and credit controls, new banking regulations and reserve requirements have strengthened the value of the kip, and reduced inflation to 10.4% in 1991, and 6% again in 1992. Annual inflation stabilized to below 10% between 1991 and 1995 (Kittikhoun 1996), and should remain below 10% in coming years.

Under the supervision of the IMF, Laos has tried to control central government spending, but still needs to borrow to keep the central government operable. Fiscal reforms have progressed, and efforts to fight inflation have focused at the state-enterprise and large-organization levels, with positive effects. Inflation performance improved markedly as the government realized the danger of loose monetary and fiscal policy controls (Keoboula 1995; Lenosavad 1995), and adopted a macro-economic stabilization program. With the availability of foreign exchange, the supply of consumption goods has increased to meet the growing demand. The Bank of Laos has also been exerting more active control over monetary growth and credit extension to public enterprises by permitting real interest rates, encouraging savings deposits, and controlling inflation (Frontier Funds Management Company 1997). Note, however, that a small portion of GDP remains in the formal banking system, which has helped businesses finance activities, and that banking reforms have only recently permitted consumer finance and consumer friendly banking services. (Clifford Chance 1997; Frontier Funds Management Company 1997). If Laotian consumers continue to increase their wealth, but do not trust banking reforms enough to save more, inflation may increase again at a rate greater than 10%.

The Lao government has worked to fight inflation, with success through 1997. However, inflationary pressure has been building, as the money supply grew rapidly through 1995–1996. Inflation and the dollar/kip exchange rate both remained fairly stable through that period, which demonstrates confidence in economic reforms enacted by the government (see Table 10.5). The IMF and other international bodies continue to assist Laos with economic stabilization policies; however, the central government remains short of necessary funds for making the improvements in education and infrastructure needed for integration into the ASEAN region. The current economic slowdown in Asia should dampen inflationary pressures for a time, but Laos is very dependent on external sources of aid to balance its government budget. If donor aid or foreign investment begin to drop due to regional economic crises, the central government may be tempted to permit an overly rapid growth of the money supply, which could trigger additional inflation as the year 2000 approaches.

Table 10.5 Lao PDR key economic indicators and Consumer Price Index change (US$ million)

Year	*1990*	*1991*	*1992*	*1993*	*1994*
Total exports	146.0	97.0	132.1	247.9	305.4
Total imports	276.0	228.0	253.0	431.9	564.1
Total balance	-130.0	-131.0	-132.9	191.5	263.7
Current account balance	-72.0	-47.0	-41.0	-60.0	-42.1
Overall balance of payments	-14.6	-2.7	15.7	–	18.7
Official reserve	64.8	57.2	52.0	98.8	80.7
(in months of total imports)	3.9	3.0	3.7	4.6	5.0
Growth of US$ supply (%)	7.8	15.7	49.0	54.8	61.2
Official exchange rate (kip/US$)	669.0	700.0	705.0	717.0	725.0

% change	**1990**	**1991**	**1992**	**1993**	**1994**	**1995**	**1996**
CPI	17.7	10.4	6.0	6.3	7.0	7.0	7.0

Source: Clifford Chance (1997), *Asian Financial Services Newsletter*, Clifford Chance Solicitors, London.

The demographic and cultural environments

Population

The population of Laos is relatively small–4.4 million people–and widely dispersed. In fact, Laos has the lowest population density in all of South-East Asia, with about 18 persons per square kilometer. Over half of the total population lives in the three lowland provinces of Vientiane, Savannakhet and Champassack (see Table 10.6) (LPDR Foreign Investment Management Committee 1995). In addition to being dispersed and relatively young, Lao consumers from all ethnic groups tend to be traditional and, historically, unlikely to migrate. We have hinted that NEM and its socio-economic outcomes will affect substantially extant traditions and migratory patterns, but, currently, the population consists primarily of peasant households working to meet subsistence requirements.

Table 10.6 Population by province

Province	*Population*
Savannakhet	673 000
Champassack	477 000
Vientiane Prefecture	489 000
Luang Prabang	355 000
Vientiane Province	321 000
Oudomxay	188 000
Khammouang	258 000
Houaphan	232 000
Saravane	237 000
Xieng Khouang	191 000
Sayaboury	195 000
Borikhamsay	151 000
Phongsaly	149 000
Huang Namtha	125 000
Attapeu	83 000
Bokeo	104 000
Sekong	59 000
Special Region Xieng Hongsa	73 000

Source: Laos United Nations Mission (1996), "Basic Data and Economic Indicators", Permanent Mission of LPDR to the United Nations and Vientiane, the Statistical Center of the LPDR, New York.

Age is an important demographic variable (see Table 10.7). Almost half of the population is under 16 years of age, and the population is growing at a rate of 2.9%. This statistic is particularly troubling because it suggests that the number of young Laotians will exceed the capacities of health and education systems and, perhaps, the nation's projected employment capabilities. Official statistics provided by the LPDR (LPDR 1994, p. 12) reveal fears that the large proportion of young people in the existing population composition will spur even further growth. This demographic pressure will be felt gradually; in the not too distant future, however, people in the age group 0–14 will enter the education system and labor markets; they will form families, seek housing and generally exert pressure on the physical and institutional infrastructures.

Table 10.7 Age distribution in Laos

Age group	%
0–19 years old	55
20–34	21.4
35–59	17.4
Over 59	13.2

Source: Laos United Nations Mission (1996), "Basic Data and Economic Indicators", Permanent Mission of LPDR to the United Nations and Vientiane, the Statistical Center of the LPDR, New York.

Sex roles

The ratio of men to women is approximately 1 to 1, but Laos is a patriarchal country, and sex roles are traditionally defined, hence another important factor is the secondary role played by women, especially in rural areas. At present, "[F]ertility is high, and the dependency ratio is high, women have low levels of education, infant and maternal mortality is high, and labor force participation is low" (LPDR 1994, p. 20). Female students account for only 37% of middle-school pupils, and under 20% for most technical training programs and higher education. Until Laotian social and economic institutions provide more educational and professional opportunities for women, especially in the upland and central regions, women will continue to take a secondary role in the economic transformation. Recent trends suggest that such opportunities are forthcoming (Kittikhoun 1996). For example, women have had leadership roles in the creation of small service and tourism businesses in Vientiane and other towns bordering Thailand. As income to (mostly male) state workers is eliminated or declines, or if it remains stagnant, women will have marginally greater freedom, at least in terms of economic development as defined by opportunities for employment.

Ethnicity

Laos is ethnically diverse, with ethnic Lao comprising 60% of the population, Phoutheng "Khan" minorities 15%, tribal Thai 20%, and Hmong, Yao and others making up the remainder of the population (see Table 10.8). But, essentially, there are three "broad consumer cultures" in Laos, namely peasant culture, upland tribal culture, and a modernizing urban culture. This urban culture is being pushed into a modern "free" market for many reasons. First of all, the state is reducing salaries and jobs as part of the NEM reforms, leaving citizens to rely more heavily on the market for jobs and wages. Second, regional integration has permitted more non-Lao, and indeed non-Thai, goods to enter Laos. Western brands can now be purchased in Laos, as can goods from China and other regional economies, whereas Laos consumers have historically consumed Lao goods, or goods brought in (legally or illegally) from Thailand.

Table 10.8 Ethnic groups in Laos

Ethnicity	*%*	*Characteristics*
Lao Loum	60%	Occupy lowland plains and Mekong river valley; dominant ethnic group, involved in government and trade.
Lao Theung	22%	Mountain slopes and uplands; moderate contact with monetized economy and consumer culture, along with subsistence agriculture.
Lao Soung	10%	Mountain-top dwellers, cut off from standard education and monetized economy, save for small pockets of narcotics and precious-gem smugglers.
Other	8%	Hmong tribes, returning exiles, smaller ethnic groups, Thai families, ethnic Chinese traders and immigrants, and expatriates.

Source: Laos United Nations Mission (1996), "Basic Data and Economic Indicators", Permanent Mission of LPDR to the United Nations and Vientiane, the Statistical Center of the LPDR, New York.

Despite non-discriminatory economic policies, there is a gap between lowland Lao and upland/mountain tribes in terms of income, political power, and culture. The Lao Loum, or lowland Laotians, are the larger ethnic group. They live in the river valleys along the Mekong, practice wet-rice agriculture, and are beginning to comprise the new urban culture. The Lao Loum have more access to markets and services. The mountain tribes can be divided roughly into two groups, Lao Theung and Lao Soung. The Lao Theung, or upland Laotians, are generally continuing with their slash-and-burn agricultural and other traditional practices in spite of government attempts to resettle them. The Lao Soung peoples live in the mountains, are continuing their cultivation of opium and cash crops and also tend to hold on to their traditional practices (LPDR Foreign Investment Management Committee 1995, p. 3).

Many government officials are males of Lao Loum origin, as are members of the ruling party. The minister of the interior is from an ethnic minority, and ethnic Hmong who supported the Lao Communist movement before 1975 continue to hold official posts. Minority tribes have recently been encouraged to participate in government. According to one senior official (Kittikhoun 1996):

> Although Laos is a multi-ethnic country which has 68 ethnic groups, the Lao government does not practice any discriminatory policies. It

> consistently pursues the policy of promoting unity and equality and prohibits all acts of creating division and discrimination. At the present time, most government officials are males of the Lao Loum who have had more advantages of education . . . For this reason the government pursues a policy facilitating representation of all ethnic groups on different government bodies.

Religion

The principal religion of Laos is Buddhism. Almost all Lao Loum are Buddhist. All Christian seminaries were closed in 1975, although a few churches in Vientiane have opened since 1990. In 1991, the Constitution of the LPDR (Article 9) protects "all lawful activities of Buddhists and other religions' followers." Lao Theung and Lao Soung are a mix of Christian, Moslem and animist. The government is presently working to continue demonstrating its respect for the Buddhist clergy, which it reorganized in 1975. As there is no formal opposition to the government, the party is working to forestall any opposition by taking proactive measures to make religion legitimate. According to a recent human rights report by the US Department of State (1994):

> The government now tolerates and encourages the open practice of Buddhism, and it has openly supported Buddhist organizations in the last few years. High-ranking government officials routinely attend Buddhist functions, and Buddhist clergy are prominently featured at important state and party functions . . . many temples are being repaired and restored (p. 4).

This trend is not particularly surprising, because Buddhism has a great history in Laos and Buddhist symbols have been powerful and enduring traditions in the countryside and among the common people (cf. Swearer 1981, p. 3). The practice of Buddhism is on the rise in Laos, with over 30 000 Buddhist monks practicing throughout the country (Marukathat 1993). On a somewhat cynical note, it can be argued that, since Buddhism is an egalitarian religion, with an emphasis on sharing and group values, the government may wish to encourage this religion in order to counterbalance the possibility of a pure consumer culture.

Cultural protectionism

An important cultural factor that will affect consumer behavior, marketing management, continued liberalization and greater exposure to the outside world is the concern about cultural imperialism or, worse, de facto annexation. Laos is surrounded by relatively powerful and influential neighbors, and most of the country is unified in its fear of cultural and economic domination by Thailand, which has a similar language and culture. Laotian political leaders and consumers want the consumer goods Thailand can provide, but also wish to assert Laotian culture and independence. Consequently, Laos will "balance" its liberalization: that is, it will continue to cultivate ties with China and Vietnam and thus counterbalance the Thais. To these ends, Laos signed a historic border agreement with China in 1993, and has been quick to praise the "priceless lessons" (Economist Intelligence Unit 1995, p. 21) of Chinese economic reforms. So, while consumers may wish to buy Thai products, the government will be pushing trade and infrastructure links with China and Vietnam, to create a counterbalance of additional influences. Laotian government policy is to promote economic openness at the same time that it protects cultural traditions (Kittikhoun 1996).

Household size

The average Laotian family, because of both tradition and encouragement by the government, is very large. Three generations typically form one household in Laos; even more can be found in the upland and remote regions, and household size varies somewhat from province to province. Laotian women, for example, bear an average of 6 children, but women in the Luang Namtha province typically bear 4 children; in Vientiane, 7 children are more the norm (LPDR 1994, p. 4). A Laotian household generally includes more than 10 people; very few men, and even fewer women, live alone or without children.

In a subsistence society, large households are generally helpful for managing agricultural tasks. However, Laos currently has a high "dependency ratio" of 93, which means that, "in Laos society, every hundred people in the age group 15–64 have to support 93 children and elder persons" (LPDR 1994, p. 4). Over two-thirds of Laotian households remain in rural areas, depending on agriculture for income. It is worth noting that the Central Committee, at the Fifth Party Congress held in March 1991, spoke directly on the issue of household economy:

> Our Party's basic policy in this agricultural field is to strongly promote the farmer's household economy, aiming at gradually shifting from subsistence production to commodity production . . . the peasant family is, and will clearly remain, the basic unit in Lao agriculture (Ljunggren 1992, p. 72).

Recent trends indicate that this policy has not changed substantially. The family unit tends to make group- or household-based consumer decisions. That is, a single household can pool resources for a single scooter, television set, or other relatively expensive household items. The high dependency ratio would indicate that households cannot afford the excessive consumption of non-essential items.

Immigrants and returning refugees

Laotians who fled the country in the 1970s have been encouraged by the government to return, and over 26 000 refugees have returned under the auspices of the UN High Commission for Refugees; perhaps as many as 60 000 have returned both officially and unofficially from neighboring countries. Many Laotians abroad have begun returning to visit families, and to investigate business possibilities (cf. US Department of State 1994). Those who fled were often educated or technically trained, and the government has encouraged these expatriates to invest in Laos. A Bangkok-based diplomat comments: "Ironically, these exiles and former political prisoners are becoming the propelling force behind Laos' economic reconstruction" (Gorman 1995, p. 9). As has happened in similar cases, for example Vietnam and China, refugees may return with cash gifts for family members and investment capital, and influence purchasing patterns and consumer values within their referent groups.

Another important development is the immigration of non-Laotians. In northern Laos, there has been an influx of Chinese workers from Yunnan Province looking for economic opportunities. The Chinese government will capitalize on improved relations and the trend toward Mekong-region integration. This will enable China to have a well-developed road-link into Laos for the first time. This scenario, while potentially beneficial economically, will likely be viewed by Lao officials as threatening to Lao sovereignty and cultural identity: "Once the Chinese workers start coming in large numbers or become squatters, then don't want to go back, how are the Lao going to police them without upsetting the Chinese or members of their own elite?" (Lintner 1995, p. 18). In southern Laos, many families migrate to and from Thailand, bringing more Thai products and cultural influences to Laos. Vietnamese migration and cultural influence may also increase. In the end, more trade and softened authoritarianism will accelerate the inflow of immigrants and returning exiles, and increase the concerns of Lao authorities that the country's culture and geographic boundaries are being rendered irrelevant.

Education

Because of war disruptions and political discord, the national education system has never been fully established, and it continues to be adversely affected by the transition policies of NEM. Budget allocations for education declined in the early stages of reform, and in the immediate future the central government will lack the resources needed for funding planned increases. Not surprisingly, the literacy rate in Laos is fairly low; it is optimistically estimated to be between 60% and 83%, depending on region; women tend to be less literate than men. Primary education (beginning at age 6), secondary school (beginning at age 11) and technical training are widely available. Laos also has one medical school, a university, and other institutions that train teachers and medical technicians, and students in other vocational areas. Details of the educational environment are provided in Table 10.9. Education is supposedly compulsory from ages 6 to 15, but not everyone attends school. The dominant Lao Loum ethnic group comprises 60% of the population, but over 70% of primary school enrollment. In rural and upland areas, many children have difficulty accessing schools, and, typically, only 25% of them continue their education beyond the primary level.

The trend in education is not promising for a growing economy dependent upon a literate and skilled workforce. Teachers with marketable skills are leaving government teaching jobs for better opportunities, and qualified candidates are sometimes not filling the vacuum created by their departures. Although these career-switching teachers may add to the extant skilled workforce, the next generation of Laotian workers will lack the necessary skills for succeeding in those technical and multiskilled jobs that help to form the backbone of economic development. A major focus of government policy has included the improvement of human resource skills and training (Frontier Funds Management Company 1997).

Health

Generally, health conditions are also not good, as indicated in Table 10.10. War has adversely affected public health, and the government continues to lack the resources for serious improvement. Trained doctors have fled the country; US and Thai aid and technical training ceased in the late 1970s. The population dispersal and poor transportation facilities throughout the rugged, mountainous countryside also hinder medical care. Poor sanitation and nutrition throughout rural Laos have resulted in high infant mortality rates (91/1000) and low life expectancy (51 years). There is also a low people-per-doctor ratio. Although there has been some improvement in overall statistics in recent years, tropical and water-borne diseases are on the increase. Finally, low population density and a lack of trained personnel make public health very expensive.

Since 1975, the public health service has grown; by 1990 there were 2100 hospitals, with over 12 000 beds in total. However, recent reductions in the government payroll have affected state health workers. The combination of high fertility and low life expectancy means Laotian households could be expected to spend a growing portion of their incomes on sanitation improvements, medicines to improve health (especially anti-malarial drugs), and family-planning products (in urban areas, large families are not as desirable). Donor aid will cover most of the costs of these medical products, but low state salaries force medical workers to charge—either officially or unofficially—for medical services.

Table 10.9 Education in Laos

Feature	%
Net school enrollment	
Primary school	69%
Secondary school	26%
Tertiary institutions	1%
Adult literacy	**50%**
Female	42%
Male	65%
Employment	
Male	55%
Female	45%

Source: LPDR (1995), "World Summit for Social Development: National Report", Vientiane, courtesy of the Permanent Mission of the LPDR to the United Nations.

Table 10.10 Health and nutrition indicators in Laos

Indicator	*Value*
Life expectancy at birth	52 years
Infant mortality	91/1000
Under 5 yr mortality	134/1000
One year immunization	98.46%
Access to safe drinking water	52%
Access to health services	67%
Access to sanitation	28%
Population per doctor (Vientiane)	1:1 089
Population per doctor (elsewhere)	1:12 600

Source: International Monetary Fund (1996), *The Lao PDR: Systemic Transformation and Adjustment*, IMF Publications, Washington.

Environment

As a resource-rich but poor country, Laos has difficulty ensuring that its businesses and development projects are all environmentally friendly; without proper regulation mining, logging, power-generation and light industry will likely harm the environment. Laotian economic planners, for example, are hoping that exports of hydro-electric power will boost the economy. Consequently, the Ministry of Industry in Vientiane has recently proposed over 50 hydro-electric projects. Environmentalists, however, have warned that "power projects, if not handled properly, will cause irreparable damage to some of continental South-East Asia's last virgin forests" (Kopitts & Offeerdal 1994; Lintner 1994, p. 70). So Laos faces problems that many developing countries face, and will be forced to balance the needs of the economy with environmental factors. In the short run, policies could be expected to favor employment and development over conservation, but, to its credit, the government has formed the Organization of Science, Technology and the Environment, as well as the Agricultural and Forestry Ministry, which is intended to co-ordinate environmental policies. Additionally, the Laotian government and international organizations are funding training programs to reform "slash-and-burn" agriculture practices that destroy the natural environment.

Despite such efforts, however, fewer factories and hydropower stations mean less hard currency for this poor nation, and a growing population will demand more land for cultivation, which will impact on rain forests, watersheds, and the environment in general. Note, too, that at this juncture Laotian consumers do not clamor for "green" policies. Consumers in Laos are generally not aware of or do not favor "environmentally friendly" products and consumer goods. Therefore, as Laos remains desperate for economic growth, it is unlikely that environmental policy will profoundly affect development plans or consumer decision making in the near term.

Changes in consumer behavior

Materialism

The extent to which Laotians are embracing consumer culture and becoming more materialistic varies considerably throughout the country, but in the accessible, wealthier lower regions around the Mekong River basin a fledgling consumer culture is emerging, along with greater interest in material possessions. This consumer culture along the Mekong and on the Chinese border is assisted by neighboring states. Laos has evolved from a strategic buffer, sandwiched between rivals Vietnam, China and Thailand, to "a link among these growing economies" (Kittikhoun 1996).

> Now, driven by the force of free markets, Laos is becoming a land bridge between China and Thailand, while Vietnam's influence is waning . . . Hundreds of cars imported through Thailand stand in the fields awaiting re-export to China . . . Construction workers from China's Yunnan province mingle with Lao townspeople, wandering among stalls run by Chinese migrants and jammed with Chinese-made goods (Lintner 1995, p. 18).

It would be premature, however, to suggest that a consumer culture is firmly entrenched. Indeed, while Laos is rich in raw materials and is evolving as a distribution hub for its neighbors, "(it) is not exactly teeming with consumers with strong purchasing power" (Lintner 1995, p. 19). This may change, however, and as the country becomes less isolated Laotians will become increasingly aware of how well their neighbors live—or at least aware of what they have.

Several factors will affect the evolutionary processes of consumerism and materialism. Among them are regional and cultural differences, political forces, and religious influences. The Lao Loum, the largest ethnic group, with the greatest purchasing power and urban representation, can be expected to become the most materialistic. In the upland cultures, materialism is not yet an option. At present, ethnic groups and remote villages still make many of their own clothes and tools, and barter to exchange goods. Their focus is on obtaining basic clothes and foodstuffs for survival, and adapting to a cash economy. Moreover, overt materialism is generally discouraged by the government in a number of ways, not the least of which is the socialist philosophy it advocates. Although market forces are now accepted in Laos, and the country's leadership realizes that economic development is necessary, conspicuous consumption will be discouraged on an ideological basis. The Laotian government, which "fears widening economic inequalities and resultant social friction" (Rigg 1995, p. 164), has not hesitated to "re-educate" its citizens, and this legacy will tend to discourage conspicuous consumption. High-profile corruption trials have also been used as a general deterrent to excesses of capitalism such as embezzlement and bribery (Dommen 1995, p. 85). More ethereal cultural forces such as Buddhist and co-operative ideals, or perhaps simply resistance to change, may also slow materialism. Lao villagers, for example, "welcomed the additional opportunities for economic enterprise [but] they were at the same time concerned about the effects of the NEM on village support networks and communal solidarity" (Rigg 1995, p. 161). Lastly, fears of Thailand will play a role in Laos' evolution. Thailand is seen as a pure consumer culture. Most consumer products, local television and media, and common cultural exchanges come from Thailand. While Thai products may be desirable, Laos retains a conservative culture that sometimes portrays the Thais—not the West, as is the case in many other countries in the region—as the "Great Polluter of cultural identity" across the "AIDS Bridge" (the new Friendship Bridge) spanning the Mekong River. And Laotians, generally, tend to view Thai merchants and businesspersons as "rapacious, mercenary and duplicitous" (Rigg 1995, pp. 161–5). We would therefore expect Thai-based materialism and consumer values to be discouraged.

Consumer expectations

If the experiences of Vietnamese and Chinese consumers are accurate indicators, Laotian consumers will expect a higher standard of living, and more goods on which to spend their income. Author observations suggest that the more favorable economic environment, less repressive political climate, and greater exposure to foreign ideas and products after years of hard-line Communist rule and economic disaster are beginning to change expectations among many Laotian consumers.

Difficult long-term problems remain, however, including, for example the previously discussed low per-capita income, inadequate infrastructure, population dispersion and largely uneducated workforce. These problems will obviously affect the purchasing power of and choices faced by consumers. Indeed, a substantial adjustment process by all consumers has accompanied reform. Furthermore, not all consumers will have the same expectations. As previously noted, Laos' fate as a landlocked country with many inaccessible areas will create pockets, or rudimentary "segments," of consumers with varying expectancies.

Consumer expectations in Vientiane and the border towns will rise most rapidly. Again, the government will try to *dampen* the desire for Thai goods, for fear of being overwhelmed by the strong economy and culture of Thailand. Thai goods, however, are generally perceived by Laotians to be of a higher quality than either Chinese goods or the few available goods from Vietnam. And, since Thai goods are considered to be reasonably priced and packaged in a language and form they understand, consumers will expect more goods from Thailand. Demand for Western goods among the newly emerging pockets of wealthy, urban, and elite consumers who are profiting from the NEM will also increase as Laotian policy cautiously fosters the growth of wealthier market segments. Rural consumers, who were able to participate in the economic renaissance because farmers and commodity producers were allowed to sell products at market prices and thus to accumulate some disposable income, have also raised their expectations. Only the most remote tribal groups have tended to maintain modest expectations, or, perhaps more accurately, have not at all changed expectations. Nevertheless, a critical mass of Laotians expect their lives to improve through consumption. Whether purchasing power will enable consumers to meet expectations remains to be seen. If it does not, dissatisfaction and, ultimately, discord are probably inevitable. As new roads and other rudiments of infrastructure are built, rural communities and remote regions will have more contact with the rest of Laos and the infusion of goods and ideas from other countries. Consumers, generally, will expect more sophisticated products, and only the most remote hinterlands will remain dependent on subsistence living, stay outside the growing sphere of consumer culture, and therefore maintain their present expectations.

Market-segmentation trends

We have alluded to emerging market segments, most notably urban vs rural consumers, varying geographic regions, Lao Loum vs other ethnic groups, and persons of political influence vs those without political influence. As Laos becomes more prosperous and experiences social changes forced by the market, consumption patterns are becoming diverse, and the number and complexity of market segments is increasing. Some segmentation examples (and trends) are shown in tables 10.11 and 10.12.

Table 10.11 Emerging market segments

Segment	*Principle of segmentation*
Geographic	Northern vs Southern Thai Border Town/Chinese Border Town/Vietnamese Border Town Urban vs Rural Highland vs Lowland
Ethnic	Lao Loum/Lao-Thai/Lao-Chinese/Hinterland tribes
Purchasing power and political influence:	State salaried workers Joint-venture employees Small entrepreneurs Wealthy traders, newly rich, party officials
Societal orientation	Buddhist vs former Communist vs secular urban elite
Age	19 years or younger 19–35 35 and above
Sex	Male vs female

Regional differences, differences in political influence, professional standing (and hence purchasing power), and presence in urban centers will continue to be consequential in the foreseeable future. Indeed, southern urban consumers who are in favor with the government consume most NEM-inspired products and services. Sex roles will become increasingly important, but, if trends in other transition countries are an indicator, perhaps age will be the most important segmentation schema. Over half of the population is under the age of 16, and the 16-and-under group in other South-East Asian transition economies has readily embraced the products and norms of consumer culture.

Although segments are still somewhat nebulous, trends suggest that there are attractive market segments in Laos, and somewhat predictable buyer behaviors from which astute marketers can profit. Economic conditions are such that many consumers are buying more than the basic food, clothing, shelter and transportation items that the government hopes market reform will provide. Moreover, many Laotians are wealthier than the macroeconomic statistics indicate, since only a fraction of commercial exchanges are transacted with money (LPDR 1994, pp. 6–8). Estimates of purchasing

Table 10.12 Market segments under NEM reforms

Segment	*Characteristics*
New entrepreneurs	Service sector & tourism Businessmen, foreign joint venturers, urban women
New private-sector employees	Garment manufacturing Transportation Contractors to donor agencies Tourism Factory workers in joint ventures
Traders and middlemen	Border residents exposed to foreign goods, traders, exporters, "smugglers"
Private agricultural workers	Increased "cash" earnings from reforms, few choices of goods in the countryside, spending preferred to uncertain savings opportunities
State workers	Salaried workers with little opportunity to keep up with inflation and uncertain prospects
Collective state farmers	Salaried workers paid in kind or with ration coupons, little opportunity in money economy, underutilized and underemployed

Note:
The new economy of Laos has moved from two classes of consumers–state workers and collective farmers–to a number of market segments, including those shown in this table.

power place the amount of money at the disposal of a small number of urban dwellers and successful farmers at over US$1200 per capita. The presence of computers, electronics equipment, motorcycles, automobiles, and other "high-ticket" items in the shops of Vientiane and border provinces indicates that pockets of wealth exist, and that many consumers do have purchasing power.

Consumer credit

Credit in Laos has been rationed as part of the drive to control inflation. State enterprises have been hardest hit, but consumer credit has not, until recently, been part of government plans. To complicate the credit situation, consumers do not look to banks as safe places to put their savings (see Table 10.13). Wealth is kept in gold, hard currency, or desirable consumer goods, all of which will hold their value over time. The Lao goverment has undertaken measures to make credit available to consumers, and especially entrepreneurs, from state and joint-venture banks. The government has also encouraged banking reform, and has begun offering consumer financial products such as loans and banking services. The Lao National Bank, the Military Bank,

Vientiane Bank and others have carried out ambitious reforms, and now make loans to cash-crop agriculture and even service businesses. Since 1995, entrepreneurs have been able to attract the funding necessary to purchase durable goods and to acquire business loans. Major international credit cards can now be used in parts of Laos, and retailers of the more expensive items such as new and used cars, motor scooters, and durable goods have begun offering "installment finance" programs whereby large down payments are accepted, and the balance is financed. Informal agreements among private citizens and citizen groups are also an important source of consumer credit. The Chinese community, for example, continues to offer informal banking and moneylending in Laos (cf. Mackie 1992, p. 163).

Table 10.13 Banking in Laos

Bank type	*Examples*
State banks	The Bank of Laos
	Bank for Foreign Trade
	Agricultural Bank
	Laos Commercial Bank
Foreign bank branches	Siam Commercial Bank
	Thai Farmers Bank
	Thai Military Bank
	Krung Thai Bank
	Bangkok Bank
	Public Bank (Malaysia)

Note:
The banking system in Laos has undergone recent reforms, raising the savings rate from 3% to 10% of GDP in the formal banking system.

Sources: United Nations (1995), "The Least Developed Countries, 1995 Report/Midterm Review", UNCTAD, New York; Frontier Funds Management Company (1997), *The Vietnam Frontier Fund: Placement Memorandum,* Frontier Funds Management Company and Nomura International, Bangkok.

Changes to the macromarketing mix

The implementation of NEM has substantially changed the macromarketing mix. Below is an overview of what marketing managers can expect with respect to macromarketing trends for products, prices, distribution, marketing communications and market research.

Products

Except for a few black market goods, prior to NEM Lao consumers had few product and service choices. This condition has rapidly changed in Vientiane, Luang Prabang and some border provinces. Consumerism is emerging, more goods are available and inflation has been kept in check.

Prosperity, albeit gradual, brings more choices–and different goods to meet the different wants and needs of different market segments. Now consumers are being presented with numerous choices, and these choices include, primarily, local goods, inexpensive Chinese products, inexpensive and moderately priced Thai products, expensive foreign goods from many sources, and services. Some details follow.

Local goods

Most staples, such as unprocessed food products and simple clothing, are produced domestically. Laos imports most finished products, but manufacturing capability for these kinds of products for domestic consumption (in addition to export) is a government priority. To date the Lao garment industry produces shirts and shoes of acceptable quality. Beverages such as "Beer Lao" and the less expensive "Fresh Beer" are becoming favored alternatives to Thai and Western imports.

Chinese products

Increased road links and trade with China have led to a flood of imports across the northern border. China buys 5% of Laos's exports, but officially accounts for 11% of Laos's imports. Much of this is construction equipment and labor, but much is also in the form of cheap consumer goods–again, in the North in particular.

Thai goods

Thai products present a problem for Laotian consumers. Because of the proximity of Vientiane to Thailand, the similarity of Lao and Thai languages and cultures, and the generally favorable attitude toward Thai goods, an array of Thai products in different product categories are sold in Lao markets. However, despite this favorable attitude and because of the growing number of products from other countries, a general bias against Thais means Laotian consumers are beginning to look to goods from other countries as product alternatives.

Expensive foreign imports

The small segment of more wealthy consumers prefers foreign goods associated with or produced in developed countries, as these are symbols of high status. Foreign goods are also generally perceived to be better, with Japanese and Western goods considered to be of the highest quality. But many Asian companies are now beginning to view Laos as a potential market. Hong Kong firms, for example, have had success selling office equipment and imported consumer goods in Laos, and the number of motorcycles in Laos, manufactured throughout East Asia, increased over 30 000 in 1992 alone. Current trends indicate that, despite Laos' relatively small population, more expensive goods from several countries will find their way to Laotian markets and consumers. Ironically, at this time many of these goods are simply in transit; they are frequently "smuggled" goods on their way to China or Vietnam via Laos. Nevertheless, Laotians are increasingly being exposed to these goods, and they are often preferred (even if not affordable).

Services

The services sector has flourished under NEM. Before NEM, services were generally not seen as productive and were discouraged. Now, taxi services, construction services, domestic and international air travel, hotels, cafés, telephones, and the media are increasingly available to the Laotian consumer. Increasing the scope and availability of services is a priority of the government of the LPDR; services are a priority for development between 1997 and the year 2000. Increases in domestic and international air traffic, investments in hotels, and tourism have brought the service share of the GDP to almost 25%. Over US$280 million was invested by foreigners in this sector in 1994, with additional domestic and foreign investment planned as part of the National Development Strategy for the year 2000.

Entertainment

Entertainment, like services, has also shown signs of life in the past 5 years. In the countryside, entertainment is as simple as buying a ticket to watch Thai Television for a few hours. In the cities, movies, icecream shops, dance halls, videos, and video games are now available for consumption.

In summary, some domestic products, especially garments, soft drinks and beer, will begin to gain even wider acceptance; what Laos does manufacture domestically meets international standards. The garment industry, for example, now exports to Canada and other Western countries. Careful strategies to manufacture locally, or to construct joint ventures to make and market goods with local content, will be successful. At the same time, Laotians will learn to discriminate better between high-quality goods (foreign imports), medium-quality goods (Thai consumer goods) and cheap goods (often imported from China) when making purchase decisions. Since so many goods are being smuggled through Laos, consumers are being exposed to more goods, even if they cannot afford them for local consumption. This exposure, coupled with actual purchases by wealthier Lao consumers, will also stimulate the demand for more expensive foreign products.

Successful product management in Laos should consider the following recommendations:

- Products should be durable and have long shelf lives, as they may take weeks to reach the intended consumers.
- Labels should clearly identify what the product does, and which segment is being targeted.

- Information on labels should be easy to comprehend; few Laotians are familiar with languages other than Lao and Thai.
- New-product introductions should preferably not be identified with Thailand. There will be continued preference for non-Thai goods at the government level, and among more conservative elements of the population. At present, language and proximity makes Thai goods easy to use, but an alternative to Thai products, with clearly understandable labels, would be welcomed by the government and Lao consumers.
- Joint-venture products, those partially made in Laos, should be identified. When they can, consumers will buy local products. Products sold in Laos may be consumed in Laos, or exported or smuggled to or used in neighboring countries.

Prices

Price policy has been one of the most significant outcomes of NEM. As Ljunggren (1992, p. 73) notes, "(D)omestic prices of most goods and services are market determined. Prices are negotiated freely, and administrative bodies are forbidden to interfere in the market mechanism."

However, as discussed previously, many Laotians are just now coming to grips with this policy change, and high prices for some products discourage general consumption. It is also important to note that, although consumer prices have been freed, procurement prices used by state trading firms "rationalized" and subsidies drastically reduced, the presence of a truly free market has been hindered by weak support services, shortages, and difficulties in obtaining needed imports. Therefore, although a free market legally exists, Laos remains an underdeveloped country with an economy that cannot always respond to free-market signals.

Segmentation and pricing strategies are clearly linked, and in Laos foreign firms must be sensitive to this relationship. Additionally, and as discussed earlier, the institutionalization of consumer credit for more expensive items, such as motor scooters, will dramatically increase sales. Indeed, consumers for these products are in more need of credit than they are of the "best" price.

Unfortunately, without banking reform in Laos, there is a danger that consumer prices will rise. Currently there is no mechanism except consumption to absorb increased wealth. The local currency, the kip, has been stable for the past few years, and convertible into hard currency, but inflationary pressures seem never to be far removed from Laos, and when products are priced locally, the close monitoring of inflation is vital.

Distribution

As previously discussed, geographic constraints, the land-to-population ratio, poor infrastructure and government policy have created distribution difficulties in Laos. Much of the population is not served by modern roads or rail links; upland tribes have little contact with the outside world. Markets remain highly fragmented, and lack communication systems. There are numerous intermediaries involved in the distribution process, which tends to be inefficient and labor intensive. Laos also suffers from high internal transportation costs, and even domestic products have difficulty in reaching all areas. Moreover, the country's nascent manufacturing capabilities often render distribution even less efficient than we could initially imagine. For example, consumer goods are often transported by truck from Thailand, but trucks must return empty as Laos has few manufactured goods to trade.

The net effect of these realities means consumer products are generally distributed through small, family-owned shops or travelling peddlers. Consequently, marketing managers would probably do best by targeting major distribution points, then using the traditional distribution customs and practices, and routeing the products to end users.

The preceding information depicts today's Laos, but note that infrastructure is a government and foreign-investment priority. Foreign businesses looking to penetrate the Laotian market should be aware of numerous road and infrastructure projects aimed at linking different provinces internally, and joining neighboring countries into a "Greater Mekong Sub-Region" co-operative arrangement for transportation, power and communications (Brimble 1994). The linkages are in place for closer regional transportation co-operation, and significant investment is being made in local and international infrastructure projects. Remember, too, that Laos is also considered to be at the heart of regional distribution networks, so that distribution costs should drop in Laos in the near term. Improved infrastructure and distribution mechanisms will probably have the following effects:

- *Product reach:* Forest products, other crops and raw materials businesses are currently profitable, with few places for sellers to spend the cash. Better infrastructure will lead to the delivery and purchase of goods in the countryside.
- *Trading center development:* As towns become more accessible along new roads, more goods will eventually be available in shops, and more business will be done with travelers as well as with villages not directly served by roads.
- *Exposure to more types of goods:* To date, Thailand has been the only cost-effective venue for routeing trade. With trade growing, and transportation links to China, Cambodia and Vietnam, consumers in Laos will be exposed to more types of goods.
- *Greater consumption of goods generally,* and the growth of a consumer culture.

Marketing communications

In Laos, the formulation and implementation of marketing-communications strategies are affected by government policy, the existence of the media, and consumer capabilities—for example, literacy, and familiarity with and exposure to various media. The government now accepts the necessity of private advertising, and laws have been changed to enable this. In fact, the government has begun to accept private advertising for television and for state-run newspapers. Consumer capabilities are now a more pressing concern. Laotian consumers are similar to many other South-East Asian consumers, but may be more receptive than their neighbors to many foreign brands, since their country has little domestic industry to protect and their historical isolation has made them more impressionable.

Most strategies have attempted to create brand awareness. The quintessential brands of South-East Asia, such as Darlie, Marlboro, Honda, JVC, Samsung and Coca-Cola, are all recognized brands in Laos. With more than half of the population under the age of 16, brand loyalties are just forming. Consequently, brand promotion is crucial, and should be rewarded in future years.

However, reform efforts in Laos are lagging behind those in China and Vietnam, and many consumers do not know what products they want, have not been exposed to many brands, and will have difficulty discriminating among product offerings. Again, this suggests that marketing communications are crucial.

Media selection is also an important consideration. The government has experimented with private and joint-venture ownership of a television station, and local newspapers. Thai television and periodicals are widely circulated in Laos. At the present time, outdoor advertising is favored, and billboards remain the primary method for communicating advertisements. Point-of-purchase materials are also an important part of the marketing communications mix, as are free samples, and the sponsorship of local sporting or cultural events. Other print media—especially newspapers, which are rapidly expanding in circulation—will be increasingly important to a firm's marketing-communications mix. Detailed print advertising is more effective in the cities, however, because of the illiteracy problem, and because newspapers are rarely circulated outside metropolitan areas. Electronic media are beginning to influence consumers, and the provinces now have radios and televisions, although they are often communally owned. Laotian towns bordering Thailand receive Thai TV broadcasts and advertising messages, and a Thai–Laotian joint-venture television station, Channel 3, recently began operation. If Laos replicates other South-East Asian economies, we would expect the electronic media to become an increasingly important element in marketing-communications strategies.

Market research

Market research is in its infancy in Laos. The government has begun to measure market trends, although most measures examine macro-economic activity rather than consumer inclinations and behavior. Some international marketing research firms have also begun to examine the Laotian market, as have international-aid donors. Their efforts have helped to give a more accurate picture of the Laotian market than was available in previous years, but data are often neither accurate or reliable. Consumers are sometimes difficult to assess; they are not familiar with obtrusive instruments used to collect data, and are still not completely comfortable speaking to others about personal issues such as money accumulation and consumption patterns. Managers and owners of private businesses, having learned to avoid taxes and regulations whenever possible, are also reluctant to provide accurate information.

Given these problems, we may well ask how an operable understanding of the Laotian market could possibly be gained. It has been suggested that the Indochinese condition requires companies to place employees in-country to collect primary data relevant to company specific needs and objectives (Shultz 1994). And Laos is not an exception. Laotian consumers need many things, but the majority of them often do not value, or cannot afford, many items companies wish to sell. Determining which products will sell is important, but determining where to sell them, and how to transport, promote and price them, is equally important. In-country assessments by investing firms that have examined country conditions in relation to company capabilities have led to successful product introductions. Indeed, many have been able to profit from understanding infrastructure needs and from the construction boom, by selling materials and machinery. An awareness of consumer preferences and extant distribution mechanisms has enabled American firms, for example, to sell soft-drink manufacturing equipment to local Thai–Lao joint ventures. Japanese motorcycle manufacturers and parts distributors are profiting from an understanding of the transportation in Laos. In summary, certain segments are profitable within the Laos market at this time, and thorough site research that goes beyond an examination of economic indicators will be able to pinpoint trends and opportunities.

Future trends and expectations

An analysis of historical events and more recent marketing and consumer activities leads us to believe that Laos is a small but promising market that is likely to continue to follow the transition models initiated in China and Vietnam. If further progress is to be assured, then Laos is dependent upon political stability—perhaps more so than for other countries in the region except Cambodia and Myanmar. Continued regional harmony will permit consumer markets to evolve as aid, foreign investment, and domestic industry and services combine to raise national income. This investment and development is critically important because Laos has been blessed with natural resources but cursed with limited extraction capabilities. It has also been historically dependent on neighboring and foreign powers; Laos's relations with Thailand, France and Vietnam have always been such that Laos has been the weaker of the parties, unable to extract needed resources, infrastructure and technical skills from the others.

Consumer behavior

Consumer behavior in Laos will be affected by two major trends. The first is the gradual increase in the purchasing power of Laotian consumers, which is coupled with the increased ease of obtaining goods in shops. Retail outlets will remain small and family owned in the immediate future, and most goods beyond those items that could be categorized as subsistence goods will be imported. The most significant market-segmentation trends will be the growth of segments that are determined by disposable income and purchasing power. Purchases of necessities such as clothing and housing amenities, transportation (whether bicycles, scooters or automobiles) and medicines will be coupled with more purchases of soft drinks, imported beer and cigarettes, movie tickets and goods generally associated with hedonic consumption. Because Laos is a geographically disparate and relatively small market, products and product information will filter in from neighboring countries. Products will not typically be labeled for and marketed specifically to Laotian consumers.

The second major trend is the overall integration of South-East Asia, which includes all of Laos's neighbors, including Southern China, into a "Golden Quadrangle" (Rigg 1995, p. 164). Rail and road links will bring historically isolated and antagonistic peoples together through trade, and create new market opportunities. This trend has been ongoing for at least a decade, but is now being accelerated by mutually beneficial trade and commerce. Products that are accepted into one country's market in South-East Asia can usually be extended with ease into neighboring markets. As transportation links improve, consumption values meld, distribution costs decline, and marketing opportunities increase. Compare a prognostication from nearly a decade ago:

> Linguistic, religious, ethnic, and social isolation within each of the countries [in South-East Asia], if not always between them, has been lessened. As a result, each society has undertaken a search for a new and broader consensus, one that would harmonize established social institutions with changing conditions. Increasingly, as people participated in a range of new organizations and activities, they broadened their frame of reference from the village or province to the nation. The

> new congruence of values are restructured allegiances, challenging primordial loyalties. Earlier distinctions of culture, society and state have become blurred . . . the importance of genealogical and geographical origins has lessened, for some if not for all (Steinberg 1987, p. 6).

Changing government role

Leaders of the Laotian government understand that Laos needs foreign investment and assistance, but they do not want to let the country be dominated by any one power or group of nations. The central government expects to be the leading force as the economy continues its reformation, and it will manage the process of opening the country gradually to the outside world. Economic prosperity will come long before multiparty democracy. In some cases, this will lead to inefficiencies, such as the initial and poorly run state monopoly over transportation on the new Friendship Bridge, where only government trucks are permitted to transport goods into Laos. But the government has remained committed to its NEM policies, and is resigned to the fact that not everyone will be a "winner" under free-market conditions.

Both the military and the philosophy of socialism continue to have a strong ideological influence, especially at the elite level. Lao officials, not unlike their Chinese and Vietnamese counterparts, may be concerned about the Western "spiritual pollution" that often accompanies imports of Western products and knowhow. Official ideology could affect the consumer revolution, and the government would prefer to manage it gradually to prevent gross inequalities and social and political discord.

To achieve these objectives, leaders will continue to encourage the development of consumer markets so that Laotian citizens can obtain a "standard package" of clothes, better food and medicine, and basic transportation. As Laos imports most manufactured necessities and consumer goods, part of its liberalization policy has to include trading links with neighboring economies. Aiming to stimulate the market economy, the government has generally not restricted entrepreneurs from starting businesses, corporations from investing, or consumers from acquiring more expensive goods—when they can afford them. Still, the government has further reforms to implement, and tough policy decisions to make on resource allocation. It must also contain inflation, attract investment, fight corruption, and protect Laotian culture. But, if its consumption trends continue to mirror those of its neighbors, and regional integration proceeds, Laos will increasingly become an attractive market to regional and multinational firms.

Implications for marketing management

The Laotian consumer market is relatively small, and lags a few years behind neighboring China and Vietnam—and certainly many years behind Thailand.

Yet, rather than ignoring Laos, it may be worthwhile to include the penetration of the Laotian market as part of a South-East Asian strategy for the emerging Golden Quadrangle. The following suggestions may be helpful to marketing managers interested in pursuing this objective.

Broadly defining the market

Most economic and commercial activity takes place in the South. Laotians buy goods for themselves, and also consumer goods and durables to export—legally or illegally—into neighboring countries. This trend of South-East Asia's Greater Mekong Sub-Region as a market will continue. A strong presence in Laos will provide entry to, or supplement marketing efforts in, Myanmar, Vietnam, Yunnan Province of China, Cambodia and Thailand. The growth of consumer culture in Laos and integration into the Golden Quadrangle are both recent occurrences. This new, enlarged market may have greater primary and selective demand for consumer products than macro-indicators and government statistics reveal.

Riding the demographic wave

Laos has a young population, one that is growing in affluence and sophistication. Although still relatively poor, it is developing fast enough to warrant simple, specific advertising and promotions to Laotian consumers. Billboard advertising and promotions used now will pay off later; educational advertising used now will inform consumers about the benefits and advantages of foreign products, and lead to increased sales.

Extending brands to Laos

The Laotian market is similar enough to its neighbors to create the expectation that products that have been successful in other South-East Asian markets should succeed in the LPDR. In 1995, Laos imported almost US$500 million in consumer goods from China alone (Economist Intelligence Unit 1995, p. 24). There is clearly an opportunity for more established brands in this market.

Expecting government involvement

The Laotian government, like governments in China and Vietnam, wants to be seen as leading or managing the reform process. Companies of all sizes need to develop contacts with the government and nurture relationships with government agencies that affect investor outcomes, not only for the purpose of managing regulation, but also if they wish to exploit opportunities within Laos and among neighboring states. To these ends, investors should remember that:

> [T]he industrial development that has fanned South-East Asia's recent growth has depended greatly on arrangements negotiated at the top

> level between entrepreneurs, bureaucratic chiefs, and foreign sources of aid, investment and markets. Small producers may supply the major firms which made the deal, and pathways to investment and markets, once opened up, may become directly accessible to middling businesses, but their opportunities arose from the groundwork laid at the national government/big business level (McVey 1992, p. 9).

Seeking good local partners

Corruption and over-regulation have not been major impediments to investment and business development in Laos, but firms have been most successful when they have teamed up with reliable local partners. Loose clan, political and family networks are often more important in Laos than in Western culture, and the military is playing an increased role in the economy (Dommen 1995, p. 85). Furthermore, in an economy where annual wages rarely exceed US$500, appropriate compensation schemes for valuable services can greatly facilitate operations.

Investment in training

Laotian education is weak, and there is a clear shortage of trained personnel. However, as local breweries and garment firms have found, investments in Laos can be profitable. And, just as American firms were welcomed into Vietnam to counterbalance Chinese and Japanese influence, so Laos wants to learn from foreign—especially non-Thai—investors.

The evolving marketing and consumer-behavior phenomena in Laos replicate in many ways the evolutionary processes still unfolding in China and Vietnam, but Laos' land mass, low population density, cultural and physical proximity to Thailand, and location as the center of the Golden Quadrangle also make it unique. As in neighboring countries, consumer demand will increasingly dictate government policy. Prudent investment and marketing savvy are needed if firms hope to be successful in Laos, but successful market penetration, while sensitive to Laotian uniqueness, should be also part of a broader investment strategy to exploit the Golden Quadrangle market as a whole.

References

Asian Development Bank (1992), *LPDR: Economic Review and Bank Operations*, ADB, Manila.

— (1993), *LPDR: Economic Update*, ADB, Manila.

Bangkok Post (1994), "Laos Drafting New Laws for Trade", *Reuters Textline*, December 24.

Brimble, Peter (1994), "From Thailand to the Greater Mekong Subregion: The Challenges for Private Business", Paper presented 5 January, Brooker Group Limited, Bangkok.

Clifford Chance (1997), *Asian Financial Services Newsletter*, vol. 1, Clifford Chance Solicitors, London.

Dommen, Arthur J. (1995), "Among Generals, Among Friends: Laos in 1994", *Asia Survey*, vol. 35, no. 1, January, pp. 84–91.

Economist Intelligence Unit (1994), *Indochina: Vietnam Laos Cambodia*, EIU, London.

— (1995), *EIU Country Report: Laos*, EIU, London.

Frontier Funds Management Company (1997), "The Vietnam Frontier Fund: Placement Memorandum", Frontier Funds Management Co & Nomura International, Bangkok.

Gorman, Julius (1995), "Laos Ousts Vietnam as Regional Darling", *Thailand Business Day*, January 13, p. 9.

International Monetary Fund (1996), *The Lao PDR: Systemic Transformation and Adjustment* , IMF Publications, Washington.

Ismartono, Yuli (1993), "Laos: Conflict Free Laos Slowly Races Ahead of Neighbours", Interpress Service, May 12.

Keoboula, M. (1995), Speech before the 29th Plenary Meeting of the United Nations General Assembly, 50th Session, October 11.

Kittikhoun, A. (1996), Permanent Mission of Lao Peoples Democratic Republic to the United Nations: Interviews with authors 12/94 and 12/21/96.

Kopits, George & Offeerdal, Erik (1994), "Fiscal Policy in Transition Economies: A Major Challenge", *Finance & Development*, December, pp. 2–24.

LPDR (1994), "LPDR Socio-Economic Development Strategies", 5th Round Table Meeting, Final Draft, LPDR, Geneva.

— (1995), "World Summit for Social Development: National Report", LPDR, Vientiane.

LPDR Foreign Investment Management Committee (1995), Raw data, Vientiane.

Lao Peoples' Democratic Republic UN Mission (1994), "LPDR Population & Development", LPDR UN Mission, NY, March.

Laos Statistical Survey, 1992 (1993), Service National de la Statistique, Vientiane.

Laos United Nations Mission (1996), "Basic Data and Economic Indicators", Permanent Mission of LPDR to the United Nations and Vientiane, the Statistical Center of the LPDR, New York.

Lengsavad, Somsavat (1995), "Statement of the LPDR Foreign Minister to the 28th ASEAN Ministerial Meeting", Bandar, July 29.

Ljunggren, Börje (1992), *Market Economies Under Communist Regimes: Reform in Vietnam, Laos & Cambodia*, PhD Thesis, Southern Illinois University, Carbondale.

Lintner, Bertil (1994), "Add Water: Laos' Hydroelectric Plans Seem Overambitious", *Far East Economic Review,* October 13, pp. 70–1.

— (1995), "Laos: Ties that Bind", *Far East Economic Review,* February 9, pp. 18–19.

Mackie, James (1992), "Changing Patterns of Chinese Big Business in South-East Asia", in ed Ruth McVey, *South-East Asian Capitalists,* Cornell SEAP, NY, pp. 163–87.

McVey, Ruth (1992), "The Materialization of the South-East Asian Entrepreneur", in ed Ruth McVey, *South-East Asian Capitalists,* Cornell SEAP, NY, pp. 7–33.

Marukathat, Saritdet (1993), "Laos: Whether Fast or Flawed, Vientiane's Drive to Privatize Goes On" *Bangkok Post,* Reuters Textline, October 26.

Rigg, Jonathan (1995), "Managing Dependency in a Reforming Economy: The Lao PDR", *Contemporary South-East Asia,* vol. 17, no. 2, September, pp. 147–72.

Shultz, Clifford J. (1994), "Balancing Policy, Consumer Desire and Corporate Interests: Considerations for Market Entry in Vietnam", *Columbia Journal of World Business,* vol. 29, Winter, pp. 43–52.

Steinberg, David Joel (1987), *In Search of South-East Asia: A Modern History,* University of Hawaii Press, Honolulu.

Swearer, Donald K. (1981), *Buddhism and Society in South-East Asia,* Anima Books, Chambersburg, PA.

Tilleke & Gibbins (1997), "The ASEAN Challenge", Client editorial paper presented by Tilleke & Gibbins Consultants Ltd, Bangkok, December 15.

United Nations (1995), "The Least Developed Countries, 1995 Report/Midterm Review", UNCTAD, New York.

US Department of State (1994), *Foreign Economic Trends: Laos,* US Embassy, Vientiane.

Xinhua General Overseas News Service (1991), "Laos Produces More Consumer Goods", February 23.

Notes

1 The authors thank Alounkeo Kittikhoun, the Ambassador of Lao People's Democratic Republic to the United Nations and ASU FGIA and SRCA programs for their support. The views expressed herein are those of the authors.

2 It should be noted that, in Laos, the term "urban" is relative; even Vientiane resembles and functions like a large town rather than a city.

CHAPTER 11

Malaysia

Consumer behavior and the future

ALIAH HANIM MOHD. SALLEH, BIANCA TEO &
ANTHONY PECOTICH

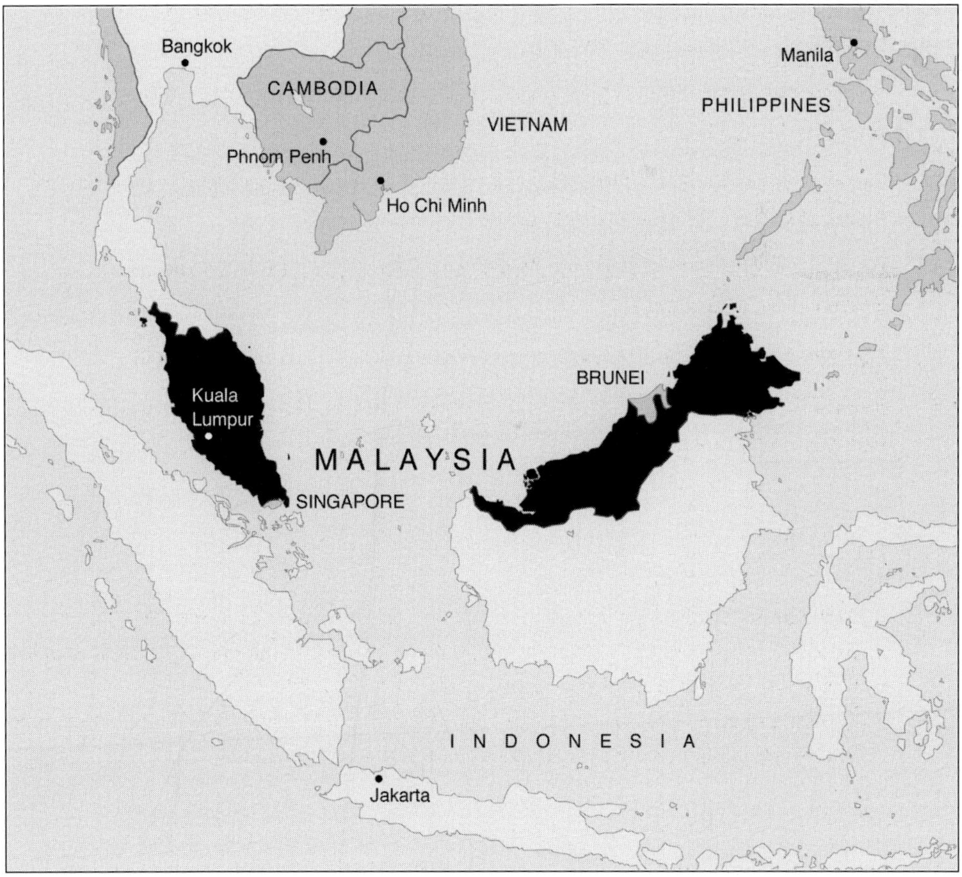

Abstract

Malaysia, Asia's "tiger with a vision," has just completed a period of remarkable economic development (7 consecutive years of growth above 8%), followed by a financial crisis, which together have changed the nation forever. This chapter attempts to identify and explain the sources and the nature of these changes. Their impact and likely future manifestations are also evaluated, with a particular emphasis on the consumer-behavior and marketing aspects. The general conclusion is that, despite the major financial and economic crisis, Malaysia is in a unique position of political stability and national unity that forms a solid platform for the future.

Introduction

The Federation of Malaysia came into being in 1963. The history of independent Malaysia has been influenced by the need to reconcile the interests and ambitions of the principal ethnic communities. The 1957 Constitution sought to balance Malay political and administrative power against the Chinese and Indian economic dominance. (In the Malaysian context, "Indian" is an ethnic term that refers to people from India, Pakistan or Bangladesh.) In essence, a gradual harmonization of interests was the goal (Moore 1994; Cribb 1997). Although, due to its dependence on commodity exports, Malaysia is vulnerable to world recession, its recent history has shown sound economic growth and development, followed by the surprising currency crisis. Nonetheless, because of its natural endowments, it has one of the best economic prospects of any Asian economy (Rafferty 1990).

Further, Malaysia was until mid-1997 an attractive place for foreign investment due to its political stability, competitiveness, and, as sometimes arrogantly described by its leadership, strong economic fundamentals. But the shock of the currency crisis cannot be underestimated. The events of mid-1997 came after a period of unprecedented growth, when the nation was confidently approaching the 40th anniversary of independence. The currency devaluation, the stockmarket crash and the resultant indefinite delay in, or even abandonment of, a number of megaprojects have shattered that confidence as the nation proceeds to implement tough measures in an attempt to stem the tide. However, the present situation may be viewed as providing a challenge, and an opportunity for alert marketers with long-term vision.

Physical environment

Malaysia has an area of over 300 000 km^2, and its territory is made up of 2 distinct regions: Peninsula Malaysia (previously known as Malaya), which has 11 states, and east Malaysia, which comprises the states of Sabah and Sarawak in northern Borneo (Kalimantan). Geographically, Peninsula Malaysia forms the southern end of the Asian mainland, with Thailand on the north and Singapore on the south. It is flanked by "one of the oldest and most frequented maritime highways of the world" (Demaine 1997, p. 565). The non-peninsular states of Sabah and Sarawak are positioned along the northern fringe of the island of Borneo, bordered by Indonesia. The major seaports of Peninsula Malaysia are those at Penang and Port Klang. Kuching, Sibu and Miri are the main ports in Sarawak, and Labuan is the principal port of Sabah (Demaine 1997).

There is great geographical difference between the peninsula and the rest of the country. Although the majority of the population is concentrated on the peninsula, the greater part of the land is in east Malaysia, consisting of rugged terrain with valuable forest and jungle. Though much of the country is mountainous, with dense tropical forests, most of western Peninsula Malaysia has been cleared and developed. The most well developed part of Malaysia is the area between the mountains and the west coast. These "western lowlands" are close to the sea routes and contain vast mineral deposits (alluvial tin) (Demaine 1997).

Malaysia has an extremely rich natural-resource base, and is often referred to as a "Garden of Eden." Its main wealth remains in its coastal and offshore deposits of hydrocarbons and its extensive tin deposits. However, before the rise of petroleum, Malaysia's main economic resource was the Peninsula's agricultural output (rubber, oil palm and tropical timbers). The rate of extraction of timber has been so rapid that the situation is serious, and major efforts will be necessary to prevent total depletion and ecological disaster.

Malaysia has an equatorial climate with high temperatures coupled with rain during all seasons. The relative humidity averages 80% year round and temperatures vary between 22°C and 33°C.

Demography

In Malaysia, geographical variety is matched by racial richness. As will be discussed later, the population is composed of Malays and other indigenous people (officially termed *bumiputras*—a word meaning "sons of the soil"), Chinese and Indians, who account, respectively, for 62%, 29% and 9% of the population. The country is predominantly rural, with the total population at mid-1995 estimated to be 20 103 000 as compared with 13 764 352 in mid-1980 (see fig. 11.1). Of these, 83.1% were in Peninsula Malaysia (the most urbanized part of the country, where the average density was 86.9 per km^2), 7.3 % were in Sabah (13.7 per km^2), and 9.6% were in Sarawak (10.5 per km^2) (Demaine 1997) (see fig. 11.2).

The unemployment rate stood at a high of 7.9% in 1989 (Hong Kong and Shanghai Banking Corporation 1991), despite a growth of 3.2% in employment. However, this unemployment rate has been drastically reduced, to 5.1% in 1990 and 3.0% in 1993; it fell to a low of 2.8% in 1995 (*Mid-Term Review of the Sixth Malaysia Plan* 1993; Demaine 1997). Malaysia's population is relatively young, with some 40% in the under-14 age group and about half in the working age group of 15–64 years (see fig. 11.3). As a consequence, Malaysia's labor force (estimated to be 8.07 million people in 1995) is young, with about three-quarters of employees under the age of 40. Current policy aims to boost the population growth rate by offering tax benefits to larger families (Hong Kong and Shanghai Banking Corporation 1991; Demaine 1997).

As in most developing nations, there is an income disparity between urban and rural households. A principal cause is the division of agriculture

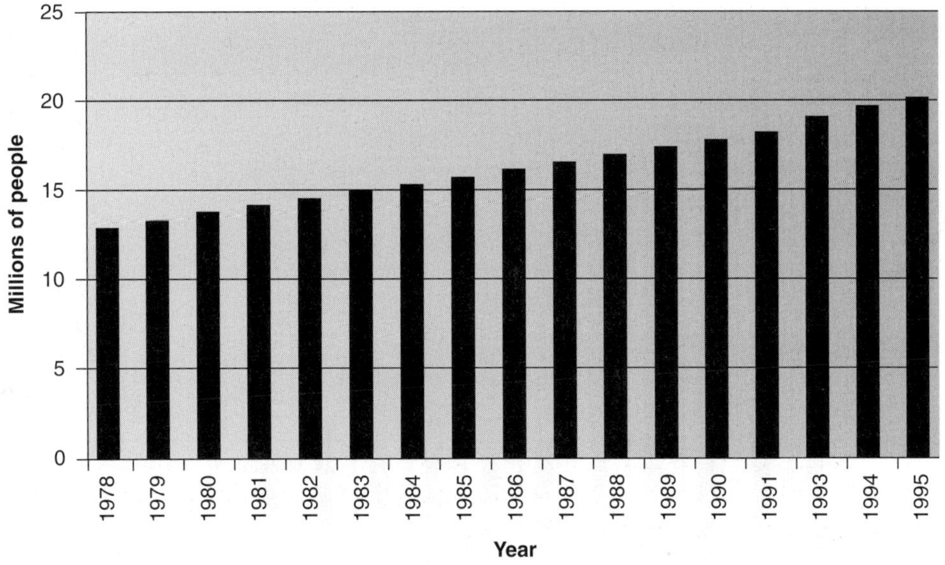

Fig. 11.1 Malaysia's population (1978–1995)

Sources: Based on the 1991 census; Europa Publications (1997), *The Far East and Australasia*, 27th edition, Europa Publications Ltd, London.

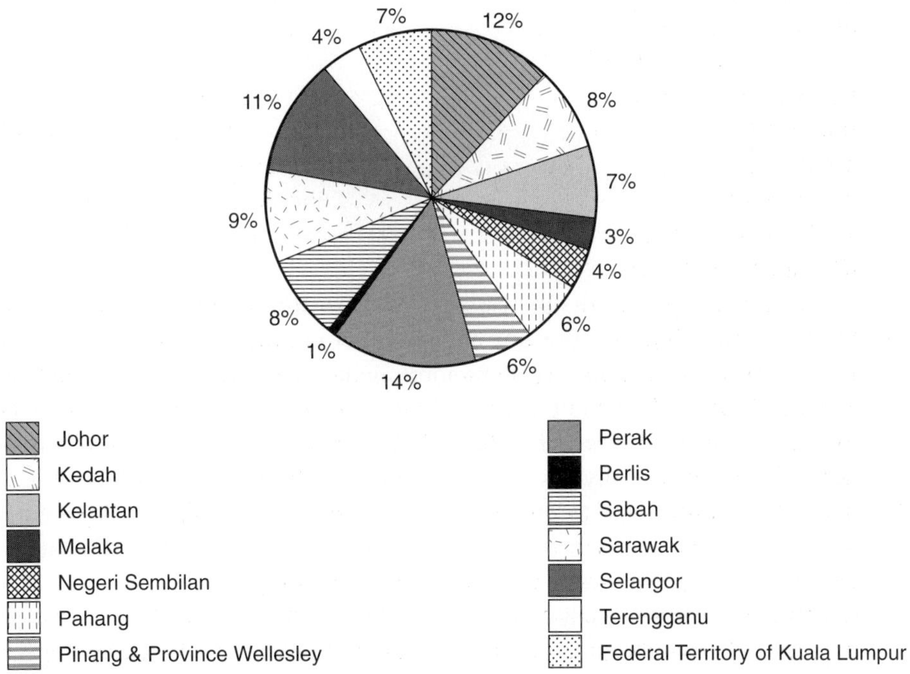

Fig. 11.2 Distribution of population among Malaysia's states (mid-1990s)

Source: Europa Publications (1997), *The Far East and Australasia*, 27th edn, Europa Publications Ltd, London; based on 1991 census.

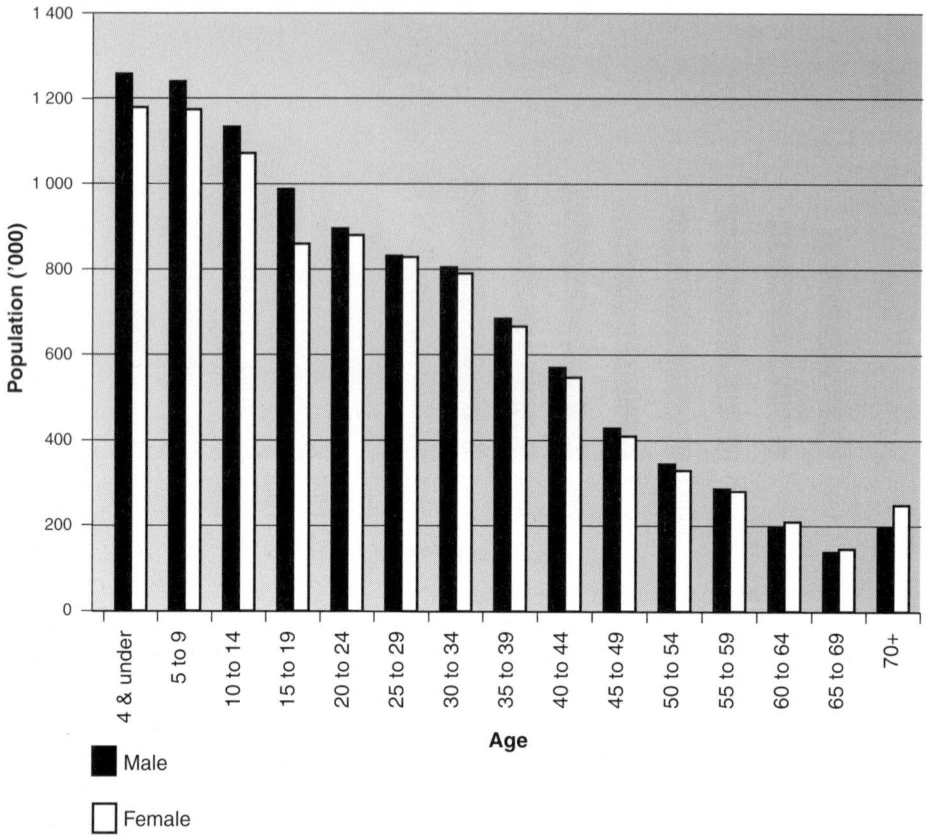

Fig. 11.3 Population by age and gender (July 1994)

Source: United Nations (1996), *Statistical Yearbook for Asia and the Pacific*, UN, New York.

into a relatively high-income estate sector, predominantly owned by ethnic Indians and Chinese, and a low-income, low productivity traditional sector composed of *bumiputras*. This economic imbalance of the racial groups is a significant feature of the economy, and a major aim of government policy has been to redress this imbalance to the advantage of the numerically superior but economically disadvantaged Malays (Moore 1994). However, the transfer of state assets to *bumiputra* ownership has resulted in the creation of a wealthy elite within the Malay community, where income disparity is now greater than in other ethnic groups (Demaine 1997).

Unique features of Malaysia's economic development policy are the objectives of poverty alleviation and wealth distribution. For instance, the incidence of hardcore poverty (households earning less than RM250 a month) has dropped from 5.2% of total households in 1990 to 4.3% in 1993. The following programs have contributed to this progress:

1 the Development Program for the Hardcore Poor
2 the "Amanah Saham Bumiputera" unit trust scheme (launched in 1992 to enable the hardcore poor to supplement their income through participation in this investment scheme; by 1993, RM700 million[1] had been fully disbursed to 140 000 of the hardcore poor)
3 programs of non-government organisations by "Amanah Ikhtiar Malaysia" and state "Yayasan Basmi Kemiskinan" (Poverty Eradication Schemes), providing various assistance in the form of bank loans, training opportunities, better housing and educational support.

From 1991 to 1993, a 10.2% increase in mean monthly household income was registered, with all ethnic groups recording increases. *Bumiputra* household income, for instance, increased by 10.1% annually, three times its rate during the 1987–1990 period. The Chinese income increase was 10.4% per annum, and the Indian income increase 9.5% per annum for 1991–1993. Over this period, rural household income grew at a much faster rate of 8.4% per annum, compared with 3.9% growth per year over the previous three years, though it is still slower than the 9.4% growth of urban income. The different rates of growth resulted in an increase in the rural–urban income disparity ratio from 1:1.70 in 1990 to 1:1.75 in 1993. This reflects Peninsular Malaysia's pattern of urban income growing faster than rural income. However, in Sarawak and Sabah, a reverse situation prevailed over this period (*Mid-Term Review of the Sixth Malaysia Plan* 1993). The political aim has been to gradually narrow the income disparity along urban–rural and ethnic lines. The economic progress has to a certain extent assisted in the achievement of this aim, as each gets a bigger share of the expanding economic cake. However, although the proportion of households classified as "very poor" declined from 3.9% in 1990 to 2.2% in 1995, relative poverty across ethnic lines appears to have increased (Edwards 1997).

Political environment

Though a discussion of the history and political background of Malaysia is not the primary purpose of this chapter, it is necessary to sketch an outline to enable an assessment of the country in terms of political risk. Malaysia has enjoyed a long period of democracy and stability since independence in 1957. The same government has been voted into power through a democratic process, and it retains important political and economic links both within and outside the Asia Pacific region (*Asia Pacific: An Investment Guide* 1990).

Since independence in 1957, the 3-party multiracial Alliance and its successor, the 12 party National Front (NF), have retained political power (Asia 1993 Yearbook). The United Malays National Organization (now known as New UMNO) is the dominant party in the ruling NF coalition. Each of the main races has tended to congregate in its own racial political party. The government has maintained racial harmony, despite UMNO and the Malays remaining in power (Rafferty 1990). Malaysia has political concerns, as a result of the delicacy of racial relations between the Malays, Chinese, and Indians (Rafferty 1990). Like many things in Malaysia, politics is complicated by the great ethnic and racial diversity and economic disparity of the country. Malaysia's recent history has been peppered by serious inter-communal rioting due to racial and religious tensions between the ethnic groups, which has, more than once, severely threatened the country's political stability.

In Malaysia, the business sector may be the ground on which the silent battle for ethnic dominance is fought. The comparatively late Malay entry into the business corporate sector and their supposed lack of business heritage are weaknesses that are assailed by their established competitors. Talk about the "incompetent Malay business professionals" is among the many tacitly used folkstories with damaging implications. Khairudin Damhoeri et al.'s (1994) study provides evidence from the Malaysian general insurance industry that refutes this myth. Their study demonstrates that Malay CEOs, despite the myth and despite market perceptions, do not affect corporate performance any differently than their non-Malay counterparts.

One important development has been the formation of a strong regional grouping of key South-East Asian Nations (commonly referred to as ASEAN) in 1967. Though ASEAN was primarily concerned with economic development, co-operation in foreign policy issues increased rapidly (Moore 1994). There was also the formation of the East Asian Economic Caucus (EAEC), which operates as an East Asian interest group within the US-inspired Asia-Pacific Economic Cooperation (APEC). In January 1992, the members of ASEAN agreed to establish an ASEAN Free Trade Area (AFTA) within 15 years from January 1993 (Moore 1994). However, Malaysia has not made substantial progress toward a common market. Most of Malaysia's partners in ASEAN compete in export markets and for foreign investment. Hence, though much has been achieved in terms of political unity, there is little cohesion in developing strategies and policies. The competition among the 6 states is thought likely to continue to stand in the way of closer unification in the 1990s (*Asia Pacific: An Investment Guide* 1990).

Investment climate

Introduction

Prior to the currency crisis of 1997, international confidence in the Malaysian economy was high, as indicated by the increase in foreign investment. Although statistics of foreign investment are either crude or not available, US investment at the end of 1983 amounted to US$2.8 billion, and in general the flow of investment has been high–just under 5% of GDP between 1967 and 1986 (Bair 1988; Demaine 1997). The country has been helped by its good infrastructure, widespread knowledge of English, plentiful land, and lower labor costs than either Japan or Singapore (Rafferty 1990). The business and investment climate in Malaysia was hence attractive until mid-1997. Despite the government's austerity program in development spending, its efforts to privatize traditional services have opened up many opportunities for foreign businesses. The Malaysian government has encouraged foreign investment in order to generate industrial growth, and is seeking, in particular, vertical integration in the electronics industry and investment in resource-based industries. Complementing the investment incentives to the foreign investor is an increasingly sophisticated banking and financial system. To encourage greater efficiency, the government has implemented measures to deregulate the banking sector and has encouraged competition (*Asia Pacific: An Investment Guide* 1990).

Riots in May 1969 forced a major re-adjustment in the terms upon which communal interests and aspirations were accommodated, and in the manner in which that accommodation was negotiated between the major communities. The New Economic Policy (NEP) had as its objectives the eradication of poverty (irrespective of race), and of the identification of race with economic function. The latter objective implied securing, for the Malays, not only a far greater share in the country's wealth, but also a far wider range of educational and employment opportunity. Immediately after the 1969 riots, new legislature removed from public discussion such sensitive issues as the power and status of the Sultans, Malay special rights, the status of Islam as the official religion, and citizen rights (Demaine 1997). The policy offers affirmative action in favor of the Malays, and has had partial success. Share-ownership by Malays, the main indicator of the extent of economic backwardness of the group, has risen from 2.3% in 1970 to more than 20% in 1990, though this is still short of the 30% target. Despite this, Chinese businesspeople remain Malaysia's liveliest entrepreneurs. Unfortunately, the Chinese in particular have been leaving the country or sending their children abroad for education, claiming that Malaysia is too small and too racially oriented for them to really prosper. The Indians fare even worse, contributing approximately 9% of the population and still possessing only 1.5% of the country's corporate assets.

The other achievement of the NEP has been to reduce the foreign ownership of corporate assets from 62% in 1970 to 26% in 1990, well below the 30% envisaged in the original NEP. The government, sensitive to the NEP implications for new investments, adopted measures to liberalize foreign equity participation (Moore 1994). Understandably, the Malaysian authorities regard the continued inflows of foreign investment as one of the key factors in sustaining economic growth and the development of the economy, and have an active program of encouraging foreign investment in conformity with Malaysia's economic development goals (Bair 1988). Hence, the government has sought to create a favorable environment for private-sector initiatives through a liberal investment code, selective tariff protection, moderately expansionary fiscal and monetary policy, the establishment of free trade zones, and the creation of a productive infrastructure. Its privatization policy is further evidence of the bigger role it wants the private sector to play in the economy (Bair 1988).

Foreign investment accounted for 56.7% of total investment in 1991, with major investors including Taiwan, Japan, the USA, the Republic of Korea, Indonesia and Singapore. Traditionally, foreign investment has been mainly in the electrical and chemical sectors, as well as the food-manufacturing industries. However, between 1987 and 1989, rubber-based and wood products emerged as important export-oriented industries, and both have since enjoyed significant foreign participation in direct response to increased international demand. Continuing strong investment in the manufacturing sector is reflected in the pace of demand for manufacturing licenses, with the rubber-products sector dominating the applications (*Asia Pacific: An Investment Guide* 1990). Opportunities for foreign participation are abundant, as evidenced by the amount of foreign equity in approved manufacturing projects. In general, the outlook for foreign investment remains good, though increasing infrastructure deficiencies and power shortages (the result of 6 years of rapid growth) are likely to affect investor confidence. A further problem is the shortage of labor, which allows workers to change jobs frequently and continues to exert upward pressure on wages (Bair 1988).

Government policy on investment

An integral part of the NEP are the government's guidelines for regulating the acquisition of assets or interests, mergers, and takeovers of companies and businesses. They are used to redress imbalances in the distribution of corporate wealth, and apply to several categories of investment. Any proposed acquisition by foreign interests of any substantial fixed assets in Malaysia is subject to them, as is any proposed acquisition of assets or interests, or any merger or take-over that results in ownership or control passing to foreign entity. While the targets of the NEP of 1971–1990 have remained broadly applicable, the Malaysian authorities have relaxed the constraints imposed on foreign investment, and a greater flexibility has characterized the investment code since late 1986. To encourage foreign investment, the government has introduced legislation relaxing foreign equity rules (1986) and freeing credit restrictions (1987), and has withdrawn its proposals to abandon tax incentives for foreign firms.

Malaysia's readiness to conclude investment-guarantee agreements testifies to the government's desire to increase the confidence of foreign investors in Malaysia. Under the terms of an investment-guarantee agreement, the foreign investor is provided with protection against nationalization and expropriation, allowed the free transfer of profits or capital and other fees; and entitled to settlement of investment disputes under the Convention on Settlement of Investment Disputes, of which Malaysia has been a member since 1966 (*Asia Pacific: An Investment Guide* 1990). Foreign investors in Malaysia therefore have a degree of protection if an investment-guarantee agreement exists with their home country (Hong Kong and Shanghai Banking Corporation 1991).

Exchange controls

The present Malaysian exchange-control regime is very liberal, and applies uniformly to transactions with all countries. No permission is required from the Controller of Foreign Exchange for a non-resident to undertake direct or portfolio investment in Malaysia (Bair 1988). In principle, there are no exchange controls on foreign persons investing in Malaysia, and dividend income, profits and capital can be freely repatriated to any country, provided that the relevant forms are completed if payments exceed the equivalent of RM10 000. Thus, payments, repatriation of capital and remittance of profits can be made in any foreign currency, though payments within Malaysia must be made in Malaysian ringgit. Further, export proceeds must be repatriated to Malaysia within 6 months of the date of exportation.

It should be noted, however, that both foreign persons borrowing local funds in Malaysia and Malaysian companies borrowing in foreign markets require the approval of the Controller of Foreign Exchange in certain circumstances. Though a company controlled by a non-resident may borrow up to a total of RM10 million from Malaysian sources without the permission of the Controller of Foreign Exchange (provided that it obtains at least 60% of its credit facilities from financial institutions incorporated in Malaysia), borrowings in excess of RM10 million require the approval of the Controller (Hong Kong and Shanghai Banking Corporation 1991). A resident company that requires additional financing for business purposes may borrow in foreign currency from banks, whether to pay for imports or to sell to a bank for Malaysian ringgit, but the foreign currency may not be retained for temporary investment abroad except with the permission of the Controller of Foreign Exchange. For Malaysian resident companies, borrowing from non-residents requires the approval of the Controller of Foreign Exchange if the total foreign borrowing exceeds the equivalent of RM1 million (Hong Kong and Shanghai Banking Corporation 1991).

Protection

Malaysia is a good market for foreign exports, particularly food, computer systems, telecommunications equipment, specialized manufacturing equipment, petroleum production, and refining and defense equipment. Significant demand will also continue for engineering and architectural skills. However, the level of protection can be high. The Malaysian customs tariff structure is based on the 1978 Customs Corporation Council Nomenclature (CCCN). This tariff structure applies to all of Malaysia, and all items, with the exception of certain goods, mainly petroleum products and live animals. The exception also extends to goods manufactured locally or abroad that are transported among the 3 areas of Malaysia (Peninsula Malaysia, Sabah and Sarawak).

Import licenses fall into three categories:

1 no restrictions on issuance of license, no restrictions imposed on import
2 quantitative restrictions: import on a quota basis
3 nil issue of any license: no import license will be issued

Most goods enter Malaysia under an open general license, but some are admissible only under a validated license that is issued by the Comptroller of Customs, who administers trade controls (Bair 1988). The open general license is an authorization by the government of Malaysia to import (or export) specified goods without recourse to a specific validated license for each transaction.

Investment regulatory agencies

The *Industrial Coordination Act, 1965* (ICA) requires that all manufacturers with capital of RM250 000 or more and at least 25 full-time workers obtain a license from the Ministry of Trade and Industry for each manufacturing site. The Minister may exempt a manufacturing activity from any or all of the provisions of the Act, as well as attaching any condition deemed suitable to the license. Conditions imposed may include the proposed venture's location, equity structure, and the use of local raw materials. Further, the number and type of goods manufactured under a license may not be changed without the Minister's approval (Bair 1988).

Besides the Ministry of Trade and Industry, there are a number of regulatory agencies that are concerned with the operation of businesses in Malaysia (Hong Kong and Shanghai Banking Corporation 1991). Foreign firms interested in investing in Malaysia should consult initially with the MIDA, which is primarily concerned with providing information on Malaysian investment, and serves as a liaison between foreign investors and the government of Malaysia. Other agencies involved in approving foreign investment in Malaysia may include the Ministry of Finance, the Central Bank, the Ministry of Agriculture, and the Ministry of Primary Industries. Depending on the location of the proposed investment, a local State Economic Development Corporation may also be involved in the approval process. The most important of these regulatory agencies from the foreign investor's standpoint is the Foreign Investment Committee (FIC). This was established in 1986 to formulate policy guidelines on foreign investments in Malaysia in order to ensure that the social and ownership objectives of the

NEP were achieved. The FIC has also been given the responsibility of supervising all government actions relating to foreign investment. Currently, FIC approval is required in the event of any proposed acquisition by foreign persons of substantial fixed assets in Malaysia (*Asia Pacific: An Investment Guide* 1990).

Although foreign investment in Malaysia is encouraged, the Malaysian government is concerned with increasing indigenous Malaysian participation in the overall ownership of the Malaysian economy. For this reason investment in Malaysia, both foreign and local, is subject to governmental review and approval. However, with respect to companies whose shares are listed on the Kuala Lumpur Stock Exchange (KLSE), the approval procedures for foreign investment have been relaxed so that there appear to be no substantive limits on foreign persons buying KLSE quoted shares (*Asia Pacific: An Investment Guide* 1990). All shareholders, whether foreign or local, must comply with the Malaysian *Companies Act,* the Malaysian Code on Takeovers and Mergers and the *Banking and Financial Institutions Act* (*Asia Pacific: An Investment Guide* 1990).

Employment policy

Malaysia's policy is to ensure that Malaysian citizens are trained and employed at all levels. Foreign companies are allowed to bring in essential expatriate personnel for key posts and other positions, for which there is a shortage of trained Malaysians. They are, however, expected to train *bumiputra* personnel so that employment patterns at all levels of the company reflect the multiracial composition of the country (Bair 1988). For new investments with foreign paid-up capital of US$2 million or more, a company is automatically allowed 5 expatriate posts. However, the employment of expatriates is flexible, and numbers are negotiable, particularly in export-oriented industries.

Wages in Malaysia are lower than wages in the industrialized countries, and toward the lower end of wages in the NECs of East Asia. Wages are set in various ways:

- by individual companies
- through collective bargaining between unions and management
- by minimum wage legislation
- for government employees, after consultation between unions and the government, conducted every 5 years (Bair 1988)

The Trade Union Ordinance of 1959 provides safeguards against excessive militancy and unlawful activities of trade unions.

A potential problem that was frequently highlighted in the 1990s was the growing labor shortage, which was anticipated to lead to a rise in wages above productivity level, thus reducing Malaysia's competitiveness in relation to other countries in the region such as China and India. While the supply of skilled and unskilled labor is still fair, there is a lack of technicians (Hong Kong and Shanghai Banking Corporation 1991). To combat this, in 1992 the government lifted restrictions on the employment of foreign workers, and placed an emphasis on shifting industrial production toward skill-intensive high-technology products. Given the country's dependence on foreign companies for investment, technologies and skills, the government also increased investment in vocational and technical training (Moore 1994). In late 1997 these problems seem far away as economic downturn precipitates all of the problems associated with unemployment, and the repatriation of guest workers.

Investment incentives

Malaysia's tax system applies on a territorial basis, and a non-resident is taxed only on income derived from Malaysia. A resident company is defined as one that is managed and controlled in Malaysia at any time during the financial year, irrespective of where it was incorporated (Hong Kong and Shanghai Banking Corporation 1991). Malaysia's investment incentives are designed to provide, to companies investing in new enterprises or expanding existing ones, total or partial relief from the payment of income tax, development tax and excess profits tax.

The tax incentives offered differ according to the form of investment. Firms that invest in free trade zones and whose products will be exported, and firms that introduce new technologies or manufacture products that further Malaysia's economic development goals, may obtain as much as an 8-year exemption from corporate income tax, developmental tax and excess-profits tax (Bair 1988). The following are the 4 investment incentive programs most widely used: Pioneer Status, Labor Utilization Relief, Location Incentive, and Investment Tax Credit (Bair 1988). There are also 5 incentives designed to encourage companies to export products manufactured in Malaysia:

1. an export credit re-financing scheme
2. an abatement of adjusted income for exports
3. double deduction on export credit insurance premiums
4. additional deductions for the promotion of exports
5. export allowances

Free Trade Zones

The aim of these is to encourage the dispersal of industry, especially to less developed areas. They enable export-oriented industries to enjoy minimum customs control and formalities in their import of raw materials, parts, machinery, and equipment (Bair 1988). Free Trade Zones (FTZs) are especially designed for manufacturing establishments that produce or assemble products essentially for export. Investors who apply for sites in an FTZ must be prepared to export the entire output of their plants or, in exceptional circumstances, not less than 80% of production, and must use imported raw materials and components. Goods exported from an FTZ are free from customs duty, but those manufactured there and subsequently imported into the principal customs area for home consumption are subject to the prevailing tariffs (Hong Kong and Shanghai Banking Corporation 1991). So far, 9 FTZs have been set up, in the states of Johor, Malacca, Penang and Selangor. Where the establishment of an FTZ is neither practical nor desirable, the government permits the setting up of licensed manufacturing warehouses which enjoy concessions similar to those accorded to factories in the FTZs.

Business organization

Four types of businesses may be set up in Malaysia: public companies, private companies, sole proprietorships and partnerships, and branches of foreign companies. Three types of public companies may be incorporated: a company limited by shares, a company limited by guarantee, and an unlimited company. For most foreign investors, a company limited by shares—which may be public or private—is the most appropriate form of business organization to set up (Hong Kong and Shanghai Banking Corporation 1991). Foreign investors also have the choice of establishing a branch of a local company or entering into a joint venture with local businesspeople. The formation of joint ventures is particularly welcome, since it involves Malaysian participation. In keeping with the objective of ensuring increased Malaysian participation in the corporate sector, it is the government's general policy to encourage projects to be undertaken on a joint-venture basis.

The term "non-residents" refers to any resident of a country other than Malaysia, including a company incorporated outside Malaysia. A company is considered to be non-resident where non-residents hold 50% or more of the paid-up capital. Also, the company will be considered non-resident if it is a branch of a company that is incorporated outside Malaysia. The conduct of business operations in Malaysia by non-residents may be undertaken by the establishment of a Malaysian subsidiary of a non-resident company. It may also be carried out by the acquisition by a non-resident company of an existing Malaysian firm, or by establishing a branch of a non-resident company in the country. Approval must be obtained from the Domestic Trade Division of the Ministry of Trade and Industry, with documents then lodged with the Registrar of Companies. As already stated, businesspeople who intend to set up manufacturing or assembling units or plants in Malaysia are required to apply for a manufacturing license from the Ministry of Trade and Industry (Hong Kong and Shanghai Banking Corporation 1991). Finally, business can be carried out in Malaysia by establishing an agent of a non-resident company so that it does not require registration as a branch–that is, a corporation does not necessarily have to incorporate in Malaysia.

Infrastructure

Owing to the NEP's emphasis on the private sector, a privatization master plan was launched in late 1989. There have been plans to privatize the national airline, telecommunications, railways and the container port (Rafferty 1990). In 1991, the sixth Malaysian Plan (1991–1995) placed a major emphasis on upgrading infrastructure and improving productivity (Brown 1994). However, questions about the adequacy of the physical infrastructure were highlighted in 1992 by a near-nationwide power blackout. Bottlenecks in Malaysia's network of roads, ports and utilities also intensified in 1992, and were cited as a major reason for the foreign investment decline by some 33% (*Asia 1993 Yearbook*).

The capital markets in Malaysia are also relatively unsophisticated. Some attempts have been made to rectify this through the liberalization of securities trading (*Asia Pacific: An Investment Guide* 1990). In 1995 the capital market was liberalized further, and in 1996 an operating license was granted for the second financial futures exchange (Edwards 1997). The government has declared the island of Labuan an international offshore financial centre, but its failure to attract significant investment was again due largely to a lack of basic infrastructure and efficient telecommunications (Brown 1994).

Malaysia's government-owned telecommunications system is modern and efficient, but is one of the government services that is a candidate for privatization. All of the principal cities are linked by telephone, and calls may be placed immediately to most points via direct dialing. Overseas radio and telephone service is available between Malaysia and most foreign countries.

Ocean shipping is vital to Malaysia, due to its heavy dependence on foreign trade and the separation by water of the Peninsula from the east Malaysian states. Malaysia's shipping capacity has been increased by the completion of new shipping facilities (Bair 1988). Malaysia's highway network generally serves all the settled areas and connects principal commercial centres, reaching into the newly settled land development areas opened up by the Federal Land Development Authority. Road and rail communications are more highly developed in Peninsula Malaysia than in Sabah and Sarawak (Brown 1994).

The demand for electricity grew by approximately 13% per year in the 1970s, and exceeded 10 000 million kilowatt-hours in 1983. Around 89% of Malaysia's generating capacity is located in Peninsula Malaysia, and the government-owned National Electricity Board operates virtually all facilities. In 1983, generating capacity was 2 400 megawatts, exceeding the required level by 1 100 megawatts (Bair 1988). However, power shortages have affected Malaysia since 1991, and seemed likely to continue (Brown 1994). To remedy this, a major hydro-electric dam in Sarawak was begun (Edwards 1997). The concern that the economy would overheat as a result of this and other grandiose schemes has been realized, and the project has been delayed indefinitely.

Economic environment

Throughout the 1970s, the country achieved high rates of growth, which were sustained primarily through its rich endowment of resources. Overall economic performance since 1980, especially up to 1986, was more erratic, with sharp fluctuations in growth, investment, and the fiscal and external balances. This was primarily a result of cyclical changes in commodity prices and rapid fiscal expansion to support a development strategy led by the public sector (*Asia Pacific: An Investment Guide* 1990).

Aside from Singapore, Malaysia has been the most dynamic and the fastest growing economy in South-East Asia (Moore 1994), averaging growth of more than 8% a year. Since the 1980s, Malaysia has slowly shifted from a commodity-based economy to one built around light industry (*Asia 1993 Yearbook*). It has a good foundation and is one of the wealthier developing countries, with a per-capita income of around US$3300 a year in 1993, as compared with US$700 in 1970 (Sheridan 1994a). It is also the world's leading exporter of palm oil and a major producer of rubber and tin. Oil palm products and rubber accounted for 5.3% and 2.8% respectively of total exports in 1991 (Moore 1993). In addition, it is a principal exporter of tropical hardwoods and has large petroleum and natural-gas reserves. Other important cash crops include cocoa, pepper, coconuts, tea, and pineapples. Sawlogs also remain an important source of foreign exchange (4.3% of total exports in 1991) (see fig. 11.4).

In general, Malaysia is heavily dependent on exports, with an export-to-gross domestic product (GDP) ratio of 80.9% in 1991 (Moore 1994). During the period 1980–1990, agricultural GDP increased by an annual average of 3.8% (Moore 1993) (see fig. 11.5). Despite the decline of the agricultural sector, agricultural products are still a leading source of export earnings. In 1992 they provided 15.7% of GDP and engaged 26.2% of the workforce. By 1995 the figures had declined to 13.9% of GDP and 18.4% of the workforce. Since 1987, however, the manufacturing sector has become the leading source of revenue for the country, providing an estimated 28.8% of GDP and 20.5% of employment in 1992, and 32.3% and 24.8% respectively in 1995. Industry (including mining, manufacturing, construction, and power) contributed an estimated 43.3% of GDP, and engaged about 27.9% of the employed labor force in 1992; in 1995 the figures were 47.2% of GDP and about 33.2% of the labor force. During 1980–1990, industrial GDP increased

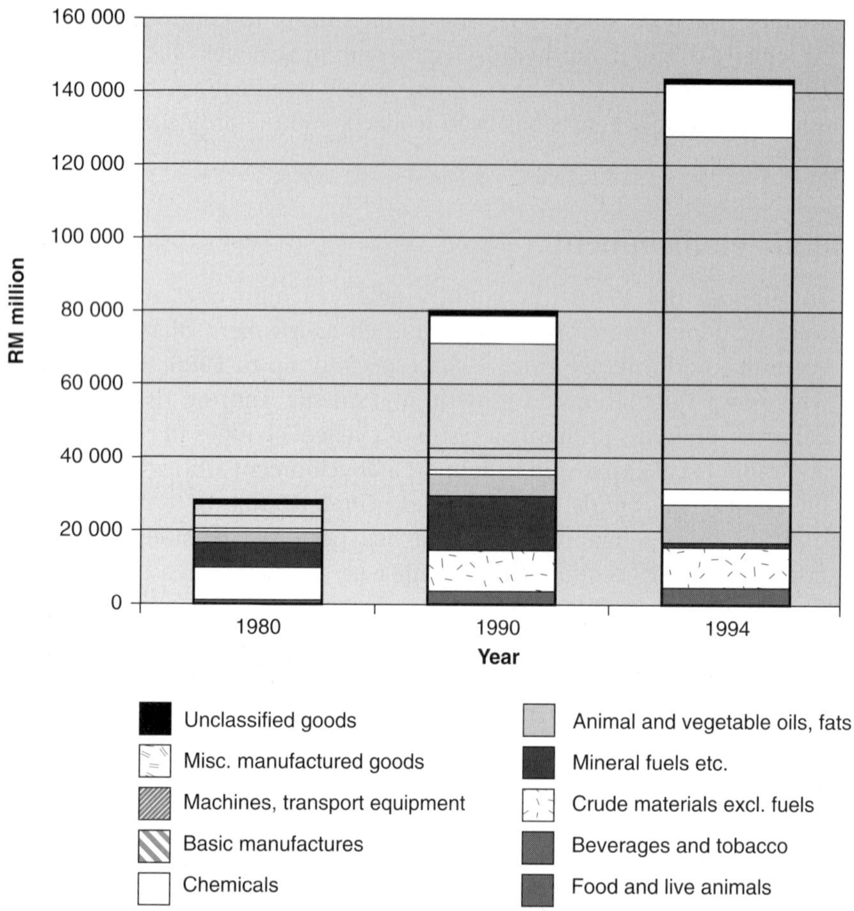

Fig. 11.4 Principal export commodities, 1980–1994

Source: Europa Publications (1997), *The Far East and Australasia,* 27th edn, Europa Publications Ltd, London.

by an annual average of 7.1% (see fig. 11.5). Mining contributed about 8.6% of GDP. Malaysia is one of the world's leading producers of tin, though in 1991 sales of this commodity accounted for only 0.7% of total export revenue. This was because in the 1980s these exports of primary products were equaled, and in 1987 superseded, by the export of a growing amount of manufactured products (Moore 1994). The decline in the proportion of exports of mineral fuels, lubricants and related minerals from 12.9% in 1993 to 7.3% in 1995 provides further strong evidence of the extent of the restructuring of the economy (Edwards 1995).

The *Mid-Term Review of the Sixth Malaysia Plan* reported a GDP growth of 8.1% for 1991–1993, and of 8.0% for 1994–1995. Between 1988 and 1992, GDP increased between 8 and 10% each year—remarkably, achieving over 8.0% growth for 8 consecutive years up to 1995. Specifically, over the

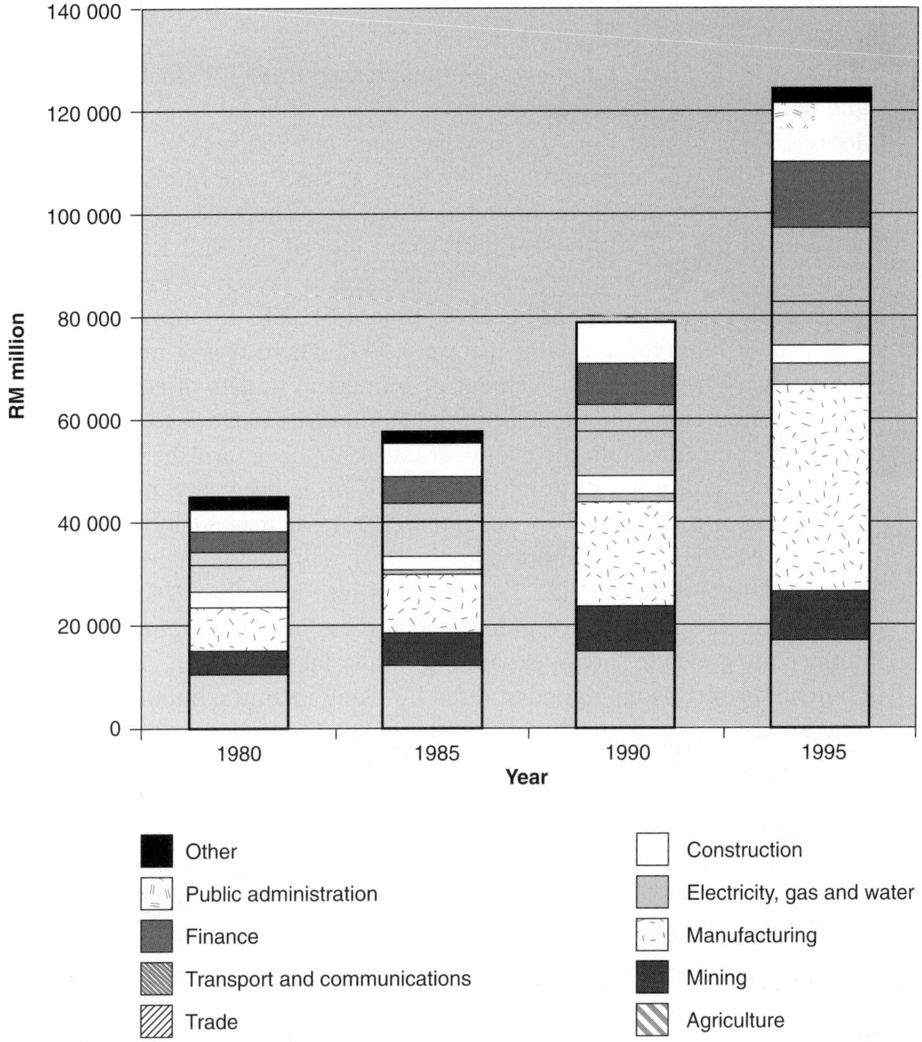

Fig. 11.5 GDP by industrial origin, 1978–1991

Sources: Asian Development Bank (1992), *Key Indicators of Developing Asian and Pacific Countries*, vol. 23, July, Manila; Europa Publications (1997), *The Far East and Australasia*, 27th edn, Europa Publications Ltd, London.

period 1991–1995, GDP in real terms grew at 8.1% per year, the highest growth rate relative to other ASEAN and Asian countries, with the exception of China. The average annual growth rate of GNP at purchasers' value has been 8.0% for 1991–1993, and 8.5% for 1994–1995. During 1980–1991, GNP increased in real terms at an average annual rate of 5.6%, while real GNP per capita increased by 2.9% per year. Over the period covered by the NEP, the level of poverty in Malaysia was reduced from 52% of all households in 1970 to 17% by 1990 (Moore 1994). The *bumiputras'* share of the corporate sector increased from 2.4% to 20.3% between 1970 and 1990.

Chinese and Indian equity ownership increased from 32% to 46% over the same period, while that of foreign investors was reduced from 63% to 25% (Moore 1994). In June 1991 the New Development Policy (NDP), the successor to the NEP, was announced as the basis of the Prime Minister's "Vision 2020," the date by which he intended Malaysia to be a developed country. The focus of the NDP differed slightly from that of the NEP. Racially based economic and social engineering were relaxed in favour of national unity, and emphasis was placed on the development of skills to promote the consolidation of *bumiputra* wealth (Brown 1994). There was a major shift in strategy away from the achievement of numerical targets of equity ownership to strengthening the capacity of the *bumiputras* to manage, operate and own businesses. Although the events of late 1997 have tarnished the "Vision 2020," the situation is still promising; a revision is necessary, however.

Gross imports continued to expand in 1991, increasing by 27.8% from 1987 figures. The rise in import value in 1991 was predominantly due to an increase in import volume (22.3%) as prices rose by only 4.5%. This rise in imports was due to intensive public and private investment, an increase in intermediate goods to satisfy expanding industrial production, and a growth in purchases of consumer goods caused by rising incomes. Imports of investment goods recorded the highest growth (37.7%) followed by consumer goods (24.8%) and intermediate goods (21.1%). However, in terms of total import value, intermediate goods accounted for the largest share with 43.2%, compared with 40.7% and 15.6% for investment and consumption goods respectively (Moore 1994). This trend continued from 1992 to 1994, when imports increased by 53.7%, thereby providing an indication of the possibility of future balance-of-payments problems (Edwards 1997).

The pressure on price stability has made it harder to sustain the high growth rates that have energized the nation for the past 8 years (1990–1997). High growth rates have helped fuel inflation, which rose from 2.5% in 1988 to 4% in 1989 (Rafferty 1990). In 1989, prices for most consumer items registered increases, with food showing a 3.7% rise, as against 3.8% in 1988. Similar figures were recorded in 1995 when the food price index rose by almost 5%. In particular, transport and communication costs rose at an annual rate of 6.9%. Further cost-of-living increases were fueled by conspicuous consumption and other forms of excessive spending as Malaysia's expanding middle class splurged on luxury items. The devaluation of the Malaysian ringgit, which was worth 25% less in 1989 than its level of 1986, further accentuated this trend.

The period of the early 1990s was characterized by labor shortages that became more protracted and deepened in 1992 as the country's well-trained but relatively small workforce failed to keep up with the demands of new manufacturing operations. Tight labor supply-demand conditions have pushed up wages for both skilled and unskilled employees, succeeding in further complicating inflation problems and increasing the costs for foreign investors of doing business. In 1992, the average wage bill per employee rose by 6% (*Asia 1993 Yearbook*). As a result of the higher costs for labor and raw materials, producer prices increased by 4.5% in 1991 (Moore 1994). Strict monetary and fiscal measures successfully slowed the growth of the economy in 1991–1992, relieving inflationary pressures, and the government removed restrictions on the use of semi-skilled and unskilled foreign workers, a policy that is now showing indications of reversal.

The long-term solution to labor shortages proposed by the government was to move into more capital-intensive value-added industries. Improvements in education were vital to produce the necessary qualified personnel to service these industries, and Malaysia also needed to maintain its competitiveness in order to secure the requisite foreign investment.

The inflation rate (up to 4.4% in 1991 and 4.8% in 1992, compared with less than 1% during 1985–1987) and the growth in the money supply (11% in 1991, compared with 3.6% in 1987) have continued to increase. The renewed inflationary pressures were a consequence of the strong domestic demand for credit and the sharp increase in liquidity, caused by inflows of foreign capital related to Malaysia's rapid economic growth.

During 1992, high interest rates and restrictions on credit resulted in a slowing of consumer spending. High interest rates also attracted funds from abroad, accelerating the appreciation of the ringgit (Moore 1994). By mid-1992, the economy was showing signs of stability, notwithstanding the spectacular rise in the value of the ringgit against the US dollar. The ringgit had depreciated significantly against the currencies of Malaysia's trading partners in the 1980s, due to falling prices for major export commodities and political uncertainty. This depreciation reduced the growth in demand for imported goods, and enabled manufacturing exports to become more competitive, thereby encouraging domestic and foreign investment. Figure 11.6 shows rather starkly the effect of the 1997 currency crisis, with an over 37% drop in the value of the ringgit from July 1997 to January 1998.

GDP has a projected growth average of 7% per annum from 1991 to the year 2000. Malaysia is expected to achieve Newly Industrializing Country (NIC) status by the end of the century, by which time industrial production is targeted to account for 80% of GDP. This is in sharp contrast to the present level of only about 18%. The greatest opportunities are in industry and manufacturing, particularly in the downstream processing of raw materials.

Culture

The total population of Peninsula Malaysia is formed from three main ethnic groups, with the indigenous population (consisting mainly of Muslim

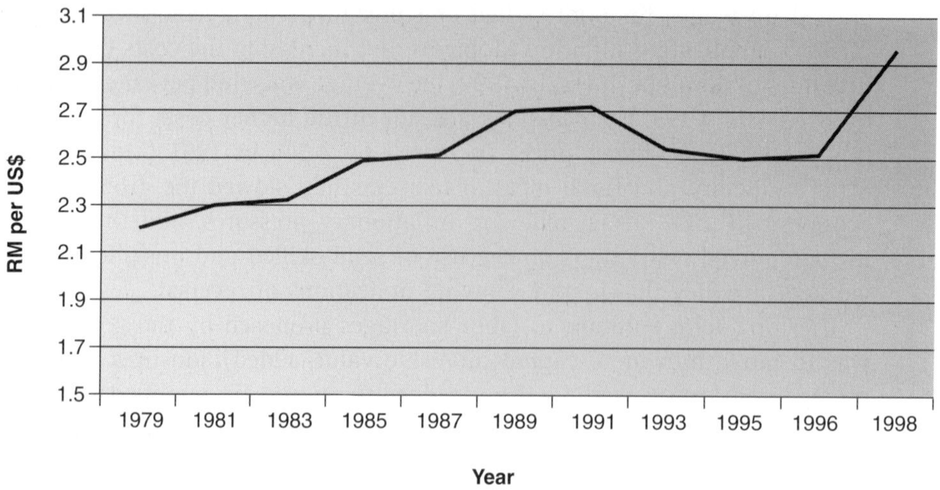

Fig. 11.6 Exchange rate, 1979–1998

Sources: Asian Development Bank (1992), *Key Indicators of Developing Asian and Pacific Countries*, vol. 23, July, Manila; Chris Edwards (1997), "Malaysia: Economy", *The Far East and Australasia*, 28th edn, Europa Publications Ltd, London.

Malays) contributing 58%, while the Chinese and Indians account for approximately 31% and 10% respectively, based on the 1991 census (Demaine 1997). In Sabah and Sarawak, Malays and Muslim peoples are confined mainly to the coast, while other ethnic groups occupy the interior. The Chinese element is large, amounting to 29% of the population in Sarawak and 14% in Sabah. During 1980–1991, the population increased by an annual average of 2.6% (Demaine 1997).

In the whole of Malaysia, the population is broken down along ethnic lines into 61.9% *bumiputra*, 29.5% Chinese and 8.6% Indians, as of the 1991 census. Hence, the majority of the population consists of Malays and other indigenous people (the *bumiputras*). The Chinese and Indians are mostly concentrated in the cities and towns and make up a higher proportion of the population in the Peninsula than in Sabah or Sarawak, where the indigenous groups tend to predominate. The population is mainly rural, but urbanization is increasing: the rate moved from 29% in 1970 to 41% in 1990, and to 51% in 1995, at an average of 4.0% a year (Demaine 1997).

A country's language is the key to understanding its culture, as spoken language is an observable cultural manifestation (Terpstra & Sarathy 1991). The impact of language on international marketing is twofold: it affects the communication program of marketers, and a foreign language may contain different thinking patterns or indicate varying motivations of prospective customers (Jeannet & Hennessey 1988). The official language is Bahasa Malaysia, based on Malay, but English is also widely used, as well as various Chinese dialects. Minorities speak Tamil and Iban. Islam is the established religion, practised by around 60% of the population (including virtually all Malays), while about 19% (including most of the Chinese community) are Buddhists. The Indians in the population are predominantly Hindus. Despite the predominance of Islam, Malaysia is not officially an Islamic state, and has remained committed to freedom of religion. Like Indonesia, it has avoided the excesses of Islamic extremism evident in parts of the Middle East (Sheridan 1994b).

There are many religious customs that remain a major factor in marketing today, and local variations of religious traditions can have a substantial impact on international marketing activities (Jeannet & Hennessey 1988). For instance, religious holidays vary greatly among countries. Religious requirements or taboos may also affect consumption patterns. Further, the economic role of women varies from culture to culture, and religious beliefs are an important determinant of this. Women may be restricted in their capacity as consumers, purchase influencers, workers, or respondents in a marketing study. Also, the caste system restricts participation in the economy, and hence affects a company's staffing practices, distributional and promotional programs, as it must deal with the market segments set up in the system. For instance, the Hindu joint family has economic effects: nepotism is a characteristic of family business. A joint family is a group in which all are descended from the female and/or the male line, and who live together with their spouses and offspring in one homestead under the authority of one of the members. The group members share the tasks of food gathering, trade, food preparation, and childrearing, and form a highly cohesive group. Other factors include differing consumption and decision-making patterns, and pooled income, which causes differing purchase patterns by allowing the purchase of relatively high-priced items. Religious institutions themselves can also block new products or techniques if these are seen as a threat (Terpstra & Sarathy 1991).

For the purpose of gleaning some insight into Malaysian culture, the main tenets of these religions will be briefly outlined. A common dictum of Hinduism is that it is not a religion but a way of life; a Hindu is born, not made. Modern Hinduism is a combination of ancient philosophies and customs, animistic beliefs, legends and, more recently, Western influences. Hinduism tends to assimilate rather than exclude, though an important Hindu practice is the caste system. Each member of a particular caste in Hindu society has a specific occupational role that is hereditary, as the system is aimed at preserving the status quo of society at large. Other elements include *baradari*, or the joint family, which is aimed at preserving the family, the restriction of women and the attainment of Nirvana.

Buddhism is derived from Hinduism, and is a reformation of it to some extent. Buddhists were released from caste restrictions, and its openness to all classes and sexes has been a major reason for its growth in popularity. While accepting the philosophical insights of Hinduism, Buddhism seeks to avoid the dogma and ceremony, stressing tolerance and spiritual equality. At the heart of Buddhism are the Four Noble Truths, which in essence state that suffering is omnipresent and part of the very nature of life, and that its cause is the desire for possession and selfish enjoyment. Nirvana is the ultimate goal of both the Hindu and Buddhist, and represents the extinction of all desires, and hence the final release from all suffering. To the extent that such an ideal reflects the thinking of the mass of the people, goals of acquisition, achievement, and affluence would be considered antithetical to the society, and this would be an obvious constraint on marketing (Terpstra & Sarathy 1991).

Muslim theology, *Tawhid,* defines all that a person should believe, whereas the law, *Shari'a,* prescribes all that he or she should do. The Koran is accepted as the ultimate guide, and anything not stated in this is likely to be rejected by the faithful. It is apparent that introducing new products and techniques would be difficult in such an environment, given that fatalistic beliefs tend to restrict attempts to bring about change in Muslim countries. The Five Pillars of Islam include recital of the creed, prayer, fasting, alms giving, and the pilgrimage. The Islamic value system requires a commitment to God and a constant awareness of God's presence. The Malaysian government has tried to make Islam a force for modernization by linking its conservative social values of abstemiousness, frugality, family and diligence with economic productivity. It also seeks to promote an element of spiritual reflection in Malaysian society in a partial response to modernization and increasing affluence.

The international marketer must also understand the educational situation in a foreign market: it is a key determinant of the nature of the consumer market and the kind of marketing personnel available. In a developing nation such as Malaysia, education may present major problems. Though the educational system of a country largely reflects its own culture and heritage, education can have a major impact on how receptive consumers are to foreign marketing techniques. Education shapes people's outlooks, desires and motivations. It not only affects potential consumers, it also more generally shapes business practices and competitive behavior. Participation in secondary education affects literacy levels and economic development. The extent of education thus affects marketing at two levels. Low levels of participation in education generally means low levels of literacy, which not only affects the earning potential of people and thus their consumption, but also determines the communication options for marketing programs. Illiteracy and an overall low level of education lead to (Terpstra & Sarathy 1991):

- the need to adapt package labels and advertising programs
- problems with conducting market research, as a result of communication difficulties and a lack of qualified researchers

- problems with complex products, particularly those requiring instructions to be followed
- difficulty with obtaining co-operation in the distribution channel
- a lower quality of marketing support services

In 1989, the total enrollment at primary and secondary schools was equivalent to 77% of the school-age population. In 1980, the average rate of adult illiteracy was 30.4% but, according to UNESCO estimates, in 1990 the rate had fallen to 21.6% (Demaine 1997).

Employment is greatest in agriculture (33%), government services (15%), and the manufacturing sectors (22%)—the last is deemed to be the largest employment growth area (Bair 1988). Migration to industrial centres such as Kuala Lumpur has led to an imbalance of the labor supply. The overall unemployment rate was 9% and rising in 1986, but in 1992 the rate was estimated at 4.1%, and in 1994 at 2.8%.

Malaysian social problems stem from the rural-urban drift, undercurrents of racial sensitivities, and the presence of possibly as many as 2 million illegal migrant plantation workers in Peninsula Malaysia and in Sabah (*Asia 1993 Yearbook* 1993). Recent dilemmas faced by Sabah exemplify the struggle of the people against notions of political and cultural correctness (Vatikiotis 1994a). Malaysia's national culture has tended to be dominated by the Muslim Malays, who are most significant in number and, given the government's plans to redistribute wealth, notably significant in corporate ownership. To fuel the racial sensitivities further, politics is also dominated by the Malays and their ruling National Front coalition. This has led to a national cultural policy in favor of the Malays which is not always well regarded by the other ethnic and religious groups. Though there are many facets to Malaysian culture, much of the country's richness has been detracted from by official moral strictures that too often restrict creativity and the full development of cultural interchange. Further, some have suggested that there is a grave problem with the way culture has been officially promoted in Malaysia, where "there must always be a moral, something to teach the masses," the government seeing art "as a tool most often to promote morality or tourism" (Vatikiotis 1994b).

The multiracial nature of Malaysia has led to the development of a rich distinctive culture that is unique in its diversity. To illustrate, eating is a critical component of cultural expression, and yet dietary habits differ from race to race. For example, Muslims do not generally eat pork, while the Chinese feature it among their culinary delights. Malaysians are sensitive to such differences. Similarly, race and religion are intertwined, and racial-religious differences also tend to affect the business environment.

However, having lived side by side for generations, the multiracial people of Malaysia also display some common traits. Malaysians are known to be warm and hospitable, as well as being generally well educated and culturally sensitive. The Malaysian culture stresses courtesy, respect and the importance of performing good deeds (*budi*), etiquette, gentleness and good manners (Harris & Moran 1987). Politeness and patience are important attributes, and relationships built on trust are a necessary prelude to the conduct of business. Malaysians dislike the Western legalistic approach, and look for sincerity and flexibility. They also place great importance on the correct use of titles, as they are generally status conscious (Tan & Lim 1992).

Within the multiracial structure, common traits tend to present themselves in the different major ethnic groups in Malaysia. *Bumiputras* usually prefer the indirect approach, with the aim of building up trust and confidence. In this respect, the personal touch and contacts tend to override the written word or contract, which is not viewed as very important. Further, compromise is preferred to confrontation. Business with the *bumiputras,* especially the Malays, must be guided by the customs, traditions, and religion of the Malay society. The Malays tend to be collective decision-makers, reminiscent of the village practices of *gotong royong* (mutual co-operation) and *mesyuarat* (problem solving by consensus) (Tan & Lim 1992).

The government's restructuring of the corporate sector to increase *bumiputra* ownership has reduced the influence of the Chinese at the professional and technical levels. However, the Chinese still occupy the majority of middle-level managerial positions. As with the Chinese in other parts of Asia, dealing with this group requires establishing a *guanxi,* or "relationship." Religion does not play an important part, but knowledge of Chinese customs and culture is an advantage. Traditionally, the Chinese are not strong on individualism, due to the predominance of Confucianism, the Chinese philosophy that is based on the family rather than the individual. The Chinese have a great sense of pride and do not like to "lose face." They are also more commercially minded, with a profit-seeking, self-promotion orientation, display a sense of pragmatism, and are known for being aggressive and shrewd (Tan & Lim 1992).

The Indians in Malaysia are underrepresented in business, and tend to concentrate in the textile, wholesale, and retail sectors. Most of the educated Indians are professionals in law and medicine. Personal relationships are also important to this group, who tend to be more litigious and to prefer low-profile negotiations, often making them appear disinterested (Tan & Lim 1992).

Marketing infrastructure

The market

Consumer spending in all sections of the economy—especially the retail and service industries—has continued to rise, and will continue to do so despite the current crisis. Spurred by private-sector spending, domestic demand has replaced external demand as the major contributor to growth. This spending has been supported by rising consumption and investment. The government has introduced tax and other incentives favoring large families, aiming for a fourfold increase in population by 2000, and so increasing domestic demand even further (Rafferty 1990).

Distribution

Trading companies

The marketing of imported goods in Malaysia is primarily conducted by trading companies that operate sales outlets in principal cities. Peninsula Malaysia, Sabah and Sarawak are treated as a composite market to be cultivated by branches and travelling salespersons. Although some of these trading companies are headquartered in Singapore with branches in Malaysia, many have head offices in Kuala Lumpur. The entire range of importing services is available, with the larger importers providing the full range of marketing services. A few of the small and medium-sized firms offer the same services, but most operate as indent merchants, placing and handling imports ordered on the account of others. It is mainly the role of a few large, foreign-owned and managed trading companies to move as much as one-half of the import trade of Malaysia. Among the major trading companies are several foreign firms that operate mostly as branches. These include several branches of US-owned firms, though their marketing role in Malaysia is secondary to that of the large British companies. A typical major trading company may represent several hundred foreign suppliers and be involved in the marketing of several thousand individual product items. It may sell to factories and other producing enterprises, to government agencies owning and operating public facilities, to construction and building companies, and to wholesale and retail outlets (Bair 1988).

A large number of small and medium-sized firms, as well as a smaller number of locally owned major firms, now account for about one-half of Malaysia's foreign trade. Such firms are usually owned by Chinese Malaysians and, to a lesser extent, by Indian Malaysians. Participation in foreign trade by Malays is small, despite government encouragement. Many of the small and medium-sized firms are diversified in the range of products they handle, though some tend to prefer specialization. These firms also take orders from customers and engage in wholesale and retail trade, and are mainly located in the Peninsula Malaysian cities of Ipoh, Penang, and Malacca, and in the East Malaysian cities of Kuching and Kota Kinabalu. Their import activities are for the benefit of local customers in these cities and adjacent markets.

There are other variations in Malaysia's distribution patterns. A large department store may operate as an importer–retailer, and also import through indent orders placed with trading companies representing foreign suppliers whose merchandise the store requires. Retail dealers specializing in food and other shelf goods follow the same pattern. There are also instances of local sales branches maintained by foreign manufacturers, who staff them with local management and technical personnel. However, branch sales offices of Malaysian and Singaporean trading firms are often given autonomy in arranging import transactions with foreign suppliers who have agency contracts with the parent firms or on a single basis.

Wholesale and retail facilities range from the most modern warehouses and department stores to small individually owned shops. Modern, Western-style retail outlets are increasing in popularity, as are US merchandizing methods. Wholesalers usually grant credit to those retailers who agree to stock their products. Generally, the trading companies handle the wholesaling and, to some extent, the retailing function. They maintain large warehouse complexes in connexion with their trading activities from where the retail market is supplied (Bair 1988).

Direct procurement

Direct infrastructure equipment procurement by government agencies for power, water, irrigation, and transport development still takes place. These purchases are arranged with foreign suppliers in response to international tendering. However, the number of direct transactions has waned as it has become clearer to foreign suppliers that dealing through a competent local agent or distributor will greatly enhance their chances of making sales to government agencies.

Using an agent

Trading companies in Malaysia are competent, and generally have a good knowledge of the market; however, foreign suppliers often face the problem of inadequate agency-selling performance. A contributing factor is the overcommitment by local distributors, particularly the larger firms, in representing foreign suppliers. The result is that they give appropriate attention only to some of the more saleable products they handle, and ignore those that require more effort to sell. Marketers must therefore search for more flexible agents, often among the less committed trading agents, and must be prepared to provide their own market promotion and development. The agent should be a local–not a third-country–agent. A visit to Malaysia by a company executive to select an agent and to learn firsthand the subtleties of the culture, government policies, and the market is a wise investment of company resources, particularly in the light of increasing competition (Bair 1988).

Despite the problems with finding a suitable marketing outlet, foreign suppliers are making successful representation arrangements and selling their products. This success is based largely on the suppliers' genuine interest in exporting, an awareness of the market situation, the careful selection and training of agents, active support in sales campaigns, and the appropriate monitoring of distributor performance (Bair 1988). While follow-up evaluation of distributor performance is a key factor in the success of an agency arrangement, an important and probably more difficult requirement is to make the distributor feel he or she is a member of the supplier's firm. All of the support elements are needed in such a relationship, with probably the most vital element being technical and training support. Effective marketing of hard goods (durable machines and equipment) demands full assistance from the supplier in all phases of selling, particularly in the identification of requirements, installation, the operation and maintenance of facilities and equipment, and sales training. Frequent contact between the supplier and the local distributor is also essential.

Import and distributing firms that have advanced to the role of "selling the market" have often had the benefit of advice and help from foreign suppliers who already understand and apply this concept. The conversion from a habit of order filling to a role of finding buyers has been, and continues to be, a gradual process, and success is achieved in proportion to the competitive spirit and market-development interest of the supplier. Hence, a foreign supplier who has found a likely agent in these markets should anticipate working with the agent to advance selling techniques, so that an effective market-development program can be pursued (Bair 1988).

Foreign trading firms have gradually substituted locals for foreign sales staff, and have trained them in selling methods and product know-how. They frequently supplement on-the-job sales training with training abroad in the corporate headquarters. This training, generally financed by suppliers, includes product orientation and application, by exposing trainees to the manufacturing process in the plants of suppliers. In addition, local talent for selling positions in foreign-owned and local establishments is increasingly being drawn from college graduates who have received degrees in business administration and other specialties from universities in Malaysia, the USA, the UK, Canada, or Australia. Sales training of local sales staff is also provided by company representatives of foreign suppliers who are stationed in Malaysia, or make frequent visits to the area from company headquarters or from regional marketing offices.

Regional warehousing

Foreign exporters of a variety of products may be able to overcome the time–distance delivery problem by developing facilities for regional marketing and distribution in a single commercial centre. Such practices may improve the foreign firm's competitiveness by enabling the earlier delivery of goods ordered in Malaysia and other Asian market areas. Malaysia is well suited for this type of operation.

A basic element in a regional marketing operation is the storage of selected products in warehouses for future delivery to customers in markets located a reasonable distance from the distribution point. Other basic elements for this operation are adequate port and warehouse facilities, inland transportation, frequent shipping connections with market areas in the region, capable trading establishments, and banking services. Malaysia has an abundance of these basic elements, and is being used increasingly by foreign suppliers as a regional distribution and marketing centre.

Advertising

Advertising is widely used in Malaysia, and there are many advertising and public-relations firms that will assist the foreign exporter or his or her agent in media presentations. The most effective advertising medium is the newspaper. Newspapers have a wide circulation, and reach readers in the major local languages. While Malay is the national language, most of the business community can be reached in the English language press. The principal English language newspapers are the *New Straits Times* and the *Sunday Times*. Advertising in US publications also reaches the Malaysian market. US consumer and trade journals have a wide circulation, and often reach a worldwide readership, which includes the more affluent business-people and professionals in Malaysia (Bair 1988). Most Malaysian periodicals accept advertising, but regulations can restrict content and presentation.

The government controls most of the 42 daily and periodical publications, as well as the radio and television stations (Rafferty 1990). The broadcast media are government owned, while the privately owned press is forbidden, by law, from publishing any matter considered harmful to security, order, or morality. The Commercial Division of the Ministry of Information is responsible for radio and TV advertisements. Movie advertising is limited to consumer goods. Outdoor advertising and posters are widely used. Direct marketing is available, though the need for multilingualism restricts its use. Radio and TV are being used increasingly by distributors to advertise consumer goods, with both media offering commercial "spots." The rise in family incomes has made these media very popular. The majority of the population listens daily to Malaysian radio broadcasts, while TV operates on 3 channels, which offer a full range of programming. In general, all types of advertising familiar to the exporter are available in Malaysia—the type of medium used will depend upon the product and the target market. The Code of Advertising Practices (1972) sets guidelines for "legal, decent, honest and truthful" advertising. Recent revisions in the code ban all television liquor advertisements, place time restrictions on advertising certain products, and ban, in general, advertisements that feature scantily dressed women, Malaysians who look like foreign celebrities, and children.

Market research

Market research is being utilized with increasing frequency, with very satisfactory results. Several firms, including Asian ones, have been established to supply this necessary service, and have developed an acceptable competence in professional market research. These firms are constantly expanding their activities to meet the growing demand for their expertise. Market research firms based in Singapore and Hong Kong also take on commissions in Malaysia. Although professional market investigation services are available, many local trading firms conduct market enquiries on a rule-of-thumb basis–that is, they do not follow any formal research practices. Results vary according to the competence of the firms and the staff responsible for market planning and development.

Important trends and their marketing implications

There are numerous demographic and economic trends that will have important implications for marketers in this country. Malaysia's population is relatively small compared with that of its neighbors such as Indonesia and Thailand, hence the perceived need for a relatively large population growth rate, which is being encouraged by the government. This will mean that, in time, marketers will have a greater market, in terms of both size and potential. Malaysia also has a relatively young population; this, like its small population size, is contrary to world demographic trends, which show an overall ageing of the population. Distinct demographic trends that have significant implications on Malaysia's consumer-buying behavior are:

- a dominantly younger population
- the increasingly prominent role of women
- the existence of ethnically segmented consumer markets

Dominance of the young population

In 1995, Malaysia's population was estimated to be 20.1 million, with 84.2% under 45 years old (Edwards 1997). In 1994, of the total, over 36% were under 15 years, and over 47% were in the 16–44 year age group. It is estimated that, at the end of 1992, about 7.1 million Malaysians were gainfully employed. This number has been growing at an average of 4.1% annually since 1986; on average, the economy can provide new employment to about 290 000 people annually.

A survey of household members by Zaharah Bakar (1991) on the characteristics of the family lifecycle in the Klang Valley (whose distribution closely resembles the national racial composition) reveals that a majority, or 58.4% of the 1500 families sampled, are in the "full-nest with children" categories. The average household size is 5 members (2 adults, 3 children). Twenty-nine per cent of the total are aged 25–35 years, have been married less than 10 years and have several children, with the youngest child under 6 years old. Another 29% are older, married, and have older children, while the third largest category is that of the singles, aged between 25 and 35 years, with over half of this subgroup earning over RM1500 in monthly income, and one-third being full-time students.

The *Star* (1995) reported that the children's market in Malaysia is worth, annually, RM28.38 billion in the influence market, and RM1.548 billion in the primary market–the estimated amount spent on 8.5 million children. With its predominance of younger households, Malaysia is a good market for education, nursery care, household cleaning products, children's and teenagers' clothes, cars, sports and recreational goods and services, child education policies, savings plans, and fast-food outlets.

Increasing women's role in purchasing decisions

There has been an upsurge in the number of women pursuing college and university education, as well as those entering the workforce. Their role in household purchasing behavior is increasingly significant. In studying marital role consensus in 22 household purchase decisions, Osman and Salleh (1986) found that the following purchasing decisions have been confirmed to be made jointly by husbands and wives in Malaysia: forms of savings, family medical care, TV sets, children's schooling, children's toys, refrigerators, and the hiring of domestic help. While purchasing decisions on wives' cosmetics and personal items are clearly the wives' domain, surprisingly, Malaysian wives are found to exert a strong influence on the purchases of even their husbands' clothes and personal items.

Across all races, both the husband and wife agree that automobile purchase decisions, especially on what type to buy, the price and the timing of purchase, are clearly very husband dominant. Only in the choice of color does the wife seem to have a share in the automobile-purchase decision. This concurs with a previous study by Nik Rahimah Nik Yacob and Ismail Rejab (1984), suggesting that role specialization in purchasing decisions among Malaysian families tends to vary by product type. Knowing precisely who is relatively more dominant at particular consumer decision stages for specific products can certainly help marketers to devise more targeted promotional campaigns and make the other marketing mix decisions more effectively. Merely assuming that Western consumer behavior will also prevail among Malaysians would certainly be misleading, and it is essential that the uniqueness of the local context be well understood.

Ismail Rejab and Nik Rahimah Nik Yacob (1986) investigated the use of the AIO (activities, interests and opinions) inventory in studying Malaysian women's lifestyles. Eight distinct lifestyles were identified:

1 traditional mothers
2 fashion-conscious women
3 innovative opinion leaders
4 feminine women
5 liberated women
6 economically conscious women
7 socially active women
8 women with basic role orientation

For international marketers, this stresses the need to be sensitive to local cultural variations. Specifically, Malaysian women ought to be viewed as distinct population segments identifiable through lifestyle dimensions or other segmentation bases. It would certainly be presumptuous to adopt a stereotype approach in developing undifferentiated marketing strategies aimed at this population sector.

Studying the influences of women's lifestyle patterns on family role structure, Yacob Nik Rahimah and Noor Sallehuddin (1993) found that Malaysian women who view equal decision making and responsibility sharing between married couples as acceptable tend to lead a different lifestyle from those who find the same to be unacceptable. They differ in degree on their attitudes to housekeeping, cooking, sewing, performing religious activities, attending formal functions, and being involved in social and political activities. Clearly, research is called for to foster a better understanding and identification of Malaysian women's lifestyle segments, so that this market can be better served.

Ethnically segmented/differentiated consumer markets

Because of the differing religious and cultural needs in the country, several types of goods and services require segmentation along ethnic lines. Certain packaged foods, for example, are differentiated based on language-specific brand names, with different packaging and color. Muslims can only consume "halal" foods and services (products permissible by Islamic standards). All fast-food franchise businesses in Malaysia, including McDonald's, Kentucky Fried Chicken and A & W are gazetted under Malaysian law to serve only "halal" food and non-alcoholic beverages.

In a similar fashion, goods colored or packaged in black wrapping are not as readily accepted by the Chinese as those using red or gold, which signify good luck and prosperity. The Chinese also favor the number 8. This psychological pricing tactic is also used by some housing developers to set prices for residential properties.

Among Malaysian-manufactured chili sauces, brands such as Aminah Hassan and Besta cater largely for the Malay consumer segment, whereas Maggi and Ayamas are more popular national brands catering for all ethnic groups. Lingam sauce, though originally Indian by inspiration, is geared for the export market, in view of the insufficient size of the Malaysian Indian domestic market and other market considerations. These are examples of the degree of preference toward certain products by different ethnic groups; marketers need to exercise some sensitivity to these differences.

Through a study of Malaysian lifestyles by Survey Research Malaysia (1990), 7 lifestyle segments were identified. These are:

1 the "not-quite-there's" (largely Malays aged 20–29 years, white-collar workers)
2 the "upper echelons" (largely Malay males, high income earners, city dwellers)
3 the "rebel hang-outs" (largely adult Chinese, high income earners, singles, city dwellers)
4 the "sleep-walkers" (largely Chinese housewives with lower education)
5 the "inconspicuous" (largely Malay housewives)
6 the "kampong trendsetters" (largely rural Malay males under 30 years)
7 the "rural traditionalists" (largely Malay rural residents over 30 years).

Knowledge of these lifestyle segments offers an opportunity—and a challenge—to marketers to reach and serve these market segments.

M.Z. Osman (1994) examined the relationship between lifestyles and loyalty patronage behavior of Malaysian shoppers at retail stores. Ethnicity was found to exert some influence on loyalty toward a particular store. (Previously, Yacob's (1991) study on the influence of ethnicity on product symbolism had reported positive effects across both the Malay and Chinese ethnic groups.) This implies that retail store managers should endeavor to break this "ethnicity restriction" by most customers. Breaking this polarization would enable them to offer merchandise to target consumers who are not necessarily limited to a certain ethnic group.

Marketers should first be aware of the underlying racial and religious sensitivities. Malays are predominantly Muslims, but there are other races and religions that exist and must be catered to. Such differences have implications for product packaging and labelling, as well as the type of promotional strategy used. For instance, multilingualism generally prevents the use of outdoor advertising. Terpstra and Sarathy (1991) argue that packaging should be labeled in at least Chinese and Malay. Further, as the distribution of wealth continues to change, different groups will become more attractive target markets. The *bumiputras,* now no longer economically disadvantaged and still numerically superior, are a much more viable target market than they were perhaps 20 years ago. Given all this, marketers should also realize the potential for conflict in this country.

Though Malaysia is predominantly rural, urbanization is increasing. It is recommended that marketers take advantage of the urban–rural split, which makes it easier to target different ethnic groups in terms of packaging and point-of-purchase advertising. Further, the Chinese and Indians contribute a higher proportion of the population in the Peninsula than in Sabah and Sarawak (where the indigenous groups predominate), and are concentrated in the cities and towns of Malaysia.

In countries such as Malaysia with lower income levels and in rural areas, the extended family still plays a major role, and increases the size of the average household. Because the family plays such an important role as a consumption unit, marketers need to understand family roles and composition as they differ across countries. The primary emphasis for successful marketing is on the roles of individual family members, their respective influence on each other, and the society's expectation as to what role each should play. Such an understanding is crucial for the marketing of consumer products, and tends to affect both communication and product policy (Jeannet & Hennessey 1988).

An overall increase in consumer spending has caused inflation, and this has been further fueled, prior to the financial crisis, by increasing shortages of labor and the resulting increase in wages. Among other things, this will mean that prices will be set as high as necessary to combat inflationary pressure. At a general level, it is Kreutzer's (1988) assertion that consumers in developing Asian countries can be classified into three broad segments. The *elite segment* is typically a small segment in developing countries and NICs. Consumers in this segment have a strong tendency toward a Western orientation, and are mainly interested in prestige products that offer the opportunity for conspicuous consumption. These products often cross national borders without being strongly supported by marketing activities. The *segment of change* refers to those consumers who have a large income compared to the general community average at their disposal, and spend to improve their standard of living. This segment will be of the greatest importance in the future, as these consumers, mainly living in urban and suburban areas, display very dynamic consumption behavior. Further, the growth of this segment is strongly related to the economic development of the country as a whole, as this group participates in economic progress. These consumers are still rooted in the national culture, but are open minded about Western consumption norms. Finally, the *segment of tradition* constitutes the major market in both developing countries and NICs. Consumers in this segment possess limited purchasing power. Some of these consumers live in rural areas, where they have less contact with change agents and are hence less receptive to new products, being firmly rooted in cultural traditions. Others live in the suburbs surrounding the major cities, and have closer contact with sources of information on new products and the way of life in other countries (Kreutzer 1988).

In terms of marketing implications, the elite segment is mainly covered by importers and trade agents, while other supplier groups are less important.

Here, there is only a highly competitive situation within the group of importers. The most competitive segment is that of the segment of change, where all supplier groups are active, and global strategies of industrialized multinational corporations (MNCs) are increasingly challenged by developing countries' MNCs as well as by local brands. The traditional segment is still the domain of local producers. Access to this group must be gained in the long run, due to its potential for being the mass market of the future. A co-operative strategy with local producers (as in a joint venture) may be a promising way of gaining a foothold in these markets (Kreutzer 1988).

Other business-economic developments

The development of new "alternative Islamic" products

While advocating religious freedom for its multiracial populace, the government is sensitive to the needs of the Muslim majority. It strives to offer goods and services conforming to Islamic principles, as an alternative to conventional offerings. These "Islamic alternatives" are, in most cases, offered to Muslims and non-Muslims alike, thereby generally offering greater consumer choice as they compete on fair terms. However, they would certainly appeal strongly to the more Islam-conscious consumers. Two recent significant developments are the growth of Islamic financial instruments (see below), and the recognition of the need for the production and marketing of "halal" products, particularly food.

In the financial services industry, Malaysia is reported to be the only country in the Middle East and Asia to be given an "excellent" rating for government support in developing an Islamic banking industry, based on a *New Horizon* survey (*New Straits Times* 1995d).

Precisely, indications are that the banking and other financial authorities have been successful in using various government ministries and Bank Negara (the Central Bank), to promote Islamic banking as a viable alternative to conventional banking. New Islamic financial products have been rapidly developed by removing the non-"halal" elements such as *riba* (primarily the interest element), from savings and loans, combined with the redesigning or repackaging of existing conventional product features. These Islamic financial instruments are frequently managed through distinctly separate funds that provide services alongside existing counters in banks.

For instance, with 167 branches nationwide, Bank Bumiputra Malaysia Berhad, the commercial bank with the largest branch network in Malaysia, has introduced up to 10 basic interest-free banking services, ranging from savings accounts to trade financing facilities. Its one-stop Muamalah Banking Center, which handles its interest-free banking operations, amassed RM615 million through several accounts up to December 31 1994. This is about 32% of the more than RM1.8 billion in total deposits accumulated by

37 commercial and merchant banks and finance companies through various interest-free banking services (*New Straits Times* 1995b).

Examples of interest-free banking facilities introduced include elements of *al-mudharabah* (profit-sharing) and *al-Bai Bithaman Ajil* (deferred payment sale). General and family *takaful* (insurance) plans, unit trust investments based on Syariah (Islamic legal) principles, and interest-free pawnbroking services constitute other new Islamic financial services created. This "Islamization innovation process" is expected to penetrate into the share-brokerage, real estate/property and other related businesses within the next decade.

The trend toward greater Islamic consciousness requires marketers to be more receptive to consumers who want at least some degree of religious product assurance. This, coupled with the task of targeting a potentially large (possibly global) Islamic market, makes it commercially imperative for companies to promote their food products as "halal." Certification of "halal" food is issued by Pusat Islam Malaysia (Islamic Affairs Division Malaysia) upon verification of the ingredients used, production processes, storage systems, and other considerations. This issue will continue to be a major concern for scientists, manufacturers, suppliers, marketers, and regulatory agents serving the food, hotel, and catering-service industries.

The post-Proton era of heavy industrial growth

From the time it started production in 1986 to March 1995, Perusahaan Otomobil Nasional Berhad ("Proton") had exported 115 000 units of Proton cars to the UK, Singapore, New Zealand, Mauritius, Jamaica, Brunei, and Malta. Unit sales reached 160 000 per year in 1995, including 20% for the export market (*Berita Harian* 1995). In the domestic market, Proton had a 74% market share, offering the Saga, Iswara, Wira, and Satria models to cater for different segments within the passenger-vehicle market. The Proton has been complemented by the introduction of the second Malaysian national car, the Perodua Kancil, a compact, value-for-money model in the under 1000 cc segment.

The Malaysian luxury sports car, the Proton Perdana, was introduced in 1995 with high expectations. It was an attempt to penetrate the 2000 cc market, and was designed to add prestige and glamor to the national automobile line spearheaded by the Proton Saga. Unfortunately, the Perdana had problems with quality, and sales have not come up to expectations. Sadly, the indications are that the heady days of rapid growth are over and there is evidence of a slowdown in sales. Edaran Otomobil Nasional Berhad (EON) management is "expecting the local car market to enter a phase with sales dropping off a little as a result of the economic problems" (*Straits Times* 1998, p. 25).

Other projects in the pipeline are the first Malaysian 2-seater aerobatic trainer aircraft, national motorcycles and small engines, and a national van.

The spinoffs for the economy as a whole have been considerable. The implementation of these projects helped lift Malaysia out of the mid-1980s' recession, while strengthening its emergence as "Asia's Tiger with a vision" (Selvarajah 1993). Insistence by the government on the gradual increase in the proportion of local content in the national car has nurtured the emergence of home-grown light-engineering manufacturers. This strategy has prevented Proton from becoming merely an assembly plant of foreign components. Instead, through integrated industrial plans such as the vendor development program, it has sparked off remarkable growth for small and medium scale industries, particularly those supplying production parts in the passenger-vehicle, electronic- and electrical-appliances industries.

Malaysia, with its export-driven economy, requires a faster technology transfer and enhanced R&D if it is to remain competitive globally. Growth in this direction has brought a corresponding increase in the pool of highly skilled labor, and this in turn has resulted in improvement in living standards as better products have been produced (*New Straits Times* 1995b). The International Trade and Industry Ministry is currently conducting a comprehensive study that will chart the growth of the country's industrialization program from 1996 to 2005. The new industrial strategy will develop a dynamic, integrated, and diversified manufacturing sector, as well as new subsectors of industries, and will expand market opportunities under the ASEAN Free Trade Area and the World Trade Organisation and enhance the export capabilities of small- and medium-scale industries. New efforts will also be made to forge linkages among MNCs, large local corporations and small- and medium-scale industries, to prepare them to spearhead the globalization drive (*New Straits Times* 1995a).

The future

Malaysia is a good market for exports, particularly food, computer systems, telecommunications equipment, aircraft, logging equipment, petroleum production and refining equipment, and defense equipment. Significant demand will also continue for engineering and architectural skills. Development projects throughout Malaysia also present opportunities for foreign firms. Prior to the crisis of 1997 there were many mega-projects of interest, including the Railway Modernization Project, the Kelantan Paper Mill, Kuala Lumpur City Center, Kuala Lumpur International Airport and the Aerospace Industries of Malaysia (AIM). Four equipment categories offering excellent prospects for foreign exporters are aircraft and parts, computers and peripherals, medical equipment, and process control instrumentation (Bair 1988).

The interpretation of the NEP, launched in 1970, and the lack of cohesion in its implementation, have long been a source of anxiety and uncertainty for foreign businesspeople (*Asia Pacific: An Investment Guide* 1990). Other government priorities include the removal of any overhanging threats in the form of unexercised options for the state to take a stake or set participation ratios, and the setting of a quality of treatment once a foreign business has been restructured. To a foreign investor, an unexercised option hanging over a business venture with no time limit to it is a major uncertainty. Once a foreign business has complied with restructuring targets, the quality of treatment is vital to convince overseas shareholders of the benefits of divesting a proportion of ownership. However, while compliance with the new NDP is important, the Malaysian government welcomes foreign investment, and the conditions imposed on such activities are generally flexible and based on the merits of individual projects (*Asia Pacific: An Investment Guide* 1990).

The change in Malaysia's fortunes has been difficult to predict. Even as recently as 1996, Malaysia was the rampant tiger whose grandiose projects (e.g. the world's tallest building, Petronas Towers, the longest building under construction on the Kuala Lumpur River, a new airport due to open in 1998, and a technology and intellectual property zone) displayed a confidence that made it highly visible on the world economic stage. This confidence has been shattered by the almost 38% drop in the value of the ringgit in the six months following July 1 1997. The current-account deficit is approaching $US6 billion. The list of problems is getting longer, and includes difficulties with the national steel company, lagging sales on the national car, the Proton, and the question of migrant workers.

Many Malaysians are having difficulties coming to terms with the evolving situation, and it has not been easy to put aside the natural desire to blame outsiders. There has also been a reluctance to take the necessary tough actions to address the economic shortcomings. Pulling out of the crisis will not be easy. Malaysia is only one of a number of nations competing for foreign investment, and with considerable debt. With only 20 million people, there is much work to be done.

Nonetheless, foreign investment has been drawn by the progressive stability of Malaysia relative to other South-East Asian countries and, as neighboring markets change radically in complexion, Malaysia will have to ensure that it retains its attractiveness. Certainly, the Kuala Lumpur Stock Exchange offers considerable incentives to foreign investment, and the government remains committed to ensuring ease of access and operation for direct investors. In this time of difficulty it is too easy to forget that Malaysia has made considerable progress, and that the spirit within the nation was, until very recently, upbeat, with strong optimism about the future. Indeed, the 1995 re-election of the UMNO government indicated a degree of national unity that was remarkable, and that augured well for the future. It is likely that, with good management, Malaysia's growth will resume, although perhaps at a slower rate, and that the nation will once again move forward toward the vision of a new century.

References

Asia 1993 Yearbook: A Review of the Events of 1992 (Far Eastern Economic Review) (1993), Review Publishing Company Ltd, Hong Kong.

Asia Pacific: An Investment Guide (1990), Euromoney Publications PLC, London.

Asian Development Bank (1992), *Key Indicators of Developing Asian and Pacific Countries*, vol. 23, July, Manila.

Bair, F.E. (ed.) (1988), *International Marketing Handbook*, 3rd edn, vol. 2, Gale Research Company, Detroit, Michigan.

Bakar, Zaharah (1991), "Ciri-ciri kitaran hayat keluarga: suatu tinjauan keatas keluarga-keluarga diLembah Kelang", *Jurnal Pengurusan*, Universiti Kebangsaan Malaysia, vol. 10, July, pp. 75–94.

Berita Harian (1995), "Proton yakin jual hingga 160 000 unit", 11 February, p. 17.

Brown, Ian (1994), "Malaysia: History", *The Far East and Australasia*, 25th edn, Europa Publications Ltd, London, pp. 511–25.

Cribb, R. (1997), "Malaysia: History", *The Far East and Australasia*, 28th edn, Europa Publications Ltd, London, pp. 566–71.

Damhoeri, Khairudin, Mashori, Fuat, Muhamad, Jaafar & Sharif, Kamaruddin (1994), "Corporate leadership and the myth of the incompetent Malay chief executive officer: Evidence from the Malaysian general insurance industry", *Jurnal Pengurusan*, Universiti Kebangsaan Malaysia, vol. 13, July, pp. 47–62.

Demaine, Harvey (1997), "Malaysia: Physical and Social Geography", *The Far East and Australasia*, 28th edn, Europa Publications Ltd, London, p. 565.

Edwards, Chris (1997), "Malaysia: Economy", *The Far East and Australasia*, 28th edn, Europa Publications Ltd, London, pp. 572–90.

Engel, J.F., Blackwell, R.D. & Miniard, P.W. (1993), *Consumer Behavior*, 7th edn, The Dryden Press, Sydney.

Handbook of the Nations (1986), 6th edn, Gale Research Co., Detroit, MI.

Harris, P.R. & Moran, R.T. (1987), *Managing Cultural Differences*, Gulf Publishing Co., Houston.

Hong Kong and Shanghai Banking Corporation (1991), *Business Profile Series: Malaysia*, 6th edn, Hong Kong.

Jeannet, J.P. & Hennessey, H. (1988), *International Marketing Management*, Houghton Mifflin Co., Boston.

Kreutzer, Ralf T. (1988), "Key Factors for the Development of Marketing Strategies for West Asia", *Singapore Marketing Review*, vol. 3, pp. 61–70.

Mid-Term Review of the Sixth Malaysia Plan, 1991–1995 (1993), Percetakan Nasional Berhad, Kuala Lumpur.

Moore, Spencer (1994), "Malaysia: Economy", *The Far East and Australasia,* 25th edn, Europa Publications Ltd, London, pp. 526–32.

New Straits Times (1995a), "Of success, glory and prosperity", February 18, p. 10.

— (1995b), "Comprehensive Study to Chart Industrialization" and "One-stop centre for interest-free banking", February 22, pp. 14, 18–19.

— (1995c), "Higher growth forecast", March 30, p. 1.

— (1995d), "Malaysia gets excellent rating", April 13.

Osman, M.Z. (1994), "The influence of lifestyles on loyalty patronage behaviour", in eds Nik Hashim Mustapha, Jaafar Muhamad, Aliah Hanim Mohd. Salleh & Zaini Mahbar, *Pascasidang Seminar Antarabangsa Prospek dan Cabaran Ekonomi dan Pengurusan dalam Pembangunan Abad ke-21*, Universiti Kebangsaan Malaysia and Universitas Syiah Kuala, Indonesia.

Osman, M.Z. & Salleh, Aliah Hanim Mohd. (1986), "Husband-wife influence in purchasing decisions: a research using the Delphi technique", in eds Chin Tiong Tan et al., *Emerging International Strategic Frontiers—Proceedings of the American Marketing Association International Marketing Conference in Singapore*, American Marketing Association, pp. 331–6.

Rafferty, Kevin (1990), "Malaysia: Country Profile", *The Asia and Pacific Review,* 11th edn, Hunter Publishing Inc., Edison, NJ.

Rejab, Ismail & Yacob, Nik Rahimah Nik (1986), "An application of AIO inventory in delineating patterns of women's lifestyles in a non-western culture", in eds Chin Tiong Tan et al., *Emerging International Strategic Frontiers—Proceedings of the American Marketing Association International Marketing Conference in Singapore,* American Marketing Association, pp. 48–52.

Selvarajah, C.T. (1993), "The opening of strategic windows for Australia and New Zealand in the Asia-Pacific: Focus on Malaysia: The Tiger with a vision", in eds Nik Yacob et al., *Proceedings of the International Symposium on Gaining Competitive Advantage Through Marketing—Current Issues and Future Challenges for Small and Medium-scale Enterprises,* Kuala Lumpur, pp. 29–42.

Sheridan, G. (1994a), "Campaign Aims to Lift Learning Curve", *The Australian,* August 31, p. 17.

— (1994b), "Islam Chases an Identity", *The Australian,* August 31, p. 19.

Star (1995), "Little Big Spenders", March 27, section 2, pp. 2–4.

Straits Times (1998), "EON Sees Slowdown in Proton Car Sales", January 21, p. 25.

Survey Research Malaysia (1990), *The Malaysian lifestyle study*, Survey Research Malaysia, Kuala Lumpur.

Tan, Cheng Leong & Lim, Terence T.S. (1992), *Malaysia: Business and Investment Opportunities*, Cassia Communications Pty Ltd, Singapore.

Terpstra, Vern and Sarathy, Ravi (1991), *International Marketing*, 5th edn, The Dryden Press, Hinsdale, Ill.

United Nations Yearbook (1996), *Statistical Yearbook for Asia and the Pacific*, UN, New York.

Vatikiotis, Michael (1990a), "A Mirage Market", *Far Eastern Economic Review*, vol. 148, May 17, p. 48.

— (1990b), "The Late Starter", *Far Eastern Economic Review*, vol.148, May 17, pp. 46–8.

— (1994a), "A Matter of Identity", *Far Eastern Economic Review*, vol. 157, March 17, p. 18.

— (1994b), "Morality Plays", *Far Eastern Economic Review*, vol. 157, March 10, pp. 40–1.

Yacob, Nik Rahimah Nik (1991), "Gender and ethnic-subcultural influences on product symbolism", *Jurnal Pengurusan*, Universiti Kebangsaan Malaysia, vol. 10, July, pp. 13–26.

Yacob, Nik Rahimah Nik & Rejab, Ismail (1984), "Pemilihan responden bagi mengukur struktur peranan keluarga dalam keputusan membeli", *Jurnal Pengurusan*, vol. 3, July, pp. 77–84.

Yacob, Nik Rahimah Nik & Noor, Sallehuddin M. (1993), "Influences of women's lifestyle patterns on family role structure", *Malaysian Management Review*, vol. 28, no. 2, December, pp. 8–15.

Notes

1 US$1 = RM2.51 at October 11 1996.

CHAPTER 12

Myanmar

From an isolated past to a golden future?

MAY LWIN & ANTHONY PECOTICH

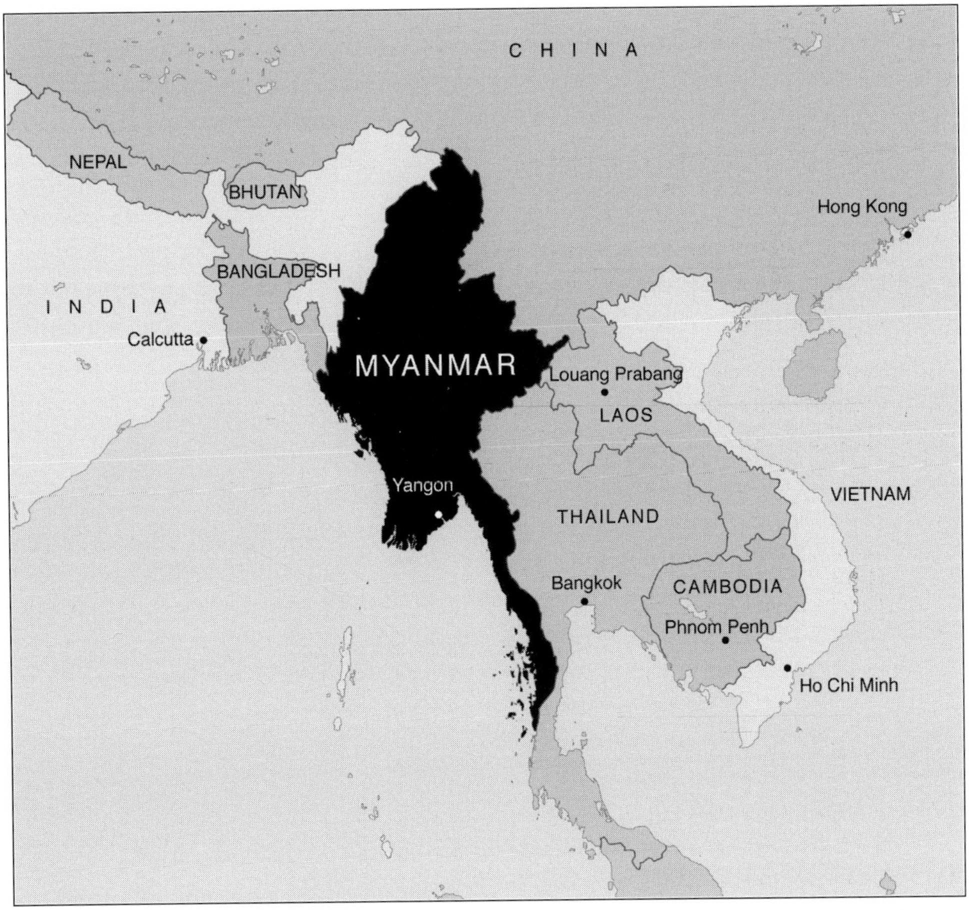

Abstract

Myanmar is a South-East Asian nation which, although it was never involved in a destructive, all-encompassing war, is still emerging from a period of political unrest and seeking to re-establish itself as an economic force in the region. To achieve this end, the major thrust of reform has been directed toward opening up the economy and allowing the market forces to work, and thus improving the economic and social conditions of the people. In this chapter we provide an overview of the historical nature of these developments and evaluate some of the current conditions leading to what we hope will be a successful transition to a prosperous future.

Introduction

The union of Myanmar, known until 1989 as the Socialist Republic of Burma, is a South-East Asian nation that, after a post-colonial period of devastation and poverty, is moving forward with the hope of one day taking its place as one of the strong, progressive nations of the region. Myanmar is located between China and India, and shares borders with Bangladesh, Thailand and Laos, with a long coastline that provides access to the Bay of Bengal (Demaine 1997). It is one of the most promising and exciting markets. This is accentuated by the strong indications that it intends to join the emerging developing economies in South-East Asia by emphasizing market reform as it moves its economy into a transitional phase.

In the past 6 years, the country has undergone radical changes, which have transformed the once sleepy, underdeveloped backwater to a budding economy capable of giving tough competition to neighboring markets such as Vietnam and Cambodia.

Some may argue that the economic reforms have been gradual and somewhat slow, but they have had the effect of generating a great deal of overseas business interest. The basic reason for this is simple: in terms of mineral and agricultural resources, Myanmar is one of the region's richest and least exploited countries. In the 1950s, it was among the most economically promising South-East Asian nations, and the largest exporter of rice in the world. It has attracted the attention of international managers who have become aware of the marketing potential of its large population—although poor, this population has knowledge of Western brands, through the country's colonial history and the black market, and harbors a high degree of latent demand.

Our purpose in this chapter is to introduce the reader to the Myanmar consumer market. Taking a marketing perspective, we will discuss the nation's background and economic conditions, and, in particular, the Myanmar people and their customs and consumer habits, as well as the marketing conditions facing both the consumers and marketing managers. It is our hope that, by providing information on marketing areas such as product options, pricing levels, distribution alternatives, and promotion modes, we will encourage and assist entities wishing to market products in Myanmar.

Background

Prior to the Second World War and its independence in 1948, Myanmar was under the influence of Britain, its colonial ruler since 1885. In 1962, political turmoil led the military to seize power and introduce "the Burmese Way to Socialism," a unique blend of self-reliance, socialism and national ethos. For the past three decades, Myanmar has been in a state of self-imposed isolation described as a period of "hibernation" by many outsiders. It has been described as a place "where people haven't heard of Pepsi-Cola," and "East Asia's last frontier after Vietnam" (Hirsh & Moreau 1994). During this period, the country has experienced decreasing levels of economic output, coupled with falling imports and exports. Across towns and villages, the consumers have coped with product shortages by turning to the emerging black market.

Although the once-thriving economy had been reduced to one of the most backward in the world, change is under way since the State Law and Order Restoration Council (SLORC) took over the government in 1988. While the country continues to face internal political problems and external pressure, the SLORC has attempted to move the economy from one based on a socialist command philosophy to one driven more by market forces, and so, it hopes, to create in Myanmar a land of opportunity. This "open-market" policy has attracted foreign investment, which is changing the nature of Myanmar society. However, for tourists travelling to Myanmar, the fascination of the country is not only that of taking a backward step in time into a world of another generation, but also that of experiencing the unique cultural and environmental beauty.

Environment

Comprehending fully the nature of the consumers of Myanmar requires an open mind, and empathy for a people who, although relatively advanced in the 1950s, were at that time isolated from the rest of the world. Unlike other parts of South-East Asia, which are still recovering from the ravages of recent wars, Myanmar went through a unique period of self-imposed solitude. Today, this is reflected in the aged look of the intact cities, and the timeless character of the environment, which have contributed to the Myanmar people's particular pattern of consumer behavior. The following sections describe the recent natural, economic, demographic, and cultural factors that are critical to an understanding of the nature of the Myanmar market.

Natural environment

Myanmar is strategically located on the Bay of Bengal and the Andaman Sea, and borders Bangladesh, China, India, Laos, and Thailand. Surrounded by mountains, it is blessed with great alluvial lowlands through which the river Ayeyarwaddy (previously Irrawaddy) with its two tributaries (Chindwinn and Sittoung) flow, so forming the cultural and economic centre of the nation (Demaine 1997, p. 611). Although its climate may be classified as "tropical monsoonal," it has important climatic variations, including a dry zone caused by a rain shadow area from the south-western monsoons.

Traditionally, Myanmar has been most dependent on its agricultural resources. Although rice exports have diminished, Myanmar was once the world's greatest rice exporter. About 33% of the population is still employed in agriculture, which include the production of oil-seed and cotton as well as rice. On the mountainsides the greatest resources are timber, and a variety of metallic minerals such as silver and zinc. Similarly to the rest of Asia, the timber holdings are under pressure. Although almost half of Myanmar is forested, if current rates of depletion (legal and illegal) continue, an environmental disaster could be the result. Due to the nation's long period of isolation, the mineral resources have not been fully exploited, and prospects for the petroleum and related industries are bright.

Economic environment

During the 1970s and the 1980s Myanmar was economically poor, and considered among the least developed nations of the world. As recently as 1990, based on the traditional measure of development, Myanmar, with a per-capita income of about US$200,[1] was among the 46 lowest-income countries with per-capita income below US$500 (Kyaw 1995). While its South-East Asian neighbours Singapore and Brunei lead the GDP Purchasing Power Parity Dollars (PPP$) index, followed by Malaysia, Thailand, the Philippines, and Indonesia, Myanmar lags behind with a PPP$ figure of 659. While accurate figures are hard to obtain, there is evidence that unemployment and underemployment are quite high in both urban and rural areas, and are dependent on the season. Further, estimates based on population projections suggest that unemployment may be as high as 34% (Economist Intelligence Unit 1995).

In an attempt to remedy this situation, the SLORC initiated, in October 1988, economic reforms with the aim of decontrolling and deregulating a wide spectrum of economic activities. The SLORC enacted new liberalizing laws and regulations designed to encourage economic activity by enabling extensive private-sector participation (Kyaw 1995). The main components of this policy were:

1. adopting a market economy
2. encouraging private investment and entrepreneurial activity
3. allowing foreign trade and investment

This resulted in a turnaround of the Myanmar economy as the country entered into an era of "Market Economy System." After 2 years of negative growth, a recovery followed in 1989/1990. The growth of Myanmar's gross domestic product (GDP) initially declined to 2.7% in 1990/1991 and to 1.3% in 1991/1992, before rising to 10.9% in 1992/1993 and 9.8% in 1995/1996 (Vokes 1997). Social conditions also improved, as measured by various indicators such as the death rate (number of deaths per 1000), which fell from 14.1 in 1980–1985 to 11.1 in 1990–1995 (Vokes 1997); life expectancy, which increased from 44 in 1960 to 57 in 1992, and the infant mortality rate, which fell from 121 per thousand live births in 1970 to 72 in 1992 (Economist Intelligence Unit 1995, pp. 63–4).

The greatest economic impact on Myanmar has come from foreign trade and investment. The entry of potential foreign investors exploring possibilities has increased between 1990 and 1997, and deals have been struck on hotel, gas and oil projects. Conventional trade (export and import) has also been promoted to a great extent. From 1989, exports have steadily grown in almost all sectors (see Table 12.1).

Table 12.1 Value of foreign trade (million kyats)

Year	*Export*	*Import*	*Balance of trade*
1983–1984	3 386.4	5 197.3	–1 810.9
1984–1985	3 134.3	5 041.2	–1 906.9
1985–1986	2 566.1	4 802.0	–2 235.9
1986–1987	2 418.5	3 936.1	–1 517.6
1987–1988	1 655.2	4 065.7	–2 410.5
1988–1989	2 168.9	3 443.0	–1 274.1
1989–1990	2 834.1	3 395.0	–560.9
1990–1991	2 952.6	5 522.8	–2 570.2
1991–1992	2 925.9	5 336.7	–2 410.8
1992–1993	3 590.0	5 365.3	–1 775.3
1993–1994	4 227.8	7 923.3	–3 695.5

Sources: Government of the Union of Myanmar (1994), *Statistical Yearbook 1993*, Ministry of National Planning and Economic Development, Central Statistical Organization, Yangon; Government of the Union of Myanmar (1995), *Statistical Abstract 1994*, Ministry of National Planning and Economic Development, Central Statistical Organization, Yangon.

Foreign direct investment has grown more than 10 times since 1992, when economic reforms began in earnest, to US$2.6 billion in 1994, and US$3 billion as at August 1995 (Kyaw 1995). The oil and gas sectors have attracted the most foreign investment. Six multinational oil and gas companies are involved in production-sharing projects in 7 offshore and 5 onshore areas (see Table 12.2). One of the most visible investments is a US$1 billion natural-gas pipeline being built by France's Total with a US partner, Unocal. When it opens, it is expected to bring in annual revenue of US$400 million—enough to balance the country's current-account deficit (Hirsh & Moreau 1994). Following the energy sector is the hotels and tourism sector, which alone has the most ongoing projects (31), with a forecast addition of over 5000 rooms when all projects are completed. However, Agriculture, the mainstay of Myanmar's economy in the past, has attracted only one major investment so far.

Table 12.2 Foreign investment in Myanmar by sector, at August 31 1995

Sector	*No.*	*Foreign capital (US$ million)*
Oil and gas	24	1 435.42
Hotels and tourism	31	603.88
Fisheries	15	252.04
Real Estate	5	224.45
Mining	25	192.51
Manufacturing	51	178.30
Transport	5	113.21
Agriculture	1	2.69
Total	**157**	**3 002.50**

Source: Thane Kyaw (ed.) (1995), "Golden Opportunities for Investment in Myanmar", *Golden Myanmar,* Uniforce Co. Ltd, vol. 2, no. 4, p. 5.

Investment in Myanmar is headed by the UK, with US$642.47 million (see Table 12.3), followed closely by Singapore with US$548.32 million. With 33 investments, Singapore leads in terms of total number of investments. In fact, regional neighbors such as Singapore, Thailand, Malaysia, and Hong Kong comprise the bulk of investors in Myanmar in terms of the number of investments. Given the country's colonial history, the high investment from the UK is to be expected, but the high proportion emanating from the South-East Asia region not only provides a new economic facade for Myanmar (a more Asian character as opposed to a Western profile), but also underlines a new-found regional confidence. The increase in foreign-related businesses is visible from 5-year data showing the number of registered companies (see Table 12.4).

However, it is not just foreign-related companies that have developed in Myanmar. Business enterprises have mushroomed in all sectors. For example, domestic Myanmar limited companies increased by over 30% in 1994 alone, while tour-guide businesses have more than doubled. This has occurred because the government has encouraged the private sector and foreign investment in an unprecedented manner. Many private companies, enterprises and agencies have emerged—12 807 registered by 31 December 1994 at the Ministries of Trade, National Planning, and Development. More specifically, there are 6032 exporters/importers, 1225 business representatives, 949 partnerships, 3401 Myanmar limited companies, 296 foreign companies and branches, 90 joint ventures (Myanmar and foreign organizations) and 31 chambers of commerce.

Heeding advice from the World Bank and the IMF, the government has installed foreign-investment laws that make it attractive for foreign businesses

Table 12.3 Foreign investment in Myanmar by country of origin, at August 31 1995

Sector	*No.*	*Foreign capital (US$ million)*
UK	16	642.47
Singapore	33	548.32
France	1	465.00
Thailand	27	418.26
USA	14	241.07
Malaysia	9	227.27
Japan	6	106.86
The Netherlands	2	83.00
Austria	1	71.5
Hong Kong	17	64.44
Others	31	334.31
Total	**157**	**3 002.50**

Source: Thane Kyaw (ed.) (1995), "Golden Opportunities for Investment in Myanmar", *Golden Myanmar,* Uniforce Co. Ltd, vol. 2, no. 4, p. 5.

to venture into Myanmar. For example, foreign firms are eligible for a 3-year tax holiday. Although inflation remains high (35%), and the local currency, the kyat, is currently pegged to artificial high levels, the government has instituted foreign-exchange certificates similar to those once used by China to facilitate capital flows. The extent of the overvaluing of the currency is underlined by the fact that, in 1996, black-market value was as much as 19 times the official rate (Vokes 1997). Border trade with Thailand, China, India, and Bangladesh has also been legalized. This has resulted in a wide range of commodities–except some that are prohibited–being traded across these borders.

Another noteworthy fact is that foreigners of all nationalities are now commonly seen in both Yangon and smaller cities. This increase in foreign visitors (see Table 12.5) has given further momentum to the hotel and tourism business, which was boosted when the Ministry of Hotels and Tourism was instituted in September 1992. Prior to this, there were 4 foreign companies that had signed contracts to build and operate hotels in Myanmar. Since September 18 1995, the total number of licenses issued to local entrepreneurs to operate motels and inns totalled 248, and 32 foreign-invested hotel projects worth over US$1 billion and providing over 8000 rooms have also been approved (*Business Indochina* 1996, p. 13). Such well-known giants as the Shangri-la and Idris Hydraulic are involved in large projects worth over US$200 million (Naw 1994). The government has sought

Table 12.4 Number of registered exporters, importers, limited companies

S.N. Enterprises	Number of registered exporters, importers, limited companies, partnerships and joint-venture companies limited 1989–1990	1990–1991	1991–1992	1992–1993	1993–1994
1. Exporters	770	1 777	2 103	–	–
2. Importers	216	900	1 503	4 813	6 032
3. Business reps	183	480	768	947	1 225
4. Myanmar ltd companies	174	816	1 308	2 269	3 401
5. Partnerships	376	565	727	850	949
6. Foreign companies & branches	39	80	133	183	296
7. Joint-venture companies ltd (not under foreign investment law)	15	18	24	26	29
(a) state-owned economic enterprises & private entrepreneurs	7	10	12	13	16
(b) state-owned economic enterprises & foreign companies	8	8	12	13	13
8. Joint-venture companies ltd (under foreign investment law)	0	14	18	23	32
9. Other organizations	3	5	27	29	31
10. Tourist enterprises	0	0	0	69	145
11. Tourist transport businesses	0	0	0	71	287
12. Hotel businesses	0	0	0	27	71
13. Lodging-house businesses	0	0	0	19	62
14. Tour-guide businesses	0	0	0	87	247
Total	**1 776**	**4 655**	**6 610**	**9 413**	**12 807**

Sources: Government of the Union of Myanmar (1994), *Statistical Yearbook 1993*, Ministry of National Planning and Economic Development, Central Statistical Organization, Yangon; Government of the Union of Myanmar (1995), *Statistical Abstract 1994*, Ministry of National Planning and Economic Development, Central Statistical Organization, Yangon.

to increase tourism by opening up border areas with China and Thailand, extending tourist visas from 14 to 28 days, and simplifying entry formalities. The resulting increase in the arrivals of tourists and business travellers is sure to place great pressure on the hotel and tourism industry. In 1993 there were only 1477 hotel rooms in the whole country, and the estimated need in Yangon alone for 1996 was 2000 to 4000, giving some indication of the investment potential (*Business Indochina* 1996, p. 13).

Table 12.5 Number of tourist arrivals at Yangon, 1981–1994

Nationality	*1981*	*1986*	*1991*	*1992*	*1993*	*1994*
North America						
1 American	2 730	5 875	677	953	1 474	3 052
2 Canadian	673	1 400	132	110	277	536
Europe						
3 British	1 934	3 694	491	722	1 182	2 240
4 French	4 960	4 726	870	887	1 187	2 254
5 German	4 258	5 943	1 606	1 253	1 656	2 355
6 Italian	–	2 680	1 213	1 144	1 563	1 903
7 Russian	–	25	1	1	7	16
8 Swiss	1 385	2 524	453	392	448	820
Asia						
9 Chinese	–	93	6	33	220	322
10 Indian	352	389	4	27	162	271
11 Korean	–	104	51	516	1 149	1 633
12 Japanese	3 164	2 999	1 051	819	1 987	4 557
13 Pakistani	231	266	15	27	324	257
14 Thai	–	913	172	186	1 848	4 684
15 **Australian**	1 846	2 043	174	191	384	745
16 **Other**	6 546	6 931	1 145	1 683	7 471	13 548
Total	**28 079**	**40 605**	**8 061**	**8 944**	**21 339**	**39 193**

Sources: Government of the Union of Myanmar, (1994), *Statistical Yearbook 1993*, Ministry of National Planning and Economic Development, Central Statistical Organization, Yangon; Government of the Union of Myanmar (1995), *Statistical Abstract 1994*, Ministry of National Planning and Economic Development, Central Statistical Organization, Yangon.

Table 12.5 shows that much of the visitor growth stems from Asian countries such as Thailand and Korea. While separate figures are not available for Singapore and other ASEAN countries, it is anticipated that a great deal of the growth in the "Others" group is from these sources. Between April 1993 and February 1994, 52 998 foreigners (including 16 123 businesspeople) entered Myanmar through Yangon airport alone. International promotions such as the Visit Myanmar Year 1996 have attracted attention, and the number of visitors is expected to continue to rise in the future. Over one-third of the visitors are businesspeople intent on exploring business opportunities.

These activities have transformed the economic and demographic environments. The signs can be seen most clearly in a large city such as Yangon.

Cities that in the last few decades looked like sleepy, unchanging hollows are now bustling with activity as the construction of hotels, new buildings and roads accelerates. Observers (e.g. Than & Thein 1995) have noted some signs of increasing affluence, such as the following:

- an increasing number of automobiles in Yangon, Mandalay and other big towns
- widened roads and highways, with advertising billboards lining them at intervals
- new buildings and private houses in urban centers and new satellite towns
- new stores, stacked with imported goods
- new and more sophisticated advertisements on television and in the press
- the appearance of numerous satellite dishes in many cities

New shops stocked with Western products now line city streets, and many people have found employment with foreign businesses. These economic changes are not as obvious in the rural areas, however, except for towns on the border trade route; these show signs of a newfound prosperity. Examples are cities such as Mandalay, which provides a possible transhipping point for Chinese merchandise to Yangon and beyond. While Mandalay's city business center features largely Chinese immigrants, Monywa, linked to the Indian border trade, is thriving on trade with India (Moreau 1995). These activities have resulted in varieties of cheap consumer goods swamping the market.

Demographic environment

The population of the country was estimated to be about 44.74 million at the end of 1995, an increase of 0.82 million over the figure of 43.92 million at the end of 1994. With a population growth rate of 1.88%, there appears to be a steady increase in numbers at every lower-cohort level (see Table 12.6). For example, in 1994, 35% of the population was between the ages of 0 and 14. This increase in the numbers in younger age groups is expected to have significant impact on marketing trends in Myanmar in the future. Unlike other countries in South-East Asia, the rate of urbanization in Myanmar has been slow. Only 33% of the population was classified as urban in 1992—a small increase when compared to the proportion of 23% in 1970. Unless Myanmar is contrary to regional trends, this is likely to accelerate as the nation develops.

The number of students enrolled at institutes of higher education (see Table 12.7) have remained relatively constant over the past 10 years, especially in the professional institutions. The total enrollment of 101 826 in 1993–1994 is less than the 1985–1986 figure of 117 246, indicating that the population growth may yet have to impact on the limited spaces at these institutes. The percentage of graduates in the entire population has actually decreased over the last decade. A comparison with the regional countries (see

Table 12.6 Estimated population of Myanmar by age group ('000)

Age group	*1973*	*1983*	*1989*	*1990*	*1991*	*1992*	*1993*	*1994*
0–4	28 083	4 502	5 178	5 238	5 276	5 301	5 319	
5–9	3 929	4 388	4 755	4 799	4 859	4 925	4 984	
10–14	3 481	4 268	4 657	4 664	4 667	4 676	4 698	
0–14	*35 493*	*13 158*	*14 590*	*14 701*	*14 802*	*14 902*	*15 001*	*14 847*
15–19	2 931	3 735	4 448	4 505	4 554	4 594	4 627	
20–24	2 309	3 286	3 977	4 077	4 176	4 268	4 353	
25–29	1 795	2 763	3 415	3 513	3 615	3 723	3 832	
30–34	1 664	2 152	2 867	2 960	3 051	3 145	3 244	
35–39	1 594	1 667	2 304	2 401	2 501	2 601	2 700	
40–44	1 470	1 480	1 815	1 887	1 969	2 055	2 147	
45–49	1 159	1 414	1 513	1 543	1 582	1 631	1 688	
50–54	1 043	1 299	1 363	1 369	1 379	1 393	1 415	
55–59	781	995	1 202	1 217	1 232	1 247	1 260	
15–59	*14 746*	*18 791*	*22 904*	*23 472*	*24 059*	*24 657*	*25 266*	*25 808*
60–64	662	830	960	987	1 013	1 040	1 066	
65+	1 031	1 340	1 580	1 626	1 678	1 734	1 796	
60 +	*1 693*	*2 170*	*2 540*	*2 613*	*2 691*	*2 774*	*2 862*	*3 267*
Total	**28 083**	**34 119**	**40 034**	**40 786**	**41 552**	**42 333**	**43 129**	**43 922**

Source: Government of the Union of Myanmar (1995), *Statistical Yearbook 1994*, Ministry of National Planning and Economic Development, Central Statistical Organization, Yangon, p. 14.

Table 12.8) shows that, while Myanmar lags behind its neighbors in terms of absolute GDP indicators, the literacy rate of 81.5% in 1992 (an increase from 71% in 1970) is high when compared to countries such as India (52.0%) and some of the lesser-developed South-East Asian countries (see Table 12.8). This is a result of government policy to eradicate illiteracy by innovative programs such as encouraging students to spend their holidays in rural literacy programs. Despite problems, the tertiary-education system appears to be expanding (e.g. in 1993 Yangon's second arts and science university opened), and public expenditure on the educational sector is increasing.

There are about 135 ethnic groups in Myanmar. The Bamah, Kachin, Kaya, Kayin, Chin, Mon, Rakhine, and Shan are the predominant groups. The Bamah are the majority (69% of the total population), and mainly inhabit the large cities such as Yangon and Mandalay. While attention is paid to the

Table 12.7 Enrollment at institutes of higher education, 1983–1994

Institutes	*1983–1984*	*1984–1985*	*1985–1986*	*1986–1987*	*1987–1988*	*1990–1991*	*1991–1992*	*1992–1993*	*1993–1994*
Professional institutes									
Medicine 1	2 303	2 527	2 431	2 310	2 073	1 434	1 510	1 499	1 862
Medicine 2	932	906	943	1 004	900	684	832	820	1 234
Medicine Mandalay	1 085	1 102	1 118	1 099	1 009	736	856	855	1 113
Dental medicine	313	428	412	405	353	291	327	326	330
Paramedical sciences	61	67	70	83	83	70	40	40	88
Inst. of Nursing	–	–	–	–	–	–	–	67	106
Inst. of Pharmacy	–	–	–	–	–	–	25	25	65
Technology	5 324	5 395	5 289	5 128	4 863	–	4 429	5 066	5 428
Economics	5 447	5 183	5 265	5 229	5 065	–	4 773	4 593	4 380
Education	515	630	614	554	620	–	1 273	1 477	1 703
Agriculture	1 574	1 835	1 996	1 919	1 574	–	1 159	1 101	1 087
Forestry	–	–	–	–	–	–	261	259	249
Animal husbandry & Vet.	873	878	870	849	828	–	743	759	717
Computer science & Tech.	–	–	–	–	261	–	271	519	497
Subtotal	**18 427**	**18 951**	**19 008**	**18 580**	**17 629**	**3 215**	**16 499**	**17 406**	**18 859**
Others: Arts & Science	65 790	78 008	98 238	129 028	112 327	–	90 814	93 453	82 967
Total	**84 217**	**96 959**	**117 246**	**147 608**	**129 956**	**3 215**	**107 313**	**110 859**	**101 826**

Source: Government of the Union of Myanmar (1995), *Statistical Yearbook 1994*, Ministry of National Planning and Economic Development, Central Statistical Organization, Yangon, p. 277.

Table 12.8 Comparison of vital statistics for selected countries

Country	*Population (millions)*	*Population growth (%)*	*People per doctor*	*Literacy rate (%)*	*GDP (per capita)*	*GDP growth (%)*	*Inflation (%)*
Bangladesh	122.7	2.2	12 500	36.6	1 290	4.5	6.4
Cambodia	9.8	2.5	9 523	37.8	1 266	4.9	18
India	927.8	2.1	2 165	52.1	1 280	5.3	8.2
Laos	4.8	2.9	4 447	83.9	2 071	8	6.7
Malaysia	20.1	2.4	2 063	89.3	8 763	9.3	3.4
Myanmar	**46.7**	**2.1**	**12 500**	**81.5**	**676**	**6.4**	**27.9**
Philippines	67.7	2.3	1 016	93.5	2 660	5.7	11
Singapore	3.1	2	711	91.6	21 493	9	1.1
Thailand	60.6	1.5	4 361	93.8	6 816	8.5	10.2
Vietnam	74.6	2.3	2 298	88.6	1 263	8.5	13.8

Source: Asiaweek (1995), December 22–9.

preservation of the culture of each group, the Bamah language is the official language. This is a monosyllabic tonal language that Westerners find difficult to hear correctly (Maung 1991). About 89.4% of the population, mainly Bamahs, Shans, Mons, Rakhines, and some Kayins, are Buddhists, while the rest are Christians, Muslims, Hindus, and Animists. The Christian population is composed mainly of Kayins, Kachins, and Chins. It is mainly the people of Indian origin who practice Islam and Hinduism.

Cultural environment

The Myanmar society of today has developed from about 15 centuries of a rural, agricultural way of life in which the village, and, within the village, the family, were the controlling units (Khaing 1994). The Myanmar national character is certainly distinct, produced, as it is, through an interaction between the peaceful landscape of green paddy fields, palm groupings, low roofs, high pagodas, and monasteries. Some of the key ingredients of Myanmar's culture include the following.

The influence/dominance of religion

It is said that Myanmar is one of the few places where pure Buddhism is still practiced. Over 85% of the citizens are practicing Therevada Buddhists, and the lives and values of the people are greatly intertwined with the Buddhist religion. Every Myanmar Buddhist tries to live a life based on the Buddhist principles of a simple lifestyle, and to fulfill the requirements of merit. It is, indeed, a religion that affects both the social and psychological aspects of Myanmar life. The belief in "karma," that of present life being due to deeds in the past lives, is also strong. The Myanmar Buddhists hold all persons, places, and things associated with religion in much veneration (Pe 1996).

Marketing managers should be aware of certain codes of conduct to which Buddhists adhere, in order to avoid seeming disrespectful. For example, images of Buddha and photographs of pagodas should not be used in advertisements, except for tourism purposes. Uniforms or cloth of saffron colour should be avoided, as this color is used for religious purposes only.

Strength of family ties

The components of a Myanmar family are mirrored in the 3 ages that Buddhist teaching apportions to a human being: the first of acquiring knowledge (in youth), the second of building up material resources (in middle age), and the third of devotion to more spiritual things (in old age). Family ties in Myanmar are strong—not so much as a result of rigid traditions as of allowing natural affections full play. A typical family living in one household includes the children, the parents—both of them usually working to support the home—and old men and women, who give much time to prayer and daily offerings at the altar for the entire family. The family structure is loosely defined, its membership varying according to circumstance. Sons and daughters and sisters, aunts, and uncles acquired by marriage may be incorporated in the family. The Bamah word for "relative" has the same root as "friend," and most Myanmar people have a warmhearted desire for as many relatives as possible. Such a concept extends the family naturally to friends and neighbors—in the country to the whole village, and in the city to the whole yatkwet (residential district). The community elders share with the heads of family the privileges of giving guidance and being kept informed. Marketers should therefore mirror such values in advertising concepts; for example, by using elders as central figures in advertising campaigns.

Customs and beliefs

Within the Myanmar society, a great deal of respect is accorded to the elders, teachers (*sayah*) and religious authorities such as monks. There exists a nexus of obligations, due by the young to the old and the old to the young, that bonds all generations of Myanmar people (Pe 1996). Many unspoken rules exist with respect to interaction between various types of people. For example, one should not offer to shake hands with monks, but instead observe "gadaw" with clasped palms at forehead level. Neither should one touch any person on the head, or step over any part of a person. One should also seek permission before retrieving an article above a person's head. In addition, when using the Myanmar language, suitable words or phrases should be used when addressing others based upon the relevant relationship and social position. There is a very strong sense of "ar-nah" among the Myanmar. Loosely, this refers to a feeling of being beholden, and as such they shy away from imposing on others, or from actions that require a favor in return. Care is often taken not to create the loss of "face." This is somewhat, though not quite exactly, similar to the Thai concept of "krenjai." Spiritual beliefs are also strong, and blend harmoniously with religious beliefs. These include giving offerings to the "nats," or spirits before any ceremony or major undertakings, for example, the purchase of a car.

Ceremonies and festivals

There is hardly any activity, apart from routine work, in which all neighbors do not participate. Myanmar life is rich in opportunities for communal experience. Due to the semi-tropical climate, the Myanmar people enjoy being outdoors–except during the monsoon months–and the cultural traditions provide many opportunities to join festival processions to the monastery or the pagoda, all participants dressed in their best and bearing gifts or offerings.

The Myanmar calendar is lunar, and liberally sprinkled with holidays such as Thingyan, the New Year Water Festival, Kason, the watering festival of the Bodhi tree, and Thadingyut, the festival of lights. Thingyan is celebrated merrily and noisily, while Kason is a more somber religious occasion (Thein 1995). At Thadingyut, the young pay respect to their elders.

There are a myriad of sports activities and cultural events, held almost every month of the year, ranging from boat-racing festivals to soccer matches. In addition to such occasions, there are many reasons for social gatherings. For example, there is always a gathering for the naming ceremony for a month-old child, when the baby's hair is cut and washed for the first time. And far more elaborate preparations are made for the ceremonies that mark the passing from childhood into adolescence. Almost all young boys go through a *shinpyu* ceremony, in which they spend a period of time as novice monks. Other occasions of celebration include house-warmings, weddings, birthdays, paying gratitude to the dead; or any time a person feels good or, alternatively, low in spirits, and needs the blessings for a righteous deed done.

Historical characteristics

Myanmar's history stretches back many centuries, at least to the Pyu Kings in the 5th century AD. There is an invisible web, comprising cultural pride, awareness of legends and folklore, and a strong sense of history, that binds the people.

Myanmar people are proud of their history. The greatest period of cultural activity began with King Anawratha in the 11th century. His legacy can be seen in the ruins of Bagan with its magnificent temples and pagodas. This was the time at which Theravada Buddhism and the Myanmar language, art, and culture began flourishing (Thein 1995). Since then, a long list of kings, queens, heroes, battles, conquests, and legends have been part of the Myanmar collective past. After the fall of Bagan to the Mongols in the 13th century, the Ava Dynasty (1364–1555) was followed by the Toungoo Dynasty (1486–1752). The most prominent member of the latter dynasty was King Bayinnaung, who forged Myanmar into a strong, respected nation. The final days of this dynasty also saw Myanmar at war with neighboring Thailand, and the infamous sacking of the Thai capital of Ayutthaya in 1767. Another dynasty followed under King Alaungpaya in 1752. During this time, the Myanmar kingdom conquered distant regions such as Arakan, Manipur, and Assam. These victories were followed by wars with the British in the early 19th century, leading to Myanmar's defeat, and the eventual annexation of Burma. In 1886, King Thibaw, the last king of the dynasty, was deported to India. Myanmar gained its independence only after two World Wars, on January 4 1948.

The strong influence of history is apparent not only in the Myanmar religious and cultural systems, but also in the more tangible elements such as architecture, arts and crafts, dance and drama, and the Myanmar language and literature. There are 2217 historical monuments and temples under the care of the Archaeological Department in Bagan alone. Today, large audiences even in small towns enjoy the performance of Ramayana in Myanmar drama, said to be adopted from the Thais in the 18th century.

The role of women

Compared to other developing nations, and even some more developed Asian nations, Myanmar women enjoy a fairly high status in society. An unmarried woman is not necessarily considered an "old spinster." Myanmar women also have an active say in household and purchase decisions. Gender bias against women is neither apparent nor acute (Thein 1996). In the cities and the countryside, there is a fair share of participation by women in economic activities, such as production, service, and agriculture. The women also enjoy shopping of any nature, and are therefore an important target for marketing activities. Nevertheless, and despite the positive aspects discussed above as Buddhist doctrine, women are considered to be on a plane of lesser "existence" than men. Education and choice of profession are regarded as less important for a girl than for a boy. Child rearing and food preparation are still mainly the domain of women.

Overall, Myanmar life can be seen as one of goodwill and fraternity, with its spirit of generosity and relaxation resulting from the different elements of society being well-adjusted to each other (Khaing 1994). For instance, the old neither feel unwanted nor have an urge to behave like the young, as there is a definite function for them in every festivity, and a role in the home routine. So it is with the role of both sexes. There also exists the pride to be expected by an isolated inland culture that for many centuries did not experience a feeling of inferiority toward anything in the outside world. This pride will be hard to eradicate even with the entrance of Western materialism. Despite economic difficulties, the people of Myanmar live within a social system that promotes a sense of both spiritual and worldly fulfillment. Their self-confidence in their own standards allows for sufficient amusement at their own shortcomings to take the edge off economic hardship—without, however, giving them any sense of inferiority to any other race of people.

Consumer behavior

The economic, cultural, and demographic environments have an important bearing on the consumer behavior of the Myanmar people. Class structures exist within Myanmar, and consumers can be roughly divided into two types: the well-educated and wealthy upper class, and the much larger and poorer lower class.

In Myanmar, unlike most other developing countries, a large middle class of consumers did not exist until recently. With the influx of foreign capital and growth in the economy, there now appears to be the beginnings of a middle class of consumers who have benefited most directly from the economic reforms. This phenomenon is, however, confined mainly to the cities and certain rural areas. For example, a village called Ywatharnyunt near Nyaungdon, with approximately 275 households relying mainly on the cultivation of beans and pulses, had about 30 radios and 2 bicycles before 1988. Now it has 1 television set, over 80 radios and about 60 bicycles (Than & Thein 1995).

The small upper class consists of the ruling elite, the traditional nobility that remains a vestige of the past, and some wealthy families of overseas workers who have repatriated their earnings. They mostly dwell in the cities such as Yangon, Mandalay, and Mawlamyaing, own property, and have the means to buy any of the consumer products that are available in these large cities.

The lower class consists of both city dwellers and farmers. In the city, lower-class members tend to be small traders, manual and salaried workers, and the unemployed; in the rural areas, this class consists mainly of farm workers. While the nominal incomes of the city workers have probably just kept pace with the increase in the general level of prices, some of the workers are able to earn additional wages by "moonlighting." As for the farmworkers, those who do not have surplus to sell on the open market are expected to have little discretionary income. Their purchase cycles also tend to be seasonal, with harvest period late in the year being a good time for targeting marketing activities. As rural consumers are currently unreceptive targets of Western consumer marketing, it may be of greater value to concentrate on city consumers, principally those in Yangon and Mandalay.

Despite the barriers to external influences, Myanmar's city dwellers are surprisingly well informed about the outside world—though their knowledge may be somewhat dated. The infiltration of foreign influences has been aided by several factors, which are discussed below.

Myanmar people abroad

A large number of Myanmar emigrants work and live abroad. Unlike the refugees originating from Indochina, they are mostly professionals, with high levels of skill and/or education. Most of them send food, clothing, and other necessities to relatives and friends in Myanmar, thus keeping the recipients in touch with foreign goods. This has created a latent demand for foreign brands.

Knowledge of English

For the marketer, one of the most striking features of the Myanmar people, especially the older generation, is their ability to understand English. Most Myanmar schooling was conducted in English until 1962, when this language was banned as "representative of a degenerate and decadent culture" (Maung 1991, p. 222). Nonetheless, the decades of British rule have ensured that many older people are fluent in the English language. After a lapse of about 30 years, English has been reintroduced in schools as a second language. In the cities, there is a great demand for English-language books, CDs, magazines, videotapes, and movies.

Intact brand profiles

The Myanmar consumer is surprisingly brand conscious. The British influence created consumer habits that many of the upper class retained; these habits have recently started to re-appear. Therefore, brands that were strongly represented in Myanmar during the 1940s to the 1960s continue to have strong "share of mind," and are widely popular on the black market. For example, food giant Nestlé has had its products in Myanmar homes for generations, and even today consumer preference leans toward Nestlé products such as Nescafé coffee.

Thriving black market

Contrary to popular belief, the "black" market in Myanmar is a thriving and perfectly "open" business. For example, in the Mingala Bazaar in Yangon town center there is a large mall of small shops where almost any Western item, from toothpaste to TV sets, can be bought. The government policy is based on the notion that, once the goods are moving through the legal channels, the black markets will disappear. Until that time, however, the strong presence of these markets has provided consumers with a continuous link to the products and fashions of the outside world, despite the years of isolation.

Given the above knowledge, the consumers tend to be rather selective in their shopping habits. They tend to prefer well-known labels over cheaper versions, and familiar makes over newer ones (for example, a "Made in England" label is perceived to be better than a "Made in Hong Kong" label). However, because of tight budget constraints, Myanmar consumers often settle for cheaper, less desirable brands. They tend to be very careful when selecting a product to meet their needs. While some forms of impulse purchases do exist, consumers tend to consider all aspects of product benefits before a purchase decision is made, often going back to the shop for a second look.

In addition, the close social ties create an environment where entire clans remain faithful to a brand, unlike a Western family, where each individual in the same household may prefer or use a different brand. Furthermore, word-of-mouth recommendation plays an important role in determining the success of a product, especially from family members. Women, especially, play an important role both as purchase decision makers and influencers.

There is also a great deal of receptivity to foreign goods and advertising. This has been explained by suggesting that Myanmar is in the initial stages of development, and therefore its consumers tend to be less cynical about marketing practices. Recent studies have indicated that Myanmar consumers tend to have a much stronger positive response to advertising than consumers in more developed countries (Lwin 1997).

Trends in the macromarketing mix

Consumer products

Almost anything and everything a consumer could want is quite easily available in Myanmar—at a price. Imported cooking aids, food, toiletries, electrical goods, and many other products are available not only at the central Mingala Market, but also in all small provision stores—even those on the outskirts of Yangon. Most "imports" appear to have originated from Thailand, Hong Kong and Singapore, although, of late, cheap products from China and India have infiltrated the market as well. In Yangon and Mandalay, there are also larger department stores carrying various types of foreign goods.

A wide variety of local products are also available, a few of which are direct imitations of foreign goods, right down to the packaging. The products available in the markets follow a clear trend, with market leaders being the most visible and well stocked. Lesser-known brands, imitations, and even totally unknown brands are also widely available. For example, among cigarette brands, 555 is the most well known and the best seller, followed by Benson & Hedges and Marlboro. The consumer outlook has obviously been so good that foreign companies like Rothmans of Pall Mall are in the process of opening factories in Myanmar. Duya, a local cigarette brand, is also very popular because it is much cheaper than the foreign brands. Besides these brands, cigarettes produced locally by joint-venture companies, such as Polo and Sampoena, are also selling well. In addition, a typical cigarette seller might stock virtually unknown brands such as KKK and American Club. The clear market leaders in other categories are always available in stores, on sidewalk stalls, in homes, and on the black market. This exclusive club includes Colgate toothpaste, the beverage Ovaltine, Johnny Walker Red Label and Nescafé coffee powder. There is also a great demand for electrical and high-technology products such as computers.

As Myanmar opens up more to the outside world, most consumers are eager to show their modernity by acquiring products such as TV sets, cameras, videocasette recorders and home computers. Two decades ago, these products had almost no penetration in the Myanmar market.

Pricing

Pricing of foreign goods follows similar processes (i.e. as a function of supply and demand), and prices are usually quite uniform across institutions, but fluctuate, sometimes daily, according to the erratic supply situation. Taking into consideration the official exchange rate of approximately 1 US$ to 6 kyats and a black-market rate of 1 US$ to over 110 kyats, in 1995 a few black-market selections were priced approximately as shown in Table 12.9.

Table 12.9 Pricing of consumer products in Yangon (kyats)

Product	*Price*
Colgate Toothpaste (large)	90
Darlie Toothpaste (small)	40
Lux Soap Bar	40
Kleenex Tissue Box	55
Carnation Evaporated Milk	40
Nescafé (large tin)	300

The pricing of local produce has been much more predictable, with food and many other commodities being locally produced. With the high inflation rates, the consumer price index (CPI) has reflected rising costs over the years. Between 1986 and 1994, the CPI rose more than fivefold to 571.5. This problem is even more acute in the food and beverages category (CPI = 658.4) and the fuel and light category (CPI = 613.6), while tobacco and education have been more controlled, at lower CPIs of 244.7 and 113.7 respectively (see Table 12.10).

Table 12.10 Consumer price index, Yangon, 1984–1994*

Particulars	*1984*	*1985*	*1986*	*1987*	*1988*	*1989*	*1990*	*1991*	*1992*	*1993*	*1994*
A General Consumer Price Index	85.7	91.6	100	123.9	144.8	184.1	216.6	286.5	349.2	460.4	571.5
Food & Beverages	85.9	94.1	100	126.7	152.9	196.4	234.2	322	394.4	547.7	658.4
Tobacco	87.3	84.3	100	146.8	152.1	153.7	160.8	186.7	230	272.2	284.7
Fuel & light	88.5	86.8	100	118	134.6	172.7	210.8	267.9	336.8	380.3	613.6
Clothing & apparel	82.6	90.7	100	122.1	120.9	134.9	174.6	218.7	289.4	345.7	382
House rent & repairs	87.2	92.7	100	102	102.1	111.8	133.6	186.7	216	245.4	292.8
Education	90.3	96.1	100	100.3	99.9	99	102.9	104.2	105.9	108.4	113.7
Medical care	58.6	74.1	100	145.7	164.2	203	239.2	323	321.3	327.9	329.7
Conveyance	100	100	100	137.4	223.7	223.7	223.7	223.7	223.7	241.8	529.8
Cleansing & toilet	100.3	85	100	142	143.6	187.7	186.8	212	227.9	289.5	277.55
Annual change in CPI(%)	4.84	6.81	9.21	23.94	16.81	27.19	17.63	32.27	21.91	31.83	24.11

Note:
*Base year 1986 = 100.

Sources: Government of the Union of Myanmar (1994), *Statistical Yearbook 1993*, Ministry of National Planning and Economic Development, Central Statistical Organization, Yangon; Government of the Union of Myanmar (1995), *Statistical Abstract 1994*, Ministry of National Planning and Economic Development, Central Statistical Organization, Yangon.

Recently, the influx of foreign goods through legal retail outlets has made many consumer products readily available to consumers. A sampling of the prices of consumer electronic products, which until very recently were not easily available, is shown in Table 12.11. While these products are readily available, their price does place them out of reach of ordinary citizens, whose household income is well below 2000 kyats per month. Nevertheless, sales have been brisk, as many households have supplementary incomes from second jobs or part-time work. Marketers are therefore advised to consider the total household income, including secondary incomes, when deciding on pricing issues, rather than simply individual incomes (Bin et al. 1995).

Table 12.11 Pricing of electronic products in Yangon (kyats)

Product	*Cost*
National Cassette Player RX. C51DF	15 300
Sanyo (SR17NE) Refrigerator	51 000
Toshiba Aircon (30BA)	97 000
Sony Color TV (KV 1485)	35 000
Sony Video Player (SLV 710)	45 000
National Washing Machine (250 OH)	18 500

Source: Myanma Dhana (1994), "Top Ten Survey", no. 47, May, p. 10.

Distribution: The retail market

Traditionally, there existed only two types of distribution outlets in Myanmar—government-run stores and small private bazaars. Most of the private bazaars sold illegal black-market goods. At the government stores a quota was often set for each family for the purchase of products.

Today, however, this system has been discontinued. With the opening up of the economy, there has been a systematic entry of larger trading houses-cum-stores as well as provision shops. The division between the various types of establishments is somewhat blurred. The government-run stores continue to be poorly stocked. They sell mainly commodities (sugar, rice, unbranded soap, textiles). In some outlets, foreign goods, imported by the government, are available. For example, Medicines and Medical Equipment Trading (a government instrumentality) imports large quantities of pharmaceuticals and medical supplies that are available through hospital outlets. Many consumers continue to purchase items from this source, as prices are stabilized, and well below market costs.

The bazaars continue to thrive. They range from open-air market stalls, and provision shops that are family owned and operated, to the newer department stores. Many stock both local and Western goods, while some "specialize" in only a few types of products. Their supply of merchandise comes from seamen, returning residents and foreigners, as well as from direct illegal imports. A number of these stores are housed in a few major "shopping centers," in Mingala Zay, and the old and new areas in Bogyoke Zay.

There has also been a proliferation of new stores, run by Myanmar traders or foreign investors, in response to the government's more liberal trade and investment policies in recent years. They aim at local consumers, and their pricing structure sometimes varies to accommodate taxes and other costs. However, the need to make a profit is the same, and, at many of the stores, items are for sale in US dollars, credit cards or Foreign Exchange Certificates (FECs). As ordinary citizens are allowed to handle FECs (US dollars are illegal for locals) an FEC market has been created where FECs can be traded.

Examples of new retailing developments include the Myanmar-Singapore Emporium, run by Singapore entrepreneurs, Sony Electronics, the Toshiba outlet, which sells all types of electrical appliances, Apple Computers, which sells the latest software and hardware, and National Trade Union Congress supermarket. Even though this channel may not provide large short-term profits, investors clearly see it as a good and legitimate way to enter the market and establish their presence and leadership. These stores are run in a more "Western" manner than the black-market outlets. Products such as refrigerators, TV sets and household appliances are "departmentalized" by product category, and prices are fixed, with no bargaining taking place. Most also provide product guarantees and after-sales service. Toshiba, for example, boasts of having over 30 technicians among its after-sales service staff.

Promotion and advertising

The major media–TV, radio, and newspapers–are state owned. There are numerous private publications: mainly feature magazines, comics, cartoons, and novels. The local media, the majority of which use the Myanmar language, dominate the general communication scene in Myanmar. In a 1994 survey, the "Top Ten" lists of best-selling books, magazines, videocassettes and laser disks, cassettes and CDs found that locally produced Myanmar language titles occupied the entire 10 positions in each category (*Myanma Dhana* 1994). The Myanmar Television and Radio Department controls radio and TV broadcasting. It has 5 divisions: Information, Radio Broadcasting, Engineering, Television and Administration. Television currently airs approximately 3 to 5 hours of programs on weekdays, and 7 hours on weekends. Television transmissions are now beamed to almost every corner of the country through a network of recently built repeater stations–television is the most effective medium for creating advertising impact, if cost is not a factor. A 30-second TV spot advertisement–exclusive of agency commission, which can be negotiated on a project basis–ranged from US$360 to US$760 in 1995, with prime-time slots commanding the highest premium.

According to the Department, TV currently reaches 80% of the country's households. This is expected to grow to 90% in the near future. The ownership of TV sets is much smaller, however, and is limited to better-off consumers; it totaled 225 477 in 1994. Radio has a much higher reach of 95%, airing approximately 10 hours a day in English and Myanmar. In 1995 there were also an estimated 50 000 video sets in Yangon, which represents a 150% increase over the 20 000 sets in 1988; and ownership is fast increasing, as a result of aggressive marketing campaigns by foreign brands. Technical transmission data for Myanmar television are the following: video system–Umatic 3/4–NTSC 3.58–525 lines, with audio frequency of 4.5 megahertz.

Myanmar TV broadcasts both English and Myanmar programs, although the news, documentaries, variety shows and dramas are mainly in the Myanmar language. Some Western shows, such as "Silk Stalkings," are also shown. Weekday programs on TV are confined mainly to the evenings, with the highlight being an hour-long news program at 8 p.m. Direct transmission is limited only to major events such as important soccer matches. Most television advertisements are shown in commercial breaks during the prime-time periods. The majority of commercials are locally produced, although some foreign advertisements also appear. Western television commercials must be approved by the censorship board. The Myanmar Television and Radio Department also administers radio advertisements. These are mostly in Myanmar, with the range of products advertised being similar to that on TV. Prime time for radio is 8 a.m. to 9 a.m.–before work–and 7 p.m to 8 p.m.

The News and Periodicals Corporation publishes and/or distributes national and international newspapers as well as periodicals, books, and other literature. Newspaper advertising is currently the most far-reaching and cost-effective medium available in Myanmar. There are only 3 newspapers in the country, and they have a very wide readership. At present, *The New Light of Myanmar* (*NLM*) is the only English-language newspaper. There are two Myanmar-language newspapers–*Kyemon Daily* and NLM's *Myanmar A-Lin*. Daily newspaper circulation figures indicate a tremendous increase in circulation between 1990 and 1995, even surpassing the pre-1988 figures when more newspapers were available. Approximate circulation figures for the 3 newspapers in 1995 were as follows: *NLM* (English)–24 000+; *Kyemon Daily* (Myanmar)–180 000+; *Myanmar A-lin* (Myanmar)–220 000+. The base rate for newspaper advertising is US$15 per inch per column. The base rate for a half-page advertisement in the *NLM* is about US$1100, and a half-page advertisement in the tabloid-sized *Kyemon* is about US$700. Discounted rates are available from the official advertising agents.

There is a wide range of local reading material. Those published by the government-controlled Printing and Publishing Corporation include

Forward Magazine, People's Army Magazine, Workers Journal, Shwe Thway Journal (comics and features for young people), texts, schoolbooks, and many local magazines. Myanmar people and visitors to the country read many magazines, particularly as TV viewing time is limited. There are about 40 monthly magazines, ranging from children's magazines to magazines devoted to selective translations of *Time, Newsweek* and *Asiaweek.*

The majority of publishing companies are privately owned. Magazine publishers are often quite flexible, and willing to discuss various promotional ideas. All printers and publishers are required to register annually with the General Administration Department, Ministry of Home Affairs, for permission to operate. They also have to submit regular information to the Registration Office on books and magazines published. Registered books are classified under 9 subjects. Authors wishing to publish books have to obtain permission to do so.

Print advertising is abundant in local magazines, although both print and paper quality are poor. For newspapers and magazines, the printing is acceptable, but the paper used is often of inferior quality. However, magazines do provide great flexibility in terms of color and space, and seem to be favored by the smaller local advertisers. Less common, though growing, is newspaper advertising, which is confined to regular black-and-white spaces in the Myanmar or English editions of the national newspaper. Recently, however, desktop publishing has been introduced to Myanmar's newspapers, and is set to revolutionize newspaper advertising by enabling the use of modern computer-based techniques.

The Motion Picture Corporation is the state agency responsible for the operation of cinemas in major cities as well as the procurement of films. There are over 20 cinemas in Yangon showing local movies and a potpourri of English, Indian, Chinese, and Japanese movies. The movie is a popular entertainment medium; a large cinema complex that can show five movies simultaneously was opened in 1995.

In Myanmar, billboards are a popular and effective advertising medium, especially in strategic locations. Two decades ago, these were almost nonexistent in Yangon, but today billboards are present both within and outside city limits. Billboards can serve as a year-round awareness generators on major roads and inter-city "highways," at a fraction of print-media costs. They are available at specific sites in the cities, in a wide variety of sizes. The jurisdiction of these sites falls under city municipalities. While most of the billboards are in the Myanmar language, some foreign brands such as airlines are advertised in English.

An important factor to note is the overall lack of regulation on advertising claims. This has created many advertising opportunities for advertisers of products such as cigarettes and medicinal products who face restrictions in other countries.

Other popular promotional activities include sports sponsorships (the most popular being soccer and golf), beauty contests or pageants, festival participation, and celebrity endorsements. Most of the events tend to be seasonal, to take advantage of the cool dry season (October to February) and to avoid the monsoon or the wet season (July to September). Some of the important festivals include the New Year Water Festival (Thingyan) in April, and the Light Festival (Thadingyut) in October.

Future trends: The potential

There is little doubt that the potential for marketing of foreign products exists in Myanmar, with its relatively large population and attractive location. Initially, however, consumer markets may have to be confined to the major cities.

Certainly the Myanmar people are aware of many Western brands, and are anxious to purchase them–provided the price is within their means. In the early 1990s, the United Nations Development Program worked out a Human Development Index (HDI) that combined life expectancy, education, literacy, and GDP, to show how well people live in 130 different countries. According to the HDI ranking, Myanmar, with a life expectancy at birth of 61.8 years, adult literacy rate of 80.6%, 2.5 mean years of schooling, and an adjusted real GDP per capita of PPP$ (Purchasing Power Parity Dollars) 659, rates an HDI index of 0.390, and ranks 123rd among 197 countries (Tun 1995). This index ranks Myanmar only just behind Indonesia and Vietnam, and much further ahead than India, Laos, and Cambodia. In fact, many businessmen with whom the authors have spoken consider Myanmar to have as good a potential as Vietnam, although it is less developed–it is a nation that needs the development of all types of infrastructure and institutions.

On the downside, managers need to be aware of the risk factors involved in marketing in Myanmar. There are a host of uncertainties, ranging from lack of consumer information to foreign-exchange problems when dealing with pricing. Interested marketers are advised to familiarize themselves with various business and social issues involved in marketing to the Myanmar people. Despite the presence of many private companies and enterprises engaged in various kinds of trade, it is obvious that much remains to be done. Investment by foreign organizations has so far been small when compared to the available resources and investment potential. South-East Asian governments and investors have taken a pragmatic approach to Myanmar, in the hope that economic development will lead to other improvements. In particular, the members of ASEAN have welcomed Myanmar into their forum, indicating their faith in the nation's future. If the political situation remains stable and continues to develop along democratic lines, and especially if a mineral deposit such as oil is discovered by the major foreign oil companies, then the life of the people will become much better, and consumer marketing in the Western sense will blossom. It is hoped that economic development in Myanmar will provide an opportunity for a peaceful transition from an undeveloped to a developing country, and to prosperity.

References

Asiaweek (1995a), October 13, p. 78.

— (1995b), December 22, p. 9.

Bin, Hee Jun, Kwok, Kenneth, Lau, Kok Chiang, Then, Joon Boo & Yap, Kuan Sze (1996), "Marketing in Myanmar", in ed. Myat Thein, *Business Opportunities in Myanmar,* Prentice Hall, Englewood Cliffs, NJ, pp. 217–30.

Business Indochina (1996), "Special Issue on Myanmar", Indochina Project Management Ltd, Hong Kong.

Demaine, Harvey (1997), "Myanmar: Physical and Social Geography", *The Far East and Australasia*, 27th edn, Europa Publications Ltd, London, pp. 633–4.

Economist Intelligence Unit (1995), *EIU Country Profile—Myanmar,* EIU, London, pp. 1–71.

Government of the Union of Myanmar, *Review of the Financial, Economic and Social Conditions for 1993/1994,* Ministry of National Planning and Economic Development, Central Statistical Organization, Yangon.

— (1994), *Statistical Yearbook 1993,* Ministry of National Planning and Economic Development, Central Statistical Organization, Yangon.

— (1995a), *Statistical Yearbook 1994,* Ministry of National Planning and Economic Development, Central Statistical Organization, Yangon.

— (1995b), *Statistical Abstract 1994,* Ministry of National Planning and Economic Development, Central Statistical Organization, Yangon.

— (1995c), *Statistical Abstract 1995,* Ministry of National Planning and Economic Development, Central Statistical Organization, Yangon.

Hirsh, Michael & Moreau, Ron (1995), "Risky Business", *Newsweek,* June 19, p. 10.

Insight Guide to Burma (1994), APA Publications Ltd.

Investing in Myanmar (1994), The Union of Myanmar Foreign Investment Commission, Yangon. p. 2.

Khaing, Mi Mi (1994), "Myanmar Character and Customs", *Golden Myanmar,* vol. 1, no. 4, p. 3.

Khin, Maung Kyi (1994), "Myanmar: Will Forever Flow the Ayeyerwady?", in ed. Chan Heng Chee, *South-East Asian Affairs 1994,* Institute of South-East Asian Studies, Singapore.

Kyaw, Thane (ed.) (1995), "Golden Opportunities for Investment in Myanmar", *Golden Myanmar,* Uniforce Co. Ltd, vol. 2, no. 4, p. 5.

Lwin, May (1990), "Myanmar: Coming Out of its Shell", Ogilvy & Mather Worldwide Publication, Singapore.

— (1997), "The Effect of an Audio Stimulus: Accents in English Language on Cross-cultural Consumer Response to Advertising", unpublished doctoral thesis, National University of Singapore, Singapore.

Maung, Mya (1991), *The Burma Road to Poverty,* Praeger, New York.

Moreau, Ron (1995), "Mandalay: The Next Chinese Province?", *Newsweek,* June 19, p. 13.

Myanma Dhana (1994), "Top Ten Survey", no. 47, May, p. 10.

Naw, Angeline (1994), "Hotel Fever", *Today* Magazine, Today Media & Information Ltd., April, p. 55.

Pe, Win (1996), "Dos and Don'ts in Myanmar", Amarin Printing and Publishing, Bangkok.

Silverstein, Joy (1997), "Myanmar: History", *The Far East and Australasia,* 27th edn, Europa Publications Ltd, London, pp. 634–44.

Than, Mya (1995), "Economic Outlook, Myanmar 1994–95", *Regional Outlook South-East Asia 1994–95,* in ed. Chan Heng Chee, Institute of South-East Asian Studies, Singapore.

Than, Mya & Thein, Mya (1995), "Transitional Economy of Myanmar: Performance, Issues and Problems", *Asian Transitional Economies —Challenges and Prospects for Reform and Transformation,* Institute of South-East Asian Studies, Singapore, pp. 211–61.

Thein, Mya (1996), "Socio-economic and Cultural Background of Myanmar", *Business Opportunities in Myanmar,* Prentice Hall, pp. 17–24.

Tun, Thet (1995), "International and Regional Perspective for the Development of Myanmar", *Myanmar Business and Economic Review,* vol. 1, no. 5, May–June 1995.

Vokes, Richard (1997), "Myanmar: Economy", *The Far East and Australasia,* 27th edn, Europa Publications Ltd, London, pp. 644–55.

Notes

1 US$1 = K5.94.

CHAPTER 13

New Zealand

Consumers in their market environment–Profiles and predictions

ROGER MARSHALL, CHRISTINA KWAI-CHOI LEE & KIM MARSHALL

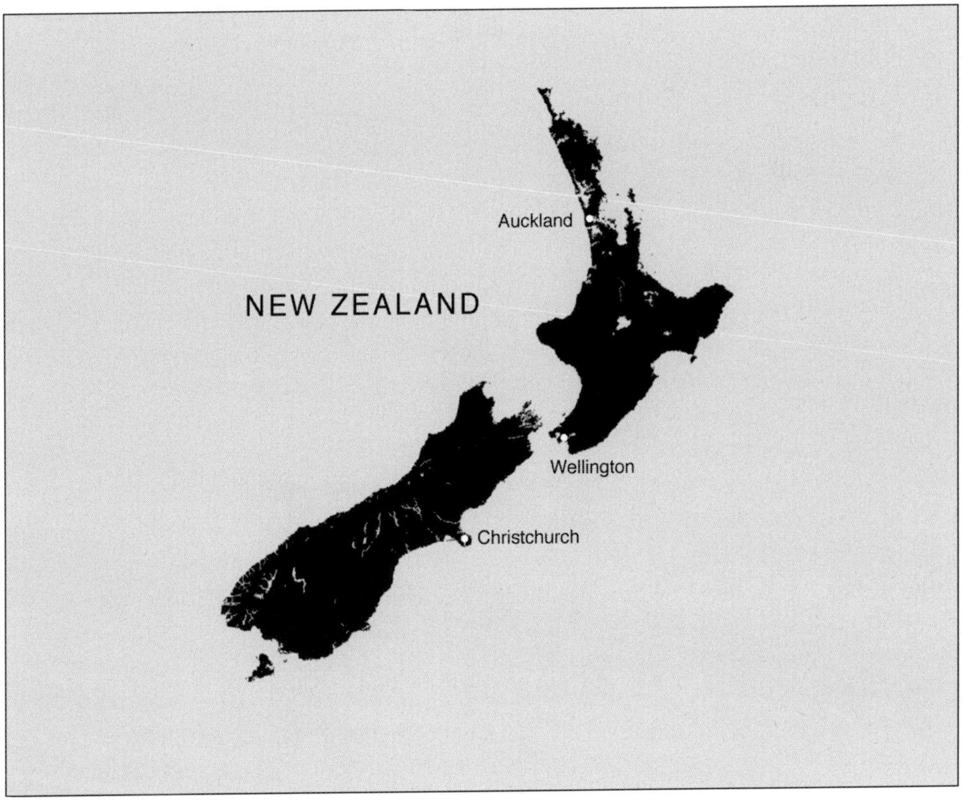

Abstract

New Zealand is a small country, on the southernmost tip of the South Pacific region. It is a country dominated by its British heritage, the multicultural nature of its population, its larger, more powerful northern neighbors and its geographical isolation. Marketers coming into the region will find the country is distinctly different from any other, even her closest neighbor, Australia. This paper provides an overview of the New Zealand environment and a profile of the New Zealand consumer. First the economic, demographic, and cultural environments are discussed, then implications are drawn from the trends noted, in order to provide a guide for potential marketers.

The economic environment

The political environment in New Zealand has, historically, provided a stable, small, democratic commercial arena in which market forces have been able to function. This has proved both advantageous, in that the country is attractive to investors, and disadvantageous, in that the economy has been very susceptible to external shocks. For this reason, mainly, there have from time to time been swings toward protectionism. The latest and most powerful protectionist lobby dominated the nation's politics and economy for many years, up to the late 1970s. During this time New Zealand's international trade consisted largely of unprocessed agricultural products, sold mostly to the UK. Inefficient import-substitution activities were supported, and the national debt figures began to climb alarmingly.

Although strongly democratic in orientation, New Zealand has always had a "first-past-the-post" party-based voting system, which gives full powers to one of the two major political parties for a 3-year term. Traditionally, this political system has tended toward a stable, strong government. It was the agriculture-based, traditional, right-wing National Party that led the protectionist movement mentioned above, while the left-wing Labour Party was dedicated to the maintenance of the welfare state established by Labour in the immediate post-War years. Ironically, it was the Labour Party that, when it gained power in the 1980s, began massive restructuring to make New Zealand a more competitive economy. This restructuring embraced the privatization (or at least corporatization) of many public utilities, including the welfare-state establishments of health and education. The irony of this is even more poignant if we consider that, when the National Party regained power and continued the economic restructuring process during the second half of the decade, this led inevitably to a massive loss of the collective bargaining power of the Labour unions.

New Zealand's political system has undergone a dramatic change, however, following a national referendum abandoning the "first-past-the-post" system in favor of proportional representation. This system came into effect in 1996, and its longer term impact is not yet fully understood. Certainly, it will be harder to push through strong, radical changes as previous governments have done, because the coalitions that will inevitably form (or the minority government party that rules) will not have the same mandate of power accorded the victor in the 2-party system. The inability to make radical, rapid change in the near future is rather more a comfort than a worry in short-run economic terms, as the present economic direction seems successful, and will probably be continued. It is only in the reaction to external shocks or internal pressure groups that the new form of governance could, in the longer run, be less positive for the economy than the old.

New Zealand is now in the midst of a long, steady economic recovery. Twin economic shocks were sustained when England joined the European

Common Market–the traditional outlet for New Zealand's vital agricultural exports consequently disappeared–and when intense pressure was exerted on the country to remove protectionist measures. Both have led to a trade (and attitudinal) re-alignment toward the Asia-Pacific region. The transition of New Zealand from a Euro-focused to an Asia-focused economy, from unprocessed agricultural exports to technological, processed agricultural and light manufactured exports, involving such significant and painful restructuring, is seen by most to have been successfully managed to date.

Overall, the indicators for the New Zealand economy are positive. The GDP growth rate peaked in 1995 at 6%, and although it fell to 2.7% in 1996, all the signs are that there will be a steady rise in that figure to around 4% in 1998 (National Bank 1996). These figures have been fueled by the highest household income and consumption figures for 20 years. In fact, New Zealand–and her key trading partner, Australia–have experienced the fastest growing GDP among all the OECD countries in recent years.

An NZ$190 million surplus for the fiscal year 1993/1994 was followed by one of NZ$2600 million (3% of GDP) in the fiscal year 1994/95, and a surplus of NZ$4900 million (5% of GDP) is expected in 1997/98. This surplus can be attributed to a sharp recovery in direct-tax receipts, significant growth in both company taxation and source deductions, and a nominal decline in financial net expenditure. Sustained economic growth is principally a result of robust export performance, especially in manufacturing, tourism and business investment, and booming household expenditure. Assuming that there is no change in government policy, the New Zealand Institute of Economic Research (NZIER 1994) forecasts that tax receipts will continue to exceed government spending, which will result in a fiscal surplus of over NZ$6 billion in 1998/1999.

These steady growth rates have been accompanied by low inflation, which peaked in June 1995 at 2.2%, and slumped in 1996 at 1%–this is expected to rise through 1997/1998, but to stay under 2%. In fact, the *Reserve Bank Act* (1990) adopted an official target of 1% for inflation, with an upper limit of 2%, so New Zealand economic policy has been dominated by the need to adjust the rate of growth to keep inflation in check. Again, the effect of the 1996 elections in this regard are not yet fully understood, but most observers anticipate that there could be some movement in both inflation and interest terms around that period. Most analysts do not expect a change in the longer term underlying trends, however, as the 1% target rate is contained in the Act, monitored by Treasury, and woven into development plans.

Trading

The volume of exports of goods and services rose by 8.9% in the year ending March 1994, and 7.1% in the year ending March 1995. In 1996 the figure fell to 3.4%, but there are clear signs of a 6–7% sustained export growth rate over the following few years. The major contributors have been dairy products, wool, basic metals, non-commodity manufacturing goods, and tourism. Optimism is high in the agricultural sector, with expected positive outcomes now the GATT Uruguay Round has been settled. Tourism is expected to continue to be an important driver of growth, with annual visitor numbers expected to reach 2 million by the year 2000. The growth in imports of goods and services–12% in the year ending March 1994 and 18.1% in 1995–has countered export growth (NZIER 1994).

Finance

The tight monetary policies adopted by New Zealand have been reflected in a slowly appreciating currency against both the US and Australian currencies (although no such appreciation has occurred to date against the pound sterling or yen), and a general upward trend in interest rates. Monetary conditions tightened over 1995 as inflation increased, and have not slackened even after inflation (and GDP growth) fell in 1966. This balancing act is all part of the ongoing recovery process, so that sustainable levels of growth in competitive sectors can be managed with as little assistance from government as possible, and without allowing the economy to overheat.

Regional differences

Despite the positive economic indicators, business confidence is mixed. The sector with the most optimistic outlook is services, with several surveys in 1995/1996 showing that a majority of the respondents expected business conditions to improve. Furthermore, general business confidence varied on a regional basis, with the northern regions the most confident. This is hardly surprising, as Auckland and Hamilton (in the North Island) are the two fastest growing areas in the country; Auckland is by far the largest city, the most vigorous business centre and the strongest in the growing services sector (employment is expected to come through increased tourism from, *inter alia*, the Country's first casino, and from the preparations for and running of the Americas Cup yacht races). For the country overall, growth is heavily dependent–in a regional sense–on investments. Hence, the west coast (with the Reefton Gold Mine), the Southland (with the Tiwai Point smelter upgrade, and the Rayonier fibreboard plant in Matura) and Gisborne (with the Juken Nissho expansion) are expected to lead the way, and the provinces most heavily dependent on agricultural products, and lacking specific investment projects, are likely to experience much slower growth in employment and exports.

Employment

Employment has been a key economic, social, and political factor for the country for the last 2 decades. The immediate effect of the depression that struck the country after the British realignment to Europe was widespread unemployment. This had a strong impact on the financially strapped social services; these services have been deliberately pruned in recent years, and more public money has been spent on job-creation schemes and retraining exercises.

The reduction of unemployment to the current, more acceptable, levels has been a major achievement (the unemployment rate as at March 1994 was 9%, but this had fallen to 6.3% by 1996 and is expected to reach 5% by 1998). One of the key devices used to achieve economic efficiency in labor markets—required to support New Zealand's economic recovery—was the *Employment Contracts Act* of 1991. This Act effectively curtailed the collective bargaining power of organized labor, and created a more flexible employment environment that was advantageous to business generally. The NZIER (1994) has speculated that the Act has led to stronger cyclical elements to wage movements by ensuring that wage growth is restrained during a period of high unemployment, but facilitated during periods of expansion. As demand for labor increases, relative bargaining power could shift to employees, especially for those with skills.

Income

Rising employment, combined with moderate wage increases, has led to a growth in household incomes. Real household incomes increased by 3.3% annually over the 3 years to 1996, and figures of 4.5% and 5.5% for 1997/98 have been predicted by the National Bank (1995). Large tax cuts announced in 1996/1997 will be mainly responsible for this predicted growth, and the further encouragement of consumer spending is designed to provide an internal stimulus to growth without fueling import-led inflation.

The residential sector

In September 1994, building permits rose 22.6% over the previous year. This is a reflection of the growth in the economy, as well as the increasing pressure of a growing population. The increase in building permits fell sharply in 1996, however, to 10%, in line with the national growth pattern. It is expected that this trend will continue until recovery, to around a steady 5% growth in 1998/1999 (National Bank 1996). Growth in the residential real-estate market has not been evident in all parts of New Zealand, but is manifest chiefly in the main cities, Auckland in particular. The current trend toward inner-city living has seen the conversion of many office blocks into apartments. Demand has waned slightly with the rise in interest rates, and the general overpricing of the apartments, but the trend toward inner-city living is likely to remain, as inner-city living is attractive to investors, young professionals without children and older couples.

The retail sector

As previously mentioned, retailing is fairly buoyant in New Zealand at this time, with consumer spending set to rise further in the near future. The nature of shopping has also changed, both in concert with the economy and with the new internationalism experienced by the country as a whole. Economic pressure has forced retailers into competitive innovation, and often into outright price competition—all of which work to the consumer's advantage. The entry of overseas competitors such as FAL, the Australian retail food giant, has also added to the intense competition in this sector. Table 13.1 shows that supermarket sales are still growing—at the expense of smaller food retailers, whose sales are being further eroded as pharmacists and gas stations encroach on their traditional, convenience-type general-merchandise territory. As in other developed nations, information technology has allowed retailers unprecedented opportunities to understand their customers, and local companies have not been slow to take advantage. Similarly, the style of retailing has developed, to satisfy not only local customers with increasingly sophisticated tastes, but also the many shopping-oriented Asian tourists. Perhaps as a consequence of the increased participation of women in the workforce, retail shopping hours have been extended. Indeed, weekend shopping—not so long ago an impossibility even in the large cities—is now a major leisure activity with the extension of trading hours.

The demographic environment

Population

Population growth in the 1990s has been steady and, at a 1% annual growth rate, relatively faster than that experienced in the 1980s (see Table 13.2). For example, the New Zealand population increased by 1.4% over the year to March 1995, and rose by 1.3% over the following year.

The volatility in this growth is mainly due to migration. The 1991 *Amendment to the Immigration Act* allowed a target of new residents to be set; this is currently set at 25 000 persons per annum. Permanent and long-term arrivals are expected to exceed departures over the next 5 years. By the year 2031, the population is projected to increase to 4.5 million. (This is assuming medium fertility and mortality, and a net migration of 5000.) Although predominantly European, New Zealand is a multicultural society, with the subcultures consisting mainly of Maoris (9.5% of the total population), Pacific Islanders (3.7%), and Asians (Chinese 1.1%, Indians 0.8%). The influx of Asian immigrants over the past 5 years has made this a significant group in the community; between 1986 and 1991, the Chinese population increased by 92% (see Table 13.3).

Table 13.1 Retail sales by store type, 1986–1993 (NZ$ million)*

Store type	*1986*	*1987*	*1988*	*1989*	*1990*	*1991*	*1992*	*1993*
Butcher	488.7	463.7	495.3	479.4	479.9	426.9	363.0	347.7
Supermarket	2 288.6	2 686.0	3 181.9	3 667.4	4 100.9	4 442.6	4 535.4	4 810.0
Other Food	1 809.0	1 907.4	1 996.1	1 949.5	1 985.4	1 978.7	1 880.9	1 771.7
Footwear	278.7	222.0	286.9	270.3	269.5	282.0	267.6	253.8
Clothing and textiles	963.5	1 183.3	1 282.8	1 227.8	1 382.5	1 350.7	1 352.4	1 390.1
Furniture	804.4	936.1	905.1	852.1	859.3	777.4	673.1	702.1
Household appliances	996.7	1 208.1	1 238.3	1 237.1	1 349.7	1 219.5	1 260.3	1 305.9
Hardware	408.3	474.4	506.6	529.6	553.6	596.6	648.6	717.3
Chemist	587.1	672.1	749.7	821.4	820.5	882.4	906.3	957.9
Department and General	1 234.0	1 345.0	1 364.7	1 301.5	1 328.2	1 294.7	1 278.2	1 385.5
Restaurants and Take-aways	1 052.5	1 183.0	1 245.0	1 197.1	1 244.1	1 375.5	1 420.7	1 536.7
Liquor and Accommodation	2 270.9	2 506.0	2 775.0	2 839.4	2 940.9	2 795.9	2 751.7	2 751.0
Other stores	1 463.0	1 746.1	1 805.0	2 000.5	2 028.8	2 217.4	2 330.1	2 440.8
Subtotal	**14 645.0**	**16 607.5**	**17 833.0**	**18 373.0**	**19 343.0**	**19 640.4**	**19 668.3**	**20 371.2**
Automotive–Vehicle sales	6 395.3	6 856.7	7 235.5	6 169.4	6 450.0	5 653.6	5 114.2	5 576.9
–Fuel & Repairs	2 999.9	3 004.7	3 167.4	3 314.4	3 542.5	3 668.1	3 657.5	3 884.8
All stores–total	**24 040.8**	**28 235.9**	**26 468.9**	**27 856.9**	**29 335.8**	**28 962.0**	**28 440.0**	**29 792.9**

Note:
* $1 (US) = NZ$1.44

Source:: New Zealand Department of Statistics (1993), *Consumer Expenditure Statistics*, Wellington.

Table 13.2 Population growth in New Zealand, 1989–2031

Year	*Population*	*Annual growth rate (%)*
1989	3 347 100	0.7
1990	3 373 400	0.7
1991	3 418 300	1.3
1992	3 454 900	1.0
1993	3 494 300	1.1
1994[a]	3 541 600	1.3
2001[b]	3 820 000	
2011	4 120 000	
2021	4 364 000	
2031[c]	4 584 000	

Notes:
[a] Estimate only
[b] Based on medium fertility and mortality rates, with migration of 5000
[c] Rate of change, 1991-2031 is 0.7% pa

Source: New Zealand Department of Statistics (1994), *Key Statistics*, Wellington, November.

Table 13.3 Ethnic composition of the New Zealand population

Census	*Total population*	*Maori*	*Pacific Island*	*Polynesian Chinese*	*Indian*	*Fijian*	*Other*
1936	1 573 812	82 326	988	2 943	1 200	109	1 486 246
1945	1 702 330	98 744	2 159	4 940	1 554	185	1 594 749
1951	1 939 472	115 676	3 624	5 723	2 425	277	1 811 747
1956	2 174 062	137 151	8 103	6 731	3 151	479	2 018 447
1961	2 414 984	167 086	14 340	8 524	4 179	746	2 220 109
1966	2 676 919	201 159	26 271	10 283	6 843	1 323	2 431 040
1971	2 862 631	227 414	40 918	12 470	7 140	1 147	2 573 542
1976	3 129 383	270 035	61 354	14 860	9 247	1 548	2 772 339
1981	3 175 737	279 252	89 697	19 248	11 580	1 908	2 774 052
1986	3 307 084	295 659	99 135	20 259	12 843	2 127	2 877 421
1991	3 373 929	323 493	123 183	37 689	26 979	2 760	2 589 825

Source: New Zealand Department of Statistics (1993), *Demographic Trends*, Wellington.

Age distribution

The population of New Zealand follows a pattern typical to maturing societies, with an increasing number of people in the older age group. This is not, however, true for the NZ Maori and Pacific Island population, whose age distribution is less mature (see fig. 13.1). Currently, 61% of the population is within the productive age range of between 15 and 59 years, which represents an increase of 2% since 1980. The younger age group—those under 15 years—has shrunk from 27.8% of the population in 1980 to 23% in 1994. In the next 20 years, the older age group will move toward retirement age, putting more stress on the social system. Department of Statistics figures indicate that the elderly population (those aged 60+) will double from 502 000 in 1988 to 1 090 000 by 2031. In 1993, the median age of the population was 32 years; this is set to increase to 41 years by the year 2031.

Household size

The growth rate for family households in New Zealand is very slow. Family households grew 6.1% in 1993 compared to 1986, while the rate for non-family households increased by 6.5%, and for sole-person households the increase was 15.9% (see Table 13.4). Although families are still an important unit in New Zealand, the composition of a "typical" family has changed—families are smaller than in the past, there are more families without children, and 1 in 4 families with children is headed by a single parent.

Table 13.4 Household type

Household type	*1989 (%)*	*1991 (%)*	*1993 (%)*
Young one-person household*			8.1
Older couple with no children*	26.0	25.2	17.5
Couple with one child	11.5	11.0	9.9
Couple with two children	14.4	13.3	13.8
Couple with three or more	10.8	9.0	10.7
One parent with children	8.6	9.4	9.6
Family with others	4.4	5.93	5.5
Non-family households	24.0	26.0	24.9

Note:
* In 1993, the category "Couple with no children" was divided into these two categories.

Source: New Zealand Department of Statistics (1993), *New Zealand Population, Labour Force and Household Projections 1991-2031*, Wellington.

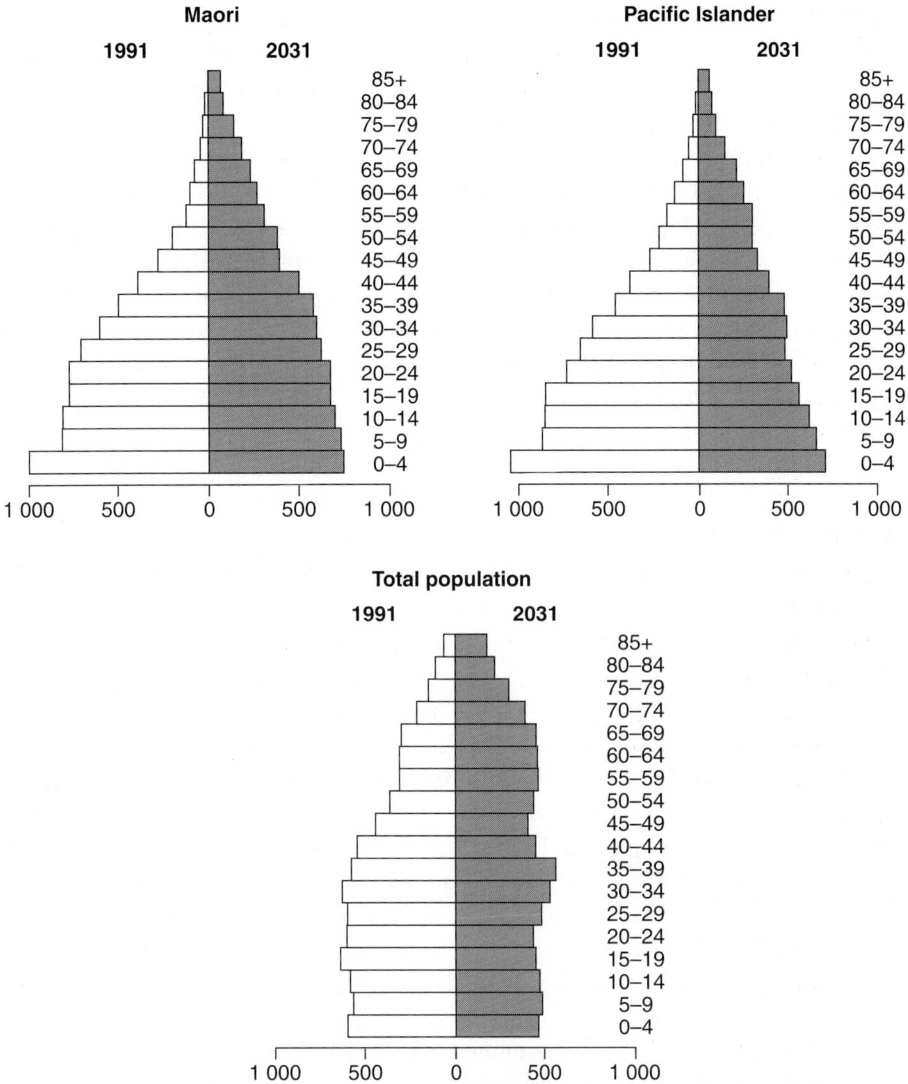

Fig. 13.1 Age distribution: NZ Maori, Pacific Island and total populations, 1991 and 2031 (projected)

Cultural environment

New Zealand has been described in the past as an England of the South, but this is even less true today than it was previously. Although it is dominantly English, the earliest settlers were, of course, the Maori people. There were also Scottish, Dutch, French and Scandinavian settlers; several areas in New Zealand still recognize their non-English roots and have a distinctly non-English flavor.

It is true that the Maori were not considered New Zealanders in the early recorded history of the country, but this has changed very significantly over the last few decades. Toward the turn of the 20th century, at the cessation of the Maori Wars, the Treaty of Waitangi was drawn up between Queen Victoria's New Zealand representative and a consortium of Maori chiefs. The Treaty was designed to safeguard Maori interests from exploitation. As a result of legal action, it has recently been re-recognized, and a series of lawsuits have seen large settlements (mostly in terms of land) made to various Maori tribes. The question of a Maori identity within the national identity is being vigorously pursued at this time by both Maori and non-Maori New Zealanders.

Another potent agent for cultural change has been the economic imperative that New Zealand has increasingly to turn to Asia for new trading partners. Consequently, New Zealand businesspeople travel more frequently than ever before within the region, both inbound and outbound Asian tourism have mushroomed, and there have been significant increases in Asian immigration. This has all led to the development of a less ethnocentric New Zealander, and a more cosmopolitan shopping and living environment, particularly in the larger cities.

Women in New Zealand

There is an increase in women's participation in the workforce overall, and a corresponding deferral of childbearing to a later age. In 1994, for the first time ever, more women than men graduated from New Zealand universities. The percentage of professional women in the workforce has increased in recent years, women now comprising 54% of professionals. Women, therefore, are an important force in the marketplace, both as consumers and as a major influence in family decisions. Moreover, a high percentage of single-parent families are headed by females. It is important that marketers do not neglect to target women in their product advertising, even for product categories not traditionally targeted to women. The increase in the level of education attained by this gender group, and the emergence of active consumer-rights groups, have also brought about an increasing awareness of consumer rights in terms of quality, service, sales, and purchases of goods and services.

Sales of take-away foods and restaurant meals indicate a growing trend in consumption of food outside the home, from $1 052.5 million in 1986 to $1 536.7 million in 1993. This is a result of the increase in the number of double-income families, time pressure, and affordability of food outside the home. The influence of the overseas trend of cafés and breakfast bars is also evident, especially in the major cities of New Zealand.

Education

New Zealand has a strong tradition of accessible education (see fig. 13.2), and follows the British model. One repercussion of changes in the Government's competitive philosophy and policy is that schools have been given more autonomy to manage their own affairs. This has meant, though, that different standards of equipment and teaching have emerged for schools located in suburbs with differing degrees of wealth among their population. Thus the quality of education does depend, to a point, on the financial status of parents.

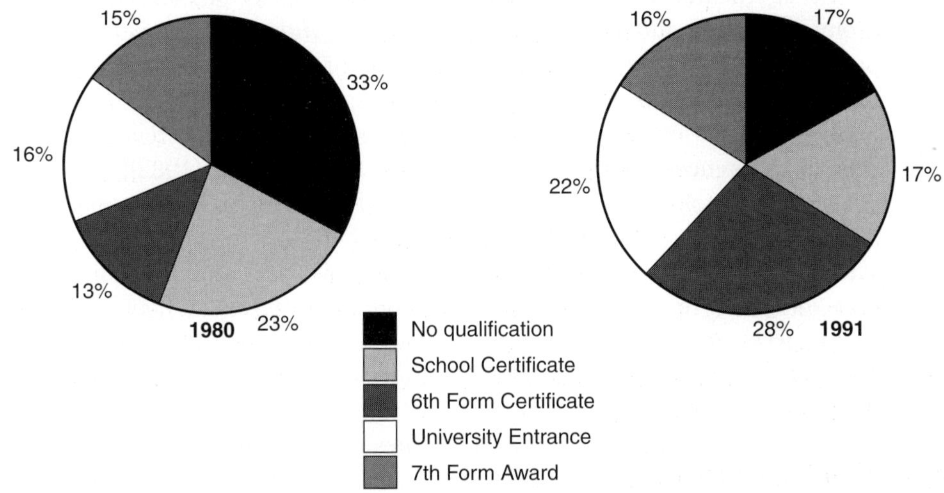

Fig. 13.2 Highest educational attainment of secondary-school leavers

However, teenagers are being encouraged to stay back in school to receive further training because of the government's stated intention not to provide unemployment benefits to persons under 18. This move is in response to the growing need for a more skilled and educated labor force.

Similar changes are being made to the tertiary system. The open-door university policy of the 1960s and 1970s no longer pertains, and there are clear differences in the standard of degree awarded by various universities—often reflected in the stringency, or otherwise, of entry requirements.

Social-class structure

In the 1950s, Keith Sinclair (1959) expressed the sentiment that New Zealand is a relatively classless society. But this has long been forgotten—although New Zealand's society is egalitarian in nature, the society is becoming more stratified. As with other Western cultures, a person's social class is measured in terms of economic success—that is, the amount of wealth and property owned, either inherited or through one's occupation.

Although this is not directly related to any hierarchy of social class, Statistics New Zealand uses the International Standard Classification of Occupations (ISCO) to provide information on the different sectors of New Zealand. The most prominent work on socio-economic status measurement is that of Elley and Irving (1976; 1985), who have produced an index of occupational status using census data based upon the income and education of the people in the various occupations. This categorizes a person into the upper, middle or lower socio-economic class. However, New Zealand is predominantly middle class–Johnston (1983) notes that more than 54% of New Zealanders can be categorized as part of this class.

The significance of social class in consumer behavior has been questioned (Coleman 1983), and interest in this issue has waxed and waned over the past 30 years. In any event, the importance of social class as a marketing tool will continue to increase in New Zealand, given both the current and predicted social and economic environments. Social class is related to attitudinal differences. Martineau (1958), and later Coleman (1983), have proposed that social class reflects psychological differences in consumers, and is therefore better as a predictor of behavior than of income. Lawson and Winzar's (1994) study on social class in New Zealand and Australia shows that there are real and significant attitudinal differences between social classes in New Zealand. In this study, social class was measured using the Elley and Irving scale. The authors found that lower classes were oriented to the shorter term, for example being less career motivated, and less focused on the local community. Table 13.5 presents the attitudinal differences among differing social classes in New Zealand, based on the findings of Lawson and Winzar (1994) that families in the lower social class are more conservative about roles within the family. In the view of this class, father should be "boss," and that the woman's place is at home. This finding is confirmed by Lee (1994), who notes that fathers in the lower social class have more influence in family decisions when their wives do not have paid employment outside the home.

Changes in family structure and decision making

Changes in the New Zealand family structure are similar to those being experienced in other Western societies: families are becoming smaller, with an average of 2 children, and there is an increase in the number of single-parent families and families where both parents work outside the home. These trends have encouraged greater participation by children in the family decision-making process–they have been given more responsibility for the family's grocery shopping. Also, the increasing affluence of the society has meant that children as well as adults have become more discerning in their consumption habits (Boland 1994; Lee 1994).

The marketing environment

Distribution

The geography of the country makes trade awkward: although it is impossible to be more than 75 km from the sea anywhere in New Zealand, its 5 main

Table 13.5 New Zealand consumers—attitudinal differences among social classes

1. Upper classes
—feel less alienated in society than middle and lower classes
—are more likely to regard themselves as leaders
—are less conservative
—feel less attracted to simplicity and more drawn to sophistication
—attach higher importance to education
—attach less importance to children's obedience

2. Middle classes
—are less concerned with appearance and fashion than upper and lower classes

3. Lower classes
—are less career minded
—are more likely than middle and upper classes to be "do-it-yourselfers"
—are more interested in local-community events than national or international events
—exhibit more traditional attitudes toward roles within the family

Source: Rob Lawson & Hume Winzar (1994), "Social Class and Consumer Behaviour in Australia and New Zealand", paper presented at the New Zealand Marketing Educators Conference, Hamilton, New Zealand, November.

centers are strung across two large islands, from Auckland in the north to Dunedin some 1358 road kilometers to the south. More than half of the population lives in the relatively industrialized northern half of the North Island. Other than the capital (Wellington) at the southern extremity of the North Island, and the South Island cities of Christchurch and Dunedin, the rest of the country is fundamentally rural, hence distributional possibilities are constrained.

A recurring theme running through this chapter has been the increasing competitiveness in all facets of New Zealand business life, and the transport sector is no exception. Rail services for freight are excellent, along the north–south axis at least, and the roads and road services are well developed. Rail and road compete directly on most major routes, and this keeps service and price strategies to the fore. Similarly, air services have moved away from a monopoly situation, where the government-backed national carrier provided the only regular internal freight and passenger services, to a competitive situation, where two major international carriers compete in an open-market situation.

The major cost problem associated with transportation comes back to the population density, and the small size of the country. Hence, at this time, and under some conditions, it is cheaper to air-freight goods from Auckland to Sydney (Australia) than from Auckland to Dunedin. The Cook Strait also acts as an impediment to the flow of vehicles and trains between the North and South Islands; although ferries do ply the route regularly, waiting is inevitable at peak demand periods, and there has been a long history of industrial action plaguing the ferry services. However, with the introduction of two new fast ferries, as well as further competition, this situation may improve.

Pricing

At various points above we have referred to price-related factors—New Zealand's generally low inflation rate, its relatively low and stable labor rates, and the generally competitive environment. All of these have acted to keep prices in check.

However, the low (but slowly appreciating) value of the New Zealand dollar is countering this pressure on prices. Although the low "kiwi" (dollar) does assist exporters, and consequently makes a major contribution to the overall economic welfare of the country, it also makes the cost of imported goods high. This becomes particularly significant when imports have to be freighted over great distances.

Consumer watchdog organizations are active, and the government has enacted strong legislation—*The Consumer Guarantees Act, 1994*—which can affect manufacturers' approach to pricing. For instance, all consumers are guaranteed financial redress if they are not satisfied with their purchases, and traders are not permitted to trade-off this legislated right within their pricing strategies.

The government levies a 12.5% goods and services tax on all goods and services, and this tax must be included in the advertised price of the item. The tax was introduced in an effort to lower income tax, introduce more equity into the system, and make taxation changes more readily visible to the constituency.

Communications

Communication technology is well advanced in New Zealand. There are 3 competing telephone services, a very competitive national and local radio network, a thriving print-media industry, and many television services—these include 2 government and 1 private television station, as well as several regional and special-interest and 5 satellite channels. The technological advances in telecommunications have had their most visible impact in the areas of direct mail and telemarketing. Direct mail comprises a huge 6.7% of total media advertising expenditures, and is set to grow; however, telemarketing is picked by some marketing pundits as the medium of the future (Teutenberg 1994).

As it is in most developed countries, the advertising industry is thriving in New Zealand. Table 13.6 shows the expenditure rates on the various media for 1993, which total $1 1670 million. Fifty-two per cent of this sum was placed through advertising agencies, of which there were 70 operating in March 1993. These agencies employ over 900 people directly, and many

Table 13.6 Media advertising, 1993

Media	*Expenditure (NZ$ million)*	*Share (%)*
Newspapers	361	29.9
Television	423	35.0
Radio	139	11.5
Magazines	77	6.4
Direct mail	81	6.7
Telemarketing	9	0.7
Outdoor	6	0.5
Cinemas	3	0.2
Community newspapers	110	9.1

Source: New Zealand Department of Statistics (1993), *New Zealand Year Book*, Wellington.

more in related activities. Almost two-thirds of the agencies are local, although all of the large multinationals are well represented among the larger companies in the industry. Expenditure by industry, reported in Table 13.7, reflects both international and local patterns–respectively, high expenditures by retailers, and high expenditures by the agricultural and leisure/travel/entertainment sectors.

Table 13.7 Advertising expenditure by selected industries

Industry group	*Expenditure (NZ$ million)*
Agricultural/industrial/office	78
Automotive	54
Beverages	54
Clothing	19
Foodstuffs	142
Household	100
Investment/finance/banking	74
Leisure/travel/entertainment	148
Miscellaneous	68
Pharmaceuticals	30
Retail	195
Toiletries/cosmetics	52

Source: New Zealand Department of Statistics (1993), *New Zealand Year Book*, Wellington.

Table 13.8 Magazine circulation, consumer titles

Publication	*Circulation*	*Published*
Direction	533 341	Bi-monthly
TV Guide	232 686	Weekly
Woman's Day NZ	204 166	Weekly
Reader's Digest	154 065	Monthly
NZ Women's Weekly	150 633	Weekly
Australian Women's Weekly	122 632	Monthly
Listener, TV & Radio Times	115 470	Weekly
Grapevine	114 451	Monthly
New Idea NZ	103 549	Weekly
Little Treasures	63 298	Bi-monthly
Next	43 186	Monthly
Superannuant's Lifestyle	42 121	Quarterly
Time	41 370	Weekly
North & South	39 904	Monthly
More	39 761	Monthly
Metro	29 432	Monthly
Fashion Quarterly	28 813	Quarterly
NZ Home and Building	27 489	Bi-monthly
Your Home	24 190	Quarterly
RTR Countdown	15 077	Monthly

Source: New Zealand Department of Statistics (1993), *New Zealand Year Book*, Wellington.

It is worthy of note that New Zealanders read a great deal—28 daily newspapers are published in the country, although 2 large publishing groups account for 90% of their ownership. In addition, there are over 2300 magazines available, of which 58 are published locally (Table 13.8). For a nation with a population of a little over 3 million, these are interesting figures. They show that:

- New Zealanders are aware of their isolation, and seek to follow the news and trends of the rest of the world
- markets are highly segmented, and marketers quite sophisticated
- although there are strong efforts to keep markets competitive, concentrations of marketing power are not unusual because of the small overall size of the market

Product

The *Consumer Guarantees Act* mentioned above also affects product issues, in that all providers of goods and services must meet basic quality standards—although it has yet to be decided by the courts exactly what the concept "what reasonable people might reasonably expect to receive for the amount they pay" actually means (Mackay 1994). Whatever else the Act achieves, it has placed a spotlight on consumer rights with respect to product quality standards; these cannot be ignored by marketers.

Also discussed above is the high level of mass-communication integration enjoyed by the country. This factor contributes to the high rate of adoption of new technologies in New Zealand. There is also a high level of general education and a large middle class; these factors all contribute to a positive attitude to change, and a willingness to try new products. The latter trait has been noted by both the local media (Young 1993) and some multinationals, who have chosen to test their new products in New Zealand before rolling them out to the rest of the world.

Consumer lifestyles

This topic has already been introduced in the discussion above about social class in New Zealand. However, specific research, carried out over a number of years, is also of interest, because of the trends that can be extrapolated from it. New Zealand researchers are challenged by the small market size—there is an important trade-off between more detailed (but smaller) segments, and larger (but more generalized) groups. A 1989 Lifestyle Survey sponsored by Readers Digest and conducted by University of Otago academics (Feigler et. al 1989) identified 6 clusters—see Table 13.9. A follow-up study, sponsored once again by Readers Digest, but this time carried out by a professional research company (AGB McNair 1993), chose to consider only 3 segments, on the grounds that the previously identified 6 lacked viability in terms of buying power (see Table 13.10).

Table 13.11 provides the segment demographics for the more detailed, earlier study. The breakdown of demographic groups into lifestyles is interesting, but hardly surprising. That most of those households earning over $60 000 annually contain "Success driven" people and "Educated greens" follows intuition. In addition, there is, of course, much variation in lifestyle within each demographic category. However, the business problem is minimized in that the country has a well-integrated communication system and is small, and it is therefore quite feasible to reach either a demographic or a psychographic segment with relative ease.

There is evidence in Table 13.11 (p. 544) of a social phenomenon readily observed in the everyday life of the country: the growing divide between rich and poor. Although this division still falls far short of that evident in the USA and many of the neighboring South-East Asian countries, it is still noticeable

Table 13.9 New Zealand lifestyle segments

Lifestyle segment	*% of population*	*Brief description*
Success-driven extroverts	8.9	Career and social players Living it up, socializing Excitement and pleasure focus Free enterprise . . . self (me) —Impressing people —Money and modernity
"Educated Greens"	12.4	"Societal reformers" Supporting topical causes —Intellectual and educational focus Modern naturalists Culture, fashion, sophistication Secure, well-off future
"Active family people"	21.9	"Family-life enthusiasm" Active, warm togetherness Child-development focus Protective of family health, environment and heritage Family activities, outings
"Traditional-values family people"	20.3	"Orderly family life" Discipline and obedience Parental-role focus Traditional institutions Spiritual values, trust Local-community activities
"Envious strivers"	21.1	"Give me a break" Life's a struggle Ambition-achievement focus Cautious and conformist Wanting life's "essentials" Escapist activities
"Friendly quiet-lifers"	15.4	Enjoyment of neighborly chats Familiar, hassle-free life Friendly, close-to-home focus Elderly and nostalgic Companionship Continued good health

Source: Bruce Feigler, Rob Lawson, G. Mueller-Heumann & Amy Rummel (1989), "New Zealand into the 1990s: A comprehensive Survey of New Zealanders' Opinions and Lifestyles", University of Otago and Marketing and Diagnostics Department, Auckland.

because of the extreme egalitarianism that was once experienced in New Zealand under so many years of welfare economics. The study by AGB McNair (1993), reported in Table 13.10 above, shows the divide very clearly. For many consumer durables, purchasing power clearly lies with the 35% of the population ("Powerful families") that is heavily overrepresented by the professions, the top income earners and those with a higher education level. The same trend can be seen, to a lesser degree, in Table 13.11, in which the segment demographics for the earlier study (Feigler et al. 1989) are presented. Further illustration is provided in tables 13.12 and 13.13 (drawn from the 1993 study), where the proportion of new products purchased by the "Powerful families" segment is compared to the proportion purchased by the general population.

Table 13.10 Three lifestyle clusters in New Zealand

Cluster name	*% of population*	*Brief description*
"The strugglers"	25	Resist the rate of change Shop for bargains Find it hard to make ends meet Believe they have a "raw deal" from life Lower income, high unemployment Many between 15 and 44 years old Heavy television viewers Low social participation rate
"Comfortable conservatives"	40	Conservative attitude Middle to low household income Believe the Law should be tougher on law-breakers Believe racial problems in NZ are getting worse Anxious about future of the country 39% over 55 yrs of age 49% live in 1–2-person households 73% have no children living at home
"Powerful families"	35	Optimistic Positive attitude to change Lead active lives Early adopters Family-oriented Success-driven In business and the professions Higher incomes 69% live in households with 3 or more people

Source: AGB McNair (1993), *The Changing Fabric Of Society*, Reader's Digest, Auckland.

Table 13.11 Segment demographics, 1989 study

	"Quiet lifer"	*"Envious striver"*	*"Active family"*	*"Trad. family"*	*"Success driven"*	*"Educated Greens"*	*Total*
% of population	15	20	23	21	9	12	100
Sex							
Male	55	43	34	46	66	40	45
Female	45	57	66	54	34	60	55
Age							
under 25	8	26	11	23	28	15	18
25–34	10	22	20	25	28	28	21
35–54	26	25	42	34	32	45	34
55+	56	27	27	18	12	12	27
Household income							
Under $30 000	56	41	40	44	25	26	41
$30 000–$60 000	36	37	39	40	32	42	38
Over $60 000	8	22	21	16	43	32	21
Education							
School exams	44	38	30	29	13	11	30
SC/UE/Trade	41	40	41	43	45	37	40
Prof./Uni.	15	22	29	28	42	52	30
Occupation							
Prof./Managerial	28	28	41	37	50	51	38
Clerical/Sales	29	32	22	25	25	27	27
Trades/Manual	31	25	29	25	15	14	24
Children at home	21	41	49	50	32	50	41

Source: Bruce Feigler, Rob Lawson, G. Mueller-Heumann & Amy Rummel (1989), "New Zealand into the 1990s: A comprehensive Survey of New Zealanders' Opinions and Lifestyles", University of Otago and Marketing and Diagnostics Department, Auckland.

Discussion

New Zealand business has to operate in a dynamic social, demographic, technological, and economic environment, and as a result any new entry into the marketplace will find at least basic market research a necessity. In reality it is somewhat artificial to discuss these environments separately, as they interact so closely. The economic drive and the changing immigration patterns that have forced New Zealanders to become world citizens have resulted in a less ethnocentric attitude in all walks of life. Again, the advances in communications technology, which have created such a strong marketing tool for advertisers, researchers and marketers, also influence the shopping habits of consumers.

Table 13.12 Purchasing pattern of "Powerful families"

Product	*% share of purchasing population represented by "Powerful families"*
Washing machines	41
Ground/real coffee	51
Microwave ovens	44
Hot milk-based drinks	42
Camcorders	46
Canned & dry catfood	41
VCRs	43
Icecream novelties/blocks	41
Color TV sets	42
Potato/corn chips	42

Source: AGB McNair (1993), *The Changing Fabric Of Society*, Reader's Digest, Auckland.

Table 13.13 Shopping habits of "Powerful families"

Type of store	*% share of total custom represented by "Powerful families"*
Women's wear	50
Jewellery	53
Travel agencies	48
Children's wear	51
Footwear	48
Records	53
Men's wear	48
Photographic equipment	53
Video libraries	54
Sports goods	51
Health food	52
Furniture	50
Florists	56

Source: AGB McNair (1993), *The Changing Fabric Of Society*, Reader's Digest, Auckland.

What are the important trends that will change the face of consumer behavior in New Zealand over the next few decades? Technology changes will clearly have an impact—on advertisers, retailers, researchers, and consumers. This is a worldwide phenomenon, however, and by no means unique to New Zealand. The drives toward privatization and internationalization are also shared by other countries, although it is hard to find an example of another country that has moved from the extremes of protectionism and isolationism to open markets and globalization quite so quickly and dramatically.

The signs are positive. New Zealand does seem to be on a sustainable economic growth curve, one that is founded in a competitive attitude and a willingness to seek business wherever it comes from, rather than a desire simply to tag along as a protected little speck of pink on England's trade map.

The demographic trends noted are also of interest and importance, but hardly unique. That the population is ageing, that the structure of family groups is changing, even that the (northward) urban drift does not seem to be slowing much, are all significant trends, but are also prevalent in other developed nations in some form or another.

In contrast, however, it does seem probable that the social trends identified in this chapter are unique to New Zealand. The struggle to find a clear national identity has been going on for many years. The peculiar local aspects of this problem lie with the indigenous Maori people, the immigrant Asians, and a new awareness by the population at large that the country really is more part of the Asia-Pacific region than of any other grouping of nations.

Predictions are available, but are not actually a great deal of help. Buchanan-Brown (1993) talks of "the browning of New Zealand," seeming to suggest that the country may go through some melting-pot cultural transformation. This cry, however, echoes the words of Sir Keith Holyoak, Prime Minister in the 1950s, which were succeeded by louder and louder cries from the Maori people for a separation of the Maori from the dominant European culture in order to retain and develop their fast-disappearing cultural identity. The Chinese, too, are hardly noted for a tendency to compromise with their cultural values and habits, so the views of the melting-pot theorists lack conviction.

Whatever the outcome, in the coming years businesspeople interested in the New Zealand market will not only (as always) have to complete their segmentation studies before launching their products or services, but will also have to pay attention to ensure that the super-sensitive cultural dimension is not neglected.

Concern for the environment is another issue that echoes some overseas trends, but has a unique local flavor as well. The issue of Maori claims to fishing rights and land adds another dimension to the usual concerns, and the increasing number of tourists tramping through the country is yet another. The Green lobby is strong. The demographic profile of the

"Educated greens" in Table 13.11 above shows clearly that the Greens are indeed educated, and that they have considerable political leverage in terms of both their ability to understand and work the system and their possession of enough money to back their concerns with action. What is not shown in the table is the fundamental concern with the environment that is part of the Maoris' cultural-value system—the group of citizens concerned with what happens to New Zealand's waterways and forests is far larger than the numbers reveal.

Probably the only trend that can be predicted with any real degree of confidence is that the rate of change enjoyed (or suffered, perhaps) by New Zealanders will continue to increase. This is a small, rapidly maturing nation blessed with a well-educated, positive-thinking, competitive population and a fundamentally sound economy. The country is poised to make a significant contribution to the Asia-Pacific region, to which it so clearly belongs.

References

AGB McNair (1993), *The Changing Fabric Of Society*, Reader's Digest, Auckland.

Boland, Mary J. (1994), "Teens in the Marketplace", *New Zealand Herald*, August 6, Section 3, p. 3.

Buchanan-Brown (1993), in *N.Z. Business*, October, p. 16.

Business and Economic Research Limited (1994), *Berl Monthly Monitor*, Wellington, November.

Coleman, Richard P. (1983), "The Continuing Significance of Social Class to Marketing", *Journal of Consumer Research*, vol. 10, December, pp. 265–79.

Craig, Duncan (1994), "Banks Warn Clients to Dump Apartments", *National Business Review*, 2 December.

Elley, W.B. & Irving, J.C. (1976), "Revised Socio-economic Index for New Zealand", *New Zealand Journal of Educational Studies*, vol. 11, no. 2, pp. 25–30.

— (1985), "The Elley-Irving Socio-economic Index 1981 census revision", *New Zealand Journal of Educational Studies*, vol. 20, no. 2, pp. 115–28.

Feigler, Bruce, Lawson, Rob, Mueller-Heumann, G. & Rummel, Amy (1989), "New Zealand into the 1990s: A comprehensive Survey of New Zealanders' Opinions and Lifestyles", University of Otago and Marketing and Diagnostics Department, Auckland.

Johnston, Raylee (1983), *A Revision of Socio-economic Indices for New Zealand*, New Zealand Council for Educational Research, Wellington.

Lawson, Rob & Winzar, Hume (1994), "Social Class and Consumer Behaviour in Australia and New Zealand", paper presented at the New Zealand Marketing Educators Conference, Hamilton, New Zealand, November.

Lee, Christina K.C. (1994), "Influence of Children in Family Purchase Decisions: The Development and Use of an Observational Scale as a Method of Measuring Influence", unpublished PhD thesis, Department of Marketing and International Business, University of Auckland, New Zealand.

Martineau, Pierre (1958), "Social Class and Spending Behavior", *Journal of Marketing*, vol. 23, pp. 121–41.

National Bank of New Zealand (1994), *National Business Outlook*, Wellington, November.

— (1995), *National Business Outlook*, Wellington, November.

— (1996), *National Business Outlook*, Wellington, November.

New Zealand Department of Statistics (1991), *Consumer Expenditure Statistics*, Wellington.

— (1993a), *Consumer Expenditure Statistics*, Wellington.

— (1993b), *Demographic Trends*, Wellington.

— (1993c), *New Zealand Population, Labour Force and Household Projections 1991-2031*, Wellington.

— (1993d), *New Zealand Year Book*, Wellington.

— (1994), *Key Statistics*, Wellington, November.

New Zealand Institute of Economic Research (1994), September.

Sinclair, Keith (1959), *A History of New Zealand*, Penguin Books, Harmondsworth, New Zealand.

Teutenburg, Penny (1994), "Fast forward—focus on the future", *Marketing* (Market Research Conference Report), October, pp. 37–42.

Young, Christine (1993), "The new megatrends, what's in store for business", *New Zealand Business*, October, pp. 12–20.

CHAPTER 14

Papua New Guinea

An overview of the marketing environment

GABRIEL O. OGUNMOKUN

Abstract

Papua New Guinea is a developing nation with a small population spread over a large area. It has relatively unexploited natural resources and a stable government structure, although it is not without political problems. Marketing knowledge and infrastructure are both in the embryonic stages. The nation has considerable potential, and there exist many opportunities for international marketing corporations.

Introduction

In Papua New Guinea (PNG), the practice of professional marketing is at the initial stages only (see Farbood 1995; Thomas 1996). As with many third-world countries, PNG is generally a seller's market, with only a limited range of manufactured goods available for consumption, and minimal competition between brands. Also, as Thomas (1996, p. 78) claims, PNG is occasionally a dumping ground for failed products from elsewhere.

Before the marketing activities in PNG are discussed in this chapter, a brief history of the country will be presented. Other areas will also be discussed: population, languages, education, geographical environment, climatic conditions, political/legal systems, the economy, investment climate, types of industries, living standards, transportation, communication facilities, religion, and social activities.

Historical background

Papua New Guinea is an island nation, located just north of Australia in the south-west Pacific Ocean. The country is composed of the eastern half of the island of New Guinea, and a chain of tropical islands, including the Bismarck Archipelago and Bougainville. Port Moresby is the capital, and the largest city. Mainland cities include Lae, Madang, and Wewak (Compton 1993). With a land area of approximately 465 000 square kilometers (179 490 square miles), PNG is one of the largest countries in the South Pacific (Price Waterhouse 1990).

According to Ntumy (1993), humans have lived in PNG since about 25 000 BC (see Table 14.1, which supplies a dateline). The earliest migrations, from South-East Asia, brought to the country people similar to those who settled in Australia. A later migration, perhaps 8 000 to 10 000 years ago, brought a people who subsequently spread out across the South Pacific. This second migration, according to Ntumy (1993), was also responsible for the introduction of agricultural techniques still widely used in the country, including the domestication of the pig, and the cultivation of taro and other root crops.

In 1949, the Territory of Papua and New Guinea came into being under one administration, and Australia announced its intention to lead the Territory forward to self-government and independence. The handover of most Australian-held powers took place at the start of self-government on December 1 1973. On September 16 1975, PNG became an independent state (Price Waterhouse 1990).

Population, languages and education

Papua New Guinea's population is about 3.5 million; of this figure, approximately 30 000 are expatriates. The population is made up of many distinct

Table 14.1 A dateline for Papua New Guinea

Date/period	*Events*
25 000 BC	Earliest evidence of settlement in New Guinea region.
8000 BC	Rising sea level separates New Guinea from Australia, eventually differentiating their cultures.
6000 BC	New wave of Austronesian migration from South-East Asia; first evidence of domestication of pigs.
1512	First European sighting of New Guinea, by Portuguese explorer Antonio d'Abreu.
1873	London Missionary Society starts first European settlement in Papua New Guinea, at Port Moresby.
1884	Britain declares a protectorate over south-eastern New Guinea. Germany annexes north-eastern New Guinea and grants a charter to the New Guinea Company to administer the colony.
1888	Britain formally annexes south-eastern New Guinea, naming the colony British New Guinea.
1899	German government takes over the New Guinea Company's administrative role in north-eastern New Guinea.
1901	Britain transfers British New Guinea to the new Commonwealth of Australia.
1905	Australia formally accepts control of British New Guinea and renames it Papua.
1914	Australian army takes control of German New Guinea. Military administration lasts until May 1921.
1919	New Guinea becomes a mandate of the League of Nations, administered by Australia. Its administration and laws remain separate from those of Papua.
1921	Civil administration by Australia begins under mandate.
1942	ANGAV, the Australian Army, administers both territories during the Second World War.
1945	Australia establishes a single civilian administration of the two territories.
1973	Papua New Guinea gains self-governing status.
1975	Papua New Guinea becomes an independent nation.

Source: Michael A. Ntumy (1993), *South Pacific Islands Legal Systems,* University of Hawaii Press, Honolulu.

ethnic and cultural groups (Ntumy 1993). Geographical extremes have kept the groups separate, and this has resulted in more than 700 languages being spoken in the country. Although English is the official language of government and commerce, Melanesian Pidgin and Motu are used by half of the populace. Education is free for the primary and secondary levels (Compton 1993).

There are two universities in Papua New Guinea—the University of Papua New Guinea at Port Moresby, and the University of Technology at Lae. Education is not compulsory, and a large number of school-leavers do not complete their primary education.

Geographical environment and climatic conditions

The mainland (the eastern half of the island of New Guinea) and the larger islands are mountainous and rugged. The highest mountain range rises to more than 4700 meters. Interspersed in the complex of ranges on the mainland are large upland valleys. The mountains are the sources of fast-flowing rivers, which descend to the coastal plains to form some of the largest river systems in the world. The largest in PNG, the Sepik and the Fly rivers, are navigable for upward of 800 kilometers, and their estuaries are marked by extended coastal swamps (Price Waterhouse 1990). A line of active volcanoes stretches along the north coast of the mainland, and through the island of New Britain. The coastline is ringed by coral reefs. The vegetation changes from swamps and savanna grasslands on the coast, through tropical rainforest, to moss, alpine forest, and grasslands in the highlands. The dominant vegetation is dense tropical rainforest (Price Waterhouse 1990). The climate is tropical and monsoonal, with only two seasons, the wet and the dry; these are regulated by the north-west and south-east airstreams respectively. Temperatures vary significantly between the coast (20–35°C) and the highlands (10–30°C). Rainfall varies from 102 centimeters per annum in the Port Moresby area to over 510 centimeters per annum in some localities (Price Waterhouse 1990).

Political environment and system

According to Price Waterhouse (1990), with independence PNG adopted a Constitution that established a parliamentary democracy based on the Westminster model, but excluding an upper chamber. The National Parliament comprises 109 members, elected by universal suffrage. The two other tiers of the government are local government councils and provincial governments. Local government councils have varying degrees of responsibility for the provision of health services, local infrastructure development and other related services, such as schools, welfare work and recreation facilities.

Revenue sources available to councils are limited, and consist mainly of head taxes, land taxes, court fines, license fees, and government grants. Each province has an elected provincial government operating under a constitution similar to that of the national government. The provincial governments have responsibility for functions delegated by the national government, which include the development of natural resources, including agriculture, fishing and forestry, education, and industry (Price Waterhouse 1990).

Legal system

The legal system in PNG is the common-law system, based on the English and Australian codes (Price Waterhouse 1990). Most civil matters can be dealt with through the district courts or, ultimately, the national court. The final appeal for any civil or criminal matter is to the Supreme Court of Appeal in Port Moresby. To supplement this, village courts and the local village administrator settle many local matters.

Company law also follows the English and Australian systems. The *Companies Act* effective at present is an adaptation of the 1948 English act (Price Waterhouse 1990; see also Ntumy 1993).

Investment climate and the economy

Subsistence agriculture remains the principal economic activity for most Papua New Guineans, despite the increase in the numbers entering the cash economy. During the 1970s, there was rapid growth in the cash economy, largely in response to the development of primary export industries and an expanding public service. During the 1980s, growth continued, but at a more steady pace, reflecting increased competition and some lower commodity prices (Price Waterhouse 1990).

Mineral and energy resources

Copper is a major contributor to the country's economy, particularly in the areas of domestic revenue and foreign-exchange earnings (Price Waterhouse 1990). The largest mine is currently at Panguna on Bougainville Island. Due to the enclave nature of the project, the effect on employment, service industries and infrastructure has been relatively small.

Another large mineral project is the Ok Tedi copper and gold mine in the Western Province. This, together with recent discoveries of gold and oil in the highlands and on some islands, has boosted the potential of these areas for future development and further foreign investment (Price Waterhouse 1990).

Population issues

Over 85% of Papua New Guineans live in rural areas in clan or village communities. Population densities vary considerably, from 0.6 people per square kilometer in the Western District to more than 37 per square kilometer on the highlands of the Gazelle Peninsula on the island of New Britain. The highlands on the mainland are the most populous area, containing approximately 40% of the population. However, in recent years there has been a marked population drift to the urban areas (Price Waterhouse 1990).

According to Price Waterhouse (1990), Port Moresby has a population of approximately 158 000. The population of Lae, the second major city, is estimated at 83 000. Other main centers include Rabaul (15 000), Madang (25 000), Wewak (23 000), Goroka (22 000), Mount Hagen (20 000), and the Arawa-Kieta-Panguna urban area (16 000).

Agriculture, industries and exports

Agriculture is the largest segment of the economy, and consists mostly of the subsistence farming of sweet potatoes, taro, yams, and bananas (Compton 1993). About 75% of the people live in rural areas, where subsistence farming is their main occupation (Ntumy 1993). Exports include coffee, copra, palm oil, cocoa beans, rubber, timber, tuna, copper, gold, and silver. Manufacturing is limited to the small-scale production of foods and beverages, textiles, chemicals, and metal products (Compton 1993).

High-technology, service and manufacturing industries

High-technology industries do not form part of the economy of Papua New Guinea, and there is no basis established for such innovation and development (Price Waterhouse 1990). Service industries have developed in all the major centres. The main business services of computing, consulting and financial services are generally provided by subsidiary companies or branches of larger overseas organizations.

Wholesale distribution and retail trading are dominated by two large companies. Government pressure to have such activities restricted to nationally owned companies is increasing.

The manufacturing and construction industries continue to develop, although at a slow pace. However, they remain of secondary importance to mining and agriculture as sources of income generation. Many basic raw materials for manufacturing and construction still have to be imported (Price Waterhouse 1990).

Living standards

Most native Papua New Guineans do not have a very high standard of living. However, according to Price Waterhouse (1990), most expatriates working in Papua New Guinea enjoy a high standard of living, with housing, car and cost of utilities provided as part of their remuneration package. Most housing for expatriates is spacious, well ventilated and with adequate security, and many expatriates' houses are on large properties, with gardens and pools. In Port Moresby, there is a growing movement toward accommodation in self-contained apartment blocks, most of which have swimming pools, tennis courts, barbecue areas, and 24-hour security.

Transport and communications

Papua New Guinea has relatively good infrastructure, facilities and services, with the exception of its road network, which is in the early stages of development. Because of the mountainous nature of the mainland and the number of island provinces, almost all travel from Port Moresby is by air and sea. Harbor facilities are generally adequate for present traffic, and trunk and local air services are well developed. Small privately owned buses operate in all provincial centres. The telecommunications network is good, with most businesses and government organizations having facsimile and telex facilities. Electricity serves all major centers and is expanding to rural areas, and water supply is relatively good in most towns. The greatest needs, according to Price Waterhouse (1990), appear to be for road development, housing, and health and educational facilities.

Religion and social activities

According to Price Waterhouse (1990), Christianity is the dominant religion, and has been spread throughout the country by an influx of missionaries since the early days of exploration. Religious customs have little direct influence on business activities, except that the popular Seventh Day Adventist church observes Saturday as a holy day, and discourages the practice of working on this day. There are sufficient social and recreational facilities (e.g. movie houses, theatres) to cater for everyone's needs, especially in Port Moresby and Lae (Price Waterhouse 1990). In most of the major cities, the main social activity centers around sporting clubs, although private entertaining among expatriates is an active part of the social life in these cities. In the more remote areas, the lack of facilities is compensated for by opportunities to explore the bush and countryside. Some coastal areas offer very good opportunities for fishing and diving (Price Waterhouse 1990).

The macromarketing mix

Marketing research

According to a recent study by Farbood (1995), few companies get seriously involved in researching the true requirements of the market. Instead, most of the companies in PNG use the "selling approach" to marketing, rather than the "marketing concept." The latter approach calls for companies to look at the real needs of customers, and the satisfaction of such needs through the right products–which should be priced reasonably, as well as distributed and promoted efficiently and effectively. Problems (see Farbood 1995) that currently hinder effective marketing research in PNG include the following:

- a lack of very good marketing research facilities
- the unavailability of helpful data
- cultural and illiteracy barriers

An important example of the cultural barrier is the tendency of many Melanesian respondents to give the researcher what he or she thinks the researcher wants to hear, rather than the correct answer (Farbood 1995). Such a tendency reduces the reliability of the information gathered in surveys.

Promotion and pricing

Advertising blunders can occur because of a failure to understand fully the cultural and social norms of the PNG people. This can take many forms, ranging from a rejection of existing customs to an unwitting insensitivity to the environment. Advertisements that somehow fail to reflect the local lifestyle may wind up as wasted effort. For example, according to Farbood (1995), a promotional decision on the use of wood for billboard advertisements may be the wrong decision in terms of security: such billboards may sometimes end up as firewood.

Papua New Guineans are group-oriented people. Sponsorship events that bring people together, and promotion activities conducted during such events, are techniques that work well.

Most of the problems in the area of advertising and promotion relate to the fact that, in spite of the recent expansion of the EM TV network, marketing-related concepts and tools are heavily dependent on foreign agencies and consultants, or the parent companies of the Papua New Guinean subsidiaries. Often, the marketing efforts of such foreign agencies or parent companies do not take into consideration the key Papua New Guinean social and economic facts (Farbood 1995).

However, there have been some recent improvements, mainly in terms of the availability of the television media in many of the new provincial capitals (Farbood 1995). But the problems of advertising and promotion are not restricted merely to the availability of the media—as mentioned earlier, serious problems still exist in the development of the advertising art and message that matches Papua New Guinean cultural and other preferences.

The relatively efficient postal and telecommunications systems, and their recent improvement, allow a fair degree of promotion, mainly in the urban regions. At village level, however, such facilities are inadequate. According to Thomas (1996), innovative marketing systems adapted to the sociocultural environment of PNG, such as Wokabaut Marketing, seem to be the basis for business success today and possibly a foundation for future developments in PNG.

But what *is* Wokabaut Marketing? According to Thomas (1996), the term "wokabaut" is Pidgin for "walkabout," the aboriginal practice of periodic nomadic wandering. Wokabaut Marketing is the brainchild of the managing director of an advertising agency based in Port Moresby. This method of promotion combines sales-promotion techniques with cultural entertainments, produced by the group known as Raun Raun (Pidgin for "itinerant"), to create a new advertising medium for the predominantly rural population which is largely unreachable by the conventional mass media, whether broadcast or print.

The Wokabaut Marketing Agency currently has 2 troupes, which tour most of the Highlands and part of the northern coast of New Guinea Island; they cover 6 provinces, which account for about 57% of the country's population. Each province is visited for a total of 4 to 5 weeks during the 12 separate tours undertaken annually by the troupes. About 15 locations are visited on each troupe's tour, with some repetition of location over the course of the year to reinforce learning. The troupes usually perform in town centres, high schools, urban squatter settlements, villages and markets. They also perform at major tribal shows in various towns, drawing thousands of visitors from the neighboring regions. The total audience in the first year of operation was estimated at 252 000, making the Wokabaut troupe a quasi-mass media (Thomas 1996).

Wokabaut Marketing Agency has a policy of marketing only those products that it claims will benefit the villagers (e.g. biscuits, toiletries, pharmaceutical products, rice, canned corned beef, coffee, chewing gum, automobiles, rubber boots, paints, insect repellents and tools), and will not adversely affect their lifestyle (Thomas 1996).

In PNG, price is still a major factor affecting buyer choice. This is particularly true on most of the poorer islands, among poorer groups and with commodity products. However, for some consumers in the major cities, particularly the expatriates, non-price factors may be more important in buyer-choice behavior.

Distribution

In most parts of the country, distribution is affected by problems with a breakdown in law and order. These problems can cause delays, and inefficiencies in distribution.

In the urban centers, retail distribution is dominated by some chain supermarkets and department stores such as Burns Philp, Steamship, Papindo and Carpenters, and some Chinese and other trade stores.

Many of the markets in rural areas are not accessible by road, and sea and air transportation are, respectively, slow and expensive. In general, the underdeveloped state of the transportation structure, especially the road-transport system, greatly restricts the extent of markets and their growth.

Relative to many other countries, the retail outlets in PNG are very small, and numerous. As a result, few individual firms succeed in developing an effective distribution and marketing system on their own, and have to rely on many middlemen in the channel. However, as the distribution system improves, more and more manufacturers (mainly the larger ones) may try to bypass the wholesale system, and sell directly to retailers (Farbood 1995).

Summary and conclusion

From an investor's point of view, PNG may be described as a country where:

- there is a stable government relative to that of other developing nations
- the workforce in the major cities is mostly educated, although very few have university-level qualifications
- there is heavy reliance on air transport for communication links, with only a partially developed road system
- the currency is stable
- there are significant mineral resources

These are some of the benefits available to investors:

- tax incentives for new businesses in rural development areas
- export-sales incentive
- a wage subsidy for the manufacture of new products by new businesses
- accelerated depreciation rates for new manufacturing and agricultural plant
- generous deductions for capital expenditure on land used for primary production
- accelerated deductions for mining and petroleum companies

In the area of marketing, as mentioned earlier, most of the companies still use the selling orientation instead of using the marketing concept. Since the marketing environment within which marketing activities are conducted in PNG–a composite of the economic, financial, political, technological and cultural environments–is constantly changing, firms need to study it in order to develop effective and efficient strategies. Sources of information about the PNG environment may be obtained from various overseas diplomatic missions.

Table 14.2 provides a list of other organizations that may be able to offer information to foreign businesspeople.

Table 14.2 Organizations that may offer information to foreign businesspeople

Organization	*Address*
1. Bank of Papua New Guinea	PO Box 121 Port Moresby National Capital District
2. Department of Minerals and Energy	PO Box 352 Konedobu National Capital District
3. Department of Trade and Industry	PO Wards Strip Waigani National Capital District

continues

Table 14.2 Organizations that may offer information to foreign businesspeople—*continued*

Organization	*Address*
4. Institute of National Affairs	PO Box 1530 Port Moresby National Capital District
5. Lae Chamber of Commerce	PO Box 256 Lae
6. National Investment and Development Authority	PO Box 5053 Boroko National Capital District
7. National Statistical Office	PO Wards Strip Waigani National Capital District
8. PNG Chamber of Mines and Petroleum	PO Box 7059 Boroko National Capital District
9. Port Moresby Chamber of Commerce and Industry	PO Box 1764 Port Moresby National Capital District
10. Registrar General's Office	PO Box 1281 Port Moresby National Capital District

References

Compton (1993), *Interactive Encyclopedia,* Compton's NewMedia, Miriam Webster, New York.

Farbood, Ali (1995), "Marketing in Papua New Guinea", Marketing Educators and Researchers Conference Proceedings, Gold Coast, Queensland.

Ntumy, Michael A. (1993), *South Pacific Islands Legal Systems,* University of Hawaii Press, Honolulu.

Price Waterhouse (1990), *Doing Business in Papua New Guinea,* Price Waterhouse, New York.

Thomas, Amos Owen (1996), "Advertising to the Masses without Mass Media: The Case of Wokabaut Marketing", *Journal of Global Marketing,* vol. 9, no. 4, pp. 75–88.

CHAPTER 15

The Philippines

Marketing and consumer behavior, past, present and future

BIANCA TEO, ANTHONY PECOTICH & ALBERT F. CELOZA

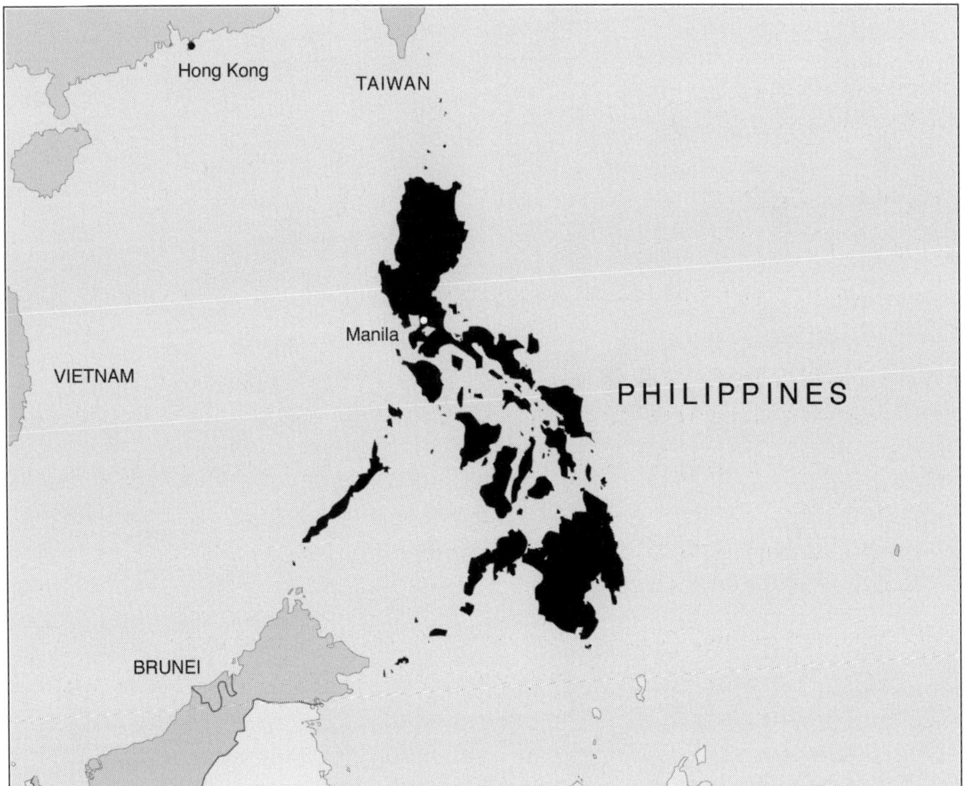

Abstract

The Philippines is an Asian nation with strong connexions to the West; these were established through colonialism first by Spain and then by the USA. The country is emerging from a period of political and economic unrest to join the ranks of the fast-growing developing nations. The journey, however, is not yet complete, and although the most recent signs have been very promising, despite the mid-1997 crisis, the nation is still facing many political and economic problems. In this chapter we attempt to provide a brief historical introduction to the marketing, consumer and economic environments of this evolving nation, a nation that has the potential to provide a positive model of successful economic development by a democratic Asian country.

> There is an old joke in Manila that says that God made a mistake when he put the Philippines in South-East Asia. What he intended was to place Chile next door to the Asian "Tiger" economies and the Philippines on the western strip of South America. But he got the two mixed up.
>
> The joke—which aptly highlighted the Philippines' role as the 'sick man of Asia' and Chile's equally incongruous success among the laggards in Latin America—no longer quite hits the mark in the mid-1990s. Although it remains a very different society from countries such as Indonesia and Malaysia, the Philippines has arguably cast off the stigma of its past (Luce 1996, p. 24).

Introduction

The Republic of the Philippines is an Asian country, shaped by its colonial past of more than 300 years of Spanish regime and half a century of US rule. Its population is predominantly Catholic Christian (many are English speaking), yet its underlying culture and mores are South-East Asian.

Western observers are able to understand the country's society and politics more easily because of the predominant use of a familiar language. Yet appearances may be misleading, because a Chinese heritage, as well as the many indigenous regional ethnic groups that compose the archipelago, also shape the culture. Therefore, the surface familiarity of Filipino culture to the West should not lead to overconfident generalizations; rather, it should be viewed as a good starting point for a deeper exploration of the intricacies of Philippine society and its consumer behavior.

Historically, the Philippines has maintained close ties with the industrialized West, in particular the USA, and has enjoyed a steady pace of growth and relative domestic stability (Doronila 1992). However, increasing political turmoil in the 1970s and the 1980s brought serious economic instability, and loss of international confidence. Its modern history has been dominated by the struggle against Marcos and the need to provide the foundations for economic growth and development within a democratic framework (Rivera 1996). The murder of opposition leader Benigno Aquino in 1983 signalled the end of the Marcos era. Although the full extent of the economic damage caused during the Marcos years is not yet completely understood, the struggle for economic development continues, and after a period of political turmoil the Philippines appears to be emerging as "Asia's next tiger" (Luce 1996). If this transformation is successful despite the currency crisis of 1997, it will provide a powerful argument against the widely promulgated belief that, for Asia's developing economies, democracy is a luxury they cannot afford.

Physical environment

The Philippines, strategically placed in the western Pacific Ocean, with access to the other ASEAN nations and with a tropical climate, fertile soil, and a hard-working population, appears to have excellent prospects for the future (*Asian Economic Handbook* 1987). The nation consists of 7107 islands, the combined land area of which amounts to 300 000 km^2; about 880 of these are inhabited. The two largest, Luzon in the north (covering 104 688 km^2) and Mindanao in the south (94 630 km^2), account for 66.4% of its territory (Europa 1994; Demaine 1997). The climate is maritime and tropical, the seasons varying more in the amount of rainfall than in temperature. Due to its mountainous character and position, the Philippines exhibits large regional variation in both the total amount and the seasonal incidence of rainfall (Demaine 1997, p. 907). The climatic vagaries of the wet and dry seasons, typhoons and high temperatures (rarely much below 26.7°C) place considerable pressure on the farming community, many of whom lead a marginal existence (Europa 1995).

The chief food-producing area may be found in the central lowlands of Luzon; however, despite poor soil quality, much of the smaller lowland areas are also highly cultivated (Demaine 1997, p. 907). The only lowland area offering scope for further cultivation is on the southern island of Mindanao. However, rapid population growth has placed great pressure on the available resources of this island, and environmental degradation is clearly visible (Demaine 1997, p. 907).

Rice is the most important single crop, although, on some of the islands, because of low rainfall, maize is the leading food crop. Major export crops are sugar, coconuts, bananas, and pineapples.

A wide range of metallic mineral deposits exist, the most important being copper, chromite and nickel. Unfortunately, despite a market improvement since 1973, when the figure was 95%, the country is still deficient in energy-producing minerals, with 60% of its energy requirements (mostly petroleum) imported in 1990—and 70% in 1994 (Hodgkinson 1997). The increasing costs of oil-based imports motivated the search for and discovery of petroleum on the island of Palawan in 1977. Nonetheless, domestic production remains relatively insignificant. In contrast, proven reserves of coal and lignite were estimated at 1.458 million metric tons in 1994. Further, hydro-electric power (which contributes about 8% of domestic energy requirements), and geothermal energy (which provides about 5%) are useful supplements for the country's energy requirements (Europa 1997).

Demographics

The population of the Philippines has shown steady growth (see Fig. 15.1), and reached 71.7 million in 1996, compared with 68.4 million in 1995, 67.04 million in 1994 and 48 million in 1980 (*Asian Business* 1996; Economist Intelligence Unit 1996; United Nations 1996; Europa 1997). The population growth rate of 2.1% in 1995 was lower than the rate of 2.5% in 1985, 2.7%

in the 1970s and 3% during the 1960s (see fig. 15.2). Despite the birth-control programs implemented by the Marcos government, the average growth rate was one of the highest in Asia (Hodgkinson 1997). Concerned about the growth rate (in contrast to his immediate predecessor), President Ramos has pursued an active population-control program with the aim of reducing the growth rate to less than 2% by 1998. Nonetheless, the projections are alarming, with an anticipated population of over 85 million by 2010.

The average population density in 1996 was 239 per km^2, which is nearly double the South-East Asian average, and is exceeded only by Vietnam and

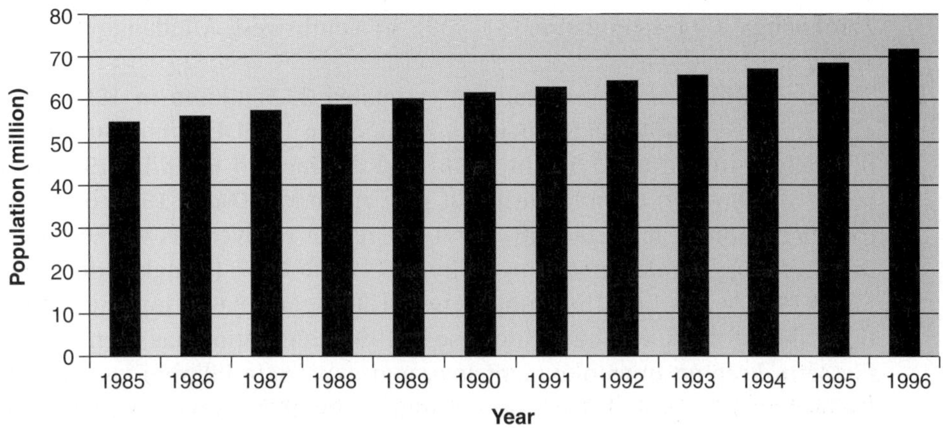

Figure 15.1 Population

Sources: United Nations (1996), *Statistical Yearbook for Asia and the Pacific*, UN; Europa (1997), *The Far East and Australasia*, 27th edn, Europa Publications, London.

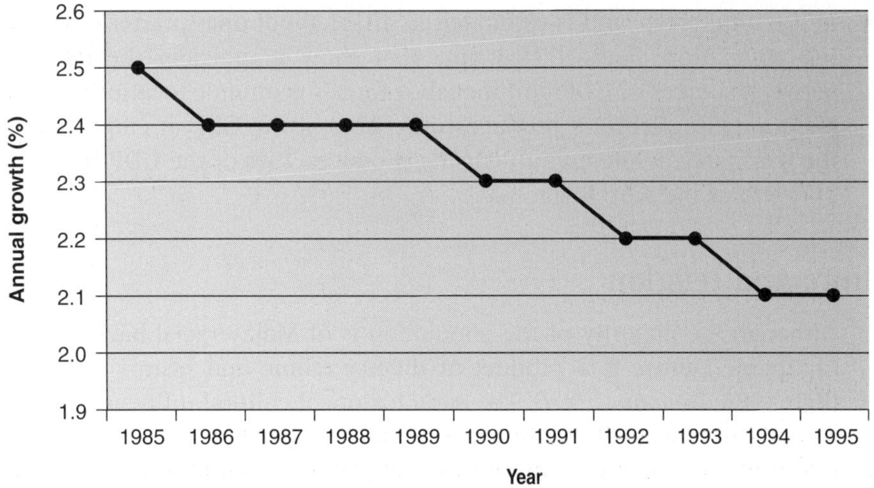

Figure 15.2 Population growth

Sources: United Nations (1996), *Statistical Yearbook for Asia and the Pacific*, UN; Europa (1997), *The Far East and Australasia*, 27th edn, Europa Publications, London.

Singapore (Europa 1995). Both this factor, and the high rate of population growth, are placing increasingly severe pressure on the available productive land resources, particularly in central Luzon (Europa 1997). Though the majority still live in rural areas, there has been an ever-increasing urban drift since the mid-1970s. Manila, the nation's capital (population of more than 1.6 million in 1995), is the core of an extensive, densely populated area called the National Capital Region of Metropolitan Manila (*Financial Times* 1995). It is one of the busiest and most congested cities of South-East Asia. Other major urbanized macro-regions are: Cebu City (population 662 299) in the Visayas, Davao City (population 1 006 840) in south-east Mindanao, and Zamboanga City (population 511 139) in south-west Mindanao (Europa 1997).

The workforce has risen from an estimated 23.5 million in 1990 (*Asia and Pacific Review* 1990) to about 25.7 million in 1995. Unemployment was officially recorded as 11.1% in 1986, and declined to 8.1% by 1990 as a result of growth in manufacturing. It rose again to 9.0% in 1991, owing to the stagnation of manufacturing and the return of overseas workers from the Gulf area, but declined marginally in 1992 to 8.6% (Hodgkinson 1997). Since 1993 it has been hovering between 8.1% and 8.6%, but the indications are that there will be an increase in 1997. Emigration has been a major factor in keeping unemployment low, and expatriate Filipino workers are visible through the ASEAN region (Hodgkinson 1997) as well as the Middle East. Population growth has not been matched by employment opportunities; the constraint of land caused a significant migration to the urban areas, which has failed to provide enough new jobs to absorb these workers (Hodgkinson 1997). Underemployment is also very extensive, especially in the rural areas, and is estimated to affect about one-quarter of the working population. Figures 15.3 and 15.4 show graphically the relationship between sources of GDP and the labor force's economic location. For example, though agriculture produces only 22% of the GDP, it employs 42% of the workforce, while manufacturing produces 25% of the GDP but employs only 9% of the workforce.

Culture and religion

Although the majority of the population is of Malay racial background, the Philippine culture is a product of diverse ethnic and historical influences (Bair 1988; Demaine 1997). The early historical cultural influences emanated from Chinese and Hindu-Arab merchants, who entered the country for trading purposes. In the 16th century, the Chinese began to settle in the Philippines, and started exercising economic influence by accumulating capital, and dominating commerce, trade and the market for skilled labor. The Spaniards, in turn, dominated the islands for 300 years, followed by the

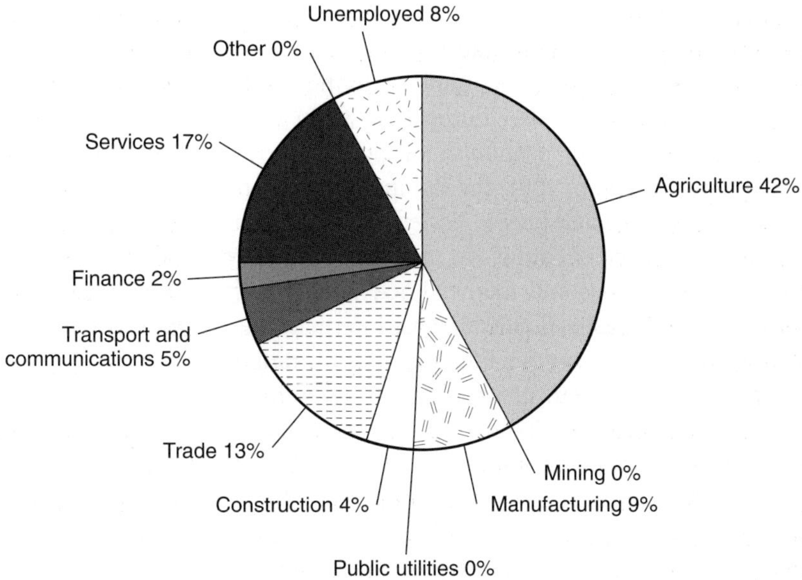

Figure 15.3 Labor-force economic activity (Oct. 1994)

Sources: United Nations (1996), *Statistical Yearbook for Asia and the Pacific*, UN; Europa (1997), *The Far East and Australasia*, 27th edn, Europa Publications, London.

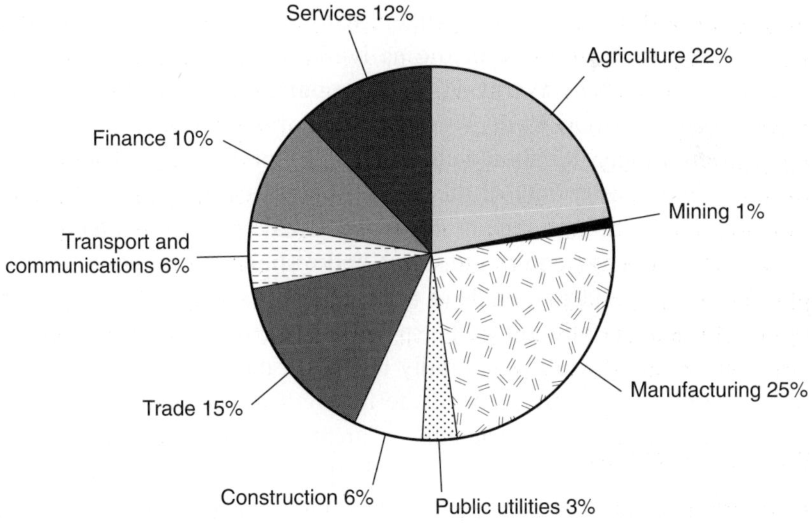

Figure 15.4 Structure of GDP (Oct. 1994)

Sources: United Nations (1996), *Statistical Yearbook for Asia and the Pacific*, UN; Europa (1997), *The Far East and Australasia*, 27th edn, Europa Publications, London.

USA, whose colonial rule lasted another 50 years. During the post-colonial period, US language and cultural forces have remained highly influential despite strong nationalistic tendencies.

Reflecting the country's past as a former Spanish colony, over 80% of the population practice the Roman Catholic faith, with around 2 million Muslims (about 5% of the total population) living in the southern islands (*Asian Economic Handbook* 1987; Europa 1997). In Luzon and Mindanao there are smaller communities of animist hill peoples, who comprise about 6% of the total (Europa 1997, p. 908). The Philippines is the only predominantly Christian state in Asia (*Asia and Pacific Review* 1990; Demaine 1997). The Chinese population is small and accounts for only about 1% of the total (Europa 1997), but its share in business and financial activities is proportionately greater than its number. There has been considerable intermarriage between the various ethnic groups, resulting in unique Filipino cultural traditions.

Roman Catholic culture and traditions dominate the nation, particularly in the lowlands. Significant minorities exist, and the divisions in 1995 (Europa 1977) were as follows (1) *ethnic*–Christian Malay 91.5%, Muslim Malay 4%, Chinese 1.5%, other 3%; (2) *religious*–Roman Catholic 83%, Protestant 9%, Muslim 5%, other 3%. The official language is based on Tagalog, which is progressing toward becoming the national language (Filipino). However, English is still widely used in business and politics, and by the largely mestizo (half-caste) elite elements of the population (Europa 1997). Despite this ethnic and linguistic dominance, it is important to recognize that the Philippines is an archipelago, where 11 Malayo-Polynesian languages and 87 dialects are spoken, with over 90% of the population also being conversant with one of the native languages (e.g. Tagalog, Cebuano, Hiligaynon, Bicolano, Waray-Waray, Pampangan, Pangasinan).

Given its Christian Roman Catholic majority, it is expected that strong kinship and family ties should characterize Filipino society. The family structure does not consist only of the husband, wife, children, and close relatives, but may be enlarged to include male and female godparents *(compadres* and *comares),* who may acquire the status and responsibilities equal to those of a blood relative such as an uncle or aunt. Divorce is still banned by the church, and annulment is difficult and expensive. Parental authority is strong, and children may stay within the family unit until married. Sacrifices are continually made for the betterment of the family, and the maintenance of family unit and harmonious relationships is an important social motivating force. *Pakikisama,* or the necessity to "get along", and *utan na loob,* or the repayment of a debt of gratitude, are two important principles that guide social action in the Philippines. Politics and business are strongly influenced by family ties, and arranged political marriages still occur.

The Philippines has one of the most highly educated populations relative to other nations in ESEA and is the third-largest English speaking country in the world (Bair 1988; Europa 1997). Well-educated college graduates provide a steady source of highly trained personnel for managerial and technical positions. Compulsory elementary education begins at 7 years of age and lasts for 6 years, with 97% of all children in the relevant age group enroled in primary schools, and 56% in secondary schools. Instruction is in both English and Filipino. Among the population aged 15 and over, the average literacy rate in 1990 was estimated at about 94% (males 94%, females 93%), reflecting a relatively high rate of literacy. The 1993 budget allocated 41 982 million pesos (14.9% of total expenditure) to education, culture and sports (Europa 1997).

Government and politics

The Philippines is unusual in the region in that its government is characterized by a weak state embedded in an often "intractable society" within which institutions have a high degree of autonomy (Rivera 1996). The Constitution, which was approved by a national referendum on February 2 1987, provides for a bicameral Congress comprising of a directly elected, 24-member Senate, and a House of Representatives (with a 3-year mandate) that has a maximum of 250 members (200 are directly elected). Executive authority is vested in the president and cabinet, but power is separated under the Constitution, with legislative power held by the elected Congress, and judicial power by the Supreme Court and lower courts. Local government exists in the 13 regions, with provincial, city, and municipal councils (*Asia and Pacific Review* 1990). The President is Head of State, Chief Executive of the Republic, and Commander-in-Chief of the Armed Forces (Europa 1997). Presidential term (6 years without further eligibility) and other powers are limited to prevent the rise of another autocrat.

Historical background

Historically, 1996 was an important year for the Philippines, because it was the centennial of the first anti-colonial revolution in 1896 against the Spanish, as well as the 50th anniversary of formal independence from US rule.

Prior to Spanish colonization in 1565, the indigenous population was poorly organized and fragmented, and incapable of repelling the invaders (Brown 1997). Under the Spanish regime, the Philippines became the bridge for the China–Acapulco trade as goods crossed the Pacific, until Mexico became independent in 1821. The colonial initiatives led to the development of agricultural commodities such as sugar, coconuts, Manila hemp (abaca), and tobacco, which formed the foundation of the economy during both the colonial and post-independence period (Brown 1997, p. 908).

The economic progress during the Spanish colonial period influenced both social and economic development. For example, the increase in agricultural production brought another invader: the economically aggressive, entrepreneurial Chinese began settling into the country from the middle of the 19th century. They intermarried and formed the mestizo, or half-caste, elite (sons of Chinese fathers and native mothers, brought up as natives and Roman Catholics). The mestizo became wealthy landowners who valued education and had the resources to educate their children. And it is these children, labeled the *ilustrados* (enlightened ones), who formed the intellectual basis for cultural definition, and eventually sought reform from Spanish political domination (Brown 1997).

The Spanish drive for religious conversion allowed for a philosophical domination despite some resistance to Roman Catholicism by the Muslims of Mindanao and Sulu, and the retention, even, of some animist beliefs. The *ilustrados* assisted this domination by propagating the Spanish culture, although by the end of the 19th century they were challenging aspects of Spanish rule and advocating reform through the "Propaganda Movement." However, the more impoverished major elements of the rural and urban Filipino population, tired of exploitation, were moving toward more radical action, and the revolution erupted in 1896.

After the entry of the USA into the war, General Emilio Aguinaldo, leader of the revolutionary movement, proclaimed the independence of the Philippines on June 12 1898, with the support of the USA. This support did not last, and conflict developed between the USA and the revolutionaries. The result, after some double-dealing, was that in December 1898 the Spanish ceded the Philippines to the USA following a compensatory payment (Brown 1997, p. 908).

On January 23 1899 the Philippine Republic was inaugurated, and for a year the new republic resisted the USA forces (Brown 1997). However, though President Aguinaldo took his oath of allegiance to the USA in 1900 and urged his fellow Filipinos to do the same, sporadic fighting by guerrillas continued.

Rule by the United States

Although at first colonization by the USA appeared to be a break with the past in many respects, this soon proved not to be the case: it was more of the same. The Philippines became even more heavily dependent economically on agricultural exports, reform did not come, and exploitation in the rural regions continued (Brown 1997, p. 909). The new US administration, with its domestic democratic traditions, did make some reformist motions, and, for example, took action to open up the political and bureaucratic positions and processes to Filipinos. That early progress was made is shown by the fact that by 1903 Filipinos occupied 49% of bureaucratic positions, and that by 1928 Filipinos controlled, in essence, the whole colonial government (Brown 1997, p. 909). However, this did not involve a change in the social structure, because the Filipino appointees were almost entirely from the *ilustrados,* whose main objective was to protect the interests of their class.

Therefore, land reform was not on the agenda, and as the dependence on the USA as a source of export revenue increased, colonial dominance became more and more visible to the public. The inevitable entry of US culture, with its visible impact on Filipino values, precipitated a fear of cultural destruction, which was a further motivating factor toward unrest. During the 1920s and 1930s, deterioration in landlord–tenant relations in the principal regions of export production provoked an emotional reaction among the peasants, and led to further turbulence (Brown 1997).

The continuing turmoil, and domestic democratic considerations in the USA, resulted in the preparation of a new Constitution that was ratified by plebiscite in May 1935, and gave the Philippines internal self-government as well as providing for independence after 10 years (Europa 1997). During the Second World War, in early 1942, Manila was invaded and occupied by the Japanese (Brown 1995). After Japan's surrender in 1945, US rule was restored. The political and bureaucratic elite remained largely intact during this occupation (Brown 1995).

The Republic of the Philippines and the Marcos years

The occupation and liberation resulted in a severely damaged physical-capital infrastructure, and the economy in general needed urgent reconstruction. However, this was difficult to achieve with Filipino political life full of conflict and chaos, and it was inevitable that the movement toward independence—attained on July 4 1946—was going to be a difficult process (Brown 1997, pp. 911–12). A succession of governments manipulated by US economic interests failed to break the power of the land-owning class. The peasant majority remained poor and without real political power, and unrest continued. Ferdinand E. Marcos came to power on a pledge to restore the economy after the obstructionist political wrangling of his predecessors. In his early years of power, he had many successes, transforming the economy with agricultural improvements and initiating the process of industrialization (*Asian Economic Handbook* 1987; Brown 1997). However, by the end of the 1960s, the country faced a balance-of-payments crisis that was aggravated by massive election spending and vote buying in the 1969 election. At the end of this election Marcos was entrenched as president for his supposed last term in office.

Economic problems and civil unrest plagued President Marcos's second term, and the social fabric of the Republic became unraveled. To restore order and to introduce drastic reforms, Marcos declared martial law in September 1972, giving as the reason the existence of subversive activities by both the left and right. The economic strategy of the Marcos administration emphasized an expansion in exports, a reduction of tariffs and an increase in foreign investment. By the early 1980s, this economic strategy was in serious difficulties, as a worldwide recession sharply reduced the

Philippines' export earnings and produced a chronic balance-of-payments crisis (Brown 1997; Hodgkinson 1997). As a result, large loans with stringent conditions attached to them were negotiated with the IMF and the World Bank.

Bureaucracy and corruption masked a system in which true power lay with a small group of the President's business associates who were willing to use force against dissenters and critics. Criticism of President Marcos became more widespread after November 1977, and although martial law ended in January 1981, Marcos remained in control, and the situation appeared unchanged. The assassination of the opposition leader, Benigno Aquino Jr, in 1983, precipitated a major economic, social, and political crisis (Brown 1997). Even before the assassination, the national economy was already on the verge of collapse. Domestic political instability caused foreign creditors to suspend the short-term loans that had sustained the economy. The US government brought pressure to bear on Marcos, urging him to hold an election. He did so in an attempt to establish the legitimacy of his regime, but the writing was on the wall as the splintered opposition rallied behind Corazon Aquino, widow of the assassinated opposition leader. The international community did not endorse the Marcos claim of electoral victory as a result of widespread electoral fraud, and a group of reformist military officers withdrew support for the regime. This spelled the end of the regime as hundreds of thousands protested in the streets and defied loyalist forces. Marcos fled to the USA with his family and friends (Celoza 1992; 1993) and died there in exile 3 years later. Corazon Aquino was sworn to the presidency of the Republic.

The Aquino government

In February 1986, Cory Aquino was inaugurated as president. The early years of the Aquino government were very difficult, accentuated as they were by the rebellion led by the banned communist NPA, and by Muslim unrest in the south (*Asia and Pacific Review* 1990). Civil unrest and instability continued, with attempted coups in July and August 1986. Lack of cohesion and continuing dissension within government ranks, as well as deplorable economic conditions, fed grave doubts about Aquino's capacity to survive. However, progress was also made, and by 1987 Aquino's position was strengthened when the new Constitution was approved in a national referendum by 76% of voters (Brown 1977).

Although the GDP growth was in the vicinity of 6% in both 1987 and 1988, there was concern for the future, as the expansion was considered artificially fueled by consumer spending on imported goods following implementation of an import-liberalization program (England 1990). While the lot of the urban middle class appeared to be improving, the agricultural lower classes remained in poverty. By 1990 economic growth had slowed (see fig. 15.5), and the government was once again facing serious economic problems.

Discontent in urban areas was increasing due to power-supply stoppages and water shortages, while in the agriculture sector, where about 70% of the population lived, the impact of the declining economic conditions was heavily felt. Despite a genuine attempt at reform by the government, which launched new programs to alleviate poverty, generate employment, and promote social justice, improvement was not fast enough for some, and instability continued as the country lurched forward. Both new problems and traditional sources of friction such as corruption, human rights abuses, the communist insurgency, vast-scale poverty, and continued indebtedness were threatening to overwhelm the government despite the progress (Brown 1997).

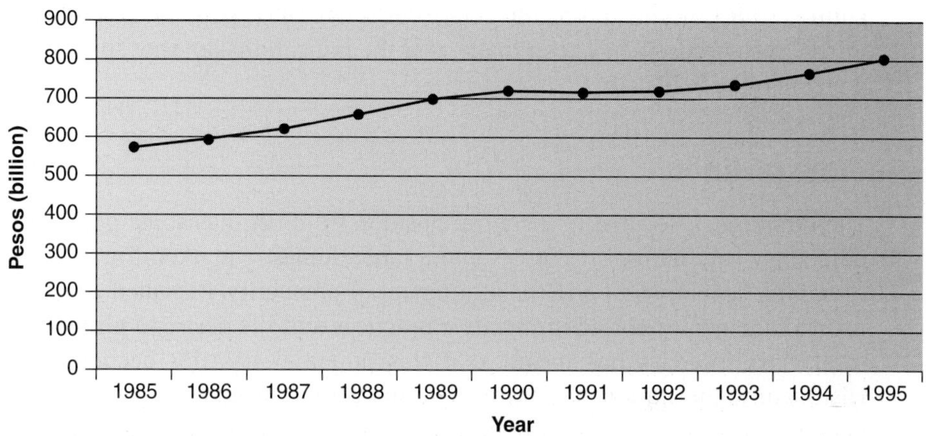

Figure 15.5 GDP at constant 1985 prices (1985–1995)

Sources: United Nations (1996), *Statistical Yearbook for Asia and the Pacific*, UN; Europa (1997), *The Far East and Australasia*, 27th edn, Europa Publications, London.

The Ramos government: a brief overview

General Fidel Ramos was elected to the presidency and inaugurated on 30 June 1992 with the support of both Cory Aquino and the major political groups within the nation (i.e. the military, the industrialists, and the traditional politicians). Ramos declared that his aims were:

1. to restore stability through national reconciliation and an amnesty program
2. to deregulate the economy and encourage foreign investment
3. to reduce crime and corruption (Brown 1997; Europa 1997)

In an effort to achieve this he began a major privatization program. So far the results of the privatization drive have produced very promising results (*Asian Business* 1994). The assessment prior to mid-1997 was that the economy was in good shape and the country was moving forward with confidence as export and investments increased (*Asian Business* 1996).

Since mid-1997, the currency crisis has taken effect, but the indications are that the Philippines may suffer less than the other ESEA nations.

Although strongly committed to ASEAN and the ESEA region, the Philippines still has special relations with the USA. These relationships have undergone periods of unease and difficulty, and the Philippines has taken an independent position on foreign relations as it pursues its own national interests. The potentially volatile international political issues confronting the Philippines include the Spratly Islands sovereignty question and rights over oil and other marine resources.

President Ramos instituted the "Philippines 2000" program in 1993 with the aim of raising the Philippines to the level of a newly industrializing country (NIC) by the end of the century (Brown 1997, p. 915). Despite some misgivings, progress has been made, and the indications are that some of the goals may be achievable.

Economic position

The Philippines, located in a central position in ESEA, has some of the fundamentals (e.g. natural resources and a large domestic market) for sustained economic development and the attainment of prosperity. Repeated economic mismanagement, poor administrative practices and the desire to protect sectoral class interests has meant that this potential has not been fulfilled. Historically, the nation has suffered from continuing balance-of-payments deficits caused by structural deficiencies. The burden of servicing the large foreign debt, natural disasters, electrical power disruptions and the dependence on imported goods have clearly been major causes of discontent (Europa 1997). Poverty and a concentration of wealth in the hands of few are also continuing sources of problems. As markets consist of people and money, the existence of large pockets of the poor, particularly in the agricultural regions (47% of the agricultural population was classified as poor in 1994 as compared with 24% in urban areas and 35.5% overall—National Statistics Office 1997), severely limits domestic market development. The government's attempts to deal with these economic difficulties are frustrated by corruption, monopoly ownership, and patronage, which subvert national performance (Hodgkinson 1997).

Both the Aquino and the Ramos governments have appeared to be genuinely committed to reform. Assets corruptly acquired during the former Marcos era were seized, and policies designed to reduce corruption and to ensure a more equitable distribution of wealth were implemented. Despite the pressure of external debt deregulation, rationalization and privatization programs were instituted. Further policy directives included reductions in government spending, the depreciation of the peso, the abolition of subsidies, and the liberalization of laws on foreign investment (Europa 1997). As expected there were problems, for example with privatization, where considerations such as national security (the sale of the Philippine National Oil Corporation was postponed indefinitely) and heritage status (e.g. the Manila Hotel) held up projects. Poor profitability of privatization targets and pricing, particularly for inefficient industries, engendered much debate and public opposition (*Asia Pacific: An Investment Guide* 1990).

With support from the international community, the various governments of the Philippines have attempted to introduce responsible economic programs, and have, in particular, increased spending on infrastructure and introduced an emergency rural employment program (Hodgkinson 1997). When this took effect, GDP at constant 1995 prices (see fig. 15.5) increased from 571.9 billion pesos in 1985 to 720 billion in 1990 (*United Nations Yearbook* 1997), and both inflation and unemployment fell. Private consumption rose, improving the capacity utilization of domestic manufacturing, and the crime rate decreased to just over 15%. The March 1989 agreement with the International Monetary Fund (IMF) aimed at achieving an average annual growth rate of 6.5% in real terms between 1990 and 1992 (The Hong Kong & Shanghai Banking Corporation 1990).

The attempted coup of late 1989 appeared to precipitate a difficult socio-economic period for the Philippines. The disproportionate growth of imports over exports caused the current-account deficit to escalate (*Asia Pacific: An Investment Guide* 1990), and, unfortunately, the community had also to face unforeseen problems in 1990 (droughts, power failures, and earthquakes) (Hodgkinson 1997). As could have been expected, GNP growth declined to 4.5% in 1990 from the 5.9% achieved in 1989. The government responded by introducing the Memorandum of Economic Policy (MEP) in 1989–1992 to reduce the deficit and foreign-debt dependence (*Asia Pacific: An Investment Guide* 1990). This and other actions had some effect, and by 1993 the foreign-exchange situation improved and there were signs of recovery.

A summary of the pre-1997 currency crisis economic indicators is shown in Table 15.1. At that time, due to the structural reforms of the Ramos administration, the prognosis was optimistic, with the possibility of even higher rates of growth. Among other actions, foreign-exchange controls were removed, the telephone monopoly was terminated, and foreign banks were allowed to enter and trade. Privatization, which had been a major feature of the Aquino administration, was being pursued with increased vigor, and the economical goals remained those of alleviating poverty, creating more employment opportunities, promoting equality and social justice, and attaining sustainable economic growth (The Hong Kong & Shanghai Banking Corporation 1990).

Although the currency crisis has had a major impact on the economy, it seems likely that the Philippines will weather the storm better than other ESEA economies such as Thailand. After years of battling economic adversity, the government is experienced in instituting reform, and is willing to apply hard economic measures, thus avoiding the mistakes of its neighbors. It is anticipated that GDP growth will be down to somewhere between 4% and 5.5% in 1997/98; although lower than in the past, this may nonetheless be perceived as highly satisfactory given current conditions. The National Statistics Office (1998) reported that in the first 10 months of 1997 exports showed a growth of 23%. The devaluation of the peso appears a two-edged sword: on the one hand it could lead to increased profit if export prices are maintained or improve competitive position if they are not; on the other hand it presents serious cost problems for manufacturers using imported products such as those in the garment industry. The optimistic predictions for the future of the Philippino government need to be tempered with the IMF evaluations that are more pessimistic and suggest that the regional crisis will deepen, and slow the economy even further.

Table 15.1 A summary of economic indicators

Economic indicators	*1991*	*1992*	*1993*	*1994*	*1995*
GDP at current prices (Pbn)	1 248.0	1 351.6	1 474.5	1 688.5	1 893.9
Real GDP growth (%)	-0.5	0.1	2.1	4.3	5.4
Consumer price inflation (%)	18.7	8.9	7.6	9.3	5.4
Population mid-year (million)	62.87	64.26	65.67	67.04	68.6
Exports fob ($m)	8 840	9 824	11 375	13 433	16 750
Imports fob ($m)	12 052	14 519	17 597	21 231	25 550
Current account ($m)	−1 034	−1 000	−3 289	−3 002	−3 900
Reserves excl. gold ($m)	3 246	4 403	4 676	6 017	N/A
Total external debt ($bn)	32.2	32.6	34.3	37.7	41.9
Total external debt service ($bn)	3.40	4.89	3.83	4.19	N/A
Fiscal balance as % of GNP	−2.1	−1.2	−1.4	0.9	N/A
Exchange rate (av., P:$)	27.48	25.51	27.12	26.42	27.50

Source: The Economic Intelligence Unit (1996), Philippines Country Report.

An overview of the major industrial sectors

Agriculture, fishing, and the environment

The agriculture, forestry and fishing sector plays a vital role in the Filipino economy. In 1994 it contributed 22.5% of GDP while employing about 42% of the working population (see figs 15.3 and 15.4) (*United Nations Handbook* 1994; Hodgkinson 1997). Rice, maize, and cassava are the main subsistence crops, while coconuts, sugar cane, bananas, and pineapples are mainly grown for export. About 35% of the total land area is cultivated, and consists mainly of smallholdings (*Asia and Pacific Review* 1990). The Philippines is the world's leading exporter of coconut products, supplying up to three quarters of total world demand (Hodgkinson 1997, p. 923).

Despite the growth in manufacturing, and particularly electronics (which accounted for 47% of the exports in 1997), agriculture remains critical to the welfare of the nation, and there exists considerable concern about its productivity. In the first 9 months of 1997, the nation was hit by a drought, and agricultural production growth declined from 5.5% to 0.9% (National Statistics Office 1998). If this decline continues, agricultural prices will rise, and food will have to be imported; serious economic pressures will resurface. Despite the fact that diets are changing, rice remains an important staple, and there is a need to improve its production at least in the short term.

In the agricultural context, land reform has been a fundamental source of conflict since independence. While all administrations have been aware of the need for reform and Aquino introduced the Comprehensive Agrarian Reform Program in 1988, resistance by the landed elite has delayed real progress. The objective of redistribution of all public and private agricultural land to farmers and farm workers within 10 years is significantly behind schedule, although there is hope that the program will be completed by the year 2000 (Hodgkinson 1997, p. 222).

The forests, which contain a large quantity of precious timber and cover about 51% of the land area, although a source of wealth, also present major environmental problems (*Asia and Pacific Review* 1990; Hodgkinson 1997). Population encroachment and, often, illegal exploitation as well as poor reforestation practices, continue to have a severe impact despite government action. Although the export of logs and sawn wood has been banned both to preserve the environment and to increase the value of forestry-related exports, deforestation continues at an alarming rate. If economic conditions decline it is quite likely that legal and illegal exploitation of the hardwoods will accelerate and present a serious environmental problem for the government.

The Philippines has extensive fishing resources, both marine and inland waters. Production increased rapidly, to account for about 5% of GDP in the late 1980s. The fishing sector became a major source of foreign-exchange earnings, principally through the export of shrimps and prawns to Japan, and ranked ahead of coconut oil in 1991 (Hodgkinson 1995). While both freshwater ponds and most of the marine waters have not been fully developed, productivity in some areas has deteriorated because of poor infrastructure and pollution.

Mining and energy

Mining contributed 1.4% of GDP in 1990, and engaged 0.4% of the employed labor force in 1994 (*United Nations Yearbook* 1996; Europa 1997).

Its small contribution belies its potential, with about a quarter of the nation still not fully explored. The Philippines possesses large deposits of gold, silver, copper, nickel, iron, lead, and chromium, as well as lesser amounts of zinc, cobalt, limestone, and manganese. Some of the richest deposits have yet to be exploited. The mining sector, therefore, has considerable potential, and there are many opportunities–but these are not without risk.

Power shortages have become a characteristic of the Filipino landscape. In an attempt to remedy the shortage of generating capacity, investment in plant has been considerable (e.g. in 1993, 11 new plants, with a total capacity of 1074MW, were put into operation). Power generation is mostly oil based (roughly 10% from domestic sources, implying a great reliance on imported petroleum), although hydro-electric power, geothermal and coal production also exist. The government has actively sought to decrease its dependence on imported energy sources and has achieved some success in this area through the use of the private sector in a build, operate, transfer (BOT) program.

Manufacturing

The manufacturing sector, although employing only about 9% of the labor force, contributed 25% to the GDP in 1994 (Europa 1997). Although the performance of this sector has, historically, at best been mixed, the recovery begun in 1986 appears to be continuing despite strikes and temporary slowdowns. Recent governments have slowly been dismantling the legacy of protected, domestic-oriented, inefficient industries, and have implemented import liberalization and tariff- and quota-reduction measures. These have had some impact; for example, the electronics industry has developed rapidly. In November 1996 it accounted for about 43% of exports, and this figure was 46% in November 1997, when exports increased by 24% (National Statistics Office 1998).

Tourism

The Philippines places much hope on the tourism industry. In recent years the country has consistently attracted over one million tourists annually. The first half of 1997 was highly successful, and 1.23 million tourists visited the country–an 11% increase over the same period in 1996. The figure is remarkable given the political uncertainties, crime and natural disasters. This has resulted in a highly optimistic forecast that the 1997 figure of 2.5 million visitors will be exceeded. The benefits of a lower peso are not consistently passed on to tourists because prices are often quoted in US dollars, particularly for hotels and resorts. Despite this, hotel occupancy rates for the first half of 1997 exceeded 74%. The visitors are mainly from the USA and Japan (25%), although Germany has been noticeable in recent times, and Filipinos from overseas (Balikbayans) are also prominent, accounting for around 10%. The tourism industry is not without serious difficulties—for example, a major tourist attraction, the Banawe rice terraces, are being threatened by soil erosion. The future may well be in ecotourism, careful control, and the promotion of domestic inter-island visitors.

International trade

The Philippines' major trading partners are the USA (25% of total trade in November 1997) and Japan (20%) (National Statistics Office 1998). Although there is an element of tradition in these figures, the trading patterns have undergone a transformation as a result of recent government initiatives. Export markets have been developed in Eastern Europe and the People's Republic of China, while trade with ASEAN and other Asian countries has increased in both absolute and relative terms. For example, ASEAN's share of imports increased from 2% in 1973 to 12% in 1994, and its share of exports from 2% to 10% (Hodgkinson 1997). The indications are that the Philippines, besides maintaining its traditional trading links, has expanded into new areas, and that it is looking more and more to its Asian neighbors for both investment and trade.

The structural composition of trade has also been transformed: in the 1970s, exports consisting mainly of primary commodities—coconut products, sugar, timber, and copper—accounted for over 50%. In 1995, primary commodities accounted for only 10% of the total, while manufacturing accounted for almost 80% (Hodgkinson 1997, p. 925). Two strong export performers are the garment and electronics industries, which accounted for over 50% of exports in October 1996. The garment industry's share of exports has dropped about 11% as a result of increasing competition from other Asian manufacturers able to source raw materials from their national domestic sources. The import structure has not changed as drastically, although the devaluation of the peso will increase the attractiveness of domestic supplies.

Important sources of foreign exchange are remittances from Filipino workers abroad. These totaled US$10.7 billion from 1992–1995 (*Far Eastern Economic Review* 1996). The tragic legacy of national poverty has meant there have been as many as over 700 000 Filipinos working abroad (Hodgkinson 1997), often under exploitative conditions (*Asia and Pacific Review* 1990; Europa 1997). The conditions of these "guest workers," and some spectacular events such as the execution of a Filipina maid in Singapore, as well as the ongoing legal and cultural clashes experienced by Filipino labor in Middle Eastern countries, have placed the long-term viability of exportation of labor in question. The currency crisis of mid-1997, and increasing unemployment levels in ESEA, have made the repatriation of "guest workers" a major social issue in the region.

Elements of the macromarketing mix

Product

The *Consumer Act* of July 1992 was designed to protect the consumer and to establish standards for business and industry. Among the broad-ranging issues covered by the Act, the agencies that implement and enforce the Act are listed. The Act also lists the procedures and processes that are expected to be followed. Specifically, the Act sets out legal and procedural requirements in relation to:

1 Consumer product quality and safety
2 Deceptive, unfair, and unconscionable sales acts and practices
3 Weights and measures (metrication)
4 Consumer products and service warranties
5 Regulations in relation to the price tag
6 Labeling and packaging
7 Liability for products and services
8 Service and repair shops
9 Advertising and sales promotion
10 Consumer education and information

Many aspects of the Act relate to products and to the responsibilities associated with marketing within the Philippines.

For corporations wishing to enter the Philippines, labeling and packaging laws are of particular relevance; with certain exceptions, every imported or locally manufactured product must be labeled to indicate brand, trademark, or trade name; country of manufacturer; physical or chemical composition; net weight and measure if applicable; and address of manufacturer or repacker. In recognition of the multi-lingual nature of the Philippines, it is expected that labels should be either in Filipino, English, or Spanish. Misleading the consumer or misrepresentation may subject the perpetrator to prosecution, and may even result in seizure and disposal of the goods. Aggrieved consumers have the full range of remedies available to them, including replacement or repair, refund of payment made, restitution or rescission of contract, reimbursement to the complainant of the amount spent in pursuing the complaint, and award of damages. In a criminal action the defendant, if found guilty, may even be imprisoned.

Channels of distribution

Both its geographic characteristics and its underdevelopment have caused the Philippines to have a very poor infrastructure. Physical distribution essential for marketing development has been difficult because of inadequate transport and communications systems. It is to be expected that the Philippines, as an archipelago, has unique distribution problems. These have been accentuated by years of neglect, owing to both a lack of investment during the mid-1980s' austerity program and the tendency to focus on new projects to the detriment of maintenance programs (Hodgkinson 1997).

The focus of land transportation is on roads that carry about 60% of freight and 80% of passenger traffic. There is considerable diversity, and the most developed road system is found around the most economically developed areas such as metropolitan Manila and the nearby regions. By 1995 there were 187 608 km of roads, more than 50% of which were in poor condition and not suitable for all-weather traffic (Hodgkinson 1997). The rail system is also poorly developed, and maintained with only a single-line track in Luzon, which does not have a major impact on the traffic patterns in the Philippines. A light railway system (LRT) does exist in Manila, and was built mainly to provide mass public transportation in the city. Improvements in the mass transport and highway system are projected to meet increasing transportation needs. The current government seems aware that full marketing development cannot take place without investment in infrastructure, and has set the year 2000 as a goal for the achievement of major improvements (e.g. the Subic motorway extensions).

Sea transport plays a major part in international and inter-island trade, carrying about 40% of the freight and 10% of the passenger traffic (Hodgkinson 1997). Most of the over 473 ports do not have modern container facilities (fewer than half of the national ports are open to international shipping), and the inter-island fleet is in a very poor state. As with the road system, the government is encouraging the upgrading of facilities through the BOT system, and expansion and rebuilding projects are under way (e.g. in the Manila port area).

Air transport is in better shape, and appears to be the mode that is most likely to undergo extensive development in the future. Over 84 national airports exist, with the major international ones located at Manila and Cebu. Air freight and air express shipments are becoming more economical for imported merchandise, and there are extensive plans for further development.

Private and public communications companies are investing heavily in improvement. For example, the Philippine Long Distance Telephone and Philippine Telegraph and Telephone (PTT) are both investing heavily in expansion, and demand for long-distance communications is expected to increase by as much as 30% annually. The Philippines has access to satellite communications, telex lines, microwave relay stations, and underwater cable systems, with which it is linked to the international community. The full range of telephone, telegraph, and postal services exist, although their quality and availability are not consistent.

Administratively, the nation is subdivided into 13 regions: Ilocos, Cagayan Valley, Central Luzon, Southern Tagalog, Bicol, Western Visayas,

Central Visayas, Eastern Visayas, Western Mindanao, Northern Mindanao, South Western Mindanao, and the National Capital Region (Metro Manila). The Manila region forms the cultural, industrial, and national center, with about 90% of all industries located in the greater Manila area, in three locations: heavy industries along the banks of the Pasig River, medium-sized plants at Antipolo, in the Marikina Valley, and the Makati main business district (Bair 1988). The other major interregional centers are Cebu City, Iloilo, Davao, and Zamboanga. There are also about 40 major and 35 secondary smaller centers (with populations of up to 60 000), which provide essential retail and other urban services to their particular trading regions (Bair 1988).

The retailing and wholesaling system is undergoing rapid development, particularly in the Manila region, where major shopping centers and other retailing configurations are developing. The proposed liberalization of the retail structure has resulted in considerable controversy, and resistance from the retail associations. Nonetheless, the sector is moving forward, with innovative developments such as the Makro membership wholesaler, and the entry of the major US retailer JC Penney.

Promotion

Although there is considerable variation in the degree of sophistication, all elements of the communication mix are visible in the Filipino market place. Within the population there is considerable brand consciousness, and advertising therefore plays a significant part in influencing buyer behavior. Advertising agencies are often modeled on their US counterparts, and multinational agencies have a significant share of billing. The estimated national media expenditures suggest that 50% is spent on television, 29% on print, 20% on radio, and the remaining 1% on cinema and outdoor advertising (Beyer 1988; Europa 1997). Relatively inexpensive mass-produced transistorized radio receivers have flooded the market, and as a result radio is more important as an advertising medium than in more developed nations. It is the least expensive medium for reaching the rural population. Television is growing rapidly, but is concentrated in the urban areas, particularly Manila. More than half of Manila's families own a TV set, while the national average is only 1 per 10 people (Europa 1997). The expensive nature of television sets and the lack of broadcasting facilities in many parts of the country (particularly in rural areas) reduce the usefulness of TV as a medium, although this is rapidly changing.

There were 43 daily newspapers with a circulation of over 3.2 million in 1992, and 11 of the 20 published in Manila are English (Europa 1997). The *Manila Bulletin* is the largest and most widely circulated English-language national daily newspaper (*Asia and Pacific Review* 1990). Magazines have a wide circulation, and are consistently used by local advertisers.

Conclusion

The Philippines was considered one of the most promising countries in Asia in the early 1960s. It had the region's most advanced education infrastructure, a vibrant economy, and a stable political system. In 1965, it was ahead of South Korea in economic terms and was second only to Japan (Celoza 1993; *Far Eastern Economic Review* 1996). However, disturbances and upheavals in the 1970s and 1980s put the Philippines behind its Asian neighbors in terms of economic progress. With the demise of the Marcos dictatorship and the revitalization of democratic structures, optimism has been restored in the 1990s.

Indeed, the headline in *Asian Business* in 1994 stated: "Philippines–the only way is up"; there was a high degree of optimism at that time, and many agreed with this statement. Whatever the problems associated with the currency crisis, the Philippines has entered a new era of development and economic growth. Industry secretary Rizalino Navarro was quoted as saying, "Our economic fundamentals are in place, political stability is here, and we have been attending to our infrastructure problems" (*Asian Business* 1994, p. 45). Indeed, after bad times and the low point of 1993, "Hopes are high that the Philippine economy is, at last, starting a growth trend" (*Asian Business* 1994, p. 44). It appears that these hopes are being fulfilled, and, despite the currency crisis and further major economic problems, the nation is being transformed from one of the world's problem areas (with a growth rate of 1% in 1992) into an ordered democratic state with one of the highest economic growths of 7.1% in 1996 (Luce 1996).

References

Asia and Pacific Review (1990), 11th edn, Hunter Publishing Inc., Edison, NJ and World of Information, Essex, UK, pp. 195–9.

Asia Pacific: an Investment Guide (1990), Euromoney Publications PLC, London, pp. 159–79.

Asian Business (1994a), "Philippines–the only way is up", January, pp. 24–38.

— (1994b), "Time to Bet Again on the Philippines", February, pp. 36–8.

— (1996), "Philippines–The Bandwagon is Rolling", January, pp. 40–7.

Asian Economic Handbook (1987), 1st edn, Euromonitor Publications Ltd, London, pp. 70–127.

Bair, F.E. (1988), *International Marketing Handbook,* 3rd edn, vol. 2, Gale Research Company, Detroit, Michigan, pp. 2030–71.

Brown, I. (1997), "Philippines History", in Europa, *The Far East and Australasia,* 28th edn, Europa Publications, London, pp. 908–19.

Celoza, Albert F. (1992), "The Ambiguities of Modernization: The Political Class and Regime Change in the Philippines", in Brown, R. & Liu, W., *Modernization in East Asia: Political, Economic and Social Perspectives*, Praeger, New York.

Celoza, Albert F. & Sours, Martin (1993), "Philippine and South Korean International Relations in Post-Cold War Asia Pacific", in Hsiung, J., *Asia Pacific in the New World Politics*, Lynne Rienner Publishers, Boulder, CO and London.

Demaine, Harvey (1997), "Philippines: Physical and Social Geography", *The Far East and Australasia*, 28th edn, Europa Publications Limited, pp. 907–8.

Dolan, Ronald (1993), *The Philippines: A Country Study*, Federal Research Division, US Library of Congress.

Doronila, Amando (1992), *The State, Economic Transformation and Political Change in the Philippines, 1946–1972*, Oxford University Press, Oxford.

Economist Intelligence Unit (1996) *Philippines EIU Country Report 1st Quarter 1996*, EIU, London.

Europa (1994), *The Europa World Yearbook 1994*, vol. 2, Europa Publications Ltd, London, pp. 2378–84.

— (1997), *The Far East and Australasia*, 28th edn, Europa Publications Limited, London.

Financial Times, "Financial Times Survey: The Philippines", October 2 1995.

Gale Research (1993), *Handbook of the Nations*, 13th edn, Gale Research Company, Detroit, Michigan.

Hodgkinson, E. (1997), "Philippines Economy", in Europa, *The Far East and Australasia*, 28th edn, Europa Publications, London, pp. 920–47.

Hong Kong and Shanghai Banking Corporation (1990), *Business Profile Series: Philippines*, 6th edn, Hong Kong Bank, Group Public Affairs, HK.

Luce, Edward (1996), "Asia's Next Tiger?", *Accountancy International Review*, December, pp. 24–8.

National Statistics Office (1998), "Population Census", Manila.

Rivera, Temario C. (1996), *State of the Nation Philippines*, Institute of South-East Asian Studies, Singapore.

United Nations Yearbook (1996), *Statistical Yearbook for Asia and the Pacific*, UN, New York.

CHAPTER 16

Singapore

An analysis of changes in the marketing environment and their implications for marketing management

JOCHEN WIRTZ

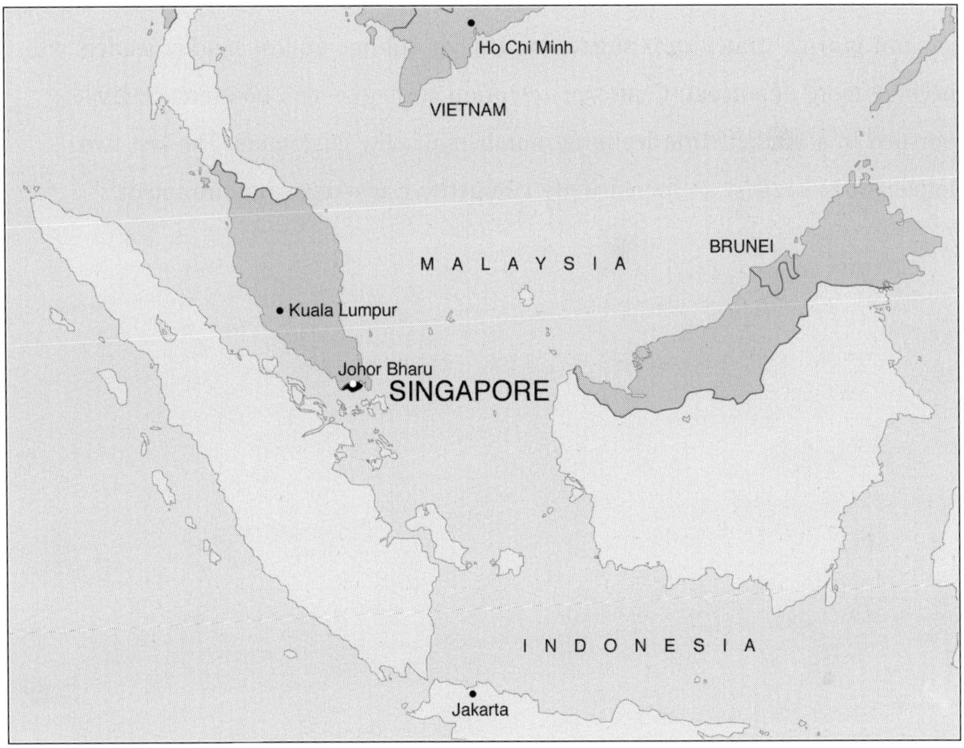

Abstract

Trends in Singapore's marketing environment are analyzed in terms of economy, demographics, and culture, as well as from a consumer-behavior and marketing-mix perspective. The analysis provides a picture of a wealthy society with good prospects. Singapore has an interesting mix of cultures with distinct languages, religions and customs. The main demographic trends follow those of more developed nations, with a low population growth, rapid ageing and smaller household sizes.

Education levels will continue to improve quickly. These macro-economic trends are reflected in consumption behavior, with increasing overall consumption, an increasing share of higher level goods such as recreational, education and health services, and changing consumer values and lifestyles. Singaporeans have become more brand and status conscious and more discerning, quality oriented and health conscious. Trends in the marketing mix are a direct reflection of the macro-environment.

Three implications for marketing strategies are highlighted. The pursuit of general growth strategies is suggested. Higher volume and/or market leaders will become more important. Customer-retention strategies will be increasingly pursued in a market with declining numbers of new customers. The last two implications suggest an increasingly competitive marketing environment.

Introduction

Singapore is a small city state approximately 641 km^2 in area, consisting of the main island of Singapore and some 60 islets within its territorial waters. Singapore has a tropical climate, which is warm and humid. The temperature is uniform throughout the year, ranging between 24°C and 31°C, and moderated by sea breezes.

Singapore was founded in 1819 by Sir Stamford Raffles as a trading post for the East India Company, and became a British colony in 1867. It was an important British trading post and military center in 1900, with a population of about 220 000. At the end of the Second World War, its population was still less than 1 million. The economy showed little development from the end of the war until the early 1960s under British rule, and in 1970 its GDP per capita was still only US$950.

In 1963, Singapore joined Malaya as one of the constituent states of a new Federation of Malaysia, with virtual freedom from colonial rule. In 1965, Singapore was separated from Malaysia by mutual agreement and became a fully independent republic (Ministry of Information and the Arts 1994). Its astonishing transformation into a modern industrial society began in the early 1970s. Since then, Singapore has enjoyed impressive rates of economic growth and achieved higher GDP per capita (c. US$20 000 by 1994) than some developed countries such as Canada, England and Australia. In fact, the World Bank (1995) ranked Singapore as number 9 on its list of the world's richest countries, measured in terms of purchasing-power parity. This has been achieved with full employment, budget surpluses, low pollution, and, by the standards of most industrial countries, with few social problems.

This Chapter analyzes trends in Singapore's marketing environment, and is structured into 7 sections. The first presents background information on Singapore's political system, some reasons for its rapid development, and its position in the region. The second discusses the economic environment, which is expected to remain favorable, with high growth, low inflation and virtually no unemployment. The demographic environment, showing rapid ageing and continuing low birth rates, is examined in the third section. The next section describes the cultural environment as a stable multicultural society, with Chinese, Malays, and Indians as the main ethnic groups, each with their distinct languages, religions and customs. Other trends examined here are increasing education levels and decreasing household sizes. Then trends in consumer behavior are discussed, including macro-economic consumption patterns, consumer values and lifestyles. Changes in the macro-marketing mix are examined next, including trends in product and service design, consumer reactions to price and promotions, distribution channels, advertising, and marketing research. Finally, the last section integrates the findings of the environmental analysis and assesses their implications for marketing management.

Political and historical background information

Singapore's political structure and its position in ASEAN and the region are discussed, and a brief analysis is made of the reasons behind Singapore's success, to provide a platform for a more detailed analysis of trends in the economic, demographic, and cultural environments in subsequent sections.

Political structure

Singapore is a parliamentary democracy. The executive, comprising of the Prime Minister, at present Mr Goh Chok Tong, and 14 ministers, are appointed by the President and are responsible to the Parliament. The head of state, the incumbent President Mr Ong Teng Cheong, is elected directly for a 5-year term by the citizens of Singapore. The President has certain veto powers, primarily related to the appointment of senior civil servants, the protection of reserves, internal security detentions, investigations into corruption, and restraint orders connected with the maintenance of religious harmony.

The national legislature comprises a unicameral parliament, with 21 members who are directly elected from single-member constituencies and 60 who are elected in teams of 4 to represent the 15 group representation constituencies (GRCs). At least one member of any GRC must be from an ethnic minority, usually Malay or Indian. The ruling People's Action Party (PAP), which has been in power since separation from Malaysia, won 61% of the 1991 vote, and holds 77 of 81 seats in parliament (Ministry of Information and the Arts 1995, p. 280). The parliamentary opposition consists of the Singapore Democratic Party (SDP), which holds 3 seats, and the Workers' Party, with 1 seat in parliament. Judicial power is vested in the Supreme Court and the Subordinate Courts. The Judiciary administers the law independently of the Executive. The Chief Justice and the other judges of the Supreme Court are appointed by the President, acting on the advice of the Prime Minister, who in turn consults the Chief Justice for appointments of judges other than the Chief Justice.

Some explanations for Singapore's rapid economic development

The reasons for Singapore's rapid economic development are manifold, and closely related. At least 4 factors are significant. These are:

1. good governance and political stability, including efficient and effective institutions and a policy of export orientation
2. favorable starting conditions in comparison to other developing economies
3. external factors such as world market developments and geopolitical constellations
4. cultural values (Menkhoff 1995)

Good governance and a high level of political stability are considered to be important factors in Singapore's success (*Sunday Times* 1995). Singapore managed to achieve political stability and a macro-economic management which can implement policy changes fast and address problems effectively; this achievement was probably facilitated by the city state's small size. Its stability enabled it to pursue an export- and growth-oriented development strategy, and as the World Bank (1993, p. 5) formulated it, Singapore "[got] the basics right." The World Bank (1993) has concluded that the success of high-performing Asian economies is due largely to private investment financed by high levels of savings–both initiated and fostered by various government policies, such as opening the economy to attract foreign direct investment, integration into the world trade, and high savings via the Central Provident Fund (CPF)–and a rapidly growing human capital (mainly via substantial investment into housing, health, and education).

Good governance is also reflected in the low level of corruption. In contrast to other developing countries, corruption is not a concern in Singapore. Civil servants receive competitive salaries, which are regularly adjusted to private sector levels, and corruption is vigorously policed. The results can be seen in international rankings of corruption: Singapore has consistently been ranked as the country with the least corruption in Asia (Kraar 1995), and as a country with less corruption than most American and European countries, including the USA, England and Germany, as shown by a joint research report by Transparency International and the University of Göttingen (Sim 1995).

McRae (1995, p. 3) suggests that the level of efficiency of an economy as a whole has to be considered when looking at its long-term international competitiveness. One important factor, of course, is the efficiency and effectiveness of public services. In recent years, Singapore's civil service has been an example to local firms in terms of service quality. In this area, Singapore seems to be at the same level as, if not at a higher level than, many developed countries. The latest knowledge and technologies in the area of quality management are applied, ranging from overall quality programs such as the Public Service 21st Century (PS 21) initiative, to micro issues such as advanced queue management systems in hospitals or the immigration office, and, increasingly, service provision via telecommunications and other electronic means such as ATM-type interfaces, the Internet or services provided via dedicated networks (e.g. Tradenet for import/export transactions). This dedication to public-service quality has been reflected by the evaluations of international bodies, which have awarded to a number of Singapore's services the number-1 position in quality in their respective industries. Examples are the Singapore Port, Changi Airport, the Mass Rapid Transport system and Singapore Airlines (which is still more than 50% state owned). In conclusion, looking at past performance, it appears that the Singapore government has been doing a good job in supporting and managing the astonishing transformation of its city state into a modern industrial economy.

A second reason for Singapore's success has been its favorable starting conditions. It has had distinct location advantages: it is centrally located on world trade routes for shipping, air transport and trade, and has a natural deep-sea port. These factors were the key reasons in the first place for the British interest in establishing Singapore as a trading post in 1819. Other important favorable starting conditions include the well-functioning public administration structures, the efficient civil service, which were left behind by the British and were developed further after independence, and the traditional free-trade status of the country, as well as its ideology of a liberal economic order and free-market orientation. Furthermore, in contrast to many other Asian developing countries, Singapore as a city state has had no socio-economic problems with rural populations pushing into the city. The immigration of workers from Malaysia, Thailand, Indonesia, Bangladesh and other countries has been effectively controlled since independence. As a city state also, it has experienced no economic conflicts of interest between regions with different levels of development. Another starting advantage has been its population of largely dynamic and achievement-oriented immigrants.

Third, external factors such as world market developments and geopolitical constellations have also contributed to Singapore's success. Singapore's outward-oriented policies with respect to trade and foreign direct investment, its tax concessions, good infrastructure and low wages, have attracted multinational corporations. These policies were pursued at a favorable time in world history, when world trade was growing rapidly. The US foreign policy and its interests in the region were further factors. The USA provided substantial support to the founding of ASEAN in 1967. Singapore, one of the founding members of this alliance against Communism, received much economic and military support from the USA.

Finally, cultural values have to be considered when explaining Singapore's economic development. It is easier for a government to be successful in encouraging savings and education, if these are already engrained in the value system of its people. Singaporeans show strong commitment to education, high savings, and evident discipline and industriousness. These factors are considered important drivers of economic development (World Bank 1993; McRae 1995, p. 70).

Singapore's position in the region

Singapore's foreign policy emphasizes the enhancing of security and prosperity through regional co-operation, of which the Association of South-East Asian Nations (ASEAN) remains a central pillar (Ministry of Information and the Arts 1995, p. 52). The government also aims to consolidate its relationship with other ASEAN countries, especially its immediate and by far larger neighboring countries, Malaysia and Indonesia (EIU 1994, pp. 7–8). In July 1995 the ASEAN Regional Forum (ARF) was inaugurated; it laid the groundwork for regional security co-operation.

Against the backdrop of an increasingly important Asia-Pacific in the global economy, a major objective of Singapore's foreign policy will continue to be the strengthening of economic relationships with those regional countries that Singapore sees as important future export markets or investment locations. The emphasis is on regional direct investments, projects and initiatives, with the underlying objective of generating economic spin-offs in Singapore (Ministry of Information and the Arts 1995, p. 106). This is hoped to be achieved by promoting Singapore as a regional gateway for mainly Western companies, by encouraging private local firms to invest in the region, and by supporting relationships between MNCs and leading local firms for regional investments.

Background information—summary and conclusions

The background information presented here is aimed at putting the recent economic developments described in the next section into a wider perspective, and also indicates future directions. Singapore's stable democracy is expected to continue, providing a favorable political environment for further economic growth. The success factors of the past will remain important drivers of growth in the future. They include:

- good governance, political stability, and a public sector that works vigorously toward efficiency and service quality
- favorable base conditions such as the country's natural deep-sea port, and its British-inherited free-trade mentality with its liberal economic attitude
- the favorable timing of its development efforts during a period of rapidly increasing world trade and, now, increasing focus on Asia
- its cultural values, which emphasize saving, education, and discipline and industriousness

Singapore's recent significantly increased efforts to use its expertise and capital to build an external wing of its own economy in the region will also impact on its economy. Low-value-added jobs will be increasingly exported into low-cost countries in the region, and more highly skilled jobs will be created in Singapore.

The next section describes key economic variables at a more microeconomic level. Trends in income, employment and inflation, as well as trade policy and future developments, are discussed.

Economic environment

Singapore's economic environment has been improving rapidly over the past 2 decades. Table 16.1 provides an overview of selected macro-economic variables such as GDP growth, GDP per capita, wage increases, unemployment rates and the like. In general, the economic environment is expected to remain favorable, with continuing increases in personal income, virtually full employment and low inflation rates. A more detailed discussion of these trends is provided in the sections below.

Table 16.1 Developments in selected macro-economic variables, 1988–1994

	1988	*1989*	*1990*	*1991*	*1992*	*1993*	*1994*
Population ('000)	2 598.5	2 647.6	2 705.1	2 762.7	2 818.2	2 873.8	2 930.2
% change over previous year	+1.7	+1.9	+2.2	+2.1	+2.0	+2.0	+2.0
GDP growth (real, %)	+11.3	+9.4	+8.8	+6.7	+6.0	+10.0	+10.1
GNP per capita (S$, current prices)[a]	15 841	18 095	20 578	21 870	24 100	26 395	28 820
Employment ('000)	1 331.6	1 394.1	1 469.2	1 524.3	1 576.2	1 592.0	1 649.3
% change over previous year	+5.2	+4.7	+5.4	+3.8	+3.4	+1.0	+3.6
Unemployment rate (%)	3.3	2.2	1.7	1.9	2.7	2.7	2.6
Private consumption (at current market prices, S$ million)[b]	23 911	26 710	29 810	32 562	35 081	39 070	42 342
Change in private consumption (real, %)	+13.5	+8.4	+7.5	+5.4	+5.0	+8.1	+4.3
Consumer price index	+1.5	+2.4	+3.4	+3.4	+2.3	+2.3	+3.1

Notes:
[a] Exchange rate as at 7 October 1995: US$1=S$1.43.
[b] Private consumption excludes residents' expenditure abroad, and includes non-residents' expenditure locally.

Sources: Singapore Statistical Highlights (1993), Department of Statistics, Singapore; *Report of the Labor Force Survey of Singapore* (1994), Research and Statistics Department, Ministry of Labor, Singapore; *Yearbook of Statistics* (1994), Department of Statistics, Singapore.

Income

There has been a significant improvement in the income of the workforce. Real wages have increased between 5.2% and 7.4% annually since 1988. These increases are also reflected in the income distribution of the workforce. In 1983, 78.5% of the workforce earned less than S$1000,[1] and this proportion fell to only 38.9% in 1994 (see Table 16.2). Mirroring this development, significantly more households earned incomes in the highest wage category of the Labor Force Survey: in 1983 only 3.6% earned S$3000 and more, whereas in 1994 13.3% achieved these income levels.

Incomes of skilled workers and professionals seem to increase faster than those of unskilled workers. In a recent study, Abeysinghe (1994) claimed that Singapore has a wider earnings gap between department managers and workers in various occupational groups than cities in all other countries examined, which included not only key Western cities, but also Asian cities such as Hong Kong, Seoul, and Taipei. Although hampered by lack of data, the author argues that the available evidence suggests this wide gap may be explained by the fact that professionals and executives in Singapore earn internationally competitive remuneration packages (Union Bank of Switzerland 1991), whereas wages of low-skill workers are held back as a result of foreign workers coming to Singapore from largely low income countries in Asia (Abeysinghe 1994). The National Trade Union Congress chief, Mr Lim Boon Heng, also emphasized in a recent interview that unskilled and cheap labor is plentiful in the region, and that, for Singapore to remain competitive, the earning capacity of low-skill workers will have to be raised through retraining and the upgrading of skills rather than salary growth over and above productivity increases (*Straits Times* 1995a).

Table 16.2 Income distribution

Gross monthly income	*1983 (%)*	*1988 (%)*	*1993 (%)*	*1994 (%)*	*Change in % points from 1983 to 1994*
Below S$1 000	78.5	68.5	45.6	38.9	-39.6
S$1 000–1 999	14.0	20.5	32.9	35.7	+21.7
S$2 000–2 999	3.9	5.6	10.3	12.1	+8.2
S$3 000 and over	3.6	5.4	11.2	13.3	+9.7
Total workforce (%)	**100**	**100**	**100**	**100**	**–**

Sources: Report of the Labor Force Survey of Singapore (1993), Research and Statistics Department, Ministry of Labor, Singapore; *Report of the Labor Force Survey of Singapore* (1994), Research and Statistics Department, Ministry of Labor, Singapore.

Employment

Singapore has one of the highest labor participation rates in the world, higher than all Asian newly industrializing countries (NICs), and higher than the three developed countries, Japan, the USA and the UK, which were also included in a study by the Ministry of Labor (*Straits Times* 1995g). In spite of its high level, the overall labor-force participation rate has continued to edge higher. It grew slightly over the last decade, by 1.1 percentage points, to 64.9% in 1994 (see Table 16.3).

Two underlying trends could be observed. First, whereas the participation rate of males was slightly lower (79.6% in 1994 vs 81.6% in 1983), the participation rate of females increased significantly, from 45.7% in 1983 to 50.9% in 1994. Second, the participation rate of the 15–19 age group decreased from over 40% in 1983 to less than 30% in 1993 (*Report of the Labour Force Survey of Singapore* 1993). This decline can be attributed mainly to an increase in the proportion of this age group that remains in the educational system.

Unemployment does not pose a problem in Singapore. The unemployment rate of 2.6% shown in Table 16.1 is somewhat inflated by the number of university, polytechnic and school leavers who entered the labor market during May and June of the year, which coincides with the annual survey period. It is estimated that the true unemployment rate for 1993 was around 2%, with a declining tendency. The median duration of unemployment was only 5.2 weeks, which indicates that most unemployed find jobs quickly (*Report on the Labor Force Survey of Singapore* 1993, p. 24).

Table 16.3 Labor-force participation

Labor-force participation rate, %	*1983*	*1988*	*1993*	*1994*	*Change in % points, 1983–1994*
Total	**63.8**	**62.9**	**64.5**	**64.9**	**+1.1**
Male	81.6	78.5	79.1	79.6	-2.0
Female	45.7	47.8	50.6	50.9	+5.2
Participation rate of married females	33.6	–	44.1	–	–

Sources: Singapore Statistical Highlights (1993), Department of Statistics, Singapore; *Report of the Labor Force Survey of Singapore* (1993), Research and Statistics Department, Ministry of Labor, Singapore; *Report of the Labor Force Survey of Singapore* (1994), Research and Statistics Department, Ministry of Labor, Singapore.

Inflation

Inflation was below 3.5% for the period 1988–1994 (see Table 16.1). Generally, it is not expected that the sustained high economic growth will lead to increased inflation. Rather, consumer price inflation is expected to drop back to the 2–2.5% range per year after being slightly higher in 1995 because of the introduction of a 3% Goods and Services Tax (GST), levied on most goods and services sold in Singapore since April 1994. The GST has failed to produce the surge in consumer prices that many had anticipated. In the long run, inflation is expected to remain low, supported by public budget surpluses and sustained high private savings rates.

Trends in trade policy

The movement of goods, services and capital in and out of the country is not hampered by trade or exchange controls. A few exceptions are restrictions on the import of goods mainly for, in the main, health, safety or security reasons. Singapore is essentially a free port, and most goods can be imported and exported freely. This situation is unlikely to change, because Singapore has derived considerable benefits from its role as the regional trading center. Rather, continued efforts are being made to make trading in Singapore more efficient and cost effective by, for example, further simplifying trade documentation and rationalizing customs operations. Import duties are mainly revenue duties on such items as alcoholic beverages, tobacco, petroleum products, motor vehicles, and a few categories of products that are manufactured in Singapore (e.g. cosmetics and furniture) (Wood 1993, p. 66).

As a result of the liberal trade policy, Singapore already enjoys a competitive market environment in most consumer markets. An opening of the markets in its neighboring ASEAN countries will therefore not have much impact on Singapore's consumers, who already enjoy the full range of goods from all over the world at competitive international market prices.

Future trends in the economic environment

It is generally expected that Singapore will show high growth rates throughout the rest of this decade (Fernandez 1995a). Deputy Prime Minister Mr Lee Hsien Loong estimates the real GDP growth potential to be around 7% up to the year 2000 (Chuang 1995), whereas the Economist Intelligence Unit (EIU 1994, p. 9) is slightly more optimistic, with real GDP growth forecasts of around 7% to 8% annually until 1999. These positive assessments are shared, even for the longer timeframe, by McRae (1995, p. 258), in his analysis of world trends in *The World in 2020*, in which he states, "Singapore's achievements are so remarkable that it is hard not to continue to be optimistic."

The growth in economic activity will mean that:

- current labor shortages will continue
- wage increases will be high
- other costs of doing business in Singapore will continue to rise (e.g. office space)
- the Singapore dollar will be strengthening against most major currencies

At the moment Singapore still seems very competitive, as many companies place a high premium on efficient air and sea transport, telecommunications and other supporting services and facilities (Richardson 1995). In fact, US-based Business Environment Risk Intelligence (Beri) ranked Singapore as the world's number-2 investment spot—after Switzerland, but before countries such as Japan, the USA and Germany (Cherian 1995).

The anticipated high rates of wage growth and other business-related costs have to be seen against a background of Singapore working rigorously toward increasing the value-added provided by its small workforce. The

Singapore Government has published a number of long-term plans and visions, of which the most important is the Strategic Economic Plan, published in 1991. It provides the master plan into which a range of other plans fit. These other plans look at more specific issues affecting economic growth and international competitiveness, such as the future role of telecommunications and information technology. The underlying objective of these plans is to maximize the value-added generated by Singapore's labor, land, and capital resources. The strategies currently being implemented to achieve this overall objective can be broadly categorized into two groups (EIU 1994).

Strategies in the first group aim to increase the value-added per unit of each resource in Singapore. They include investments in Singapore's people through programs to upgrade skills and education levels, and in its infrastructure. Other strategies in this group include attracting skilled workers and professionals to Singapore to supplement the city state's own workforce. In contrast to most other Asian countries, it will remain easy to hire expatriates and obtain employment passes for professionals and skilled workers in Singapore.

The second group of strategies aims to take advantage of resources in Asia. Singapore possesses capital and specialist management skills in some areas, and many other Asian countries are capital short, but have the land and labor resources Singapore lacks. Furthermore, they represent markets that are larger than, and will in the longer term grow faster than, Singapore's. One example of government initiatives to take advantage of these factors is the use of government-linked companies to develop flagship projects that put in place the infrastructure required by private sector companies before moving to these countries. Examples of such projects are the Batam Industrial Park in Indonesia, the industrial park being developed in the Fujian Province in China, and the technology park under development in Bangalore in India. One of the objectives of these projects is to move labor-intensive operations out of Singapore while retaining high-value-added, skill intensive operations (EIU 1994).

The upgrading of Singapore's workforce and value-added jobs, coupled with the outsourcing of low-end labor intensive work to other countries, should result in substantial increases in income for Singapore's population. The EIU expects average hourly earnings in manufacturing to increase between 7.5% and 8.5% annually until 1999.

Summary—economic environment

The economic environment is expected to remain favorable, with sustained income growth, low inflation, virtually no unemployment, and a liberal trade policy. Future trends indicate a further upgrading of the workforce, with the objective of keeping and creating high value-added activities in Singapore while exporting low-end jobs.

The sections that follow, on the demographic and cultural environments, help to paint a more complete picture of Singapore's marketing environment. Many trends mirror those in developed Western countries, such as low population growth and ageing, but others show the distinct features of a multicultural Asian society with its various ethnic groups, religions and languages.

Demographic environment

Long-term demographic developments are powerful change agents in any society. Changes in size of population and age distribution have a profound impact on any economy and its consumption patterns. Singapore seems to follow the demographic trends of developed nations. The population is growing slowly, and ageing fast. Both trends seem to be partially due to a tendency toward delayed marriage and childbearing, as well as a sharply reduced fertility rate. Increasing life expectancy contributes further to the ageing of the population. These trends are discussed in more detail below.

Population size

Singapore is a small city state, with a population of only some 3 million (including citizens and permanent residents, but excluding foreigners). Its population is growing slowly, mainly through immigration. However, the growth rate accelerated recently: from 1.7% in 1988 to 2.0% per year in 1995 (see Table 16.1). This acceleration is probably due to two factors. First, the government allows large numbers of skilled workers, professionals, and their families to migrate to Singapore. Second, the government, long concerned about a sluggish birth rate below reproduction, has in recent years put in place a number of incentives for couples to have children, and these incentives seem to have had some impact (EIU 1994, p. 19). The EIU expects that the growth rate of the resident population will remain around 1.75% annually until the year 2000.

The expatriate population may increase up to twice as fast as the resident population (EIU 1994). Singapore will continue to use such workers for both specialized skills not available in Singapore and for unskilled work, such as work on construction sites and basic assembly work in electronics factories. Foreigners accounted for more than 300 000 of the total workforce of about 1.7 million in mid-1994 (*Straits Times* 1995d).

Age distribution

Singapore is one of the fastest-ageing countries in the world (*Straits Times* 1995a). The proportion of elderly residents aged 60 years and above increased from 7.8% in 1983 to 9.7% in 1994. A significant increase was also observed for the 25–59 age group. In contrast, the proportion of residents aged 5–24 years decreased from 39% to 30% over the same period (see

Table 16.4). These trends are reflected in the increase of the median age of the population from 26.1 years in 1983 to 31.4 years in 1994 (see Table 16.5).

Some reasons for the ageing of Singapore's population are an increased life expectancy, lower fertility rates, and the trend toward delaying marriage and childbirth. Life expectancy of Singaporeans has increased dramatically, from 63 years in 1957 to 76 years by 1992, and the fertility rate dropped sharply from about 3.1 per female in 1970 to only 1.7 in 1992 (*Straits Times* 1995b). Finally, mean marriage age increased from 27.4 to 29.3 years for males between 1983 and 1993, and from 24.9 to 26.3 years for females during the same period (*Singapore Statistical Highlights* 1993). The EIU (1994) expects that the number of elderly people will increase at about twice the rate of the population as a whole. It is projected that the ageing process will continue for at least the next 40 years, peaking in the years 2020 to 2030, when between 24% and 27% of the total population will be 60 years and older (Fernandez 1995b).

Table 16.4 Age profile of the resident population

Age distribution (%)	*1980*	*1990*	*1994*	*Change in % points, 1980–1994*
0–14	27.6	23.2	23. 0	-4.6
15–59	64.9	67.7	67.3	+2.4
60+	7.5	9.1	9.7	+2.2
Total	100	100	100	–

Source: Singapore Census of Population 1990, Statistical Release 1, Demographic Characteristics (1992), Census of Population Office, Department of Statistics, Singapore; *Monthly Digest of Statistics* (1994), Department of Statistics, Singapore, November.

Table 16.5 Median age and life expectancy*

Life expectancy in years	*1983*	*1988*	*1993*	*1994*	*Change in years from 1983 to 1993*
Male	70.5	72.6	74.1	–	+3.6
Female	75.7	76.9	78.4	–	+2.7
Total	73.1	74.8	76.3	–	+3.2
Median age (to 1994)	26.1	28.8	31.0	31.4	+5.3

Note:
* For 1994, median age computed, but life expectancy figures not available.

Sources: Singapore Statistical Highlights (1993), Department of Statistics, Singapore; *Yearbook of Statistics* (1994), Department of Statistics, Singapore.

In summary, Singapore's demographic environment resembles that of older industrialized societies with a stagnating or only slowly growing, and rapidly ageing, population. The next section describes Singapore's multicultural environment.

Cultural environment

Singapore's people are largely descendants of immigrants from China, the Malay Peninsula, the Indian subcontinent, and Sri Lanka. They have gradually developed a Singaporean identity while retaining their cultural heritage (Ministry of Information and the Arts 1995, p. 29). As a result, Singapore has become a multicultural society, dominated by Chinese, with Malays and Indians as its two other main ethnic groups. Each ethnic group has its own cultural background, and its own languages and religions. The main religions remain Buddhism, Chinese traditional beliefs/Taoism, Islam, and Christianity.

Other aspects of Singapore's cultural developments resemble those of older industrialized countries in the past 40 years. In particular, education levels show rapid improvement, with more and more entrants into the workforce having university and post-secondary education. Reducing household sizes are another factor, as is an increasing workforce participation rate, which is one of the highest in the world. These cultural trends are detailed further in the sections below.

Ethnicity

The population in Singapore is predominantly Chinese; the Chinese population constitutes some 77.5% of the total population, followed by 14.2% Malays and 7.1% Indians. The racial mix has been relatively constant over the past decade (see Table 16.6).

A recent study on ethnicity and ethnic relations in Singapore shows that the various groups have learnt to be quite tolerant of one another (Chua 1995; Lai 1995). An analysis of inter-ethnic contacts during activities, such as daily marketing, eating in the hawker centers, chatting, playing in public places and other similar activities, suggests a harmonious society. This inter-racial harmony in everyday life also shows tolerance for one another's festivals and ritual practices, as well as a preference for multiracial living (although the main reason for this preference seems to be the wish to escape the excessive, even claustrophobic, closeness to one's own community). However, Lai concludes that Singaporeans have not achieved much depth of mutual cultural understanding; this was manifested in interviewee statements on wedding customs, such as: "We have our own way of doing ours, they have theirs."

Languages

The official languages of Singapore are English, Chinese (Mandarin), Malay, and Tamil. English is the language of administration, and Malay is the

Table 16.6 Ethnicity in Singapore

Resident population group	*1980 (%)*	*1990 (%)*	*1993 (%)*	*1994 (%)*
Chinese	78.3	77.7	77.5	77.5
Malay	14.4	14.1	14.2	14.2
Indian	6.3	7.1	7.1	7.1
Other	1.0	1.1	1.2	1.2
Total	100	100	100	100

Sources: Yearbook of Statistics (1990), Department of Statistics, Singapore; *Yearbook of Statistics* (1994), Department of Statistics, Singapore.

national language. Mandarin is being increasingly used among Chinese in place of Chinese dialects such as Hokkien, Teochew, Cantonese, Hakka, Hainanese, and Foochow. Most Malays speak Malay, while Indians speak mainly Tamil, but also other Indian dialects such as Telegu, Malayalam, Punjabi, Hindi, and Bengali.

Singaporeans are becoming increasingly multilingual. The proportion of people speaking only their own language or dialect has decreased sharply. More and more people speak their own dialect plus English and/or Mandarin (see Table 16.7). In particular, literacy in English (English only, and English and another language) has increased significantly, and English has become the most widely spoken language. This is the result of wider usage of English in commerce and the adoption of English as the main medium of instruction in schools and other educational institutions. Also, English is used almost exclusively for communication across ethnic groups. Greater usage of Mandarin instead of Chinese dialects reflects the success of the government's "Speak Mandarin Campaign," as well as the emphasis on Mandarin as the second language among Chinese pupils (Singapore Census of Population, Statistical Release 3 1990, p. 5).

The term "household language" refers to the language or dialect that is used most frequently among family members. In general, the use of English when speaking to family members has become more prevalent (see Table 16.8). Among Chinese, there has been a significant shift away from dialects to English and Mandarin as the predominant household languages. The number of English-speaking households increased from 11.6% in 1980 to 20.8% in 1990, while the number of those using Mandarin increased from 10.2% to 23.7%. Consequently, the use of Chinese dialects dropped from 59.5% in 1980 to 38.2% in 1990.

Religions

Religious background and ethnic group are interrelated. Many Chinese follow Buddhism and Taoism, and more are following Christianity. The vast

Table 16.7 Literacy in the official languages

% of resident population aged 10 years and older	*1980*	*1990*	*Change in % points from 1980–1990*
English only	18.8	18.2	-0.6
English and Chinese	23.5	32.2	+8.7
English and Malay	11.5	11.6	+0.1
English and Tamil	2.1	2.3	+0.2
English and other	0.1	1.2	+1.1
English total	**56.0**	**65.5**	**+9.5**
Chinese only	36.1	29.5	-6.6
English and Chinese	23.5	32.2	+8.7
Chinese total	**59.6**	**61.7**	**+2.1**
Malay only	5.1	3.7	-1.4
English and Malay	11.5	11.6	+0.1
Malay total	**16.6**	**15.3**	**-1.3**
Tamil only	1.2	1.0	-0.2
English and Tamil	2.1	2.3	+0.2
Tamil total	**3.3**	**3.3**	**0.0**

Source: Singapore Census of Population 1990, Statistical Release 3, Literacy, Languages Spoken and Education (1993), Census of Population Office, Department of Statistics, Singapore.

Table 16.8 Household languages spoken

% of resident households	*1980*	*1990*	*Change in % points from 1980–1990*
English	11.6	20.8	+9.2
Mandarin	10.2	23.7	+13.5
Chinese dialects	59.5	38.2	-21.3
Malay	13.9	13.6	-0.3
Tamil	3.1	3.0	-0.1
Other	1.7	0.7	-1.0
Total	100	100	–

Source: Singapore Census of Population 1990, Statistical Release 3, Literacy, Languages Spoken and Education (1993), Census of Population Office, Department of Statistics, Singapore.

majority of the Malays in Singapore are Muslims, and the Indians are predominantly Hindus, but also Buddhists and Muslims. With the Chinese comprising 77.5% of the resident population, Buddhism and Chinese traditional beliefs/Taoism are the predominant religions in Singapore, followed by Islam and Christianity (see Table 16.9).

Traditional beliefs/Taoism are rapidly losing "share." Kau and Young (1991) conducted a large-scale survey on the values and lifestyles of Singaporeans. They observed that the major shifts from parents' religions to those of children have been in favor of Christianity and free thought (no religion), mainly at the expense of Buddhism and Taoism (see Table 16.10). A monograph by Kuo and Tong (1991), based on 1990 census data, concludes that better educated Singaporeans, in particular Chinese, tend to abandon their traditional beliefs and become Christians or non-religionists (see Table 16.11). Education seems to be a contributing factor to the abandonment of the traditional beliefs/Taoism, which have commonly been perceived as superstitious and antiquated (*Straits Times* 1995c).

Table 16.9 Religion

% of resident population aged 10 years and over	*1980*	*1990*	*Change in % points from 1980–1990*
Buddhism	26.7	31.1	+4.4
Chinese traditional beliefs/Taoism	30.0	22.4	-7.6
Islam	16.2	15.4	-0.8
Christianity	9.9	12.5	+2.6
Hinduism	3.6	3.7	+0.1
Other religions	0.5	0.6	+0.1
No religion/free thought	13.1	14.3	+1.2
Total	100	100	–

Source: Singapore Census of Population 1990, Statistical Release 6, Religion, Childcare and Leisure Activities (1994), Census of Population Office, Department of Statistics, Singapore.

Education

Current education levels in Singapore are still far behind those in developed countries. Only 3.4% of the population aged 25 years and above have tertiary education (Fernandez 1995b). This is in contrast to figures for the USA and Japan—about one-third of the population has tertiary education in these countries; the figure for Germany was 22% in 1995. Nevertheless, education levels in Singapore are improving fast. For example, the *Report on the Labor Force Survey of Singapore* (1993, p. 17) showed that, with new entrants into the work force being better educated, and with the continual upgrading of the workforce, the overall education level of the workforce continues to improve. The proportion of the workforce with primary education or less decreased 11.3 percentage points, from 54.5% in 1983 to 43.2% in 1994, whereas the proportion of the workforce with university degrees increased more than twofold from 4.5% to 9.8% (see Table 16.12).

Table 16.10 Shifts of religion from parents to children

Parents' religion	*Shifts to:* Buddhism (%)	*Taoism (%)*	*Islam (%)*	*Hinduism (%)*	*Christianity (%)*	*Free thought (%)*
Buddhism	52.5	8.0	0.0	0.0	0.6	4.2
Taoism	0.3	35.5	0.0	0.0	0.0	1.8
Islam	0.3	0.3	99.1	0.0	0.6	0.0
Hinduism	0.1	0.3	0.0	84.4	0.0	0.0
Christianity	15.2	21.5	0.0	5.2	89.9	31.9
Free-thought	30.4	32.6	0.3	3.1	4.7	60.8
Others	1.2	1.8	0.6	7.3	4.2	1.3
Total	**100**	**100**	**100**	**100**	**100**	**100**

Source: Ah Keng Kau & Charles Yang (1991), *Values and Lifestyles of Singaporeans,* Singapore University Press, National University of Singapore, Singapore.

Table 16.11 Religion of non-student population aged 10 years+

Religion	*Below primary level (%)*	*Primary level (%)*	*Secondary level (%)*	*Upper secondary & polytechnic level (%)*	*University level (%)*	*Total (%)*
Buddhism	34.7	33.0	30.5	25.0	15.1	31.3
Taoism	33.5	23.7	14.6	12.6	7.4	22.8
Islam	15.5	20.3	16.0	7.2	2.6	15.6
No religion	7.2	10.5	17.6	25.3	31.1	13.6
Christianity	5.3	7.5	16.8	26.1	39.4	12.3
Hinduism	3.4	4.6	3.8	3.1	3.5	3.8
Other religions	0.4	0.5	0.7	0.7	0.9	0.6
Total, %	**100**	**100**	**100**	**100**	**100**	**100**
Total, '000	**599.1**	**566.1**	**471.4**	**188.4**	**84.9**	**1 910.0**

Source: Eddie C.Y. Kuo and Chee Kiong Tong (1991), *Religion in Singapore,* Singapore National Printers, Singapore; *Straits Times* (1995), "Christianity here has Strong 'Social, Political Influence'", April 26, p. 25.

Households

Households in Singapore are getting smaller. The average number of persons per household declined from 4.9 in 1980 to 4.2 in 1990. This is due to the decline in the number of children per family, and the desire of young couples to set up homes of their own rather than stay with their parents (*Singapore Census of Population 1990, Statistical Release 2* 1992, p. 3).

The participation rate of females in the labor force increased significantly from 45.7% in 1983 to 50.6% in 1993 (see Table 16.3). This is also reflected

Table 16.12 Education

Highest education level attained, % of labor force aged 15+	*1983*	*1993*	*1994*	*Change in % points from 1983–1994*
Lower primary and less	23.2	15.4	15.7	-7.5
Primary	31.3	29.2	27.5	-3.8
Secondary	30.4	29.9	30.2	-0.2
Post-secondary/diploma	10.6	16.4	16.8	+6.2
Tertiary	4.5	9.1	9.8	+5.3
Total	100	100	100	–
Literacy rate (% of population 10 years+)	85.5	91.6	–	–

Sources: Yearbook of Statistics (1993), Department of Statistics, Singapore; *Report of the Labor Force Survey of Singapore* (1993), Research and Statistics Department, Ministry of Labor, Singapore; *Report of the Labor Force Survey of Singapore* (1994), Research and Statistics Department, Ministry of Labor, Singapore; *Singapore Statistical Highlights* (1993), Department of Statistics, Singapore.

in a trend toward double-income households. The participation rate of married females rose from 33.6% in 1983 to 44.1% in 1993 (see Table 16.3). This increase can be attributed, in part, to the better education of younger married females (*Report on the Labor Force Survey of Singapore* 1993, p. 16). Furthermore, the availability of parents, other relatives, a large number of foreign maids and a wide variety of childcare centers allows Singaporean women to continue working after having children (Kau, Yeong & Richmond 1993, p. 26).

Table 16.13 Private households, by size

Household size (persons)	*1980 (%)*	*1990 (%)*	*Change in % points from 1980–1990*
1	5.7	5.2	-0.5
2–3	23.8	28.5	+4.7
4–5	36.7	45.6	+8.9
6+	33.8	20.7	-13.1
Total	100	100	–
Average household size	4.9	4.2	-0.7

Source: Singapore Census of Population 1990, Statistical Release 2, Household and Housing (1990), Census of Population Office, Department of Statistics, Singapore.

Other aspects of Singapore's cultural environment

There are other aspects of Singapore's cultural background that are less well documented in statistical data, but still have significant impact on values systems, consumer behavior, and marketing management. Some of these features include the lifestyle of Singaporeans in a high-density city state with no hinterland. This means that nearly all of the population (over 95%) lives in high-rises, and leisure activities are shaped by the urban environment and the surrounding sea.

Tropical weather is another aspect of life in Singapore; it discourages strenuous outdoor activities but allows sitting outside at one of the many hawker centers all year round. The confluence of rich and diverse cultural influences has endowed Singaporeans with both a traditional and a contemporary outlook, which is reflected in many aspects of local life, including the wide variety of food available at almost every street corner, the architectural styles ranging from traditional Chinese to hypermodern skyscrapers, and the arts and culture scene, encompassing both Singapore's Asian heritage and Western plays and music.

We present some hints at the diversity of Singapore's cultural environment, to show some of the features of life in this city state. Where considered important, these features are elaborated in the following sections on consumer behavior and marketing.

Cultural environment–summary and conclusions

This section discussed the cultural environment of Singapore, which is characterized by its population of descendants of immigrants mainly from Asia. Chinese constitute the main ethnic group, with Malays and Indians as its two other important groups. Singapore has managed to create a social environment of racial harmony and mutual acceptance. The various groups have kept their cultural heritage, which includes their language and dialects, religions and customs. The main languages spoken are Mandarin and various Chinese dialects by the Chinese, Malay by the Malays, Tamil and other Indian dialects by the Indians, and English across all ethnic groups. The extent of cultural identity by the various groups is reflected in their use of their own languages and dialects at home, whereby only 21% use English as their household language. Nevertheless, Singaporeans are becoming increasingly multilingual, with an increasing proportion of people speaking English (66%), the language of administration and main medium of instruction in educational institutions, and an increasing number of Chinese speaking Mandarin (62% of the total population) on top of their own dialects. Religious background is also closely related to ethnic group, with many Chinese following Buddhism and Taoism, and recently Christianity, the vast majority of Malays practicing Islam, and Indians mainly following Hinduism.

Other developments in the cultural environment resemble those of older industrialized countries over the past 40 years. In particular, education levels show rapid improvement with more and more entrants into the work force having tertiary education (although the proportion of the total population with tertiary education is still far below those of older developed countries); household sizes are getting smaller, and the workforce participation rate has been edging up to one of the highest in the world.

Some indication has been given of everyday life in a high-density city state on a tropical island. The next section examines macro-economic trends in the consumption behavior of Singaporeans.

Consumer behavior

Singapore has become an increasingly affluent society. This has been reflected in the high real growth rates of private consumption, as well as the increasing share of higher level goods such as recreational, educational, and health services, and a declining share of total consumption by basic goods such as food and beverages. This increasing affluence is also reflected in recent consumer value and lifestyle studies, which show that Singaporeans have become more brand- and status-conscious, more discerning and more health-conscious consumers. Increases in consumer spending and the trends observed in values and lifestyles are expected to continue for the coming years, and are discussed in more detail in the sections below. Relative to its population, Singapore welcomes a large number of visitors, many with substantial spending power. Therefore, key data on Singapore's visitors are also presented.

Consumption

Private consumption has been growing rapidly in real terms. Between 1988 and 1994, the annual increase was between 4.3% and 13.5% (see Table 16.1). It is expected that these high growth rates in consumption will continue. The EIU expects private consumption expenditure to grow at an average annual rate of nearly 7% until the year 2000. The main driving force is likely to be the continuing rapidly rising per-capita income (EIU 1994, p. 13), as discussed in the section on the economic environment.

Tangible evidence of increasing wealth are household penetration rates of consumer durables, which have increased significantly during the years 1983 to 1992. The most noticeable increase has been in the proportion of households with washing machines, air conditioners and VCRs sold (see Table 16.14). For example, the penetration rate for washing machines increased from 46.8% in 1983 to 80.5% in 1992.

Increasing affluence is also reflected in changing consumption patterns. The share of total consumption of basic goods such as food and beverages, furniture and household equipment, and clothing and footwear, has been declining from 1983 to 1994. For example, food and beverages had a share of 25.1% of total consumption in 1983, and this figure fell to 16.0% by 1994 (see Table 16.15). In contrast, services such as transport and communications, recreation and education, rent and utilities, and medical services showed slight increases in their share of total private consumption. As Singapore's real wages are set to keep rising, these trends can be expected to continue, and private consumption growth will tend to be driven by spending on services rather than on goods.

The household penetration of automobiles is low in comparison with countries of similar GDP per head. This is due to an excellent public transport infrastructure, and probably more so to the fact that Singapore has the world's heaviest rate of taxation on automobile ownership (a customs duty of 42% plus a so-called Additional Registration Fee of 150% on the value of the car) and on automobile usage (relatively high road and gasoline taxes,

Table 16.14 Possession of consumer durables, 1983–1992

% of households with consumer durable	*1983*	*1988*	*1992*
Refrigerator	96.1	98.3	97.8
Washing machine	46.8	73.5	80.5
Air conditioner	11.2	19.4	35.3
TV set	95.2	97.9	97.5
VCR	27.7	71.0	75.1
Piano/organ	9.8	11.4	11.8
PC	N/A	11.2	20.2
Automobile	25.5	29.8	31.1

Source: Singapore Statistical Highlights (1993), Department of Statistics, Singapore.

Table 16.15 Consumer expenditure in Singapore as % of total

Private consumption item	*1983 (%)*	*1988 (%)*	*1993 (%)*	*1994 (%)*
Food & beverages	25.1	21.9	17.1	16.0
Transport & communications	14.0	13.4	14.9	14.7
Recreation & education	12.3	14.2	14.0	14.6
Rent & utilities	8.9	10.7	13.7	14.2
Furniture & household equipment	8.8	8.9	8.4	8.0
Clothing & footwear	8.6	7.6	6.5	6.1
Medical services	2.9	4.2	4.5	4.6
Other goods & services	19.5	19.0	20.9	21.6
Total	**100**	**100**	**100**	**100**
Consumer expenditure at current prices (S$)	19 640	27 923	45 411	48 829

Note:
Consumer expenditure excludes residents' expenditure abroad, and includes non-residents' expenditure locally (e.g. spending by tourists).

Sources: Yearbook of Statistics (1993), Department of Statistics, Singapore; *Yearbook of Statistics* (1994), Department of Statistics, Singapore.

extra fees of S$3 per day to enter the Central Business District, and high parking fees throughout the city). Furthermore, to avoid the heavy costs of traffic jams to the economy as a whole, as can be observed in many other cities in the region, the Singapore government controls the automobile population via a license system. Every month a fixed number of licenses for new automobile registrations are released. Prospective automobile owners then have to bid for such a license, called Certificate of Entitlement, in a monthly auction before being able to purchase an automobile. Prices for these licenses vary by engine size, and in February 1995 ranged from around S$22 000 for automobiles with engines of 1000 cc and less to S$50 000 for automobiles with engines of 2001 cc and more. This means that a Honda Accord with a 2000-cc engine had an on-the-road price of some S$160 000 in March 1995. The government policy of encouraging the use of public transport and discouraging the use of private cars is unlikely to change in the foreseeable future.

Unlike in many Western industrialized countries in Singapore, private consumption does not seem to be driven much by credit availability and affordability. For example, a recent survey found that more than 90% of credit-card holders pay on or before the due date, and that more than 70% said that, rather than borrow, they would save until they had enough money to buy what they desired (SRS Adex 1994). On the whole, Singaporeans can be described as financially sober, if not conservative. This is further supported by the current government's ideological promotion of so-called Asian values as social ethos, with frugality being promoted as one of the highest virtues. In concert with this ideological promotion, local newspapers frequently report as bad examples instances of "excesses" of consumption, such as the propensity of a small group of young people to buy branded goods on credit; the newspapers also carry commentaries on the moral issues related to living beyond one's means (Chua 1994).

Expectations in terms of consumer values and lifestyles

Kau, Yeong and Richmond (1993) conducted a Delphi study with 150 participants. The authors concluded that future Singaporeans will be characterized by the traits described below.

Increasing individualism

It is felt that increasing affluence, and living in a highly urbanized society, will make consumers want to differentiate themselves from society in general.

Remaining very status conscious and materialistic

This is reflected in the infamous "5 Cs," said to be aspired to by all young professionals: career, cash, credit card (the issue of credit cards is strictly regulated, and cards are issued only to individuals with an annual income of S$30 000 or more—an amount difficult to achieve for many non-university graduates), condominium (instead of the state subsidized HDB flats in which more than 90% of the population lives), and a car (see the previous section on automobile-population regulation).

More brand consciousness

Respondents believed that future consumers will be increasingly concerned with buying well-known brands across a wide range of product categories, from cosmetics and food to jewelry and cookware. It appears that brands associated with high income, status, and sophistication will show the highest growth.

More discerning consumers

For example, consumers are expected to value more and more, and be more and more willing to pay for, higher quality products. They are also expected to want more and more detailed and accurate product information (e.g. information on materials used in clothes, expiry dates and ingredients in food), and their appreciation of art and culture is expected to increase.

More health-conscious consumers

As the population ages and affluence grows, consumers are expected to pay more attention to their health. For example, this will show in an increased demand for fitness and health clubs, as well as for health food with lower cholesterol, fat, salt and sugar content, but more vitamins, fiber, and natural ingredients.

More emphasis on leisure activities

Pastimes such as traveling, watersports, golfing and cultural activities will become increasingly important.

More demands on time

The recent increase in the labor participation rate of women will lead to more time pressure, particularly for working women. However, time pressure will not reach levels such as those in the USA, as Singaporeans frequently live within an extended family, and maids and other household helpers are readily available.

Tourism

Singapore has more than 2 visitors a year for every resident. Many visitors have come to Singapore to shop, and have consumed a variety of recreational and business services; some key data on trends are shown in Table 16.16. The number of visitors increased steadily from 2.9 million in 1983 to 6.9 million in 1994. The majority of visitors (71.3%) came from Asia, with ASEAN, Japan, and

Taiwan being the most important markets. The share of Asian visitors increased significantly from 60.1% in 1983 to 71.3% in 1994, and the European share fell from 20.6% to 14.6% in the same timeframe; the shares of Oceanian and US visitors declined to 6.3% and 5.0% respectively. These data suggest a shift for businesses, from targeting tourists to offering more goods and services that meet the tastes and preferences of Asian tourists rather than Westerners. The majority of visitors came for holidays (58.3%), and only 13.5% came exclusively for business purposes. The average length of a stay was relatively short—3.6 days—which indicates the stop-over character of most visits. The mean age of visitors was 37.9 years (Singapore Tourist Promotion Board 1994).

Despite increasing numbers of visitors, the importance of tourist spending has been declining for Singaporean retailers. The annual Survey of Overseas Visitors to Singapore conducted by the Tourist Promotion Board shows that in 1994 visitors to Singapore spent 50% of their total expenses of around S$5.15 billion on shopping, followed by accommodation, and food and beverages. This compares to a higher share of shopping (56%), of a higher total expenditure (S$5.49 billion) in 1993 (*Straits Times* 1995f). Singapore is no longer the shopping paradise it once was for Asian tourists, mainly because of a strengthening Singapore dollar. Taiwanese tourists complain that Singapore is just as expensive as Taipei, and Japanese save only about 20% to 25% in comparison to prices back home, rather than around 50% as in the past. At Isetan, one of Singapore's upmarket departmental stores, tourist expenditure is falling to about 15% of total sales, from 18% in 1994 and 25% in 1991 (Mark 1995). It seems that retailers will have to focus more and more on local business, and less and less on tourist dollars.

Consumer behavior—summary

Macro-economic trends of increasing prosperity are reflected in the consumption behavior of Singaporeans. Overall consumption has been increasing fast, with a declining share of basic goods such as food and clothing, and increasing shares of higher level goods and services such as recreational, educational and health services, as well as transport and communications. Increasing affluence is also reflected in changing consumer values and lifestyles, which show that Singaporeans have become more brand and status conscious, more discerning, quality oriented and health conscious. Although the number of tourists has been increasing, their relative importance in terms of retail sales has been declining, partially due to a lower price differential to their home countries. It seems that tourist shopping is becoming less and less important in Singapore.

The next section examines trends in the marketing mix, many of which are a reflection of trends discussed in previous sections on the economic, demographic and cultural environments, as well as the trends in consumer behavior presented in this section.

Table 16.16 Tourism, 1983–1994

	1983	*1988*	*1993*	*1994*
Visitor arrivals, '000	2 853.6	4 186.1	6 425.8	6 899.0
Growth in % over previous year	–	+13.8	+7.3	+7.4
Share of arrivals by continent:				
Asia	60.1	57.4	64.4	71.3
Europe	20.6	24.3	20.5	14.7
America	8.5	7.4	6.6	6.2
Oceania	10.0	9.2	6.3	6.3
Other	0.9	1.7	2.1	1.5
Total	**100**	**100**	**100**	**100**
Share of arrivals by key countries:				
ASEAN	32.5	25.0	27.8	31.0
Japan	13.4	16.7	15.9	16.1
UK	10.0	9.8	8.6	4.4
Taiwan	2.4	3.7	6.7	7.4
Australia	8.0	7.3	5.2	5.0
USA	6.9	5.8	5.1	5.0
Other	26.8	31.7	30.7	31.1
Total	**100**	**100**	**100**	**100**
Purpose of visit:				
Holiday only	62.8	66.6	58.4	58.3
Business only	13.2	12.7	13.4	13.5
Business and holiday	5.6	4.5	3.2	3.1
In transit	9.8	8.4	9.7	9.1
Other	8.5	7.8	15.3	16.0
Total	**100**	**100**	**100**	**100**

Note:
The data exclude arrivals of Malaysians by land.

Sources: *Yearbook of Statistics* (1993), Department of Statistics, Singapore; *Yearbook of Statistics* (1994), Department of Statistics, Singapore; Singapore Tourist Promotion Board (1994), "Survey of Overseas Visitors in Singapore", Market Planning Department, Singapore Tourist Promotion Board, Singapore.

Changes in the macromarketing mix

This section examines past and anticipated changes in the macromarketing mix, based on statistical data and anecdotal evidence. Many of the trends identified are either a direct reflection of the macro-economic environment discussed in previous sections, or are shaped by this environment. Product and service trends emphasize the upmarket shift identified in previous sections, reflecting the increase in the sophistication and the educational levels of Singaporeans, as well as the increase in their incomes. Pricing strategies go hand in hand with the higher quality of goods and services on offer.

Distribution is becoming more competitive, with retail space increases far outpacing sales increases, the continuing concentration of retail outlets in supermarket and other retail store chains, and discount stores gaining share. The importance of advertising in the marketing mix is set to increase further. With increasing competitiveness and sales volume, market research will increase in importance and sophistication. These trends are presented below in more detail.

Products and services

The trends identified in the previous sections have a profound impact on the type of products and services gaining a share in, and being launched into, the Singapore market. In particular, rising incomes and increasing status and brand consciousness have led to a proliferation of branded goods, which seem to have become prevalent in every aspect of people's lives. Rising educational standards have brought with them more discerning and informed consumers, who ask for attributes such as high quality and healthiness.

These trends are expected to continue, with increasing market shares being predicted for branded goods, in particular brands that are associated with high income, sophistication and status (Kau et al. 1993). One example showing this trend is the gourmet-food industry, which has had growth rates of between 30% and 40% a year in the past few years (*Asian Retailer* 1994b).

Health aspects of products will continue to receive greater consumer attention. In the past, health food showed relatively low growth rates, of around 10% annually. Taste seems to be the main hindering factor, as a perception exists among consumers that health food does not taste as good as less healthy food; another view is that health food is expensive. However, a recent survey suggests that this is going to change, and foods with reduced sugar, salt, fat, and cholesterol content and/or increased natural-food and vitamin content are expected to increase their market share (Kau et al. 1993). For example, hawker-center stalls have started displaying stickers with slogans such as "No monosodium glutamate (MSG)," "No added meat fat" (which is being replaced by vegetable oils) and "Reduced sugar." This program has been promoted by the Ministry of Health, and has been shown to be popular with hawkers and customers. Other examples are recent successful product launches focusing on health aspects, such as Naturel, a margarine that is high in mono-unsaturates rather than the less healthy polyunsaturates. The product has been extremely successful with consumers, and was given an "Award of Excellence" by the Ministry of Trade and Industry in 1992 (*Advoice* 1994). Also, the health-supplement (e.g. vitamins) and diet-food segments have already shown long-term growth rates of about 20% per annum. The market for health supplements in Singapore was worth some S$4 million in 1982, and about S$30 million in 1994 (*Asian Retailer* 1995a). These trends are expected to accelerate further.

Although environmental consciousness is not yet strong in Singapore, it is expected to become, slowly, a more important purchase factor. "Green" consumers have been studied by Shamdasani, Ong and Richmond (1993), who have concluded that if both "green" and "non-green" consumers perceive a lack of promotion of environmentally friendly products, this deters their adoption. The promotion of such products includes the dissemination of information, a distinctive labeling scheme and special displays. However, with the increasing environmental awareness of Singaporeans, and the immediate and growing concern of the government about environmental issues translating into pro-environmental legislation, the market for environmentally friendly products is expected to grow from its existing small base. The government introduced the Green Labeling System in 1992, which sets specific guidelines for the manufacture, distribution, usage, and disposal of products. Other governmental efforts, such as an annually organized campaign called the "Clean and Green Week," and the efforts of the Waste Minimization Department and the Singapore Retailers Association, are expected to increase consumer awareness of "green" issues in the years to come (*Asian Retailer* 1994d; 1995b). Manufacturers of environmentally safe products and packaging are expected to gain from this shift in consumer values.

Religious and ethnic background idiosyncrasies often have to be considered when designing and marketing new products. For example, non-halal food is not acceptable to the Muslim community; this has led gourmet shops to offer halal fruit cakes which have no brandy. Kau and Yang (1991) conducted a lifestyle analysis with 2126 respondents, and found significant differences between the ethnic and religious backgrounds on nearly all aspects of consumer behavior and the marketing mix, including need perceptions, leisure activities, media exposure, and shopping-center and department-store patronage. It is not expected that cultural and religious differences will assimilate much in the near future; these will therefore remain a key consideration in any marketing mix.

Consumer reactions to price and promotions

Low- income households and affluent households will co-exist for the foreseeable future in Singapore. This means we will continue to see highly priced high-quality and expressive products (e.g. very expensive watches and designer clothes) for high-income households alongside low-priced, low-quality products for low-income households. However, it can be expected that the high-quality segment will grow significantly, whereas the low-quality segment may actually see a decline, as a result of the decreasing number of low-income households. Education and skill upgrading will improve the earning power of many currently low-income households.

However, even for high-quality goods, such as gourmet food, Singaporeans are considered price conscious. Royal Gourmet's marketing manager Shirley Lim said in an interview that Singaporeans are completely governed by price considerations—a price difference of 50 cents between two products can affect buying decisions even on expensive items such as smoked salmon (*Asian Retailer* 1994b).

This perception of consumer-price consciousness by the Singapore marketing community has led to a large number of sales (after Christmas and Chinese New Year, The Great Sale in August, and numerous store-wide sales) and promotional activities (ranging from lucky draws and patronage rewards to tie-in promotions). Whether this perception of extreme price consciousness is correct is somewhat questionable. A recent study comparing Singaporean with American shoppers showed that Singaporeans were less sensitive to price-related costs and more sensitive to certain non-price related costs (e.g. time, effort and risk) than Americans (Funkhouser, Parker & Chatterjee 1994). Although the samples are not representative for the two countries (a convenience sample of 315 was used of undergraduate MBA students and their family members and friends), it clearly contradicts the general perception of Singapore's practitioners. There are grounds to suggest that, in the future, the focus should be shifted from sales and promotions to reducing non-monetary costs.

Distribution

The Singapore retail market is intensely competitive, as a result of only marginal revenue growth in 1994, and slow growth in 1995, combined with rapidly expanding shopping space. The low sales growth appeared to be due to increasing consumer spending on housing, automobiles, travel, education and health services rather than other goods, as the decline in tourist shopping (*SES Journal* 1995; *Straits Times* 1995e).

The amount of store space in Singapore is small—only 0.57 m^2 per person. Hong Kong, a city state with similar retail conditions to Singapore's, has more than twice this amount (1.28 m^2), and the USA has nearly 4 times Singapore's retail space per capita (2.01 m^2) (Yap 1994). Singapore's retail space shows high growth, and, according to the Monetary Authority of Singapore, will increase by almost 40% from the end of 1994 to the end of 1998 (*Straits Times* 1995e).

The Singapore retail scene is experiencing a concentration of market share, with larger supermarket and retail store chains growing at the expense of smaller independent shops. For example, the number of independent provision stores shrank by 50% from some 4000 stores in 1985 to only 2000 stores in 1994 (Yap 1994). Many of these are small independent shops with low efficiency and productivity, and offer a rather similar range of goods. In an interview in early 1995, the retail research director of SRS, Mr Martin

Talacko, said that he expected another 25% of these remaining shops to close down within the next 5 years. In contrast, the number of supermarkets, most of which belong to chains, increased sharply: there were 84 in 1985, 102 in 1990, and 144 in 1995 (see Table 16.17). Apart from supermarkets, there is also an increasing number of department stores and convenience stores (e.g. 7-Eleven, Shell Select and Esso Tigermarts) (Survey Research Singapore 1995).

Table 16.17 Trends in retail-outlet type

Outlet type	*End 1990*	*End 1993*	*Jan 1995*	*Change in no. of outlets (1990–1995)*	*Change in % points (1990–1995)*
Major supermarket	102	129	144	42	+41.1
Major mini-market	504	583	632	128	+25.4
Gas (petrol) station	171	236	196	25	+14.6
General mixed goods	409	458	458	49	+12.0
Western pharmacy, Chinese medical hall	562	613	622	60	+10.7
Provision shop	2 432	1 986	1 986	–446	–18.3

Sources: SRS Adex (1995), *Annual study, Singapore*, Survey Research Singapore, Singapore; Survey Research Singapore (1995), "Singapore Retail Scene", Survey Research Singapore, Singapore.

It is expected that the more competitive environment, as well as the availability of more retail space, will eventually lead to shops with a sharper merchandising mix, including an increasing number of specialty shops (Yap 1995). It is anticipated that more specialized shops such as maid, travel, and real-estate agencies, as well as sports, diving and golf shops, gymnasiums and learning centers for children and adults, will show good growth potential in the future (Yap 1995).

Large discount stores, such as Kmart and Toys "R" Us, selling branded goods, have entered the Singapore market only recently, and seem to be successful (*Asian Retailer* 1994c). For two reasons, however, it is anticipated that they will not capture as high a market share as in the USA (Kau et al. 1993). First, daily need items, particularly food, are currently purchased at convenient locations daily or at least several times a week. This practice is not expected to change markedly in the near future, particularly as only 1 in 3 households owns a car. Second, due to a generally perceived lack of leisure activities in this small city state, shopping is an important leisure activity conducted mainly downtown in dominant, classy department stores such as Yaohan and Takashimaya. Discount stores do not compete well in providing those shopping experiences (Kau et al. 1993).

Due to low motor-vehicle ownership and increasing demand for convenient locations, decentralization of shopping may be observed. Large shopping complexes offering pleasant shopping environments will move closer to their customers. The government is pursuing a policy of decentralization to avoid overload of the central area. Regional centers are being developed in the east, north, north-west and west of the island; each will be a self contained mini-downtown which provides similar-quality facilities to those available in the central area. From 1995 to early 1996 alone, 7 large suburban shopping centers were completed, with a total floor space of some 0.5 million m^2. These 7 centers account for about 35% of all new retail space, and more retailers are expected to move to the suburbs (*Asian Retailer* 1994f).

Convenience is often one of the key factors motivating consumers to shop at home via telephone, computer and catalogue. However, these new forms of shopping have been slower to catch on in Singapore than initially expected. This may be attributable to the fact that shopping in Singapore is already relatively convenient, with competitively priced and comprehensively stocked retail shops in most housing estates, and given the small size of the island as well as an excellent public transport system. Working women in Singapore do not seem to be as pressed for time as those in other (Western) countries, and shopping as a recreational activity is not easily replaced by direct marketing channels (Kau et al. 1993). A recent study confirms the notion that convenience is a less important motivator for the adoption of direct channels in Singapore's concentrated retail environment, with no significant difference being found in convenience orientation between in-home and non-in-home shoppers (Shamdasani & Ong 1995). Nevertheless, in-home shopping is expected to show moderate growth from a low base, driven by new technology, new market entrants and improved marketing strategies. The penetration of Teleview (videotex) and the Internet are expected to grow rapidly, and more and more retailers are offering their products via these electronic shopping facilities. Foreign retailers with substantial direct marketing experience have entered the market (e.g. Takashimaya, Japan's largest mail-order retailer), and can be expected to upgrade the marketing to home shoppers (Shamdasani & Ong 1995).

In summary, Singapore's retail environment will become increasingly competitive. The rapid increase in retail space will be combined with only moderate sales-volume growth; there will be continuing concentration of the marketplace, with chain stores and supermarkets gaining share. The increased competition and increasing demand for higher-end and more specialized goods will induce smaller stores and chains to move toward more distinctive, deeper merchandise mixes. Large discount stores will be successful, but probably will not obtain shares as high as those in the USA. Low automobile ownership and demand for convenience will see a decentralization of shopping from downtown areas to the densely populated housing estates. In-house shopping via the telephone, Internet and the like is expected to grow slowly, from its present low level.

Advertising

Advertising has become a more important variable in the marketing mix. Advertising spending increased from S$407.5 million, or 1.7% of total consumption expenditure, in 1988, to S$976.3 million, or 2.3%, in 1994 (see tables 16.1 and 16.18). This trend is set to continue.

No major shifts in the usage of media could be observed from 1990 to 1994. The largest increase in the share of total advertising expenditure was achieved by television, which increased its share slightly, from 32.4% in 1988 to 34.8% in 1994. The only other media that increased their shares were radio and cinema. In the medium term, TV may further increase its role, as a result of the introduction of cable TV, and an increase in the number of channels available. Even satellite TV may become available in the long-term future. At the moment, the reception of satellite TV, such as programs broadcast from Asia Sat, is restricted, and is not available to the general public.

The main languages for advertising on TV and in newspapers are English and Mandarin. The role of English seems to be increasing slightly, at the expense of Mandarin. For instance, the share by English language newspapers of total circulation increased from 45.8% in 1988 to 50.0% in 1994, whereas the share of Chinese-language newspapers slipped from 47.7% to 43.8% during the same period. Another trend seems to be toward comparative advertising, which is allowed, although this is subject to strict codes of practices detailed in the Singapore Code of Advertising Practice (Lim 1994).

Advertisers will need to continue incorporating an awareness of cultural sensitivities in the content of their advertisements. These sensitivities include a general sense of modesty about using sexual stimuli, a wide variety of superstitious beliefs such as the belief in lucky and unlucky numbers, and the prohibition of the consumption of alcoholic beverages by Muslims. Although some of these sensitivities (e.g. sexual explicitness in advertisements) seem to be reducing in intensity, others are still taboo, such as showing alcoholic beverages when targeting Muslims, or showing dogs (which are considered impure) to Malays. It is of no surprise that the mostly foreign advertising agencies (only 1 of the top 10 agencies is a local firm) employ Singaporeans who specialize in advertisements with a local flavor and can immediately assess the repercussions of creative ideas in Singapore's cultural context (Saini 1994).

Market research

Market research services are readily available in Singapore. They are offered by international heavyweights such as AC Nielsen and Information

Table 16.18 Share of advertising expenditure, by media

Medium	*1988*	*1993*	*1994*	*Change in % points, 1988–1994*
Newspapers	50.3	52.6	49.8	-0.8
TV	32.4	31.6	34.8	+2.4
Periodicals	8.3	7.3	6.3	-2.0
Radio	3.5	4.3	5.1	+1.6
Posters	2.1	1.5	1.5	-0.6
Back of bus/top of taxi	2.2	1.6	1.4	-0.8
Movies	0.6	0.8	0.8	+0.2
Rediffusion (independent network)	0.5	0.3	0.3	-0.2
Total	100	100	100	–
Value, S$ million	407.5	824.4	976.3	–
% change over previous year	–	+11.4	+18.4	–

Sources: SRS Adex (1994), *Annual Study, Singapore*, Survey Research Singapore, Singapore; SRS Adex (1995), *Annual Study, Singapore*, Survey Research Singapore, Singapore.

Table 16.19 Newspaper circulation—% of total, by language

Language	*1988*	*1989*	*1990*	*1991*	*1992*	*1993*	*1994*
English	45.8	46.7	47.4	48.2	48.9	49.2	50.0
Chinese	47.7	47.1	46.5	45.7	44.8	44.4	43.8
Malay	5.7	5.5	5.5	5.5	5.8	5.9	5.8
Tamil	0.8	0.7	0.6	0.6	0.5	0.5	0.5
Total	100	100	100	100	100	100	100
Number of copies sold daily, '000	743	777	814	878	916	978	1 029
% change over previous year	–	+4.5	+4.7	+7.9	+4.4	+6.7	+5.2

Sources: Singapore Facts and Pictures (1994), Ministry of Information and the Arts, Singapore; *Yearbook of Statistics* (1994), Department of Statistics, Singapore.

Resources Inc. (IRI), as well as a large number of regional and local firms. The Survey Research Group (SRG), a 30-year-old Asian market research firm with some 2200 full-time staff, has been taken over by AC Nielsen (*Asian Retailer* 1994g). SRG's subsidiary in Singapore, Survey Research Singapore, has so far been the largest player in terms of broadcast ratings, customized research and retail market research. Through the take-over by AC Nielsen, more advanced technology, in particular technology for the analysis of scanner data, has been introduced to the Singapore market.

It is generally expected that the next significant development in market research in Singapore will be the more efficient use of scanner data. Barcode scanning has been adopted by most large retailers in Singapore. With the introduction of the GST in 1994 and the need to keep track of the tax due on the various tax categories, scanning has also become more widespread with smaller retailers. At the beginning of 1994, 85% of all products sold had a bar code affixed, and approximately 60% of all products had been source-marked by manufacturers (*Asian Retailer* 1994e). The Singapore Article Numbering Council has started trials using electronic data interchange to retrieve bar-code data at the point of sale to predict demand, track stock levels and order electronically.

The rapid penetration of bar-code scanning and the introduction of advanced market research products and services will further improve the availability of market information and also reduce its price; in this way, the application of more formal and reliable market research tools will be increased. For example, in Singapore there are currently no data publicly available on channel shares, shares of branded private labels, and unbranded products. This situation may change within the next 1 to 5 years.

This trend may have positive impact on the utilization of market research data and tools in Singapore. Currently, Singaporean firms tend to use informal market research, such as feedback from the salesforce and customers, for identifying market opportunities, and hardly any quantitative techniques (Shamdasani, Wirtz & Chong 1995). Also, when monitoring the performance of their products, many firms, particularly the smaller and medium sized ones, still rely mainly on informal checks with their distributors rather than supplementing their current data with more formalized and quantitative research.

Marketing mix—a summary

Trends observed in the marketing mix are a direct reflection of, and/or are shaped by, the Singaporean macro-environment. Product and service trends emphasize the upmarket shift identified in previous sections on consumer behavior, which has resulted from the increasing sophistication and education of consumers, as well as rising income levels. Pricing strategies will go hand in hand with the higher quality of goods and services on offer, and non-monetary price-reduction strategies may become increasingly attractive to follow.

The retail environment in Singapore will become more competitive, with the growth in retail space far outpacing sales growth, with the continuing concentration of retail outlets in supermarket and other retail store chains, and with discount stores gaining share from a low level. The importance of advertising in the marketing mix is set to increase further, and successful advertising in Singapore will continue to be highly localized to the city state's cultural environment. Market research is expected to become more formalized and sophisticated in its application.

Implications for marketing management into the next century

Trends in Singapore's marketing environment have been described and analyzed in previous parts of this chapter. This final section brings together the main themes in Singapore's marketing environment, which include trends in the economic, demographic, and cultural environments, and trends in consumer behavior and the marketing mix. The findings are integrated, and key implications for marketing management are derived and discussed. The first part of the discussion deals with implications for the marketing mix, and the second with more general marketing strategies.

Conclusions on Singapore's marketing environment

Singapore's marketing environment represents an interesting case: a high-growth, so-called "Tiger" economy in a diverse multicultural society. There are 4 key conclusions to be drawn about future developments in Singapore's marketing environment that will have an important bearing on marketing management.

First, Singapore's economic environment has reached the level of that in a developed country at rapid speed over the past two decades. It is expected to remain favorable, with continuing high increases in personal income, virtually full employment and low inflation rates.

Second, Singapore's demographic environment will continue to follow the same trends as the less recently industrialized countries. The population will grow slowly, due to low fertility rates, late marriages, and delayed child-bearing. These factors, as well as an increasing life expectancy, contribute to the rapid ageing of the population.

Third, Singapore will remain a multicultural society with Chinese, Malays and Indians as the dominant ethnic groups, each with its own strong cultural background, its own languages, religions and customs. Nevertheless, Singaporeans are becoming increasingly multilingual, with more people speaking their own dialects plus English and/or Mandarin. Significant changes will also occur in other areas of Singapore's cultural environment. In particular, education levels will continue to improve rapidly, with more Singaporeans receiving university and post-secondary education. The female workforce participation rate, which has increased to one of the highest in the world, will remain at high levels. Household sizes will continue to become smaller.

Fourth, Singapore's development into an increasingly affluent society has had a substantial impact on consumer behavior. Real growth rates of private consumption have been high and the share of total consumption by basic goods such as food and clothing has been declining. Consumers are becoming more and more brand and status conscious, more discerning and health conscious. These trends are widely expected to continue for the coming years.

A summary of the detailed trends discussed in this paper is provided in Table 16.20. For ease of reference, these trends are presented in the same order as they have been discussed in the main body of the paper. The anticipated impact of each of these trends on marketing management is outlined in the same table.

Table 16.20 Changes in the marketing environment, and implications for marketing management

The marketing environment by the year 2000, and beyond	*Implications for marketing management*
Economic environment	
• Wages continue to increase • Continuing full employment • Low inflation	Increasing disposable income and high consumer confidence should set the scene for marketing strategies aimed at achieving high growth
Demographic environment	
• Small population • Low population growth	The small market size may suggest that economies of scale, such as those in advertising, distribution, and import/logistics, will drive marketers toward a more competitive environment, with a focus on obtaining volume and market share; the limited number of new consumers may suggest marketing strategies aimed at creating loyal customers, or even at entering more formalized relationships with customers
• Ageing population	Older customers will provide a fast-growing market segment; marketing strategies targeted at babies, children, and young adults have to work in low growth if not stagnating markets
Cultural environment	
• Improving education levels	Marketing strategies aimed at more sophisticated segments will be placed in fast growing markets
• Increasing proficiency in English and Mandarin	It will become increasingly possible to communicate with the majority of the population in English and Mandarin
• Smaller household sizes	Smaller package sizes, and perhaps convenient retail locations, will become more important
• High female participation rate in the workforce	Products that deliver time saving (ready-made meals, laundry services, etc.) and convenient retail locations (to reduce shopping time) will become more important
• Three main ethnic groups with their own languages and religions	Marketing strategies will have to continue to take cultural, language and religious variables into account

Table 16.20 Changes in the marketing environment, and implications for marketing management—*continued*

The marketing environment by the year 2000, and beyond	*Implications for marketing management*
Consumer behavior	
• Increasing total consumption	
• Declining share by basic goods of overall consumption	All main goods categories will show growth, but the market for basic goods such as food and beverages will grow slower than that for goods satisfying higher level needs. For example, entertainment, education and health have been increasing their share of total consumption
• Increasing brand and status consciousness	Branding and positioning will become increasingly important, and advertising expenditure will increase over and above increases in total consumer expenditure
• Increasingly discerning consumers	More sophisticated products will gain market share
• Increasingly health-conscious consumers	"Healthy" products (health food, exercise equipment, sports clothes etc.) will gain market share
• Declining importance of tourist shopping due to declining price differential to their home countries	Sales to tourists will grow slower than overall consumption; marketing strategies based predominantly on price advantage over tourist home countries will become increasingly unfeasible

Trends in the marketing mix	*Implications for marketing management*
Product	
• Consumers more quality conscious	
• High price/high quality segments growing fast	
• Low price/low quality segments will decline but not vanish altogether	High-quality segments are in high growth areas, whereas the low-quality end will at best stagnate
• Consumers becoming more health conscious	Health products (health food, exercise equipment, sports clothes, etc.) will gain market share
• Consumers becoming somewhat more environmentally aware	Environmentally friendly product attributes will become more important in consumer decision making
• Cultural differences will remain, not much assimilation anticipated	Segmentation by cultural division will remain important

Table 16.20 Changes in the marketing environment, and implications for marketing management—*continued*

Trends in the marketing mix	*Implications for marketing management*
Price and promotion	
• Consumers are more sensitive to non-monetary costs (from anecdotal evidence)	
• Sales and promotions remain an important component of the marketing mix, as marketers, whether rightly or not, perceive their consumers as very price sensitive	Sales and promotions will remain important components of the marketing mix; strategies reducing non-monetary costs rather than prices may be employed more than in the past
Distribution	
• Retail floor space continuing to grow from a relatively low level	Specialist retailers will grow, and increasingly serve the sophisticated/high end of many markets
• Shopping as a leisure activity to remain important	Creating a conducive shopping and entertainment atmosphere will remain important
• More shopping centers opened in suburbs	The latent demand for shopping convenience will be better satisfied
• Large discount stores making limited inroads into the Singapore market	Discounters will not become as important channels as they are in many Western countries
• Penetration of direct marketing channels is low, will not grow significantly over the coming years	Direct marketing will not become an important channel in the medium-term future
Advertising	
• Advertising expenditure continuing to grow faster than total consumer expenditure	The role of advertising in the marketing mix will become more important as the importance of branding increases
• No major shifts expected in media shares of advertising revenue in the medium term	Newspaper and TV will remain the most important advertising media
• Cultural segmentation, beliefs, sensitivities and superstitions remain important	Culturally targeted and sensitive advertising will remain crucial
Market research	
• Scanner data to become increasingly available to the public	
• More sophisticated research methods to be introduced to the Singapore marketplace	
• Indigenous Singaporean firms may increasingly use market research techniques	Marketing decisions will be increasingly based on more quantitative market research; the methods employed will become more sophisticated

Implications for the marketing mix

In general, the implications presented here fit into the overall picture of a high-growth environment with a focus on quality and upgrading rather than just more of the same. Implications for the marketing mix are presented below.

Product

Although Singapore's private consumption is growing fast, this does not apply equally to all areas of the market. Table 16.20 shows a number of trends in the environment that will have significant impact on the growth prospects for various product types. For example, high-quality, high-end and more sophisticated product markets are anticipated to grow faster than the overall market, while low-quality, low-end and basic product markets are expected to decline. Drivers of this trend include rising disposable incomes, combined with improving education levels, and more discernment on the part of consumers. Shifts in consumer values toward more emphasis on health and environmental concern will lead to high growth for health-improving and environmentally friendly products, whereas low growth or declining markets can be expected for goods being perceived as unhealthy and environmentally unfriendly. Table 16.21 provides an overview of product types that are expected to show higher growth than the overall market. The table is based on trends highlighted in Table 16.20.

Table 16.21 Trends in consumption

Expected high-growth products	*Expected low-growth products*
Products catering for needs of older consumers	Products catering for needs of younger consumers
High-quality products	Low-quality products
Branded products	Products that are not branded
Sophisticated products	Basic, coarse products
Products offering convenient purchase, consumption and disposal	Products not offering convenience
Products that help to save time	Products that do not help to save time
Products that maintain or improve health	Products that do not help to maintain or improve health
Environmentally friendly products	Environmentally unfriendly products

Pricing and price promotions

It is not clear whether Singaporeans are actually more price sensitive than, for example, US consumers. However, preliminary evidence suggests that, if there is a difference, it seems Singaporeans are more sensitive toward non-monetary costs than Americans. Combining this with anticipated trends toward higher quality products, we may expect that pricing may not increase in importance. Strategies focusing on lower non-monetary cost (e.g. product-feature bundling) may be increasingly attractive to follow, rather than those that continue to focus predominantly on monetary pricing, as is currently the case.

Communications

The role of communications in the marketing mix will become even more pronounced. In particular, branding and brand image are likely to become more important. It can be expected that advertising expenditure will continue to increase in relation to overall consumption expenditure.

Distribution

Convenience, specialist and discount shopping are expected to show strong growth. Convenient shopping locations are important in Singapore, as more than two-thirds of all households do not own automobiles, and are unlikely to be able to acquire them in the foreseeable future due to government regulation. Large shopping complexes are currently being built in the suburbs, to benefit from the trend toward more convenient retail locations. Specialist retailers will develop as demand for more high-end and sophisticated products increases. Discount stores are expected to grow fast from a small base and capture market share, but are not expected to obtain a strong position as they do in many Western countries, mainly because of limited automobile ownership in Singapore.

Each of the trends shown in tables 16.20 and 16.21 has many more marketing-mix implications than are discussed here. These general trends relate to various levels of marketing: market segmentation and product development, packaging, pricing, distribution, advertising, and promotions. For example, an increase in the demand for healthier products, as well as a more educated consumer base, will mean that food marketers are required to display much more information on ingredients on their packaging, and that they will need to focus their advertising and promotions strategies on positioning these products as health improving. Smaller household sizes may require smaller package sizes, and so on. The implications are numerous, and often product-category specific, and cannot all be enumerated here. However, it is hoped that this chapter will provide interested readers with the necessary background information for easing the first steps of developing and assessing their own specific marketing mix for the Singapore marketplace. Implications for more generic strategies are discussed in the following paragraph.

Implications for overall marketing strategies

A number of implications for overall marketing strategies can be derived from the environmental analysis. Three main implications are outlined below; they refer to growth strategies in higher end market segments, high-volume/market-leader strategies in a tiny marketplace with country-specific costs, and finally, to customer-retention strategies in a market with declining numbers of new customers entering the market.

First, marketers in Singapore can expect to operate in fast growing markets for some time to come; this growth will be fueled mainly by increasing disposable income rather than population growth. This suggests the pursuit of growth strategies in general, but with a focus on growth in quality rather than quantity. There will be high growth in better quality products and products that are consistent with a higher standard of living, rather than growth in numbers of units sold. For example, it will not be more television sets that will be sold, but better quality home entertainment sets.

Second, the Singapore market in absolute terms is small, with less than 3 million consumers. This is further aggravated by the existence of very distinct cultural differences, which often require segmentation along cultural lines (e.g. the food preferences of Malays and Chinese can vary substantially). There are a number of country-specific costs that cannot be shared with neighboring-country markets. These costs may include the costs of advertising in Singapore's media, salesforce expenditure, and logistics costs. Trends toward branded goods, and the often related increase in advertising, channel-management and market research expenditure, will further increase country-specific costs. However, worldwide future markets are expected to become more competitive, with continuing pressure on both prices and costs (Lazer et al. 1990, pp. 102, 140), and Singapore will be no exception. This has to be seen in the light of the current competitive environment, which is not nearly as harsh as that in more developed economies such as the USA and Europe, and margins for all channel members can still be considered quite generous. Nevertheless, it seems clear that, to achieve long-term profitability in an increasingly competitive marketplace, economies of scale on those country-specific costs will become more important. This is particularly so in Singapore as the small volume achievable in its market may mean that many firms are actually quite high on the sales-volume/unit-cost curve, with strong incentives to increase volume. Therefore, higher volume and/or market-leader strategies seem to be even more attractive than in larger economies, and, for many products, follower or "me too" strategies with low market share may become unsustainable as country-specific unit costs render these players uncompetitive. It seems that, as in Singapore's retail sector, further concentration of market shares can be expected. Exceptions to this rule may be high-end, sophisticated, image products where margins remain high and snob appeal favors low volumes.

Third, as in many older industrialized countries, the pool of new consumers entering the market in Singapore is getting smaller. This is a result of the ageing of the population, and the increasing saturation of markets that serve basic needs becoming increasingly saturated. As generally known, it is expensive to switch consumers from competitors. Although marketing strategies achieving customer retention and loyalty are not yet as vital in Singapore as they are in more saturated, older industrialized economies, they will also become increasingly important for maintaining market share and profitability. An increased pursuit of membership and relationship marketing strategies, combined with competitive strategies aimed at switching customers from competition, would seem appropriate.

In conclusion, prospects in general, and for goods and service categories catering for higher needs in particular, remain excellent. However, the environment will become more competitive, although still not at all to the same degree of intensity as in the USA and Europe. Nevertheless, soon it will no longer be sufficient merely to appoint importers for Singapore. Integrated marketing strategies, with increasing investment in brand equity, and increasingly sophisticated channel management, supported by cost-effective logistics and market research, will increasingly be needed to ensure success.

Conclusion

Over the past several months, Asia has suddenly been plunged into turmoil due to the plummeting of Asian currencies. This is a result of debt deflation, excessive private-sector leverage and weak financial systems (Rohwer 1998). Though Singapore has reasonably sound monetary policies with zero foreign debt and US$81 billion in reserve, it has also been affected by the region's collapse. This is because Singapore's total trade with its South-East Asian neighbors makes up 27% of exports (Shari 1997).

The Asian currencies turmoil has begun to affect Singapore companies. To date, there have been several lay-offs by companies in Singapore, such as Seagate Technology. This is bound to affect the Singapore consumer market. Singaporeans will become more prudent in their spending and will therefore cut down on buying luxury goods and unnecessary items. This was highlighted when two Valentino boutiques in Singapore recently closed down (Menkes 1997). The property market is also experiencing a slump period, with developers finding it hard to sell all of their newly built condominiums.

The number of tourists from nearby Asian countries is expected to decrease because, though Singapore's currency depreciated about 11% with respect to the US dollar (Richardson 1997), other currencies in the region had fallen by more than 20% to 40%. Therefore it is much more costly for these tourists to visit Singapore. However, tourists from the USA and Europe may be attracted by the depressed currencies, but the return of the haze may put an end to this. All of this points to a worsening retail market, and it is expected that many retailers may be driven out of business before long. The region is not expected to recover very fast. Economists believe that it will take at least 2 years before complete recovery. Singapore companies that are well managed are expected to be able to weather this storm better than their rivals who have diversified unwisely and have high debts. It is believed that, at the end of the turmoil, companies will emerge smaller and more focused in their strategy.

References

Abeysinghe, Tilak (1994), "Why a Wider Wage Gap in Singapore?", paper presented at the ESU Mid-Year Review of the Singapore Economy, in eds Tilak Abeysinghe, Ng Hock Guan, Anthony Ngerng, and Amina Tyabji, *Proceedings*, Economic Studies Unit, Department of Statistics, National University of Singapore, and Economics Society of Singapore, Singapore.

Advoice (1994), "Singaporeans' Appetite for Healthier Fare Makes Naturel a Hit", April, p. 1.

Asian Retailer (1994a), "Store Space Glut—A Blessing in Disguise?", February, p. 14.

— (1994b), "Price-Consciousness Affects Gourmet Food Sales in Singapore", February, pp. 42–5.

— (1994c), "Singaporean Retailers Face a Year of Changes and Challenges", March, pp. 28–33.

— (1994d), "Manufacturers Gear Up for the Green Crusade", April, pp. 26–7.

— (1994e), "Singapore's Smaller Retailers Now Scanning", May, pp. 28–31.

— (1994f), "Retailers Look Towards Singapore's Suburbs", July, pp. 24–7.

— (1994g), "Rocky Road to Marriage for Market Research Firms", October, pp. 32–6.

— (1995a), "Vitamins Boost Singapore Health Food Market", January, pp. 26–8.

— (1995b), "Eco-aware Shoppers Fail to Take Action", May, pp. 24–6.

Cherian, George (1995), "Beri Rates Singapore As No. 2 Investment Spot in the World", *The Straits Times*, September 13, p. 1.

Chua, Beng-Huat (1994), "Responses to Culture of Consumption in Singapore", paper presented at Workshop on Social and Cultural Dimensions of Market Expansion, Batam, Indonesia, October.

— (1995), "Ethnic Groups Tolerant but Lack Mutual Understanding", *The Straits Times*, September 23, p. 28.

Chuang, Peck Ming (1995), "Singapore Can Grow 7% a Year up to Year 2000: BG", *Singapore Business Times*, July 11, p. 1.

EIU Country Forecast Singapore (1994), Main Report 4th Quarter 1994, the Economist Intelligence Unit, London.

Fernandez, Warren (1995a), "What Limits Singapore Growth?", *The Straits Times*, March 4, p. 34.

— (1995b), "Those 'Vulnerable Years' Ahead", *The Straits Times*, April 8, p. 32.

Funkhouser, G. Ray, Parker, Richard & Chatterjee, Anindya (1994), "A Cross-cultural Comparison of Source and Brand Choice as a Function of Consumer Price and Non-price Cost Sensitivities", in eds Joseph A. Cote and Siew Meng Leong, *Asia-Pacific Advances in Consumer Research*, vol. 1, pp. 140–7.

Kau, Ah Keng & Yang, Charles (1991), *Values and Lifestyles of Singaporeans*, Singapore University Press, National University of Singapore, Singapore.

Kau, Ah Keng, Yong, Yeong Wee and Richmond, Daleen (1993), "A Delphi Study of Future Lifestyles and Consumption Patterns in Singapore", DNC Advertising and Singapore Center for Business Research and Development, National University of Singapore, Singapore.

Kraar, Louis (1995), "How Corrupt is Asia", *Fortune*, August 21, p. 18.

Kuo, Eddie C.Y. & Tong, Chee Kiong (1991), *Religion in Singapore*, Singapore National Printers, Singapore.

Lai, Ah Eng (1995), *Meaning of Multiethnicity: A Case-Study of Ethnicity and Ethnic Relations in Singapore*, Oxford University Press, Oxford.

Lazer, William, LeBarbera, Priscilla, MacLachlan, James M. & Smith, Allen E. (1990), *Marketing 2000 and Beyond*, American Marketing Association, Chicago.

Lim, Kevin (1994), " Comparative Ads Gain Popularity in Singapore", *The Straits Times*, May 23, p. 36.

Mark, Jeremy (1995), "Tough Times Rattle Singapore Retailers", *The Asian Wall Street Journal*, February 20, p. 1.

McRae, Hamish (1995), *The World in 2020—Power, Culture and Prosperity*, Harvard Business School Press, Boston.

Menkes, Suzy (1998), "High Fashion and the Asia Effect", *International Herald Tribune*, January 20.

Menkhoff, Thomas (1995), "Vom Entrepot zum Neuen Industrieland—Zu den Ursachen des erfolgreichen Werdegangs Singapurs (From a Storehouse to a New Industrial Nation—The Reasons for Singapore's Successful Development)", unpublished working paper, National University of Singapore, Singapore.

Ministry of Information and the Arts (MIA) (1994), *Singapore 1994*, MIA, Singapore.

— (1995), *Singapore 1995*, MIA, Singapore.

Monthly Digest of Statistics (1994), Department of Statistics, Singapore, November.

Report of the Labor Force Survey of Singapore (1993), Research and Statistics Department, Ministry of Labor, Singapore.

— (1994), Research and Statistics Department, Ministry of Labor, Singapore.

Report on Wages in Singapore, Annual Survey (1993), Research and Statistics Department, Ministry of Labor, Singapore.

Richardson, Michael (1995), "High-Cost Singapore Keeps its Cachet", International Herald Tribune, May 6–7, p. 11.

— (1997), "Singapore: The Blow Softened", *International Herald Tribune*, November 3.

Rohwer, Jim (1998), "Asia's Meltdown—The Risks are Rising", *Fortune*, February 16, pp. 32–8.

Saini, Rohanlah (1994), "Singapore Ad Agencies Play up their Pluses", *The Straits Times*, April 8, p. 8.

Seah, Lyn (1995), "Sticker Drive for Healthy Dishes", *The Straits Times*, September 28, p. 3.

SES Journal (1995), "Retail Sector Performance: Problems & Prospects", vol. 23, no. 7, July, pp. 4–14.

Shamdasani, Prem, Chon-Lin, Gloria Ong & Richmond, Daleen (1992), "Exploring Green Consumers in an Oriental Culture: Role of Personal and Marketing Mix Factors", in eds Leigh McAlister & Michael L. Rothchild, *Advances in Consumer Research*, vol. 20, Association for Consumer Research, Provo, UT, pp. 488–93.

Shamdasani, Prem & Yeow, Ong Geok (1995), "An Exploratory Study of In-home Shoppers in a Concentrated Retail Market", *Journal of Retailing and Consumer Services*, vol. 2, no. 1.

Shamdasani, Prem, Wirtz, Jochen & Chong, Michael (1995), "An Exploratory Study on New Product Development Activities of Singapore Firms", *Proceedings of the Academy of International Business Conference on Asia-Pacific Business*, Murdoch University, Perth, pp. 327–30.

Shari, Michael (1997), "Singapore: Storm Clouds over Asia's Safe Haven", *Business Week International Editions*, August 11, p. 23.

Sim, Susan (1995), "Corruption Index Based on 7 Polls of Businessmen, Newsmen", *The Straits Times*, August 26, p. 2.

Singapore Census of Population 1990, Statistical Release 1, Demographic Characteristics (1992), Census of Population Office, Department of Statistics, Singapore.

Singapore Census of Population 1990, Statistical Release 2, Household and Housing (1992), Census of Population Office, Department of Statistics, Singapore.

Singapore Census of Population 1990, Statistical Release 3, Literacy, Languages Spoken and Education (1993), Census of Population Office, Department of Statistics, Singapore.

Singapore Census of Population 1990, Statistical Release 6, Religion, Childcare and Leisure Activities (1994), Census of Population Office, Department of Statistics, Singapore.

Singapore Facts and Pictures (1994), Ministry of Information and the Arts, Singapore.

Singapore Statistical Highlights (1993), Department of Statistics, Singapore.

Singapore Tourist Promotion Board (1994), "Survey of Overseas Visitors in Singapore", Market Planning Department, Singapore Tourist Promotion Board, Singapore.

SRS Adex (1994), *Annual Study, Singapore*, Survey Research Singapore, Singapore.

— (1995), *Annual Study, Singapore*, Survey Research Singapore, Singapore.

Straits Times (1995a), "7000 Jobs Lost Last Year but 46 000 New Ones Created", January 31, p. 16.

— (1995b), "Rationale Behind the Revision of the CPF Minimum Sum Scheme", in Special Feature on the Revision of the CPF Minimum Sum Scheme, February 24, p. 12.

— (1995c), "Christianity here has Strong 'Social, Political Influence'", April 26, p. 25.

— (1995d), "More Foreigners will be Allowed to Work in Republic", May 6, p. 26.

— (1995e), "Domestic and Tourist Spending Remains Weak", June 29, p. 36.

— (1995f), "Visitors Reaffirm Singapore's Reputation as Shopping Haven", July 18, p. 2.

— (1995g), "Singapore has Highest Rate of Labour Participation among NIEs, other Economies", September 13, p. 38.

Sunday Times (1995), "Government as Trustee", September 24, pp. 1–5.

Survey Research Singapore (1995), "Singapore Retail Scene", Survey Research Singapore, Singapore.

The Strategic Economic Plan (1991), Economic Planning Committee, Ministry of Trade and Industry, SNP Pte. Ltd., Singapore.

Union Bank of Switzerland (1991), *Prices and Earnings Around the Globe 1991*, Union Bank of Switzerland, Geneva.

Wood, Richard ed. (1993), *Doing Business in Singapore*, Price Waterhouse, Singapore.

World Bank (1993), *The East Asian Miracle: Economic Growth and Public Policy*, Oxford University Press for the World Bank, Oxford.

— (1995), *World Bank Atlas*, Oxford University Press for the World Bank, Oxford.

Yap, Corinne (1994), "Store Space Glut—A Blessing in Disguise?", *Asian Retailer*, February, p. 14.

Yap, Evelyn (1995), "HDB Shopping to Change by Year 2000", *The Sunday Times*, February 12, p. 2.

Yearbook of Statistics (1990), Department of Statistics, Singapore.

Yearbook of Statistics (1993), Department of Statistics, Singapore.

Yearbook of Statistics (1994), Department of Statistics, Singapore.

Notes

1 Singapore currency (S$) is used throughout this chapter wherever it is necessary to avoid distortions due to fluctuations in exchange rates. The exchange rate at time of writing is US$1 = S$1.41.

CHAPTER 17

Taiwan

Changing marketing and consumer behavior

Y. EDWIN TANG & JEANNE LIU

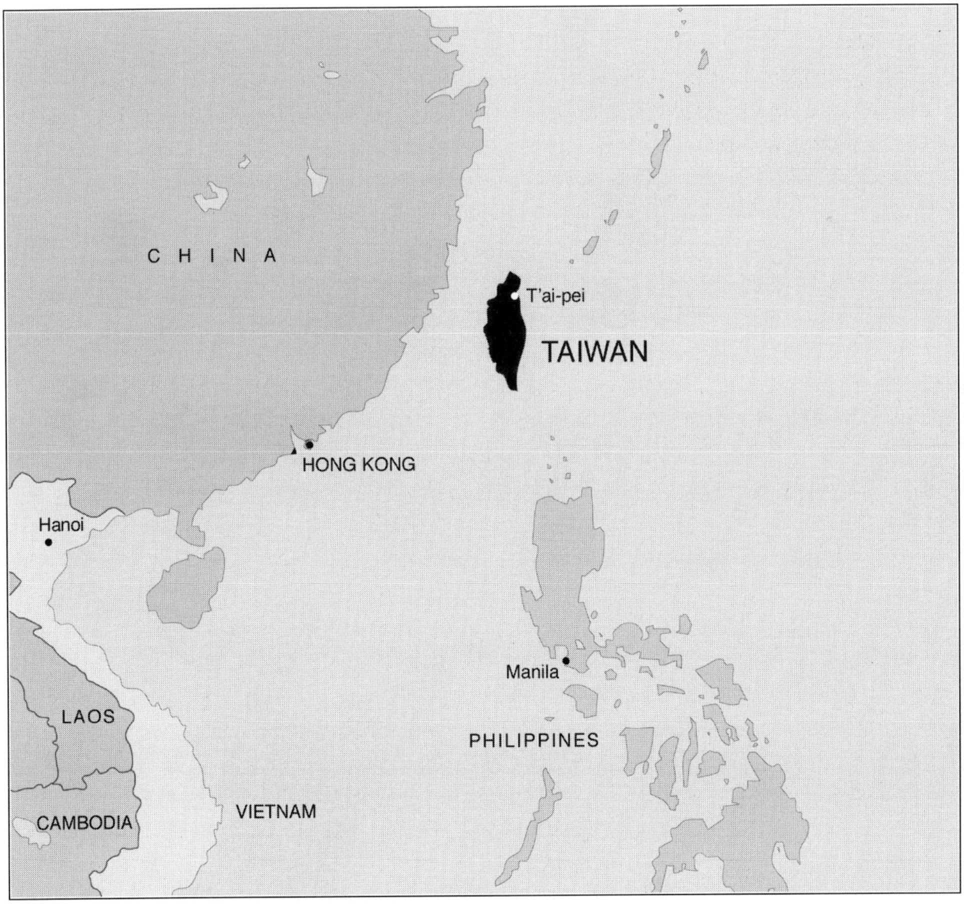

Abstract

Taiwan has undergone a dramatic transformation, from an impoverished agricultural economy to a relatively affluent industrial and service economy. The historical, social, and political bases of this change are explained, with an emphasis on marketing and consumer behavior. The present state of the cultural, social, demographic, and general marketing environments are described, and the possible future trends enumerated.

Introduction

Taiwan, officially called the Republic of China, lies south-east of the People's Republic of China across the Taiwan Strait. It has an area of about 36 000 km^2 (and as such is slightly smaller than the Netherlands), and a population of approximately 22 million, Taiwan was called Formosa in the Portuguese ruling period, which means "beautiful island." Its recent economic growth, associated with that of the other nations collectively known as Greater China (Hong Kong and China), means that it is well on its way to becoming an economic superpower. With Taiwan's technology and financial power, Hong Kong's international financial and marketing skills, and China's supply of labor, land, natural resources, and the huge potential market offered by the combined areas, its complementary strengths seem destined to drive this great economic frontier toward the 21st century. The World Bank predicts that Greater China's GDP will rank far ahead of both Japan's and Germany's, and approach that of the USA by 2002 (Hamlin 1994).

While the economic boundaries between Taiwan and China are fading, and Hong Kong is now a part of China, no one can foresee whether the whole of Greater China will become politically integrated. Prior to integration, Hong Kong fought for assurance from Beijing of the promised "One nation, 2 systems for 50 years." Taiwan has dropped the myth that it is China's legitimate government, and has begun to seek its own independent identity from international organizations such as the United Nations, GATT, WTO, and APEC, in order to protect itself against Beijing's constant embargoes and military threats (Baum 1995). Despite these political shadows, it seems that the marketplace and economics are the driving forces that keep pushing the growth of the de facto Chinese commonwealth.

After years of export surplus, combined with high saving rates and a prudent fiscal policy, Taiwan has one of the world's first or second largest foreign-exchange reserves. To continue accumulating wealth, both in this and the next century, Taiwan has laid out an ambitious plan that will take advantage of its financial power, as well as the booming economies of Greater China and South-East Asia. It plans to turn the island nation into a multipurpose Asia–Pacific regional operations center (ROC). This is a scheme that will enhance Taiwan's capacity to act as an intermediary for foreign and domestic companies in high-tech and value-added manufacturing, finance, air cargo, shipping, telecommunications, tourist transshipment and specialized services (Shapiro 1994).

The transformation of Taiwan from a manufacturing to a service economy is similar to what Hong Kong and Singapore have experienced in their attempts to restructure their economies. But the plan is on a larger and more extensive scale. Taiwan is advocating the ROC plan as a means to integrate Greater China and to compete directly with the world's three major economic zones: North America, Europe, and Japan (Abegglen 1994). Although many have criticized the scale of the plan, it is not too far fetched. Taiwan is already a major manufacturing powerhouse in Asia. With its geographical advantage of having Japan to the north and the Chinese mainland to the west, Taiwan's Kaohsiung is among the top 5 busiest harbors in the world (Neilan 1995). And if transit passengers are taken into account, Taipei's international airport is also among the top 5. As long as the Taiwan government is willing to continue its democratic reform and economic liberalization, and China agrees to resolve the reunification issue peacefully, Taiwan could conceivably turn itself into a transport hub and regional operating center for the new Asia by the beginning of the next century.

Economic environment

Having few natural resources and little arable land, Taiwan has astonished the world by creating such an economic miracle. It was ruled by the Dutch in the 17th century, by the Chinese in the 18th and 19th centuries and then by the Japanese from 1895 to 1945. The story of Taiwan's modern-day success begins with Japanese colonization. Under Japanese rule, Taiwan was first looked upon as an agricultural colony and later as an industrial supplier to support the Japanese war effort during the Second World War. The infrastructure, including manufacturing, transportation, education, banking and finance, put in place during the colonization period, enabled post-war Taiwan to make such spectacular economic progress (Barclay 1954).

The fast pace of economic growth in post-war Taiwan has dramatically transformed the nation from a relatively impoverished agricultural economy to a relatively affluent industrial and service economy. This transitional growth can be characterized by three distinct subphases: the agriculture and import substitution phase from the end of the Second War World to the 1950s, the export-oriented industrialization (EOI) phase from the 1960s to the early 1980s, and the technologically sensitive external orientation phase from the late 1980s to the present (Li 1988; Fei 1992). In 1995, only 3.4% of Taiwan's GDP emanated from agriculture (compared with 35.9% in 1952), 35.2% from industry (21.9% in 1952), and 61.4% from the services sector (42.2% in 1952) (Myers 1997). This transformation is surprising, because it was accompanied by rapid population and income growth (Myers 1997, p. 262).

As many have claimed, EOI strategy was the basic cause of the rapid growth of Asia's "Four Little Dragons"—Taiwan, South Korea, Hong Kong, and Singapore. But two additional forces were essential to Taiwan's economic success: first, there were no strong opposition groups, thus enabling the government to pursue effective growth and export-oriented policies. Second, a large amount of foreign aid, including military support, had been received from the USA in the 1960s and 1970s, and thus Taiwan was helped to obtain the necessary financial capital and military protection during the transitional growth period (Gulati 1992).

Not only did the influence of Japan and the USA condition Taiwan into an industrialized nation, but these countries have also become Taiwan's top 2 trading partners in the last several decades. In 1994, the trading volume with the USA and Japan was US$42.4 billion and US$35.0 billion respectively. In 1994, Taiwan was the 12th or 13th largest trading nation in the world. Its major exports are machinery, computers, electronic products, textiles, auto parts, and plastic and rubber products, while the major imports are telecommunications, agricultural products, medical equipment, aerospace products, and high-value textiles, electronics, and furniture (CETRA 1995).

Changes in income

Taiwan's per-capita income was US$10 566 in 1993, which gave it 25th place worldwide, but also made it large enough to be placed in the World Bank's category of high-income nations (see Table 17.1). The corresponding figure 5 decades ago at the end of the Second World War and the period of Japanese colonization was approximately US$150. This remarkable economic growth is accompanied by the equitable distribution of income. The income difference between high-income Taipei and the poorest region, Yunlin, is about fivefold. It is a relatively small difference in comparison with many Asian nations, and has contributed greatly to social and political stability; these, in turn, have created the necessary conditions for rapid economic development. For marketers, the equitable distribution of income also makes the income figure a very meaningful guide to the configuration of the market.

Table 17.1 Economic profile, 1970–1993

Year	*1970*	*1980*	*1990*	*1993*
Exchange rate (with US$)	40	36	27	26.6
GNP growth (%)	11.3	7.1	5.2	6.5
Trade surplus (US$ million)	43	1 350	12 490	7 855
Per-capita disposable income (US$)	361	2 149	7 248	10 566

Source: Republic of China (1994), *National Income in Taiwan Area,* Kwang Hwa Publishing, Taipei.

Changes in saving rate and credit spending

Taiwan is in a spending mood. At the national level, the Taiwanese government sits uncomfortably on an all-time high of foreign-exchange reserves, and is eager to dispose of them. Several economic reform programs, such as the ROC plan, the "Buy America" campaign, and the US$2 trillion 6-year development plan in infrastructure, technology, and the environment, are examples of the attempt to recycle the surplus. This desire for spending has passed down from the government to the individual. Taiwan's affluent consumers have increasingly embraced a "spend more and save less" philosophy. The overall consumption rate has increased by an average of 12% a year in the 1990s, while the savings rate dipped from the all-time high of 35% in the 1970s and 1980s to an average of 28% in 1994. Many Taiwanese economists and politicians have been alarmed at such a deteriorating rate. Yet, compared to the current average of 15% in the USA and a world average of 23%, the 28% saving rate is still very impressive (*Economic Yearbook* 1994).

Although the saving rate has declined, real purchasing power has been both compensated for and accelerated by the increase in discretionary income. Current projections suggest that purchasing power will continue to rise modestly through the 1990s. From Table 17.2, we can see that average family expenditure has increased nearly twentyfold in the past 20 years. Family expenditure on transportation, communication, recreation, and entertainment has gained the most from this growth (see Table 17.3).

Table 17.2 Average family propensities for consuming and saving (US$)

Year	*1970*	*1980*	*1990*	*1993*
Average family's disposable income	1 044	6 208	18 017	27 364
Average family expenditure	953	4 727	12 536	18 952
Average family saving	80	1 481	5 480	8 412
Average propensity to spend (%)	91.3	84.4	69.6	69.3

Data Source: Bureau of Statistics (1994), *Market Annual Report of Taiwan Area*, Taipei.

Another noticeable trend for Taiwanese consumers is that they are increasingly buying on credit. Combined domestic and international spending rose from US$3.65 billion in 1993 to US$5.77 billion in 1994. This makes incumbent card issuers, such as Citibank and American Express, the beneficiaries of the Taiwanese spending spree. Citibank alone issued more than 700 000 cards to Taiwanese in 1994, second only to the US market in the number of cards issued.

Changes in consumer consumption patterns

Another change that has accompanied the rapid growth in per-capita income is in consumption patterns. And consumption-pattern changes have a large impact on the economy and the overall marketplace. The most significant change is in food spending, which declined from 62% in 1951 to 27.39% in 1993.

Table 17.3 Consumer spending at different income levels (% of purchasers' expenditure at current prices)

Items	*1951*	*1972*	*1980*	*1991*	*1993*
Food, Beverage, Tobacco	62.01	49.54	41.38	29.26	27.39
Housing, Rent, Utility, Water	13.32	16.92	16.12	18.81	19.44
Clothing and Footwear	5.45	5.18	5.29	4.67	4.68
Furniture, Housing equipment	2.56	4.83	5.42	4.98	4.96
Medical care, Health expenses	2.59	4.24	4.57	5.06	7.06
Transportation, Communication	1.39	3.78	7.77	13.60	12.55
Recreation, Entertainment, Education, Cultural services	6.12	7.99	12.36	16.77	17.28
Miscellaneous goods and services	6.56	7.52	7.09	6.85	6.64

Bureau of Statistics (1994), *Market Annual Report of Taiwan Area*, Taipei.

In contrast, spending on transportation, telecommunications, education, and entertainment has risen the most, while spending on necessities such as clothing and furniture has remained constant. The increases in spending on transportation and telecommunications are the most drastic, showing a tenfold increase. According to Engel's laws, as family income rises, the percentage spent on food declines, the percentage spent on housing remains constant, and the percentage spent on other items such as transportation, clothing, education, and recreation increases. The changes in Taiwan's consumption pattern correlate quite well with these laws (see Table 17.3).

However, an exception has been expenditure on housing. From 1951 to 1970, housing expenditure remained around 13%, but after the real-estate boom of the 1970s it jumped to a constant rate of 17%. A possible explanation is that the housing expenditure share has not fully grown to a state of equilibrium (e.g. the ratio in the USA is about 24% for all income levels). In addition to this, the dense population in Taiwan has contributed to the increased housing costs. And this incremental rate is expected to grow, since there is no long-term solution for the problem of high population density in Taiwan.

Inflation and unemployment

Rapid economic growth has been accomplished with little inflation or unemployment. The unemployment rate, despite population growth, has rarely been above 2% since 1964; in 1994 it was 1.57%, and in 1995 1.8% (Myers 1997). This reflects well on the tightly controlled political system, as well as on the efforts by the government to promote financial stability and foster economic development. An important vehicle to help control inflation and generate employment opportunities is high-yield government bonds, which have been designated for land reform, massive infrastructure spending, and monetary sterilization (Chang 1994). Total outstanding central government bonds rose from US$5 billion in 1990 to US$21 billion in June 1993. High interest rates have not only encouraged high saving rates and a choice of investments that have high returns, but have also contributed to the choice of labor-intensive industries that have contributed to Taiwan's comparative advantage and have led to an equitable distribution of income (Balassa 1991).

The demographic environment

Changes in population size

The rate of Taiwan's population growth has dropped from 3.8% in the 1950s to 1% in recent times, and zero growth is forecast by 2035. Taiwan has a population of 21.5 million (see Table 17.4). About 40% of the total population—that is, 8.5 million—is in the labor force, which corresponds to the natural growth of the population. With 587 people per square kilometre, however, Taiwan has the second highest population density in the world after Bangladesh. This dense population has put a lot of pressure on the environment, infrastructure, and public health system. Part of the Six-Year Development Plan is devoted to resolving this problem (GIO 1995).

Since the growth of the working population cannot keep pace with economic expansion, Taiwan has recruited workers from overseas, for instance Thailand, the Philippines, and other Asian countries. An estimated 270 000 foreign workers have been brought in since October 1989. This figure does not include many Chinese smugglers who have entered illegally along the West coast. However, foreign labor is yet to be a significant factor in the make-up of Taiwan's labor force.

One unique characteristic of the population is the gender ratio. In 1995 the current ratio of males to females was 106 to 100, a decline from 111 to 100 in 1970. This reflects an interesting Chinese traditional value in that sons in general have more favorable status than daughters (Parish & Willis 1993). Since modern medical technology provides the means to detect the gender of the fetus in early pregnancy, some parents, by choice, abort baby girls before birth. Such preference has created an unbalanced gender-structure problem. In the population of 15 years of age and above, the gender ratio for singles is 137 males to 100 females. Finding a mate is often a highly skilled and complex task for the Taiwanese male. This problem of unbalanced gender structure is doomed to surface in the years to come when mate-search becomes a social issue.

Age distribution

In Taiwan, the age structure can be classified according to the country's historical and economic development. People who were born before 1945,

Table 17.4 Population growth in Taiwan

Year	*1970*	*1980*	*1990*	*2000*
Population (millions)	14.6	17.8	20.4	22.8
Annual growth (%)	2.2	1.9	1.1	0.5
Gender ratio (females =100)	111	109	107	105

Source: Bureau of Statistics (1994), *Demographic Statistic of Taiwan-Fukien Area*, Taipei.

referred to as the "Japanese Colonial generation," hold most of the personal wealth, land, and political power in the country. Because of the Japanese cultural influence, the value system, living habits, and consumption behavior patterns of this group tend to be pro-Japanese. The second group is Taiwan's "Baby Boomers," now 30–49 years old, who comprise the bulk of the Taiwanese population. The majority of today's workforce and corporate leaders come from this group. The third group is the "Bean Sprout" generation, who were born after 1971, the year Taiwan was exiled from the UN. This group is the counterpart of the "Dust Generation," or "Generation X," in the USA, who enjoy better economic and material lives than their parents. The term "Bean Sprout" implies that this youngest group is like the greenhouse-nurtured bean sprout–well protected, yet feeble and vulnerable.

Like the "demographic-imperative" scenario that most industrialized nations are now facing, the "graying" of the population will also present a threat to Taiwan (see Table 17.5). This is due to the decreasing fertility rate, which dropped from an average number of 5.5 children per couple in the 1960s to 1.7 in 1994 (Myers 1997). However, the graying of the population is occurring in a rather modest way in Taiwan. In 2020, the estimated median age will be 39, which is young in comparison with that in other developed countries. The coming of age of new-generation baby boomers will fill the void left by aged baby boomers.

Table 17.5 Age distribution of the population (%), 1975–2040 (projected)

Age group	*1975*	*1985*	*1995*	*2000*	*2020*	*2040*
0–14	35.3	29.9	24.9	23.0	18.3	17.7
15–64	61.2	65.2	67.8	68.9	67.8	62.3
65+	3.5	4.9	7.3	8.1	13.9	20.0
Median age	21	25	30	32	39	41

Source: Republic of China (1994), *Statistical Yearbook of the Republic of China*, Kwang Hwa Publishing, Taipei.

Household size

The average Taiwanese household is shrinking. In 1976, the average household contained 5.5 people. In 1993, the figure stood at 3.82. In 1996, the percentage of small households, those containing 2 people or less, was expected to rise from 8.6% to 19%, and a rise of almost 16%, from 27.2% to 43%, was expected for the household size of 3 to 4 (see Table 17.6). Household size is shrinking because the traditional concept of the "big family," where all the members of an extended family live together in one household, has been challenged by the emergence of a modern, post-agricultural economy. Many young people have left family farms to establish nuclear families in urban areas. This metamorphosis has resulted in the rising number of small families, including young families with only 1 or 2 children, single-parent families, senior citizens living alone, and non-families.

Although the number of small families has increased, the percentage of people who live in households of more than 5 people remains high. One reason for this high percentage is that the traditional conception of "family-derived nurturing" still exists; therefore, many young families still prefer to live with parents, and sharing the same dwelling. Another reason is economic necessity. As a result of high real-estate prices, many young Taiwanese families consider the ideal ratio of one person to one bedroom a luxury. The housing problem is especially serious in big cities such as Taipei and Kaohsiung. Expensive real estate and housing are also causing the erosion of the equitable distribution of income. An easy way to distinguish the rich from the poor in Taiwan is to classify them according to the "have" and "have-not" categories.

Because of social pressure, the divorce rate and the number of single-parent households was low in the past. But this has changed, and the growth of single-parent families has become a noticeable social phenomenon. Single-parent families accounted for an estimated 3.5% of total families in 1992. Prior to 1975, the divorce rate was around 0.4%, but in 1993, the figure increased to 2.6%, and the second-marriage population was 10.6%. The figures are 5.2% and 15.6% respectively in Taipei, the major metropolis in Taiwan.

Table 17.6 Household size

Size	*1976*	*1986*	*1996*
No. of dwelling households (DHs)	3 470 293	4 165 060	5 800 000
No. of occupants per DH (%)			
2 or fewer	8.6	14.5	19
3–4	27.2	36.5	43
5–6	41.6	36.7	31
7+	22.6	12.3	7

Source: Jen-sen B. Lim (1991), *Collections for Taiwan Market Research*, Taipei, Taiwan, Business Strategy Press, p. 47.

Ethnicity

The majority of the people in Taiwan are ethnic Chinese who came to settle to avoid civil wars on the mainland during the past 400 years. There are 4 ethnic groups in Taiwan. The Aborigines are a minority, with an estimated population of 357 600 in 1993. The Aborigines belong to 9 tribes, and live scattered in the island's mountain areas. The earliest immigrants were Hoklo people from Fukien coastal districts and Hakka people from the Kwangtung hinterland in the 17th century, most of them peasants and merchants. The Hoklo and Hakka make up about 65% and 20% of the total population respectively. The third wave of immigrants was in the late 1940s; when the ROC government withdrew from China, some 2 million Chinese, predominantly military officials, bureaucrats, and businesspeople, settled on the island. These mainland Chinese now make up about 15% of the population (Wachman 1994). Originally, these ethnic groups were notably different in terms of dialects, living habits, socio-economic status, and political ideology. However, after 50 years of integration efforts by government propaganda, the educational system, and interethnic relations, ethnic difference has diminished.

Cultural environment

The Chinese culture promotes hard work, industriousness, and thrift, all of which contribute to entrepreneurial activity. The doctrine of Confucianism, which places a high value on education, individual responsibility, the unity of the family, and the harmony of society, is deeply embedded as the nation's social norm. Without doubt, these cultural factors played a significant role in the success of the entrepreneur in Taiwan. In addition, the limited natural resources, the "islander" personality, and the large number of monopolized state-controlled industries have produced many adventurous and risk-taking businessmen seeking overseas opportunities.

However, one thing worth noting is that, similarly to many other Asian nations that have been influenced by Western culture, modern Taiwanese culture has gradually walked away from its past conservative and modest path. This is especially evident among the teen subculture, the "New Mankind" or the "Global Villagers," who are surrounded by MTV, Nintendo games, Hollywood movies, and the Internet Relay Chat.

Education

Since the Chinese culture values education highly and grants educated people a high level of status and respect, pursuing higher-level education for children has never ceased to be a major concern for Taiwanese parents. After the government made 9 years of primary and junior high schooling compulsory, the illiteracy rate for people aged 25 and above dropped, from 30% in the 1960s to 8.6% in 1993. The proportion of primary-school graduates increased from 35.6% in 1953 to 99.8% in 1983, and has since remained at that level, and the number of college graduates has increased nearly thirty-fold in the same period (see Table 17.7).

Growth in the education of the labor force has been one of the most important determinants of economic growth in Taiwan. To increase productivity and, hence, stimulate economic growth, the educational system in Taiwan is focused on developing a workforce with a sound basic education and sound vocational skills.

The development of education in Taiwan can be divided into the following periods. During the 1950s and 1960s, the emphasis was on the popularization of primary-school education. Following the rapid growth of the economy and the high demand for a labor force, emphasis in the 1970s shifted from academic to vocational education at the more senior institutions. To meet the growing demand for workers with a higher education and to keep pace with the development of high-tech industries–and, partly, to keep students from going abroad to study for their degrees–the late 1980s and the early 1990s saw the development of higher education. As a result, a large number of scholars and professionals have returned from abroad and the brain-drain problem has been alleviated. Taiwan currently has 125 universities and colleges. Together, these institutions ran 566 graduate programs in 1993, and produced 36 000 masters-degree candidates.

Table 17.7 Educational attainments of population aged 25+

Attainment	*1980*	*1985*	*1990*	*1993*
Average length of education (years)	6.25	7.15	8.03	8.55
Illiteracy rate (%)	17.83	13.41	10.07	8.62
Primary school graduation	49.53	44.23	37.48	32.60
High school graduation	24.25	31.96	40.10	44.51
College graduation	8.39	10.40	12.35	14.27

Source: Bureau of Statistics (1992), *Educational Statistics of the Republic of China*, Taipei.

Liberalization

Taiwan functions effectively in the modern world, but claims to the effect that the country displays a high degree of Westernized liberalization may be mistaken. Compared to the freedom Westerners enjoy, Taiwan is yet to be a fully democratized state, since leaders in political and social movements are still liable to prosecution.

Associated with the liberalization of other parts of Taiwanese culture, the newly aroused awareness of women's rights emerged after the lifting of Martial Law and the eruption of Sunism (Dr Sun Yi-sen's Three Principles of the People) in the late 1980s (Lu 1994). The rise of Women's Liberation came with women's greater participation in the labor force, economic activities, and even politics. A great number of well-educated and well-trained women now make their competitiveness keenly felt in every business sector. The percentage of working women in the total female population was 54.1 in 1993.

However, in the traditional Confucian and male-dominated Chinese culture, the economic autonomy and independence of women is always related to rebellion, liberated sex, and irresponsible motherhood. The stereotypical role expectation of women as the grocery shoppers, cooks, and nurses remains high, and the idea of androgyny for either female or male is still difficult to accept. The economic role of Taiwanese women may be drastically modernized, but social and family roles still remain significantly traditional.

The identity of Taiwanese culture

Along with Women's Liberation came other social movements, including consumer protection, environmental protection (promoting the need to protect ecological systems), anti-pollution protection (against environment-polluting industries), anti-corruption (against governmental officials), labor protection, free press (against government-controlled mass media), and the movement of students for campus democracy (against the KMT-controlled educational system—KMT is the Kuomintang, the Nationalist Party) after the lifting of Martial Law. On the surface, these movements were aimed against the inefficient governmental structure that could not keep pace with the growth of the economy, but the real objective was to break the KMT's claim on its legitimacy over mainland China, which has given it an excuse to maintain a monopolizing power over the island state (Chu 1994).

Since the ruling party, Kuomintang, has recognized that Taiwan and China are two separate political entities, it has gradually moved from a mainland-based government body to a Taiwan-based new nation. Whereas "Taiwanese" used to refer to immigrants from the early days, nowadays everybody, particularly those who were displaced from the mainland with the ROC government around 1949, all claim the identity of Taiwanese. Studying Taiwanese history, culture, literature, and folk art has become popular. Nostalgia has become very popular in advertising appeals and fashion design, while dictionaries on the Fukienese dialect and publications on the Hoklo and Hakka cultures are year-round best sellers.

As the concept of "Taiwan identity" expands, manufacturers that used to concentrate only on exporting in the international market for a quick return have shifted gear: the "Made in Taiwan" label is no longer seen as a symbol of inferiority. Many Taiwanese companies, such as Acer Computer Inc., Evergreen Shipping Co., and Kennex sportswear, have shown the potential for being world-class brands.

The environment and public health

During the Martial Law period, the KMT government's slogan was "Construct Taiwan, Retrieve Mainland China." This clearly indicates that its interest was in using Taiwan as a stepping stone to building up economic and military power, with the aim of retaliating against mainland China as opposed to protecting the island's environment.

After decades of virtually unheeded environmental regulations, Taiwan is among the most polluted countries in the world. For example, in 1994 an estimated 38% of the main rivers in Taiwan were polluted, while over 50% of underground water has been seriously polluted by heavy metals. Despite public outcry and the many grassroots environmental movements, the government has been slow to awaken to the need for policy change. It was not until 1987 that the government promoted its Bureau of Environmental Protection to cabinet level in order to oversee environmental issues. An estimated US$1.5 billion had been spent by 1997 in the cleanup effort. With such a high amount of expenditure, measures of the quality of the living environment such as PSI (the pollutant standard index) do not seem to have improved (see Table 17.8).

Table 17.8 PSI (Pollutant Standard Index)

	1983	*1986*	*1989*	*1992*
PSI*	97.4	100	103.6	118.4

Note:
* The PSI is calculated by air pollutants such as suspended particles with a diameter less than 10 mm, including sulfur dioxide density, nitrogen dioxide density, and ozone density.

Source: Economic Yearbook of the Republic of China 1994 (1994), Kwang Hwa Publishing Company, Taipei, p. 177.

The tension between the government and the general public is extremely high. Many foreign companies, such as GE (nuclear plant) and Du Pont (CFC), and local companies such as Taiwan Electricity (radio-active waste), China Petroleum (naphtha cracker), and Formosa Plastics (hazardous waste), have found themselves frequently caught at the center of the public debate on environmental issues. The environmental movement has devoted much attention to the petrochemical industry, which accounted, in 1994, for 25% of Taiwan's GNP (Cohen 1995). Waste management is also a serious problem for the government. Taiwan can only process 67% of the waste produced. About 6000 tons of garbage are left untreated each day, waiting for proper handling (BEP 1995).

Life expectancy in Taiwan is 72.01 years for men and 77.39 years for women. The top 5 causes of death in Taiwan are cancer (19.26%), cerebrovascular diseases (13.17%), accidents (12.09%), heart disease (11.94%), and diabetes mellitus (4.49%). A total of 15 208 public and private hospitals and clinic centers provide a comprehensive health-care service. The government mandated an "All People" medical care insurance program covering the entire population of Taiwan.

Changes in consumer behavior

The average household consumption expenditure was US$15 000 in 1992. The consumption percentage spent in the non-durable goods category on items such as foods, beverage, and grocery products has declined, whereas the percentage spent on durable goods and services, including medical expenses, travel, entertainment, education, banking and financial services, transportation, and telecommunications, has increased (see Table 17.3). Among these changes, the most significant is the food, beverage and tobacco category, which dropped from 62% in 1951 to 27% in 1993.

But this does not imply that Taiwanese consumers eat less or drink less. On the contrary, because the increase in real purchasing power has also increased discretionary income, Taiwanese consumers consume and demand more in both quantity and quality. In 1994, agricultural imports amounted to US$8 billion, up 11.3% from the previous year. The popularity of American restaurant chains and the more Western food items such as cheese, beef, and wine, in the daily diet, indicates that Western foods are gradually changing dietary consumption patterns. Similarly, consumption patterns in other industries, such as durable goods, automobiles, and telecommunications, have changed drastically as a result of increased purchasing power and more sophisticated buying behavior.

Consumption of durable goods

Durable goods were considered the symbol of family wealth in Taiwan 30 years ago, but this is no longer the case. Goods such as color TV sets, refrigerators, and washing machines are necessities for Taiwanese families; more than 90% are in possession of these electronic appliances (see Table 17.9). Following the worldwide trend, home computers, fax machines, and cordless phones are now the new status symbols for younger generation families. An estimated 15% of families own a home computer, and about 40% own a fax machine. According to the Information Industry Institute (CETRA 1995), Taiwan is currently the world's top producer of motherboards, computer mice, scanners, monitors, keyboards, network cards, and notebook computers. These items account, respectively, for 80%, 80%, 61%, 56%, 52%, 34%, and 28% of worldwide production. The computer and information products trade shows constantly held in Taipei's World Trade Center help to promote not only exports, but also the domestic market.

Transportation vehicles

The motorcycle has been the major transportation vehicle in Taiwan. With 7 million motorcycles and a population of 21 million, Taiwan boasts more motorcycles per capita than any other country in the world. In the late 1970s, when the North–South Freeway was completed, the demand for automobiles

Table 17.9 Penetration rate (%) of major household appliances

Household appliance	*1980*	*1985*	*1991*	*1993*
Color TV set	69.3	92.3	99.1	99.3
Refrigerator	92.3	96.7	99.0	99.1
Air conditioner	14.4	23.9	52.4	60.7
Washing machine	64.7	77.8	89.5	91.5
Telephone	51.1	82.1	94.8	96.0
Home computer	–	2.3	9.6	15
Electricity	99.7	99.7	99.7	99.7
Tap water	66.8	77.9	84.2	86.2
Total household (unit = 1000)	3 675	4 288	4 896	N/A

Source: Bureau of Statistics (1994), *Report on Survey of Personal Income Distribution in Taiwan Area*, Taipei.

started to pick up. In recent years, higher living standards and the redistribution of wealth, promoted by the booming stockmarket and real-estate markets, have further stimulated growth in the automobile market. The percentage of families owning cars increased from 5% in 1980 to 43% in 1993 (see Table 17.10).

Table 17.10 Number of (registered) automobiles and motorcycles and vehicle ownership

Transportation mode	*1980*	*1985*	*1989*	*1993*
Passenger vehicle (auto)	424 443	915 598	1 969 291	3 416 800
Motorcycle	3 965 515	6 588 854	7 619 038	N/A
Bus & truck	254 731	429 371	595 428	790 770
Ownership (per 1000 pop.)				
Passenger vehicle (auto)	24.1	47.8	98.4	162.7
Motorcycle	224.8	344.3	380.8	N/A

Source: Bureau of Statistics (1994), *Report on Survey of Personal Income Distribution in Taiwan Area*, Taipei.

New-auto sales in Taiwan, 400 000 a year by 1994, are likely to reach 600 000 by the end of the decade. Although the demand for automobiles remains strong, factors such as insufficient numbers of car parks, poor road-traffic design, and inflated gasoline prices have hindered such growth. Also, with a nearly tenfold increase in automobile usage, most road systems are overloaded. The ongoing Six-Year National Development Plan is aimed at relieving the congestion problem.

Mass-media services

Since 1987, the demise of Martial Law in Taiwan has spawned vigorous growth in each of the media channels, including many new magazines and newspapers and the entry of satellite television and cable channels. The number of newspapers increased from the regulated 31 to 288 in 1994, and at the same time the number of news agencies increased from 44 to 231. However, for national security and other reasons (Berman 1992), the ruling party, KMT, strictly regulates Taiwan's electronic media, including TV and Radio. As a result, there were about 60 underground radio stations, and about 380 Community Antenna Television outfits using unauthorized frequencies to broadcast. These include NHK from Japan, STAR-TV from Rupert Murdoch, and CNN from the USA, all of which broadcast through illegal channels. This situation was finally legitimized when the Government Information Office passed the Broadcasting and Television Operational Regulation in 1994.

Television is the most popular mass medium, with a 99% penetration rate in Taiwanese families, followed by 68.6 newspaper copies per 100 households and 17.1 copies of magazines (see Table 17.11). Although the number of newspapers has increased almost eightfold, the number of households buying newspapers has decreased. The electronic mass media, especially satellite TV programs such as CNN, BBC, and NHK, and underground radio stations such as TNT, seem to attract educated people aged between 20 and 44 (Leo Burnett 1994). Taiwan currently has two types of TV programming sources–satellite TV channels and local channel operators. Among the basic satellite channels received free of charge are NHK, STAR-TV, Prime Sports, MTV, and TVBS. Pay satellite channels that require authorization from local operators after the payment of subscription fees are HBO, CNN, Discovery, ESPN from the USA, and many other infotainment channels that carry Japanese movies and soap operas, and Mandarin movies and musical-entertainment shows. It is estimated that 60% of total households can receive satellite TV through the direct-broadcast system of Cable TV.

Taiwan's 3 TV stations, TTV, CTV, and CTS, dubbed the "Three Blind Mice" because they are out of touch with market demand and competition, are facing the same challenge. First, because of the pressure from the public, the government finally agreed to allow a fourth, privately owned TV station to begin operating in 1997. Second, since the KMT government controls the 3 other stations, their TV news looks more like propaganda. This has opened up a huge market for the Taiwan audience, who thirst for genuine TV news. The most recent development is satellite TV news. Many local satellite TV stations, including TVBS, CTN, and Super-TV, have rushed in to take advantage of this opportunity. Third, the growing cable TV channels, such as CNN, HBO, Discovery, and Disney, offer a variety of programming that is refreshing to the Taiwanese, tired as they are of homogeneous programs broadcast by the 3 major stations. The fact that cable channels aim at a more segmented audience, and offer more competitive advertising rates, is also posing a threat to the 3 state-operated channels.

Table 17.11 Saturation of TV, newspaper and magazines (number per 100 households)

Mass-media source	*1980*	*1985*	*1991*	*1993*
TV	69.3	92.3	99.1	99.3
Cable TV	–	–	51.3*	60*
Newspapers	58.9	72.7	68.6	63.0
Magazines	9.9	16.7	17.1	16.5

Note:
* estimated figures

Source: Bureau of Statistics (1994), *Report on Survey of Personal Income Distribution in Taiwan Area*, Taipei.

Changes in the macromarketing mix

Trademark and patent protection

The US Trademark Association has identified Taiwan as one of the most problematic countries for protecting trademark rights. Prodded by threats of trade sanctions from the USA, as well as by the motive of continued access to the Western market, Taiwan has implemented extensive regulations on intellectual property rights. The most recent amendment to the Trademark Law, which became effective in December 1993, is intended to overhaul the old system to meet international standards (Yang 1994). The International Classification of Goods and Services under the Nice Agreement has been adopted in the new Enforcement Rules, which became effective in July 1994. This new law intends offering protection to holders of rights that is on a par with international standards. In addition, the Fair Trade Law, the Integrated Circuit Protection Law, the Industrial Design Law, the Cable TV Law, the Video Reproduction Law, and the Trade Secrets Law provide intellectual property protection.

The enforced intellectual property protection laws do not only help foreign companies, as many domestic firms have benefited as well. Consumers are now paying more for higher quality publications. Companies and authorized dealers need no longer fear competition from "pirated" versions of cheaper and low-quality products. Higher royalties and profit margins have helped publishers to reinvest in R&D and come up with more new products. The immediate impact is visible in Taiwan's computer software industry, which has become a major Chinese software supplier (Wang 1995).

In 1994, there were more than 40 companies in CD-ROM products alone; together they developed 160 CD titles in that year.

Products

Imported products have long dominated Taiwan's luxury-goods market. High-price-tag consumer items, such as cognac, perfumes, and jewelry from France, leather and clothing from Italy, video games and automobiles from Japan, and computer and medical products from the USA, have long dominated this elite segment. And, with the further opening of the Taiwanese market and the increasing number of retailing channels, the demand for foreign goods will continue to grow. Taiwanese consumers are highly fashion conscious and somewhat insensitive to price. Innovative Western products with strong brand images will continue to fulfill their needs, if consumers can be assured of reasonable quality.

A recent study on women's sweaters indicated that the country of origin significantly influences Taiwanese consumers' perception of product quality. The sweater with the "Made in Japan" label received the highest ranking, while the sweater labeled "Made in Taiwan" had the lowest rating. The labels "Made in the USA" and "Made in Italy" were rated somewhere in between (Lin & Sternquist 1994). Although the result cannot be generalized to cover all goods, the demand for snob-appeal goods in Taiwan remains at an all-time high.

The private-product label started with a local company, the Far East Department Store, selling men's shirts some 20 years ago. Today, many foreign-invested retailers, such as Watson's personal stores, Wellcome and Park'N Shop supermarkets, and Carrefour discount stores, have introduced their own private-label products at a fairly aggressive pace. In the long run, the private label could be a threat to advertised brands, especially local ones.

The costs of pollution were very rarely taken into account in the past. However, environmental awareness has now arrived, bringing with it new pressure on both the government and business sectors. Several demonstrations have been held by environmental groups against polluters such as nuclear-power reactors and landfill sites. Yet green marketing is still on a self-regulatory basis, as the government has not enforced any mandatory programs on the business sector.

The concern for a healthier diet has long been a tradition in Chinese culture. The only difference is that the Taiwanese definition of "healthy" is very different from that of Westerners. The Western standard of low calories, low sodium, low cholesterol, low caffeine, and high fiber are well accepted among consumers, but the philosophy of choosing healthy food is Taoism or Yin-Yang oriented. Many people believe that any natural foods, from the mountain or the sea, have tonic and curative effects, and that products with artificial colors and flavors, chemical additives, preservatives, and special treatments are not considered healthy.

Distribution

The number of supermarkets, department stores and convenience stores has increased rapidly in recent years. In the past, most department stores were small, with a fairly limited cashflow and a poor product assortment; the "Mom and Pop" corner grocery stores and traditional markets were noted for their unpleasant sanitary conditions and limited store hours. Many of these are now giving way to clean, convenient, and efficiently run Western-style chain stores (Lim 1991; Chang & Sternquist 1993). A large proportion of traditional grocery stores have disappeared in the urban area, with many of them being converted to franchisees of large convenience stores or supermarket chains. It has been estimated (Lim 1991) that the opening of one new convenience store would cause 6 adjacent independent stores to close.

Since the first supermarket chain store (Taipei Agri Produce) and the first 14 convenience stores (President Enterprise) were opened in 1980, Taiwan has experienced tremendous growth and modernization in its retailing sector. In 1993 there were over 2000 supermarkets, which took in an estimated US$2.9 billion in sales. Major players include the market leader Wellcome (Hong Kong), Park'N Shop (Hong Kong), Yac's (Japan), Matsusei (Japan), and local chains Taipei Agri Produce, Weichuan, and Huei-yang.

Because of the limited availability of store sites, high real-estate prices, and the high population density in Taiwan, the expansion of convenience stores is the fastest growing type of retailing. The market leader, President Enterprise, has more than 1400 stores in Taiwan, and had sales of US$665 million in 1993. Its stores include 500 President Bakery Shops and 1000 convenience stores joint ventured with 7-Eleven (Liu 1992; Lee 1995). President's major competitors include Weichuan (with ARCO), Circle K (USA), Sunshine, Family Mart (Japan), and drugstore chains Watson (Hong Kong) and Mannings (Hong Kong). In 1993, there were already more than 2500 convenience stores in Taiwan.

Like other retailing businesses in Taiwan, the department store is also undergoing major revamping. The country's biggest department store, Far East Department Store (25% of market share), has had to contend with elite Japanese groups such as Sogo, Isetan, Tokyu, Mitsukoshi, and Yaohan, and discount store giants such as Carrefour (France), Makro (the Netherlands), and Price Costco (USA). Taiwan had 3582 department stores islandwide, with estimated sales of US$5 billion, by 1993.

With the rapid transition in the distribution industry, however, independent stores still remain a major force in the retailing business. The total sales of independent stores is greater than that of department stores and supermarkets combined (see Table 17.12). One reason, perhaps, is that traditional shopping habits are not easily changed. For Taiwanese consumers, the corner stores still offer the highest utility in terms of convenience, shopping efficiency, and friendliness. Furthermore, many independent stores have linked with large wholesalers to form de facto chains that compete with convenience stores and supermarkets in pricing and product assortment.

Table 17.12 Number of sales establishments, and sales volume (US$ billion), for retailing and wholesaling

	1990	*1991*	*1992*	*1993*
Wholesalers	72 412 ($100 m)	78 397 ($108 m)	86 017 ($119 m)	93 212 ($130 m)
Independent retailers*	336 164 ($427 m)	346 482 ($478 m)	359 313 ($498 m)	366 820 ($511 m)
Department stores	3 289 ($4.5 m)	3 484 ($4.8 m)	3 510 ($4.9 m)	3 582 ($5.0 m)
Supermarkets	720 ($1.0 m)	1 148 ($1.6 m)	1 596 ($2.2 m)	2 052 ($2.9 m)

Note:
* Convenience stores are classified in this category.

Source: Economic Yearbook of the Republic of China (1994), Kwang Hwa Publishing Co., Taipei.

Price

While the business cycle and income elasticity may have a direct impact on the demand for luxury goods and necessities, the factor with the greatest influence on consumption is government regulation. In Taiwan, licenses for imported goods are grouped into three distinct classes: prohibited, controlled, and permissible. As Taiwan moves toward greater trade liberalization, an increasing number of goods will be able to be traded freely. More than 6000 items can now be imported without permits. Apart from certain traditional areas such as agriculture, telecommunications, and electricity supply, where higher tariffs apply, non-tariff barriers are minimal. In general, consumers benefit from greater trade liberalization. From 1989 to 1993, the consumer price index fluctuated between 3% and 4%, showing steadiness in the price of consumer products (see Table 17.13). This figure is lower than that for either China or Hong Kong.

However, non-tariffs do not necessarily imply that all goods are permissible. A very unique industrial feature in Taiwan is the existence of state-run companies, including more than 100 companies with total estimated assets of US$7.4 billion (1994 estimate). These state-run conglomerates (which operate in industries such as petroleum, construction, telecommunications, steel, transportation, electronic mass media, real estate, and financial services) control more than 20% of Taiwan's GNP. Taiwan enacted the Fair Trade Law (similar to the Antitrust Law) in 1991 to prohibit monopolistic and oligopolistic enterprises from unfairly excluding others from the market and thus maintaining unfair pricing policies. Yet the majority of state-run companies have been excluded from the Fair Trade Law. This has made the price of some necessities artificially high.

Table 17.13 Consumer Price Index (rate of annual increase, %)

	1975	*1980*	*1985*	*1990*	*1993*
CPI	47.14	71.45	6.58	96.51	107.54
Commodities (excluding food)	65.13	92.57	104.56	98.05	99.67
Services	32.54	55.81	75.99	93.16	110.47

Source: Republic of China, *Statistical Yearbook of the Republic of China*, Kwang Hwa Publishing, Taipei.

Advertising

Since deregulation in 1988, the mass-communication media have shown unprecedented growth. In the area of electronic media, cable TV was finally legalized in 1994, after many years of government bans. The new services, which include STAR-TV, NHK, CNN, MTV, and TVBS, offer viewers more diversified programming than that offered by the 3 homogenous state-controlled TV stations. The Government Information Office has agreed to liberalize the electronic media. Yet intellectual property protection, the expansion and integration of channels, fees charged, and rating audits still remain problematic areas in this new medium.

Advertising expenditure has grown significantly, with an average growth rate of 16%. In 1994, total expenditure was US$3.0 billion, which ranks around 14th or 15th worldwide. Of the 4 major media, television has become the leading advertising medium for the first time in advertising history, followed by newspapers, magazines, and then radio (see Table 17.14).

The "Other" category, which makes up 19% of media expenditure, includes direct mail, outdoor billboards, newspaper inserts, and the Yellow Pages. The annual growth rate in this category is 12.61%, which is lower than that for the 4 major media. In 1993, expenditure was ranked in the following order:

1 direct mail (US$65 million)
2 outdoor billboards (US$60 million)
3 newspaper inserts (US$57 million)
4 electronic spot advertisements (US$49 million)
5 flyers (US$45 million)
6 the Yellow Pages (US$45 million)

Table 17.14 Advertising expenditure by media, 1983–1992 (US$ billion)

	1983	*1984*	*1985*	*1986*	*1987*	*1988*	*1989*	*1990*	*1991*	*1992*
Total	**0.64**	**0.64**	**0.76**	**0.84**	**1.09**	**1.39**	**1.78**	**1.84**	**2.02**	**2.60**
Growth rate (%)	**20.8**	**15.1**	**2.6**	**11.9**	**28.5**	**27.6**	**28.1**	**3.8**	**9.8**	**28.3**
Newspaper	0.27	0.30	0.28	0.34	0.47	0.58	0.77	0.73	0.78	1.03
TV	0.19	0.23	0.27	0.29	0.33	0.42	0.52	0.59	0.66	0.84
Radio	0.05	0.06	0.06	0.06	0.06	0.07	0.08	0.12	0.10	0.16
Magazine	0.04	0.04	0.05	0.06	0.08	0.10	0.11	0.09	0.11	0.10
Other	0.10	0.11	0.10	0.11	0.14	0.21	0.29	0.31	0.34	0.47

Source: Advertising Agencies Association (1994), Report, Taipei.

7 public transit (US$42 million)
8 other (US$172 million)

Flyers, newspaper inserts and direct mail showed dramatic increases over the previous year (1992)—41.2%, 36.4%, and 29.6% respectively—while the Yellow Pages and exhibition spending had a minimum growth of around 4%.

The top 10 advertising companies in Taiwan are President Enterprise (food and convenience chain stores), Ho-Tai Auto, P & G, Unilever, Kao, King Car Soft Drink, Nan-Yang Auto, Yu-Long Auto, Ford Auto, and Anchor (daily products). The top 8 product advertisers are Nan-Yang Automobile (US$5.9 million), Anchor Daily Product (US$4.9 million), Hitachi Air Conditioner, Tiger Coffee, Yamaha Motorcycle, Unilever Detergent, China Airline, and Kai-Shu Wu Loong Tea (Leo Burnett 1994).

Zandopour, Chang and Catalano (1992) have carried out research in the USA, France and Taiwan to compare advertising strategy, content, and form of execution. Commercials from Taiwan tend to present facts about the availability of the products and special offers without being conceptually or thematically integrated, and are also more likely to make explicit promises that offer more than the product can produce. Taiwanese consumers are more accustomed to subtle and symbolic presentation that links the product to a place, an event or a person.

Direct marketing

Although the expenditure on direct marketing has experienced a tremendous growth in Taiwan, it is yet to be a significant force in integrated marketing communications. The major players, which include Ogilvy & Mather Direct, and locally listed brokers Auto-mail, Showline, and Response, offer direct marketing and telemarketing services; however, there are several reasons the growth of direct marketing could be hindered. First, in terms of business customs, personal contact and familiarity in a traditional shopping environment are important for earning trust from and acceptance by customers. Telemarketing and TV home shopping are viewed as a nuisance, and considered untrustworthy. Second, database marketing relies heavily on customer information, in the form of geodemographics and purchase histories. The necessary information bases, such as GIS (Geographical Information System), single-source data, credit-card purchase records, and census data, are either not easily accessible, or simply do not exist. Third, the telephone network (which provides the 1-800 and 1-900 numbers), postal service (low-cost bulk rate), private transportation operators (Federal Express's overnight delivery), and also TV stations (the home shopping channel) are tightly regulated by the government. There is no significant cost advantage in direct marketing, as opposed to using the traditional mass media.

Market research

Increased foreign participation has transformed both the advertising and marketing research industries in recent years. Global giants such as Saatchi & Saatchi, Dentsu, Leo Burnett, and McCann-Erickson, have all rushed to capitalize on Taiwan's growing consumerism. Along with the booming number of foreign advertising agencies is the marketing concept they have brought with them. Many companies have increased their emphasis on the significance of marketing as a driving force for business operations and strategic planning. As a result, more companies in Taiwan now appreciate the importance of market research, consumer studies, advertising research, and media-habits research. The major players here are A.C. Nielsen, Burke, INRA (International Research Associates), SRG (Survey Research Group), and Redwood Market Research Center; their total expenditure in 1994 was an estimated US$30 million.

Since Taiwan is an economy oriented to international trade, business-to-business marketing research is essential. The China External Trade Development Council (CETRA), a non-profit, independent trade-promotion organization supported by government and local business associations, offers market information to companies doing business in Taiwan. Information items include how to do business with Taiwan, and news on Taipei International trade shows and trade opportunities in Taiwan; trade enquiry services are available at its World Wide Web Homepage, http://tptaiwan.org.tw/.

Future trends and expectations

Economic trends

Economic growth in Taiwan has been projected at 7% per year for the period 1995–2001. This is lower than the boom period of 1960–1987, which saw growth of 10% per year, and also lower than the figure for the transition period (the period that followed the lifting of Martial Law) of 8% in

1988–1994. The appearance of this new growth rate suggests that Taiwan has passed through the high growth phases of the Japanese agriculture-colonialism period (1895–1947) and also the labor-intensive manufacturing period (1960–1980), and is now heading toward a mature services- and technology-oriented economy. Taiwan is expected to join the ranks of the industrially advanced countries by the end of the year 2000.

In order to sustain these economic growth rates of 7% or above, several new economic policies are now under way. These include:

- government spending on the Six-year Plan
- encouraging domestic and private investment
- reforming the financial system and consumer credit
- plans to modify the current tax system (such as tax on deposit interest and dividend income) to encourage consumption

The newly revised Six-year National Development Plan (1997–2003), proposed by the Council for Economic Planning and Development, plans to boost per-capita income to US$20 000 by the end of the year 2000. Other missions include reinforcing industrial potential, promoting balanced suburban development, and improving the quality of life, including infrastructure and the living environment.

Another major initiative is the Going-South Investment Strategy. This policy was proposed with the aim of cooling down the fever of investing in China, and redirecting the capital to South-East Asian nations, including Vietnam, Indonesia, the Philippines, Malaysia, and Thailand. In 1993, investment in China reached its all-time high of US$9.97 billion. As China continues the military threat to underscore its sovereign claim to Taiwan, many businessmen worry about the risk of confiscation of assets in a takeover situation. Taiwanese investment in China dropped to US$5.4 billion in 1994. But the real concerns are not political; rather, they are both legal and economic. Political instability, out-of-control regional governments, inadequate legal guarantees, frequently changed legal and taxation policies, wage hikes, and inflation have stirred up the fearfulness and uncertainty arising from doing business with China (Mainland Affairs Council 1995).

Demographic trends

The major demographic trends in Taiwan include the following:

1. suburbanization
2. a declining population growth
3. an ageing population

Suburbanization is a major trend in Taiwan, especially for those young families who live in northern Taiwan and the greater Taipei area. Taipei's mass transit system and the new islandwide highway system will facilitate this process. This change will mean success for most business sectors, including durable goods, housing and construction, financing, retailing, and other services.

The combination of a declining population growth and an ageing population is not as alarming as it sounds. This is because Taiwan will remain a very densely populated country even with zero growth rate in the future. Yet ageing may be a problem after 2030, when the proportion of the population aged 65 and above is predicted to reach 20% (the figure for 1993 was 8%). This could cause the build-up of a financial burden, in that the government must meet the elderly's social subsidy. Contrary to past family-planning programs aimed at trimming population growth, the government now has a more moderate slogan, "Two is just right and three is not too many," to boost the fertility rate.

Cultural trends

Women's liberation in Taiwan continues. The most current reform, the "New Warm Life" package, prompted by the feminist Awakening Foundation, aims to grant equal rights in marriage, to protect the rights of women and children, and to set up a new system for divorce and separation. The existing code, which has legitimized male domination by measures such as requiring the wife to take her husband's surname, giving control of the couple's assets to the husband, and denying child visitation and custody rights to mothers after separation, will be dropped.

Environmental and health concerns remain an area of conflict between the general public and the government. While the ruling party, KMT, is eager to effect the economic plan, which includes building the new nuclear plant, the electric rail system, and new harbors, many environmental activists risk the danger of being arrested in their efforts to protect the wetlands and rivers.

Since President Lee Deng-Hui took office, and even allowing for political liberation, the ethnicity issue has been intensified. In all political elections in Taiwan, the population is clearly divided into 2 ethnic groups in terms of support for the 3 political parties, CNP, DPP, and KMT. The CNP, whose members are mainly from mainland China, insists on future unification with China. The opposition, the DPP, with the majority of its members native Taiwanese, advocates Taiwan independence. The ruling party, the KMT, whose members are a mix of Taiwanese and mainland Chinese, has shifted from reclaiming the mainland to a somewhat confused identity: "One country, Two Chinas" (i.e. the PRC and the ROC). Both the DPP and the CNP have gained a steady increase in the number of supporters, while the ruling party has lost out (Strasser 1994).

Consumption

Because of population pressure and the increasing number of new families, the expenditure on housing and gross rent will continue to grow. The growing number of working women, single families, and new families in suburban areas means the demand for child care, 24-hour convenience stores, transit services, and other services will increase. The increase in this "new-family" population segment has been accompanied by a rise in the teenage market. The youth segment—age group 10–19 years—represents 18% of the total population. Teens influence family purchases. In Taiwan, in particular, the highly fickle and fashion-oriented teens influence clothing and footwear, recreation, entertainment, and other services.

Taiwan is home to 11 automobile manufacturers, all of them joint ventures with foreign makers. Ford and Yulon are two main players in the local market, followed by imported automobiles from Germany and the USA. Because of the large trade surplus with the USA, the Taiwan government has encouraged a "Buy America" program. Yet Taiwanese consumers have a long tradition in favor of Japanese goods. As a result, the US-made Toyota and Honda models accounted for more than 50% of imported automobiles (1993 data), posing a serious threat to the local automobile industry as well as other imported models.

Political and diplomatic trends

Not only has the search for a true and individual identity resulted in a domestic social movement, but Taiwan has also reached out aggressively for recognition as an independent country in the international arena. One long-term effort has been the joining of GATT. Even though this involves an extensive modification of the present economic system in order to deregulate foreign imports, and thus depress certain domestic industries to varying degrees, the government considers the goal as a top priority. In addition, participation in the UN is also a major focus of Taiwan's plan to enter into the international community.

In order to achieve its diplomatic goals in many areas, Taiwan must give up its official "Republic of China" title and settle for a less formal name; in this way it will be able to make an appearance on the international stage. Nevertheless, these aggressive moves have only served to irritate China, which has claimed that it will unify Taiwan by brute force if necessary. Yet China is hurting itself by failing to understand Taiwan's most important driving force: seeking UN membership and, thus, the democratization of Taiwan. The 1996 Presidential Election was the first time in history that the Taiwanese people had the right of self-determination, and the right to determine their own future—with or without China's endorsement.

Marketing management in the late 1990s

Internationalization

Taiwan depended on its close relationship with the USA to create its "economic miracle" in the 1960s and 1970s. This era is drawing to an end as dependence on the US market diminishes and the need to remedy US trade deficits becomes more urgent. The development in China's coastal provinces and in various other South-East Asian nations, including Thailand, Malaysia, Indonesia, the Philippines and Vietnam, has seen the combination of these places into a single region of economic growth. Taiwan has poured capital, technology, people, and international trade knowhow into this new economic region where cultural, religious, ethnic, linguistic, and subregional identity are often similar to its own.

However, the reason for Taiwan's success may also be the cause of its downfall. Taiwan has created many new competitors in labor-intensive industries such as textiles, apparel, leather, lumber furniture, toys, computer keyboards, and agricultural products from neighboring nations. The low-cost pressure from the region will become greater as bilateral trading between those nations increases. As a result, Taiwan has been forced to upgrade its manufacturing and service sectors so that they are more capital, technology, and marketing oriented.

Taiwan's competitive-advantage industries include machine tools, integrated circuits, personal computers, electronics, and shipping. As both the government and the country's companies are eager to enhance their competitiveness in the global market, both government and companies are seeking to form strategic alliances, mainly with Western companies using Taiwan as a foothold into mainland China, as a way of business expansion and technology exchange in the region. Some successful business ventures include Microsoft, Texas Instruments, UFOC (AT&T), TECO (Westinghouse), AMBIT (Daimler-Benz), and MTI (HP and Digital Microwave), all of which have taken advantage of Taiwan as a regional business center (GIO 1995).

Marketing managers must prepare themselves to deal with the consequences of a regional economy and the reality of global competition. These new business ventures are accompanied by a new marketing management philosophy. Rapid changes in manufacturing and design technologies have led to a shorter product lifecycle. Growing computer network integration and advancements in decision-support systems have made the distribution channel more efficient and compact. The efficiency of mass distribution systems will drive the already low prices even lower. For large and small companies alike, the traditional view, which assumes that labor is the major cost component, has to be changed. This is especially important for the original-equipment manufacturers, which represent the majority of Taiwanese companies. More emphasis should be placed on the changing competitive and technological environments, and also on the importance of marketing value-added services such as customer needs, product quality, distribution efficiency, and relationship marketing.

Products

As the country-of-origin effect continues to play an important role to Taiwanese consumers, it is expected that foreign brands will become more important in the late 1990s. Furthermore, with greater protection of intellectual property rights, it is expected that demand for upscale goods, sophisticated capital goods, and franchised products and services will continue to grow. Entertainment and cultural services, telecommunications, finance, education and training, medical and hygiene services, and information services are expected to have the highest growth.

Distribution

Supermarkets will enjoy continued growth. There were 2052 stores in 1993, up from 1260 in 1991 and 126 in 1986. Because of increasing competition, the major trend is toward self-managed alliance stores that control the product selection, quality, and price. Since the market in metropolitan Taipei is mature, the expansion trend is toward the suburban areas in north Taiwan, and mid- and south Taiwan. The growth of convenience stores will level off. It is estimated that a population of 6500 is needed to support one convenience store in Taiwan. There were 2400 stores in 1993, which is close to the maximum level of 3000 stores.

Despite an increase in the number of new department stores in recent years, these stores are at a stage of maturity and decline. Most of the island's department stores posted sales increases of less than 10% in 1993, while revenues for many stores virtually dropped.

As the retailing industry is in a transition period, wholesaling and physical distribution are changing as well. In Taiwan, 5 popular physical distribution systems are TDC (Distribution Center built by Trucker), MDC (Distribution Center built by Maker), RDC (Retailer Distribution Center), WDC (Distribution Center built by Wholesaler), and PDC (Process Distribution Center). In terms of industry trends, the wholesaling industry has developed automated product distribution centers that have the potential to increase customer service capabilities while simultaneously decreasing operating costs. The nation has intensified the application of the bar-code system, the electronic ordering and inventory system, the point-of-sales (POS) system, and the computer aided picking system (CAPS) (Lee 1995).

Problems with land are the most serious difficulty confronting the industry. Under the new ROC plan, the distribution centers are allowed to utilize the 11 transfer facilities for distributors and 7 warehousing zones along the areas near the ramps of the North–South Freeway. It is expected that the wholesaling and distribution industry will record a prosperous growth in the next few years.

Accompanying this growth is the blending of retailer and wholesaler type stores in the same designated zone, so that warehouse clubs and wholesaling outlets have resulted. This blending has resulted from increasing automobile ownership in Taiwan, the near-completion of the public transit system, and the increasing average size of household dwellings; all of this will enhance consumers' shopping efficiency. The new main highways are the second Northern Freeway between Chunan and Chungho, Taipei–Ilan Freeway, and Taipei's mass transit system, which will resolve the serious congestion problems in the greater Taipei metropolitan area.

Advertising

After Japan, Taiwan has the most highly developed communications system in Asia. This government-operated system includes extensive microwave transmission links, and submarine cable links to Okinawa, Guam, Hong Kong, most South-East Asian nations, and Australia. The mass media has had much more room for expansion since the government lifted the ban on the establishment of new broadcasting companies. It is expected that major growth will be seen in the electronic media, including new air waves for radio stations, new public TV stations, the cable TV industry, and the newest form of computer networking–the Internet.

One industry that may benefit from the opening of the electronic media is that of TV home shopping. Since the cost of advertising on the 3 state-controlled TV stations is very high, the opening of cable TV stations, with their narrower target consumers and lower fees, will provide cost leverage with which direct marketers can operate. In 1993, Taiwanese consumers spent US$12 million on home shopping, whereas in 1994 annual sales reached as much as US$38 million. The current market leader is Unlimited Express, with estimated monthly sales of US$1.2 million. Among the fast-selling products are cookwares, small appliances, fashion, and jewelry. It is expected that TV home shopping will grow further with the full liberalization of the cable-TV industry. The print media of newspapers and magazines may continue to grow, but at a lower rate. Another new development is the newly established ABC (Audit Bureau Circulation). It is expected the ABC will help provide advertisers and consumers with verified and accurate circulation figures for the print media.

Conclusion

The impact of the currency crisis of July 1997 has yet to hit Taiwan, whose robust economy seems to be coping thus far. The Taiwanese dollar has dropped in value by about 16%, but inflation is only about 0.3%, and at time of writing Taiwan has a current-account surplus of $US9.7 billion. However, despite this positive picture, there is little doubt that if the crisis continues it will have an impact on the Taiwanese economy. In terms of exports, Taiwan is competing with other ESEA nations (particularly Korea), and, if these nations undergo sharp evaluations, Taiwan may have to follow suit in order to remain competitive. However, the large reserves held by the central banks suggest that Taiwan will weather the storm better than its neighbors.

References

Abegglen, James C. (1994), *Sea Change—Pacific Asia as the New World Industrial Center,* The Free Press, New York.

Advertising Agencies Association (1994), Report, Taipei.

Balassa, Bela (1992), *Economic Policies in the Pacific Area—Developing Countries,* Macmillan, London.

Barclay, George W. (1954), *Colonial Development and Population in Taiwan,* Princeton University Press, Princeton, NJ.

Baum, Julian (1995), "Lee's Challenge—Taiwan, Price of Defying Beijing", *Far Eastern Economic Review,* vol. 158, no. 37, pp. 20–6.

Berman, Daniel K. (1992), *Words Like Colored Glass,* Westview Press, Boulder, CO.

Bureau of Environmental Protection (BEP) (1995), *Taiwan Environment Protection Annual Report,* BEP, Taipei.

Bureau of Statistics (1992), *Educational Statistics of the Republic of China,* Taipei.

— (1994a), *Demographic Statistic of Taiwan-Fukien Area,* Taipei.

— (1994b), *Market Annual Report of Taiwan Area,* Taipei.

— (1994c), *Report on Survey of Personal Income Distribution in Taiwan Area,* Taipei.

CETRA (China External Trade Development Council) (1995), WWW Homepage: http: //tptaiwan.org.tw/

Chang, Hua-Jen (1994), "Impact of Inflation, Output, Employment, and Income Effect in Budget Deficits for Taiwan: A Forecast of Regional Input-Output Approach", *Journal of Policy Modeling,* vol. 16, no. 3, June, pp. 345–51.

Chang, Li Dong & Sternquist, B. (1993), "Taiwanese Department Store Industry: An Overview", *International Journal of Retail & Distribution Management,* vol. 21, no. 1, pp. 26–34.

Chu, Hai-yuan (1994), "Taiwanese Society in Transition: Reconciling Confucianism and Pluralism", in ed. M.A. Rubinstein, *The Other Taiwan—1945 to the Present,* East Gate Book, Armonk, NY.

Cohen, Marc (1995), "Choking on Growth", special issue on the East Asian Economic Miracle, *New Internationalist,* January, no. 263, pp. 22–3.

Economic Yearbook of the Republic of China (1994), Economic Daily News, Taipei.

GIO (Taiwan Government Information Office) (1995), WWW Homepage: http://gio.gov. tw/info/.

Gulati, Umesh C. (1992), "The Foundations of Rapid Economic Growth: The Case of the Four Tigers", *American Journal of Economics & Sociology*, vol. 51, no. 2, April, pp. 161–72.

Hamlin, Kevin (1994), "Greater China", *International Business*, vol. 7, no. 2, February, pp. 66–76.

Lee, Zen-fung (1995), *7-Eleven takes over Taiwan*, Yuan-liu Publishing Inc., Taipei (in Chinese).

Leo Burnett (1994), *Report*, Taipei.

Li, K.T. (1988), *The Evolution of Policy Behind Taiwan's Development Success*, Yale University Press, New Haven.

Lim, Jen-sen B. (1991), "Retailing and Channel Distribution", *Collections for Taiwan Market Research*, Business Strategy Press, Taipei, pp. 643–72.

Lim, Li-wen & Sternquist, Brenda (1994), "Taiwanese Consumers' Perceptions of Product Information Cues: Country of Origin and Store Patronage", *European Journal of Marketing*, vol. 28, no. 1, pp. 5–10.

Liu, Shuei-Shen (1992), "7-Eleven in Taiwan", in ed. N.T. Wang, *Taiwan's Enterprises in Global Perspectives*, East Gate Book, Armonk, NY.

Lu, Hsiu-Lien A. (1994), "Women Liberation: The Taiwanese Experience", in ed. R.A. Rubinstein, *The Other Taiwan—1945 to the Present*, East Gate Book, Armonk, NY.

Mainland Affairs Council (1995), *Taiwan-China Economic Development Statistics Annual Report* , Taipei.

Myers, Ramon H. (1997), "China (Taiwan)", *Far East and Australasia*, 28th edn, Europa Publications, London.

Neilan, Edward (1995), "Kaohsiung: New Trade and Shipping Hub of Greater China", *Tokyo Business Today*, vol. 63, no. 3, March, pp. 42–4.

Parish, William L. & Willis, Robert J. (1993), "Daughters, Education, and Family Budgets: Taiwan Experiences", *Journal of Human Resources*, vol. 28, no. 4, pp. 863–98.

Republic of China (1994a), *National Income in Taiwan Area*, Kwang Hwa Publishing, Taipei.

— (1994b), *Statistical Yearbook of the Republic of China*, Kwang Hwa Publishing, Taipei.

Shapiro, Don (1995), "Transforming Taiwan", *Asian Business*, vol. 31, no. 4, April, pp. 24–8.

Strasser, Steven (1994), "Taiwan's Destiny—Will it become Independent?", *Business Week,* December 5, pp. 8–15.

Wachman, Alan M. (1994), "Competing Identities in Taiwan", in ed. M.A. Rubinstein, *The Other Taiwan—1945 to the Present,* East Gate Book, Armonk, NY.

Wang, Zuei-Chi (1995), "Computer Networking and Telecommunication Softwares in Future Office", special issue on Office Automation and Computer Applications, pp. 21–4 (in Chinese).

Yang, Joseph S. (1994), "New Trademark Law and Enforcement Rules", *East Asia Executive Reports,* vol. 16, no. 6, pp. 9, 19ff.

Zandpour, Fred, Chang, Cypress & Catalano, Joelle (1992), "Stories, Symbols, and Straight Talk: A Comparative Analysis of French, Taiwanese and U.S. TV Commercials", *Journal of Advertising Research,* vol. 32, no. 1, January/February, pp. 25–38.

CHAPTER 18

Thailand

Consumer behavior and marketing[1]

NITTAYA WONGTADA, OROSE LEELAKULTHANIT &
ANUSORN SINGHAPAKDI

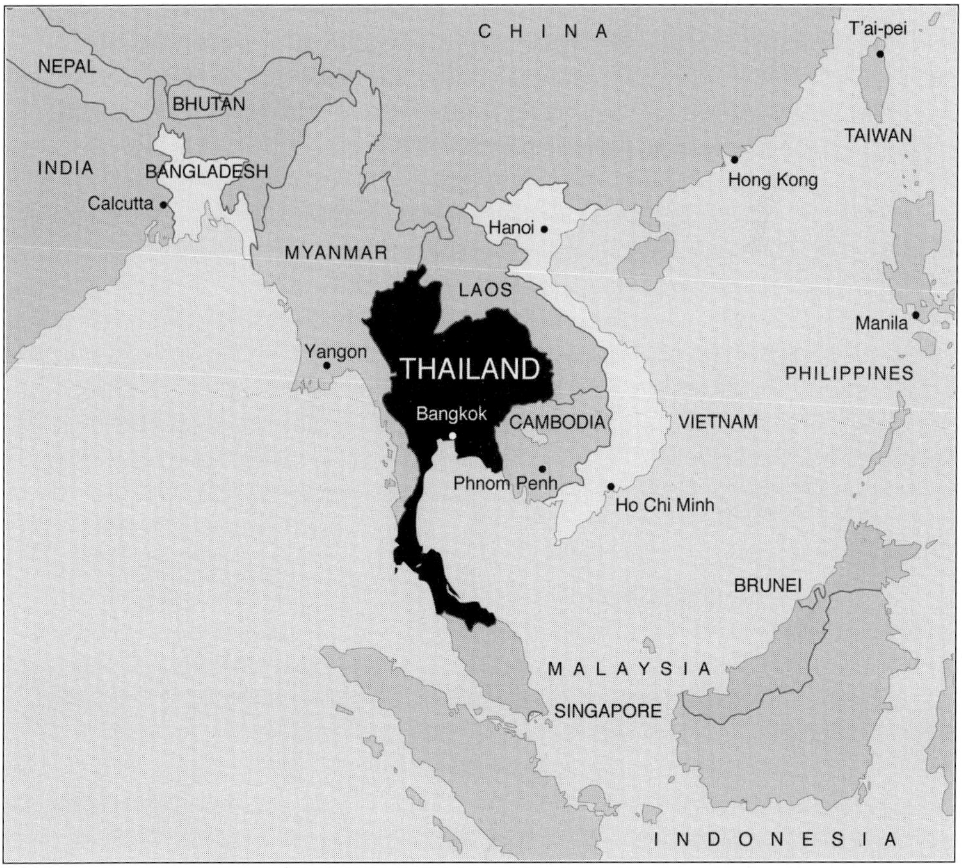

Abstract

Changes in consumer behavior and marketing practices in Thailand are the main focus of this chapter. The description of these changes is divided into 4 sections. The first presents an overview of the geography, history, and prevailing culture of Thailand. The second looks at the main driving forces of modern marketing practices in Thailand. These include economic, sociodemographic and cultural changes, and changes in consumer behavior. The third section discusses the emergence of new patterns of marketing management. The last section provides the implications for marketing management arising from these transformations.

Introduction

The Asian region has received a great deal of attention in recent years as one of the fastest growing market areas (*Marketing News* 1993). Prior to the currency crisis of mid-1997, Thailand was reported to be enjoying one of the highest economic growth rates of all the ESEA nations. Based on a recent estimate, the Thai economy was growing at rates often exceeding 8.5%. In 1995, although growth was slowing to about 8%, it was fourth in terms of growth in Asia after China, Singapore, and Malaysia (*Bangkok Post* 1994). Thailand's exports were also growing at a double-digit rate (Schwarz 1994). However, disaster struck in mid-1997; the baht dropped by 6.0% from July to November, and growth slowed to less than 1%. Nevertheless, given the emergence of Thailand as an important international market in recent years, it is appropriate to examine consumption and marketing in this country.[2]

The main purpose of this chapter is to examine Thailand from a marketing perspective. More specifically, the authors want to show that marketing practices in Thailand have changed dramatically during the last decade, and will continue to advance in the future. To show this, we have divided the text that follows into 4 sections. The first section provides a general overview of the geography, history, and prevailing culture of Thailand. The second covers the changes in environmental factors in Thailand that affect marketing practice: economic, sociodemographic and cultural changes, as well as changes in consumer behavior. The subsequent section discusses the impact of these changes on marketing management. Finally, the last section outlines the implications for marketing management.

General overview

Geography

Thailand has a total land area of 514 000 square kilometres, which makes it about the same size as France. It is situated in the center of the Indochinese Peninsula, and is bordered by Burma, Cambodia, Laos, Malaysia, and the Gulf of Thailand and the Andaman Sea. Its population of approximately 60 million is predominantly ethnic Thai. The largest non-Thai ethnic group is formed by the Chinese, who make up about 15% of the population; most of them live in the commercial center of Bangkok. Through successive waves of immigration and intermarriage, however, the ethnic Chinese are little different than ethnic Thais in terms of cultural practices and national identity.

Approximately 70% of the population lives in rural areas and the rest in the capital city, Bangkok, its surroundings, and other major provincial cities. Bangkok is located in the lower Central Plains, and the traditional language of this region has been adopted as the national tongue. The Thai language is tonal—that is, the same word can have differing meanings if the tone differs.

Bangkok serves as the administrative, financial, industrial, and commercial center of the country, with a population varying from 6 million to as many as 10 million after harvesting when agricultural labor migrates into the city seeking work to supplement income from farming. The other major regional centers are Chiang Mai in the north, Name Ratchasima in the north-east and Songhla/Hat Yai in the south.

History

Throughout its history, Thailand has been influenced by foreign cultures. The Thais themselves are descended from an ethnic group closely related to the Chinese. They originated in South China and then migrated southward in successive waves into South-East Asia during the 11th and 12th centuries (Vandenboshch & Butwell 1967; *Doing Business in Thailand* 1991). Their social and cultural influence interacted with the society and culture of the Khmers, Mons, Malays and other regional groups, and eventually evolved into the one homogeneous Thai culture. The first Thai Empire, Sukhothai, was established in the 13th and 14th century. The Thai monarchy and Buddhism are as old as the Thai nation itself. Starting from King Ramkhamhaeng, who led Sukhothai to growth and prosperity to the current Chakri dynasty, the monarchy has continued to lead the country, and to patronize Buddhism. The status of the monarchy has changed, however, from absolute monarchy to a constitutional one since 1932 (Vandenboshch & Butwell 1967).

The capital city of Thailand moved from Sukhothai to Ayutthaya, Thonburi and eventually to Bangkok, the current capital city. By the time Bangkok became the capital in 1782, contacts between the Europeans and Thais had already begun (Vandenboshch & Butwell 1967). During this Western colonial era, Thailand was the only South-East Asian country that retained its independence. However, part of its historic territory was forfeited in treaties that assured its sovereignty. During the 19th century the Thai monarchy started programs and policies to modernize the nation. The influence of Western culture was evident. The abolition of slavery, the end of the absolute monarchy, and the modernization of the educational system are among the examples of Western influences on Thai culture.

Prevailing culture

The following traits and institutions may be used to define the modern Thai culture.

Buddhism

Ninety-five percent of all Thais practice Buddhism, a religion that emphasises co-existence, tolerance and individual initiative. As a result of this open-mindedness, other religions are also freely practiced. There is a large Muslim community in the south, and the precepts of Christianity, Confucianism,

Hinduism, and Sikhism are celebrated and practiced by various minorities throughout the nation (*Doing Business In Thailand* 1991). The influence of Buddhism on daily life in Thailand is evident. The many temples, the saffron-robed monks making their daily early-morning alms rounds, and the medallions bearing Buddha images worn by most Thais, are but a few indications of their strong faith. Although Thais use the Western calendar, they also use a Buddhist calendar. Many of their holidays reflect the influence of Buddhism.

Monarchy

Currently, Thailand is governed by a constitutional monarchy with the king as head of state. Sovereignty is derived from the Thai people and exercised by the king through the National Assembly, the Council of Ministers (Cabinet) and the courts under the Constitution. Despite the many changes in the country's political scene, the Royal Family provides a unifying and stabilizing force in Thailand.

Thailand developed into a constitutional monarchy in 1932 when King Prajadhipok (Rama VII) introduced a more democratic form of government. The present monarch, Rama IX, is a direct descendant of Rama V, who began the modernization of many Thai institutions in the 19th century. Rama IX, crowned on May 5 1950, is the longest reigning monarch in Thai history.

Hierarchy and seniority

Thai society is organized in a hierarchical fashion: people occupy differently ranked positions (Mulder 1992). Superior versus inferior relationships, therefore, characterize most relationships. There are several overlapping hierarchies in Thai culture, based on such factors as age, social class, education, and position. Examples of hierarchy relationships include parent–child, teacher–student, and patron–client. In all cases, people of lower status are expected to pay courtesy to those of higher status (Aufrecht & Ractham 1991; Mulder 1992). When dealing with new acquaintances, most Thais will try to place them in the hierarchy of social status. As a result, Thais tend to be respectful in order to avoid misplacing status (*Doing Business in Thailand* 1991).

Loyalty

Within the Thai culture, the sense of reciprocal loyalty and responsibility for family and close friends is strong (Aufrecht & Ractham 1991). This obligation means that a person must be available, when asked, to offer assistance within his or her ability. Similarly, family and friends are obligated to reciprocate when the person is in need.

Avoiding confrontation

Open disagreement among Thais is rare. Thais are supposed to be polite and to avoid open conflict (Mulder 1992). "Face" is important; therefore, conciliatory compromise is always the best approach when conflict exists.

Resilience

Thais believe that they may be able to interact with foreign influences without diminishing the role of their own culture. They also believe their history shows that they have successfully achieved this balance in the past (Vandenboshch & Butwell 1967).

Thailand was the only free country in South-East Asia during the Western colonial era. The nation emerged victorious after the Second World War, even though it declared war on the Allies. These events have convinced many Thais that their culture is resilient enough to be able to incorporate and accommodate any foreign influence (Mulder 1992).

Changes in the environment

Economic environment

As shown in Table 18.1, the Thai economy has experienced drastic changes in its economic situation. From the 1980s to the early 1990s, the economy grew rapidly. However, in the latter half of this decade, the country has faced a severe economic recession; this recession is expected to last for two or three years. In this section, only the changes in some important economic variables that directly influence the consumption of Thai consumers will be described. These variables are economic growth, decline and recovery, changes in real income, employment rate, international trade, and an overburdened infrastructure.

Economic growth

From the 1980s until the first half of the 1990s, Thailand was one of the fastest growing economies in the world. The country enjoyed double-digit annual growth rates. In 1993, its economic growth slowed to about 8%; this rate, however, was still impressive when compared to other key industrial countries, which had expected growth rates of 3.6% (*Bangkok Post* 1994).

With this rapid economic growth, the country's GNP almost doubled—from US$1292 in 1989 to US$2371 in 1994 (*BOI Investment Review* 1994). It was forecast (see *Bangkok Post* 1994; Schwartz 1994; Thai Military Bank 1995) that the future of the Thai economy would continue to be vibrant. Moreover, Thailand was anticipated to achieve newly industrializing country status in as little as 5 years (*Consumers of Southeast Asia* 1994).

Economic decline

However, economic growth was overhauled by decline in the second half of the 1990s. Based on the report in the *Bangkok Post Economic Review* in

Table 18.1 Key economic indicators (%)

Indicator	*1993*	*1994**	*1995**
GDP	**8.2**	**8.5**	**8.5**
Agriculture	0.0	3.6	3.4
Commodities	-1.7	3.6	3.5
Non-agriculture	9.4	9.2	9.2
Industries	11.5	11.4	11.5
Construction	8.3	8.1	9.3
Trading	7.3	7.6	7.5
Other	8.9	8.3	7.9
Consumption	7.6	7.9	7.7
Private sector	7.9	8.5	8.2
Investment	8.7	10.8	11.5
Private sector	8.6	8.1	10.6
Government & state enterprises sector	9.6	21.2	14.8
Price level	**3.3**	**5.0**	**4.8**
Food	2.1	6.9	5.0
Non-food	4.2	3.8	4.7
International trade			
Exports **(Bt bn)**	921.4	1 096.5	1 277.8
% change	13.0	19.0	16.5
Imports **(Bt bn)**	1 143.1	1 337.0	1 543.0
% change	12.0	17.0	15.4
Trade balance **(Bt bn)**	-221.7	-240.5	-265.2

Note:
* Estimates

Source: Bangkok Post (1994), "Thailand Set to Rank 4 in Asian Growth", *Bangkok Post Weekly Review*, December 30, p. 11.

1998, the economy grew by 0.6% in 1997 and by 0% to 1% in 1998, compared with 6.4% in 1996. Heavy reliance on external funds is a main reason for this downturn. After the liberalization of the financial market in 1993, companies in Thailand rushed to take advantage of cheap foreign credits. Few borrowers sought to hedge their foreign-currency exposure because, among other reasons, the Thai baht was essentially pegged to the US dollar. The newly acquired funds were invested in such non-productive activities as property and equities. Speculation drove up the market price, and perpetuated the oversupply of housing. This led to an excessive external debt.

Then the rosy economic picture turned bleak. In 1997, the country's external debt was about $99 billion, or about 55% of GDP. The majority of this debt, privately incurred, was $71.7 billion. Moreover, the strengthening of the US dollar against other currencies caused Thai exports to be non-competitive in the world market. The export growth rate decreased from 23.6% in 1995 to zero in 1996. Thailand's deficit was 8% of GNP in 1995, and 7.9% in 1996.

Eventually, the confidence of foreign and domestic investors disappeared when several market signals gave warning of trouble. Some developers and financial institutions defaulted on their loans. To reduce the current-account deficit, the Bank of Thailand tightened monetary policies. International currency markets speculated that the Thai baht would be devalued, and the Bank of Thailand lost a lot of its foreign reserve in attempting to preserve the country's existing exchange rate. US credit agencies Standard and Poor's and Moody's Investor Service reduced Thailand's credit rating for the first time, indicating future macro-economic difficulties.

Finally, the central bank of Thailand was forced to adopt a "managed float" exchange system, which automatically devalued the baht. Being unable to pay its foreign debts, the Thai government requested the assistance of the International Monetary Fund (IMF).

Economic recovery

Based on the information in the *Bangkok Post Economic Review* (1998), it is expected that the current recession will be over within 2 to 3 years. Export revenue will be the main engine for this recovery. With the depreciation of the baht, Thai exports of labor-intensive products, in particular, have increased. For example, in the first 3 quarters, shipments of garments increased by 8%, and the figure for agricultural products rose by 4.1%. The Commerce Ministry expected exports for 1997 would increase by 3.5% to US$57.87 billion. With a recorded trade surplus in the third quarter of 1997, Thailand's current-account balance has improved dramatically.

Inflation

Before 1997, while high inflation was a problem for Thailand, this did not hinder the rise of real income, because the country's productivity exceeded its inflation rate. As compared with the expected rate of inflation of 2.5–2.6% for developed countries, Thailand's overall inflation level was relatively high: 3.3% in 1993. However, because the country's GNP growth rate has been higher than its inflation rate, its real-income gain was substantial (Schwartz 1994).

Under the current situation, despite the fact that the baht has been devalued by over 50%, the annual inflation rate is predicted to be only 10–12%

(*Bangkok Post Economic Review* 1998). This is due to strong price competition among businesses in the context of shrinking market demand. Moreover, the strong agricultural sector is keeping food prices down.

International trade

As previously stated, the international trade sector is crucial to the country's economy. During the past two decades, the high economic growth has been credited in part to Thailand's international trade. Thai international trade moved toward high value-added transactions and away from traditional agricultural products.

Thais were exporting more industrial goods that brought more foreign exchange, and experienced fewer market fluctuations (*Summary on Economic Situation in 1994 and Trends in 1995* 1995). Some industrial goods rivaled agricultural product exports. In 1993, Thailand's top five exports were electronics and components, textiles, frozen seafood, canned and processed food, and gems and jewelry. Some traditional export products, such as rubber, rice, and tapioca have become less important. In fact, agricultural exports as a group fared poorly; the total value in 1993 was only 13.3% (*BOI Investment Review* 1994). At the same time, the country imported more high-tech goods such as telecommunications equipment, computer equipment, medical equipment, and food processing and packaging machinery, in preparation for future exports (*Consumers of Southeast Asia* 1994).

During the peak time, the volume of export and import trade expanded at the rate of more than 10% annually. As a whole, the country continued to have a negative trade balance. Nevertheless, the Thai balance of payments remained positive for two reasons.

First, the Thai government deliberately encouraged more foreign investment by liberalizing international trade and investment regulations (*Summary on Economic Situation in 1994 and Trends in 1995* 1995). The government was aggressively courting foreign investors by various methods (Pinkerton 1992). For example, in 1991 Thailand implemented several economic reforms, including tariff reduction and foreign-exchange liberalization, as part of its overall national economic and social development plan. The removal of such foreign-trade and investment barriers greatly accelerated foreign direct investment and the concomitant economic growth.

Second, after the introduction of the *Securities and Stock Exchange Act* and the establishment of the Securities and Exchange Commission in 1992, confidence in the Thai market increased. This led more large foreign financial institutions to invest in the Thai financial market (*Bangkok Post Economic Review* 1993).

The situation has changed drastically under the current recession (*Bangkok Post Economic Review* 1998). Foreign capital has dried up. Imports of both consumer and industrial goods have slowed down for the first time. Exports of agricultural products and other previously non-competitive manufactured goods, such as textiles and leather goods, have surged upward. This has led to a reassessment of the country's international trade policy. Instead of promoting manufactured products, for which Thailand has to depend on technologies from abroad, developing value-added farm products could be the international direction for the future. The agricultural sector has been the country's economic backbone. Unlike the manufacturing sector, it depends very little on imported raw materials. Therefore, it can benefit fully from the devaluation of the baht. The government is assessing how to develop this sector so that it becomes a sustainable competitive advantage for Thailand.

Employment

During the period of economic prosperity, the unemployment rate in Thailand was less than 1% (*Bangkok Post* 1994). Although this figure compares favorably with the statistics for Western economies (e.g. 5–6% in the USA), an unemployment rate this low creates a labor-scarcity problem.

Much of the Thai industrial and services sector at this time faced a problem of labor shortage, especially skilled labor. In the past, the country's growth has been based on industries that require low skill levels, such as textiles, food processing, and canning. Industry's labor needs were satisfied by transferring people from the agricultural to the industrial sectors. However, several industries have evolved into new higher-technology production, and services that require a better trained labor force (*Summary on Economic Situation in 1994 and Trends in 1995* 1995).

The current recession puts the known unemployment rate at over 3%, or approximately 2 million people (*Bangkok Post Economic Review* 1998). This new unemployed workforce is not limited to unskilled labor, but is also composed of highly educated groups who lost their jobs as a result of the closing of financial institutions and of corporation failures or downsizing. Interestingly, unskilled laborers who had moved to urban centers to work in factories or low-paid service jobs could be reabsorbed by the resurging agricultural sector with relative ease. The skilled laborers, however, have had a tougher time finding compatible jobs. Many have been forced to accept lower paid positions, or to become petty cash vendors. As a result, individual earning has declined, which has had a strong impact on consumer spending.

Income distribution

The previous rapid industrialization in Thailand provided more household income (see Table 18.2), but this was not equally distributed. Except for the northern area of the country, households throughout Thailand experienced some increase in annual income. The most significant increase in household income occurred in the metropolitan Bangkok area. However, the gap between the lowest 20% and the top 20% income brackets was high. Had economic growth continued, the income disparity between Bangkok residents and the rest of the country would probably have continued to widen.

Table 18.2 (a) Annual household income (in bahts); (b) Income distribution

(a)

Area	*1990*	*1993*
North	67 224	61 164
North-eastern	51 564	55 728
Central	76 008	83 304
South	62 172	73 860
Bangkok Metro Area	148 308	182 880

(b)

	1975/76	*1981*	*1986*	*1990*	*1995**	*2000**
Top 20%	42.26	51.47	55.63	56.48	58.74	60.95
Lower 20%	6.05	5.41	4.55	4.05	3.48	2.96
Top/lower	6.99	9.51	12.23	13.95	16.88	20.59

Note:
Figures for top and lower 20% are in 1000 Bt.

Source: Faculty of Economics, *Thai Economy in the Year 2000*, 17th Annual Symposium, Faculty of Economics, Thammasat University.

Income distribution by economic sector is presented in Table 18.3. From the information shown, it is evident that the income of the manufacturing sector gained more than the other sectors. Again, if economic growth had continued, the average per-capita income of the manufacturing worker would have continued to rise. A comparison of the projected figures for the year 2000 with those for 1990 suggests that the average per-capita income of workers in the manufacturing sector would increase by 87.8%, compared to 30.9% and 62.1% for the agricultural and services sectors.

However, the impact of the existing economic decline could distort the current pattern of income distribution. Although it is still uncertain, the income of the agricultural sector could surpass that of the manufactured-products sector. Since the agricultural sector is located outside of metropolitan Bangkok, it is possible that some regional locations will experience a higher income gain. For instance, the price of rice has been unprecedentedly high since its export demand has surged due to the devaluation of the baht. Thailand produces over a quarter of the world's rice-paddy production

Table 13.3 Distribution of income (in Bahts) by economic sector

Sector	*1990*	*1991*	*1992*	*1993*	*1994*
Agriculture	7 661.86	7 974.16	8 091.98	8 167.68	8 289.65
Manufacture	87 507.40	96 471.67	103 314.68	111 222.44	119 991.83
Services	71 718.08	70 543.40	74 643.74	79 377.84	85 430.64
Average	34 845.30	37 043.25	39 207.94	41 671.67	44 595.65

	1995	*1996*	*1997*	*1998*	*1999*	*2000*
Agriculture	8 692.25	9 017.07	9 169.13	9 370.43	9 766.50	10 027.10
Manufacture	122 720.31	125 310.78	134 432.60	143 871.61	153 495.62	163 437.80
Services	87 885.41	94 218.36	100 883.74	107 727.93	109 669.32	116 229.66
Average	47 780.08	51 020.09	54 399.04	57 909.31	61 489.97	65 135.83

Source: Faculty of Economics, *Thai Economy in the Year 2000*, 17th Annual Symposium, Faculty of Economics, Thammasat University.

(*Bangkok Post Economic Review* 1998). Fearing a rice shortage, the Thai government launched an investigation to see if the middlemen were driving the price up. To the government's surprise, it was the farmers who were hoarding rice for more profits.

Infrastructure

Rapid economic growth in Thailand has created a drain on the country's infrastructure. Power shortages, an inadequate telecommunications system, chronic urban traffic jams, and port congestion are among the main problems (Ungphakorn 1993; *Summary on Economic Situation in 1994 and Trends in 1995* 1995). These problems are most acute in Bangkok, and are appearing in other major cities as well. Traffic in Bangkok approaches gridlock. The city has only 112 main roads, with a total length of 524 km, and 4280 smaller roads. Its road surface area is less than 11% of the city's land area, compared with 23.2% in New York and 13.6% in Tokyo. The number of vehicles in Bangkok increased from 1.1 million in 1984 to 1.7 million in 1989. This rapid increase in the number of automobiles causes chronic traffic jams in Bangkok and other large provinces. For instance, the average speed of traffic in the business areas is less than 7 km per hour, and less than 20 km per hour in other parts of Bangkok (*Consumers of Southeast Asia* 1994).

Communication services are also inadequate. In 1993 there were only 3 lines per 100 people in Bangkok (Chantranontwong 1993). New telephone installations in Bangkok have progressed slowly. It is difficult to meet current demand. Similarly, with the boom in construction, water and utility shortages have become common.

Pollution

Another problem associated with rapid economic development is pollution. Over the past decade, the environment of the country's large cities has deteriorated. Air pollution, water pollution, solid waste, and excessive noise are the most acute environmental problems (Thailand Development Research Institute 1990; Clifton 1994). Because of heavy traffic congestion, air pollution has worsened in the big cities. Noise pollution in Bangkok also exceeds by several times the recommended environmental standard. Water has become heavily polluted due to the waste discarded from households and factories. Solid waste frequently accumulates faster than the collection capacity. More than 5000 tons of waste are generated daily in Bangkok, whereas its collection capacity is about 4000 tons per day (Petmark & Unksutannasombat 1990). The uncollected solid waste is often disposed in undesignated areas, including canals. Pollution in Bangkok's canals and the canals of the large provinces has killed off the fish and other water animals.

Corruption

In addition to producing congested streets, strained communications, and inadequate infrastructure, the nation's economic advancement has also affected corruption. The acceptance of widespread corruption by up-coming middle-class Thais has been declining because such practices have frightened off large foreign investment (Ston & Janssen 1991; Harley 1992a). This group, which has gained the most from the decade of economic prosperity, views the corruption as a roadblock to economic advancement.

The uprising against the Thai military government in 1992 by the middle-class workers proves this attitude change (Crossette 1992). The majority of the demonstrators were middle-class workers, who carried cellular phones and used facsimile machines to spread news when other mass media were censored. The following year marked the first time in Thailand's political history that the country elected a Prime Minister who was not tainted by either corruption or authoritarianism (Tasker 1993).

Paradoxically, the economic downturn has resulted in increased public disapproval of corruption. After the strong resistance, the government eventually yielded to widespread public pressure, and the Thai parliament successfully passed a new Constitution in 1997 (*Bangkok Post Economic Review* 1998). Under this constitution, the government's cabinet members must report their financial status and sources of wealth. Those suspected of being corrupt will be investigated and prosecuted.

Demographic environment

The demographic structure of Thailand is moving closer to the pattern that is commonly found in developed countries. That is, the country is experiencing slower population growth, and now has more older people, a larger number of urban residents, and smaller household sizes.

Population size

With a 1997 population estimate of approximately 60 million, Thailand's population is expected to reach 65 million by the year 2000. Population growth rate in Thailand during the end of the last decade averaged about 1.5% yearly. Even though this average is considered high by Western standards, the country's population growth rate declined drastically from 2.27% in 1986 to only 0.74% in 1990 (see Table 18.4). Approximately 27% of the population resides in urban areas (see Table 18.5). More people in the central region of the country live in urban areas. Bangkok, the nation's business and industrial center, is located in the central portion of the country.

Table 18.4 Population growth rate (%)

Area	*1986*	*1987*	*1988*	*1989*	*1990*
Whole country	2.27	1.71	2.02	1.69	0.74
North	0.95	0.91	1.38	1.32	1.11
North-east	2.72	1.79	1.96	1.67	1.29
Central	2.7	1.92	2.64	1.72	1.67
South	2.59	1.64	2.15	1.97	1.67
Bangkok Metropolis	1.97	2.57	1.92	2.03	–4.9

Source: Office of the National Economic and Social Development Board (1990), *Social Indicators 1990*, Human Resource Planning Division, Bangkok.

Age distribution

Thai demographic trends mimic those of many Western countries such as the USA and European countries, where the population is getting older due to slowdown in the birthrate and increasing life expectancy. As shown in Table 18.6, the population group under 15 years of age has decreased slightly, while the older population group of over 60 years of age has experienced an increase of almost 4% annually.

Household size

Although the average household size in Thailand is large by Western standards, family size is shrinking. Information on average household size for

Table 18.5 Percentage of population in urban areas

Area	*1986 (%)*	*1987 (%)*	*1988 (%)*	*1989 (%)*	*1990 (%)*
Whole country	26.2	26.6	27	27.4	27.8
North	16.4	16.7	17	17.3	17.6
North-east	10.3	10.5	10.7	10.8	11
Central	29	29.9	30.9	31.9	32.8
South	15.6	15.8	16	16.2	16.4

Source: Office of the National Economic and Social Development Board (1990), *Social Indicators 1990*, Human Resource Planning Division, Bangkok.

different geographical areas of Thailand is given in Table 18.7. The average household size for the whole country was 4.9 persons per household in 1990. There are no profound differences in household size throughout the nation. It is estimated that Thai households will decline to an average size of 3.1 members by 2015 (*Consumers of Southeast Asia* 1994).

Changes in the cultural environment

Rapid economic development and changes in the socio-economic situation have dramatically altered Thai culture. These changes have resulted in a larger number of educated consumers, more openness to the liberalization of modern practices, the increase of materialism, and the deterioration of environmental and population health.

Education

Literacy in Thailand has improved significantly because of governmental educational policies and the widespread belief in the value of education. The Thai government policy has been to promote education. As seen in Table 18.8, more than 90% of Thais finished the 6th grade to satisfy the compulsory requirement. After this level, however, the enrollment rate drops dramatically, to the 30% range for junior high school and the 20% range for high school. After graduating from high school, many students will take the national entrance exam in order to be accepted at one of the national universities. The competition is high, and the number of places is limited. Only 5% of high-school graduates are accepted at universities.

Fortunately, Thai government policy is trying to ameliorate this situation. The current national economic and social development plan (1991–1996) will extend compulsory education from the 6th to the 9th grade (*Consumers of Southeast Asia* 1994). The government plans to further foster higher education by sponsoring Open universities and allowing private universities to

Table 18.6 (a) Population by age group ('000 persons), and (b) Change in population distribution between 1990 and 2000

(a)

Age group	*1986*	*1987*	*1988*	*1989*	*1990*
Total	**52 511**	**53 427**	**54 326**	**55 214**	**56 082**
0–14	18 630	18 570	18 500	18 418	18 325
% change	-0.3	-0.3	-0.4	-0.5	-0.5
% of total	35.5	34.8	34	33.3	32.7
15-59	30 865	31 734	32 589	33 440	34 278
% change	2.9	2.8	2.7	2.6	2.5
% of total	58.8	59.4	60	60.6	61.1
60+	3 016	3 123	3 237	3 356	3 479
% change	3.6	3.6	3.4	3.7	3.7
% of total	5.7	5.8	6	6.1	6.2

(b)

	1990 (%)			*2000 (%)*		
Age group	*Female*	*Male*	*Total*	*Female*	*Male*	*Total*
Total	**49.88**	**50.12**	**100**	**49.89**	**50.11**	**100**
0–14	16.07	16.6	32.67	13.08	13.58	26.66
15–29	15.24	15.76	31	14.14	14.52	28.66
30–49	11.77	11.74	23.51	14.67	14.83	29.5
50-64	4.65	4.28	8.93	5.22	4.96	10.18
65+	2.15	1.74	3.89	2.78	2.22	5

Source: Office of the National Economic and Social Development Board (n.d.), *Population Projection For Thailand 1980-2015*, Human Resource Planning Division, Bangkok.

compete with the national universities. High-school graduates who are not accepted into the national universities can enroll in one of two governmental Open universities or in several private universities. These Open universities raised the higher education level to 20% in 1992.

The value attached to education by the family also contributes to the higher literacy rate. Education is perceived as the major avenue to advancement in

Table 18.7 Population per household (no. of persons)

Area	*1986*	*1987*	*1988*	*1989*	*1990*
Whole country	5.6	5.4	5.3	5.1	4.9
Bangkok	5.7	5.5	5.3	5.1	4.7
Vicinities	5.8	5.3	5	4.8	4.5
Central	5.6	5.4	5.3	5.2	5.0
East	5.7	5.4	5.2	4.9	4.7
West	5.6	5.4	5.3	5.0	4.9
North	4.9	4.8	4.7	4.5	4.4
North-east	6.2	5.8	5.7	5.6	5.5
South	5.5	5.3	5.2	4.9	4.3

Source: Office of the National Economic and Social Development Board, *Social Indicators 1990*, Human Resource Planning Division, Bangkok.

Table 18.8 Enrollment and school-age population ratio (%)

Age group	*1986*	*1987*	*1988*	*1989*	*1990*
Pre-primary (3–5)	30.39	35.04	37.60	38.55	40.43
Primary (6–11)	95.45	94.75	93.73	93.79	93.70
Lower secondary (12–14)	34.27	32.58	32.62	34.22	37.30
Higher secondary (15–17)	24.27	24.09	23.25	22.55	22.47
Higher education*(18–24)	4.77	4.54	4.41	4.55	5.06
Total	40.97	40.74	40.39	40.46	41.05

Note:
* Excludes students at Open universities

Source: Office of the National Economic and Social Development Board, *Social Indicators 1990*, Human Resource Planning Division, Bangkok.

career, income and social status. Thai parents who can afford the expense often place their children in the best elementary schools so that they have a better chance of entering the national universities. Spending the summer abroad attending school is now common among the younger generation of the wealthy. And parental responsibility does not end at basic education. Many Thai students are sponsored by their parents through masters and Ph.D. degrees, taken either domestically or abroad.

Liberalization

The extensive economic growth of Thailand has most certainly changed the ways many Thais view their environment, and consequently, consumption patterns in the country. Two major forces account for the movement toward Western-style liberalization. First, with their higher disposable income, many Thais have travelled or studied abroad, especially in the USA and Europe. As a result of their international exposure, they have adopted Western values, including egalitarianism and individualism. According to Komin (1990), the liberal Thais differ from their conservative counterparts. They place less emphasis on obedience and respect for traditional ways, and more on egalitarian and intellectual values.

The second force influencing liberalization is the increasing number of working women. With high economic growth and the labor shortage, women have gained more income, and more freedom. Those who are less educated have shifted from working in the field or household to employment in factories. For women with more education, management and other professions are more accessible, even though bias toward males is still prevalent. This movement allows women financial independence, and provides additional financial support for their families.

However, the increase in the numbers of women in the workforce does not of itself mean that the liberalization of women follows. Social values and gender-role expectations requiring women to take charge of the household remain strong (Siengthai & Leelakulthanit 1994). Thai working women have searched for ways to cope with this dual responsibility. When housemaids or part-time helpers cannot be found or are too expensive, they delegate household responsibilities to their children, or use more time-saving equipment such as washing machines and other kitchen gadgets. Some working women prolong their single status, or avoid marriage entirely. Others divorce their spouses to gain freedom from being a wife. The divorce rate is expected to increase by 30%, from 9.7% in 1990 to 13.4% in 2000 (National Economic and Social Development Board 1990). In fact, many women in Thailand find being single is as fulfilling as being married (Leelakulthanit & Day 1992).

Materialism

Materialism has been a part of the Thai social structure, and the rise in wealth has accentuated this and allowed the people to consume even more conspicuously. As previously stated, Thai society is not stratified, with simple upper/middle/working-class distinctions. Rather, a person's social status depends on the perception of his status in relation to the person with whom he or she is interacting (Terwiel 1984; Cooper & Cooper 1990). To behave appropriately, a person must accurately assess the other's social position. When introduced to someone new, a Thai will quickly try to establish the relative status of the person he or she is meeting. The first impression will often dictate the relationship between both people.

Appearance and material possessions are commonly used as assessment criteria. In the West, a person has freedom in choosing his or her attire—especially during leisure time. In Thailand, however, a person's ranking is expressed through his or her attire, actions, mannerisms, and speech (Cooper & Cooper 1990). It is not surprising to see Thais who place great pride in "conspicuous consumption" (Thorelli & Sentell 1982). Thais are particular about their appearance (Komin 1990). They buy many outfits, and often dress themselves in quality clothes with designer labels. Such material-possession oriented behaviors are evident in all social classes. Rich people buy what they do not really need, just to show their wealth. Those who cannot afford genuine items buy imitation merchandise. Material possession brings satisfaction in life to Thais (Leelakulthanit & Day 1992).

Interestingly, although the impact of the economic recession on Thai materialism is still uncertain, it is expected to alter behavior. In the early 1990s, Thais became known as 'global shoppers par excellence'. Signs in Thai could be seen posted on shop windows in Switzerland, France, and Hong Kong. But possessing foreign luxury items is no longer seen as positive, since it is cited as a fundamental reason for the current economic crisis (*Bangkok Post Economic Review* 1998). An extravagant demonstration of wealth by using foreign products is blamed as a cause of the depletion of precious foreign currencies.

Health

Economic expansion has occurred to the detriment of the Thai environment and the general health of the population. Modern Thailand has many pollution problems. The effect of pollution on the nation's health is evident. Close to one-eighth of Bangkok residents suffered from respiratory illness in 1989 because of air pollution. In 1994 it was reported that sixty per cent of Bangkok's traffic police had serious hearing loss and respiratory illness because of exposure to noise and air pollution in the course of their duties (*Consumers of Southeast Asia* 1994).

Thais are aware of these problems, especially those who have a higher education and a higher income (Leelakulthanit & Wongtada 1993). Health issues are considered important, and influence consumption. With their increased knowledge about the harmful effects of certain products, educated Thais are willing to purchase environmentally friendly products even when they have to pay higher prices or sacrifice quality (Leelakulthanit & Wongtada 1993; Wongtada, Leelakulthanit & Rice 1994).

Enormous market opportunities exist for products and services for individual use that prevent or treat environmental problems. For example, home and automobile air-purification devices are popular items. The demand for better health care in Thailand is on the rise. Modern hospitals with the latest medical equipment are being built. Many Thai physicians who were working abroad have moved back to the country to provide expensive but advanced medical services.

Another important health issue that should be discussed here is the AIDS epidemic in Thailand, as well as its potential impact on the Thai economy. It is believed that few countries outside Africa face the potential public-health catastrophes that Thailand does with the AIDS epidemic (*Economist* 1990). One of the commonly cited causes of the AIDS problem and its rapid spread is the thriving sex industry in Thailand (e.g. Handley 1989; Lintner & Lintner 1992). Although Thailand has made great strides in building AIDS awareness in recent years, the disease is still considered to be a serious health problem in the country. In fact, AIDS is considered to be the biggest problem facing the health profession in Thailand (Chow 1994). The number of cases of HIV-infected people has been increasing. It was estimated in a 1994 report that 600 000 Thais are already infected (Pinkney 1994). The problem is so serious that it has been reported that AIDS claims the life of at least one Thai each week (Handley 1992b; 1992c). Interestingly, some demographers even cite this epidemic as one important factor that could lead to a possible negative population growth for Thailand by 2010 (Backhaus et al. 1994). It is believed that the AIDS problem could seriously affect the Thai economy (e.g. Handley 1992c; *Economist* 1993). One estimate is that this epidemic, if untamed, could cost Thailand roughly US$8 billion before the year 2000 (Handley 1992b). Obviously, if the problem is not recognized as serious and solved by the Thai government, it will have a major negative impact on the future of the Thai economy.

Changes in consumer behavior

Naturally, higher income and liberation from traditional practices as well as the current economic recession have led to changes in consumption behavior in Thailand. In particular, new behavior can be observed in terms of the increase in consumer credit usage, the changes in consumption patterns, and the favorable attitude toward locally made products.

Consumer credit usage

Traditionally, the use of credit was limited. Most transactions were accomplished using cash and, to a lesser extent, personal checks. However, in recent years credit cards have gained popularity among Thai consumers because of their convenience and because they grant freedom from carrying cash. It is estimated that US$6.2–6.5 million was spent daily by holders of credit cards in 1991 (*Bangkok Post* 1992). Sixty per cent of Bangkok residents and 40% of the non-Bangkok population use credit cards (Yeedin 1994). Credit-card consumption for all Thais is expected to be on the increase, due to the predicted rise in income for all segments, and aggressive strategies by banks.

Consumption

Consumer confidence in the country's economic growth has led to increased consumer spending. During the late 1980s, Thai consumer purchasing power averaged only US$8–12 per shopping trip. In 1992, each shopper increased his or her spending to an average of US$24–32 per purchase in upscale department stores, and US$20 in general department stores (*Business Review* 1992a). In fact, the growth rate of spending in Thailand exceeds that for earnings as well as savings (see Table 18.9). The savings rate declined in 1990 despite the fact that disposable income increased by 10%.

Table 18.9 Personal income, personal outlay and personal savings (in bahts)

Item	*1986*	*1987*	*1988*	*1989*	*1990*
Disposable income per capita **(bahts)**	15 987	17 826	20 422	23 734	26 189
% change	4.1	11.5	14.6	16.5	10.1
Personal outlay per capita **(bahts)**	13 421	14 809	16 536	19 140	22 732
% change	3.7	10.3	11.7	15.8	18.8
Personal saving per capita **(bahts)**	2 566	3 018	3 887	4 644	3 457
% change	6	17.6	28.8	19.5	–25.6

Source: Office of the National Economic and Social Development Board, *Social Indicators 1990,* Human Resource Planning Division, Bangkok.

Existing studies suggest there are 3 consumption patterns for Thais. First, Thais are spending more on imports. According to *Business Review* (1992b), in 1986, Thailand imported about US$11 million worth of foreign goods, about 24.4% of its GNP. However, in 1990, the figure jumped to about US$36 million, amounting to 43.5% of GNP. Second, the changes in the Thai economic and demographic environments have caused some items previously regarded as luxuries and as a display of wealth to be seen as necessities. For instance, the rapid sales growth of cellular phones is due to the desire of the people to be accessible. This is especially important because the public telephone system is unreliable and inadequate (*Bangkok Post Economic Review* 1993). Many businessmen, housewives, students, and food vendors now have these cellular phones where in the past owning such a phone was an indicator of status. Likewise, the labor shortage-problem is severe. Families find it difficult to get domestic help. Using their increased income, many middle class households have bought kitchenware and electrical appliances to ease daily domestic chores. The sales of electric kitchenware reached an estimated

US$100 million in 1991, and are expected to grow between 30% and 40% during the 1990s (*Business Review* 1992a).

The worsening pollution problems have increased the health concerns of many Thais. As a result, they are spending money on health foods, vitamins, exercise, and vacations to less polluted areas. Interestingly, a study on beverage consumption found that milk, unusual as a table staple in the past, was the top ready-to-drink beverage in a recent survey (*Consumers of Southeast Asia* 1994). Furthermore, milk has become the most commonly available beverage in Thai households—50% of the households surveyed kept milk on hand, while only 42% had soft drinks.

Third, for most Thais, the higher-priced consumer goods are still out of reach. Despite the fact that personal income has risen, Thailand is still a long way from achieving Western-style standards of living as in Hong Kong and Singapore. Moreover, income distribution is skewed toward certain consumer groups and industry sectors. Therefore, the majority of Thais have experienced only limited benefits from the country's economic progress. They can only afford, for example, standard electrical appliances and the lower end of the toiletries and cosmetics range (*Consumers of Southeast Asia* 1994).

This does not indicate that a wealthier segment cannot be found. Survey Research Group Ltd. (*Consumers of Southeast Asia* 1994) carried out a survey in the 7 capital cities in the region—Hong Kong, Singapore, Jakarta, Manila, Kuala Lumpur, Taipei, and Bangkok—on the consumer behavior of the elite segment defined as "men and women aged 25 and older who are currently employed in senior positions in business, the professions, government, and education, and who live in the capital cities". The survey found that this group is fairly young: 55% of this segment is less than 40 years old, and highly educated; 44% have a university degree. The Thai elite seems to possess consumer durables that are similar to those of the elite in the neighboring nations (see Table 18.10). The Thai elite also travels abroad frequently, and brings back items it cannot find in the country. This segment is familiar with the latest fashion trends, new electronic gadgets, and other popular items in the West and Japan. Therefore, its consumption patterns are closer to its counterpart in other countries than they are to the consumption patterns of other Thai market segments.

Changes in marketing practice

Marketing practices in Thailand are changing rapidly in response to new market developments. During the last 2 decades, Thailand has experienced high economic growth, which has made it attractive to many international companies such as Proctor & Gamble and Motorola. These companies have entered the market with advanced product technologies and marketing

Table 18.10 Percentage of ownership of consumer durables by the elite segment

Country/City	*Automobile (%)*	*SLR camera (%)*	*Personal computer (%)*	*VCR (%)*	*Video camera (%)*	*Cellular phone (%)*
Hong Kong	39	43	34	93	22	24
Singapore	78	33	42	88	11	13
Kuala Lumpur	92	20	21	75	4	9
Taipei	65	44	35	86	21	13
Manila	91	14	18	83	18	7
Bangkok	68	30	8	79	4	8
Jakarta	85	19	30	65	9	11

Source: Consumers of Southeast Asia (1994), vol. 1, Dynamic Markets Reprint Series, W-Two Publication, Ithaca, NY.

knowhow. They have forced established companies such as Sahaphat, Kao, and Lever Brothers to re-examine their strategies in order to maintain their leading positions. Almost all of these changes are concentrated in Bangkok—the largest city, and the center of business of Thailand. The city's dwellers here are the first to enjoy a wide product assortment from all over the world (*Consumers of Southeast Asia* 1994). Outside the capital and the large provinces, however, the average Thai has begun only in recent years to experience modern marketing practices. Therefore, the discussion below on changes in macromarketing practices covers the situation in Bangkok, except when stated otherwise. This transformation is found in the macromarketing mix as follows.

Product

As never before, Thai consumers have profited from the new product strategies employed in the Thai market, gaining more benefits.

More products and services

New products, services and ideas have been imported from around the world, especially from the USA, Europe, and Japan. Moreover, existing manufacturers are introducing new products faster than they did in the past. With more disposable income, Thai consumers are finding that new products and new services are being flooded into the market to make their daily life easier. As mentioned earlier, the problems of overcrowding, heavy traffic, and pollution in Bangkok are severe. This has led to the success of many new products that are aimed at helping individual consumers to cope with these problems. Examples of these products are personal portable toilets used in passenger vehicles, cellular phones, air and water purification products for home and automobile use, and vitamins to fortify consumers' health.

New service ideas are also found in the fast-food industry (Upananchai 1994), because consumers have less time to prepare meals. For instance, mobile fast-food vans park at business centers during lunch hours, and at closing times. The food containers are designed for convenience of consumption in a motor vehicle or at home. Some mobile fast foods are found at small portable retail stands suitable for crowded streets and sidewalks. Within these areas, food can be prepared on the spot.

Better fit for market needs

With more disposable income, Thai consumers now have more product choices. Unlike in the past, new products are launched to satisfy unfulfilled needs in the market. For example, "Naturalizer" shoes were imported because women wanted comfortable working shoes, while local shoes brands were concerned with fashion and price. Thai consumers were receptive to this appeal, and became loyal to this new brand (Doungmanee 1994). A similar phenomenon can be observed in the personal-care market. A long-time market leader in the shampoo-product market, "Sunsilk" of Lever Brothers, addressed specific market needs when P&G entered the market. P&G introduced "Rejoice" as the first convenient shampoo that contained shampoo and conditioner in one bottle. It was an immediate success, gaining about 20% of the market share. Next, P&G launched another successful product, "Pantene," as the first shampoo developed for the beauty-shampoo segment. To regain its market share, Lever Brothers offered new Sunsilk shampoos formulated for different types of hair, and introduced its "Organic" shampoo for hair-loss prevention (Plubpleng 1994). As mass marketing has lost its effectiveness in Thailand (Gatedee & Upananchai 1993), businesses have turned to more modern marketing practices and market research. Psychologists and sociologists are being employed to help businesses study Thai consumer behavior. Modern research methods, including the projective technique, focus-group discussions, and voice-pitch analysis have been employed (Gatedee 1994c).

Better warranties

Because of the competition to satisfy consumer needs, the commonly accepted notion of "caveat emptor" has been challenged. Many sellers now use product-quality guarantees to gain consumer trust. For instance, Amway, the largest direct-sales operation for consumer goods in Thailand, has employed this strategy in selling convenient items such as toothpaste and shampoo. The company assures Thai consumers that, if its products are unsatisfactory, they can return the unused portion for refund. Other companies, such as Mistin cosmetics products sold through direct sales, Central supermarket, and Pan athletes' shoes, have followed suit (Plubpleng 1994). Some companies that already provide warranties have made them better. The Molinex vacuum cleaner, for example, offers a 3-year warranty although the customary practice is only 1 year (Plubpleng 1994).

Lower brand loyalty

With this new market development, some original leading brands are now at a disadvantage. Several new product introductions using these brand names have been unsuccessful because Thai consumers view the brands as outdated and of poor quality (Gatedee 1994c). For example, efforts to use the brand name "Breeze," the leading brand detergent for several decades, flopped when a new concentrated detergent was launched. Consumers perceived the brand as an ineffective cleaning product. Similarly, Sunsilk, the leading brand for shampoo, began to strike buyers as ordinary. After several unsuccessful trials to introduce advanced-formula hair-care products under this brand name, new brand names were used.

Interestingly, foreign words, especially English words, are employed for new brand names despite the fact that Thai consumers often mispronounce and do not understand them. For instance, some consumers only recognise Vidal Sassoon shampoo by the color of its package (*Report on Marketing Plan for "Vidal" Sassoon Haircare Products* 1995). An advertising campaign for Crystal drinking water aimed at educating Thais on the correct pronunciation of the brand. The translation and adaptation of foreign brand names are not common practice, however, since foreign names may indicate better quality and image than Thai ones to Thai consumers (*Report on Marketing Plan for Poa Detergent* 1995).

Existence of private brands

An indicator of the declining loyalty toward existing brands is the emergence of private brands. As in developed countries, private brands belong to large resale businesses. These businesses do not have their own production facilities; instead, their products are ordered from manufacturers (Tongmara 1993). Prominent resale operations such as Central Department stores, Makro Wholesale Warehouse, and 7-Eleven convenience stores were among the first to use this strategy. Makro, especially, has elaborated upon the private brand strategy by using various brands to indicate different levels of product quality–Safepack is for good quality, Makpack for better, and M&K for premium quality.

"Made in Thailand"

The impact of the economy on Thai consumer behavior can be seen in the trend toward favoring locally produced goods and services. A consumer survey indicated that more than 70% of respondents would stop buying imported food and clothing (Tan Settakit 1997). This could be the result of imported products suddenly becoming more expensive with the currency devaluation. However, Thais may have realized that their individual consumption behavior could contribute to an economic downturn (*Competitors* 1997). Since the recession is a recent phenomenon, it is uncertain whether this consumer behavior change will be permanent, or will last only until economic growth resumes its course.

For whatever reason, the prevailing recession has brought about a resurgence of nationalism that is favorable toward Thai products. Several businesses have grasped this new opportunity (*Competitors* 1997). For instance, a soap with the "Nok Kaew" (parrot) brand faced difficulties with expanding its market share into the capital market because more wealthy Thais viewed it as an outdated product, despite its low price and its suitability for hard water. This product was the first to advertise nationally that it was a Thai product. Subsequently, other locally made products, which had previously disguised their Thai identity by using foreign brands, have revealed their true origin. In addition, foreign-owned companies such as P&G and Unilever are stressing their "Thai-ness" in order to reduce the backlash from this movement.

Channels of distribution

The most dramatic change in Thai macromarketing is evident in the rapid emergence of modern channels of distribution at all levels of distribution. At the retail level, there are various modern outlets. For many manufacturers and wholesalers, vertical and horizontal integrative distribution have become major competitive strategies.

More modern retail outlets

Bangkok consumers not only enjoy more product choices, they also have more retail outlets to shop at. And environmental factors affecting new-product development have also influenced the evolution of retailing in Thailand. Among them, traffic jams seem to be the most important factor. An average Bangkok consumer spends from 4 to 6 hours a day in traffic, traveling to and from the workplace. With growing pressures on time and more disposable income, Thais have altered their shopping habits. So they spend less time on daily shopping. Many Thais have switched from open-air markets to the convenience of shopping at department stores and supermarkets for their everyday grocery needs. Supermarkets now take more than 30% of the sales of personal products (*Consumers of Southeast Asia* 1994).

New retail methods are being developed to accommodate this new behavior, which is a response to a reduction in shopping time. Three patterns of development have become obvious in recent years: one-stop shopping, convenient-store shopping, and home shopping or home delivery.

One-stop shopping

One-stop shopping can reduce the amount of travel time spent searching for products and services. Consumers can find everything they need in a large retail complex. A large department store, a beauty salon, dentistry practice, movie theater, computer school, playground, billiards hall, and car repair store, for example, are commonly located in a complex (Plubpleng 1991b). Between 1986 and 1994, 37 such new large-scale retail centers were opened in the Bangkok area (*Consumers of Southeast Asia* 1994). Most of these new shopping centers were constructed in the suburban residential areas. The largest one, Seacon Square, opened at the end of 1994, and was advertised as one of the 5 largest shopping centers in the world.

A hypermarket is another form of one-stop shopping. Unlike a large retail complex, where numerous independent retailers are located, a hypermarket is a single large retail operation. This type of retailing was developed to reduce the difficulties, for a retail store, of accommodating a large number of consumers shopping at one time during certain hours of the weekday, weekends and holidays. This causes long delay at checkouts, and out-of-stock product problems; as a result, disgruntled consumers shop at retail stores instead. To improve consumer service, hypermarkets therefore offer more variety of products, and more checkouts than in the existing supermarkets. On-line inventory control and order are implemented to help consumers easily find more brands and more sizes in a store (Plubpleng 1991b).

Convenience stores

While one-stop shopping outlets reduce travel time by making the retail operation larger, convenience stores provide the ease of shopping closer to home. Convenience stores such as 7-Eleven and AM-PM have seemingly sprung up on every street corner, particularly in Bangkok. As in the USA, these convenience stores are open 24 hours, and carry only necessary grocery items. Take-home foods are the most popular items in these stores. Stores such as AM-PM have increased the amount of space for food items from 30% to 50% (Upananchai 1994).

Home shopping

Unlike one-stop shopping and convenience stores, home shopping allows consumers to eliminate travelling entirely. Home shopping is in its early stages of development, but sales are expanding rapidly (Gatedee 1994b; Upananchai 1994). Even though the current volume is only US$20 million, its annual growth rate is 20%. Of the various methods of home shopping, such as TV shopping, radio shopping and newspaper shopping, mail order is the pioneer, and the most successful. This type of home shopping business started in Thailand in the late 1980s. American Express (Thai) Company was the first to introduce this method in the Thai market, as a service provided to its card members (Upananchai 1994). Other credit-card companies and department stores have participated in recent years, because of the attractive industry growth potential.

However, most consumers are still unfamiliar with the practice of purchasing through mail order. As in other countries, some common misperceptions limit buying from mail-order houses (Wongtada & Zerio 1993; *Report on Marketing Plan for "Selective" Catalog* 1994). For Thai consumers, the limitations of the system include the inability to observe the product prior to the purchase, the perceived difficulty of returning unsatisfactory items, and time delays between placing an order and receiving a product. Mail-order companies have tried to solve these problems by offering more extensive warranties, providing generous return policies, and charging no interest for purchase on credit (Gatedee 1994b). In addition, some department stores allocate shopping areas in their stores to display items on their direct-mail catalogs, to allow consumers to observe products prior to the purchase.

Modern wholesale distribution

Similarly to the retailing industry, with more competition at all levels of distribution, wholesaling methods have experienced rapid changes. The conventional method of channel of distribution has given way to a more integrated one. Traditionally, wholesalers operate independently of manufacturers (Wongtada 1993). Retailers place an order at the wholesaler's office and pay for the transportation. Retailers may patronize a wholesaler because the latter may extend generous credit terms, and also because they may trust the wholesaler as a result of prior experience.

As a result of the changes in wholesaling methods, the relationship among channel members has evolved into two extremes. In the first, personal relationships among channel members have disappeared. Retailers no longer know their wholesalers: cash-and-carry wholesale outlets are invading this industry. In the second, the informal connexions among trade members have been replaced by formal ones when vertical integration is employed.

Cash-and-carry wholesale

This type of establishment operates in a large modern warehouse. Only retailers with membership cards are allowed to enter the premises. Members purchase from these warehouses, and pay cash immediately. The personal relationship between the wholesaler and retailers is not a part of this distribution, since retailers do not get in touch directly with the management of the wholesale operation. The main contact is through cashier clerks, at checkout points similar to supermarket checkouts.

These cash-and-carry wholesalers can offer a wide assortment and lower prices. Makro is the most successful operation in this category in Bangkok and provincial markets. Some cash-and-carry wholesalers, however, aim at a narrow product assortment. For instance, Clip concentrates only on wholesaling office-supply products (Loawakul 1991), and Home Depot only on home construction and furnishing items.

Vertical integration

While cash-and-carry wholesaling reduces the connexion between trade members, many channel members try to formalize their trade relations. Some manufacturers prefer working closer with fewer wholesalers, who will distribute their products. In this situation, wholesalers own warehouses, manage inventory, and provide credits to retailers, while the manufacturers handle the shipping and manage the salesforce that will restock products for retailers. Wholesalers receive compensation of 2–3% of the total sales volume.

Some variations of this relationship do exist. For instance, Colgate Palmolive Company requires its wholesalers also to invest in vehicles and salespeople (Loawakul 1991). Others demand that their wholesalers and retailers handle their product lines exclusively (Plubpleng & Gatedee 1992). For example, the market beer leader, Boon Rawd Brewery, which has controled the domestic market for almost 6 decades with Shigha beer, adjusted its strategy as a result of the entrance of Carlsberg, a Danish brewer (*Bangkok Post Business Review* 1993). Boon Rawd strengthened its distribution with 340 agents nationwide by asking them to form regional clubs to ensure that Boon Rawd agents do not sell beer made by other companies. A violation means an end to the right to distribute Boon Rawd products. In addition, the company urged its agents to adopt more consumer-oriented marketing by being more aggressive in selling and in servicing their clients.

Like manufacturers, many wholesalers are attempting to integrate vertically by strengthening their relationship with their retailers. Some wholesalers provide new services to their retailers so that the retailers will not switch to cash-and-carry rivals. One of these services is the creation and operation of convenience stores. Convenience-store franchises such as 7-Eleven and AM-PM have been very successful, and have sparked the interest of local retailers, who see an opportunity in copying this operation (Rujikajorn 1994). Several wholesalers provide consulting services to their retail clients who want to modernize their operations. These services include investment analysis, equipment selection, inventory control, and use of computers.

Rise of horizontal integration

In addition to the emergence of vertical integration, horizontal integration is found among traditional wholesalers. They have seen their position deteriorate because of the developments discussed above. Some wholesalers concentrate on only a few product lines, and distribute them in a larger area.

Others respond by joining forces and pursuing some of the following strategies (Loawakul 1991):

- setting up large wholesale stores that cater only to cash-and-carry retailers like Makro
- combining their orders to increase their purchasing and negotiating power
- locating next to each other in a wholesale complex

Promotion

As with other marketing-mix practices in Thailand, businesses have experienced changes in terms of promotion. These changes are discussed below.

More commercials

In addition to increased product variety and increased retail outlets at which to shop, Thai consumers are being exposed to more commercials. According to *Consumers of Southeast Asia* (1994), advertising expenditures in Thailand are rising rapidly, with a projected annual growth rate of 35% in the year 2000. The advertising sector in Thailand is among the largest in ASEAN countries. Businesses find commercials effective because Thais are still receptive to advertising. Most Thais believe that commercials are a valuable source of information on new products, styles, and trends (*Consumers of Southeast Asia* 1994). Also, advertisers can target the audience relatively easily because channel surfing is not common, and consumers prefer to watch particular programs and to read particular magazines and newspapers.

The increased importance of non-television media

Currently, TV is the most popular medium. Thailand's 9 TV channels account for more than half of total advertising expenditures in the country. Furthermore, the lack of a TV set in the home is not much of an impediment either. Although half of Thai households owned TV sets in 1989, 75% of all Thais also watched regularly at a relative's house, at a neighbor's, in the marketplace, or even in the temple (*Consumers of Southeast Asia* 1994). However, the importance of TV advertising has started to decline. Advertisers have found that other media are gaining popularity, and can target particular market segments more effectively. For instance, most Bangkok residents spend a considerable amount of time waiting for buses, using buses, and sitting in their vehicles in traffic. Therefore, outdoor advertisements have wider exposure in this urban market. Also, Bangkok has a large young population, and a growing number of professionals who like to read about both local and world events. Newspapers and magazines have accordingly been launched to serve particular markets. Moreover, many radio stations concentrate on specific interests, such as traffic reports.

New appeals in commercials

The content of commercials has become more sophisticated, in line with the changes in consumers' tastes. Many Thai consumers prefer the Japanese style of advertising to that of the USA. That is, they respond best to visual impact with emotional content, rather than written text and logical reasoning (Chumunee 1994). With more women in the workplace, smaller family size, and marriage at a later age (Pootrakul 1992), the advertisements for many products, including construction material and microwave ovens, are intended to appeal to both sexes.

Different forms of price promotion

Although an immediately available price discount on an item is the most effective way to entice consumers to buy, other forms of price discount are commonly practiced. Retailers offer membership cards that give discounts on any purchase. In addition, if a consumer buys up to a target amount, he or she can purchase promoted items at discount prices. Free premiums are often provided with purchases. Motor-vehicle dealers use several strategies, including buying a home and getting a free automobile, low down payments and low monthly payments, and sweepstakes to win an automobile (Mekruengrassamee 1994).

Price

Although Thais now have more income, price is still important in buying decisions. The reasons for this are discussed below.

Intense price competition

With more product choices, more retail outlets and more access to commercials, consumers are becoming less loyal. Retail outlets have to offer price discounts on well-known brands in order to entice consumers to shop at their stores. In the past, price discounting was impractical because suppliers would threaten to close their counters if a retailer sold below their suggested retail prices. The suppliers were afraid, in this case, that discounts would lower their profits and their brand prestige (Gatedee & Upananchai 1993). However, the bargaining power of the existing suppliers has been reduced in recent years, since their competitors have been granting price reductions. For instance, with its higher quality products, P&G gained market share by offering discounts to consumers. Other companies had to step up their offers to consumers to meet the competition, and strategies included price discounts. Now it is common to see discount coupons attached to many products on supermarket shelves.

Value for money

In the past, only the poor would buy the cheapest products. With prolonged price competition, however, middle-class Thais have learnt to be smart shoppers. They have become less brand loyal, and are looking for the best value for their money. They search for good-quality products with low prices, and will delay their purchases until they get a price reduction (Gatedee & Upananchai 1993). This behavior is expected to become more widespread as the number of middle-class consumers increases (Gatedee & Upananchai 1993).

Marketing management in the 1990s

The changes in marketing practices in Thailand have continued even during the recession. The country's strong potential for economic growth remains attractive for both local and international companies interested in expanding their operations. At the same time, Thai consumers who have been exposed to foreign products and services expect their needs to be satisfied. Therefore it is reasonable to assume that competition will intensify further.

In the latter part of this decade, successful businesses need to embrace even more modern marketing practices. Some of these practices are discussed in this section.

Precise demographic segments

In order to be more competitive, strategists will have to position their products and services to cater for the specific requirements of a target market. Demographic segmentation will be the primary basis for dividing market needs, since this reflects the different consumption patterns found in the market. Children, teenagers, and seniors, in particular, will increase in importance as market segments, and will require closer attention from marketers.

The children's market

With more disposable income and fewer children, many Thai parents are pampering their offspring. From about 5 years old, children start to influence their parents' choice of the products bought for them (Doungmanee 1993). The older they get, the more influence they have. The behavior of this group differs from that of other age groups because children are heavily influenced by premiums that come with the product. In fact, premiums may be the key buying-decision factors. Thai children are exposed to entertainment programs, and cartoon characters such as Mickey Mouse, Korebee, and Ultraman. These personalities are popular as product presenters. When a character is in fashion, Thai children want to own the products with the character in order to be a part of their group (Gatedee 1993c).

The teenage market

Thai parents indulge their teenagers as well as their young children. Teen consumers, however, often make their own buying decisions, and their peers strongly influence their choice of brands (*Report on Marketing Plan for Vidal Sassoon* 1995).[3] Even though the teenage market is large in size and in purchasing power, it is not easy to please this market because its preferences change rapidly. Teen behavior in Thailand is similar to that in the Western countries. Teens have disposable income mainly from an allowance, although a few earn money from working part time. Thai teens are fashion conscious, and popular fashions change rapidly. Teenagers do not want products that are long lasting. They would rather possess several items to suit different occasions. Any marketers who can predict the needs of this market accurately will see their sales increase rapidly–but only for a short period (Gatedee 1994d), before a new fad comes along.

The senior market

Traditionally Thais have taken care of their ageing parents. However, the lifestyle of the present generation makes it difficult to fulfill this responsibility. Urban Thais who work spend little time at home during the week. Young people tend to live in Bangkok, where there are more economic opportunities, while the old are more likely to stay in the provinces. These factors are forcing senior consumers to take care of themselves, and to rely less on their children–although the younger generation provides the financial support that allows senior citizens to make their purchases of products and services.

Compared to the child and teenager segments, the senior segment is relatively small. However, this segment will grow faster (see Table 18.11). By the year 2000, this segment will grow by two digits, while the child segment will experience negative growth rate, and the teenage market will see only single-digit growth.

The value of retail space

Currently, space-allocation and display decisions are based mostly on the hunches of the manager of a store, and his or her relationship with the supplier. However, operation costs have increased, and more new products have been introduced, causing retailers to consider the economic value of their shelf space (Plubpleng & Upananchai 1995). Some are calculating sales per square meter, and setting daily targets for sales of each product. Also, information and other tools have become available for retailers so that they can realize this concept. For example, retail audit data supplied by Demar has recently become available as a basis for comparing the sales volume of different brands. Computer programs to help retailers become more effective in merchandizing display and management are more accessible (Gatedee 1993a). In the future, any product with low turnover rate and low margin will be quickly discarded. Manufacturers will have to compete to maintain their brands on the top-3 selling lists, if they want to keep their brands on

Table 18.11 Thailand's boom years: Population

Age group	*1990*	*2000*	*% change [+/(-)]*
0–4	6 240 000	5 703 000	(8.6)
5–9	6 357 000	5 803 000	(8.7)
10–14	6 207 000	6 149 000	(0.9)
15–19	6 156 000	6 296 000	2.3
20–24	6 008 000	6 128 000	2
25–29	5 169 000	6 051 000	17
30–34	4 453 000	5 887 000	32.2
35–39	3 634 000	5 048 000	38.9
40–44	2 775 000	4 321 000	55.7
45–49	2 246 000	3 486 000	55.2
50–54	2 029 000	2 610 000	28.6
55–59	1 645 000	2 049 000	24.6
60–64	1 285 000	1 765 000	37.4
65–69	893 000	1 325 000	48.3
70–74	607 000	912 000	50.2
75+	636 000	856 000	34.6
All ages	**56 340 000**	**64 389 000**	**14.3**

Source: *Key Statistics of Thailand* (1991), National Statistical Office, Bangkok.

Note:
Thailand's population boom occurred from the 1940s through the 1960s. If the economy can remain stable and the labor force can be educated to work in a modern industrial system, the employment picture should be good for those now in their teens and twenties; this means that a very strong consumer market should emerge by 2010.

retail shelves. New products made by smaller manufacturers will have a more difficult time finding shelf space in major retail stores (Plubpleng & Upananchai 1995).

Manufacturers must build product demand at the consumer level by encouraging product trial prior to placing the product in a retail store. A pull strategy will be more important than a push strategy, because retailers want a guarantee that the new product has a good chance of being successful. Many manufacturers will begin to operate their own retail stores to compensate for their products being rejected by retailers (Gatedee 1993a). Some are already experimenting with the idea of operating retail outlets. Discount shops, for example, are found to work well for fashion producers since their products are outdated quickly. Selling through discount shops does not lower the sale of these products through regular outlets. However, because clothing for working women is less dependent on fashion, discount shops cannibalize sales through regular retail outlets (Gatedee & Upananchai 1993).

Increasing efficiency

Although the recession is expected to be temporary, only strong and efficient businesses will survive it. With declining consumer purchasing power and stronger competition, many businesses will not be able to grow without having to lower their prices in order to retain their sales (*Bangkok Business* 1997b). To survive, businesses are having to operate more effectively and efficiently.

For instance, Unilever has increased its use of inventory-control technology and logistic management. It works with its suppliers and retailers on electronic data interchanges and category and space management in order to reduce distribution costs (*Nation* 1997b). Likewise, Inchcape, a trading firm, has adopted the "just-in-time" delivery principle to avoid stocking up slow-moving items (*Nation* 1997a). PM Marketing Companies uses a mixture of space reduction, layoffs, and office operating costs (*Bangkok Business* 1997a).

"Green" marketing

High industrial growth, urbanization, and pollution will continue to dominate the Bangkok scene. Businesses have used environmental friendly appeals in their strategy. Biodegradable plastic bags and recycled packages are offered by department stores (Weerakultewan 1994). Non-water-polluting detergents and concentrated formulae for cleaning products are another example. The "green" claim by itself, however, is no longer effective. The "green" company in Thailand is perceived as one among many. Only those who were the first to be engaged in "green" activities have reaped the benefits. For example, Central department store is perceived by Thais as the first to use this "green" appeal. This gives the store a lot of goodwill—even though it uses only a few aspects of the environmentally-conscious campaign. Thai consumers perceive that Central has done more than it actually did (*Consumer Perception towards Environmentally Friendly Appeals of Large Department Stores in Bangkok* 1994).

At present, Thai consumers view the "green" marketing appeal as a sales tactic with no real value to society (Wongtada, Leelakulthanit & Rice 1994). Environmental problems in Thailand will not disappear quickly (*Consumers of Southeast Asia* 1994). Therefore, it is very likely that comprehensive "green" marketing appeals, similarly to those found in the West (Wongtada & Rice 1993), will be a new generation of environmentally friendly strategies in Thailand. Thai businesses will have to demonstrate that they have considered the impact of their practices on the environment. This covers responsibility for a product from the purchasing of supplies through production, distribution, product usage, and remains disposal (Mastrandonas & Strife 1992). A product that might save the environment in its final form but does a great deal of harm in its manufacturing process will be unacceptable (Rolfes 1990).

Symbiotic marketing

The term "symbiotic marketing" refers to co-operation among companies in order to combine their strengths and eliminate their weaknesses. Symbiotic marketing has occurred for quite some time, but in the temporary form of promotion (Gatedee 1993b). More permanent forms of symbiotic marketing are still in the early stages in Thailand. A few companies have experimented with this method in an effort to gain economies of scale in distributing goods, to increase competitive advantage, or to reduce the number of potential competitors (*Competitors* 1995). For instance, Lever Brothers (Thai) Company co-operated with Sermsook Company in selling Lipton Iced Tea. Even though Lever Brothers was capable of developing its own distribution for its first beverage product in Thailand, it relied on Sermsook's connexions, because the latter already has an effective distribution network in place for Pepsi-Cola products. Likewise, Walder arranged to have Foremost, Borneo, and Inchcape to handle the liquid form of its Ovaltine products, to prevent these companies from launching new products that would cannibalize the sales of its regular Ovaltine (Gatedee 1993b).

Globalization

Global mass communication is a major factor in the integration of Thai consumers into the international community. Satellite systems have allowed Thais to view programs from other countries. For instance, Satcom Star TV offers news from the BBC in England, and American MTV music programs to Thai viewers. Thai consumers are able to view local programs from the USA, Indonesia, Malaysia, Hong Kong, China, and Australia. Currently, the high price of the satellite dish, government restrictions and the inability to broadcast in the Thai language have limited subscription to satellite viewing to only 2000 (Plubpleng 1991a). The future is brighter, however, because the government will open up this market to more competition. Simultaneous translation machines will be installed (Chumunee 1994). This will lower the price, and gain a wider audience. Because of these trends, marketers in Thailand have to consider the following aspects.

Foreign influence

With global mass communication, different blends of foreign cultures will be seen (Plubpleng & Junghattakarnsatit 1991). The preference for foreign-made goods from the USA and Europe is rooted in Thai society, especially among middle-class and upper-class consumers between 35 and 60 years old. In recent years, however, Japanese culture has invaded the consciousness of the Thai consumer because of increasing trade between the two countries. Japanese fashion is especially popular among Thais aged between 18 and 25 years. It is not the traditional Japanese culture that is winning over young Thai consumers, but rather the one that has already been blended with Western influence.

Globalization outside Bangkok

Globalization will reach cities beyond Bangkok (Yeedin 1995). A new government policy is aimed at reducing the income gap between urban and rural Thais. To redress regional-development imbalances, the Thai government has allocated 10% of its fiscal-year budget to promoting investment in provincial areas and redistributing wealth to rural people. Although the process is slow, the government also intends to move some government agencies away from Bangkok, and to overhaul provincial governments, in order to give local governments more control over budgets and decision making (*Consumers of Southeast Asia* 1994).

With this new government direction, and strong competition in the Bangkok market, some businesses are seeking opportunities in other markets. For example, Makro, the largest wholesale outlet using the supermarket style, experienced phenomenal success when it opened an outlet in a northern province. Retailers from neighboring provinces rushed to this outlet, causing an unprecedented traffic jam near the outlet. Because of this type of success, other entrepreneurs have followed suit. Department stores in Bangkok are opening new branches in these cities. Manufacturers are setting up warehouses in various provinces in order to respond to market needs faster. In the past, these warehouses were located mainly in Bangkok. Now, companies like Nestlé and others are finding it is more competitive to own distribution centers in the main provinces of each region, including Chieng Mai, Hat Yai, and Korat (Plubpleng & Gatedee 1992). With this development, we would expect that more modern marketing practices, already found in Bangkok, will be implemented in these cities in the future (Yeedin 1995).

Trade expansion with Indochinese countries

Although the USA, Japan and Europe are still the major trading partners of Thailand, trade with its neighboring countries has increased significantly, especially with those in the Indochina Peninsula (Vietnam, Laos, Cambodia, and Burma). About 1.7% of Thai export in 1993 and 2.3% in 1994 were to these countries, representing an increase of 80% and 60% respectively over the previous years (*Summary on Economic Situation in 1994 and Trends in 1995* 1995). This increase in trade is a result of the changes in the political directions of these countries. Cambodia, for instance, ended its civil war in 1991 (Chetchotisak 1992), and the Laotian government decided to open up the country in 1980 (Malapet et al. 1992). Vietnam has been accepted as an ASEAN member country. ASEAN expects to include Laos, Cambodia, and Burma in its association in the year 2000 (*Exporters Review* 1995). Moreover, the Economic Quadrangle, an economic agreement among China, Burma, Laos, and Thailand, has plans to improve the movement of goods and people and open up the regional economy. Better roads are a priority. A circle route linking these countries is expected to be completed by 1999 (*Bangkok Post* 1995).

Since these countries are at a lower stage of economic development than Thailand, they import such products as consumer goods, machinery, equipment, and construction tools, and export raw materials such as timber, precious stones, and minerals. Currently, the infrastructure of these countries is inadequate; therefore, the trade between them and Thailand, and occurring along their joint borders, is still capable of considerable growth (Chetchotisak 1992; Malapet et al. 1992). In addition, many Thai companies have invested in these countries, in order to take advantage of lower labor costs and more abundant raw materials, service other Thai businesses and tourists in the countries, and supply products and services to these countries, where there is less competition than in Thailand (Chetchotisak 1992; Malapet et al. 1992; *Siamrat Subda Vijarn* 1992; *Summary on Economic News* 1992).

Implications for marketing management

To be successful in Thailand, marketers can no longer employ a passive strategy, or treat the Thai market as a secondary one. The current recession will last only a few years. Those companies that survive will be formidable competitors because they will have learnt how to survive in difficult market conditions. The market will be even more attractive in the near future when the infrastructure development linking Thailand with Indochina and China is completed (*Nation* 1997a). Therefore, when they are developing marketing strategies for this market, marketers should consider the following issues.

First, marketing managers should expect strong competition in many consumer markets in Thailand. The novelty of many Western products is long gone, since most major international firms have already entered the market to take advantage of its high economic growth (see Chaisen 1995; Gatedee 1995; Sintuvatin & Rujeekajorn 1995). Furthermore, competitors can be easily noticed, and imitated or their marketing strategies diffused, because all of them operate mainly in the Bangkok market.

In this situation, the need to satisfy Thai consumers becomes more important. A product or service must be aimed at the specific but unsatisfied need of a target market in order to be competitive in this crowded market. Market research will become an even more important tool for creating effective strategies than it is at present. Standard marketing strategies successfully implemented in the home market may not work well here if they have not been tested against those of their many international rivals, as well as the domestic competitors found in Bangkok market (see *Report on Marketing Plan for "Vidal Sassoon" Haircare Products* 1995).

Second, because the prevailing state of marketing practice and infrastructure is in flux, employing common methods used in the country may not be in the company's best interest. For instance, even though TV advertising is the most widely used promotion mechanism for reaching consumers, other methods have gained popularity, proving themselves more effective. Outdoor advertising may reach consumers more cheaply during the round-the-clock traffic jams in Bangkok. For the increasingly price-sensitive consumers in Thailand, discount coupons attached to products displayed on the supermarket shelf could be more appealing than an image-appeal advertising message on TV.

Similarly, although it may seem that selling a product through supermarkets or department stores would be logical since these distribution outlets are popular among Bangkok residents, other selling methods have emerged to suit the consumer lifestyle more closely. These include convenience stores, mail-order catalogs and TV shopping. After determining the distribution method, the marketer should prepare to work closely with channel members, because competing firms may employ the vertical marketing strategy.

Third, global segments such as businesspeople and teenagers (see Cateora 1993; Gatedee 1995b) may be found in the Thai market. This will facilitate the use of elements of standardized marketing strategy. The elite segment in Thailand shows a similar consumption pattern to its peers in other Asian markets (*Consumers of Southeast Asia* 1994). From our association with this group, we believe that the Thai elites have similar consumption needs and aspirations to their foreign counterparts.

We also think that many more segments found in more developed countries will become pertinent in Thailand, especially in the Bangkok market. This is because several key sociodemographic factors of Thailand have started to follow the trends found in those countries (see Gatedee 1995b; Yeedin 1995). These trends are a lower population growth rate, smaller family size, more nuclear rather than extended families, an increase in the graying population, higher disposable income, and more educated people. Furthermore, many Thais have changed their behavior from the traditional norm of submissiveness to that of being more individualistic and more outspoken.

Finally, marketers should pay closer attention to the economic situation in Thailand, since this directly affects consumers' income expectations, and, hence, their consumption (Yeedin 1995). As compared with the situation in the late 1980s, Thai economic growth has slowed. Thai consumers do not spend as fast as they used to. Although there is still some optimism, the next 5 years are likely to be difficult economically. Thailand positions itself as an international gateway to its neighboring developing countries, including Myanmar, Cambodia, Laos, Yunnan Province of China, and Vietnam (*BOI Business Review* 1994). These countries will provide a cheap labor pool, especially in light of rising labor costs in Thailand. This will strengthen Thailand's competitive position in the international market. Also, these countries will serve as additional export markets for Thai products and services. If the country's economic strategy is realized, Thai consumers will experience more rapid income increases, and will spend more.

Conclusions

The transformation of Thailand into an economic environment requiring modern marketing practices is inevitable, because of the changes that have occurred in the country in the last decade; these changes are also expected to continue, and the economy is expected to evolve further. Rapid economic expansion seems to be the main driving force that has produced other changes such as higher income, lower employment, a more educated population, an inadequate infrastructure and severe pollution. With the country's high market potential, competition among firms to satisfy the insatiable Thai consumers has increased. To be more competitive, these firms have changed their customary marketing practices in Thailand.

These changes are pervasive. Not only are they found in the implementation of the marketing mix, but the operation of all trade members has also been affected. Manufacturers, wholesalers, and retailers have found themselves employing such modern marketing concepts as product warranty and vertical integration. To be successful in this new environment, the marketing manager needs to be more alert to new opportunities, and more creative in deriving marketing strategies. The pressure of competition will come from all directions, since more companies are expanding their operations to take advantage of this market growth, and some have joined with others to strengthen their competitive position. Thailand has not yet reached its economic growth plateau, and the transformation will continue. Moreover, it will benefit from the general expansion of international trade in and with the ESEA region, because of its strategic location in the Indochina Peninsula.

References

Aufrecht, Steven & Ractham, Arun (1991), "Traditional Thai Values and the Thai Bureaucracy's Ability to Change", in eds Goraksha Bohadur, N. Pradham & Mila A. Reforma, *Public Management in 1990s: Challenges and Opportunities*, EUROPA Secretariat General, London, pp. 51–62.

Backhaus, Tara N., Belden, Peter B. & Espenshade, Thomas J. (1994), "AIDS, Low Birth Rates, and Future Growth in Thailand", *Population Today*, vol. 22, October, pp. 4–5.

Bangkok Business (1997a), November.

— (1997b), December.

Bangkok Post (1992), "Plastic Money: Card Use Continues to Soar", *Bangkok Post Economic Review 1992: Mid-Year*, Bangkok, June 30, pp. 72–4.

— (1994), "Thailand Set to Rank 4 in Asian Growth", *Bangkok Post Weekly Review*, Bangkok, December 30, p. 11.

— (1995), "Linking Laos to the World", Bangkok, September 4, p. 28.

Bangkok Post Economic Review (1993), *Bangkok Post*, Bangkok, December 30.

BOI Investment Review (1994), November 31, vol. 3, no. 4.

Business Review (1992a), April.

— (1992b), September.

Cateora, Philip R. (1993), *International Marketing*, 8th edn, Irwin, Homewood, Illinois.

Chaisen, Tippanee (1995), "Retailing Location, Bangkapi-Ramkhamhaeng, Survival of the Fittest", *Competitors*, March, pp. 83–7 (in Thai).

Chantranontwong, Pattnapong (1993), "Satellite, Phones Ring in New Era", *Economic Review, Year-end 1993, Bangkok Post*, December 30, pp. 36–7 (in Thai).

Chetchotisak, Malinee (1992), "Trade between Thailand and Cambodia—Unsettled Situation", *Economic Report*, Krung Thai Bank, vol. 25, no. 12, November, pp. 57–68 (in Thai).

Chow, Dominic Cheung (1994), "AIDS in Thailand: A Medical Student's Perspective", *Journal of Community Health*, vol. 19. no. 6, pp. 417–31.

Chumunee, Narisa (1994), "Next Century... Advertising in Thailand", *Kookengkaan*, September, pp. 50–4 (in Thai).

Clifton, Tony (1994), "Dark Satanic Mills", *Newsweek*, May 9, pp. 18–22.

Competitors (1995), "Combining Forces among Retailers", June, pp. 133–7 (in Thai).

— (1997), "Thai Products Help the Country", October, pp. 42–6 (in Thai).

Consumer Perception towards Environmentally Friendly Appeals of Large Department Stores in Bangkok (1994), report of MBA students at National Institute of Development and Administration, Bangkok.

Consumers of Southeast Asia (1994), vol. 1, Dynamic Markets Reprint Series, W-Two Publication, Ithaca, NY.

Cooper, Roberts & Cooper, Nathapa (1990), *Cultural Shock*, Times Books International, Singapore.

Crossette, Barbara (1992), "Across Southeast Asia, Awakenings to Democracy", *The New York Times*, May 24, p. 3.

Doing Business in Thailand (1991), 2nd edition, BLC Publication, Bangkok.

Doungmanee, Kokeit (1993), "Power of Children in Clothing Business", *Kookengkaan*, September, pp. 201–8 (in Thai).

— (1994), "New Face of Women's Shoes in Responding to Changes in Behavior", *Kookengkaan*, May, pp. 68–70 (in Thai).

Economist (1990), "Thailand: the New Lepers", no. 316, September 15, p. 44.

— (1993), "Termites in the Basement", no. 328, September 18, p. 42.

— (1994), "Asian Values", May 28, p. 13.

Editorial Board (1994), "The Year 2000: The Victory Year", *Manager: Monthly*, no. 370, January, pp. 3–9 (in Thai).

Educational Planning Division (1992), *Educational Statistics in Brief*, Office of the Permanent Secretary, Ministry of Education, Bangkok.

Exporters Review (1995), "Vietnam—the Most Recent Member of ASEAN and Its Business Opportunity for Thailand", *Exporters Review*, vol. 8, no. 193, July, pp. 10–18 (in Thai).

Gatedee, Rampai (1993a), "Space Management, New Technology in Getting Rid of Unwanted on the Shelf Space", *Kookengkaan*, January, pp. 147–52 (in Thai).

— (1993b), "Symbiotic Marketing, Strategy in Co-operating Strengths", *Kookengkaan*, May, pp. 210–16 (in Thai).

— (1993c), "Kid Power", *Kookengkaan*, September, pp. 195–200 (in Thai).

— (1994a), "4P's Move into Value Oriented Marketing", *Kookengkaan*, January, pp. 174–9 (in Thai).

— (1994b), "Enter the Era of Home Shopping When Goods are Available at Consumer Home", *Kookengkaan*, March, pp. 199–204 (in Thai).

— (1994c), "Psychological", *Kookengkaan*, June, pp. 185–93 (in Thai).

— (1994d), "Teen ... Boom, Win Over Teenager Segment", *Kookengkaan*, October, pp. 142–54 (in Thai).

— (1995a), "Superconcentrate—Major Revolution in Consumer Product Market", *Competitors*, February, pp. 36–8 (in Thai).

— (1995b), "Buying Power of the Single Market", *Competitors*, March, pp. 174–81 (in Thai).

Gatedee, Rampai & Upananchai, Sutinee (1993), "Value for the Money, Consumer's Dream Comes True", *Kookengkaan*, February, pp. 46–51 (in Thai).

Handley, Paul (1989), "The Lust Frontier", *Far Eastern Economic Review*, vol. 148, November 2, pp. 44–5.

— (1992a), "Catch if Catch Can", *Far Eastern Economic Review*, vol. 155, no. 10, February 13, pp. 29–30.

— (1992b), "An Ounce of Prevention", *Far Eastern Economic Review*, vol. 155, no. 10, February 13, pp. 30–1.

— (1992c), "AIDS at Work", *Far Eastern Economic Review*, vol. 155, no. 13, March 12, p. 48.

— (1992d), "Thailand: Trade and Investment—A Nap After Gorging", *Far Eastern Economic Review*, vol. 155, no. 33, August 20, pp. 40–2.

Jarujinda, Uchaporn (1994), "The Role of Private Sector According to Regulations on 1992 Environmental Preservation", *Ruthsapa Sarn*, pp. 31–9 (in Thai).

Key Statistics of Thailand (1991), National Statistical Office, Bangkok.

Komin, Suntaree (1990), *Psychology of the Thai People: Values and Behavioral Patterns*, Magenta, Bangkok.

Krongkaew, Methi & Pattamasiriwat, Direk (1994), "Thai Economy in the Year 2000", Seventeenth Annual Symposium organized by Faculty of Economics, Thammasat University, 23–24 March, Bangkok, pp. 117-25 (in Thai).

Krungtep Business (1997a), "Reveal Secret—Reduce Costs and Development", November 5, p. 8.

— (1997b), "Retailers Run out of Strategies to Lure Customers during New Year", December 17, p. 7.

Leeflang, Peter S.H. & van Raaij, W. Fred (1993), "The Changing Consumer in the Netherlands: Recent Changes in Environmental Variables and Their Consequences for Future Consumption and Marketing", *International Journal of Research in Marketing*, vol. 10, no. 4, pp. 345–63.

Leelakulthanit, Orose & Wongtada, Nittaya (1993), "Thai Consumer Behavior: Responses in Conserving the Environment", in eds Gerald S. Albaum et al., *Fourth Symposium on Cross-Cultural Consumer & Business Studies*, pp. 313–19, Hong Kong.

Leelakulthanit, Orose & Day, Ralph (1992), "Quality of Life in Thailand", *Social Indicators Research*, vol. 27, no. 41, pp. 1–57.

Lintner, Bertil & Lintner, Hseng Noung (1992), "Immigrant Viruses", *Far Eastern Economic Review*, no. 155, February 20, p. 31.

Loawakul, Somchai (1991), "Build New Barriers for Wholesalers all over the Country", *Kookengkaan*, June, pp. 247–54 (in Thai).

Marketing News (1993), "Japanese Manufacturers Look to Fast-Growing Asia", October 11, p. 12.

Mastrandonas, Andrew & Strife, Polly T. (1992), "Corporate Environmental Communications, Lessons for Investors", *Columbia Journal of World Business*, vol. 27, nos 3–4, Fall/Winter, pp. 235–66.

Mekruengrassamee, Wanida (1994), "Price War in Other Markets", *Kookengkaan*, September, pp. 146–8 (in Thai).

Malapet, Mana et al. (1992), "Feasibility and Investment Opportunity in Indochina", *Leaders*, vol. 7, no. 12, November, pp. 242–5.

Mulder, Niles (1992), *Inside Southeast Asia: Thai, Japanese, and Filipino Interpretation of Everyday Life*, Duang Kamol, Thailand.

Nation, The (1997a), "Fall Forces Expansion of Inchcape Services", October 11, p. B2.

— (1997b), "Unilever Sees Growth on Lower Costs, Technology, December 8, pp. B1–B2.

Office of the National Economic and Social Development Board (1990), *Social Indicators 1990*, Human Resource Planning Division, Bangkok.

— (1991), *Population Projection For Thailand 1980-2015*, Human Resource Planning Division, Bangkok.

Ogilvy & Mather, *Listening Post*, no. 64, Bangkok.

Pattamasiriwat, Direk (1993), "Pattern of Household Consumption: Demand, True Cost-of-Living Index and Welfare Analysis", *Journal of Economics: Thammasat University*, vol. 11, no. 2, June, pp. 391–60.

Petmark, Puntip & Unksutanasombat, Kanika (1990), *The Relationship between the Informal Sector in Dense Areas and City Economic System: A Study of Professions in Collecting and Buying Trash in Bangkok*, Center for Information Distribution, Foundation for Development of Housing, Bangkok (in Thai).

Pinkerton, Stewart (1992), "A Second South Korea?", *Forbes*, December 21, pp. 149–58.

Pinkney, Deborah S. (1994), "HIV Exploding in Asia; Projections Top Africa's Rate", *American Medical News*, vol. 37, August 22, p. 6.

Plubpleng, Patikom (1991a), "More TV Channels ... Sweet Dream or Nightmare of Advertising Industry", *Kookengkaan*, October, pp. 381–92 (in Thai).

— (1991b), "Hyper-market, New Strategy for Retailers", *Kookengkaan*, December, pp. 271–8 (in Thai).

— (1994), "Ultimate Warrantee, the Last Chip to Win over Customers", September, pp. 135-42 (in Thai).

Plubpleng, Patikom & Gatedee, Rumpai (1992), "Depot Fever", *Kookengkaan*, April, pp. 243–8 (in Thai).

Plubpleng, Patikom & Junghattakarnsatit, Teerasart (1991), "Influence of Cultures on the Behavior of Thai Consumers in the Future", *Kookengkaan*, February, pp. 243–53 (in Thai).

Plubpleng, Patikom & Upananchai, Sutinee (1995), "Superretailers", *Competitors*, June, pp. 128–31 (in Thai).

Pootrakul, Viroj (1992), "The Trend of Consumer Products in the Year 2000", *Thansaetakit*, no. 634, November 22–25, pp. 62-3 (in Thai).

Report on Marketing Plan for "Poa" Detergent (1995), marketing plan conducted by MBA students at Chulalongkorn University, Thailand, sponsored by Lion Company, Bangkok.

Report on Marketing Plan for "Selective" Catalog (1994), class project of MBA students at National Institute of Development and Administration (NIDA), Bangkok, (in Thai).

Report on Marketing Plan for "Vidal Sassoon" Haircare Products (1995), marketing plan conducted by MBA students at Chulalongkorn University, Bangkok, sponsored by P&G, Thailand.

Rolfes, Rebecca (1990), "How Green is Your Market Basket?", *Across the Board*, January/February pp. 49–51.

Rujikajorn, Somboon (1994), "Move into Regional Retail Market in Borderless Era", *Kookengkaan*, July, pp. 79–82 (in Thai).

Schwarz, Adam (1994), "Just Fine, For Now", *Far Eastern Economic Review*, June 16, p. 68.

Siamrat Subda Vijarn (1992), "Tremendous Business Benefits of Thailand in Burma", vol. 39, no. 21, October, pp. 8–10 (in Thai).

Siengthai, Sununta & Leelakulthanit, Orose (1994), "Women in Management in Thailand", in eds Nancy J. Adler & Dafna N. Izraeli, *Competitive Frontiers: Women Managers in a Global Economy*, Blackwell Publishers, Massachusetts, p. 160.

Sintuvatin, Woottikorn & Rujeekajorn, Soomboon (1995), "Competition among Movie Theaters in Upcountry", *Competitors*, July, pp. 144–54 (in Thai).

Stone, Eric & Janssen, Peter (1991), "Thailand: Indecision Comes Home to Roost", *Asian Business*, March, pp. 32–44.

Summary on Economic News (1992), "Trade between Thailand and Vietnam", vol. 23, no. 6, March, pp. 20–30 (in Thai).

Summary on Economic Situation in 1994 and Trends in 1995, Research Department, Thai Military Bank, 1995 (in Thai).

Tasker, Rodney (1993), "Thailand: the Straight and Narrow", *Far Eastern Economic Review*, August 5, pp. 18–19.

Terwiel, Barend J. (1984), "Formal Structure and Informal Rules: An Historical Perspective on Hierarchy, Bondage and the Patron-Client Relationship", in eds Han ten Brummelhuis and Jerry H. Kemp, *Strategies and Structures in Thai Society*, the Department of South and Southeast Asian Studies, University of Amsterdam, Amsterdam.

Thailand Development Research Institute (TDRI) (1990), "Urbanization and Environment: Managing the Conflict", Research Report no. 6, TDRI.

Thorelli, Hans B. & Sentell, Gerald D. (1982), *Consumer Emancipation and Economic Development: The Case of Thailand*, JAI Press, London.

Tongmara, Pranabda (1993), "Private Brands in Thai Stores", *Kookengkaan*, December, pp. 64–6 (in Thai).

Ungphakorn, Peter Mytri (1993), "Can We Manage at this Pace?", *Economic Review, Year-end 1993, Bangkok Post*, December 30, p. 11 (in Thai).

Upananchai, Sutinee (1994), "Changes in Marketing Strategies in Response to Traffic Jam," *Kookengkaan*, October, pp. 140–9 (in Thai).

Vandenboshch, Army & Butwell, Richard (1967), *The Changing Face of Southeast Asia*, University of Kentucky Press, Lexington.

Weerakultewan, Sotida (1994), "Environment Today ... Lip Service", *Rayngang Piset*, January, pp. 1–2 (in Thai).

Wongtada, Nittaya & Rice, Gillian (1992), "Emerging Issues in Green Marketing: Trends and Their Implications in Europe", for the 1992 Academy of International Business Annual Meeting, Brussels.

— (1993), "Forces Controlling the Compliance of the Gentlemen's Agreement among Overseas Chinese Businessmen", *Journal of International Consumer Marketing*, vol. 5, no. 2, pp. 69–83.

Wongtada, Nittaya & Zerio, John (1993), "Toward a Conceptual Model of Japanese Consumer Response to Direct Marketing", in eds Michael R. Czinkota & Masaki Kotabe, *The Japanese Distribution System Handbook*, Probus Publishing, Chicago, pp. 191–208.

Wongtada, Nittaya, Leelakulthanit, Orose & Rice, Gillian (1994), An Investigation of Attitudes and Environmentally Concerned Behavior of Thai Consumers, paper delivered at the 1994 Asia Pacific Advances in Consumer Research Conference, June 13–16, Singapore.

Yeedin, Apison (1994), "Credit-Card Strategies in 1994: Penetration in Rural Market", *Kookengkaan*, vol. 162, March, pp. 109–12 (in Thai).

— (1995), "Analysis of Three Forces in Shaping the Industry—Economy, Business and Politics", *Competitors*, June, pp. 50–3 (in Thai).

Notes

1 The authors thank William J. Cummings, Gillian Rice, and the editors for their valuable comments on different versions of this chapter.

2 To the best of the authors' knowledge, the only comprehensive examination of marketing in Thailand to date is the seminal work by Thorelli and Sentell (1982).

3 In a focus-group study for Vidal Sassoon, peer pressure in using particular brand names was found to be very strong among some groups of undergraduate university students. To belong to the group, one may have to wear a brand name watch such as a Hoya, or carry a Louis Vuitton bag.

CHAPTER 19

Vietnam

Market socialism, marketing and consumer behavior[1]

CLIFFORD J. SHULTZ II, NGUYEN XUAN QUE, ANTHONY PECOTICH & WILLIAM ARDREY

Abstract

Vietnam is one of the most compelling but challenging markets in South-East Asia. Since the Communist party introduced market reforms in 1986, it has been one of the world's investment favorites. With impressive growth rates and a population of almost 80 million people, many of whom are entering the consumer society, Vietnam is a country in which global organizations need to have a presence. In this chapter, we present a synopsis of the marketing and consumer-behavior phenomena that make Vietnam both an attractive and a frustrating market. We articulate the challenges that must be overcome, and share insights on strategies currently implemented by successful marketing firms competing in Vietnam.

Introduction

> We want (the world) to understand that Vietnam is a country not a war (Le Mai, Deputy Foreign Minister, Hanoi, August 6 1995).
>
> We view Vietnam as a Nation with immense potential as a partner in trade and diplomacy (William Christopher, US Secretary of State, Hanoi, August 6 1995).

These statements began a new era in international and commercial relations between two former bitter adversaries. With diplomatic relations restored on August 6 1995, and in the wake of its 1986 decision to invoke market reforms, Vietnam cleared one of the final obstacles to its full integration into the world of commerce and marketing.

Unfortunately, many people, particularly in the USA, still associate Vietnam with war. In reality, Vietnam is a country of enormous natural wealth and potential, and it is demonstrating a remarkable economic renaissance. Much of this rebirth can be explained by both this natural wealth, and the perseverance of the Vietnamese people. The country is located between China, Laos and Cambodia. It has a land area of 330 363 km^2, a coastline of over 3 444 km (longer than that between Seattle and San Diego), and a tropical monsoonal climate. Its natural assets include timber reserves, fisheries, vast oil and gas reserves, and fertile soil that has enabled Vietnam to become the third largest rice producer in the world. With a cultural wealth that includes the traditions and historical sites of 4000 years of national identity, the Vietnamese people are industrious, cheerful, and motivated to achieve a higher quality of life.

However, despite massive foreign investment and controlled marketization, Vietnam and its consumers remain an enigma that corporations must decipher in order to compete effectively. The purpose of this chapter is to help marketing managers understand better the relevant marketing and consumer behavior issues in Vietnam. To those ends, we synthesize and extend a stream of research on marketing and consumer behavior (e.g. Pecotich & Shultz 1993; Shultz 1994; Shultz & Pecotich 1994; Shultz, Ardrey & Pecotich 1994; Shultz, Pecotich & Le 1994; Shultz & Ardrey 1997), with the objective of providing insights that will assist marketing managers to be successful in this market.

Historical and cultural background

The words "struggle" and "survival" might best describe Vietnam's history and the plight of its people. Its national character and cultural institutions—indeed, its birth and present existence—have come about from centuries-long persistence, and at the price of incessant wars (e.g. McAlister & Mus 1970; Vien 1987; Karnow 1991; Sheehan 1992). The first Vietnamese were a homogenous linguistic group that inhabited the fertile Red River valley, establishing a wet-rice culture some 4000 years ago. Over the centuries,

Vietnam has been engaged in a continuous battle for sovereignty. These wars were also a source of cultural infusion, most notably by China, the Thai and Khmer kingdoms, the Mongols, France and the USA, which shaped Vietnamese culture, and continues both to shape the culture and affect the way firms currently market goods and services.

China ruled Vietnam for nearly 1000 years until 939 AD, and Vietnam continues to keep a wary eye on its formidable rival to the north (Shultz & Ardrey 1995). Despite historical antipathies, however, Chinese influence provided the impetus for a loose adaptation of Taoism, Confucianism, and a mandarin system of administration that Vietnamese feudal rulers used to expand southward in the 15th, 16th and 17th centuries to conquer the Chams of present-day central Vietnam and the Khmers of the South. The southern expansion led to a fusion of Confucian and Buddhist values that are endemic to Vietnamese culture. By the 17th century and the arrival of Europeans, Vietnam had a well-formed culture and language, and effective political and economic systems (Williams 1992, p. 7). These developments shaped the Vietnamese view of the world that in turn influences many consumer actions of today (Shultz, Pecotich & Le 1994).

In Vietnam an amalgam of early animistic beliefs, Taoism, Buddhism and Confucianism, forms the traditional world view based on the existence of two all encompassing forces—the *Yin* and the *Yang*—from which all creation emanates. Jamieson (1993, pp. 12–13, 399–400) defines their nature as follows:

> *Yang* is defined by a tendency toward male dominance, high redundancy, low entropy, complex and rigid hierarchy, competition, and strict orthodoxy focused on rules for behavior based on social roles. *Yin* is defined by a tendency toward greater egalitarianism and flexibility, more female participation, mechanisms to dampen competition and conflict, high entropy, low redundancy, and more emphasis on feeling, empathy, and spontaneity.

It is the desire for harmony and balance between these two co-existing, interlocking forces that leads to social change, particularly when the *Yang* dominance is too strong and a *Yin* reaction is necessary. Based on this foundation, the Vietnamese developed a core set of traditional values, enumerated by Jamieson (1993, pp. 16–41, 397–400) as follows:

1. *Ly* (reason or the nature of things): An overarching principle intended to provide a harmonious conformity with the structural principles governing the nature of the universe by specifying the proper form of relationships.
2. *Hieu* (filial piety) and *On* (moral debt): The parent-child relationship forms the core of the culture—children must obey, respect and honor their parents and endeavor to repay the unpayable moral debt.

3 *De* (the basis of a proper relationship between brothers): The model for societal roles, where the older brother should "teach, nurture and protect" the younger brother, who in turn should "respect, obey and support." This is an important principle, as "blood family ties" are a critical factor in social action, and to disregard them is to act contrary to the natural order. Vietnamese children learn dependence, nurturing and submissiveness rather than assertiveness and independence.

4 Sex roles: Even in the traditional context there was social tension in the roles expected of women (the *Yin* as opposed to the *Yang*). While Vietnamese history is replete with heroic, intelligent and successful women, the general expectation is that women should be submissive and subordinate. Marriages were primarily transactions between two families, with care taken not to lose face. The wife's primary obligation (*hieu*) was to provide a male heir.

5 *Nghia* (the righteous path): This emphasizes duty, justice and the fulfilling of obligations in social relations regardless of circumstances or preferences.

6 *Tinh* (emotionalism, spontaneity, or love) and *Nhan* (Compassion): These values, although subordinate to *Nghia*, provide a balance to the rationality embodied in the other values.

7 *Dieu* (relative versus absolute harmony): This moderates the absolute standards of *Ly* and emphasizes a relativist, reasonable, moderate position in social affairs.

8 Abstention versus participation: A good citizen must strive between these two extremes of social involvement.

9 The power of the natural order: The moral justice by which the universe operates guarantees the return to the natural order.

10 The family: This basic unit, reinforced by ancestral worship, forms the fundamental element of the natural order. Marriage, birth, death and other complex social interactions all occur within the family and the wider context of the village-based hierarchical society. The social and economic structure involves both "solidarity and competition," with emphasis on "face and status." *Tet*, the "annual family ritual of renewal," forms a central part of Vietnamese culture.

This traditional order, although briefly articulated, forms the basic fabric of Vietnamese society, which persists despite innovation and cultural diffusion as well as the inevitable cyclical development.

Western influence began with the French, and the cultural impact of over 100 years of French colonial rule was significant in shaping many Vietnamese institutions. The influence was particularly strong in urban areas, and among the elite and intellectuals. This impact is still seen today in the architecture, alphabet, education, social attitudes and the arts in Vietnam.

Given the failures of the traditional system, the *Yang* domination, the confrontation with the West, the economic hardships and the resulting cultural disorientation, it was not surprising that by 1932 strong voices were raised questioning traditional values. This was the beginning of the ideological struggle between the traditional values, Western ideas and the revolutionary ideals—a struggle that has continued to the present (Jamieson 1993). In the political context, the French, similar to the Chinese before them, had a precarious co-existence with the Vietnamese. They were finally expelled from Vietnam after their defeat at Dien Bien Phu in 1954, which in turn led to the North–South/Communist–Capitalist division of Vietnam until 1975.

US involvement was evident as early as the Second World War, when the Office of Strategic Services worked co-operatively with Ho Chi Minh to repel Japanese forces from Indochina. By 1968 the influence of the USA, and of Western popular culture generally, reached its zenith, with the presence of over 500 000 US, Australian, and other UN troops in South Vietnam. Williams (1992, p. 21) has articulated well the profound effect of this presence:

> In essence the (southern) cities had become a service economy for the American war effort. Countless thousands were employed by US bases and offices, while an even larger number serviced the every need of the American soldier. The consumer needs of this society were met by imports, which were financed by US economic assistance. The departure of the Americans and the removal of their substantial buying power created severe economic and psychological problems for the urban economy, and especially Saigon.

The capitulation of the Southern regime in 1975, and the defeat and final withdrawal of the USA, resulted in the unification of Vietnam. The emergence of the Socialist Republic, while an impressive military triumph, nonetheless presented the national leadership with the immense problems of peace-time government. The euphoria of victory was short lived. Vietnam was ravaged by two generations of uninterrupted war, and its infrastructure was decimated; the task of rebuilding would have been formidable even under ideal conditions.

The next 10 years saw the implementation of a devastating series of Marxist-Leninist plans and social policies that did not deliver the expected economic benefits. To exacerbate the difficulties, Vietnam became mired in protracted military actions with China and Cambodia. Given the incalculable toll that war had already taken on the Vietnamese people, these conflicts brought an additional burden on the country's depleted social and economic resources. Food and consumer goods were scarce, and living conditions became so difficult that approximately 1 million Vietnamese fled the country. Vietnam had become one of the poorest nations in the world. Cut off from US$1.7 billion of annual Soviet aid, denied access to the World Bank, the

Asian Development Bank, and the IMF, and with the Soviet Union calling for the repayment of US$15 billion in loans, the Communist Party of Vietnam (CPV) was forced to make policy changes (Shultz, Pecotich & Le 1994).

Economic environment

Rebirth through *Doi Moi*

The economic failure of the "socialist transformation" (Vo 1990) was finally recognized by the CPV in August 1986. This was ratified by the Sixth Party Congress later that year, when the old system was abandoned (although not in its entirety) in favor of a policy simply referred to as *Doi Moi*—that is, economic renovation, or change for the new. Essentially, the policy prescribed a partial turn to the market, allowing private ownership and freeing prices, among other reforms. Consequently, both the Vietnamese economy and society changed—irrevocably. The newspaper of the People's Army summarized the public sentiment and political climate that necessitated the change (*Quan Doi Nhan Dan* 1992):

> Because of irresistible demands by the people the need for social change has become a pressing question. Realities in the recent past show that the move to break from the old model in a country can be undertaken with less tension and less danger if the communists in that country know how to look squarely at the truth to actively carry out renovation themselves or to lead the entire people in this process. On the contrary, those who intentionally try to turn a deaf ear or a blind eye to the demands of the age and the wishes of the people are likely to meet a tragic end.

The impact of *Doi Moi* was felt almost immediately (Cima 1989; Pike 1991; General Statistical Office 1992; Do Duc Dinh 1993). Entrepreneurs quickly emerged to capitalize on latent consumer demand. Consumer goods channeled through Singapore, Thailand and Cambodia from the south, and Hong Kong and China from the north, became readily available. Turmoil, however, also accompanied the first signs of prosperity. Inflation rose to 800% by 1988, and the disintegration of Eastern Europe caused a conservative backlash that led to the disgrace of several reformers (Shultz & Le 1993). Still, by 1991, it became clear that economic reforms would not be suppressed, and the Seventh Party Congress solidified them (Communist Party of Vietnam 1991); it also became apparent that supporting reform would likely consolidate the party's power (Erlanger 1991). The CPV seeks to maintain its unique "third way" between capitalism and communism (Hanson 1991; Shultz & Pecotich 1997), and has been able to improve the lives of the people it governs through market reforms, while maintaining power (Shultz, Pecotich & Le 1994).

Vietnam has come a long way since the implementation of *Doi Moi*. At home, the economy continues to produce impressive, nearly double-digit growth rates, and foreign investors continue to fund projects for Vietnam's expansion. Abroad, Vietnam has achieved stable relations with its neighbors, has reduced its military expenditures, and has enjoyed recent foreign policy successes with ASEAN and the USA. These developments have facilitated Vietnam's economic boom. If this policy continues, opportunities for marketing firms will increase dramatically, though entry without full cognizance of the risks is not encouraged.

Since putting behind itself the wars with the USA, Cambodia and China, Vietnam has been able to attract significant private investment capital and multilateral aid. These developments are possible, for the fundamental reason that Vietnam is a country of immense promise. Vietnam's Ministry of Planning and Investment received license applications for US$5.4 billion in 1995, and approximately US$6 billion in 1996 (Clifford Chance 1996). And with development aid came more private business. The World Bank financed a US$2 billion highway and infrastructure project that brought many multinational companies to Vietnam. Total investment of over US$520 million from US companies alone flowed into the country by the end of 1995, making the USA the 6th largest investor despite being a relatively late player in the market. Australia, for example, has led the way in telecommunications and Singapore, Malaysia, the Republic of Korea, Taiwan, and Hong Kong are the largest investors in Vietnam, the 13th largest market in the world.

Despite its promise, however, Vietnam is not an "easy" market, not even for those with successful experience in Asia and other international markets. It is a market in the throes of economic transition, still uncertain, not only in its philosophical orientation, but also in the basic administrative practical aspects of reform implementation. Some of the major negative and positive aspects of the developments are discussed in the paragraphs that follow.

Administrative practices and regulations

Regardless of the generally favorable view created by Vietnam's market potential, it is easy to forget that economic transition is both quite recent, and ongoing. The nation is emerging from almost 50 years of war, international isolation and almost total dependence on dwindling aid from the former Eastern bloc. In addition, the US-led economic embargo, coupled with poor central economic planning at home, means that Vietnam, as of 1998, still has an annual per-capita income of less than US$400. Despite post-*Doi Moi* improvements, Vietnam's small but growing "middle class" counts on annual incomes of under half the US$2600 per year income of the emerging middle class in China (Shultz & Ardrey 1997, p. 28). It is, therefore, still a very poor nation facing major problems with its physical, legal and economic infrastructure. Economic progress is linked not only with market reform but also with the development of the infrastructure. These developments are being implemented by the CPV (Shultz, Ardrey & Pecotich 1995, p. 22), which, in seeking to find a consistent ideological direction, appears not totally comfortable in promoting "market socialism". Accordingly, regulations, laws and licenses continue to be issued and enforced at the discretion of the CPV as the reform process moves forward in the classic "two steps forward and one back" manner.

The result is that the rules always seem to change just when one is about to be profitable. Despite the efforts of senior political leaders to take a personal interest in streamlining licensing agreements and business procedures generally, the bureaucracy and red tape in Vietnam remain daunting. As a result, while license applications for investment continue to increase, the actual investment by foreign corporations in approved projects decreased by over 40% in the first half of 1996. Some foreigners have become especially wary of joint ventures with Vietnamese firms (usually state owned), and the Vietnam News Agency has reported a trend toward wholly owned foreign projects.

The private sector grew to over US$300 million in combined capital in 1993, with license applications for private businesses maintaining double-digit growth since that year. However, local, private manufacturers complain of excessive taxation, lack of capital and resources, and government favoritism for foreign investments, especially those that are joint ventures with the state. Foreigners looking to create partnerships with a private Vietnamese company must be aware that the private sector receives much praise, but few useful resources. The state-run commercial banks, which account for almost 90% of bank assets, are heavily, if not exclusively, geared toward the state enterprise sector. Few resources are left for the private sector (cf. Freeman 1996, p. 15). Many state firms have been ordered to begin "equitization," gradually selling small stakes into private hands. Unfortunately, there is no secondary market for these equity stakes. Smaller private companies, and foreign joint ventures already prepared for privatization, have been discouraged from offering shares, and management buyouts and outright acquisitions have been frowned upon as well. By 1996, 5000 of the 12 000 State-Owned Enterprises (SOEs) operating in 1993 were closed or merged as part of *Doi Moi*, but only 5 small state enterprises have "equitized" and permitted private participation (Merrill Lynch 1994; Freeman 1996).

Medium-sized firms have also felt the squeeze due to efforts by the conservatives within the CPV to keep all assets in the hands of the state. From 1991–1995, Vietnamese state and private partners were able to attract foreign investors by offering land rights directly to foreign companies as an important part of the local partner's contribution to the capital of a new business financial venture. Before the controversial Decree 18/CP in February of 1995, Vietnamese firms were also able to mortgage land use rights for loans. And while the repeal of this decree is still being debated in the National Assembly, land-use rights must be leased directly from the state. This places a significant burden on existing companies and new ventures that want to attract loans and foreign investments.

Individuals and small firms have typically been left out of plans for financial-services reform. If they can buy shares of equitized firms, they cannot trade them. The 62 foreign banks and bank representative offices in Vietnam are severely restricted in taking Vietnamese dong deposits, especially from Vietnamese citizens. The Vietnamese government has development plans, which will require between US$40 billion and US$50 billion of investment, yet it can reasonably expect only half this figure to come from foreign sources. It must mobilize domestic savings to fund the needed investments in infrastructure and key industries, if it wants the Vietnamese economy to emulate the Asian "tiger" economies.

Without banking services from foreign banks, Vietnamese citizens and small private firms are left with the state banking system (see Merrill Lynch 1994; Balfour 1996). This system has been set up to serve state enterprises, and continues to have serious service-delivery problems. Among these problems is the inability to clear checks between branches of the same bank. Even for a developing country, Vietnam has a low volume of non-cash transactions, and difficulty with checks and wire payments. In many cases, foreign firms must pay their employees and settle payroll tax liabilities in cash. Vietnam has one of the lowest deposit rates in the developing world, less than 25% of GDP (most countries average 75%, with higher rates in Asia). This is not surprising, considering that local banks charge for withdrawals, an obvious disincentive to save in the formal banking system. Memories of bank failures are also harmful. In the 1980s, state-run banks failed to honor withdrawals, informal credit co-operatives collapsed, and high inflation discouraged saving.

Not surprisingly, alternative services and sources of capital have filled the vacuum created by state-bank shortcomings. Informal credit rings are flourishing. Over US$2 billion is being hoarded outside the formal banking system in US dollars, gold, or consumer goods such as spirits (liquor) and durable goods that will hold their value over time. Viet Kieu (overseas Vietnamese) infusions also contribute. Approximately 2 million Viet Kieu bring money into the country and/or send money to families and friends. Some private banks have also been established in Vietnam, with many turning a profit from trade finance. Financial-service reforms, however, still tend to ignore small enterprises and consumers, and the institutions generally are not in step with international standards. Problems are appearing, including the following (see Chapman 1996):

- inconsistent and frequently inexplicable policies that hinder all aspects of the transition from a command to a market economy, including the legal, banking and accounting systems
- persistent and expanding trade deficits, which ballooned from US$60 million in 1992 to US$2.2 billion in 1996
- growing overseas debt
- a burgeoning current-account deficit, which hit an estimated 15.1% of GDP in 1995
- stagnating FDI realizations; while approval rates are soaring, actual realization of the projects are slowing, partly because of the frustrations presented by the bureaucracy
- inefficiencies of SOEs, as most evidenced by minimal job creation and the failure to create a large number of value-added exports

In summary, uncertainty over the pace of reforms has resulted in disenchantment with Vietnam's investment potential. Many investors entering with high expectations and hopes for quick profits have been disappointed, and some without staying power have departed.

Progressive economic results

Despite the problems, the macro-economic reforms that resulted from *Doi Moi* have spurred foreign investment and opened domestic markets (e.g. Fforde 1991; Le & McCarthy 1995; Dapice & Vallely 1996). The following fundamental economic indicators (see also Table 19.1) suggest that the economic situation is improving, and that it may continue to do so:

1. Annual GDP growth over the last 5 years has averaged 8.0%.
2. The Vietnamese dong has generally stabilized against the US dollar, and in 1998 is trading at 13 000 to 1. As a result of tough government budgets, inflation dropped from 487% in 1986 to 12.4% in 1995, and is expected to remain at low double-digit figures in the foreseeable future.
3. Agricultural production has risen 7% annually, and industrial production has risen 13–15% annually since 1988.
4. The reorientation of trade to a market-style economy has doubled exports between 1992 and 1995.
5. Registered imports are up; unregistered imports smuggled in from southern China and Thailand via Cambodia are way up.
6. Foreign Direct Investment licensing approvals totaled US$18 billion at the end of 1995, up 97% in 1995 alone.
7. Overseas direct assistance pledges remain healthy, with US$2 billion pledged at the latest donor conference in Paris, November 1995.

We believe that many of the problems are temporary, caused by rapid growth, and that action by the central government may result in their

Table 19.1 Vietnam: Fundamental socio-economic indicators

Indicator	*Details*			
Per-capita income (1996 estimate)	US$250			
Literacy rate (1989 estimate)	88%*			
Population (1997 estimate)	77 million			
Rural population :	78%			
	1991	*1992*	*1993*	*1994*
% CPI change	67.5	17.5	5.2	14.4
GDP				
current prices (VD billion**)	76 707	110 535	136 571	170 258
1989 prices (VD billion)	31 286	33 991	36 736	39 982
% change	6.0	8.6	8.1	8.8
GDP by % expenditure				
Private consumption	81.8	78.73	76.1	68.6
Govt consumption	8.1	7.6	9.8	14.4
Total investment	15.0	17.6	20.5	24.2
Exports	29.6	31.9	32.9	34.5
Imports	−34.2	−36.0	−37.3	−42.9
Statistical discrepancy	−2.0	−2.0	−2.0	−2.0
Total	**100.0**	**100.0**	**100.0**	**100.0**
Population (1991–1995) (million)				
Males	32.994	33.814	34.671	35.386
Females	34.780	35.591	36.355	37.123
Total	**67.774**	**69.405**	**71.026**	**72.510**
% growth rate	2.3	2.4	2.3	2.1

Notes :
* Recent field work by the authors indicates that the literacy rate may be declining.
** The VD (Vietnamese Dong)–US$ exchange rate is approx. 12 000:1.

Sources: General Statistical Office (1996), *Statistical Yearbook*, Statistical Publishing House, Hanoi; Economist Intelligence Unit (1997), *Vietnam*, EIU, London.

amelioration. After a decade of reforms, the direction, if not the pace, of *Doi Moi* remains focused on economic growth and expansion. Moreover, Vietnamese authorities are increasingly attempting to facilitate the foreign-investment process. Legal, tax, and financial reforms are on the agenda, and many desirable projects have had their license procedures "fast tracked" by the government. Although the recent economic tremors being felt in other parts of ESEA are bound to affect Vietnam, the economy continues to grow, inflation remains low, and some early foreign investors have begun to generate returns.

Political and ideological reform

Recent political developments are also cause for investor optimism. The period 1992–1997 has produced more sustainable progress and, therefore, more predictable economic growth than at any time in the past 50 years. Consider the following developments since 1992:

1. The USA and Vietnam established diplomatic relations in 1995, and it is expected that Vietnam will eventually be granted Most Favored Nation (MFN) status as a trade partner.
2. Vietnam has been, since July 1995, a full standing member of ASEAN, and is expected to join APEC.
3. Constructive engagement with China, Vietnam's principal rival in the region, has resulted in reduced military threats, exchanges of senior delegations, and an 80% increase in bilateral trade.
4. The emergence of the Greater Mekong Sub-region, a trading zone of 200 million consumers comprised of Vietnam, Cambodia, Laos, Thailand and southern China: the sub-region shares the costs and benefits of regional infrastructure and investment products, lowers trading barriers, and facilitates exchanges of goods and services (Brimble 1994). Vietnam, at the mouth of the Mekong, serves as the principal conduit to the entire region.
5. A 50% debt-forgiveness negotiation with the Paris Club, and rescheduling and forgiveness of over US$750 million in debt with the London Club, will permit Vietnam to tap the Eurobond market for needed capital. Vietnam has even begun to address the need to repay some of its debt to the former USSR.
6. Joint arrangements are being developed with Thai and Korean governments and banking groups to reorganize and reform Vietnam's ailing financial-services sector.

Improved relations with the USA and China have been critical to Vietnam's economic success. Further economic impetus has been provided by the pursuit of an ongoing foreign policy based on a desire to "get along well with everyone" (Le Van Bang 1992; Ha Huy Thong 1996). Vietnam now boasts of trading relationships with over 100 nations.

Vietnam continues to capitalize on its successful mix of domestic reforms and openness to foreign investment. Even though Vietnam started its reform process nearly a decade after China, the Vietnamese were able to catch up in the areas of agricultural reform, price reform, currency devaluation, and healthy growth rates of GDP and foreign investment. Similarly to China, the Communist party has remained in command, with the role of guiding the economy along the road to marketization. The Asian Development Bank and other sources predict 9–10% annual growth rates, single-digit inflation rates and exponential growth in consumption.

Marketing environment

On balance, the macro-economic and political changes discussed above, coupled with latent consumer demand, underline the vast potential that is Vietnam. Indeed, precisely because of the current uncertainty of the market, there are still many opportunities for investors who understand the unique dynamism of the environment. Entry requires commitment, perseverance, and faith in the long-term future of the country. Further, a degree of sympathy is required for a nation that is facing tough choices and appears to have reached a critical point in its development. Some of the fundamental issues that the nation faces also provide great opportunities.

Marketing institutions and infrastructure

Before the market reforms can fully succeed, Vietnam needs to develop marketing institutions and infrastructure. Retailing, although developing, is relatively primitive (Shultz, Pecotich & Le 1994), as are telecommunications, transport, and other institutions necessary for the evolution of a modern marketing system. An appropriate example is given in *Asian Business* (1995), describing the difficulties associated with the Nomura of Japan US$450 million investment in the Nomura Haiphong Industrial Zone:

> Electricity and water are to be supplied by the Haiphong People's Committee, although both are in short supply in the city. Haiphong port is also notoriously silted up and can accommodate only 7000 deadweight-tonne vessels—city officials have refused to start building a deep-water sea port elsewhere. Until a new bridge is built in 1998, all traffic between Hanoi and the zone has to cross a single-lane bridge, which is also shared by the rail line between the capital and the Haiphong port (p. 33).

Sympathetic recognition that in many respects this is the expected result of a protracted war and underdevelopment does not alter the existing situation. We reiterate that, before true, sustained progress can be made, institutions and infrastructure must be developed, and this can only be achieved by strong political will and an infusion of capital.

Potential investors need to recognize that Vietnam is in the process of rebuilding a nation, and that it has the fundamental right to achieve this in its own unique way. This way may not always suit the investor, but there are immense opportunities in infrastructure development for those who persist. Seaports, airports, highways, water-treatment facilities, buildings, dams, power stations, and other foundations to support a modern economy are being built or re-furbished. Construction, telecommunications, and transportation supplies and equipment are all not only in demand, but also desperately needed (e.g. parts of the railway system have been out of service since the war) before full progress can be made. In an effort to meet this need, the government, funded by the World Bank and the Asian Development Bank, intends to spend US$9.6 billion on infrastructure by the turn of the century. However, this expenditure is earmarked for physical facilities such as ports and irrigation systems, and there is concern that the government may not be moving quickly enough in administrative and institutional reform, particularly of the financial and legal sectors, which is necessary to sustain growth.

Reform in the banking sector in particular has been slow despite the recognition that, to meet development goals, the Vietnamese economy needs not only to attract more foreign investment, but also to mobilize over US$20 billion in domestic resources by the end of the decade. Unfortunately, savings (in the form of thrift deposits in the formal banking system) have not kept pace with economic growth. Even after a decade of economic openness, the Vietnamese seem to prefer to keep their savings in the form of gold, hoarded US dollars, or investments with risky informal credit co-operatives (*Hui*). Unfortunately, Vietnam's deposits in the formal banking system are lower than those for other transition economies such as China, Hungary, and even Mongolia and Albania.

International trade

Since the renovation policy, trade in Vietnam has been booming. The government has introduced many reforms such as tax breaks and export-processing zones, to encourage investors to initiate operations that facilitate export growth and development. It has actively promoted foreign investment, including joint ventures, 100%-foreign-owned ventures, build-own transfer (BOT) projects and co-operation agreements. This has had an effect, and much of the growth has been fueled by foreign investment, which has expanded by 50% since 1993. The major investors are regional players such as Singapore, Hong Kong, Japan, and Taiwan. Interestingly, Singapore, whose largest investment is a $US2.1 billion urban development project outside Hanoi, has recently ranked first on the list of foreign investors in Vietnam. Oil is still the major export, but garment manufacturing, aquatic products and rice are occupying an increasing proportion. Manufacture of low-tech, labor-intensive, value-added products such as textiles and furniture is growing (Shultz & Ardrey 1997). Imports in 1994 were dominated by capital and intermediate goods. The top 3 in 1994 were machinery/equipment (US$737 million), petroleum products (US$691 million) and automobiles/motorcycles (US$310 million), with Singapore, Taiwan, and Japan being the major import source (*Asian Business* 1995). Imports of heavy equipment, for example, are often duty free. The government has the avowed objective to compete in high-tech industries within a decade, and is attempting to achieve this by establishing technology parks and R&D centers as well as making a commitment to maintain low wages.

Consumer markets

The economic environment of the Vietnamese consumer has changed dramatically since the implementation of *Doi Moi*. Accompanying this change are fundamental changes in societal values, embraced by some and resisted by others. International brands are rapidly diffusing throughout Vietnam. Popular brands familiar around the globe are beginning to dominate the clothing, electronics, household-goods, and recreational-beverage markets. As in most developing nations, foreign brands are often considered of higher quality and prestige, and consumers are willing to pay price premiums for them.

An interesting aspect of branding is that brand authenticity does not seem to be important and is, if at all, a secondary consideration. Brand piracy is flourishing, and Vietnamese manufacturers seem to have no hesitation in distributing counterfeit items. Pop culture seems to have permeated the economy, and Disney characters, Ray Ban sunglasses and Nike are examples of popular trademarks that are frequently used indiscriminately.

The natural and common result of the popularity of foreign brands is concern for the progress of domestic manufacturers, which are being squeezed out of the marketplace. There is therefore a strong protectionist move within the CPV in favor of industries such as cigarettes, beverages, detergents, and paper (Clifford Chance 1996, p. 15).

Another concern is with the cultural destruction that accompanies such "social evils" as karaoke bars, outdoor advertisements, and other corrupting Western influences. Although the government has not expected demand for popular brands or non-Vietnamese ideas to disappear, it has taken steps to avoid cultural disintegration and complete dominance by foreign products. Consequently, the government has invoked regulations, for example, to ensure that advertisements for foreign products include copy in the Vietnamese language (Shultz & Ardrey 1997, p. 32). However, this battle against "cultural imperialism" may already have been lost due to rising incomes, exposure to popular culture, and product availability. The limited opportunities for other forms of recreation are making shopping and consumption popular pastimes in Vietnam. The trends affecting the shift toward a consumer culture include the 5 basic factors discussed below.

Demographics

Estimates of the total Vietnamese population vary, and have been placed as high as about 80 million, but the official, understated figures are shown in Table 19.1. Population growth declined from 3.1% per year from 1960–1970 to 2.1% in 1995, and the hope is to reduce this rate to 1.7% by 2000 (Economist Intelligence Unit 1994, 1997; *Asian Business* 1995). The population continues to increase, despite the effects of the war and emigration, mainly because of the post-war "baby boom."

Vietnam is still an agrarian society, with 78% of the population living in the countryside, but, as everywhere else in ESEA, there is large-scale migration to the cities. This migration is the result of economic growth and opportunities afforded by extensive foreign investment in Hanoi, Ho Chi Minh City (formerly Saigon), Danang, Can Tho, Hue and Haiphong, and special economic zones such as Vung Tau. It is likely that this trend will continue despite controls on population movement and low income differentials between rural and urban areas (Economist Intelligence Unit 1994).

Although the Vietnamese divide the nation into 3 main regions (North, Central and South), the population is concentrated in the 2 major fertile regions: the Red River Delta, with a population density of about 1 085 per km^2 in the north; and the Mekong River Delta, with population density of about 385 per km^2 (Economist Intelligence Unit 1994). The majority of the population live in the deltas, and are the ethnic Vietnamese (*kinh*), who constitute about 87% of the population. The minority groups are found in the mountain areas, and include the Cham, Khmer, Muong, Thai, and others with distinct cultures and languages.

Historical and other factors have provided the 2 most populous regions with distinctive cultural characteristics. The harsh conditions of the North produced a collectively disciplined, closed society as compared with the more individualistic, tolerant, and moderate society of the South. Despite these differences, it is important to realize that Vietnamese "share a core culture, have a common historical heritage, and speak mutually understandable dialects of the same language" (Jamieson 1993, p. 6).

Markets consist of people and money, and there is little doubt that for those with money in Vietnam living conditions have improved. However, for most of the population, living conditions are poor, though expenditures may often exceed official incomes. The Economist Intelligence Unit (1994) reports the result of a survey which suggests that both farmers' and state workers' families were having problems surviving. In 1990, "the average monthly income per head of the state workers' families surveyed . . . was D48 248 [about US$5.00], while expenditure was D47 835" (Economist Intelligence Unit 1994, p. 19). Farmers' families spent 94% of their income on essentials, of which 82% was spent on food, while state workers' families spent 77% and 62% respectively. These data clearly indicate that Vietnam is a poor country that has a long way to go. Nonetheless, progress has been made, and a potentially huge market exists.

Social structure

Vietnam is a nation that has been under stress from both external and internal forces. It is inevitable, therefore, that there has been pressure on the traditional values and social structures. In the wake of the recent US influence, as well as the ideologically based government influence, traditional values, although still held, have been surrounded by ambiguity. To complicate matters, the effects of these stresses and pressures in the North were different from those in the South. Jamieson (1994, pp. 300–7) summarizes these effects as follows:

> Most people still conceived of a "virtuous" or "decent" person as one who observed the time-honored conventions of traditional society, especially the 5 cardinal virtues (*nhan, nghia, le, tri, tin*) and 2 of the 3 bonds–those between parent and child and between husband and wife. The bond between subject and sovereign was so complex and emotionally charged, and the context had changed so greatly, that it was excluded from moral judgments of the kinds people continued to make in other areas.
>
> Loyalty was a prized attribute, but with such a rapid turnover of governments and leaders and so many competing claims to legitimacy in recent history, it was not always clear to whom or to what one should be loyal.
>
> ... Only among some villagers was trustworthiness insisted upon. Most of the middle-aged and younger adults said that you must expect people to do what they have to do to survive in a difficult and rapidly changing world.
>
> ... Most significant[ly], even within the context of family, the behavioral norms were perceptibly shifting as traditional values were not abandoned but redefined.
>
> ... Filial piety, the cardinal virtue of Vietnamese life, was also undergoing operational redefinition. Parents in the 1960s and 1970s neither expected nor demanded the total obedience and responsiveness that previous generations had extracted from their children.

These social changes have had their strongest impact on families that continue to be large and share small houses (urban households typically consisting of more than 7 members), but whose social cohesiveness is being challenged by modern values. The move to a market system has necessitated the redefinition of the traditional collectivist entities such as the commune and the family, and has also meant the introduction of Western legal individualism (Unger 1994; 1997). Although each family member may not earn more than a few hundred US dollars per year, household income more than exceeds expenses. Children typically live at home until marriage, contributing to the family income in addition to paying for their own needs. Viet Kieu family members also contribute significantly by sending money or gifts. So, while individual purchasing power is modest, pooled resources by families may increase purchasing power.

The economic growth has provided many Vietnamese with disposable income and, consequently, the emergence of a new class of consumers.

Official figures in Hanoi and Ho Chi Minh City indicate that incomes now often approach and exceed US$1000. Our personal interviews indicate that much larger, unreported, and untaxed pockets of wealth are springing up throughout Vietnamese cities. Many of these newly middle-class consumers can now afford relatively expensive items such as motorcycles, television sets, videocassette recorders, stereo equipment, and washing machines. A small upper class is also now emerging, and is purchasing luxury items of all kinds, including automobiles, villas, and high-fashion products (Shultz & Ardrey 1997).

Foreign invasion

Once bombarded by explosives, many Vietnamese feel as if they are now being bombarded by new products and advertising; a series of political cartoons has recently made light of this sentiment. Furthermore, tourists and expatriates visiting or working in Vietnam bring new ideas, products, consumer expectations and demands. Hotels, transportation services, discotheques, newspapers, magazines, golf courses, promotions campaigns, and satellite TV are all intended to meet the needs of this growing "foreigner" market. Vietnamese are also exposed to these new products, information, ideas and values, however, and are subsequently changing their expectations and demands.

The new generation

The combination of the impressionable nature of youth and the flood of new ideas and products into Vietnam has created a segment of "Generation X" consumers in a very short period of time. The size of the youth market is having a profound effect on Vietnamese society. Although the majority of the society is still family oriented and living under the shadow of socialist dogma, over half of Vietnam's population is under the age of 20. To these consumers, war and politics are little more than history lessons. An affluent population of teenagers in Ho Chi Minh City now has the capacity to obtain credit cards from foreign banks, and to purchase expensive imported consumer goods. In addition to being a growing market in their own right, the youth in Vietnam are becoming opinion leaders for others.

These trends all indicate radical change, rapid market segmentation and consumer power. Traditionally, segmentation schemes differentiated consumers on urban–rural and North–South dimensions, and certainly Vietnam is still a society in which approximately 80% of the population lives in rural areas and is involved in the agrarian economy. But, more recently, age, access to Western or "developed Asian" ideas and products, and increasing disposable income have become factors that produce predictable consumption patterns. It should also be noted, however, that, as in any transforming agrarian economy in which socialism and collectivism have been the norm, there is a conservative element, particularly in Northern and rural regions, which still often prefers traditional products or local Vietnamese products. Nevertheless, the sweeping trend is that of the transformation to a consumer culture, and in the cities this trend is occurring at an astonishing rate.

Regardless of the economic implications, the trend toward a consumer culture has not been universally embraced because it often conflicts with many of the values, attitudes, and behaviors associated with traditional Vietnamese culture and/or CPV doctrine. However given current trends, traditional consumption patterns and cultural idiosyncrasies will be difficult for Vietnam to sustain. Indeed, global trends suggest that items and institutions—from rainforests to traditional culture—that cannot be made into marketable commodities may not survive. Even the legendary Cu Chi tunnels have been made into a tourist attraction. For a fee, visitors now have the opportunity to crawl through the former Viet Cong stronghold, sip US soft drinks at the snack shop located mid-way, and shoot a Soviet-made rifle at the conclusion of the tour. Construction on the adjacent golf course has just been completed (cf. Shultz, Pecotich & Le 1994).

Implications for marketing management

Vietnam is a promising market, but to succeed there, marketing managers must have more than a fundamental understanding of the classic 4 Ps of the marketing mix. They must accept that Vietnam is a series of enigmas and seemingly illogical confounds. Management in Vietnam is as much art, nuance, and persuasion as science. For the most part projects do not fail because of poor market demand, but because of a management failure to comprehend and adapt to the environment. In the following we discuss some critical factors to consider during the process of marketing management in Vietnam.

Adapting to changing regulations

Managers must accept that administrative practices and regulations will continue to change. Waiting for a perfectly stable system may mean missing opportunities that already exist. Asian investors and some Europeans seem much more willing to accept this fact and spend considerable amounts of time nurturing relationships with partners and government authorities (note, too, that sometimes these two entities are synonymous). As a case in point, one European brewer was pleased to discover it would not have to remove or repaint its billboards in response to the "social evils" campaign. Its country representatives attributed this time and cost savings solely to its good relationship with government authorities. In contrast, Australian and US investors find it difficult to work on an agreement based solely on solid relationships and trust, and are inclined to ensure that all the legal issues are agreed upon before moving forward. This strategy is counterproductive, however, because the legal codes may either be non-existent, or in revision.

This is not to argue that respect for laws and the legal process in Vietnam should be abandoned. Indeed, understanding Vietnamese laws and Vietnam's legal system is very important. For example, trademarks mean nothing unless they are registered in Vietnam. If one does register a trademark in Vietnam, protection is afforded, and despite problems with brand piracy, bogus plants have been closed and purveyors of pirated goods fined when the pirated trademarks have been registered. So in Vietnam managers constantly struggle to balance home-country laws, Vietnamese laws, and social forces in addition to their responsibilities of managing the marketing mix.

The need for changes in the legal and accounting systems dominates and affects virtually all other changes needed. Observers tend to argue that infrastructure development should be the highest priority, and in a sense it should, but the need for a legal and administrative system to accompany it should not be overlooked. The most encouraging changes from the perspective of foreign investors include the formalization and clarification of legal and administrative practices—for example, investment-guarantee measures, assurances of rights and obligations of foreign organizations and individuals, contract and joint-venture guidelines, procedures for the resolution of disputes, export and import regulations, labor regulations, contracts on the lease of land and water, insurance contracts and credit, banking and financial contracts. A welcome outgrowth of the reform is the success of export processing zones, which have been given the dispensation to streamline bureaucracy and provide relief from some taxes, fixed-wage laws and land-use rights. But we cannot emphasize the following point too strongly: despite progress on law reform, as with other Vietnamese institutions, the legal system is new, and in transition. Managers must accept this fact, and adjust accordingly.

Entry strategies

A local presence and some official support are both necessary for success. Investors in wholly owned factories, joint-venture projects involving more powerful state companies, and small private companies have had some success in Vietnam. But trying to handle all business affairs from outside Vietnam generally proves to be an unsuccessful strategy. Hence, Viet Kieu and local Vietnamese who are experienced in working with foreigners may be the most desirable partners. The partner-selection process must be included as part of market research. As is the case with most endeavors in Vietnam, however, there are no guarantees, but individuals and groups who are truly committed to the project, and are not concerned with undue favors and quick returns, have typically proven to be good partners. There is another strong economic incentive to pick good partners: they are likely to be charged 10 times less than foreigners when paying "facilitation fees" and other gratuities frequently required to expedite business processes.

Good partnerships are enhanced by nurturing relationships. If a good partner has been chosen, the social institutions of honor and saving face will often suffice when no contract is available. Because of these social institutions, a company can be successful even without an intricate legal system familiar to Westerners. Instead of standard institutions of accepted business practices that Westerners tend to think are requisites for success, in Vietnam a confederation of loosely co-operative networks and relationships exist, and these help to provide much of the institutional framework.

Private and government intermediaries can help investors to find partners, but circumspection should be the norm. Current Vietnamese law still requires most firms to work co-operatively with government intermediaries such as city and local authorities, and the Ministry for Planning and Investment (MPI). This is an agency ostensibly responsible for "streamlining" the business-application process, but is in fact another bureau that is often associated with unnecessary delays. Agents and enterprises engaged in processing operations or shipping concerns can usually avoid the MPI, but will still need to work co-operatively with local authorities. Any large or "strategic" project—that is, a project that even remotely involves national security—will require MPI approval.

The channel decision

As noted earlier, Vietnam is generally divided into 3 basic cultural/commercial zones: North, Central and South. Most investors have opted to establish commercial operations in Ho Chi Minh City, the largest, most cosmopolitan urban center, and Vietnam's commercial hub. This city has a metropolitan population of approximately 5 million. The city is booming because of its intrinsic market size and the marketing acumen and consumption ethos of its population. Located on the Saigon River with a tropical climate, it is usually favored by foreign investors.

There are other promising locations in Vietnam, however, that should not be overlooked. Hanoi, for example, the capital and second largest city of Vietnam, has a metropolitan population of approximately 3 million. The city is located on the Red River, and, while most of Vietnam is tropical, its latitude causes significant changes in seasons: hot and steamy summers, and damp winters with a temperature range from 10–15°C. Although *Doi Moi* has brought new life to Hanoi, its development lags behind that of Ho Chi Minh City, and both the North and Hanoi are generally more conservative. Nevertheless, Hanoi is the political center of the country, and a viable market in its own right. The Vietnamese government is eager to develop the North and the countryside, and often offers incentives to foreigners interested in investing in these areas. Moreover, while the urban sprawl of Ho Chi Minh City may make it an attractive consumer market, rent and wage increases may make it less desirable for manufacturing. Consequently, special development zones such as Haiphong, Vung Tau and Danang, all of which also happen to be ports, may be more attractive sites for factories.

Researching the market

Market research has been, and always will be, important in Vietnam. But the dynamics of the market and the research requirements have changed considerably since the embargo was lifted. The previously discussed segmentation trends support this assertion, and urban consumers have become much more sophisticated as a result of the deluge of products and promotions. For many Vietnamese, attitudes and beliefs have changed. Understanding how they have changed will, of course, affect the decision on how to manipulate the marketing mix. Also, the competition across product categories has become much more intense. These changes collectively shape how one might now administer, for example, a promotions campaign. Unlike the early 1990s, the battle for many segments is now to differentiate products rather than to make consumers aware. Furthermore, where simple outdoor advertisements and point-of-purchase materials once sufficed, many managers will now have to consider the importance of other variables in the marketing communications mix. Several market research and advertising firms have established operations to assist with the market research process. There is still, however, no substitute for sending multiskilled employees to Vietnam to examine the market conditions thoroughly, and thereby determine the viability of the proposed product or service offering, and the appropriate management of pricing, distribution, and promotion.

Developing human resources

No matter how great the demand for a product or service, employee selection, training, and management are critical. Fortunately, the pool size and quality of applicants for many jobs has increased impressively in the last 3 years. Younger Vietnamese are scrambling to learn English and acquire computer and marketing skills. Not very long ago, it was difficult to find anyone who could operate a computer and speak English well. To compare this situation to today's employee pool, we cite the following example. A firm recently placed an advertisement in a Ho Chi Minh City newspaper announcing the opening of a clerical position that required some customer contact. The firm received 1500 applications; over 200 applicants met or exceeded the required qualifications.

Vietnamese have earned a reputation for being hard workers, and as a population enjoy one of the highest literacy rates in Asia. They are also very keen to learn contemporary business practices, and often prefer to work for foreign-based companies. The workforce is still lacking middle managers, however, and this problem can only be remedied with substantial investments in corporate-sanctioned training.

Motivation and persistence

Vietnam remains an exceptionally challenging market, where strategic focus and sound, consistent commitment to projects are the greatest predictors of success. Companies that come to Vietnam are likened to Sisyphus (the king of Corinth condemned perpetually to roll a huge stone up a hill only to have it roll on top of him when he reached the top) in that their representatives not only work arduously with little to show for their efforts, but are also constantly replicating unsuccessful strategies. However, there are some good examples of both large and small firms that have avoided the Sisyphus syndrome and have done very well in Vietnam.

One of the most frequently cited large-firm success stories is PepsiCo. Typically second in market share in the cola wars around the globe, PepsiCo arrived in Vietnam 5 hours after the US embargo was lifted. It thoroughly researched all relevant aspects of the market and in so doing determined demand; it also found an optimal partner and appropriate manufacturing sites. It kept the initial investment low, established quality controls, offered professional training and cash resources, and effectively used *Su Lua Cua The He Moi* ("The choice of a new generation") as its promotional tag line. In one year, this joint venture, in which PepsiCo holds 30% equity, had sales revenue of US$33 million and a profit of US$2.5 million. In the process, PepsiCo solidified its relationship with the government by paying US$6 million in taxes and employing 1200 people.

A second case, involving a European beverage company, provides another illustration of this strategy. First, the company acquired a clear understanding of consumer demand for a specific product. Then it entered into a cooperative agreement with a Singaporean company that had many synergies with the European firm; moreover, the Singaporean company had established regional distribution and manufacturing capabilities and good working relationships with appropriate gatekeepers in Vietnam. Next, once a "go" decision was made, the European company sent a plant manager to Vietnam during the earliest stages of the plan. This person was involved in every aspect of the project, including negotiations, site location, and employment decisions. The manager's "staying power" and commitment to the project were vital. Finally, the company used an extensive top-of-mind-awareness campaign via outdoor advertising and sponsorship of local events, as well as point-of-purchase items such as mugs, coasters, and posters. The firm maintains a very favorable brand image, and consumers are willing to pay premium prices for the product.

Small-firm success typically involves young, energetic entrepreneurs who are attacking newly emerging niche markets. From bamboo production and real-estate brokerage to trading companies and language centers, these pioneers are making a mark in Vietnam. There are interesting commonalities among these success stories. They include low overheads, flexibility, an ability to see opportunities where others see only stumbling blocks, target focus, enthusiasm, and a sense of adventure. All of these successful firms made a total commitment: they moved to Vietnam, immersed themselves in the environment, many of their staff learned the language, and they made market-opportunity discoveries that enabled them to leverage their skills.

Conclusion

The combination of policy changes, ensuing market reforms, latent consumer demand, the re-emergence of local entrepreneurs, and multinational corporations has dramatically changed the lives of Vietnamese consumers. The magnitude of the change is placed in perspective when we consider that little more than a decade ago most Vietnamese struggled simply to survive. Now they struggle to make sense of the multitude of products and brands that have flooded their markets, the obtrusiveness of advertising, retail proliferation and the confusion of consumer choice. As a result, we are currently witnessing an unprecedented social as well as economic transformation in Vietnam.

These sweeping changes have enhanced the quality of life of the Vietnamese people. Increases in the availability, variety, and quality of consumer goods are evidence of progress, as is the government's successful effort to control inflation. This advance can be sustained only if consumers have access to desirable goods and can afford to purchase them. As living standards rise, so do expectations. The mechanisms that enable the influx of desirable consumer goods also give Vietnamese greater access to information from other market economies, especially their more affluent Asian neighbors, which provide benchmarks by which Vietnam measures its progress. Ironically, the successes of *Doi Moi*, in conjunction with better information about living standards elsewhere, have raised consumer expectations, and these, in turn, have challenged the constraints of current government policies, which always seem to be a step behind consumer desires.

The transformation from a society in which harmony and collectivism were importuned–sometimes with harsh measures–into a society in which individuals are now encouraged to compete and to be profitable, has not occurred without some social costs. Anxiety about class stratification and the erosion of social programs are also accompanying the emerging consumption ethos and the state's emphasis on privatization, entrepreneurship and market-determined prices.

All of these changes spell opportunity, and Vietnam provides opportunities for marketing enterprises of all sizes and specialties. The initial reforms favored only well-capitalized or well-connected businesses that could build roads, export oil, or generate hard currency. Vietnam's transformation has created a growing appetite among both Vietnamese and the expanding foreign community for all kinds of goods and services.

Vietnam should also be recognized for its links to other promising markets in the region. Its strategic location in the Greater Mekong Sub-region make it possible for firms to enter the country as part of a larger plan to market products to the 200 million consumers in this emerging trade bloc.

But, as promising as the Vietnam market may be, it is still perilous. Bureaucratic encumbrances and other constraints one would expect to find in any developing economy are present here. Problems especially relevant to Vietnam include an absence of qualified managers, poor infrastructure, and erratic improvements of legal, tax, and accounting systems. Rent extractions and other forms of corruption by national and local authorities are also problematic. So, in addition, are occasional reactionary movements within the government as Vietnam makes its transition to a market economy. Competition has become a factor as many companies struggle to penetrate the market and to establish brand dominance.

As in the marketing environments of other transition economies in ESEA–Cambodia, Laos, and Myanmar–any serious marketing manager in Vietnam should add Prudence, Patience, and Persistence to the classic 4 Ps of the marketing mix. In Vietnam, relationships take time to nurture. Favorable brand and company images must be built and maintained. Establishing good contacts, understanding the market, incremental growth, and sound business practices that address the unique Vietnamese condition will all pay off in the long term. Although the Vietnamese government's policies can be confusing, the government has attempted to address the concerns of foreign investors about problems that need longer term solutions. Even with 10% growth rates, however, it will be a while before Vietnam joins the ranks of the "tiger" economies. But marketers would be well advised to "seize the day." Vietnam will eventually join the tigers, and failing to enter the market now will be immeasurably costly to companies that intend to position themselves in the future as significant players in Vietnam and the region as a whole.

References

Asian Business (1995), "Vietnam Politics Delay Tough Choices", vol. 31, no. 10, October, pp. 30–9.

Balfour, Frederic (1996), "Why are we in Vietnam?", *Institutional Investor*, vol. no. 1, pp. 115–16.

Brimble, Peter (1994), "From Thailand to the Greater Mekong Subregion: The Challenges for Private Business", Paper presented, Brooker Group Limited, Bangkok, January 5.

Chapman, Matthew (1996), *Vietnam: Transition Under Threat*, Peregrine Securities, Hong Kong.

Cima, Ronald J. (1989), "Vietnam's Economic Reform: Approaching the 1990s", *Asian Survey*, vol. 29, no. 8, August, pp. 786-99.

Clifford Chance (1996), *Asian Financial Services Newsletter*, July, Clifford Chance Solicitors, London.

Communist Party of Vietnam (1991), *Seventh National Congress Documents*, Foreign Language Press, Hanoi.

Dapice, David O. & Vallely, Thomas J. (1996), "Vietnam's Economy: Will It Get and Stay on the Dragon's Trail", Harvard Institute for International Development Research Report, Cambridge, MA.

Do, Duc Dinh (1993), "Vietnam's Economic Renovation to the Market Mechanism", *Journal of Asian Business*, vol. 9, Summer, pp. 17–33.

Economist Intelligence Unit (1994), *EIU Country Profile—Vietnam*, EIU, London.

— (1997), *Vietnam*, EIU, London.

Erlanger, Stephen (1991), "Vietnam's Gains Slip Away", *International Herald Tribune*, February 19.

Fforde, Adam (1991), "The Political Economy of Reform in Vietnam—Some Reflections", Harvard Institute for International Development, Cambridge, MA, March 19.

Freeman, Nick (1996), "Going for a Dong", *The Banker*, vol. 146, January, pp. 33–5.

General Statistical Office (1992), *Economy and Trade of Vietnam 1986–1991*, Ministry of Trade and Tourism, Hanoi.

— (1996), *Statistical Yearbook*, Statistical Publishing House, Hanoi.

Ha, Huy Thong (1996), "Vietnam Policy, US Relations and the Future", paper presented at the Markets and Marketing Opportunities in Vietnam Conference, ASU West, Phoenix, April 19.

Hanson, Philip (1991), "Is There a 'Third Way' between Capitalism and Socialism?", *Reports on the USSR*, RFE/RL Research Institute, vol. 3, no. 35, pp. 15-19.

Jamieson, Neil L. (1993), *Understanding Vietnam*, University of California Press, Berkeley, CA.

Karnow, Stanley (1991), *Vietnam: A History*, Penguin, New York.

Le, Dang Doanh & McCarthy, Adam (1995), "Economic Reform in Vietnam: Achievements and Prospects", in eds S.F. Naya & J.L.H. Tan, *Asian Transitional Economies*, Institute of Southeast Asian Studies, Singapore:, pp. 99-153.

Le, Van Bang (1992), Interview with Author, Hanoi, May 4.

McAlister, John T. Jr. & Mus, Paul (1970), *The Vietnamese and Their Revolution*, Harper and Row, New York.

Merrill Lynch (1994), *Vietnam*, Global Securities Research and Economics Group, Asia Pacific Series, Hong Kong.

Pecotich, Anthony & Shultz, Clifford J. II (1993), "Vietnam Revisited: Observations and Emergent Themes in Consumer Behavior Since the Implementation of Market Reforms", in eds Gary Bamossy & W. Fred van Raaij, *Advances in Consumer Research*, Association for Consumer Research, Provo, UT, pp. 233–6.

Pike, Douglas (1992), "Vietnam: 1991 the Turning Point", *Asian Survey*, vol. 32, no. 1, pp. 74-81.

Quan Doi Nhan Dan, (1992), the People's Army of Vietnam, Hanoi, February.

Sheehan, Neil (1992), *After the War Was Over*, Random House, New York.

Shultz, Clifford J. II (1994), "Balancing Policy, Consumer Desire and Corporate Interests: Considerations for Market Entry in Vietnam", *Columbia Journal of World Business*, vol. 29, Winter, pp. 42-53.

Shultz, Clifford J. II & Ardrey, William J. (1995), "Future Prospects for Sino-Vietnamese Relations: Are Trade and Commerce the Critical Factors for Sustainable Peace?", *Contemporary Southeast Asia*, vol. 17, September, pp. 126-46.

— (1997), "Asia's Next Tiger? Vietnam is Fraught with Promise and Peril for Marketers", *Marketing Management*, vol. 5, Winter, pp. 26-37.

Shultz, Clifford J. II, Ardrey, William J. & Pecotich, Anthony (1995), "US Involvement in Vietnam, Part II: US Business Opportunities in a New Era", *Business Horizons*, vol. 38, March–April, pp. 21-7.

Shultz, Clifford J. II & Le, Khai (1993), "Vietnam's Inconsistencies between Political Structure and Socioeconomic Practice, and Implications for the Future", *Contemporary Southeast Asia*, vol. 15, September, pp. 179-94.

Shultz, Clifford J. II & Pecotich, Anthony (1994), "Vietnam: New Assessments of Consumption Patterns in a (Re)Emergent Capitalist Society", in eds J. Cote & Siew Meng Leong, *Asia Pacific Advances in Consumer Research*, Association for Consumer Research, Provo, UT, pp. 222–7.

— (1997), "Marketing and Development in the Transition Economies of South-East Asia: Policy Explication, Assessment and Implications", *Journal of Public Policy & Marketing*, vol. 16, no. 1, pp. 55–68.

Shultz, Clifford J. II, Pecotich, Anthony & Le, Khai (1994), "Changes in Marketing Activity and Consumption in the Socialist Republic of Vietnam", in eds C. Shultz, R. Belk & G. Ger, *Research in Consumer Behavior*, vol. 7, pp. 225–57.

Unger, Esta S. (1994), "Gender, Land and Household in Vietnam", *Asian Studies Review*, vol. 17, no. 3, pp. 61–72.

— (1997), "Gender and Real Property in Vietnamese Law and Practice: Commune Household and the Individual", in Veronica Taylor, *Asian Laws Through Australian Eyes*, LBC Information Services, Sydney, pp. 281–96.

Vien, Nguyen Khach (1987), *Vietnam: A Long History*, Foreign Language Publishing House, Hanoi.

Vo, Nhan Tri (1990), *Vietnam's Economic Policy Since 1975*, Allen and Unwin, Sydney.

Williams, Michael C. (1992), *Vietnam at the Crossroads*, Pinter Publishers Ltd, London.

Notes

1 Portions of text in this chapter have previously been published in a different form—in Clifford J. Shultz II (1994), "Balancing Policy, Consumer Desire and Corporate Interests: Considerations for Market Entry in Vietnam", *Columbia Journal of World Business*, vol. 29, Winter, pp. 42-53; Clifford J. Shultz II & William J. Ardrey IV (1997), "Asia's Next Tiger? Vietnam Is Fraught with Promise and Peril for Marketers", *Marketing Management*, no. 5, Winter, pp. 26-37; Clifford J. Shultz II, Anthony Pecotich & Khai Le (1994), "Changes in Marketing Activity and Consumption in the Socialist Republic of Vietnam", in eds C. Shultz, R. Belk & G. Ger, *Research in Consumer Behavior*, vol. 7, JAI Press, Greenwich, CT. Some direct quotes from Clifford J. Shultz II & William J. Ardrey IV (1997), "Asia's Next Tiger? Vietnam is Fraught with Promise and Peril for Marketers", *Marketing Management*, vol. 5, Winter, pp. 26–37, are reprinted with permission from *Marketing Management* and its publisher, the American Marketing Association. We thank both the AMA and Carolyn Neal, editor of *Marketing Management*. Clifford Shultz also thanks the ASU, FGIA and SRCA programs.

Acronyms

AFTA	ASEAN Free Trade Association
AIM	Aerospace Industries of Malaysia
AIO inventory	Attitudes, Interests and Opinions Inventory
APEC	Asia-Pacific Economic Co-operation
ARF	ASEAN Regional Forum
ASEAN	Association of South-East Asian Nations
BCA	Bank Central Asia
BIMP	ESEA subregional grouping: Brunei, Indonesia, Malaysia, and the Philippines
BLD	Buddhist Liberal Democratic party
CAPS	computer-aided picking system
CCCN	Customs Corporation Council Nomenclature (1978)
CCP	Chinese Communist Party
CEO	Chief Executive Officer
CFO	Chief Financial Officer
COO	Chief Operating Officer
CPP	Cambodian People's Party
CPV	Communist Party of Vietnam
EAGA	East ASEAN Growth Area
EOI	export-oriented industrialization (Taiwan)
EPA	Economic and Planning Agency (Japan)
ESEA	East and South-East Asia
FDI	Foreign Direct Investment
FEC	Foreign Exchange Certificate (Myanmar)
FIC	Foreign Investment Committee (Malaysia)
FTZ	Free Trade Zone
FUNCINPEC	Front Uni National pour un Cambodge Independent Neutre Pacific et Cooperative

GATT	General Agreement on Tariffs and Trade
GDP	gross domestic product
GDP (PPP$) index	GDP Purchasing Power Parity Dollars index
GNP	gross national product
GRC	group representation constituency (Singapore)
GRDI	gender-related development index (UN)
GVSP	Gross Output Value of Social Production
HDI	Human Development Index (UN)
IMF	International Monetary Fund
IPR	intellectual property rights
ISCO	International Standard Classification of Occupations
KLSE	Kuala Lumpur Stock Exchange
KOBACO	Korea Broadcasting Advertising Corporation
LDC	least-developed country
LPDR	Laos Peoples Democratic Republic
MDC	Distribution Center built by Maker
MEP	Memorandum of Economic Policy (Philippines)
MFN	Most Favored Nation (status from the USA)
MITI	Ministry of International Trade and Industry (Japan)
MNC	multinational corporation
Moulinaka	Mouvement de Liberation Nationale du Kampuchea
MTR	Mass Transit Railway (Hong Kong)
NCP	National Peoples Congress
NEM	New Economic Mechanism (Laos)
NEP	new economic policy
NIC	newly industrializing country
NZIER	New Zealand Institute of Economic Research
OECD	Organization for Economic Co-operation and Development
PDC	Process Distribution Center
PLA	People's Liberation Army
PNG	Papua New Guinea
POS	point-of-sale
PRB	Brunei People's Party
PRC	People's Republic of China

PRK	People's Republic of Kampuchea
RDC	Retailer Distribution Center
RMB	Renminbi
ROC	Republic of China
SEA	South-East Asia
SEZ	Special Economic Zone
SITC	standard international trade classification
SLORC	State Law and Order Restoration Council (Myanmar)
SOE	State-Owned Enterprise
SRI	Survey Research Indonesia
TDC	Distribution Center built by Trucker
UN	United Nations
UNDP	United Nations Development Program
UNTAC	United Nations Transitional Authorities in Cambodia
VCR	videocassette recorder
WDC	Distribution Center built by Wholesaler
WTO	World Trade Organisation